# THE CLINICIAN'S HANDBOOK

INTEGRATED DIAGNOSTICS, ASSESSMENT, AND
INTERVENTION IN ADULT AND
ADOLESCENT PSYCHOPATHOLOGY

## THIRD EDITION

**ROBERT G. MEYER, Ph.D.**

**University of Louisville**

**ALLYN AND BACON**

Boston   London   Toronto   Sydney   Tokyo   Singapore

# Dedication

## To my parents, Bob and Ardelle, who gave so much.

Copyright © 1993, 1989, 1983 by Allyn and Bacon
A Division of Simon and Schuster, Inc.
160 Gould Street
Needham Heights, Massachusetts 02194

### Library of Congress Cataloging-in-Publication Data

Meyer, Robert G.
    The clinician's handbook : integrated diagnostics,
assessment, and intervention in adult and adolescent
psychopathology / Robert G. Meyer.—3rd ed.
      p.    cm.
    Includes bibliographical references and index.
    ISBN 0-205-14230-3 (casebound)
    1. Mental illness—Diagnosis.   2. Psychodiagnostics.
3. Psychotherapy.    I. Title.
    [DNLM: 1. Mental Disorders—diagnosis.   WM 100 M6134c]
RC469.M457    1992
616.89—dc20
for Library of Congress                92-21932
                                  CIP

Printed in the United States of America
10 9 8 7 6 5 4 3 2 1   96 95 94 93 92

# CONTENTS

# PREFACE

As early as my graduate training and internship, I looked for a book that had not only integrated discussion of coverage of the common symptoms, personality styles, test patterns, and treatment recommendations but had also linked these with the various major psychodiagnostic categories that clinicians use every day. These data were available, but they were only available as isolated pieces of information. Books such as Graham's (1973) *The MMPI: A Practical Guide* and Zimmerman and Woo-Sam's (1973) *Clinical Interpretation of the WAIS* took steps to incorporate the data, yet these books dealt with only a single test. Also, such texts—as well as others that do deal with a number of tests—only occasionally linked general behavior patterns to particular test results. Furthermore, the test results were seldom related clearly to specific diagnostic classifications. Finally, there were no other books that linked all of these with the next step, treatment recommendations.

*The Clinician's Handbook* integrates these distinct, but necessarily related, considerations. This book links diagnostic issues and concepts with updated correlates for the most commonly used objective psychological test, the Minnesota Multiphasic Personality Inventory (MMPI-2), as well as complementary data from other tests, such as personality information from the Institute of Personality and Ability Testing's (IPAT) Cattell Sixteen Personality Factor Questionnaire (16 PF) Test (and, analogously, IPAT's High School Personality Questionnaire, the HSPQ, for adolescents and young adults ages 12–18, because virtually the same factors are measured in each). Other psychological tests commonly used with adults and adolescents are discussed, primarily the Wechsler Adult Intelligence Scale-Revised (WAIS-R), the Millon Clinical Multiaxial Inventory (MCMI-II), the Rorschach Ink Blot Technique, and the Thematic Apperception Test (TAT) and drawing tests. This book then integrates common behavior features (and *Diagnostic and Statistical Manual of Mental Disorders* (DSM-III-R) descriptors in most instances), test data, and the most-valid treatment recommendations. This synthesis is based on the assumptions that (a) a multimodal treatment is almost always the optimal approach, (b) virtually all theories and schools are useful to some degree, and (c) that a major challenge in modern treatment is determining the best fit of client type with treatment type. The eclecticism (hopefully in the best sense of that word) inherent in the latter two assumptions dovetails with the multimodal approach to treatment recommendations. That is, it rarely appears that a single treatment approach is sufficient to treat clusters of disordered behaviors comprehensively, and the use of only one technique is seldom the best approach with any one client.

*The Clinician's Handbook* was designed first for practitioners, since they are likely to encounter the broadest variety of emotional disorders in their work. Even practitioners who do not regularly administer the tests previously noted should find this book useful, because test responses are tied to various functional aspects of each disorder and to treatment options that might be used. The practitioner can assess this information in several ways. Generally, it is most useful to begin with common initial diagnoses and to examine the book's behavioral descriptors, DSM-III-R requirements, and various personality indices that are detailed for each. The relevant treatment recommendations can then be checked and incorporated into a report or overall treatment program.

Clinicians who prefer to look at MMPI-2 data before making a tentative diagnosis can use this book by going to Chapter 12 to locate the particular high score (or two-point code) that is obtained and then, if desired, use Table 12.1 at the end of Chapter 12. The table presents a list of probable diagnoses associated with virtually all of the two-point MMPI-2 codes. These probable diagnoses can then be checked as described above.

Although originally designed for the practitioner—including clinical, counseling, educational, forensic, and industrial psychologists; psychiatrists; clinical social workers; psychiatric nurses; family and marital therapists; and pastoral counselors—*The Clinician's Handbook* is also useful as a text in graduate-level courses. The breakdown of the disorder patterns follows the same schema as that of DSM-III-R and adds material about important allied topics, such as the criminal personality, acting-out potential, malingering, central nervous system dysfunction, and legal concepts (insanity, incompetency) as they relate to diagnostic categories. Thus, a full spectrum of adult and adolescent psychopathology can be studied. Numerous instructors have used this book as a primary text, which they supplemented with readings on research relevant to the various disorder patterns and with other textbooks. *The Clinician's Handbook* can also be used to supplement a standard text on abnormal psychology or in clinical courses and practicums as an adjunct to books on specific tests, test research, or test administration.

As noted in Chapter 1, this book incorporates most modern research available on the relationship of disorder patterns to diagnostic indicators and treatment options. Table 1.1 (in Chapter 1) lists many of the standard sources for the general and developing tradition of research studies noted throughout this book. Chapter 1 also details the long process by which this book evolved; the bedrock was the available research.

It is clear that this material, like any other body of information, will change with time. It is hoped that many of these changes will be spurred on by this book itself—that is, that researchers will refine, through more practical and precise studies, the clusters of diagnostic features, test results, and treatment options that are offered in the following pages. Reports of research and feedback from clinicians as they use these formulations would be most welcome. Please send any information to the author, Department of Psychology, University of Louisville, Belknap Campus, Louisville, KY 40292.

I am grateful to the American Psychiatric Association for its permission to convey generally the essence of the DSM-III-R categories seen in this book. Readers who want a more detailed description of the behavioral and statistical correlates of these categories should consult the DSM-III-R itself.

This book has been significantly aided by the contributions of the many teachers, colleagues, and students whom I have known over the years; each has in some way been helpful. A particular debt is owed to professors Albert I. Rabin and Bertram Karon at Michigan State University, as well as to many other clinicians and colleagues, such as Norman Abeles, Curtis Barrett, Will Bickart, Vytautas Bieliauskas, Mary Clarke, David Connell, Dan Cox, Sarah Deitsch, Herb Eber, Will Edgerton, Ray Fowler, Carleton Gass, Phil Johnson, William Kronenberger, Rhett Landis, Peter Mayfield, Ken McNiel, Leonard Miller, Lovick Miller, Steve Riggert, Paul Salmon, Steven R. Smith, Harvey A. Tilker, and Wilfred Van Gorp, all of whom have been helpful and instructive throughout the years. Thanks is also owed to those reviewers who read the entire manuscript and made comments that helped to improve its quality and usefulness. They are for the second edition, Diane R. Follingstad of the University of South Carolina, Columbia; Wilfred Van Gorp of the Veterans Administration Medical Center in Los Angeles; and Harrison Voigt of the California Institute of Integral Studies. I also wish to thank Professor James P. Rafferty, Wright State University; Professor Jeffrey Hecker, University of Maine; and Dr. Joseph Poirier of Rockville, MD, for their reviews and helpful comments on the revised manuscript for this third edition.

A special thanks is due my editor at Allyn and Bacon, Mylan Jaixen. A major acknowledgment and thank-you goes to Sandy Garcia who contributed significantly to this book, and also to Jennifer Yurt, Michael Valsted, and Tonia Dean for editorial assistance.

R.G.M.

# CHAPTER 1

# Overview and Introduction

This book provides overall diagnostic concepts and observations, links these with specific assessment and test data for diagnostic categories, and then integrates all of this with recommended intervention procedures. It would be unreasonable to expect that any one treatment approach or single pattern of test responses will be specifically relevant to only one diagnostic grouping and, conversely, that individual clients in any one diagnostic category will respond to only one type of treatment or show a single pattern on diagnostic tests. Hence, there is a multimodal assessment and treatment emphasis throughout this book.

There is also an emphasis on integrating psychological test data with interview data, because the combined information is a substantial improvement over interview data alone. This is true even when the interview data are obtained in a controlled format, such as the Mental Status Examination, which includes assessment of the following: (1) identifying data—chief complaint and physical appearance; (2) personal and family history; (3) motor functions; (4) speech activity and patterns; (5) mood and affect; (6) alertness and attention; (7) content and organization of thoughts; (8) orientation and perception; (9) the general areas of memory—abstract thinking, judgment, and the client's fund of knowledge; and (10) the client's attitude toward the examination and toward his or her condition (Melton et al., 1987). Some of the questions that commonly appear in the Mental Status Examination are the following: What is this place? Who am I? What day is it? Who are you? Who is the President? Who was the President before he was? What does "Don't cry over spilled milk" mean?

Even though there is structure provided to the interview by the Mental Status Examination, the examination contains the weakness of all data obtained from interviews: there are few or no statistical or normative standards for the obtained responses on which to base a communicable inference and an eventual diagnosis. Examiners are too often left to develop their own idiosyncratic notions of what a certain response means. While this procedure may be helpful in developing beginning inferences, these first inferences are significantly strengthened (or called into question) when the more objective data of psychological testing are considered as well.

The author was confronted with the potential of idiosyncratic error in the first case conference examination of a patient that he ever witnessed. The senior clinician who was examining the client proceeded with the questions of the Mental Status Examination. The client did generally well on most questions, except that he did not remember what date it was, he had some trouble counting backward from 100 by 7s after he got to 86, and he gave a rather concrete interpretation to the "spilled milk" question. After the client left the room, the examining clinician suggested the diagnosis of schizophrenia, pointing out that the client's lack of awareness of what date it was suggested a global disorientation, the problem in counting backward from 100 by 7s suggested general confusion, and the difficulties with the proverb suggested concreteness.

By this time I was uncomfortable because I also had missed the date by a full seven days. In actuality, a simpler and better explanation for the client's behavior is available. A lack of knowledge of the exact date, even being off by a number of days, is common. In addition, people who have been in an institution for any period of time easily become confused about, if not indifferent to, the date. The problems with the other two pieces of data are explainable by the fact that this client was not very bright.

There are trends, probabilities, and even some hard data to link the categories typically used by clinicians to various patterns. This book presents these relationships to the extent they are known at this time. In that regard, it is hoped that this book will result in more research that relates patterns of responses on several tests (which is what most clinicians use in an individual case) to various syndromes. As in any other area of scientific knowledge, subsequent research may supplant little, much, or all of what is now known.

This book is based on research results that have been melded with reported consensual clinical experience. The extent of the research data and the clinical experience naturally varies, depending on the particular syndrome being discussed.

If a single author or study is the source of material leading to a diagnostic or therapeutic recommendation, it will be directly referenced. If the recommendation is the speculation of the author alone, it will be so labeled. Where two or more different sources have provided information on which a recommendation is either directly based or inferred, it will be stated in ways such as "The evidence shows . . ." or "The classic profile for . . . ," or it will be put in a direct statement such as "Clients who are low on scale 8 are. . . ." The primary sources for the inferences for each of the four major tests used in this book – Minnesota Multiphasic Personality Inventory (MMPI-2), Cattell Sixteen Personality Factor (16 PF) Questionnaire, Wechsler Adult Intelligence Scale-Revised (WAIS-R), and Rorschach – are presented in Table 1.1.

The first section of this book (Chapters 2–11) proceeds in a standard sequence for each disorder, with a number of related syndromes grouped together under an appropriate chapter heading. An overview of the material relevant to the specific diagnostic disorder being discussed is presented first. This is usually followed by a synopsis of what the *Diagnostic and Statistical Manual-III-R* (DSM-III-R) requires so that the clinician can apply this diasgnosis to a client. In some cases, where there is little detail in the DSM-III-R requirements, I incorporate this information into the first general subsection rather than having a specific DSM-III-R subsection for that syndrome.

The next subsection presents the MMPI-2 code types and scale patterns one might expect with a client who exhibits this specific disorder. In most cases, the disorder can manifest itself in a variety of ways, so the text attempts to detail the major possibilities. This same approach is used in the next subsection, the presentation of 16 PF correlates. Following the subsection on the 16 PF, corresponding information from other relevant test sources is presented, notably from the Wechsler Adult Intelligence Scale-Revised (WAIS-R) and the Rorschach.

For some of the syndromes, little information is available. If so, only a short subsection is included based on this limited information, and, combined with consensual speculation, it is presented under the heading of Diagnostic Considerations, a designation that supplants the categories usually used – for example, MMPI-2 and Other Test-Response Patterns.

The last subsection, usually entitled Treatment Options, succinctly presents a number of possible treatment methods appropriate for the particular disorder, since the clinician often faces this question. An important point is that I will not consistently mention psychotherapy, chemotherapy, or general schools of therapy as treatment options for the various syndromes. There is good reason to believe that psychotherapy is an appropriate treatment for virtually every syndrome mentioned, either as the major component or as an adjunct to other techniques (Bloom, 1992; Zeig, 1987; Landman and Dawes, 1982; Smith and Glass, 1977). Hence, it would be redundant to mention it continually as an option. On those occasions when psychotherapy is specifically mandated, this fact will be noted. Similarly, the proponents of psychoanalysis and the other major therapy schools often assert that their techniques are valid for the majority of syndromes noted in this book. Where the literature indicates that a particular theoretical approach is especially efficient, it will be noted. Also, chemotherapy may be a useful adjunct in many of the diagnostic categories. It will be mentioned only where it

**TABLE 1.1**    Primary Sources for Four Test Inferences

**MMPI-2**

Ben-Porath and Butcher (1989)
Berry et al. (1991)
Butcher (1979, 1990)
Butcher and Graham (1988)
Carson (1969)
Colligan et al. (1983)
Dahlstrom and Dahlstrom (1980)
Dahlstrom and Welsh (1980)
Dahlstrom et al. (1972)
Dahlstrom et al. (1986)
Fowler (1981)
Gilberstadt and Duker (1965)
Graham (1977, 1987, 1990)
Graham et al. (1991a)
Green (1980, 1991)
Gynther et al. (1973a)
Gynther et al. (1973b)
Kelly and King (1979c)
Lachar (1974)
Lane and Lachar (1979)
Lewak et al. (1990)
Lorr et al. (1985)
Marks et al. (1974)
Webb et al. (1981)

**RORSCHACH**

Allison et al. (1988)
Anastasi (1987)
Aronow and Reznikoff (1976)
Beck and Beck (1978)
Beck and Molish (1952)
Burstein and Loucks (1989)
Cooper et al. (1988)
Exner (1974, 1978, 1986, 1988)
Gilbert (1978, 1980)
Goldfried et al. (1971)
Groth-Marmat (1990)
Klopfer and Davidson (1962)
Klopfer and Taulbee (1976)
Levitt (1980)
Newmark (1985, 1989)
Ogdon (1977)
Phillips and Smith (1953)
Piotrowski (1979)
Rabin (1964, 1968, 1981)
Rapaport et al. (1968)
Rickers-Ovsiankina (1960)
Rorschach (1953)
Shafer (1948, 1954)
Siegel (1987)
Swiercinsky (1985)
Wagner and Wagner (1981)

**WAIS-R**

Allison et al. (1988)
Anastasi (1987)
Gilbert (1978, 1980)
Golden (1979)
Groth-Marmat (1990)
Guertin et al. (1962)
Holland and Watson (1980)
Klinger and Saunders (1975)
Kramer (1990)
Matarazzo (1972)
Newmark (1985, 1989)
Rabin (1964, 1968)
Rapaport et al. (1968)
Shafer (1948)
Swiercinsky (1985)
Wechsler (1981)
Zimmerman and Woo-Sam (1973)

**16 PF**

Burger and Kabacoff (1982)
Cattell, H. (1989)
Cattell, R. (1965, 1973, 1979, 1986)
Cattell, R. and Warburton (1967)
Cattell, R. et al. (1970)
Eber (1975, 1987)
Golden (1979)
IPAT Staff (1963, 1972)
Karson (1959, 1960)
Karson and O'Dell (1976, 1989)
Krug (1978, 1980, 1981)
Krug and Johns (1986)
Lorr and Suziedelis (1985)
Lorr et al. (1985)
Newmark (1989)
Reuter et al. (1985)

is specifically warranted, with no implied assertion that it may be inappropriate in those groupings where it is not specifically listed.

The reader will also note that specific secondary or derived MMPI-2 or 16 PF scales for the diagnosis of a pattern or type of disorder are only mentioned when they specifically and clearly apply. Many secondary scales have been derived on the MMPI-2 for almost everything from depression to potential for happiness in marriage (Graham, 1990, 1987). In fact, there are secondary scales derived by researchers for almost every type of personality or affect pattern imaginable. The problem is that some of these scales are not routinely given in standard clinical assessments, and many of the others are not well validated and/or do not measure what the scale title suggests they do.

Special topics are present in the second section of this book (Chapters 12–18). The clinical correlates of the MMPI-2 and the 16 PF scales are examined first in Chapters 12 and 13. Many researchers and clinicians have carried out similar work in this area, and much is owed to them. These chapters attempt to integrate and update previous efforts so that the reader has an up-to-date body of information along traditional lines—that is, the various behavior patterns associated with the scale patterns. For some readers much of this information will be new. For others it will be at least a short refresher and a handy section to refer to on occasion while using the rest of the book.

Chapter 14 examines issues in predicting various patterns of behavior that directly involve dangerousness to self or others. Chapter 15 discusses psychopharmacology, and Chapter 16 examines malingering. The last two chapters deal with the forensic–legal arena: Chapter 17 discusses the issues of competency, criminal responsibility, and civil commitment; Chapter 18 deals with professional case preparation for the office or the courtroom.

## ■ The Rationale for Inclusion of Certain Tests

The reader might ask why the primary emphasis is on the MMPI-2, 16 PF, Millon Clinical Multiaxial Inventory (MCMI-II), WAIS-R, and Rorschach tests. The reason is obvious with the MMPI-2 and WAIS-R: They are the most commonly used and researched objective psychological tests (Allison et al., 1988; Newmark, 1985; Piotrowski et al., 1985). Virtually every clinician, regardless of theoretical orientation or type of training, has some familiarity with the MMPI and WAIS-R. As readers are aware, a revised version of the MMPI (MMPI-2) has been developed, with alternate forms for adolescents and adults. The interpretations derived from the original MMPI hold for those scales which were retained in MMPI-2 (Graham, 1990; Ward, 1991). There also has been such an extensive amount of normative data gathered on the MMPI that is by far the most useful standard objective test among the clinician's diagnostic options.

In using the WAIS-R, variables such as sex, race, and education have to be taken into account. Some may find the WAIS-SAM version reduces testing time, and it appears to retain good validity (Cargonello and Gurekas, 1988).

Although certain clinicians question the validity of projective tests, there are data to support their usefulness in many situations, and the Rorschach has become one of the most commonly used and well known of these tests (Piotrowski et al., 1985). The Thematic Apperception Test (TAT) also is commonly used (Bellak, 1993; Piotrowski et al., 1985), and many of the observations on TAT in this book apply equally well to other, newer thematic tests.

The Cattell 16 PF test is not as commonly used as the others. However, while the MMPI-2 is particularly good at assessing severe patterns and conditions of pathology and present adjustment, the 16 PF is a useful measure of personality patterns (Cattell, 1989), and there is increasing empirical support for using such measures (Goldberg, 1992). Thus, they dovetail nicely and provide the practitioner with an effective overview of the client. This is not to say that other tests, such as the Edwards Personal Preference Test, would not be useful as an adjunct to the MMPI-2 as well. However, the validity data on the 16 PF are certainly as impressive as the data on these other tests (Cattell, 1979; Krug, 1981; Krug and Johns, 1986; Goldberg, 1992). As Karson and O'Dell (1989) note, "It is important to remember that, in the search for significant variables in personality, the 16 PF has a decided edge over other tests, in that it is deeply embedded in a data-based multivariate personality theory" (p. 50).

The Cattell group has also formulated tests (using virtually the same scales) for persons in the lower age ranges. Thus, if practitioners use these tests with adults, they begin to develop some facility with a related set of children's tests, and vice versa. Also, it is felt that the motivational distortion scores derived for the 16 PF are more useful (Winder et al., 1975; Krug, 1978; Krug and Johns, 1986) than those in other available tests, when they have them at all. Finally, from a personal standpoint, I have worked with both the childhood and adult forms of the Cattell test since internship and have gathered a great deal more data regarding this test. Like numerous clinicians, I have continually used it in conjunction with the MMPI-2 and have found the combination to be especially effective.

The MCMI-II (Million Clinical Multiaxial Inventory) was first included in the second edition of this book because of its increasing popularity with clinicians (Choca et al., 1992). It was designed primarily by Theodore Millon and first published in 1976 by National Computer Systems (NCS). The advantages of the MCMI-II, in addition to simply being "new," are (1) its brevity–175 items, (2) its coordination of scales with the DSM diagnostic system, (3) its evolution from a clinical theory (which may be a minus, depending on your view of the theory), (4) the selection of test items by contrasting responses of a diagnostic group with undifferentiated psychiatric patients rather than normals, (5) the conversion of MCMI-II scores into base rates rather than normalized standard score transformations, and (6) a three-step validation procedure: theoretical-substantive, internal-structural, and external-criterion.

The disadvantage of the MCMI-II are (1) the problem of applying scores from one set of databases to new ones, (2) the scoring of twenty scales from a very small number of questions, (3) the large variance in one factor, termed a neuroticism-distress-maladjustment factor, a problem further compounded by the small number of questions, (4) the penchant for the MCMI-II to indicate pathology where there is none, (5) the fact that the MCMI-II may be more of a direct measure of Millon's personality theories about a category than the DSM-III-R formulation of that category, and (6) the absence of clearly interpretable validity scales or scores and the definite problems in assessing "faking good" with the MCMI-II (Millon, 1985, 1986; Widiger and Sanderson, 1987; McNiel and Meyer, 1990; Can Gorp and Meyer, 1986; Retzlaff and Gibertini, 1987; Patrick, 1988). Thus, in this book the suggested MCMI-II correlates for overall diagnostic patterns—especially for specific patterns, for example, Cocaine Abuse rather than Substance Abuse—are less data based and more speculative than those listed for the MMPI-2 and 16 PF.

In addition, there is one other flaw with the MCMI-II. It is the most serious of all, and it stems from the private and proprietary evolution of this instrument. For the most part, one must take the word of NCS and Dr. Millon that their generation, selection, and in many instances, analysis and interpretation of the data, all of which seem to make the MCMI-II look "good," were carried out in the best fashion. In a related vein, it is often financially prohibitive to do research with the MCMI-II because the profile should be computer scored. Although the MCMI-II can be hand scored (this is a very cumbersome task), it is difficult to do research at times because of lack of access to certain sets of base rates or the exact research results used by NCS. After encountering some red tape, one may be able to obtain a discount to do research using computer scoring. Yet it's hard to imagine there wouldn't be even more red tape if one kept getting results pointing to problems with the MCMI-II. The results on the MCMI-II break down as follows:

## BASIC PERSONALITY SCALES

Scale 1: Schizoid
(passive-detached)

Scale 2: Avoidant
(active-detached)

Scale 3: Dependent
(passive-dependent)

## CLINICAL SYMPTOM SYNDROMES

Scale A: Anxiety

Scale H: Somatoform

Scale N: Bipolar-Manic

Scale 4: Histrionic
(active-dependent)

Scale 5: Narcissistic
(passive-independent)

Scale 6A: Antisocial
(active-independent)

Scale 6B: Sadistic
(active-discordant)

Scale 7: Obsessive-Compulsive
(passive-ambivalent)

Scale 8A: Passive-Aggressive
(active-ambivalent)

Scale 8B: Self-Defeating
(passive-discordant)

Scale D: Dysthymia

Scale B: Alcohol Dependence

Scale T: Drug Dependence

Scale SS: Thought Disorder

Scale CC: Major Depression

Scale PP: Delusional Disorder

### PATHOLOGIC PERSONALITY DISORDERS

Scale S: Schizotypal (schizoid)

Scale C: Borderline (cyclic)

Scale P: Paranoid
(irritable-aggressive)

## ■ The Information Evolution in This Book

Before proceeding to a discussion of DSM-III-R, I would like to explain the procedure by which the information in this book was gathered and integrated. The following stages were followed to bring research information into coordination with consensual clinical experience.

**1.** For about fifteen years (up to the publication of the 1983 edition of this handbook), I continually used the most-accepted diagnostic tests, especially the MMPI-2, 16 PF, and WAIS-R, in a wide-ranging diagnostic practice and kept written records that were cross-checked and compared to the research literature to develop correlations of test patterns with various syndromes and the syndromes with the most appropriate treatments. This was in keeping with the traditional admonition that too much dependence on memory quickly leads to error in clinical inference. These patterns also were used as a teaching tool in graduate courses in diagnostic testing and clinical psychopathology. Thus, the developing concepts were again continually checked against available clinical research literature and within the case itself.

**2.** A thorough formal review of the literature was instituted, and from this and the information collected in step 1, a first draft was written that correlated the patterns on the 16 PF and MMPI-2 and appropriate treatments with the diagnostic categories in the initial DSM-III.

**3.** Graduate students in sequential clinical psychopathology courses were each assigned a subset of DSM-III categories. They were asked, independent of the information in the first draft, to find correlates of the DSM-III draft categories on the MMPI-2, 16 PF, WAIS-R, and Rorschach in the research and clinical literature. Another review of the most recent literature was coordinated with the corrections and suggestions gleaned from the production of these graduate students.

**4.** As soon as the final DSM-III was published, the work that emerged from step 3 was coordinated with changes from the earlier versions to produce a polished draft.

**5.** The information derived up to that point was presented to a continuing-education seminar of twenty practicing clinical psychologists. These people responded via formal feedback procedures about the applicability and accuracy of the findings in this draft. There was substantial agreement between the views of these practicing clinicians and the draft that was produced at the end of step 4, but corrections were noted, and some interesting suggestions were incorporated.

**6.** After integrating this information, the latest draft was presented to five of the most respected practicing clinical psychologists in the region, all of whom regularly used these tests in their practices. Each carried out a thorough review of the book, and again, although there was general agreement with the material as presented to them, they did offer much helpful commentary.

**7.** After this material was integrated and amplified in accordance with the publisher's reviewers, there was a last check with the relevant research literature, and the manuscript was again considered and put into a final state.

**8.** After the publication of the 1983 edition of this book, it was used each year as the primary text in a graduate course on psychopathology and psychological testing. At various junctures, students were asked to critique and/or update subsections of the book, including new diagnostic categories proposed for and then included in DSM-III-R. More diagnostic categories specific to adolescence were added. Taking cues and new points of view from the work of these students, the author carried out similar continuing updates and critiques himself, using all of this material to keep reworking the manuscript.

**9.** The MCMI-II was incorporated into that edition because of its increasing popularity with a number of clinicians. MCMI-II diagnostic correlates of the major syndromes are now included throughout the book. After being initially generated, they were critiqued and updated by several graduate students and local clinicians who had worked extensively with the MCMI-II; they were later thoroughly critiqued and reworked by Wilfred Van Gorp, Kenneth McNiel, and John Boles, all of whom not only have extensive clinical experience with the MCMI-II but also have carried out research on the instrument.

**10.** A chapter on professional practice (Chapter 18), relevant to the courtroom as well as the office, was developed.

**11.** For each chapter, at least two (and often more) experienced practicing clinicians, each of whom is recognized as having substantial expertise in the areas covered, contributed a thorough critique and update of that chapter to aid in finalization of the manuscript.

**12.** A final reworking of the manuscript incorporated the changes from DSM-III to DSM-III-R, as well as the publisher's reviews and a thorough check on the relevant literature.

**13.** After the publication of the 1989 edition, graduate student feedback and input was again incorporated; most chapters were submitted to experienced clinicians with specific expertise in that area, and their input was also integrated.

**14.** Theodore Feldmann, M.D., Harvey A. Tilker, Ph.D., and Murray H. Rosenthal, D.O., authored Chapter 15 on psychopharmacology, as well as contributing numerous related additions to the overall text.

**15.** With substantial help from Steven R. Smith, dean of the Cleveland-Marshall Law School at Cleveland State University, Appendix B on relevant legal cases was developed.

**16.** The material on the MMPI and MCMI was revised and updated so as to make recommendations in this book consistent with the respective revisions of these tests, MMPI-2 and MCMI-II.

**17.** A final update based on the recent research, and publisher's reviews, produced the present manuscript.

Throughout this process, as much research information as possible was gathered and integrated and then complemented by consensual clinical experience.

In addition to the standard DSM-III-R categories, this book examines several other topics of interest to practitioners: the issues of acting-out potential (for example, aggression and suicide potential); the criminal personality; rape; and the legal concepts and psychological correlates of insanity, involuntary civil commitment, and competency to stand trial. Malingering is included in the DSM-III-R, but it receives relatively little notice, as it does in most diagnostic texts. I consider it to be of considerable importance to the diagnostician, so it will be dealt with in some depth in Chapter 16.

Following the main text is Appendix A, a set of paper-and-pencil test materials that I have revised and integrated over the past eighteen years. The reader can use the material as a classroom handout with the text without written permission, so long as it is not sold or reproduced for any other reason. You may want to insert a drawing test different from the Draw-A-Group Test, add some Bender-Gestalt-like figures (see the section on central nervous system impairment in Chapter 11), or

otherwise modify it. The four proverbs included were selected because
Johnson (1966) found these to be the most efficient in discriminating
between cases of central nervous system impairment and schizophrenia.
The validated short form of the Marlowe-Crowne Social Desirability
Scale would also be a useful addition, in order to get a quick estimate
of the client's response set (Zook and Sipps, 1985). As noted earlier, Appendix B presents a listing of the major legal cases relevant to clinicians.

Aside from the overall chart of DSM-III-R categories already
presented, the following summary of certain aspects of the DSM-III-R
may be useful to those readers who do not yet regularly use the
DSM-III-R.

## ■       DSM-III-R

The DSM-II-R (American Psychiatric Association, 1987) is the revised
form of the third edition of the *Diagnostic and Statistical Manual of Mental Disorders* that was published in 1980. The predecessors of DSM-III
were DSM-II (1968), and DSM-I (1952). A new edition, DSM-IV, is expected in 1993–94, timed to coincide with the anticipated publication
of the tenth edition of the *International Classification of Diseases*
(ICD-10). Compatibility with the ICD codes was markedly increased in
the DSM-III-R and is expected to be furthered in DSM-IV.

As to the definition of "mental disorder," it is conceptualized in DSM-
III-R (p. xxii) as

**a clinically significant behavioral or psychological syndrome or pat-
tern that occurs in a person and that is associated with present
distress (a painful symptom) or disability (impairment in one or more
important areas of functioning) or with a significantly increased risk
of suffering death, pain, disability, or an important loss of freedom.
In addition, this syndrome or pattern must not be merely an expec-
table response to a particular event, e.g., the death of a loved one.
Whatever its original cause, it must currently be considered a
manifestation of a behavioral, psychological, or biological dysfunction in the person. Neither deviant behavior, e.g., political, religious,
or sexual, nor conflicts that are primarily between the individual
and society are mental disorders unless the deviance or conflict is a
symptom of a dysfunction in the person, as described above. There
is no assumption that each mental disorder is a discrete entity with
sharp boundaries (discontinuity) between it and other mental
disorders, or between it and no mental disorder.**

The actual process of making that diagnosis is governed by two principles (pp. xxiv–xxv):

**1. When an Organic Mental Disorder can account for the symptoms,
it preempts the diagnosis of any other disorder that could produce**

the same symptoms (e.g., Organic Anxiety Disorder preempts Panic Disorder).

2. When a more pervasive disorder, such as Schizophrenia, commonly has associated symptoms that are the defining symptoms of a less pervasive disorder such as Dysthymia, only the more pervasive disorder is diagnosed if both its defining symptoms *and* associated symptoms are present. For example, only Schizophrenia (not Schizophrenia and Dysthymia) should be diagnosed when the defining symptoms of Schizophrenia are present along with chronic mild depression (which is a common associated symptom of Schizophrenia).

Also, current severity of disorder *may* now be indicated, by adding in parentheses the following terms after a diagnostic: mild, moderate, severe, in partial remission (or residual state), or in full remission. With some diagnoses, specific criteria for these severity levels are provided.

There were numerous changes in the categories from DSM-III to DSM-III-R. Many are semantic or not especially noteworthy, but the following are the more important category changes.

| DSM-III | DSM-III-R |
|---|---|
| Attention Deficit Disorder with Hyperactivity | Attention-Deficit Hyperactivity Disorder |
| Attention Deficit Disorder without Hyperactivity | Undifferentiated Attention-Deficit Disorder |
| *Conduct Disorder*<br>  undersocialized, aggressive<br>  undersocialized, nonaggressive<br>  socialized, aggressive<br>  socialized, nonaggressive<br>  atypical | *Conduct Disorder*<br>  isolated, aggressive type<br><br><br>  group type<br>  undifferentiated type |
| Oppositional Disorder | Oppositional-Defiant Disorder |
| Bulimia | Bulimia Nervosa |
| Infantile Autism and Childhood Onset Pervasive Developmental Disorder | Autistic Disorder |

Addition of: Developmental Expressive Writing Disorder

| | |
|---|---|
| Developmental Language Disorder | "expressive" and "receptive" subcategories |

Addition of: Inhalant Intoxication

Addition of: "dependence" subcategory for Cocaine and Hallucinogens

Addition of: Polysubstance Dependence

Deletion of: Requirement that Schizophrenia begin before age forty-five to warrant the diagnosis

| Paranoia | Delusional (Paranoid) Disorder, with specification of subtype: erotamanic, grandiose, jealous, persecutory, somatic, or unspecified |
| Shared Paranoid Disorder | Induced Psychotic Disorder (for the "receiver") |

Acute Paranoid Disorder now subsumed under Psychotic Disorders Not Elsewhere Classified

Schizoaffective Disorder to be specified as bipolar or depressive type

Major Depression to be specified as chronic, melancholic, or seasonal types

| Dysthymic Disorder | Dysthymia |
| Cyclothymic Disorder | Cyclothymia |
| Agoraphobia with Panic Attacks | Panic Disorder with Agoraphobia |
| Panic Disorder | Panic Disorder without Agoraphobia |

Body Dysmorphic Disorder, to be added—was Dysmorphobia, which was subsumed under Atypical Somatoform Disorder

Addition of: Gender Identity Disorder of Adolescence or Adulthood, non-transexual type

| Transvestism | Transvestic Fetishism |

Deletion of: Zoophilia

Addition of: Frotteurism

| Inhibited Sexual Desire | Hypoactive Sexual Desire Disorder |

Addition of: Sexual Aversion Disorder

Deletion of: Ego-Dystonic Homosexuality

Addition of: Trichotillomania

| Compulsive Personality Disorder | Obsessive-Compulsive Personality |

Provisional consideration is allowed for three patterns (they are not official categories, but they may be used by individual clinicians): Late Luteal Phase Dysphoric Disorder, Self-Defeating Personality Disorder, and Sadistic Personality Disorder. Another controversial category, Paraphilic Coercive Disorder, essentially compulsive rapists, was eventually withdrawn because, although it was felt to be valid, it was doubted that it would be useful.

One important format shift from DSM-III to DSM-III-R, and a trend that will continue into DSM-IV, is from a "monothetic" to a "polythetic" model for qualifying a diagnosis. In the monothetic model, criteria A, B, and C, for example, are specified, and *all* are required to make the diagnosis. In the polythetic model, a certain number within an array of possible diagnostic indicators (for example, five of nine for Obsessive-Compulsive Personality Disorder) are required to make the diagnosis. In a few instances, such as, Conduct Disorder, the symptoms are ranked by discriminating power, as determined by research. Spitzer (1992) is candid in observing that in some cases the required number of symptoms, or even the actual symptoms themselves, were arrived at by a relatively casual consensual model. This essentially boils down to "Well, three would seem about right for that diagnosis," and Spitzer emphasizes that more research is needed for many categories. The polythetic model is favored because, overall, it attains greater reliability, yet has more flexibility, and more effectively lends itself to empirical validation (Widiger et al., 1991).

Even though the DSM has been criticized for a number of reasons, it is the official document of the American Psychiatric Association, it has received approval from the American Psychological Association, and it has received wide international acceptance. For several reasons, the DSM-III (and now the DSM-III-R and DSM-IV) has had and will have more influence than its predecessors, and even has more acceptance at the international level than the ICD system (Maser et al., 1991). It has a more thorough and extensive description of categories and criteria for diagnosis (there is an increasing demand of third-party payers for a full diagnosis), and its influence on the types and number of health service providers is increasing. Another major reason is that there is simply no alternative system that has reached even a minimal level of usage and acceptability.

A major change in the DSM-III—continued and refined in the DSM-III-R—is the use of a multiaxial diagnostic system, which allows the clinician to provide several different types of information. Although there are five axes that can potentially be used, the first three make up the official DSM-III-R diagnostic categories. A client may receive a diagnosis on each of the first three axes:

Axis I:     Clinical Syndromes and V Codes

Axis II:    Personality Disorders and Developmental Disorders

Axis III:  Physical Disorders or Conditions

Axis V is used to denote the Severity of Psychosocial Stressors that preceded the disorder. The stressor should be noted, and it should be rated on the basis of its impact on an "average" person. Thus, it should not be influenced by the vulnerability of the individual being rated. The specific stressor should be further specified as either a "predominantly acute event" (less than six months) or "predominantly enduring circumstances" (more than six months duration). They are coded from number 1, which designates no psychosocial stressor, through number 7, with 0 referring to an unspecified stressor or inadequate information.

A second optional scale, Axis V, the Global Assessment of Functioning (GAF) Scale, refers to the highest level of adaptive functioning noted for both the year previous to the disorder and for one's condition at the time of evaluation. The rating is on a 1-to-90 scale (*DSM-III-R,* p. 12) that is an integrated judgment of psychological, social, and occupational functioning (although not for physical limitations). Most clinicians will not regularly use Axes IV and V because they are predominantly used in research situations.

The general criteria for inclusion on Axis II is that the condition be lifelong, reasonably stable, and handicapping. Yet is is interesting that the only conditions that are appropriate for listing on Axis II are the Personality Disorders and the Developmental Disorders. This limits the potential disorders for this axis to less than thirty different categories, as opposed to the substantial number of categories possible for Axis I. However, personality traits (and defense mechanisms, a list of which is supplied in an appendix in the *DSM-III-R*) rather than disorders may also be listed on Axis II. For example, if the clinician felt the client should be considered paranoid, yet did not feel a formal diagnosis of Paranoid Personality Disorder was warranted, the paranoid trait would be put on Axis II and no code number would be used along with it, because a code number indicates a formal diagnosis of disorder.

If there is no evidence of disorder on an axis, the clinician should write: "V71.09, no diagnosis on Axis I (or II)," or one of the Conditions Not Attributable to a Mental Disorder (the V codes) may be recorded. There may also be occasions when it is felt that the principal diagnosis—the one mainly responsible for the diagnosis and treatment—is on Axis II. In that case, the diagnosis listed on the second axis should be followed up with the phrase "Principal Diagnosis." Otherwise it is assumed that the principal diagnosis is the one listed on Axis I. When multiple diagnoses are made on any one axis, they are to be listed in the order of importance for attention or treatment. A number of DSM-III-R diagnoses are followed by a small *x*, indicating a place for further qualifying phrase (see *DSM-III-R*).

The clinician should take note of several categories that are available to indicate a questionable level of diagnostic certainty. For example, the clinician may put the term "Provisional" after a diagnosis to indicate a tentative formulation while more data are gathered. The designation 300.90 is used where the clinician has obtained enough data to rule out a psychotic disorder but has concluded that further diagnostic specification is not available. The diagnosis number 799.90 can be used on either Axis I or II when there is not adequate information to make a diagnostic judgment, and it is thus deferred. Most categories contain a term that is qualified by the code NOS (Not Otherwise Specified), which is used to indicate that the disorder does not fully meet the required specifications of a more refined categorization.

# CHAPTER 2

# Substance Use Disorders

Modern society provides an increasing number of substances that are abused (L'Abate et al., 1992; Blum and Payne, 1991), and this is reflected in the DSM-III-R. The drugs that are commonly abused, such as heroin, barbiturates, amphetamines, cocaine, and marijuana, are given separate subcategories in the DSM-III-R. Caffeine and tobacco use disorders are also included, the latter being especially important as a precursor to other forms of chronic substance abuse.

There are many narrowly defined substance use categories in the DSM-III-R, so many that it would be impossible to discuss each one here, especially since many of them are not often applied. The overall diagnoses of "abuse" and "dependence," as they are applied in the DSM-III-R to each of the various substances throughout this chapter, are detailed in the first specific substance to be discussed: alcohol. However, this section will first take note of some characteristics of substance use disorders in general.

A critical component of the process of evaluation is to sort out the validity of the client's various self-reports. The following schemata may help in this process:

| CONDITIONS CONDUCIVE TO INVALID SELF-REPORT | CONDITIONS CONDUCIVE TO VALID SELF-REPORT |
|---|---|
| 1. Client shows positive blood alcohol/drug concentration, is experiencing withdrawal, and/or apparent substance-related distress | 1. Client is alcohol/drug free and is not showing withdrawal symptoms or evident substance-related distress |

2. Client referral generated primarily by objective coercion, e.g., DUI, threat of job loss

2. No objective coercion

3. Client referral generated primarily by interpersonal distress, e.g., threat of divorce

3. Interpersonal coercion not primary

4. Client doubts confidentiality of information he or she provides

4. Confidentiality is assured and apparently accepted

5. Client keeps interpersonal distance and/or contacts are brief

5. Adequate rapport has been established

6. Client is unaware that self-report data will be corroborated

6. Client understands self-report will be checked against other data

7. Vague, unstructured interview techniques are used

7. Structured interview techniques and psychological tests are employed

8. Client shows psychopathic and/or antisocial personality characteristics

8. Client is relatively low on psychopathic-antisocial dimension

9. Client shows inadequate compliance

9. Client shows adequate compliance

10. Adequate attendance and/or compliance is a condition of parole, continued relationship, or employment, etc.

10. Reasons for performance compliance are minimal or do not appear to be a primary motivation

## ■ MMPI-2

Johnson, Tobin, and Celluci (1992) find the 2-4/4-2, 2-7/7-2 and 4-9/9-4 profiles to be especially common in substance abusers. Trethvithick and Hosch (1978) have noted that persons with substance use disorders in general are typically elevated on MMPI-2 scales 4, 8, 2, and 7, and others note that 9 is often high, too (Patalano, 1980). These elevations reflect the confusion, distress, and depression that are found in addition to the sociopathic traits of drug abusers. Scores on scale 9 will vary, depending on the person's need to affiliate with others and whether they are inclined toward the use of depressants or stimulants in response to their own typical physiological patterns. The rare spike-9 profile is indicative of drug abuse associated with antisocial patterns (King and Kelley, 1977).

An MMPI-2 content scale (49 items) that is particularly useful in diagnosing substance abuse disorders, especially with alcohol, but also with heroin, heavy marijuana use, cocaine, polydrug use, etc., is the MacAndrew Alcoholism Scale (MAC) (MacAndrew, 1965; Fowler, 1981). This scale is also useful with young adults in predicting later abuse patterns. When MMPI-2 was developed, four religious items were dropped, but were replaced with four items that were found to differentiate alcoholics from nonalcoholics. In general, the MAC is hard to fake unless one fakes the MMPI-2 in general, so it is usually accurate if the validity scales are within acceptable limits. A cutoff range (raw scores) at 26–28 strongly suggests past or present abuse and/or potential abusers; a score of 29–31 indicates an addiction problem of some sort is very likely; and with a score over 31, addiction is highly probable (Butcher, 1990). Since minorities (especially blacks) and obese persons tend to score a bit higher on this scale, adjusting the cutoff one to two points higher is suggested for these clients; females tend to score slightly lower than males, so reducing the cutoff score by two to three points is recommended. From a more general perspective, persons scoring high on the MAC present themselves as self-confident, are risk-taking, assertive, exhibitionistic, extroverted, and show a history of concentration and persistence difficulties and acting-out problems such as in school.

■      ## 16 PF

In the typical testing situation, when disposition is at least one of the considerations, individuals with substance use disorders tend to score high on the H, I, M, and $Q_4$ scales and low on F, which reflects their imagination and their disdain for typical societal standards, as well as their distress. They are likely to be moderately high on scale L, reflecting again their concern about arrest and the eventual disposition of their situation. They tend to be moderately low on both scales G and $Q_3$, reflecting again their disdain for the standard mores. They are also lower on scales B, C, and E, and if their distress is relatively high, they are also likely to show a lower score on scale F.

■      ## Other Test-Response Patterns

Clinicians should of course look for physical signs of substance abuse (needle marks, abscesses over veins, constriction of pupils) and make sure that adequate physiological screening, such as urinalysis, has been carried out. If the substance abuse has not been long-term, or if there is little in the way of allied psychopathology, WAIS-R scores are in the normal range and do not show marked subtest deviation (Hewett and Martin, 1980). In some instances, when clients are tested after having ingested low doses of cocaine or amphetamines, they do slightly better on certain tasks, such as digit symbol, that require speed and role learning (Washton, 1991). If individuals have been abusing drugs for some time, they do poorly on tests that reflect school achievement, such as information and arithmetic, although they still do reasonably well on vocabulary. If they have begun to develop confusion, which occurs in the polydrug abuse syndrome, they are likely to do poorly on the coding and the block design test. They do best in such subtests as similarities, picture completion, and comprehension.

Several factors on the MCMI-II have been noted (Choca, et al., 1992; Bryer et al., 1990). Scores of 75 or higher on B or T have traditionally been thought to indicate the presence of some drug or alcohol abuse, while scores of 85 indicate a more severe abuse problem (although Bryer and his colleagues (1990) report a 50% false-positive rate, and positive hit rates of 43% for alcoholics and 49% for drug abusers when using a score of 75 as a cutoff point). During periods of intoxication by drugs or alcohol, the severe symptom syndromes SS and PP may become elevated, and scale 3 and/or 5 is also high.

## ■ Treatment Options

A variety of treatment techniques has been used in substance use disorders (Barrett and Meyer, 1992; Committee, 1990; L'Abate et al., 1992). Common to most therapeutic situations involving substance abuse are (1) breaking through the denial, often massive denial, that there is a problem, (2) bolstering the often-wavering motivation, and (3) avoidance of manipulations and rationalizations. Aversive conditioning has been favored for working on the specific habits that form the matrix of substance abuse, as well as in helping develop an aversive response to the drug itself. It is also argued that relaxation training is helpful for substance abusers, particularly those who use tranquilizers or depressant drugs. Where the disorder appears to be an escape response from fears and phobias, systematic desensitization is helpful. Analogously, assertive training may be included in the treatment package if social inadequacy is evident, as is often the case in substance dependence.

In the initial stages of the treatment, when the person is being detoxified in a controlled setting, token economies are helpful in getting the client to organize his or her behavior in some effective fashion. With regard to the cognitive behavioral treatments, many feel that covert sensitization is especially useful for the substance use disorders (Cautela and Wall, 1980). Within the psychoanalytic therapies, it appears that the Adlerian approaches have the most to offer for this particular pattern, with their emphasis on personal responsibility for behavior. As the person progresses away from drug abuse, the process and existential therapies take on a particularly important role (Committee, 1990). Certainly the critical issue in treatment success in any substance abuse pattern is the client's decision to change. Since the experience-seeking subfactor of the stimulation-seeking variable particularly characterizes the substance abuser (Zuckerman et al., 1980), the therapist needs to help the client channel this need into more legitimate and constructive pursuits. Family therapy also is usually necessary (Brown, 1991).

# Alcohol Use Disorder

## DSM-III-R CONSIDERATIONS

The DSM-III-R classifies the drug use disorders either into the organic mental disorders to reflect their effect on the central nervous system or else as a psychoactive substance use disorder that emphasizes the maladaptive behavior caused by taking the substances. In an individual case, a diagnosis from both sections could be appropriate.

The subcategory diagnosis of alcoholism—the organic alcohol disorders and the substance use alcohol disorders—is very specific. The problem is that alcoholics may run the gamut of behaviors appropriate to each of several diagnostic categories in each division—and in a very short period of time. Thus, any particular observed behavior is contingent on when the diagnostician happens to see the alcoholic. It would be absurd to try to detail these subcategories here, as it would require an inordinate amount of space. However, the important differentiation between substance abuse and substance dependence is presented.

Psychoactive Substance Abuse (e.g., Alcohol Abuse, 305.00) requires that (1) the substance be abused rather often for at least one month, (2) the criteria for Psychoactive Substance Dependence for this substance has never been met before, and (3) there be evidence of either recurrent use in physically hazardous situations (e.g., driving while intoxicated), or continued use despite awareness that such use is causing or increasing persistent or recurrent psychological, physical, social, or occupational problems.

Psychoactive Substance Dependence (i.e., Alcohol Dependence, 303.90) requires that this disorder has occurred for one month, or at least repeatedly over a longer period of time, and that at least three of the following possible manifestations of this disorder be evident: (1) one or more efforts, or at least a persisting desire, to cut down or stop; (2) significant time or effort spent to get, take, or recover from the substance; (3) an increase in the amount of substance taken or the time while taking it; (4) reduction or stoppage of important social, recreational, or occupational activities; (5) frequent intoxication or withdrawal symptoms that occur during important role obligations or that put one in physical danger; (6) continued use even while aware that it causes or exaggerates another significant physical, social, or psychological problem; (7) marked tolerance for (at least a 50% increase needed to get original effects) or lessened effects with the same amount; (8) characteristic withdrawal symptoms; or (9) use of the substance to relieve withdrawal.

□    OTHER BEHAVIORAL CONSIDERATIONS

The psychological euphoria from alcohol is functionally a toxic response (Blum and Payne, 1991). Alcohol is not digested, but absorbed through the stomach and intestinal walls and metabolized in the liver by the process of oxidation. In this process, alcohol fuses with oxygen, and the resulting pure grain alcohol, or ethanol, is converted by enzymes to acetaldehyde, which is further broken down to acetic acid (vinegar). The vinegar is then broken down by enzymes into water and carbon dioxide, which are passed out of the body. The liver can only break down approximately one ounce of one-hundred-proof whiskey per hour, assuming the person is of average weight. Any excess that cannot be broken down directly affects the brain, causing intoxication. Interestingly, even when males and females are of equal weight, this process is still slower in females.

Pharmacologically, alcohol acts as a depressant that first inhibits the higher brain centers and only later depresses the lower brain centers (Blum and Payne, 1991). The resultant decrease in control of overt behavior has led to the mistaken belief that alcohol is a stimulant. With continued alcohol intake, there is a loss of the more complex cognitive and perceptual abilities and eventually a loss in simple memory and motor coordination.

It is interesting that part of the strength of the effect depends on whether people are getting drunk or sobering up. Those who are sobering up perform better on short-term memory and perception tasks than those who have the same blood level of alcohol but who are getting high.

Long-term alcohol abuse is likely to result in central nervous system dysfunction, or organicity, especially in older alcoholics (see Chapter 11 for relevant diagnostic considerations). Also, most researchers now believe that this dysfunction is not simply a result of B-vitamin deficiencies from the poor diet that often accompanies chronic alcoholism, but at least in part is caused by the effects of alcohol per se (Barrett and Meyer, 1992). The reader is referred to the important work of researchers (see review by Marlatt et al., 1988) who have indicated that the *belief* that one has ingested alcohol is often more critical than whether one has actually done so. These researchers show that both aggression and sexual behavior are highly dependent on the belief system of those individuals who use alcohol, and many times the alcohol is a learned excuse for acting-out behavior in these areas (Blane and Leonard, 1987).

Fabian and Parsons (1983) addressed the question of whether cognitive deficits (decrements in problem solving, abstracting, and spatial-perceptual skills, but with intact verbal intelligence) found in detoxified alcoholics diminish over time. Results indicated that most, but not all, cognitive deficits continued to show up, but at reduced levels, at follow-up (1.8 years later), with the greatest and perhaps the earliest improvement occurring on complex abstracting tests. Continued deficits in the four-years-sober alcoholics were most notable on perceptual-motor tasks, such as WAIS-R Digit Symbol and the Trail-Making Test. Recovery of most functions for which recovery is possible occurs roughly within the first year of sobriety. Thus, differential recovery among cognitive abilities was noted over a four-year period: Some complex cognitive abilities appear to return to normal levels, while others (perceptual-motor speed, for example) remain lower than normal.

□                          MMPI-2

As noted earlier in this chapter, the MAC is especially useful here (MacAndrew, 1965; Graham, 1990; Allen et al., 1991). The MAC seems especially effective in picking up alcoholics or those predisposed to substance abuse because of traits of extroversion and/or sensation seeking (Allen et al., 1991). The scale is somewhat less effective in spotting the reactive and/or neurotic substance abuser.

Because chronic alcohol intoxification refers to one behavior pattern within an overall personality, and because that behavior can be generated by diverse trains of personality development, what one might expect on various tests is even less clear than with a number of the other disorders that will be discussed later. Johnson, et al. (1992) find the 4-9/9-4 profile to be especially common in alcoholics. Otto et al. (1988) found alcoholics to be high on all scales except L, K, 5, and 0. Holland and Watson (1980) reported elevations above the 65-T level on F, 2, 4, 7, and 8 in their sample of MMPIs from inpatient alcoholics. They compared this group to neurotic, schizophrenic, and brain-damaged groups and found that the only marked differences from the other groups in general were the alcoholics' low scores on L, K, and 0. They assert that this is indicative of the introversion, somatization, and depression that are characteristic of this group. The 8-7 alcoholic is most likely to be psychotic and/or depressed (Conley, 1981).

The classic high 4-9 pattern that characterizes the psychopath is commonly found in outpatient alcoholics, although it is usually accompanied by a higher F score (Greene, 1991). When referring to the more acute alcoholic, people like Conley (1981), Gynther et al. (1973a), and Lachar (1974) have noted that the 2-4/4-2 profile is particularly common. The

2-4/4-2, also common here, reflects the depression that a person in an acute state of alcoholic disorder is likely to experience (Barrett and Meyer, 1992). The 4-2 is more common than the 2-4, although the two scores are closer together here than in the 4-2 obtained with other drug disorders. This 4-2 pattern is particularly noted in those arrested for driving under the influence of alcohol.

Gynther and his colleagues (1973a) have also found that the 1-2/2-1 MMPI profile is common in alcoholics, particularly for males who show an episodic pattern with numerous physical complaints. This usually represents a person who has used alcohol for a significant period of time and who primarily manifests the abuse in episodic sprees. When 3 is also elevated and 7 is one of the next highest scores, a substantial and often severe neurotic component is involved (Conley, 1981). Profiles with an elevation on 4 and 7 frequently indicate persons who manifest a cycle of alcoholic indulgence, regret and remorse, and then repetition of the acting-out, while the 2-7/7-2 is noted where remorse is more chronic and has channeled into depression.

The 4-6/6-4 profile is commonly found in alcoholics who have a long history of alcoholic problems; as the alcoholic ages, however, scales 4 and 6 decline. They are less inclined toward episodic drinking than those with the 1-2/2-1 profile, and they are likely to avoid treatment. The 6-4/4-6 alcoholics usually have very poor work histories and have had numerous marital problems, including the tendency to get married repetitively. When the 6 scale is higher, the individual is likely to be abusive, with the spouse probably the main target of this abuse. The 4-9/9-4 profile with a high F scale has already been noted; such persons tend to be long-term alcoholics.

There is also the 1-4/4-1 pattern, where the person is high on scale 9 and at least moderately low on the 0 scale. These individuals are the extroverted social alcoholics (or drug abusers in general) who do not have as severe underlying conflicts as those with other patterns.

☐            ## 16 PF

Some of the early research gathered by the people who developed the Cattell 16 PF test has delineated some characteristics on the 16 PF that are common to most alcoholics (IPAT staff, 1963). They found the alcoholic to be high on the I, M, O, and $Q_4$ scales, as well as moderately high on the L and N scales. They reported the alcoholic to be low on the B, C, and F scales and at least moderately low on scales E and G.

Gross and Carpenter (1971) found somewhat similar results in a study of 266 alcoholics who showed elevation on O and $Q_4$, with slight elevation on B and M. They also found low scores on C, E, G, H, and $Q_1$, with a moderately low $Q_3$. They assert that these profiles characterize the alcoholic as having more imaginative capacity and intellectual ability than the normative group and indicate extroversion, passivity, emotional instability, anxiety, and interpersonal undependability.

Costello (1978) found two major subtypes of alcoholics reflected in the 16 PF. The first is characterized by high scores on L, N, O, and $Q_4$, with low scores on C, E, H, I, M, $Q_2$, and $Q_3$. This group, which approximates the stereotype of the alcoholic, manifests anxiety, introversion, and ambivalent dependency. The second subtype shows high scores on G, N, and $Q_3$, with lower scores on B, C, F, $Q_1$ and $Q_2$. This group is more aggressive, more highly socialized, and has less immediate anxiety.

The scores on the O and $Q_4$ scales depend in large part on the degree of anxiety the alcoholic is experiencing at the time of the test. Some alcoholics no longer have immediately intense sources of anxiety and are involved with alcohol in a large part out of habit and personality factors. They are not likely to be as high on the O and $Q_4$ scales and are expected to be lower on the $Q_3$ scale.

☐                   OTHER TEST-RESPONSE PATTERNS

In part, the response of the alcoholic to the WAIS-R is dependent on whether there has been a development of central nervous system impairment (CNSI) (Barrett and Meyer, 1992) (see Chapter 11). It has generally been assumed that alcoholics do well on tests that measure vocabulary (which may be the highest score), similarities, information, and comprehension, but do less well on tests that tap visual motor coordination and on problems in impulsivity. They occasionally miss surprisingly easy items, reflecting a lack of attention and/or CNSI.

Holland and Watson (1980) administered the WAIS-R to alcoholic inpatients, with their subjects obtaining average scores on similarities, comprehension, information, vocabulary, picture completion, and arithmetic. Scores were significantly lower on digit symbol, block design, object assembly, and picture arrangement, which suggests the decrements in visual motor coordination to which others have alluded.

Kish et al. (1980) tested four groups of alcoholics at 6, 15, 21, and 102 days of abstinence from alcohol, using the arithmetic, digit-span, block design, similarities, and digit-symbol WAIS-R subtests. At the time of the first evaluation (6 days), the alcoholics showed scores that were deficient on all the scales used. Scores improved, however, between 6 and 21 days on digit span, block design, and similarities. This pattern continued, indicating that, with reference to the degree of alcoholism they were studying in general, "recoveries in short-term memory and attention, visual, analytic and synthesizing ability, and abstracting ability" did occur, while the decrements in learning new material or handling arithmetic or digit-symbol tasks continued.

Highest elevation on scales B and then T should occur on the MCMI-II (Choca, et al., 1992). This may be accompanied by an elevated D, reflecting the depression often occurring in chronic alcoholics or in alcoholic withdrawal. Personality types most often associated with chronic alcohol intoxication are 2, 3, S, C, and P (Craig et al., 1985). Also, those who are schizoid should score high on scale 1. A score of at least 75 might be expected on one or more of these scales. The borderline passive-aggressive mixed-personality disorder is often seen in chronic alcoholic patients drying out (see Chapter 9). Depressed alcoholics tend to score higher on D, A, 2, 8, C, S, SS, and H than nondepressed alcoholics.

On the Rorschach, a high percentage of oral responses and anatomy responses have been reported. W responses and an increment of Dd responses have been reported by Rapaport et al. (1968) to be associated with addictive tendencies. Others (Gilbert, 1978, 1980) found a high number of anatomy responses, a low F+ percentage, a number of aquatic-animal responses, and some color responses to be related to orality. Phillips and Smith (1953) found an absence and/or decrement of Popular responses in the record. Bug and/or beetle responses are alleged to denote the frustrated dependency commonly associated with alcoholism.

## ☐    TREATMENT OPTIONS

A critical first step in the treatment of alcoholics is simply getting them involved in the treatment program (Committee, 1990). Confrontation techniques are often useful here. Another helpful approach to this problem was demonstrated by Craigie and Ross (1980): They used videotape to model self-disclosing behaviors and treatment-seeking behaviors with one group of alcoholics who were in a detoxification unit. They compared their subsequent degree of involvement in treatment to those who had seen only general films about alcoholism and found that the modeling for self-disclosure and treatment seeking significantly improved the probability of staying in treatment.

Most alcoholics who have been chronically imbibing will need an initial period of detoxification, especially in light of the mild confusion and memory and concentration problems commonly found as acute withdrawal symptoms in the one to three weeks following the cessation of drinking. In addition, a period of hospitalization or other controlled-living environment keeps them from giving in to strong immediate habits that would return them to drinking (Barrett and Meyer, 1992). Drugs such as disulfuram (Antabuse), introduced in 1948 following the serendipitous discovery of its action by two researchers who became ill at a cocktail party, can also be helpful in controling the immediate impulse to drink, although the effects of the Antabuse can be bypassed in short order (Ciraulo and Shader, 1991). The implantation of time-release drugs similar in action to Antabuse is a future option, although there are potential legal liabilities if the client fatally overdosed by combining alcohol and the drug, which is possible. Aversion therapy is also helpful in giving the client additional control over impulses; aversion by electric shock can be supplemented by videotape replays of the person while he or she is drunk (Committee, 1990).

Many alcoholics, like other persons with impulse problems, are relatively unaware of their physiological reactions as they proceed in their abuse (Blane and Leonard, 1987). Analogous to obese individuals, alcoholics are less aware of how much more they drink than normal drinkers, a surprising finding in light of the alcoholic's substantial experience. Clients who are able to return to social drinking rather than to rely on total abstinence are usually better educated, have a shorter drinking history, and are more confident of their ability to avoid drinking that goes out of control (Marlatt et al., 1988). For all alcoholics there is a need for continued monitoring, supportive therapy, and work with the alcoholics' social networks well beyond the point when they have stopped drinking (Barrett and Meyer, 1992).

Continued contact is one of the advantages of Alcoholics Anonymous (AA). In addition to the group-therapy support structure, AA forces alcoholics to publicly label themselves as in need of help and gives them a new social network composed of nondrinkers. Although AA's data supporting the claim of high rates of success are highly flawed methodologically, AA is helpful to persons who have trouble with impulse drinking, who need a new social network, and who are able to work within the somewhat rigid demands of the AA belief system (Marlatt et al., 1988).

Chemotherapy can be helpful in specific instances for weaning the person away from alcohol (Poling et al., 1991), although it introduces the paradoxical problems of treating drug abuse with another drug and secondarily, the implicit message in any chemotherapy that the client's efforts to change are not the critical factor. A combination of methadone and imipramine has been useful for alcoholics where depression is a strong feature. Marital and family-help therapy are important for dealing with the disruption that has usually occurred in the alcoholic's family life and most importantly, for helping the family offer positive support to the alcoholic while not subtly encouraging a return to drinking. Such approaches may be extended beyond the nuclear family to friends and associates in order to keep them from reinforcing drinking (Marlatt et al., 1988).

■  ## Prescription Drug Abuse

The DSM-III-R discusses a number of substance abuse patterns, and the differentiation between organic and psychological patterns mentioned in the alcoholism section is continued in this section. The DSM-III-R does not specifically discuss a pattern called "prescription drug abuse." However, I feel that this is an important pattern because it focuses on the common characteristics of clients rather than making a differentiation according to the specific drug that is abused, an approach that often cuts across personality patterns. Drug companies and physicians should openly acknowledge at least some degree of responsibility for the high level of prescription drug abuse in our society.

While the barbiturates were for many years the most commonly abused prescription drugs, amphetamines and minor tranquilizers are heavily abused in our present society (Ciraulo and Shader, 1991). Since this book will discuss some of the ancillary patterns common to amphetamine abuse, the focus will now be on prescription drug abuse involving minor tranquilizers. This latter abuse pattern typically emerges in individuals between the ages of thirty and sixty, predominantly in middle-class and upper-class females. Female abusers are rather evenly divided between housewives and those who work outside the home. They take prescribed tranquilizers initially for nervousness or insomnia, gradually increase the dosage, and commonly compound the problem with an increased use of alcohol. The likelihood of abuse is further compounded because more than 90 percent of the mood-altering drugs taken by women have been prescribed by physicians who have no special training in psychological disorders (Meyer and Salmon, 1988).

☐     MMPI-2

It has already been noted that in substance abuse in general, the clinician can expect elevations on MMPI-2 scales 2, 4, and 8 (Greene, 1991). This would generally hold for the typical prescription drug abuses as well, although I would accentuate the depression reflected in the 2 scale. the 8 scale—and to a lesser degree the 7 scale—is also likely to be substantially elevated, reflecting tension, a sense of being disturbed, and allied complaints of a vague nature. At the same time, I would expect the 4 scale to be less elevated than one would find in most drug abuse patterns. It will probably be above normal, particularly because these individuals are likely to use the more simplistic defense mechanisms of denial and projection and are also narcissistic in their personality orientation (Blane and Leonard, 1987). These factors also predict moderately high scores on scales 1 and 3.

A low score on scale 5 is expected because these individuals usually identify with the female role, and lower scores on scale 5 are typical of the standard middle-class interest pattern for females. This would vary because of age and whether the woman had a paying job. Because these individuals often feel isolated, and many of them actually live alone, a moderately high score on scale 6 is not uncommon. The depression and the social isolation also suggest that scale 9 is likely to be lower than average.

□              16 PF

The 16 PF patterns should differ somewhat from the overall substance abuse pattern presented in the previous section. Similar to that pattern, a high I score likely reflects a tender-minded and somewhat dependent individual, and the $Q_4$ score, reflecting anxiety, may be somewhat higher than with the standard drug abuse pattern. I expect scale A to be only moderately high, at best, and in some individuals–possibly the housewife who is bordering on agoraphobia because of her anxiety–I expect a low A.

The M score, unlike that obtained in many drug abuse patterns, should be no higher than average. In the case of the housewife, particularly the middle-class one, it may tend toward the low end of the scale. Because anxiety is not being dealt with very well, there should be a high $Q_3$ score. I would expect at least a moderately high L scale, in coordination with a high scale-6 score on the MMPI-2. As in most psychological disorders, C should be low. Shyness and social isolation are likely to be reflected in a low H score and low F and E scores. $Q_1$ should be much lower than that of most drug abuse patterns. The B scale, measuring general intelligence, will depend on the social class and education of the individual, as well as on the degree of depression.


□              OTHER TEST-RESPONSE PATTERNS

Prescription drug abuse is likely to occur in those personality types in which anxiety and depression are major components, and this would be reflected in the MCMI-II by high scores on 2, 8A, C, and S. Those who score high on scale 7 may be more likely to turn to prescription drugs or alcohol than illegal drugs because of the high level of conformity to social rules in these individuals. Because alcohol use is often combined with prescribed medications, elevation on B is probable.


□              TREATMENT OPTIONS

Persons with a prescription drug abuse syndrome are oriented toward medical treatment and often have a middle-class value system, so hospitalization for detoxication fits well with their concept of what should occur. After the initial stage, the clinician has to deal with the tension and depression that often underlie this pattern (Marlatt et al., 1988). The development of a relaxation response is important, particularly since it teaches clients that they can exert some control over their lives and thus do not need to be so dependent on external agents, such as drugs.

Many of these people have withdrawn socially, so assertiveness training and efforts to expand their social networks are most important.

Along with this, the therapist can present the issue of taking drugs as a rational and/or existential choice (Committee, 1990), while emphasizing how the clients can determine many of the events that occur in their worlds and thus the anxieties and responsibilities concomitant with these choices.

Because insomnia and obesity are common problems that lead to prescription drug abuse, as well as to drug abuse problems in general, it is important to help the person cope with them (Hauri, 1991). With either pattern, any form of relaxation training that emphasizes deep-muscle relaxation can help, although the habit control procedures are more important. With regard to weight problems, the reader is referred to the treatment options in the section on amphetamine abuse later in this chapter.

## ■ Polysubstance Abuse

The term "polysubstance abuse" is also not included in DSM-III-R, nor was it in prior versions of the DSM. However, there is in DSM-III-R for the first time the category Polysubstance Dependence (304.90), in which a person has used at least three different substances for at least three months and no substance has predominated. The relative neglect of polysubstance abuse reflects an essential feature of our society: the belief that there is a particular remedy for virtually any physical or psychological disorder that occurs (L'Abate et al., 1992). The polysubstance abuser usually combines the expectancy that an external agent will take care of all problems with a high need for new experiences or sensation seeking (Marlatt et al., 1988; Zuckerman et al., 1980).

The use of a combination of drugs over a period of time is, of course, not new to human society, although in our present culture the pattern is magnified. The epidemic of this pattern is so recent that there are few significant data regarding how these individuals will eventually function in later life. These data are important to obtain, since polysubstance abusers appear to most clinicians to be more disturbed psychologically than those with other abuse patterns (Penk et al., 1980).

Polysubstance abusers could be described as psychotics without the loss of reality contact: They show deterioration of behavior in a wide variety of arenas—work, school performance, interpersonal relationships, and motivation—especially if they have been abusing drugs for a substantial length of time. Affect is generally flat, or when emotion is manifest, it is quite labile. Like the alcoholic, there are many protestations of future positive change, and also like the alcoholic, the promises are seldom fulfilled. This does not appear to be a manipulative deception, as the person seems intellectually committed to changing, yet the motivation and behavior necessary to actuate that change cannot be generated.

Polysubstance abusers are likely to be late adolescents or young adults (Herbert, 1987). They commonly begin ingesting some mood-altering substance in their early teens and quickly progress through the less potent substances to the point where they will use practically anything provided to them. There are some sex differences in the preferences for drugs: Males lean toward the use of alcohol, cocaine, opiates, marijuana, and hashish, and females are more prone to combine diet pills, tranquilizers, relaxants, sedatives, and more recently, tobacco.

□                    MMPI-2

As with alcoholics, scale 4 is consistently high in polysubstance abusers, as is 8, especially with late-adolescent polysubstance abusers (Archer, 1987). It is relatively lower in that subgroup of polysubstance abusers who tend to be depressed and who therefore have high 2, 7, and 8 scales as well. The more psychopathic 6-8 and 8-9-4 patterns are less likely to show depression and more likely to act-out in ways other than simply drug abuse. In those individuals who are high-sensation seekers, the F scale is consistently elevated above a T score of 70. Elevations on scales 1 and 3 are not consistently found with polysubstance abusers, although when these are at least moderately elevated, some feel it is a better prediction of successful participation in treatment programs. As a person continues in the polysubstance abuse pattern, apathy increases and scores on scale 9—and, to a lesser degree, on scales 6 and 4—will be lowered. The apathy and social problems that accompany this pattern predict a high O scale, especially if depression is still present and not diluted by the drug use.

Overall, polysubstance abusers have been found to have more MMPI-2 scores elevated over the 70-T level than do heroin abusers. The latter group on the average shows elevations above 70-T on 2, 4, and 8, whereas polysubstance abusers show them on F, 2, 4, 7, and 8 (Penk et al., 1980). As noted earlier, the MAC is useful here (MacAndrew, 1965; Allen et al., 1991).

□                    16 PF

Four factors consistently found in drug abusers are high F, low G, high H, and moderately high I. The high H measures their venturesomeness, more specifically their willingness to try nonapproved consciousness-altering drugs. The moderately high I, in conjunction with the other scores, reflects reliance and yet also the sensitivity and ambivalent dependency found in alcoholics. The low G measures the sociopathy to be expected here. The high F suggests extroversion and even a slightly manic quality; this primarily depends on when the individual is tested.

These persons' lack of a consistent value system, along with an imaginative although nonpersistent problem-solving approach, predicts a higher M score, and the orientation toward experimentation with drugs and disavowal of standard morality systems predicts a high $Q_1$ score. Similarly, emotional lability and a lack of discipline predict low scores on C and $Q_3$. In the early stages of the pattern, one could also expect relatively high scores on A, B, and $Q_4$, but with increased apathy and decreased ability to generate new behaviors, these scales should decrease. The lack of adequate social skills usually noted in this group (Washton, 1991) would suggest at least a moderately low N score and a moderately raised $Q_2$ score, although the latter is then more appropriately interpreted as group avoidance rather than self-sufficiency.

□     ## OTHER TEST-RESPONSE PATTERNS

A high score on the MCMI-II on T is indicated, and B if alcohol is involved. If psychotic symptomatology occurs, then SS, CC, and/or PP will become elevated. The lack of concern for social rules exhibited by the narcissist and the impulsivity and stimulation seeking of the aggressive and gregarious personalities predispose them toward polydrug abuse; elevations on scales 5 or 6A and sometimes 4 are likely.

□     ## TREATMENT OPTIONS

In many instances, there is an acute toxic reaction to the drug that must be dealt with first. For example, in an acute reaction to cocaine, the standard stabilization sequence may require the use of (1) oxygen to stabilize respiration, (2) Inderal for any cardiac arrhythmias, (3) a barbiturate to reduce central nervous stimulation, or (4) benzodiazepines to control convulsive reactions (Washton and Gold, 1987). This response must be short-term and very carefully monitored in order to avoid secondary abuse patterns.

Since the typical polysubstance abuser is an adolescent or young adult who is showing a deterioration of functions in a wide array of behaviors, a broad-spectrum treatment is necessary. The clinician should be aware of the probability that such clients, while in the detoxication phase, will attempt to obtain addicting drugs through manipulation of their peer group (Herbert, 1987).

Group experiences that emphasize confrontive techniques are often necessary here, so rational-emotive (Lyons and Woods, 1991) or reality therapy (Glasser, 1980) can be an important adjunct to the treatment program. Polysubstance abusers easily verbalize promises and commitments, but they seldom tie commitments to future contingencies, and these therapies, of course, emphasize this linkage. Most importantly, clients should be forced to accept responsibility for the abuse behavior, as these persons often promote the idea that they were "seduced" into the drug culture. Aversive techniques can be helpful in dealing with specific habit patterns. Because family problems may have been a catalyst for the early drug abuse, these need to be worked out via family therapy.

## Amphetamine Use Disorder

As previously noted, the DSM-III-R lists a variety of substances for which abuse can be diagnosed. For many of these substances, especially tobacco and marijuana, there is no consistent personality pattern. However, this book will comment on three diverse patterns—use of amphetamines, cocaine, and opiates—because they are so important in our society today.

The first synthetic amphetamine, a methamphetamine, was compounded in 1919 by the Japanese scientist Ogata. Amphetamines were used to combat fatigue in World War II and are used today in treating hyperactive children. They also have been too commonly prescribed as a diet aid in the past, although there are now increasing restrictions on physicians. The use of amphetamines, or other similarly acting sympathomimetic substances, is often the first step from abuse to dependence. Tolerance to amphetamines builds quickly, so abuse easily leads to increased intake and dependence. Continuation of an intake of amphetamines over a significant period of time leads to paranoid and other psychotic symptoms that may continue for some time after the drug is discontinued.

### DSM-III-R

All of the DSM-III-R diagnostic categories relevant to amphetamines include the concept "or similarly acting sympathomimetic agents," as these are thrown together in the same diagnostic category. In the section on organic diagnosis, there is the category Amphetamine Intoxication (305.70), which refers to the toxic effects of a single recent dose. Criteria include evidence of a recent use of amphetamines and two consequent (within one hour) physiological symptoms, such as tachycardia, elevated blood pressure, nausea, perspiration or chills, or pupillary dilation and such maladaptive behavioral changes as psychomotor excitement, grandiosity, or hypervigilance.

"Delirium" is the term for the syndrome that used to be called "acute brain syndrome." It involves a clouding of consciousness and memory disruption, along with evidence of two of the following: speech difficulty, perceptual problems, sleep problems, or hypo- or hyperactivity. The duration of delirium is typically short, no more than a week. In the specific instance of amphetamines (Amphetamine Delirium, 292.81), delirium lasts only about five hours, starting about an hour after ingestion of the substance, and the DSM-III-R requires evidence of onset within twenty-four hours of ingestion.

The Amphetamine Delusional Disorder (292.11) is the presence of rapidly developing persecutory delusions directly related to amphetamine abuse. Amphetamine Withdrawal requires evidence of one of the following three symptoms: disrupted sleep, psychomotor agitation, or fatigue, within twenty-four hours of the cessation of prolonged heavy use of amphetamines. Suicidal ideation and depression are also common.

Amphetamine Abuse (305.70) and Amphetamine Dependence (304.40) fit the general requirements for the abuse and dependence categories, as described in the prior section on alcohol.

□    MMPI-2

The elevation on scale 4 that is common to most drug abuse patterns is particularly evident in this syndrome. It is combined with an elevation on scale 9, reflecting the heightened activity and agitation associated with amphetamine use. There is also a significant elevation on scale 6, depending on the degree of abuse and whether paranoid ideation has begun. Elevations on scales 8 and 3 are also relatively common. Since amphetamine abuse is often a coping mechanism to deal with depression (Barnett and Gotlib, 1988), this will be manifest in a degree of suppression of scales 2 and 0.

□    16 PF

As in the other drug abuse patterns, low C and $Q_3$ scores are expected. The rejection of standard mores and the high activity level characteristic of amphetamine abuse are reflected in higher scores on E, F, M, and $Q_1$, and probably to a lesser degree on H. Prolonged abuse is likely to result in a higher L score, which reflects the development of a paranoid trend. Since these individuals, especially when they are still experiencing the effects of intoxication, are not likely to pay attention to a particular question for any length of time, scores on B should not be particularly high. A low score on G would be expected, as well as a moderately low score on H, the latter reflecting the autonomic over-reactivity generated by this particular drug.

□    OTHER TEST-RESPONSE PATTERNS

In addition to elevated T, high scores on the MCMI-II on N are likely to occur as a result of physiological arousal and hyperactivity. Since these individuals often show acute paranoia, an elevation on P is possible. As psychomotor activity increases, scores on D will decrease. Long periods of amphetamine use may lead to psychotic symptoms that will elevate PP and SS. Personality elevations that are likely to occur include 4, 5, and 6A, along with those with whom depression was initially a factor: 2, 8A, C, and S. The former will be more likely after repeated amphetamine use, while the latter may be more probable in early states or preceding use.

□         TREATMENT OPTIONS

Because amphetamine abuse or the abuse of other, similar stimulant drugs is often related to underlying anhedonia or depression, existential techniques to confront the apathy—and the cognitive behavior techniques described later for depression—are useful here. It is extremely important to teach persons that they can get involved with and control their worlds without the crutch of a stimulating drug (Committee, 1990).

Covert sensitization, a subcategory of the techniques known as covert conditioning, is useful for drug disorders (Cautela and Wall, 1980). This is an imagery procedure that asks the client to imagine a highly aversive contingency or event occurring immediately on the cessation (in imagination) of the behavior that one is attempting to eliminate (in this case, involving the specific components of the amphetamine abuse sequence). This is repeated over a number of sessions and is efficient to the degree that the client can develop adequate images and that the imagery is experienced as vivid and real.

Since amphetamine abuse is often a logical extension of an abuse of other prescription or nonprescription pills for dieting, concomitant techniques to help with obesity are often useful to prevent the return to the use of amphetamines. Supportive group therapy, teaching of a relaxation response, hypnosis (in some cases), and especially behavioral and confrontive control therapies are useful here (Ellis, 1992). For example, it is important that the person never associate eating with other activities, such as reading or watching television; the eating has to come with independent cues. Teaching the person to be able to interrupt meals for brief periods of time is a useful exercise, as well as eating a salad or small bowl of soup before meals. Analogously, the person should be admonished to take smaller portions into the mouth, chew the food much longer, keep desirable foods out of the house as much as possible, purposely slow the pace of eating, and eat in only one spot in the house. A diary of eating behaviors should be kept so that awareness increases and therefore contingency contracting can be carried out to lower the size of the food portions (Ruderman, 1986).

■         ## Cocaine Abuse

Cocaine has become a favored drug in recent years (Washton, 1991). Its abuse by many sports and entertainment idols has received much media attention. Nevertheless, cocaine has been used for centuries. It is an alkaloid derivative of coca leaves, which were chewed by the Aztecs and are still used by at least four million Indians in South America. Such diverse people as Arthur Conan Doyle's character Sherlock Holmes, John Philip Sousa, and even Sigmund Freud have sung the praises of cocaine.

A number of people became inadvertently habituated to cocaine in the United States during the late 1800s by drinking Coca-Cola. John Pemberton, an Atlanta druggist, combined cocaine with sugar and kolanut extract in a brass pot in his backyard to make the original Coca-Cola, which he advertised as a "brain medicine." When the Pure Food and Drug Law of 1906 outlawed the use of cocaine, caffeine was substituted in "the real thing." Today, refined cocaine is usually sniffed in small amounts. Most of what passes for cocaine is not pure (free-base) cocaine but cocaine hydrochloride, a salt that is approximately 85 percent cocaine by weight. Pure cocaine is sometimes smoked, a psychophysiologically more dangerous process than sniffing. When cocaine is mixed with alcohol, a new substance called cocaethylene forms in the liver, which amplifies the effects of cocaine and increases the risk of heart attack by almost twenty times.

☐     ## DIAGNOSTIC CONSIDERATIONS

The DSM-III-R diagnostic considerations that apply to substance abuse and dependence in general apply here as well. In addition, Spotts and Schontz (1984) have found that middle-class and upper-middle-class cocaine users, especially males, show an intense, narcissistic, competitive, and achievement-oriented personality, with a strong fear of intimacy and vulnerability in relationships, so diagnostic considerations for the narcissistic and obsessive-compulsive personality disorders (see Chapter 9) would also apply here. Johnson, et al. (1992) find that the 2/4-4/2, 2-7/7-2, and 4-9/9-4 MMPI-2 profiles account for 65 percent of the profiles of cocaine abusers. A stairstep progression on scales 1, 2, 3, 4, 7, and 8 has been noted in a population of cocaine abusers, with scores in general being significantly elevated above normal and with an inverted V on the validity scales (F being the highest score). Since cocaine use will often facilitate paranoid ideation (Washton, 1991), scale 6 may be elevated.

☐     ## TEST CONSIDERATIONS

MMPI-2 and 16 PF patterns are usually similar to the overall substance abuse pattern discussed at the beginning of this chapter. As in other patterns of substance abuse, a high T is very likely on the MCMI-II. To the extent that alcohol abuse is involved, B will be elevated. On the MCMI-II scales representing the persistent personality features (1–8), expect elevation on 4 and 5. Scale 4 reveals a sociable self-image and a preference for a fast-paced life style. Also, the immature stimulus-seeking behaviors and manipulation of others to receive attention will be evident here. A high 5 shows the interpersonal exploitiveness that typifies a cocaine abuser. As the chronicity of drug use increases, so, too, do the elevations on scales C and N. High C scores reflect the endogenous mood or other depressive components that often underlie cocaine abuse, while high N scores reflect hypomanic characteristics that also may accompany abuse.

On the Rorschach, a heightened level of defensiveness will be manifested by a small number of total responses (R), an increased number of W, F, and Popular responses. A disproportionately high L score is also predicted, indicating that the subject has refused to process the stimuli as requested. A high number of M and Y responses may indicate a situational crisis related to the abuse condition. Because FM answers are increased under altered states of consciousness (Exner, 1986), cocaine abusers should show a higher frequency of them.

☐  TREATMENT OPTIONS

Any inpatient treatment plan should have the goals of detoxifying the person's biological system and directly and strongly confronting the destructive psychological patterns (Barrett and Meyer, 1992). Calcium channel blockers (e.g., nitrendipine) directly act to reverse the effects of cocaine toxicity. Agonists (i.e., drugs that substitute for the effects of the drugs), such as buprenorphine, can be very helpful. Confrontation techniques, pioneered with heroin abusers by group treatment centers such as Synanon and Daytop Village, are used with cocaine addicts as well. The goal is to get the addict to assume control of his or her own decisions; to plan more adaptive behaviors to satisfy vocational, interpersonal, and sexual needs; and then to look at more characterological and existential issues.

Many such addicts need intensive psychotherapy with a focus on the avoidance of dependency and unresolved spiritual and intimacy-betrayal and intimacy-avoidance crises. Such psychotherapy should take into account the often underlying depression and at the same time allow socially acceptable outlets for the commonly higher-than-average level of stimulation seeking. As some success is attained, involvement in a group therapy modeled on AA principles can be effective (Washton, 1991).

■  ## Opiod Use Disorder

Even though the opium poppy has been used as a mind-altering substance for at least 6,000 years, two events in particular spurred the increased abuse patterns noted recently. Early in the nineteenth century, morphine (ten times stronger than opium) was isolated from the opium poppy, and approximately fifty years later, Alexander Wood perfected a more effective drug delivery system: the hypodermic needle. Morphine was soon included in many patient medicines, although it was supplanted in use near the end of the century when Wright discovered heroin, a semisynthetic opioid derived from morphine. Interestingly, heroin was at one time used to cure morphine addiction, just as another addicting drug, methadone, is now used to treat heroin addiction.

Heroin induces a warm, sensual euphoria, usually followed by sleepiness and lethargy. Tolerance develops rapidly, however, and eight to twelve hours after an injection the individual is likely to experience withdrawal symptoms, the severity depending on the amount ingested and the duration of time the person has been abusing. Even so, these symptoms are seldom as severe as the mad ravings portrayed in the media. In fact, most addicts describe withdrawal as quite similar to influenza symptoms.

Perhaps no one has expressed so clearly the reinforcement from heroin as French humanist and poet Jean Cocteau:

**Everything we do in life, including love, is done in an express train traveling towards death. To smoke opium is to leave the train while in motion; it is to be interested in something other than life and death. (Jarvik, 1967, p. 52.)**

☐             DSM-III-R

The DSM-III-R requires the same criteria for opioid abuse and dependence as it does for all the substances heretofore mentioned. In the section on organic mental disorders, the DSM-III-R lists Opioid Intoxication (305.50), which is the effects of a single dose toxic enough to produce pupillary contraction, psychomotor retardation, apathy, and the experience of either euphoria or dysphoria. Itching, flushing of the skin, nausea, and analgesia also typically occur. The diagnosis requires (1) evidence of recent use; (2) pupillary contraction, signified by at least one sign, such as drowsiness, attention or memory problems, or slurred speech; and (3) maladaptive behavioral changes, such as psychomotor retardation or dysphoria.

Prolonged or heavy use often results in Opioid Withdrawal (292.00), in which three of the following are experienced on cessation of use: nausea, muscle aches, craving for an opioid, lacrimation or rhinorrhea, pupillary dilation, sweating, diarrhea, yawning, fever, or insomnia.

☐             MMPI-2

Elevations on scales 2, 4, and 8, which are generally characteristic of the drug abuse patterns, are found in opiate abuse (Penk et al., 1980). Elevations on scales 3 and 6 are also likely, which reflects the egocentricity and problems with authority characteristic of this pattern, although it is true that the elevation on scale 6 may not be as high as it is for a person who is dependent on amphetamines. In certain opiate abusers, there is a high scale 9, indicating a person who is easily bored and has a low frustration tolerance and is in that sense narcissistic. In another subgroup, the more relaxed or bohemian opiate abuser, a 4–5 code type is common. Scores on scales 2 and 9 will vary depending on whether the person is feeling euphoric or dysphoric. Because the person is not likely to be tested while in the midst of an episode, a rise on scale 2 is more likely. It is interesting that opiate abusers seldom show a profile as pathological as most of the other significant drug abusers do. The MAC may be useful here (MacAndrew, 1965), although it is usually more effective in pointing to existent or potential substance abusers who have higher levels of extroversion and/or sensation seeking (Allen et al., 1991), which is not always the case in opiate abusers.

## 16 PF

Opiate abusers are likely to be high on scales I and M. This reflects their paradoxical indulgence in fantasy while they maintain an apathetic view of events in their world, along with their avoidance of either stress or commitment whenever possible. They are also relatively high on O, although typically not as high as alcoholics. They are relatively high on scale A, which is different from a number of other drug abuse patterns; this reflects their lack of paranoid response toward the environment, at least in relation to the amount seen in the other drug abuse patterns. They tend to be slightly above average on L, although this will vary depending on the testing situation.

Opiate abusers tend to be average on scales H, $Q_1$, and $Q_3$, and lower on N, which again differentiates them from those with other drug abuse patterns. However, like all of these patterns, they are low on scales C and E. They are also low on B, reflecting their lower socioeconomic status and educational attainment, as well as the lack of initiative found in these persons.

## OTHER TEST-RESPONSE PATTERNS

Keiser and Lowy (1980) present evidence that heroin addicts tend to be significantly higher on digit-span scores than on other WAIS-R subtests. This fits with the evidence that a digit-span score well above the mean of the client's other WAIS-R subtest scores is correlated with an interpersonal-detachment syndrome characterized by superficial and emotionally distant relationships.

## TREATMENT OPTIONS

The confrontational group experience first evolved with the opioid disorders, primarily through institutions like Synanon and Phoenix House. These groups are effective with a number of clients, although they have been burdened by problems resulting from their resistance to any reliance on professionally trained staff. As a result, there is a lack of objectivity in assessing techniques and outcomes and a lack of awareness about the wide range of treatment techniques discussed in the professional literature. In any case, a method of providing a more therapeutic social network is critical in dealing with opioid addicts, as they easily return to their destructive peer-group setting (Herbert, 1987).

Naltrexone, an antagonist, blocks the opiate from its brain receptor so the client does not get high, and it can be helpful as long as the client continues taking it. Unfortunately, many stop taking it against therapeutic advice.

Just as heroin was once used to treat morphine addiction, methadone, also an addicting drug, is now used to treat heroin addiction (Ciraulo and Shader, 1991). It appears to be effective in certain cases, although the clinician must be aware of possible secondary abuse of the drug used for treatment, particularly in addicts who are psychopathic. Methadone can be useful at least in the initial stages of treatment. Since, as an agonist, it does not cause the distinct euphoria of heroin, it can be taken orally and less often than heroin; also, its lower cost may allow the addict to move out of the criminal system.

Tranquilizers and/or antidepressants can often be helpful in reducing psychological withdrawal or allied psychopathology. While clomidine has often been cited as effective, acetorphan has also been found to be effective (Hartmann et al., 1991).

# CHAPTER 3

# The Schizophrenic and Paranoid Disorders

■  ## Schizophrenia

Many clinicians would argue that schizophrenia is the most serious of all mental disorders (Tamminga and Schulz, 1991; Bernstein et al., 1988). Although other disorders are more common or may involve more immediate distress, the pervasive effect of a schizophrenic disorder throughout all areas of an individual's functioning and the complexity of problems it presents in assessment and intervention support the assertion that it is the most serious mental disorder. About one out of every one hundred people will receive a diagnosis of schizophrenia in his or her lifetime (Myers et al., 1984). This is a percentage that is pretty stable across and within most cultures. This fits with the concept that genetic factors are critical in the development of some schizophrenics, just as there is evidence that brain dysfunction from other causes may be important in other schizophrenics. The schizophrenic who has been released after a first hospitalization unfortunately still has about a 50 percent chance of returning to the hospital within two years. It has been estimated that schizophrenics occupy approximately two-thirds of our mental hospital beds and almost one-fourth of all hospital beds. These statistics reflect the long period of time that schizophrenics traditionally spend in institutions.

Fenton and McGlashan (1991) found that negative symptoms (affective flattening, alogia, avolition/apathy, anhedonia/asociality, and attentional impairment) were directly correlated with a high rate of remission, slow onset, and higher probability of permanent disability. Positive symptoms (hallucinations, delusions, positive formal thought disorder, and bizarre behavior) predicted future hospitalizations but were relatively weak and unspecific as predictors of other variables.

Two negative symptoms, anhedonia and affective flattening, were the strongest independent predictors of negative outcome, and patients with the poorest long-term outcome tended to show an increase in negative symptoms during the early years of their illness. Early and progressive negative symptoms may signal a process leading to long-term disability.

There are a number of premorbid predictors of schizophrenia worth assessing in a client (Tien and Eaton, 1992; Tamminga and Schulz, 1991; Gottesman, 1991):

1. A schizophrenic parent or parents, a less potent variable being the presence of other schizophrenic blood relatives. There is evidence that for daughters, the earlier their mother became schizophrenic, the higher is the likelihood that they, too, will become schizophrenic. For sons, however, this is not as critical, with a more important issue being the time of separation from a disturbed mother. The earlier separation occurs, the more damaging it is for a son.

2. A history of prenatal disruption, birth problems, viral or bacterial infections, or toxic situations during pregnancy.

3. Low birth weight and/or low IQ relative to siblings.

4. Hyperactivity; cognitive slippage; any signs of central nervous system dysfunction, especially difficulties in attention tasks with distracting stimuli and/or eye tracking; convulsions; evidence of enlarged cerebral ventricles; significant reaction time problems; or an abnormally rapid recovery rate of the autonomic nervous system.

5. An early role as the "scapegoat" or odd member of the family.

6. Parenting marked by emotional and/or discipline inconsistencies, including double messages.

7. Rejection by peers in childhood or adolescence and perception by either teachers or peers as being significantly more irritable or unstable than other children.

8. Rejection of peers, especially if accompanied by odd thinking processes, ambivalent emotional responses, or a lack of response to standard pleasure sources.

9. An inability to develop a stable committed relationship, especially for men. For example, never-married men have 50 times higher odds of developing schizophrenia than men who married; for women it is 14 times higher for never-marrieds over married (Tien and Eaton, 1992).

A common cause path (Meyer and Salmon, 1988; Gottesman, 1991) for the development of a long-term schizophrenic pattern is presented in Figure 3.1.

**FIGURE 3.1**    A Common Developmental Path in Schizophrenia

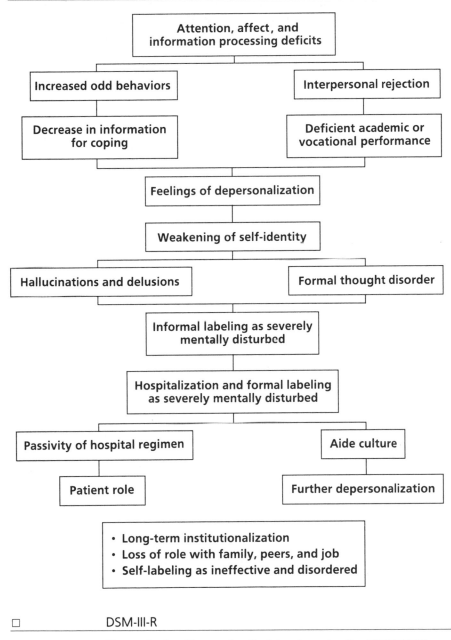

☐         DSM-III-R

To apply the diagnosis of schizophrenia, the DSM-III-R requires evidence of one of the following: either (1) two of the following: (a) delusions, (b) catatonic behavior, (c) incoherence or marked loosening of associations, (d) prominent hallucinations (throughout the day for several days or several times a week for several weeks, not just brief moments), or (2) bizarre delusions, or (3) prominent hallucinations of a voice with no depressive or elated content, or two voices, or a voice keeping up a running commentary on the person's behavior or thoughts. There must be an active phase of at least one week, and the disorder must continue for at least six months with or without a prodromal or residual phase.

Typical delusions of schizophrenics include somatic delusions, delusions of being controlled, thought broadcasting, and grandiose delusions. This symptomatology must not be directly related to a depressive or manic disorder, or else the affective disorder must be a relatively minor component. During the active phase of the disorder, there must be some significant impairment in areas of daily functioning, such as interpersonal relationships, school, or work.

Pathological hallucinations or delusions may sometimes be difficult to separate from culturally sanctioned experiences that are not particularly pathological in nature. These latter experiences are usually characterized by (1) socially appropriate, productive, and adequate coping behavior before and after the experience; (2) time limitations of a few hours to a few days; (3) a reasonable degree of family and/or subgroup support; (4) a resultant gain in social prestige or self-esteem; (5) culturally congruent experiences in the delusions or hallucinations; and (6) a relative absence of psychopathological indicators.

Auditory hallucinations, the most common in schizophrenia, are sometimes difficult to discriminate between true and faked hallucinations. They are more likely to be faked if (Rogers, 1988; Resnick, 1991)

1. they are vague or if the person reports it is hard to hear them or to understand them
2. they are reported as continuous rather than sporadic or intermittent
3. the hallucination is reported as not being associated with a delusion
4. stilted language is reported as the content of the hallucination
5. the content specifically exonerates the individual from some blame or responsibility
6. the person reporting the voices can give no strategy to diminish the voices
7. the person says that he or she obeyed all commands in the hallucinations

Delusions that are most characteristic of paranoid schizophrenia (as well as the upcoming paranoid disorders) also can be faked as part of an attempt to avoid responsibility. In general, the clues that lead one to believe that the reporting of a delusion may be faked are

1. an abrupt onset or cessation
2. if the person is eager to call attention to the delusion or leads the discussion to this topic

3. if the person's conduct is not consistent with the delusion (and the person is not a "burned-out" schizophrenic who generates few or no behaviors anyway)
4. if there is reported bizarre content in the delusion without disordered thoughts or hallucinations
5. if the delusion (or hallucination) somehow specifically reduces the relevant responsibility or culpability

The preschizophrenic personality of individuals who later become schizophrenic can often be described as eccentric and isolated, mildly confused and disorganized, suspicious, and/or withdrawn. As a result, such individuals are likely to require the additional diagnostic qualifier of such categories as schizotypal, borderline, introverted, or paranoid personality disorder (Widiger et al., 1986).

Several studies have pointed to the problems of making accurate subclassifications within the overall category of schizophrenia (Tamminga and Schulz, 1991). Most clinicians find such classification meaningful, however, because it clarifies communications and facilitates discussions of treatment and prognosis. Structured interviews, such as the Schedule of Affective Disorders and Schizophrenia (SADS), can be useful here, as well as in the overall diagnostic process (Wetzler, 1989). While relatives have a 5 to 10 percent increased risk of schizophrenia, depending on the diagnostic criteria used, well-defined subtypes do not tend to run in families. Regarding the overall diagnostic category of schizophrenia, a landmark study by the World Health Organization (1979) has demonstrated the reliability of this concept in a variety of sociocultural settings.

☐          MMPI-2

As might be expected, most clinicians agree that scale 8 is typically elevated above 65 T in schizophrenics, since this directly reflects their tendency to escape reality through fantasy behavior and to process information inadequately. Most schizophrenics tend to score in the 70–85 range, particularly as they move toward chronicity. Extremely high scores are more likely to indicate severe patterns within other diagnostic categories or to reflect an attempt to fake-bad (Graham, 1987). They tend to be high on the Bizarre Mentation (BIZ) and Family Problems (FAM) content scales.

A variety of scale patterns have been noted (Moldin et al., 1987). Lachar (1974) points out that the 7-8/8-7 profile suggests possible chronic schizophrenia, whereas the 2-7-8 code type, or a similar combination, is more likely to be associated with an earlier stage of schizophrenia (Edell, 1987; Golden and Meehl, 1979). A pattern that appears especially predictive of schizophrenia is the F scale (in T scores) being in the range 65–85; scale 8, 70–90; and scale 7 less than scale 8.

When a profile is obtained where scale 8 is high and scale 1 is around

85 T and at the same time 10 to 20 T greater than scales 2 and 3, this suggests a schizophrenic with somatic delusions. The unusual 3-8/8-3 profile, especially when 1 is also high, also indicates an individual with high somatic concerns but with a greater tendency to dissociate (Moldin et al., 1987). A primary elevation on scale 6 is not consistently obtained in schizophrenic profiles, although it is likely in paranoid schizophrenics and occurs occasionally in some catatonic schizophrenics.

The 8-4/4-8 profile also can indicate schizophrenia (Greene, 1991), particularly when hostility and anger are major components. If a 4-8 client shows an elevation on the BIZ and FAM content scales, it points to schizophrenia, whereas elevations on the Cynicism and Anger content scales should suggest an aggressive personality disorder as the first option. When the clinician sees an 8-9/9-8 profile, it is commonly that of a schizophrenic who finds it extremely difficult to vocalize the issues at hand, who is consistently problematic to work with therapeutically, and who is often disruptive in functioning.

Schizophrenics are usually elevated on the F scale, and Gynther et al. (1973b) note that a very high F scale obtained in a psychiatric population is likely to indicate a confused individual rather than one who is faking-bad. Although it does occur in certain instances, a major elevation on scale 3 is not typical in schizophrenic profiles. A particularly high scale 5 in a woman who appears to fit within the traditional femine role should alert the clinician to look for other indications of schizophrenia. In a somewhat similar vein, Holland and Watson (1980) find male schizophrenic VA-hospital inpatients to be high on F, L, 5, 6, and 8.

In this regard, Goldberg's formula (Graham, 1977) for determining psychosis using T scores should be noted. The L score must be added to the scores for scales 6 and 8, and then the scores on scales 3 and 7 must be subtracted. Using a lower cutoff point of 45, one is allegedly correct 70 percent of the time in using the label schizophrenia, although this seems to be a sign of paranoid schizophrenia more than schizophrenia in general. Newmark's formula (T on Sc > 80, < 100; total Sc raw score is no more than 35 percent of K items; T score on F > 75, < 95; on Pt > Sc) has proven to be effective, primarily with schizophrenics under forty-five years of age (Newmark and Hutchins, 1980).

□     ## 16 PF

On the 16 PF, schizophrenics tend to be high on I, M, O, and $Q_4$. This reflects their propensity to engage in fantasy as a way to control intra-psychic conflict and their tendency to withdraw and not deal in a practical fashion with the world. This pattern at the same time reflects the high level of anxiety and insecurity experienced by most of these individuals. This fits well with the concept that they are stimulation-avoidant, as opposed to the primary psychopath who is stimulation-seeking.

Schizophrenics also tend to be low on scale C though surprisingly, often not as low as many of the other psychiatric-disorder categories. They are consistently low on scales F and H, which reflects a stimulation-avoidant pattern, as well as the depression that is likely to accompany such a high level of disturbed functioning. Numerous schizophrenic individuals may score in the average range, but in general, they tend to be somewhat lower on G, $Q_2$, and $Q_3$. Corresponding with their significant inability to cope with the world, they also tend to be low on scale B. As schizophrenia becomes chronic, C, E, F, and H tend to be lower and I and M higher.

OTHER TEST-RESPONSE PATTERNS

On the WAIS-R, several patterns are commonly found in schizophrenia (Feinberg and McIlvried, 1991; Newmark, 1985; Anastasi, 1987). First, subtest scatter is common and the verbal-scaled score tends to be higher than the performance-scaled score. Within the subtests themselves, there is a tendency to succeed on harder items while at the same time, surprisingly, to fail some of the easier items. Scores tend to be higher on block design, occasionally higher on information and vocabulary, while typically lower on arithmetic, picture arrangement, digit symbol, and comprehension. A low similarities score often includes several overinclusion responses, and a low score on comprehension is usually accompanied by evidence of irrelevant associations. A high similarities score is a good prognostic sign for schizophrenia. There are often peculiar arrangements in the picture arrangement test; in the picture completion test, frequent reference is made to items not intended to be together. In addition, process schizophrenics do less well than reactive schizophrenics on the picture completion test, relative to their other scores.

Ogdon (1977) reviewed a wide range of studies that used the Rorschach and noted several response patterns found to be associated with psychosis in general and schizophrenia in particular: (1) poor quality and a low number of human movement responses (those in which humans are perceived as involved in at least some minimal action); (2) animal movement responses in which the organization of the response is very poor; (3) an abnormally high or low number of pure-form responses (in which the client made the response based simply on the form of the blot, without reference to any other aspect); (4) responses dictated only by the color of the blot (that is, pure-C responses); (5) an abnormally low number of responses in which all aspects of the blot are integrated into the response (whole, or W, responses); (6) a lower-than-average number of Popular, or P, responses (responses perceived by most people); and/or (7) perseverating by continually seeing the same or analogous responses throughout several blots in sequence.

Exner (1978, 1986) has noted several differences between schizophrenics and normals on the Rorschach. Schizophrenics obtain more F and M responses than do either borderlines or normal persons, although there may be a high percentage of F responses. Borderline individuals average 6.4 Popular responses, whereas schizophrenics average only 3.6. Not surprisingly, schizophrenics have almost twice as many unusual responses as borderline cases and certainly far more than normal individuals. Schizophrenics also give three times fewer S responses and two times fewer T determinates than normal individuals. More specifically, schizophrenics scored significantly lower than normals on R, D, DQt, Sum T, H, Xt%, Pop, and Afr and higher on Dd, (FQw) − (fQ-), Sum Y, L, Sum SP.SL (Mason et al., 1985).

Exner (1986) has developed a "Schizophrenic Index" (p. 423) that includes the following criteria:

1. $X + \% < 70$
2. Sum FQ- $>$ Sum $FQ_\mu$, or $X - \% > 20$
3. $M = O$, or WSUMG $> 11$
4. (Sum DV + DR + INCOM + FABCOM + ALOG + CONTAM) $> 4$
5. (Sum DR + FABCOM + ALOG + CONTAM) $>$ (Sum DV + INCOM), or M- $> 1$

Exner asserts that a cutoff score of 4 or 5 is indicative of schizophrenia, but this would probably not always allow an acceptable number of false-positives or -negatives, but these signs are a useful general indicator of thought/perceptual distortion.

Others have noted that schizophrenics are more inclined than other groups to show a massing of pure-color responses, and they occasionally show very arbitrary FC responses (e.g., pink rats). Color-shock or pleasantly verbalized comments about color in the cards are considered to be favorable prognostic signs in schizophrenia (Phillips and Smith, 1953). Along with the deviant verbalizations—such as fabulized responses (two rabbits with a baseball bat), contaminations (the head of a beetle-tiger), and other incongruous combinations (a woman with a head of a horse)—schizophrenics tend to show overelaborate symbolism and absurd responses in the patterns and a number of mangled and distorted perceptions. Schizophrenics are more likely to show a perseveration of Dd responses, which reflects a high degree of overcontrol in their response patterns combined with underactivity in the actual perceptions. They also may show a massing of sex responses, particularly referring more often to the sexual act rather than to sexual organs. As in most of the tests, there is a tendency for the quality of responses to deteriorate toward the end of the test. Not only do schizophrenics show a higher percentage of F responses, but they also show higher levels of articulation of the object as they perceive it within the F response. In essence, their ego resources are being channeled into fantasy behavior.

The Thought Disorder scale on the MCMI-II is designed to reflect

schizophrenic thinking, but is not always effective because it is susceptible to faking-good (i.e., schizophrenics who tend to be nonreporters of
symptoms do not show up on this scale) (Jackson et al., 1991).
Schizophrenics do tend to be higher on 2, S, 1, and 8B.

On the Thematic Apperception Test (TAT), schizophrenics are prone
to tell rambling, confused stories or to have a very restricted response
record. They are more likely to make comments of self-reference or show
personal reactions, such as disgust, in response to the cards. They make
bizarre comments and show less ability to concentrate on their responses.
From a thematic standpoint, schizophrenics are more likely than normals to show direct sexual and aggressive themes; themes of persecution and/or omnipotence; characters changing in confused, odd, or
magical ways; ideas of reference (especially linking the present card to
a prior card); juxtaposition of extremes (e.g., acts of murder and
tenderness); disorientation as to person, place, and time; lack of clear
body boundaries; gross deviation from the stimulus properties; and
grossly destructive bizarre or sexual themes (Bellak, 1993; Karon, 1981).

Proverbs have also been used to distinguish schizophrenics from other
groups. Johnson (1966) found that only those proverbs that are commonly
understood ("It never rains, but it pours") are consistently useful in
distinguishing schizophrenics from other groups, such as persons with
organic brain damage (and these are the four proverbs included in the
Meyer Information Battery listed in Appendix A). Schizophrenics are
more likely to give peculiar, abstract responses to these proverbs.
Figures on the Bender-Gestalt are likely to be boxed, to be drawn in
a confused order, and to be drawn overly large (Rossini and Kaspar,
1987).

During active phases of schizophrenia, disorientation, inappropriate
affect, hallucinations, and delusions will be represented by SS scores
above 84 on the MCMI-II. Elevations on CC and PP are likely to the
extent that depression and paranoia are present. In general, elevations
on 1, 2, 3, and 8A have been found to be characteristic of inpatient
samples, who are often schizophrenics (McCann and Suess, 1988).

Persons with basic personality patterns encompassing traits of the
schizoid, borderline, schizotypal, and avoidant personalities are more
likely to use schizophrenic patterns as coping devices or to decompen-
sate to a schizophrenic pattern. Elevations on scales 1, 2, C, and S may
be present and representative of precipitating personality styles. Scales
4 and 7 should be somewhat depressed, as these patterns are not likely
to develop schizophrenic disorders. Overall, the MCMI-II does not appear to be as effective as the MMPI-2 in assessing schizophrenia (Patrick,
1988).

Iacono (1991) notes several physiological markers for schizophrenia
that could be integrated into a specialized evaluation, e.g., dysfunctional
smooth-pursuit eye tracking, differences in event-related brain
potentials.

□    TREATMENT OPTIONS

There are several prognostic indicators that point to a positive chance of remission once schizophrenia does occur (Tien and Eaton, 1992; Meyer and Salmon, 1988; Kay and Lindenmayer, 1987): (1) sexual-marital status: being married or at least having a history of stable, consistent sexual-social adjustment, (2) a family history of affective disorder rather than schizophrenic disorder, (3) presence of an affective pattern (either elation or depression) in the acute stage of the schizophrenic disorder, (4) abrupt onset of the disorder and onset later than early adulthood, (5) adequate premorbid school and/or vocational adjustment, (6) evidence of premorbid competence in interpersonal relationships and a higher socioeconomic status, (7) a short length of stay in the hospital with an absence of electroconvulsive therapy (ECT) treatment, (8) nonparanoid subdiagnosis, (9) a family history of alcoholism, (10) psychomotor retardation, (11) a relatively high score on the WAIS-R similarities subscale score, and (12) evidence of clear precipitating factors at the onset of the disturbance. However, the clinician should note the markedly increased risk for suicide (with estimates up to 10% of lifetime prevalence rates) in schizophrenics.

More than almost any other disorder, schizophrenia warrants a multifaceted treatment plan because of its complexity. Chemotherapy—usually with the phenothiazines, the butyrophenones, or the thioxanthenes—is useful as one component in the treatment of many schizophrenics, particularly for those who are hospital-prone clients of low competence (see Chapter 17). Clozapine has been helpful for some schizophrenics who do not respond well to other medications. However, 1–2 percent of persons taking clozapine are at risk to develop agranulocytosis, a life-threatening blood disorder, so consistent monitoring is required.

"Positive" symptoms—that is, those marked by their presence, such as hallucinations, delusions, and incoherent speech—respond more quickly to chemotherapy, while "negative" symptoms—those marked by their absence, such as social-isolation withdrawal, lack of communication skills, and poverty of speech—do not respond as well. Since there can be major problems with a schizophrenic's ability to take medication after being released from the hospital, the long-acting agents, such as the phenothiazine Prolixin, can be useful, although they have a restricted range of effectiveness and there are problems with side effects.

As with all the antipsychotic chemotherapies, approximately 35 percent of the clients show muscular problems and feelings of lethargy alternating with restlessness. Approximately 5 percent (up to 40% in the elderly) develop tardive dyskinesia, a typically irreversible syndrome that involves grimacing, lip-smacking, and involuntary neck and head movements. Also, particularly with the phenothiazines (the most commonly used drug), a significant number of deaths due to aspiration asphyxiation have been noted because this drug tends to suppress the gag reflex. In addition to these side effects, there is loss of creativity and spontaneity and a reinforcement of the patient role, because the client sees treatment as totally external to her- or himself. Although chemotherapy can be useful, antipsychotic drugs are prescribed too often and/or at too high a dosage (Rifkin et al., 1991).

Electroconvulsive therapy (ECT) has been used with schizophrenics since its discovery, but it has not shown marked success. Psychosurgery, dialysis, and megavitamin therapies have been tried with increasing frequency in recent years, but as yet there is little significant evidence of their success with schizophrenia (Valenstein, 1986).

Token economies have been used effectively in bringing the disrupted and institutionalized schizophrenic back to a semblance of normal functioning, and it is in this development of simple and basic behaviors that token economies are most applicable. Milieu therapy, occasionally only a euphemism for sitting around the ward, is optimally a total treatment approach that adds the values of patient-governance and input to the concepts of group process and the "moral therapy" of the nineteenth century (Adler, 1988). Milieu therapy should also include an available combination of new and effective treatment techniques directed toward the overall improvement of schizophrenia. In this regard, occupational, activity, and art therapies can be useful adjuncts. Developing adequate vocational skills is important, and these skills should not be for obsolescent vocations, as is often the case in prison and mental hospital programs. Social-skills training is not only effective for the specific skills taught, but also generalizes to other situations outside the treatment environment. The rehabilitation techniques used for head-injury patients can also be helpful in dealing with the attention dysfunctions that are critical to the schizophrenic process. Cognitive retraining and family and group therapy as the person moves back into the home system are also important.

Ellsworth et al. (1979) thoroughly examined the issues in milieu therapy and advised that the milieu is much more effective when there is a mixture of both chronic and acute patients. They noted a cluster of specific factors that facilitate the positive effects of milieu therapy, notably the availability of a separate television room, recent magazines and other reading materials, music at meals, stalls separating the toilets, and pleasant pictures on the walls. This may only be a reflection of the Hawthorne Effect, wherein change per se—not necessarily positive change—acts to produce a positive effect. Whatever the reason, these changes promote a positive effect.

## ■ Undifferentiated Schizophrenia (295.9x)

This category is marked by prominent schizophrenic symptoms; however, there are several symptoms from various subtypes, or for some reason the criteria for one of the other categories are not quite fulfilled.

This category fits most clearly the previous comments, testing indicators, and treatment suggestions for the overall category of schizophrenia.

# ■ Disorganized Schizophrenia (295.1x)

Disorganized Schizophrenia was termed Hebephrenia in earlier DSM classification systems. The DSM-III-R diagnosis of disorganized schizophrenic denotes an individual who shows incoherence, disorganized behavior or loosening of associations, and remarkably flat or inappropriate affect, often in the form of random giggling.

Delusions and hallucinations do not show the structure or pattern common to other schizophrenic disorders. Other elements commonly associated with disorganized schizophrenia include odd facial grimaces, extreme social withdrawal, and very peculiar mannerisms. As would be expected from the preceding description, social functioning is severely disrupted.

Overall, disorganized schizophrenia is characterized by very poor premorbid adjustment, slow onset (usually starting in adolescence or early adulthood), neurological problems, and chronicity of adjustment. These individuals are likely to develop more chronic and apathetic patterns with time, and the likelihood of significant long-term remission is quite low.

## □ MMPI-2

Gynther et al., (1973a) note that the 8-9/9-8 profile is commonly associated with the behaviors typical of disorganized schizophrenia. This is particularly true if the affect is silly or inappropriate. When it is flat, scale 9 tends to be lower and scales 7 and 2 are likely to be higher. Disorganized schizophrenics are often so severely disturbed in functioning that they cannot adequately complete the MMPI-2, at least to the degree where it is suitable for scoring. The reader is referred to the section on malingering (Chapter 16), since some of that material relates to the patterns to be expected here.

## □ 16 PF

The same problems in adequately scoring the MMPI-2 also hold true for the 16 PF. In those individuals who are able to perform the task adequately, their 16 PF profile is likely to fit the overall schizophrenic pattern mentioned earlier, with only a few minor changes: Scale C is likely to be lower in disorganized schizophrenics than in others, as are scales N and $Q_3$. They also tend to be higher on scale A and lower on scale L, which reflects their willingness to interact interpersonally as expressed through fantasy, but their inability to actuate this interaction in reality.

☐          OTHER TEST-RESPONSE PATTERNS

While the overall schizophrenic pattern is most likely to be reflected on the WAIS-R, this test emphasizes the very odd response patterns to an even greater degree. Proverbs are especially peculiar, and the disorganized schizophrenic is probably not able to provide even the distorted rationale that paranoid schizophrenics may volunteer if they feel comfortable enough with the tester (Feinberg and McIlvried, 1991). If the affect of the disorganized schizophrenic is silly or incongruous, there is usually an extreme scatter in the quality of responses, and this will affect the subtest patterns and the within-test scoring. They tend to do more poorly on block design, digit symbol, and object assembly than do other schizophrenic clients, reflecting the neurologic component.

On the Rorschach, form level is very low, and although there are occasional M responses, these are likely to be of poor quality and reflective of disrupted ideation.

On the MCMI-II, elevations above 84 on C and S are most common, with elevation of P and 1 likely. Because PP and SS are partly defined by hallucinations and delusions, they are not likely to be very high in the disorganized schizophrenic, where these symptoms are not typically present, but moderate elevations (74–85) may occur. One personality pattern that is most likely to occur with the disorganized schizophrenic is the avoidant type; indeed, disorganization may be considered an extension of their characteristic protective maneuver in interfering with cognitive clarity (Millon, 1981). In this case, elevations above 74 may be expected on scale 2.

☐          TREATMENT OPTIONS

The particularly low level of functioning of the disorganized schizophrenic warrants the use of most of the techniques noted previously in the treatment option section of the category of schizophrenic disorders. Chemotherapy is commonly required, and token economies and milieu therapy are particularly useful (Adler, 1988). Until disorganized schizophrenics can develop the basic appropriate behaviors of even the most minimally normal individual, many of the other therapy techniques—such as psychotherapy, group therapy, and occupational therapy—are virtually impossible. Since disorganized schizophrenics are likely to have a markedly poor premorbid adjustment, an emphasis on vocational training is important if they are to make any ultimate transition to normal living. Thus, rigorous training in basic social skills is necessary, first via the token economy and then later through a total-milieu approach. Genetic counseling is also encouraged (Gottesman, 1991).

In choosing a specific therapist for an extremely disturbed client, the clinician might recall the classic differentiation between A and B therapists, first studied by Whitehorn and Betz (Goldstein and Stein, 1976). They found that B therapists were significantly more successful with the extremely disturbed individual. These therapists are characterized as noncoercive problem solvers; they are able to persuade while at the same time communicate a sense of acceptance of and empathy with the schizophrenic's bizarre thoughts and fantasies.

■   ## Catatonic Schizophrenia (295.2x)

Severe psychomotor disturbance is the essential feature of catatonic schizophrenia. The first of the two major traditional subdivisions is that of stuporous catatonia, in which movement is severely reduced and catatonic stupor, rigidity, or posturing is evident. Some may even show waxy flexibility, a condition in which the body is passively receptive to posture control. It is possible to manipulate such individuals physically just as one would move a store manikin, and they can remain in the manipulated position for extremely long periods of time.

The agitated catatonic, or excited type, is marked by uncontrollable verbal and motor behavior—apparently purposeless and not necessarily influenced by external stimuli. Individuals of this type can be quite dangerous and may break into frenzied violence in which they hurt or kill themselves or others. This is not an outgrowth of personal hostility, but rather a response to other persons as objects in their way. Before the use of psychomotor-control drugs, agitated catatonics would sometimes drive themselves to the point where they would die from severe exhaustion.

Two different courses are typically observed in catatonic schizophrenia. The chronic form of this disorder is primarily manifested in the stuporous types, and the progression in the disorder is slow and steady. The prognosis for remission is low, and the person may eventually develop into an undifferentiated schizophrenic.

In the periodic type, an abrupt onset is usually followed by alternating periods of agitated and stuporous catatonia. Remission is more likely, but there may be recurrences. They are particularly dangerous at the point of the shift from stupor to agitation, primarily because hospital personnel have few cues as to when the shift will occur.

☐   DSM-III-R

In addition to meeting the standard criteria for schizophrenia, a diagnosis of catatonic schizophrenia requires that at some time during the active phase of the illness the symptom picture is dominated by a catatonic pattern that includes either catatonic negativity or excitement, catatonic rigidity or posturing, or catatonic stupor. Mutism is common in this disorder. It is interesting that although the catatonic subtype was once considered to be one of the most common schizophrenic patterns, it is now relatively rare in Europe and North America, according to DSM-III-R.

☐ MMPI-2

The 2-7-8 pattern, with 2 most likely to predominate, is often reflective of the catatonic who is confused and yet oriented toward stuporous catatonia. Agitated catatonics are more likely to show an 8-9 or 8-0 pattern (Moldin et al., 1987). If this agitation has been transferred intellectually into hostility, an elevation on scale 4 is more likely and scale 6 is usually elevated. The 0 scale is high, reflecting significant discomfort with and withdrawal from interpersonal relationships.

☐ 16 PF

This pattern is similar to the prototypical pattern for schizophrenia, although it will differ on certain scales depending on whether the person tends toward stupor or agitation. This will be reflected particularly in scales F, $Q_4$, and to a degree, E and $Q_3$. Since this pattern may border on the hostility and social isolation of the paranoid, the L scale is likely to be affected more so than for other schizophrenics; to a degree, this is also evident in a higher $Q_2$ score.

☐ OTHER TEST-RESPONSE PATTERNS

The schizophrenic profile would be expected on the MCMI II, represented by elevations on SS along with the indicated patterns that seem to predispose toward schizophrenia (elevation on 1, 2, C, and/or S). Additionally, CC would be more prominent in this type of schizophrenia than in others, representing the catatonic and agitated types of motor activity. Scores on this scale of 85 or higher would not be uncommon. The overactivity factor of the excited type would be represented by an elevated N.

☐ TREATMENT OPTIONS

Agitated catatonic schizophrenics may force a coercive control of their behavior, so chemotherapy, the "modern straitjacket," is often necessary to bring a semblance of order into their worlds. Intravenous amobarbitol is often successful in breaking through the mutism seen in many catatonics. Token economies and milieu therapy are also useful for ameliorating the extremes of either agitated or stuporous catatonia (Adler, 1988). The possibility of an associated manic component in the agitated catatonic must not be overlooked, so a trial period of lithium therapy can be employed.

The stuporous catatonic is not unlike the severe depressive on several continuums, so the reader might consult some of the techniques useful for moving a person out of a depressive episode (Schuyler, 1991). Direct therapy, which can be seen as a psychoanalytic analogue to implosive therapy, is useful primarily with paranoid and catatonic schizophrenics (Karon, 1976). Through a prolonged verbal assault on the person's inner fantasies and fears, the client is goaded into at least a retaliatory response. Once this occurs, the therapist can move into more supportive and interactive roles.

## ■ Residual Schizophrenic Disorder (295.6x)

This diagnosis is applied to the individual who has already been labeled schizophrenic under the previous criteria, but in whom the disorder has lessened to the point that there are no longer any prominent psychotic symptoms.

DSM-III-R requirements for the diagnosis of Residual Schizophrenic Disorder are a previously diagnosed schizophrenic episode with symptomatology that no longer includes *prominent* psychotic symptoms. However, at least two signs suggestive of schizophrenia remain, such as difficulties in social behavior or interpersonal communications, odd or peculiar mannerisms, or inappropriate or flat affect. DSM-III-R has some difficulty with the goal of making a diagnosis operational. A judgment as to whether symptoms are still prominent is quite subjective, especially in view of the potency of certain chemotherapeutic agents to mask or suppress a wide variety of behavioral responses. Nonetheless, the category is likely to be used often since it is potentially applicable to many individuals.

☐     MMPI-2

Since the category is *residual* schizophrenia, it could be debated how much psychopathology is likely to be evident in the MMPI-2 profile. It is reasonable for the clinician to expect that in most cases the general profile of schizophrenia will be evident, but without the extremes of response. For example, a significant elevation on scale 8 would still be likely, but it should be less than in a person with active schizophrenia. Similarly, an elevation on scale F is reasonable, although on occasion this may be an individual who is trying to avoid remembering the schizophrenic episode and who becomes very defensive in that regard. As a result, scale K, and possibly L, would be high (Moldin et al., 1987).

When this happens, the person is also likely to be defensive about any kind of intrapsychic exploration.

It is typical to expect a relatively low 9 score in most residual schizophrenics, particularly since many of them are still on medication to suppress behavior. Other changes will be dependent on the specific type of schizophrenia, as well as on the premorbid personality, which is likely to come to the fore as the schizophrenic symptoms are suppressed.

## 16 PF

Much the same suppression of extreme scales would be expected on the 16 PF, C, H, M, O, and $Q_4$ should still be on the negative side of the continuum, yet they will be somewhat muted from prior levels. Scale B should be somewhat higher and now more accurately reflective of the person's actual abilities. A higher score on $Q_3$ should reflect the fact that the individuals now have more control in their worlds. Other scores will be affected by the type of schizophrenia manifested, the premorbid personality, and the feelings of security about present adjustment.

## OTHER TEST-RESPONSE PATTERNS

MCMI-II profiles of residual schizophrenic disorder may be similar to those of other schizophrenic disorders without such extreme elevations on the clinical-symptom scales CC, PP, and SS. The personality pattern elevations expected for schizophrenia—1, 2, C, and/or S—should be more elevated relative to CC, PP, and SS, in contrast to the active phases in which clinical-symptom scales are more prominent relative to personality patterns.

## TREATMENT OPTIONS

Since by definition the symptom picture of residual schizophrenia excludes pervasive and permanent psychotic symptoms, it is questionable whether any values from chemotherapy are, or could be, offset by the physical and psychological risks. It would seem that trial periods without medication and/or lower dosages of medication, such as haloperidol (Rifkin et al., 1991), should be more common for such persons than they are.

The residual symptoms are usually in the area of social and interpersonal behavior and, as such, require systems that provide adequate feedback to the schizophrenic about these behaviors. Such expatient groups as Recovery can be useful in helping previously hospitalized clients adjust, but there is the risk that mildly bizarre behaviors in the social and vocational world will be reinforced, or at least too easily tolerated, without feedback. Hence, it is important to move quickly into group therapy situations in which the predominant ethic is normality and in which feedback without inappropriate behaviors is generated in a supportive and accurate fashion. Similarly, the family can be trained to provide this feedback in a positive manner through family therapy situations.

If attentional problems persist into the residual phase, which they often do, biofeedback of electroencephalographic (EEG) patterns can be employed to increase those patterns associated with attention, such as decreasing the percentage of alpha waves, the classic indicator of non-attention. Biofeedback of muscle patterns is potentially useful to decrease the motoric side effects of tardive dyskinesia, or even to lower the excitability level of the agitated catatonic, although the latter task would indeed be challenging.

# ■   Schizophreniform Disorder (295.40)

The major substantive difference between the schizophreniform disorder and schizophrenia is duration. If the disorder lasts less than six months but the symptoms are that of schizophrenia, or if the person is symptomatic but has been so for less than six months, the term "schizophreniform disorder" is appropriate. The diagnosis of schizophrenia requires symptoms for six months or more. So, even though repeated incidents of the schizophreniform disorder may account for a cumulative duration of more than six months, the diagnosis remains the same. If the duration of disorder is less than a month, the appropriate diagnosis is usually brief reactive psychosis.

The major reason for the differential diagnosis is that the schizophreniform disorder shows several characteristics that differ from schizophrenia. There is better prognosis in the schizophreniform disorder; the individual is far more likely to recover to the premorbid level of functioning.

☐         DIAGNOSTIC CONSIDERATION

There is a high likelihood that the symptom picture is going to include much emotional upset and turmoil, reflecting the acute variable. This is opposed to chronic schizophrenic patterns, so scores on the MMPI-2, 16 PF, MCMI-II, and other tests are likely to be slightly accentuated. For example, on the MMPI-2, one is more likely to see a higher F scale than for chronic schizophrenics, but lower F, 7, 8, and 0 scales than for acute schizophrenics. This profile occurs in schizophrenia as well, although not so consistently. On the 16 PF, higher scores on scales O and $Q_4$ and lower scores on C and H are likely to be found more often than with schizophrenics.

☐     TREATMENT OPTIONS

Since the schizophreniform disorder is essentially a schizophrenic adjustment that has not yet lasted for six months, the techniques noted as appropriate for the treatment of schizophrenia are applicable here. This is particularly so for psychological techniques, as every effort should be made to help the client avoid the patient role and even worse, extended institutionalization. Hogan (1980) advises the use of an implosive technique for any brief psychotic episodes. This is possible since anxiety is high and has not yet crystallized into bizarre avoidant mechanisms.

## Brief Reactive Psychosis (298.80)

The primary distinguishing features of this psychotic reaction are sudden onset and short duration, ranging from a few hours up to one month. Once it exceeds two weeks, the diagnosis is changed to schizophreniform disorder.

This disorder is often triggered rather suddenly by an event of extreme stress: the loss of a loved one, a traumatic war experience, or other such stress. Unable to deal with the stress, the individual withdraws into a state of mental confusion, typically characterized by extreme emotional lability, bizarre behaviors, and perceptual distortions, including hallucinations and delusions. Individuals with histrionic, schizotypal, and borderline personality disorders, as well as adolescents and young adults manifesting emotional instability of various sorts, are especially prone to this reaction.

Unlike the schizophreniform disorder and the organic mental disorders that display comparable symptoms, the brief psychotic reaction is sudden in onset and of short duration. Unlike the factitious disorder, which in some respects may be considered a stress reaction, the person with a brief psychotic reaction appears to have little or no voluntary control over his or her symptoms.

☐     DSM-III-R

The diagnosis requires evidence of at least one of the following symptoms of impaired (not socially sanctioned) reality testing: (1) distorted or incoherent thinking, (2) delusions, (3) hallucinations, or (4) severely disorganized or catatonic behavior. It also requires evidence of emotional turmoil or overwhelming perplexity or confusion, a duration of symptomatology of not more than one month, and a period of clear increase of psychopathology after the stressor.

☐    OTHER TEST-RESPONSE PATTERNS

The test-response patterns are similar to the schizophrenic disorders, even more so to the exaggerated patterns of the schizophreniform disorder, particularly since acute emotional distress is apparent here. Those accentuations noted in the section on test responses in schizophreniform disorder are applicable here, with some minor exceptions. Those exceptions relate to the probability of lower ego strength and indications of a more-permanent disorder that are found in the other patterns. Hence, scales 4 and 6 on the MMPI-2 would be even less likely to be elevated, and scale 0 is not as likely to be very different from normal in these individuals, as in schizophrenia. Scale 2 is likely to be elevated, representing the present acute distress. On the 16 PF, the C and H scales are not as likely to be as low, as these are reflective of more-disturbed ongoing personality functioning. Patterns similar to schizophrenic patterns would also be expected on the MCMI-II, along with greater elevations on A, N, and to a lesser degree, D. Along with the expected accompanying personality disorders, elevation on 4 is possible since this type is related to the histrionic disorder.

☐    TREATMENT OPTIONS

Since this diagnosis is warranted when the person has shown psychotic behavior only for two weeks or less, the techniques appropriate for the treatment of schizophrenia or severe affective disorder (see relevant sections) can be supplemented by the techniques of crisis intervention. Most importantly, every effort should be made to keep clients from withdrawing from their social or vocational worlds and adopting patient roles. If at all possible, the family should be involved in the treatment, both as a mode of cutting off pathological behaviors and as a means of providing emotional support.

In addition, the brief psychotic disorder is effectively treated with covert modeling. In this technique, clients are asked to imagine a whole set of new behaviors and imagine themselves performing these behaviors. With practice, and with contracting for gradually moving aspects of the imagery patterns into their existing worlds, a positive effect can be generated.

■    **Psychotic Disorder NOS (Atypical Psychosis) (298.90)**

This category is used to designate those individuals who for some reason do not fit into any of the previous categories. For example, atypical psychosis might refer to individuals with a monosymptomatic somatic delusional system or to someone with such a confusing clinical picture that a specific diagnosis would be wrong.

# ■ Paranoid Schizophrenia (295.3x)

This disorder is discussed here because it is a juxtaposition of concepts from both schizophrenia and the paranoid disorders, the focus of the next section. Paranoid schizophrenia shows the most fragmented thought processes of any of the paranoid disorders; for that reason, it is included under schizophrenia. At the same time, however, there is a delusional system that is the mark of a paranoid disorder. In order to warrant the DSM-III-R diagnosis of Paranoid Schizophrenia, the person has to fulfill the criteria for schizophrenia and present a symptom picture dominated either by preoccupation with one or more systematized delusions or with frequent auditory hallucinations related to a single theme. There should be an absence of incoherence, marked loosening of associations, catatonic behavior, grossly disorganized behavior, or inappropriate affect.

A number of researchers (Zigler and Glick, 1988; Lazar and Harrow, 1985) have found evidence to establish that paranoid schizophrenia is a somewhat different disorder than other forms of schizophrenia. Paranoid schizophrenics show less anxiety (more of a counterphobic response to depressive ideation), relatively less judgment impairment, smaller deficits on most cognitive tests, and more concern with erecting boundaries in tasks and in their personal worlds than do other schizophrenics. There may even be differences in blood chemistry between these groups; however, these data have been contradictory to date.

In addition, paranoid schizophrenia can be contrasted with other schizophrenic disorders on the following dimensions:

| PARANOID SCHIZOPHRENIA | OTHER SCHIZOPHRENIC DISORDERS |
| --- | --- |
| Depression not that common | More often show depression or other mood disorder |
| Develop later in life | Show first manifestations in adolescence or late adolescence |
| More common in males | Approximately equal incidence in males and females |
| Often show some reasonably normal-appearing outward behaviors | Appear more disoriented or withdrawn |
| Higher intellectual ability than other schizophrenics | Often of lower-than-average intelligence |
| Seldom occurs in many rural non-Western cultures | Approximately equal occurrence rate across cultures |
| Proportionately shorter hospital stays | Tend toward long periods of hospitalization |
| More often tend to be mesomorphic (the body of a powerful athlete) | Any body build |

Although paranoid schizophrenics are typically more adequate socially than other schizophrenics, their reactions are consistently more stilted or intense than are normal responses. This is particularly so if anger and suspicion rather than grandiosity are the focus of the symptom picture. Reasonably appropriate affective responses often exist in paranoid schizophrenia, in contrast to the other schizophrenias.

Another occasionally confusing differential diagnostic problem is between the temporary psychotic state induced by severe alcoholic abuse and that of paranoid schizophrenia. Table 3.1 offers some guidelines.

☐ MMPI-2

When the profile is devoid of a T-score elevation over 70, the L score is greater than or equal to 7 (absolute values), and the person is not a minister, paranoid mentation with some delusions is likely and probability of acting-out is increased to the degree that scales 3 and 4 are high (Fjordback, 1985). The 8-4 pattern, with high scores on 2, 6, and 7, is characteristic of paranoid schizophrenia. The 8-6/6-8 and the 6-9/9-6 profiles are also typical for paranoid schizophrenics (Moldin et al., 1987), and if the 6 is the predominant scale with 4 also raised, the per-

**TABLE 3.1**  Differential Diagnosis Between Alcoholic Hallucinosis and Paranoid Schizophrenia

|  | ALCOHOLIC HALLUCINOSIS | PARANOID SCHIZOPHRENIA |
|---|---|---|
| **AGE OF ONSET** | More often 30–60 years of age | Usually less than 35 years of age |
| **ONSET** | Acute | Insidious |
| **FAMILY HISTORY** | Usually no family history for schizophrenia | Typically a positive family history for schizophrenia |
| **DISTINGUISHING CHARACTERISTIC AFFECT** | Anxiety and depression | Flat or inappropriate |
| **THOUGHT PROCESSES** | Coherent thought processes | Loose associations, formal thought disorder |
| **INTELLECTUAL FUNCTIONING** | Slight impairment of cognitive functions | No compromised cognitive functioning |
| **LENGTH OF ILLNESS** | Spontaneous improvement within days to weeks | Lifelong relapsing illness |

Adapted in part from Surawicz, F. (1980). "Alcoholic Hallucinosis, a Missed Diagnosis. Differential Diagnosis and Management." *Can J Psychiatry, 25,* 57–63.

son should be considered one of the more dangerous paranoid schizophrenics. If the 8 dominates in the profile, then prepsychotic schizoid traits are more likely.

A high F scale is typical, and an F − K (F minus K) ratio greater than 11 is not necessarily an indication of an invalid profile in a situation with high 4, 6, 8, and 9 scales. If the 7 scale is low, auditory hallucinations are particularly likely to occur. When the individual is more inclined toward grandiose rather than persecutory delusions, an 8-9/9-8 profile is more likely, with the 2 scale being lower than usual. The 1 and 3 scales are often relatively low in the protocols of paranoid schizophrenics, although Gilberstadt and Duker (1965) suggest that the 1-6/6-1 pattern with a 4 scale less than 70 T should be considered a cue to look for futher evidence of paranoid schizophrenia. They tend to be moderate to high on the BIZ (Bizarre Mentation) content scale, higher to the degree that their adjustment is fragmented and deteriorating.

□                    16 PF

The paranoid schizophrenic 16 F profile is similar to the overall schizophrenic profile, with some significant differences. Paranoid schizophrenics, especially females, are more likely to be high on the L scale, reflecting the jealous paranoid component essential to the disorder. Paranoid schizophrenics are also more likely to be high on $Q_3$, because anxiety is more controlled by projecting conflict and feelings onto other agents. As a result, the O score is less, the C and E scales higher, and the $Q_4$ scale somewhat lower than is found in the usual schizophrenic protocol. Also, because paranoid schizophrenics on the average are more intelligent, scale B is higher.

□                    OTHER TEST-RESPONSE PATTERNS

Elevations on 1 and P are expected on the MCMI-II, and to a lesser extent, 2, 6A, and/or C. MCMI-II scores of 85 and higher occur on PP, whereas the relatively less psychotic thought processes and affects exhibited by this type produce relatively lower scores on CC and SS, placing them in the 75–84 range.

On the WAIS-R, paranoid schizophrenics are likely to be higher on the similarities and picture completion subtests, while relatively lower on the digit-symbol and picture arrangement subtests. This reflects the unusual interpretations they tend to make, as well as their compulsive traits, which are usually more evident premorbidly. Because they exhibit less cognitive confusion, compared to disorganized schizophrenics, their overall scores are higher (Feinberg and McIlvried, 1991). On the comprehension subtest, paranoid schizophrenics are occasionally lower because they tend to make peculiar and overinclusive proverb interpretations. This trait is also found in the Benjamin Proverbs (Johnson, 1966).

This is one instance when the use of more exotic proverbs can be helpful. Paranoid schizophrenics, particularly if they are bright, often understand the popular interpretation of common proverbs and sayings and will state them, even though they may entertain other interpretations (Oltmanns and Maher, 1988). Exotic proverbs can bring out the delusional material more clearly.

On all tests, including the WAIS-R, paranoid schizophrenics show overconcern about the correctness of their responses and will often question the examiner as to what the correct response is. They tend to make deviant replies in response to numerous stimuli and are happy to argue about the meaning of any question presented to them (Heilbrun et al., 1985). On the Rorschach, paranoid schizophrenics are again very concerned about the meaning of the test, particularly since the ambiguous stimuli are not easily interpretable. They are more likely to look at the back of the card and to make excessive Dd responses. They show a fairly high F+ percentage, but not with the quality seen in the other paranoid disorders. If they are more oriented toward the persecutory dimension, a low number of responses is likely unless they can be made at least minimally comfortable in the testing situation.

If responsive, paranoid schizophrenics are likely to show a higher number of M responses and a lower number of C responses, particularly if there is a degree of integration in their adjustment. Responses are occasionally seen as "coming at" the person, and there are more "mask" responses than usual, as well as percepts of animals or humans being attacked or surrounded. There is an overemphasis on W responses, but often with poorer form than one would expect based on their intelligence level. Content often includes grandiose or cosmic concepts as well as responses that define boundaries, such as "edge" or "border" responses.

On the TAT, grandiose and pretentious stories are likely, with the person often being too negativistic to cooperate in pinning down details of the story. They are likely to use a story as a forum for making philosophical comments or moralizing about situations. Alternatively, if they feel threatened, they may refuse even to tell a story or will give very short and concrete descriptions of the pictures (Bellak, 1993). Gutters, fences, other indications of borders, castles, and similar concepts are found in the drawings of paranoids (Oster and Gould, 1987).

☐      ## TREATMENT OPTIONS

Several of the neuroleptic drugs have been used with the severe paranoid disorders. Although no single drug has been consistently effective, there is some evidence that chlorpromazine, haloperidol, and a trifluoperazine-amitriptyline combination may have some benefit when used as an adjunct to other treatment techniques in severe paranoid disturbance.

The significant level of disturbance and more bizarre quality of the paranoid schizophrenic, as contrasted to that of the other paranoid disorders, may warrant more intrusive methods. ECT has been used with some paranoid schizophrenics in an apparent attempt to disrupt the consistency of the belief system. However, ECT contains all the risks of any intrusive procedure, which are so important here because a fear of being intruded on in any number of dimensions is central to the paranoid disorders. In addition, there is the probability of short- and long-term memory loss, which could easily increase the sense of vulnerability so critical to many paranoids.

Chemotherapy can lessen the anxiety often found in the paranoid delusional system (Zigler and Glick, 1988). But again, there are the risks of apparent intrusiveness, plus increased delusions in response to any side effects, even those that have little long-term danger.

With the more bizarre paranoid disorders, the therapist may have to crash through the defenses erected by the paranoid system rather than wait for trust to develop in a series of psychotherapy contacts. Direct analysis (Karon, 1976) has been useful in this regard. Interpretations are forced on paranoid individuals, made necessary by their massive avoidance procedures. These interpretations usually center on what are thought to be major inner conflicts, notably in the areas of aggression, sexuality, and inadequacy. Once the person is moved into a more normal mode of functioning through any technique, approaches should then emphasize the development of trust, along with empathy for the person's distorted beliefs. (The reader is referred to the treatment techniques discussed at the end of the next section on the paranoid disorders.)

## ■    The Paranoid (Delusional) Disorders

The paranoid disorders are psychotic conditions in which the symptom picture is dominated by persistent persecutory delusions or delusions of jealousy. While the DSM-III-R emphasizes the "delusional" rather than "paranoid" terminology, I will use the traditional and still more generally accepted "paranoid" terminology. There are no significant hallucinations in the paranoid disorders, and the symptoms are not primarily attributable to a schizophrenic, affective, or organic mental disorder, or any combination of the three. Unlike paranoid schizophrenia, there is not much fragmentation of thoughts or bizarreness in the delusions. Also, there is seldom as severe an impairment in daily functioning as there is in paranoid schizophrenia (i.e., the latter show more characteristics of an "autistic retreat" from life). Paranoid schizophrenics typically have more than one delusional system, but it is not uncommon in the paranoid disorder that there is only a single focus in the delusions (Oltmanns and Maher, 1988).

The paranoid disorders can be oriented on a continuum based on the degree of integration in the delusions, with paranoid schizophrenia being the most fragmented and delusional (paranoid) disorder the least. The paranoid personality disorder can be seen as an extension of this continuum in that there is no true delusional system at all (Turkat, 1990). Although it is no longer formally included in the DSM, I will also discuss the relatively rare shared paranoid disorder, traditionally known as *folie à deux,* and now incorporated into the concept of induced psychotic disorder.

The paranoid disorders seldom show marked disruption in occupational functioning or intellectual activities, but they do show disruption in marital and interpersonal functioning. These are relatively rare disorders, and since these individuals are usually coerced into treatment, they are not always cooperative in a diagnostic situation. For that reason, the reader should consult the section on malingering (Chapter 16). Because anger is often a factor in the personality makeup, and occasionally is so extreme that there is danger to others, the reader should consult the section of this book on aggression potential (Chapter 14).

☐               MMPI-2

While one would expect scale 6 to be elevated in this disorder, this is not always the case. Paranoids with good defenses may not want to reveal their delusions and as a result may score rather low on scale 6, in some instances being inordinately low, even relative to normal scores (Heilbrun et al., 1985). It must also be remembered when making a diagnostic judgment that blacks tend to score higher on scale 6 throughout the range of normal and paranoid patterns (Dahlstrom et al., 1986). Overall, paranoids are likely to skip a number of the questions and often express irritation at being forced to make true-false decisions.

Unlike persons with other psychiatric disorders, paranoids will show a high K score and a relatively low F score and, consistent with that, a lower score on scale 4 than would be expected. The more disturbed the individual is (the more toward the paranoid schizophrenic end of the continuum), the more likely the "paranoid trough" will occur, that is, high scores on scales 6 and 8 and a relatively lower score on scale 7. Since denial and projection are common features of the paranoid disorders, reasonably high scores on scale 3 can be expected. As noted in paranoid schizophrenia, with a profile of T well below 70 and L (in absolute numbers) greater than or equal to 7, paranoid mentation is probable, and elevations on 3 and 4 increase the probability of acting-out (Fjordback, 1985). They tend to be high on the Overcontrolled Hostility (O-H) supplementary scale and the Cynicism (CYN) content scale and to the degree they approach psychosis, on the BIZ content scale.

☐ 16 PF

It was originally thought that paranoids would score high on the L scale, but this is not always so, which again reflects the situation where the client is guarded in revealing the content of his or her concerns. Hence, the diagnostician should score for faking-bad (Winder et al., 1975; Krug, 1980) in order to check for the extremity of this response pattern. On the paranoia end of the continuum, as opposed to the paranoid schizophrenic end, scores on B, N, and $Q_3$ are likely to be higher, while I is lower.

☐ TREATMENT OPTIONS

The concerns of the paranoid about intrusiveness make this set of disorders most difficult to treat, and the possibility of an underlying depression has to be kept in mind (Zigler and Glick, 1988). The therapist can crash through the defenses via techniques such as direct analysis, chemotherapy, or even psychosurgery. The consequently disrupted psychological functions then have to reintegrate—not always an easy task. In addition, the iatrogenic effect of coercively intruding on an individual who already has a low threshold for perceiving intrusiveness presents real difficulties in the later development of trust.

To the degree the paranoid individual is more integrated in functioning, intrusive techniques can be avoided and the therapist can focus on developing trust. In that manner, paranoids may gain recourse to another individual, a pattern often absent in them. Therapists must attempt to maintain their integrity and honesty while empathizing with the paranoid's delusional beliefs. The critical feat is to gain the trust of an individual who is pervasively untrusting and at the same time, accept but not participate in the paranoid's delusional system.

■ **Delusional (Paranoid) Disorder (297.10)**

Delusional (Paranoid) Disorder (DPD) is rarely observed in clinical practice for several reasons. First, DPD apparently does not exist as commonly as many other disorders. Second, the higher level of personality integration allows DPDs to avoid seeing a clinician, even when their lives are being disrupted. Since they are inclined to isolate themselves under stress, it is very hard to even coerce them into treatment.

Two well-known variations of classical paranoia are conjugal paranoia and erotomania. Conjugal paranoia is marked by delusions of jealousy that involve the spouse. This condition, sometimes termed the *Othello syndrome,* progresses from minor criticism of the marital partner through suspiciousness to full-blown delusions involving thoughts of the spouse's infidelity. Psychotic jealousy may lead to acts of violence against the spouse or lover, who is the subject of the delusional system. Conjugal paranoia should be distinguished from pathologic jealousy, which occurs simply as an accompanying symptom in many disorders, including organic mental disorders, alcoholism, schizophrenia, and the affective disorders.

Erotomania, also referred to as Clerambault's syndrome, is more often reported in women. The patient develops an intense delusional belief that a man, usually older and of higher social standing, is in love with her. One pattern, considered a subset of paranoia, is characterized by the sudden onset of a delusional belief that focuses on one object and becomes fixed and chronic. The second type, a subset of schizophrenia, is characterized by an erotic delusion superimposed on other symptoms of schizophrenia. A third type is characterized by recurrent and short-lived delusions in the absence of other symptoms of schizophrenia.

☐     DSM-III-R

DPD is marked by a structured, chronic, and nonbizarre delusional system. If auditory or visual hallucinations are present, they are not prominent. This delusional system focuses on few issues (usually just one), and after the acceptance of the first premise, the logic is reasonable and orderly and consequent behavior is not obviously odd or bizarre. To apply a diagnosis of DPD, the clinician must find that (1) the person has not met the criterion for either schizophrenia or organic disorder, (2) any mood disorder has been brief relative to the delusional behavior, and (3) there is evidence of nonbizarre delusions (those that reflect real life: being cheated on by a spouse, being followed, etc.). DPD is subdivided, based on the type of delusion, into the following types: grandiose, erotomanic, jealous, persecutory, somatic, and unspecified.

☐     MMPI-2

There are fewer data in the literature on the MMPI-2 responses of DPDs than there are for most other psychopathology groupings. On occasion, a DPD will show a spike on scale 6, with most of the other scales relatively low. This is not common, however, as the defenses usually do not allow that kind of disclosure. A moderate elevation on scale 6 along with an elevation on scale 4 is more common, reflecting the paranoid delusions and the hostility and social alienation that typically accompany them. At the same time, this suspiciousness and anger can result in a complaining attitude if the client has been forced into a diagnostic situation, and hence a higher K scale relative to other psychopathology groups, with a concomitant lower F scale, can be expected. In addition, scale 9 is usually moderately elevated.

## 16 PF

Just as with the DPD, paranoid individuals may skip many items, and the clinician should examine this closely if someone else is doing the scoring. Scale L may be elevated, although DPDs are often well-enough defended so that this is not the case. $Q_3$ is likely to be particularly high, and scales N and $Q_1$ are likely to be low. These scores reflect the guardedness and the integration around the delusional system that mark a DPD. They are likely to be lower on scale A than their behavior would suggest, which reflects the inner guardedness not always directly manifest in their initial interpersonal contacts.

DPDs are likely to be relatively low on $Q_4$, indicating the denial of anxiety, and low on $Q_1$, again indicating a conservtive and guarded approach toward the world. Scores are relatively high on B because DPD is a coping mechanism more common in brighter individuals. The chronic and unshakable aspects of the delusions are reflected in higher scores on scales G and E. Scale G points to the persistently moralistic nature of DPDs' belief systems, and scale E points to the need for dominance that is embedded in DPDs' coping strategies. DPDs are likely to be relatively low on M, as reflective inner fantasy is antithetical to the use of projection and denial (Heilbrun et al., 1985).

### OTHER TEST-RESPONSE PATTERNS

On the WAIS-R, DPDs are likely to attain high arithmetic and picture completion scores, reflecting their hyperalertness toward the environment. They also do well on similarities and comprehension, in large part because they take a meticulous approach to these tests and are thus likely to gain two-point answers. Their propensity toward abstraction also helps them in the similarities tests.

During the tests, they are likely to be argumentative, critical, and condescending about both the purpose of the test and the actual questions used. They may even object to the examiner's writing down responses or ask to examine what has been written. On the Rorschach, they are likely to attain a very high F and F+ percentage, reflecting their constriction, as well as many Dd and space responses. Unless they feel comfortable, they are likely to reject cards that the clinician is reasonably sure they could handle intellectually, and in general, the record provided is sparse. Although they characteristically have few M and color responses, the more grandiose DPDs do show M responses. Phillips and Smith (1953) suggest that any "eye" or "ear" responses, as well as any looking at the back of the cards, are indicative of a paranoid orientation. There is a concern for the symmetry in the cards, and, as in other tests, there is criticism of the test itself, particularly if the ambiguity of the Rorschach stimuli becomes threatening.

Most common in the MCMI-II is the elevated P score—at least 75 and very possibly greater than 85—because this personality type is likely to develop acute paranoid disorders; PP may be raised, depending on the extent to which the paranoid defenses allow disclosure (Choca et al., 1992). Except for the occurrence of delusions, paranoids are generally cognitively intact, so scores less than 75 on SS should occur. Elevations on scale 6A commonly occur, indicating an aggressive component of paranoia and possible acting-out. Elevations on 5 are rather common, as paranoid features are present in the narcissist; variable scores on 7 occur, depending on the degree of obsessive-compulsive features. Patrick (1988) found the MCMI to be more effective than the MMPI in assessing paranoid disorders.

☐ TREATMENT OPTIONS

DPDs will typically undergo treatment only when coerced by possible legal sanctions or the threat of the loss of a relationship. They are inclined to be condescending and only make a pretense of interest, at least at first.

Since DPD is marked by a well-integrated system of personality functioning, albeit based on bizarre premises (Oltmanns and Maher, 1988), intrusive techniques are likely to backfire and further alienate the client from the treatment process. It is hoped that consistent contact in psychotherapy will lead to a development of some minimal trust in the relationship. This trust gives DPDs a much-needed feedback resource, a person with whom they might test out the adequacy of their delusional system.

The therapist must accept and empathize with the DPD and yet not lose integrity as a therapist by participating in the delusional system. For example, the therapist may note correlates between his or her own life and the client's, which gives the client a potential new frame of reference as well as a new model for coping with vulnerability and fear. Humor, notably absent in many DPDs, can be modeled, as can other cognitive coping systems.

As they move away from their delusional systems, a variety of cognitive retraining procedures can be brought into play. The clinician might also consider group therapy; however, the transition from individual to group therapy is particularly tricky for the DPD. If it can be accomplished, an even greater potential for consensual feedback, so lacking for most DPDs, is then available.

## Shared Paranoid and Induced Psychotic Disorders (197.30)

The Shared Paranoid Disorder has traditionally been termed *folie à deux* ("the madness of two"). As noted earlier, this category is no longer included in the DSM per se. However, since it is a traditionally recognized pattern and still occurs, it is included here.This form of double insanity involves one person who is originally paranoid in some form and a receiver who passively incorporates the paranoid beliefs into his or her own system. This receiver is in an intimate relationship with the dominant individual and has a history of being psychologically dependent on the controlling person. When they break away from the relationship, the paranoid belief system dissipates.

The diagnosis of Induced Psychotic Disorder (297.30) applies specifically to the secondary individual, the receiver, and it requires that the delusion be similar to that of the sender. Since the paranoid ideation of the receiver is likely to dissipate if the reltionship is broken (Oltmanns and Maher, 1988), the paranoid elements are not the dominant focus of the personality. The need for affiliative dependency is a primary factor, usually in conjunction with passive-aggressive hostility that is expressed through the channel of the shared paranoid belief system.

## MMPI-2

The receiver is typically very defensive about the paranoid beliefs and in one sense wishes to manifest them to gain the approval of the dominant other. Thus, a raised score on scale 6 is likely. Several questions on L tape a willingness to trust others, so the receiver's dependency keeps the L scale from being extremely high.

Interestingly, depression is common here, as are psychopathic components; hence, scales 2 and 4 are likely to be raised. Males who are receivers are higher on scale 5 than other paranoids, whereas females are lower on scale 5. Scale 7 is also likely to be moderately raised, as is scale 8.

## 16 PF

Since these individuals are fairly open about their paranoid beliefs, they score high on L, and the submissiveness is reflected in lower scale E and H scores. They are also, for the same reason, relatively higher on I and N. They are not likely to show as high a $Q_3$ score as other paranoid individuals, as their personality integration derives from the other person rather than from their own personality. They are also not likely to be as bright as other paranoids; hence, B should be lower.

## OTHER TEST-RESPONSE PATTERNS

On the MCMI-II, the features of the paranoid profile are present. While elevated 5 and 6A are likely in the dominating member of the pair, elevations on 3 and 4 would be the most prominent patterns in the dependent member of the pair.

☐          TREATMENT OPTIONS

The sender, the dominant individual in the shared paranoid disorder, often manifests classic paranoia and is thus now diagnosed as having a delusional (paranoid) disorder; the reader is referred to the previous section for the modes of treating this pattern. The first issue for the shared paranoid system is to separate the parties, either by hospitalization or by some other means. At this point, the paranoid elements of the receiver are likely to dissipate since they are heavily based on the dependent relationship with the dominant personality. Cognitive retraining procedures and assertive therapy for the dependency are especially appropriate. A group therapy experience can give the person the much-needed personality support and at the same time provide access for modeling new and more appropriate belief systems (Ettin, 1982).

# CHAPTER 4

# Mood (Affective) Disorders

The mood disorders have always been a common problem, but appear especially so in modern society (Keller and Baker, 1992). In DSM-III-R, the focus is on two major subcategories: bipolar disorders and depressive disorders. It is important to note that DSM-III-R does not provide for a diagnosis where mania alone (without some evidence of depression) is found. The authors of DSM-III-R believe that such a pattern occurs very rarely, if at all. Thus, the diagnosis of whether or not there is a manic episode is useful to determine whether the affective disorder is a bipolar syndrome or depression alone.

Within the depressive disorder subcategory of the mood disorders, the formal DSM-III-R terms are "major depression" and "dysthymia." Likewise, the same differentiation is used for the bipolar disorders, substituting the terms "bipolar" and "cyclothymia" to designate the severe and the chronic behavior-problem patterns, respectively. The DSM-III-R also now provides for an optional diagnosis of late luteal phase dysphoric disorder.

■ ## Treatment Options

Treatment of the mood disorders depends on which affect is predominately manifested, mania or depression. When it is mania, the primary treatment of choice has been lithium therapy (Lickey and Gordon, 1991; Goodwin and Jamison, 1990). If this is not successful, others have used some of the antipsychotic medications, which can at least suppress the behavior. ECT has also been used, but this is only reasonable as a last resort. When the quality of the manic episode shifts toward irritability and suspiciousness, appropriate techniques for the paranoid disorders can be considered (see Chapter 3).

A wide variety of treatments have been useful for depression, yet depression still remains a pervasive problem for our society. Classic treatment wisdom advises the use of chemotherapy and/or ECT. The problems with chemotherapy are the significant side effects, the further disruption of any sense the depressives might have that they can control their destinies, the fact that they do not work in all cases (although they do in the majority of them), the delay in action of often up to two weeks, and the fact that drugs only work to improve the activity spectrum and not the interpersonal dimension (Poling et al., 1991; Haaga et al., 1991).

ECT has been recommended where immediate disruption of the depression response is required, especially when suicide is a possibility. ECT is appropriate for the severe psychotic depressions; however, the treater must consider the cost–benefit issues of short- and long-term organic dysfunction as a result of the ECT and the possible exaggeration of learned helplessness through the use of such a coersive treatment (many theories of depression emphasize learned helplessness as a generic factor).

Several studies report no detrimental long-term effects from ECT. However, such studies usually contain methodological approaches that do not deal with the actual issues involved. In the Weeks et al. (1980) study, for example, the number of ECTs received by clients was low compared to the number administered in traditional psychiatric practice, and there was no random assignments of clients to the ECT and non-ECT group. Others (Breggin, 1979; Smith and Meyer, 1987) detail substantial data to indicate that ECT can result in impaired judgment and insight, shallow emotional reactions, confusion, and global disruption of intellectual functioning, these effects being permanent and resulting from the electrical insult to the brain. And most researchers note that there is still very little informed consent obtained from patients for the use of ECT.

Existential therapies are useful where the central quality of the depression is apathy rather than psychomotor retardation. Also, the cognitive behavior therapies have been specifically helpful throughout the range of depressive disorders. Burrows (1992) recommends this follow-up treatment, after remission, if there has been either more than one severe episode or several minor episodes: use of a tricyclic antidepressant or lithium, at least a single dose at night; at least two contact visits a month; and a review of medication after a two year euthymic period. The reader is referred to the individual sections in this syndrome grouping for further elaboration.

## ■ Manic Episode

Mania has been described since ancient times. Hippocrates accurately noted many of the symptoms but attributed manic behavior to an excess of yellow bile. While depression is a common affective disorder, mania is not; it accounts for only about 4 percent of psychiatric hospital admissions. Its incidence, however, appears to be increasing in the United States. A possible explanation for this increase is that there is now a reasonably effective and straightforward cure for mania, while in the past it was considered very difficult to treat (Goodwin and Jamison, 1990), so clinicians may now be more amenable to putting borderline cases into a category that now has a better prognosis.

Throughout the literature, three cardinal features of the manic phase have been described: (1) hyperactive motor behavior, (2) labile euphoria and/or irritability, and (3) flight of ideas.

Four important behavioral variables are useful in making a differential diagnosis between severe manic episodes, schizoaffective disorder, and a more emotionally labile form of schizophrenia. First, while all three categories are distractible, schizoaffectives and schizophrenics are primarily distracted by internal thoughts and ruminations, whereas manics are distracted by the external stimuli that often go unnoticed by others. Secondly, schizoaffectives and schizophrenics during an active phase tend to avoid any true relationships with others, whereas the manic is usually profoundly open to contact with other people (Mester, 1986). Thirdly, another useful distinction between mania and schizophrenia involves language organization. Although both manics and schizophrenics may exhibit thought disorder, the incoherence in manic speech is due to shifts from one coherent discourse structure to another, while the ability of schizophrenics to construct any discourse structure is different (Feinberg and McIlvried, 1991). Fourth, while the thought problems of schizophrenics are marked by disorganization, confusion, and peculiar words or phrases, the thought problems of manics are marked by odd combinations denoted by playfulness, flippancy, and humor (Solovay et al., 1987). Additionally, supersensitivity to light (noted, for example, by a marked reduction in plasma melatonin levels upon exposure to light at night) has been found to be a marker for manic reactions (Lewy et al., 1985). Disturbance in the epinephrine–norepinephrine balance is central to the disorder, pointing to a disruption in the adrenal medulla as a likely common marker (Swann et al., 1991).

Positron-emission tomography (PET) is a radiological technique that determines patterns of glucose metabolism in the brain. These patterns can be abnormal for both manics and schizophrenics and yet still differ from each other. Schizophrenics, especially schizophrenics of low competence, show decreased glucose metabolism in the frontal cortex; manics in the midst of an attack show increased glucose activity in the right temporal region. There are some drawbacks to this diagnostic technique. First, there is little evidence that PET can make that differentiation with any consistency when the behavior patterns are somewhat similar. PET is also expensive and requires the introduction of a catheter into a blood vessel, a small but clear risk. In addition, a radioactive substance is introduced to the brain, and the long-term risks of such a procedure are not yet known.

☐          DSM-III-R

To warrant a diagnosis of manic episode, the DSM-III-R requires the existence of one or more clear-cut periods of predominantly euphoric and/or irritable mood (not due to an organic cause); in addition, the person must show a distinct period of abnormality, with episodes usually lasting from several days to a few months. There must also be evidence that contraindicates schizophrenic symptoms—for example, no delusions or hallucinations for as long as two weeks in the absence of prominent mood symptoms—and at least three of the following symptoms must be present (four symptoms if the mood is irritable rather than euphoric): hyperactivity, increased or pressed speech, flight of ideas, inflated self-esteem, less need for sleep, excessive distractibility, excessive involvement in pleasurable activities with ultimately negative payoff, and psychomotor agitation or increased goal-directed activities. These criteria constitute a hypomanic syndrome. With the addition of marked impairment of functioning in the social or occupational arena or the need for hospitalization because of dangerousness, it is a manic syndrome.

It must again be noted that the DSM-III-R does not provide for a diagnosis of mania in the absence of depression. Thus, the diagnosis of manic episode is a primary diagnostic question in the eventual decision as to whether a bipolar diagnosis or a diagnosis of depression alone is warranted. The primary diagnosis of manic episode may be further delineated by qualifiers, for example, "in partial or full remission" or "with psychotic features," the latter requiring the presence of delusions or hallucinations, which may be either mood-congruent or incongruent.

☐          MMPI-2

It is often difficult to get a true manic who is in the throes of an active episode to produce an adequate MMPI-2. But if you do, a high 9 scale and elevated scores on 6 and 8 and usually 4 are predominant (Graham, 1990). A very low 2 scale may indicate the manic component of a cyclothymic process. Winters et al. (1981) found the 9-6 code discriminated manics from schizophrenics effectively. Scales 3 and 0 are usually elevated in manics, and scale 2 is low, except in the depressive phase of bipolar disorders (Silver et al., 1981). The 6 scale is particularly related to the irritability factor. Those individuals who are not irritable but are primarily euphoric usually do not score high on the 6 scale or even on the 4 scale. Very irritable manics will occasionally have their highest elevations on scales 3 and 4, with lesser elevations on scales 6, 8, and 9. To the degree that there is an attempt to control tension and anxiety, scale 7 is higher. Severity is related to the F scale: the higher it is, the more likely the individual will manifest a psychotic level of disorder. In moderate-level manics, the F scale may be lower with the K scale raised, reflecting a denial of psychopathology.

## 16 PF

Manics score high on scales F and H and low on N. This results from their high activity levels, combined with a lack of insight about the reactions they engender in others. They also tend to be high on scales A and E.

To the degree they are euphoric, manics are a bit higher on A relative to E and lower on L, whereas they tend to be opposite to the degree they are irritable. Their high level of tense and driven behavior is reflected in a low $Q_3$ scale, with a tendency to be moderately low on C and $Q_2$, while moderately high on O.

## OTHER TEST-RESPONSE PATTERNS

The frenetic behavior patterns that mark the manic (Goodwin and Jamison, 1990) should result in higher WAIS-R scores when speed per se is an issue, such as in digit symbol. However, the lack of allowance for feedback through checking of one's own performance results in lower scores on block design, picture arrangement, and object assembly. They may often come quite close to the required response, but in their impatience offer an incomplete solution as the finished solution. If their manic behavior includes continuous talking, they may do well on subtests such as comprehension, vocabulary, and similarities, in which persistence can result in extra points. However, at the same time, if the mania takes the form of impatience, they would likely score low on these tests. Throughout both the WAIS-R and the Rorschach, they are likely to manifest a desire to move on to a new item or task.

This frenetic behavior should result in a number of poor W responses on the Rorschach, with simultaneous notice of details that others often ignore. Response latencies are typically very short, and there are usually a number of M responses (Wagner and Wagner, 1981). Shafer (1954) asserts that a high number of confabulation responses and/or shading responses, in combination with a high percentage of C, CF, Dd, S, and W responses, are indicative of mania, a result generally confirmed by Wagner and Heise (1981).

The emotional lability and ambivalence indicated by high scores on S and C on the MCMI-II suggest the predisposition of these persons toward development of manic episodes (Choca et al., 1992). During the period of mania, an N of 85 or higher should occur. Impulsive behavior during these periods may cause increase in the likelihood of drug abuse, evidenced by a T score of 74–85. The flight of ideas and sometimes confused state of the manic may produce some elevation on SS, but when it is 75 or higher, a diagnosis of schizoaffective disorder may be warranted.

☐          TREATMENT OPTIONS

The single most recommended treatment for mania is lithium therapy (Lickey and Gordon, 1991); it appears to reverse the manic factor in approximately 75 percent of the cases treated. However, research does demonstrate that combining psychotherapy with lithium therapy is superior to the use of lithium alone (Mester, 1986).

Lithium salts were originally used, but lithium carbonate is now used because it is less toxic, is chemically convenient, and contains a high percentage of lithium relative to weight. Since lithium is rapidly absorbed by the kidneys, it has to be taken in divided doses to prevent any cyclical physiological response from overwhelming the client. As a result of the need for consistently administered divided doses, education of the patient is critical. Doses must be taken on a schedule, so when a patient indicates a lack of intelligence and/or discipline, mechanisms for controlled administration of the drug are necessary.

Other drugs are sometimes used if lithium is ineffective, such as valproate or imipramine if there is a substantial depressive feature. Tranylcypromine has also been of value.

Since manics may have elaborated some negative behavioral habits in addition to the apparent physiological disorder, behavioral training is advised in addition to the lithium. It is helpful to teach the client to consider plans thoroughly before beginning to actuate them, to follow through with them once the decision is made, and to stay with interpersonal commitments (Goodwin and Jamison, 1990).

# ■  Major Depressive Episode

As with the manic disorders, depressive disorders are divided between major depression and dysthymia (or depressive neurosis), based again on chronicity and severity (Keller and Baker, 1992). It is estimated in DSM-III-R that approximately 3 percent of males and 6 percent of females have had a depressive episode sufficiently severe to require hospitalization. An important aspect of the explanation for the twofold incidence of depression in females compared to that in males is the accentuation of behavior prescribed by traditional sex-role expectations. Also, abuse early in life, other patterns of victimization, unhappy marriages, and infertility or a large number of children (especially when the latter is combined with low economic resources) are factors that predispose women to depression (McGrath et al., 1990; Meyer and Salmon, 1988).

Several other factors predict depression in women (McGrath et al.,

1990): economic deprivation, low self-esteem, a preoccupation with failure, a sense of helplessness, a pessimistic attitude toward the world, and narcissistic vulnerability. In addition to the factors just mentioned, a critical mother and a dependency-fostering father were also important in the genesis of depression in females.

## DSM-III-R

If there is a single major depressive episode, the formal DSM-III-R diagnosis is Major Depression, Single Episode (296.2x), whereas the occurrence of more than one is diagnosed Major Depression, Recurrent (296.3x). Both require an absence of any manic episodes.

The diagnosis of major depressive episode requires evidence of dysphoric mood or loss of interest or pleasure in most of one's usual activities for at least two weeks. This reaction cannot be the result of a schizophrenic or organic disorder or simple bereavement such as follows the loss of a loved one. At least five of the following consistently present depressive symptoms are required for the diagnosis: (1) sleep disturbance, (2) agitated or retarded psychomotor ability, (3) weight gain or loss of appetite, (4) loss of interest in usual activities, (5) fatigue or loss of energy, (6) guilt or sense of worthlessness, (7) slowed or disrupted thinking, (8) suicide or death ideation, or (9) depressed mood nearly every day (or irritability for adolescents).

A major depressive episode is delineated by most of the same qualifiers as used for a manic episode—e.g., "in partial remission" is between "in full remission" and "mild." The psychotic designation requires evidence of either hallucinations or delusions. The disorder can also be sublabeled as to mood-congruent or mood-incongruent psychotic features. Again, severity per se is not enough to warrant a psychotic diagnosis. There is also the possibility of a subdiagnosis of melancholic type, or a seasonal pattern referred to as Seasonal Affective Disorder (Oren et al., 1991).

## MMPI-2

Scale 2 is, of course, consistently elevated in chronic depressive disorders (Nelson and Cicchetti, 1991), as is the DEP (depression) content scale. In women, the ANX content scale is often elevated. The 2-7/7-2 combination is commonly noted across the depressive spectrum. A concomitant high scale 4 suggests possible passive-aggressive accompaniments to the depression (Anderson and Bauer, 1985), and it has been noted by several observers that a high scale 4 in depressives correlates best with both hostility and depressive thoughts rather than with psychomotor retardation. The 3-2 and the 2-8 profiles are also indicative of possible depression (Lachar, 1974; Silver et al., 1981). As the 8 score rises, the latter profile is more likely to be schizoaffective, and such persons are likely to be agitated and have a specific suicide plan. Johnson et al. (1980) found the 2-8-7 combination to be characteristic of severe depression. Overall, Winters et al. (1981) found codes 2-7-8, 2-8, and 4-8-2 to discriminate a group of depressives from schizophrenics effectively.

In all of these situations, as scores rise on both F and 8 and scores on scale 9 become lower, the depression is proportionately more severe, there is retarded motor behavior, and the depression is prone to move into the psychotic range. Scale 9 is also an indication of avoidance patterns and correlates with the depression. In some cases, a high 9 signals a frenetic counterphobic response to depression, and the 1-9 code is often a masked depression. The clinician occasionally sees a 2-0 profile, which suggests a chronic depression. Also, the profile of a high 1 and relatively low 2 scale, along with verbalizations of depression, suggests a situationally generated depression, possibly even an extended bereavement. The subtle items of scale 2 have consistently proved to be a better predictor of depression than the obvious items (Nelson and Cicchetti, 1991).

☐    ## 16 PF

In the marked and moderate range of the depressive episode, individuals are likely to score relatively high on scales I, L, M, O, and $Q_4$, particularly where there is still a degree of agitation in the depressive response. They also score high on $Q_2$. As the disorder moves toward a psychotic dimension, scores are higher on L, M, and O and lower on C, H, and $Q_3$. They revert to average on $Q_2$ and are now lower on A. Because of their apathy toward the environment, they also score low on B.

☐    ## OTHER TEST-RESPONSE PATTERNS

There are several good rating scales—e.g., the Beck, Zung, and Hamilton scales—designed specifically to assess depression, each with its own strengths and weaknesses (Lambert et al., 1986). A structured interview, such as the Schedule of Affective Disorders and Schizophrenia (SADS) can be especially useful here (Wetzler, 1989).

On the WAIS-R, the classic sign of depression has been an overall performance-scale score significantly less than the verbal-scale score, as well as generally brief responses (Swiercinsky, 1985). Depressed clients are likely to fail on WAIS-R items that they should typically be able to answer, simply because they give up on them, and they usually do poorer on the timed components of any test, including the WAIS-R. Within the performance-scale scores, picture completion is usually the highest. Within the verbal-scale scores, digit span is expected to be the lowest (Keiser and Lowy, 1980), with arithmetic also being very low, and vocabulary rather than high. "I don't know" responses and general lack of persistence are common.

Depressive inpatients, in common with other inpatients, are likely to score high on MCMI-II scales 1, 2, 3, and 8A (McCann and Suess, 1988). Both CC and D of 85 or higher should occur on the MCMI-II in most major depressive episodes, especially where there are psychotic features. The uncomfortable depressed state may be represented by some elevation on A. The intense moods and dysregulasted activation of the borderline will predispose him or her to react with a depressive episode. The emptiness and dysphoria experienced by the avoidant can often escalate to a major depressive episode. Therefore, elevations between 74 and 85 are likely on scales C and 2. Overall, the MCMI-II does not appear to be as effective in assessing depression as does the MMPI-2 (Patrick, 1988).

On the Rorschach, long reaction times to the cards and the rejection of several cards are probable. Furthermore, the number of responses is usually less than twenty. The individual is often highly self-critical while responding to the Rorschach. A low percentage of good W or original responses and high F percent and a high percentage of Popular responses are common (Swiercinsky, 1985). FY or MY responses are seen as indicative of depression (Phillips and Smith, 1953), and something like a YF response would in particular suggest depression. There are typically few C and CF responses, a low number of M responses, and a low number of W or Wt responses (Wagner and Heise, 1981). Dysphoric content is common, and cloud and vista responses occasionally occur. Within the Exner system, Mason et al. (1985) found that depressives scored significantly lower than normals on Rorschach scoring criteria M, Xt%, Pop and significantly higher on DQv, Col-Shd, Sum V, Sum SP.SC. They also scored lower than normals but higher than schizophrenics on (FQw) − (fQ-), Xt%, Pop.

Analogous to the schizophrenic index, Exner (1986) has a "Depression Index" (p. 182). Again, it is best to avoid using a hard and fast cutoff point, but simply to use the following as helpful general indicators of depression:

Sum FV + VF + V > 0

Color Sh Blend > 0

$(3r + (2)/R < .30$

Sum $FC^1 + C^1F + C^1 > 2$

Sum MOR > 3

Figures on the Bender-Gestalt are likely to be boxed, to show a confused order, and to be drawn overly large (Rossini and Kaspar, 1987). Stories on the TAT are short and stereotyped and are often only descriptions of the cards rather than an actual story. It is difficult to carry on an inquiry in either the TAT or the Rorschach since the person may give only monosyllabic portrayals of each card. Themes of guilt, lack of success and expiation through suffering are common. Bellak (1993) points out that cards 12BG, 14, 3BM, and 3BF may bring out the depressed feelings of a subject. Card 9GF can also bring out depressed feelings, even suicidal tendencies, as when a story involves circumstances in which the girl below in the picture is made into someone who panics and runs into the sea.

□          TREATMENT OPTIONS

Since the major depressive episode often involves a severe level of depression, possibly including psychotic components, more intrusive techniques are likely to be used (Burrows, 1992). However, the techniques discussed in the next subsection (Dysthymia) are useful as well.

ECT has often been used for severe depression; it is probably one of the few syndromes for which there is good evidence of ECT's effectiveness (Valenstein, 1986). Similarly, psychosurgery has been used in which a lesion is placed in areas that control emotional response, such as the limbic system. However, any effectiveness must be balanced against the high psychological and physical costs of these techniques.

Clients usually receive six to twelve ECT treatments administered every other day. The sine-wave, or brief-pulse electric stimulus, typically ranges from a minimum of ten 2-watt seconds to several 90-watt seconds. Briefer pulse stimulus is correlated with less cognitive deficit, and the lowest stimulus for an adequate seizure response should be used. ECT is strongly contraindicated if the patient (1) shows any increased intracranial pressure, (2) shows cerebral pathology, (3) shows impaired cardiac function, especially if from an aneurysm or recent myocardial infarction, or (4) is pregnant.

Since ancient times, humans have used drugs to alleviate depression, notably alcohol and other self-medications. Although new medications, such as gepirone, are constantly being developed, the two traditional major subcategories of antidepressants used in recent times are the tricyclics and the monoamine oxidase (MAO) inhibitors (see Chapter 15). Both drug classes require substantial trial-and-error adjustment on dosages (titration), and both require from several days to several weeks before any positive effects occur. Because the MAO inhibitors have more significant side effects, the tricyclics have been favored in recent years (Lickey and Gordon, 1991). They are most effective with severe depressions that have a significant endogenous component, but the rate of effectiveness is seldom better than 70 percent. When the tricyclics are administered to someone who actually has a bipolar disorder in a depressive phase, there is a very real danger of stimulating a manic episode. Some depressives have responded well to high doses (3,000 mg) at bedtime of L-tryptophan, a naturally occurring amino acid. A dose of nicotinic acid needs to be taken at the same time to protect the liver from destroying all of the L-tryptophan. Also, in a study in which imipramine and lithium were used, Prien and Klupfer (1986) found that drug therapy should be maintained for at least sixteen to twenty weeks following a cessation of significant depressive symptoms. Additionally, even mild symptoms during the period indicated that the depression had not run its course and that continued drug therapy was essential to contribute to the absence of relapse in the treatment group.

When there is a strong seasonal variation in the depression (i.e., occurs significantly more often in winter), sessions of bright, incandescent light can be effective, especially light in either the white or green spectrums (Oren et al., 1991). Treatment sessions are normally about two hours per day and delivered by a light box or light-source visor. It is equally important to avoid or remedy disruptions of the individual's circadian rhythms.

Also, there is some evidence that a certain small subgroup of major depressives may have a disturbance in rapid eye movement (REM) sleep patterns. This specific pattern is marked by an abnormal temporal distribution of REM sleep. This inadequate capacity to sustain REM sleep tends to worsen with age in all individuals and may explain why sleep problems are much more common as persons age. Vogel and his colleagues (1980) treated this subgroup of depressives by depriving them of REM sleep for short periods of time and found that this significantly decreased their depression. It is interesting that depressed patients who were responsive to this technique were unresponsive to the tricyclic antidepressives, although in a comparison among studies, REM sleep deprivation and drug treatments were equally effective. However, it takes about three weeks for the REM sleep deprivation technique to bring about improvement. When specific brain dysfunction has caused depression, the disease is more likely to be found in the left frontal region.

Any of the intrusive techniques have a number of risks, which, of course, can be balanced by gains in controlling the depression and in preventing any suicide behaviors. Yet it is most important that they be implemented in an overall treatment that includes a variety of techniques designed to control the depression psychologically and to upgrade the skills needed to prevent future depression (Haaga et al., 1991).

## ■ Dysthymia (Depressive Neurosis) (300.40)

Many of the symptoms characteristic of the depressive episode are noted here. However, they are not as severe or as common, but they are of longer duration. A duration of two years is required for the diagnosis (except for children and adolescents, where the requirement is one year and where irritability can substitute for depression), and periods of dysphoria cannot be separated by periods of normal mood of more than two months. Dysphoria and apathy are commonly noted, although neither severe impairment in social or vocational functioning nor significant suicidal preoccupation is consistently present. Along with the characteristics just noted, the DSM-III-R requires that at least two depressive symptoms occur, such as sleep disturbance, poor appetite or overeating, low self-esteem, low energy or fatigue, problems in concentration or decision making, or feelings of hopelessness.

☐          MMPI-2

Since this personality profile does not show the anxiety, agitation, and possible psychotic components of major depression, a lower overall profile is expected. For example, scale 9 is not as likely to be low nor is scale 0 likely to be as high as in the depressive episode. Yet, scales F, 2, and 7 are high. If scale 4 is raised, there is reason to look for a passive-aggressive use of the depression (Anderson and Bauer, 1985). If somatization is a major factor, scale 1 should be high. The DEP content scale is usually high.

☐          16 PF

Similarly, the 16 PF profile is not as extreme for dysthymia as in the depressive episode, yet the general outline is the same and is similar to the pattern for the more neurotic aspects of the depressive episode. With that stipulation, scale C is not as likely to be low nor is $Q_4$ likely to be quite as high.

☐          OTHER TEST-RESPONSE PATTERNS

In contrast to the profile of the major depressive episode, the highest elevation on the MCMI-II is likely to occur on D, with the more severe symptomatology of CC less prominent. To the degree anxiety is present, there is an elevated A. Borderline and negativistic personalities can be susceptible to developing this disorder, so elevations on scales 8A and C are indicated. Very low scores on 7 are expected, because the restrained affectivity and conscientious self-image of the conforming personality are not compatible with the depressive affective features of the dysthymic disorder.

Several short scales (approximately 20 questions) have been specifically designed to measure depression and can be helpful in screening procedures and measuring outcome (Lambert et al., 1986). Three of the most commonly used have been the Zung Self-Rating Depression Scale, the Hamilton Rating Scales, and the Beck Depression Inventory. All three have been found to have adequate validity, although Lambert's data seems to favor the Zung. Others have commented, however, that the Zung Scale is too age-specific for certain groups, since normals under nineteen years of age or over sixty-five unfortunately tend to score in the depressive range.

Performance on other tests will be similar to that of the depressive episode; again, the clinician should temper the interpretation of these patterns with the awareness that this is less severe than major depression, with the symptoms more integrated into the ongoing personality.

☐          TREATMENT OPTIONS

Monitoring is a worthwhile first step in any treatment of depression (Haaga et al., 1991). Simple self-monitoring of both mood and activity produces decreases in depressed mood, as well as some increase in self-reported participation in chosen activities. To aid in self-monitoring, it is useful to teach them to keep a daily log of their automatic thoughts, especially those that are dysfunctional—for example, "I can never succeed to the point that (Mommy, Daddy, or others) will love me," "If I'm alone, I'll be unhappy," "If I become unhappy, I won't be able to stop it," etc. The most straightforward method for uncovering automatic thoughts is to ask clients what thoughts went through their minds in response to particular events. Modeling the assessment on some of your own automatic thoughts can also be useful. Such thoughts can then be analyzed "scientifically" and/or confronted, e.g., via rational-emotive techniques (Lyons and Woods, 1991).

With regard to their future perspective, depressives should understand that occasional upsurges of anxiety and depression will occur throughout their lives and that these should not be construed as indications of a return to pathology. This is an important admonition for all groups with psychopathology. In many cases, as these persons move toward a cure, they develop hope that they will never encounter any experiences similar to their past disorder. Hence, when these experiences naturally emerge, even in a minor form, there is a tendency to drop their coping patterns. Adopting a cognitive set to counteract this phenomenon is most important.

Chemotherapy is often used with dysthymia, but it is not as appropriate as it is for the more severe depressive episode (Burrows, 1992; Poling et al., 1991). Since learned helplessness is often a factor in dysthymia, chemotherapy, ECT, or similar treatments can easily exacerbate this component by pointing out in a direct way that a patient cannot play a major role in redirecting their life situation. As a result, a package derived from the following psychological treatment methods is recommended.

The clinician can employ contingency management techniques, as they aid the client especially in developing a new self-percept less confounded by helplessness and apathy. It is initially advisable for the therapist to avoid reinforcing any of the client's depressive verbalizations. The clinician can use audiotapes of the sessions to indicate to a client how thoroughly he or she is inclined toward these verbalizations. This approach can be augmented by a contractual agreement with the client to avoid such verbalizations and instead to increase the number of positive verbalizations (Meichenbaum, 1985). Such behaviors can be consolidated by using the Premack Principle and, in addition, by training the family and friends of the client to reinforce positive behaviors and verbalizations.

Imagery techniques are also helpful. For example, Lazarus (1971) recommends a variation of systematic desensitization that he terms "time projection with routine reinforcement." Clients are first hypnotized, deep relaxation is induced, and then they are asked to imagine that they are in the future and are engaged in what had been previously pleasant activities. Clients are then asked to return to the present while still maintaining these positive feelings and images from the future. By continually shifting back and forth, this time-projection strategy aids depressed persons to develop more-consistent present images of pleasurable activities; Lazarus indicates that this then generalizes into behavior.

Probably the most important psychological treatment methods of depression are the cognitive-behavioral techniques (Haaga et al., 1991), derived originally from Beck (1976). Through discussion and consciousness-raising techniques, clients are taught to view their thoughts more objectively (to distance themselves from these maladaptive thoughts). Such common depressive thoughts as "I am totally worthless" are suggested as hypotheses rather than facts, a phenomenon rather than a reality. In addition, clients are taught to "decenter." Through feedback, possibly in a group, depressives learn that they are not the focal point of all events, such as a disparaging glance on the street. Implicit in all this is the need for clients to learn to validate any self-made conclusions more objectively, a behavior notably absent in depressives. The belief systems that a person lives by are then examined, since impossible standards are commonly promoted within the self-system.

Another useful cognitive-behavioral treatment for dysthymia is covert negative reinforcement, because depressed individuals often find it different to envision positive behaviors at all and therefore are not particularly responsive to covert positive reinforcement techniques. In covert negative reinforcement with depression, a highly aversive image is developed and is then terminated by the imagination of the performance of the desired behaviors. It is critical that the switchover of images take place as quickly as possible.

Finally, a number of life-style modification techniques can be used. Assertiveness training is appropriate (Wickrameseka, 1988), so that the person does not introject anger and frustration. Inducing the individual to take more frequent and more strenuous exercise can help in many cases, and if the depression has a seasonal component, sessions of bright, incandescent light can be helpful (Oren et al., 1991). Within the context of group therapy, the person can contract for a series of graded tasks, all of which are increasingly pleasurable and thus likely to change the overall negative set the individual carries. Such experiences appear especially therapeutic to the degree that they also increase the client's sense of mastery over events in the world.

# ■ Bipolar Disorder

The diagnosis of Bipolar Disorder, Manic (296.4x) requires that the individual has in the past shown a depressive episode and is now manifesting or has recently manifested a manic episode (the reader is referred to the criteria in the sections on depressive episode and manic episode previously described in this chapter).

The converse is required for the diagnosis of Bipolar Disorder, Depressed (296.5x). The diagnosis of Bipolar Disorder, Mixed (296.6x) requires that major depressive and manic episode symptomatology occur in rapid alternation or in combination and that the depressive symptoms that do occur are prominent, lasting for at least a full day. Bipolar Disorder, Mixed replaces the traditional term "manic-depressive psychosis," as it is usually understood.

The MMPI-2, 16 PF, and other test-data patterns are generally similar to what is expected in single episodes. The reader is referred to the appropriate sections for the behavior pattern manifest at the time. However, it should be noted that depressives tend to be lower on scales K, 2, 6, 7, and 8A than do bipolars (Donnelly et al., 1976). Clients with bipolar affective disorder show larger average cortical-evoked potentials than do normals, who in turn are higher than schizophrenics, with this particularly so at high stimulus intensities. It has also been found that the shift from mania to depression is physiologically marked by increases in blood levels of phosphorous and calcium, as well as differences in the epinephrine-norepinephrine balance (Swann et al., 1991). A similar phenomenon has been observed when certain withdrawn depressives move toward more agitated behavior.

□      TREATMENT OPTIONS

The treatment of the bipolar is directed in large measure toward the dominant affective mode at the time. Lithium therapy is used to alleviate severe mania and has occasionally been effective with the depressive component as well, although the standard chemotherapy for the depressive component is that noted in the previous section on the depressive episode. It should again be noted that administration of the tricyclic antidepressants to an individual with bipolar disorder who is in a depressive phase may induce a manic episode. As the person moves toward a better level of functioning, the psychological treatment techniques noted in the sections on manic episode and dysthymic disorder become the primary mode.

## ■ Cyclothymia (301.13)

Cyclothymia is the DSM-III-R term for the traditional term "cyclothymic personality." As with dysthymia, this diagnosis requires a disorder duration of two years (but not symptom-free for more than two months), and one year for children and adolescents, as well as alternating numerous hypomanic episodes and depressions or loss of pleasure that were not major depressions. The reader is referred to previous sections for those diagnoses as well as the concomitant patterns expected on the MMPI-2, 16 PF, MCMI-II, and other tests. This disorder has traditionally been thought to be very rare, but recent evidence suggests that it is at least moderately common.

### □ TREATMENT OPTIONS

In most instances, the manic phase of cyclothymia is not severe enough to warrant significant intervention. Rather, it is more like a relief stage and, at worst, requires the psychological techniques noted in treatment of the manic episode. The depressive components are appropriately treated by the techniques detailed in the section on dysthymia (Haaga et al., 1991). The clinician should be careful to watch for the possible emergence of a classic bipolar disorder, and if the client shows any increasing pathology, lithium might be considered. Some clinicians have found the use of a diary helpful with cyclothymia. When a client keeps a diary, he or she becomes more attuned to the factors that are likely to set off the pattern.

## ■ Atypical Mood Disorders

The DSM-III-R has provided categories labeled Bipolar Disorder NOS (296.70) and Depressive Disorders NOS (311.00). These are simply residual categories in which there is clear evidence of a general pattern, although it does not exactly fit the specific diagnostic requirements of any mood disorder or the adjustment disorder with depressed mood.

## ■ Schizoaffective Disorder (295.70)

This disorder was traditionally (i.e., in DSM-II) included as a subgroup under schizophrenia. It is now listed as a separate disorder, probably because of the evidence that it has several characteristics different from those disorders that remain under the "schizophrenic" rubric. Schizoaffective disorder is more likely than schizophrenia to have an acute onset, and it has a better prognosis for avoidance of a long hospitalization and recovery to a premorbid level of functioning. In addition, it has been noticed that blood relatives of persons with the schizoaffective disorder do not have a significantly higher proportion of the same disorder than do normals, a finding different from that of schizophrenia.

☐ DSM-III-R

The essential feature of this disorder is a combination of schizophrenic and affective symptoms. The affective component (either significant depression, mania, or an alternating mixture of the two) occurs before or concomitant with the onset of the schizophrenic symptomatology. Evidence for both clear schizophrenic and affective symptomatology must be present, but there is no requirement of a duration of six months to diagnose this disorder. At some point, there is at least a two-week episode of delusions or hallucinations, but without prominent mood symptoms. This is essentially a residual category, as the clinician should have ruled out the major depressive disorders, schizophrenia, and the schizophreniform disorder.

☐ MMPI-2

Because of the confluence of two pathological trends, the profiles in schizoaffective disorders are likely to appear quite disturbed. Johnson et al. (1980) find that a spike 8, with high scores on scales 2 and 7, is characteristic of the schizoaffective disorder, particularly when depression predominates. Another common pattern for the depressed schizoaffective is the 8-2 profile (Kelley and King, 1979a). It is probable that these individuals have considered suicide and even have a specific suicide plan. The possibility of acting out this plan is often related to the 9 scale. As the score moves up, it indicates an increase in the amount of available energy and makes actualization of the plan more likely.

If the affective component is more in the manic direction, a common profile is an 8-9/9-8, with a higher score on scale 4 as compared to the depressed schizoaffective. In both types, scale 7 is elevated, as is the F scale (although both are more elevated in the depressed type).

☐ 16 PF

The 16 PF resembles the overall schizophrenic profile, but with the following qualifications. In the manic type of schizoaffective disorder, a higher A, F, and H and a lower N and $Q_4$ are more probable than in schizophrenia or schizoaffective, depressed type. Conversely, depressed schizoaffectives are inclined to show the reverse profile, having a fairly low F score, as well as lower scores on A, B (reflecting less attention to the task), E, H, and M. They also manifest a lower C and a higher O score, indicating more-blatant distress and emotional upset.

On the other tests, the typical patterns obtained by schizophrenics are likely, with the added content and style factors specific to either the manic or depressed syndrome.

☐    OTHER TEST-RESPONSE PATTERNS

The characteristics of the schizophrenic and affective disorders will appear in varying combinations on the MCMI-II as well. Typically, one would expect the profile of the affective disorder that is present along with elevation above 74 on S and a higher elevation on SS. Avoidant characteristics often occur, so there may be a moderately high score on 2.

☐    TREATMENT OPTIONS

As with the bipolar disorder, the treatment in large part depends on the affective flavor of the disorder. Since it is usually depression, the reader is referred to the sections on the depressive episode and the dysthymic disorder. In those rarer cases that have a manic component, the reader is referred to the section on the manic episode. The section on the schizophrenic disorders is also relevant here.

# ■    Late Luteal Phase Dysphoric Disorder (LLPDD)

The concept of a specific syndrome related to negative mood changes premenstrually was first introduced by Frank in 1931 (Dawood, 1985). Since then, many studies have been conducted on premenstrual syndrome (LLPDD), but there is still much that is not known about the disorder (McGrath et al., 1990; Corney and Stanton, 1991). As with many syndromes, failure to agree on a definition has led various investigators to utilize different criteria, creating inconsistencies among research findings.

Traditionally termed "premenstrual syndrome," the DSM-III-R uses the term "late luteal phase dysphoric disorder" to avoid what many perceive as prejudicial implications that have encrusted on the traditional term. As noted in Chapter 1, this category is not an official DSM-III-R diagnosis, but it is included in the DSM-III-R as an optional diagnosis.

The DSM-III-R offers a rather complex diasgnostic requirement in order to make a diagnosis of LLPDD, as opposed to the more general concept of "premenstrual syndrome." At least five of the following ten symptoms must occur, with at least one of the symptoms being number

1, 2, 3, or 4: (1) persistant and significant anger or irritability; (2) marked affective lability; (3) marked tension or anxiety; (4) marked self-deprecation, depression, or feelings of hopelessness; (5) lessened interest in usual activities; (6) significant fatigue or loss of energy; (7) insomnia or hypersomnia; (8) subjectively experienced problems in concentrating; (9) marked change in appetite, such as specific food cravings or overeating; and (10) other physical symptoms, such as sensations of bloating, swollen or tender breasts, headaches, joint pains, or weight gain.

Just as importantly, these symptoms must occur during the last week of the luteal phase and be remitted within a few days after onset of the follicular phase (in nonmenstruating females, determination of these phases may require measurement of circulating reproductive hormones). Also, the LLPDD cannot be simply an exacerbation of another disorder, such as major depression (although it can be superimposed on it), and the symptoms must be confirmed by prospective daily self-ratings during at least two symptom cycles.

Some LLPDD women have been found to have personality charac teristics of instability, suspicion, guilt-proneness, apprehension, tension, and self-conflict. Women with LLPDD commonly show problems in coping successfully with environmental stress or the added stress from internal changes. On the average, LLPDD sufferers were found to have significantly lower self-esteem; more negative attitudes about their bodies, their genitals, sexual intercourse, and menstruation; and the feeling of less control over the events of their lives (Corney and Stanton, 1991; Dawood, 1985). One of the more thorough reassessments of the literature suggests that the incidence of LLPDD is about 2 to 5 percent (Dawood, 1985)—reflecting the extent to which women are seriously debilitated by the disorder.

In the past, clinicians used questionnaires that focused on premenstrual symptoms to diagnose patients with LPDD. However, these questionnaires are often unreliable because they depend on retrospective reporting of symptoms. Patients tend to remember the symptoms that occur near menstruation but ignore those symptoms during the intermenstruum.

The specific cause of LLPDD is still unknown, although numerous hypotheses have been generated, with the most popular explanations focusing on hormonal disruption. But, it appears that LLPDD is a complex disorder comprised of several overlapping syndromes. It is likely that there is more than one specific cause in any individual case.

□ MMPI-2

Stout and Steege (1985) administered the Minnesota Multiphasic Personality Inventory to women suffering from LLPDD during their nonpremenstrual phase and found that almost all of them had normal profiles. The most common feature of the profiles was a low scale 5, which reflects a strong endorsement of the traditional feminine role. This is in striking contrast to the overall characteristics of that sample. Most of the women had completed college and were working outside the home. This may suggest that this group of women is particularly stressed by role conflicts related to career goals and stereotypical female values. Along with a low scale 5, a good percentage of the women had two-point codes of either 3-4 or 3-6, reflecting strong tendencies to overcontrol or repress angry feelings. Surprisingly enough, in light of all the physical symptoms experienced during the premenstrual phase, only 3 percent of the profiles met the criteria for conversion V on scales 1, 2, and 3.

As women move into their premenstrual phase, and their LLPDD symptoms become extreme, one would expect a rise in scales 1, 2, and 3, reflecting the physical changes and symptoms: edema, weight gain, breast tenderness, headache, and depression. Scales 7 and 8 would also likely increase mildly as symptoms of anxiety, irritability, depression, and dissatisfaction increase. Scores on scale 9 should be in the moderately low range, reflecting the lethargy experienced by some women.

☐    ## MCMI-II

Women with LLPDD may show basic personality patterns of a high scale 8 with a possible increase on scale 3. This would reflect emotional lability, hypersensitivity to criticism, and a lower frustration tolerance. LLPDD women should show an average response level to the pathologic personality disorders scales C, P, and S.

On the clinical symptom scales, scale A would tend to be a bit high, reflecting feelings of restlessness, tension, and physical discomfort. Scale H would be elevated to the extent that the woman is affected by physical symptoms. Scales N and CC are likely to be mildly elevated. This may seem contradictory, but it reflects the extent to which the client experiences unstable moods, distractability, impulsiveness, and irritability, as well as depressed mood and lack of hope for the future.

☐    ## 16 PF

For the woman with LLPDD, the 16 PF profile would generally resemble a normal profile, but it might destabilize somewhat as the woman approached the premenstrual days of her cycle.

$Q_4$ and I are likely to be high, reflecting the frustrations and overall sensitivity and stress. A low score on C, combined with a high $Q_1$ and low $Q_3$, may indicate the extent to which the woman is suppressing anger. Scale F is likely to be lower, as well as scale H, consistent with her tendency to focus on the inner aspects of the self, more often with negative perceptions and a feeling that she is being threatened.

□    OTHER TEST-RESPONSE PATTERNS

If LLPDD women took the Rorschach during the premenstrual cycle, one would expect a higher CF + C response, emphasized by several pure C responses. There would be an elevation of An + Xy responses, a high F + %, and possible the presence of a V response. D would be around the −1 or −2 range (Exner, 1986). A person with this type of profile is one who is fairly intelligent but who is unable to cognitively respond as well as usual because the affective experience is so intense.

On the TAT, women with LLPDD are likely to tell stories with themes of an overall depressed mood and self-deprecation, without reference to the future. They may show affective lability, overreacting affectively to the stimulus picture. The overreacting may take the form of explanations, criticisms, affectively charged descriptions, arbitrary shaping of the story, and emotional eruptions, even to the point of crying. They may also show blocking on a picture as a result of the interference of affects or of being able to describe only the mood or affective tone of the picture. There may be plots emphasizing sudden physical accidents and emotional trauma, such as the loss of husband, mother, sweetheart, job, or house by fire.

□    TREATMENT OPTIONS

There are almost as many treatments as there are proposed etiologies for LLPDD. Since the 1950s, progesterone has been used extensively on the basis that premenstrual-syndrome patients have either progesterone insufficiency or a high estrogen-to-progesterone level premenstrually. Although results of well-controlled double-blind studies show that progesterone and drugs like spironolactone are not generally more effective than a placebo, all were better than no therapy at all (Dawood, 1985). Other common treatments include diuretics, oral contraceptives, and vitamins A and $B_6$, again with varying although not marked success.

LLPDD has biological, behavioral, and psychological components, and in that vein, an effective multidimensional biopsychosocial approach can be effective. The first step is to record daily symptoms of mood and physical well-being in order to chart out a monthly pattern. Next, the client is asked to regulate the intake of certain foods and beverages. Reduction in caffeine and nicotine can help reduce premenstrual anxiety and irritability. Women with LLPDD should avoid alcohol because it can facilitate depression and feelings of hopelessness. They can cut down on their salt intake to help reduce the physical symptoms of edema, weight gain, and breast tenderness, but they should not cut down their water intake (continuing to drink at least 6 glasses of water a day). Naturally diuretic foods, such as cucumbers, asparagus, and watermelon, can help here. Also, women with LLPDD should be encouraged to eat small, frequent meals, rich in protein and complex carbohydrates, in order to decrease symptoms of anxiety, irritability, and lethargy. This helps to keep blood glucose levels stable, which in turn stabilizes estrogen-linked increases in insulin production.

Another step is to engage in a daily aerobic (but not overly vigorous) exercise program. Exercise cuts down the amount of body fat, which in turn reduces the amount of estrogen the body produces. It has consistently been found that women who are physically active tend to suffer less from LLPDD (Corney and Stanton, 1991). Efforts should be made to decrease stress, especially premenstrually, because stress exacerbates the symptoms of LLPDD. A stress-reduction program may include yoga, meditation, or relaxation exercises.

Finally, if these measures fail to alleviate the symptoms of LLPDD, medications may need to be prescribed, often amplified by standard treatments for depression and/or anxiety (Haaga et al., 1991; Hecker and Thorpe, 1992). The choice of medication should be determined by the prominent symptoms. In this regard, clinicians group LLPDD clients into four categories, characterized by a different cluster of symptoms and thus by different therapies.

First, there are women whose main symptoms are anxiety, irritability, and mood swings. They respond best to magnesium and $B_6$ supplements and sometimes progesterone suppositories. Other women with LLPDD experience depression, insomnia, and mental confusion and are best treated with progesterone suppositories and in some cases, an antidepressant.

A third category includes women who primarily report bloating, swelling, weight gain, headaches, and breast soreness. They may be helped by the drugs bromocriptine or spironolactone or by supplements of $B_6$ or vitamin E. The fourth group of women is characterized by increased appetite and cravings for sweets. They respond well to the hypoglycemic diet and a B-complex supplement.

# CHAPTER 5

# Anxiety Disorders

This grouping of disorders is a subgroup of the disorders traditionally termed "neurosis," and indeed, this subgroup of disorders is subtitled the Anxiety and Phobic Neuroses in DSM-III-R. Many clients show symptoms from various diagnostic categories, so a single DSM-III-R diagnosis may not communicate the complexity of their disorders. The anxiety disorders in DSM-III-R do not encompass such traditionally included categories as conversion reactions or dissociative reactions, which are now dealt with in separate sections. The DSM-III-R category of anxiety disorders is meant to include only those in which anxiety is still present or at least operative. Some clinicians might argue that this is not necessarily so for the obsessive-compulsive disorder or the post-traumatic stress disorder, but they are included here nevertheless.

## ■ MMPI-2

The classic general signs for neurosis on the MMPI-2 are elevations on scales 1, 2, 3, and 7. In fact, scales 1, 2, and 3 are often referred to as the "neurotic triad." The neurotic disorders, of which the anxiety disorders are a traditional subclassification, have an MMPI-2 that slopes from left to right, whereas the psychoses are expected to slope from right to left. The character disorders tend to peak more in the middle, with emphasis on the word "tend."

The F scale is high in the neurotic profile. If it is very high, and scales K and L are 50 T or less, the clinician should look for (1) a blatant cry for help that could point to a variety of disorders, (2) faking-bad, or (3) in a hospitalized psychiatric population, the diagnosis of confused psychotic (Gynther et al., 1973b). As a result of the relative openness about anxiety, anxiety disorder profiles show some elevation on most of the scales, with the exception of 5, 6, and 9. They are typically high on the A and ANX (anxiety) scales, and to the degree the fear is specific, on the FRS (fears) scale.

# ■    16 PF

The general profile for the anxiety disorders has higher scores on I, L, M, O, and $Q_4$, with a moderately high score on $Q_2$. In addition, one would expect scores to be lower on C, E, F, G, H, and $Q_3$.

Karson and O'Dell (1976, p. 83) list the individual scales in their order of importance in contributing to the second-order anxiety scale derived from the 16 PF. They list these as $Q_4$, O, C. L, and $Q_3$. If very high, $Q_4$ can additionally be interpreted as a cry for help, as it shows an r of .75 with scale 7 of the MMPI-2. $Q_3$ is an index of emotional lability, that is, a reflection of the ability to bind up anxiety. Scales I and M pick up an ongoing vulnerability or sensitivity to stress.

The anxiety disorders, especially in males (Krug, 1980), are relatively higher on scale M than are those who suffer psychosomatic disorders. It is hypothesized that in neurotics with anxiety, the greater inclination to fantasy makes them more prone to anxiety reactions, whereas psychosomatics have a more practical and concrete cognitive process, so they are more likely to use denial (Silverman, 1976) and less prone to use fantasy behavior to cope with distress.

# ■    Other Test-Response Patterns

On the MCMI-II, the single most prominent indicator, in most cases, of the presence of an anxiety disorder is the highest elevation on A (Choca et al., 1992). Because features of somatic disorders and depression are often involved, scales D and H frequently lie in the 75-or-higher range of scores. Personality types indicated by elevated scales on 2, 8A, 8B, C, and S are subject to anxiety experiences that may develop into anxiety disorders. Scale 7 is negatively correlated with the overt experience of anxiety. To the extent to which alcohol is used to cope with chronic anxiety, high scores on B occur.

Impaired concentration from high anxiety would likely result in lower scores on arithmetic and digit span on the WAIS-R. In addition, as a result of anxiety and its accompanying inefficiency, lowered performance scores in general could be expected. In particular, awkwardness and a lack of orderly checking could lead to mistakes on object assembly and block design that one would not otherwise be expected to make. This anxiety may also result in surprising errors in the early part of the information subscale.

A classic sign on the Rorschach of high anxiety and the inability to cope with it is extreme (both ways) reaction time to the cards. Color shock, or the inability to integrate and respond appropriately to the color cards, is also commonly noted as a sign of anxiety or neurosis (Exner, 1986). The novelist Joseph Heller (1974, p. 435) described the phenomenon of color shock well:

**Some look like Van Dykes, and these I'm tempted to tug. Others have sideburns and shock me a moment like card number eight on the Rorschach test again. I was struck speechless when that damned color shock card appeared. I was stupefied.**

Poorly integrated W responses, a form level below the acceptable range of 65 to 80 percent, and vague responses—such as clouds, smoke, maps, etc.—are also a common result of the high anxiety. Shafer (1954) states that several C or P responses, a moderately low F percentage, and oral-threat-content responses (such as wolves) are indicative of potential for anxiety moving into panic. Shading, tiny figures, and fine and/or broken lines are traditionally thought to connote anxiety in figure drawings (Oster and Gould, 1987).

## ■ Treatment Options

A wide variety of techniques are used in the treatment of the anxiety disorders (Hecker and Thorpe, 1992; Hoehn-Saric and McLeod, 1988). Besides the standard reasons, treatment is critical to reduce the heretofore unrealized high rate of suicide—in anxiety-disorder clients it is almost as high as that with depressives (Allgulander and Lavon, 1991). One option is the development and maintenance of a relaxation response as an antidote. Other possible options are systematic desensitization, implosive therapy techniques, chemotherapy, and covert conditioning techniques. They aid in the avoidance of anxiety-generating situations and facilitate the ultimately critical variable in the treatment of the anxiety disorders: helping clients to confront the sources of their fears (Lyons and Woods, 1991). To the degree that the client is highly labile and physiologically reactive, the anxiety-lessening techniques, such as relaxation training, are useful; if that is not as strong a factor, an emphasis on skills training may be more productive (Cattell, 1986). Stress inoculation training and/or cognitive reframing are also effective and have been proved superior to chemotherapy, if you consider the issue of side effects (Hecker and Thorpe, 1992). Treatment requirements for the obsessive-compulsive disorder differ markedly from those of the generalized anxiety disorder or even the phobias. The reader is referred to the specific sections for treatment suggestions.

■      ## Agoraphobia

The phobic disorders in general are patterns in which chronic avoidance behavior is combined with an irrational fear of a particular object or situation. Many people experience phobias of one sort or another; for example, many people avoid extreme heights or strongly fear touching snakes. Because these types of fears can easily be controlled by environmental avoidance patterns, they are not usually disabling. A classic phobia is disproportionate, disturbing, and disabling and is marked by responses to a discrete stimulus. People with phobias may assert that their avoidance is reasonable because of the overpowering anxiety they feel, but they do not usually claim that this is rationally justified.

Agoraphobia is a more complex phobia. The essential marker is a severe fear of being left alone in unfamiliar circumstances or of being in the midst of people with no help available. Their ultimate fear seems to be that they will be left alone, with the possibility that fear or panic will occur and overwhelm them. Such individuals have a very low threshold for discomfort anxiety.

Even though agoraphobia is an important concept in DSM-III-R, it had not even been listed in DSM-I and II. It could be hypothesized that the rapid rise in the occurrence of this disorder reflects the increasing interpersonal alienation and heightened requirements for competence in vocational and social functioning that mark our society. In addition, such factors as the rising divorce rate and alleged breakdown of the family unit, along with our increased urbanization and the high level of social and geographic mobility, make it easier than ever to experience being alone in facing change and stress.

Such pressures often first coalesce in adolescence, although they may have been preceded by attacks of separation anxiety and occurrences of school phobia in childhood (Hoehn-Saric and McLeod, 1988). Social or vocational role changes make one particularly vulnerable to this disorder. Hence, women in a traditional housewife role who are going through menopause at the same time their children are leaving home are likely to be vulnerable to this pattern. Agoraphobics are prone to become housebound and attempt to break up their anxiety through manipulative behaviors toward significant others. Since these defenses are seldom effective, such individuals may with time become bothersome to those around them and consequent depression will then complicate the agoraphobia. Alcohol and other drugs may be used to dilute the anxiety, leading to an overlay pattern of addiction. Approximately 5 percent of the population has at some time suffered from agoraphobia; the disorder is common in both psychiatric and cardiac practices.

□      DSM-III-R

The two specific DSM-III-R diagnoses are Agoraphobia without History of Panic Attack (300.22) and Panic Disorder with Agoraphobia (300.21).

Agoraphobia is specifically defined as the avoidance of any situation, particularly being alone, where people fear they could not be helped or get in touch with help in the event of sudden incapacitation. These fears pervade their worlds, and as a result, they avoid being alone in open spaces or avoid public places where help is possibly not available if there is an emergency. As a result, their normal behavior patterns and experiences are disrupted.

## MMPI-2

Agoraphobics, whether or not they experience panic attacks, should score relatively close to the modal pattern for anxiety disorders presented in the previous subsection, with high scores on the A and ANX (anxiety) scales, and usually on the LSE (low self-esteem) scale. Even when the diagnosis "with panic attacks" is warranted, it is not likely that the person would be experiencing the panic at the time of testing. It would, however, suggest that the individual is not adept at binding up anxiety, so there will be some scores on the MMPI-2 and 16 PF that will differ. The 2-7/7-2 profile with scales 1 and 3 close to average is a likely one here, reflecting the high level of anxiety, the rather vague targets for the anxiety, and the absence in most cases of accompanying extensive somatic concerns or conversion reactions. Scales 4 and 9 would also be expected to be relatively low, and scale 8 would depend partially on how well the anxiety is integrated. The O scale is likely to be raised, even above the other neurotic disorders. The uncommon 7-0/0-7 profile, which reflects anxiety and inadequacy, might well suggest an agoraphobic orientation.

## 16 PF

Mlatt and Vale (1986) found that female agoraphobics who have families score significantly higher on the relaxed-tense dimension ($Q_4$) on the 16 PF, while male agoraphobics who are married with children score significantly higher on the dimension of tension ($Q_4$), warmth (A), and suspiciousness (L) and significantly lower on emotional instability (C). Generally, scales such as O and $Q_4$ will be high and somewhat dependent on whether or not there are panic attacks, with the latter suggesting higher scores. Slightly higher scores on scales I and L might also occur, reflecting the isolation of the individual who has developed agoraphobia. Similarly, scale A would probably be low in this disorder, but it is not commonly as low in the anxiety disorders.

## OTHER TEST-RESPONSE PATTERNS

The typical indicators of anxiety on the MCMI-II—great elevation on A and possibly on H and D—are expected here. With respect to precipitating personality styles, however, dependent types (scale 3) are more vulnerable to agoraphobic attacks.

☐    TREATMENT OPTIONS

Chambless (1985) points out that agoraphobia is particularly difficult to treat, with only about 20 percent of cases receiving significant, lasting relief. Chambless states that the agoraphobic very much needs to feel accepted, and the initial fostering of dependency is encouraged here more than with most other types of clients. As clients are eventually weaned from dependency, assertiveness training is useful to help them deal with their personality dependency and general lack of self-sufficient behaviors. The repressed feelings, often directed toward significant others, can be elicited by having the client write a diary with a focus on those feelings, and then catharsis techniques can be more systematically employed. Cognitive restructuring of the negative thoughts is also crucial to success (Hecker and Thorpe, 1992).

The tricyclic antidepressants, especially imipramine, which appear to block the reuptake of serotonin and norepinephrine by the presynaptic neurons and thus increase their concentration at the synaptic cleft, can help eliminate the panic aspects of agoraphobia with panic attacks, but they seldom do much for the agoraphobia (Hecker and Thorpe, 1992). Down-regulators of 5-HTZ receptors, such as busiprone, have proved helpful here, as has alprazolam.

The panic experience, so common in agoraphobia, can often be effectively dealt with by implosive therapy, or flooding. Implosive therapy can be presented either in imagination or in vivo, depending on the particular case, and it is more successful if the implosion is carried out when anxiety is not muted by tranquilizing drugs. The stimuli can be presented either live or via audiotape, although therapist presence facilitates the effects in the latter condition. The client's ability to develop vivid imagery is a positive factor (Walker et al., 1991).

Even clients who are able to approach and handle the feared object after implosive therapy may still retain a basic fear sensation. This feeling typically dissipates with time; initially it can be disconcerting to the client and even to the therapist. An in-vivo desensitization involving successfully difficult practice tasks can be helpful here. As the fears of the agoraphobic become more specific, usually as the panic recedes, techniques such as relaxation training, systematic desensitization (SDT), and other behavioral control methods offer the highest chance of a successful intervention (Foa and Kozak, 1986). In certain situations, the use of a neighborhood self-help group can reduce agoraphobia, and the training of the spouse to be a "coach" and supportive companion is also effective.

■    ## Overanxious Disorder (313.00)

If the person is under eighteen and is manifesting anxiety similar to agoraphobia, the appropriate diagnosis could be either Overanxious

Disorder (313.00) or Separation Anxiety Disorder (309.21). These two disorders are typically seen in childhood or early adolescence rather than in late adolescence. They predict later disorders, such as agoraphobia, the phobic disorders in general, the generalized anxiety disorder, or other similar patterns.

The diagnosis of overanxious disorder requires symptomatology of excessive worry or anxiety for at least six months and evidence of at least four of the following: (1) unrealistic worry about the future or past or about ability in such areas as academic subjects, athletics, and social interactions, (2) tension and inability to relax, (3) proclivity toward self-consciousness and embarrassment, (4) an excessive need for reassurance, or (5) somatic complaints without a physical basis.

Diagnosis and treatment for adolescents who show this disorder are similar to those advised for the anxiety disorders in general, the panic disorder, and the identity disorder, and the reader is referred to those sections.

## ■ Separation Anxiety Disorder (309.21)

The correlation of separation anxiety and school phobia is high and in some cases may precipitate referral for treatment (Bloom-Feshbach and Bloom-Feshbach, 1987). While refusal or reluctance to go to school often accompanies separation anxiety, the use of the term "school phobia" to describe these children is frequently misapplied. Whereas simple phobias refer to anxiety responses associated with specific stimuli, such as school, and typically involve otherwise stable personalities, disorders such as separation anxiety and agoraphobia generally suggest more deep-seated personality disorders and are characterized by an overlay of symptoms that may include generalized anxiety, depression, and somatic complaints. For the child experiencing separation anxiety, it is usually not the stimulus of school from which she or he retreats that is of clinical significance, but the attachment to parents or others that is sought. Thus, "school phobia" is a misnomer when applied to children experiencing separation anxiety associated with refusal or reluctance to attend school, and the term "school refusal" is generally more appropriate. Separation anxiety disorder commonly develops after a loss (the death of a relative or pet), after a change in the child's environment, or after a change in school or neighborhood.

A diagnosis of separation anxiety disorder requires evidence of disturbance for only two weeks, onset before age eighteen, and significant anxiety regarding separation from attachment figures, as evidenced by at least three of the following symptoms: (1) worries that major attachment figure, such as a parent, will be harmed or will not return; (2) worries about being separated from attachment figures, such as being lost or kidnapped; (3) nightmares about separation; (4) resultant school phobia; (5) resultant reluctance or refusal to sleep; (6) apparent resultant physical symptomatology at points of potential separation; (7) temper tantrums or evidence of psychological distress on potential separation; (8) recurrent signs or complaints of excessive distress when separated from home or attachment figures; or (9) reluctance to stay alone or at home without the major attachment figure.

School refusal is often hard to sort out from a normal response (Bloom-Feshbach and Bloom-Feshbach, 1987). Most school children's worst fear on entering kindergarten or the first grade is leaving their homes and their mothers. The first symptoms may include waking up in the morning with somatic complaints such as headache, stomach pain, vague "aches," or nausea, but no fever. So, after recurrences of these alleged illnesses, most parents become concerned. As school refusal worsens, actual symptoms may occur, including sleep disorders, disrupted peer relationships, low school achievement, and distinct school avoidance. Poor attendance in school naturally disrupts peer relationships and school achievement. A fear of being teased by other children and disapproval from the teacher for the child's ongoing absenteeism can cause the child to further refuse school. Such fears may also be expressed in nightmares and fantasies, resulting in requests for someone to sleep with him or her at night. School refusal is often preceded by episodes of separation anxiety.

☐ TREATMENT OPTIONS

Cases of school refusal and separation anxiety provide an opportunity for treatment from a variety of theoretical perspectives, largely due to the range of clinical symptoms that arise and the nature of etiological factors. From a behavioral perspective, treatments involving contingency management programs and systematic desensitization have been found to be successful in reducing symptoms of anxiety and improving school attendance (Dangel and Polster, 1986). In SDT, the emphasis is placed on developing a relaxation response in association with a feared stimulus—school, separation from mother, riding a school bus, etc.—in an attempt to reduce and eventually eliminate fear responses, while at the same time assessing the system of overt and covert reinforcements that is maintaining the target behaviors. In a contingency management program, reinforcers are used to reward school-approach behaviors rather than school-avoidance behaviors, and school refusal results in such punishments as time out, loss of privileges, or extra household chores.

From a psychodynamic or developmental perspective, symptoms of separation anxiety may be seen as mechanisms of defense that function to reduce the anxiety generated from intrapsychic conflict (Bloom-Feshbach and Bloom-Feshbach, 1987). Unconscious conflicts are worked through using the therapeutic relationship as a mechanism of change, perhaps involving such techniques as psychodynamic play therapy, fantasy storytelling, and art therapy to express unconscious material indirectly.

In many cases, the parent is subtly (or not-so-subtly) reinforcing the child's separation anxiety. It is always worthwhile to interview the parent for current stresses or concerns and to see if the parent is over-reliant on the child. Using a family systems model, the structure of family relationships might be emphasized, with a goal of treatment being to restructure family boundaries and communication patterns. Attempts are made to strengthen the boundary between parent and child and to more clearly establish family roles.

## ■ Social Phobia (300.23)

Social phobics are marked by anxiety about possible scrutiny of their behaviors by others, usually accompanied by clear anticipatory anxiety of panic and/or acting in a manner that will be considered shameful by others (Walker et al., 1991). As a result of the anticipatory anxiety, social phobics make strenuous efforts to avoid such situations. Social phobias are centered on such behaviors as eating or riding in public, using public lavatories, or blushing.

The most common social phobia, however, is one in which the person is acutely fearful of public speaking. This often leads to a classic vicious cycle (Hecker and Thorpe, 1992). First, such persons experience anxiety about a public performance. If they then attempt to proceed in spite of the anxiety, the upset often detracts from the adequacy of the performance, possibly even causing them to twitch or shake visibly. Their prophecy that they will perform poorly and be embarrassed is then fulfilled, and future anticipatory anxiety is facilitated.

This disorder in severe form is relatively rare; it usually begins to evolve in late childhood or early adolescence, although spontaneous eruptions in adult life are not that uncommon (Hoehn-Saric and McLeod, 1988). The disorder is rarely incapacitating, but it may stunt an individual's professional and economic advancement, particularly if the person's position requires making public presentations. Social withdrawal is not characteristic of this pattern, and if this is present in a substantial fashion, the diagnosis is not appropriate.

☐                        DSM-III-R

Social phobics show consistent avoidance of specific social situations in which they could be scrutinized and/or possibly embarrassed. Accompanying fear is disruptive and irrational, there is marked anticipatory anxiety, there is often avoidant behavior, and at some point there is an exposure to the feared situation, which in turn generates immediate distress. However, they have insight into the inappropriateness of their behaviors, and the pattern is not accompanied by severe psychopathology in other areas.

☐     MMPI-2

Since these individuals are not markedly disturbed in any area other than their social phobia, their MMPI-2 profiles are relatively normal. The F scale is at least mildly elevated, which reflects their concern about obtaining help. They are higher on the O scale, reflecting their problems in social functioning, although this elevation is not consistently high. They are a bit lower on the 9 scale, indicating their lowered interest in interacting with the environment, and scales 3 and 2 may be somewhat elevated.

☐     16 PF

Again, there is an absence of the more extreme scores that are found in the anxiety disorders, even including the obsessive-compulsive personality. Yet, scores on scales E and H are usually low, and scores on I and $Q_4$ are reasonably high. Scores on scales C and L should be more toward the average than they are in the more blatantly disturbed anxiety neurotics.

☐     OTHER TEST-RESPONSE PATTERNS

In social phobia, the related symptoms indicated by elevation on D and H are less likely to occur on the MCMI-II than in other anxiety disorders. The elevation of A may vacillate depending on the imminence of a situation in which they may be scrutinized. Social phobias are deeply ingrained in the style of the avoidant so that some elevation on 2 is probable; however, an extremely withdrawn avoidant would not receive a diagnosis of social phobia.

☐     TREATMENT OPTIONS

The standard treatments for phobias—systematic desensitization and implosive therapy—are helpful with the social phobic, especially when combined with cognitive restructuring and guided imagery (Hecker and Thorpe, 1992). Analogously, the clinician can train clients to overcome their fear in a graded-task approach, wherein they gradually develop their public presentation and social skills in front of increasingly larger groups. Role playing that develops specific skills, such as rescuing a mistake made in front of an audience (a technique refined and made famous by Johnny Carson) is helpful in giving such clients a sense of control that allows them to go on if the anticipated and feared mistake does occur.

Propranolol, as well as the standard minor tranquilizers, can at times be helpful with that anxious mood that often accompanies the social and simple phobias, although it does not cure the phobia, particularly for the subgroup of phobics who are found to have a hyperresponsive betaadrenergic system. Propranolol, however, is contraindicated when there is indication of a tendency toward asthma or congestive heart failure.

## Simple Phobia (300.29)

The simple phobias are those that most people commonly associate with the term: fear of bugs, snakes, or any other discrete objects or situations not included in social phobia or agoraphobia. The simple phobias are usually relatively chronic disorders, typically arising in childhood, and tend to occur more frequently among (or are more commonly reported by) women (Kleinknecht, 1991).

As noted earlier, most individuals have at least one mild, nondisabling phobia of one sort or another. A fear of heights or snakes is very common and usually can be easily controlled, whereas a classic phobia is a disturbing, disproportionate, and disabling response to a discrete stimulus.

### DSM-III-R

The DSM-III-R criteria for simple phobia are similar to those for the other phobias except that the targets are simple and specific. The person shows avoidance behavior, which is distressing to the individual or interferes with functioning. At some point, exposure to the feared stimulus generates an immediate anxiety response. This behavior must be in response to an irrationally feared situation or object. If there is an element of active danger in this situation or object, such as in fear of heights, the reaction must be disproportionate. It is also required that phobics recognize the irrational aspect of their anxiety.

Fear of dirt or contaminated objects may at first appear to be a simple phobia. However, such a fear is more often a sign of the complex anxieties and conflicts that suggest an obsessive-compulsive disorder.

### MMPI-2

Simple phobics are more logical and rational in their thought processes, as well as less emotionally labile, than are people with more-complex phobias, such as agoraphobia. As a result, their MMPI-2 profiles usually are not particularly remarkable. They do tend to be high on the FRS (fears) and PHO (phobias) content scale, especially if they are multiphobic. Both F and K may be at least mildly elevated, the F elevation reflecting the expression of concern and the K simultaneously reflecting an attempt to keep the disturbance compartmentalized as to type of phobia. Minor elevations on scales 2, 3, and 7 can be expected, reflecting the mild to moderate anxiety combined with the symptomatic depression that can be expected by the time they seek help. This also reflects the tendency toward denial and a lack of insight that is occasionally characteristic of such persons. If their controls appear to be breaking down and they are becoming concerned that panic will set in as a result of an expansion of the phobia, an elevation of scale 8 occurs, and possibly on scale 6, too.

☐     16 PF

As with the MMPI-2, it would be extremely difficult to differentiate a simple phobic based on the 16 PF profile, since such phobics are so common and so close to normal functioning. However, following the theory that the individual has attempted to provide a focus for vague anxieties with the phobia, I would hypothesize at least some elevation on the $Q_3$. Yet the fact that it has not been entirely successful should lead to a mild elevation on O and $Q_4$. The H scale has been hypothesized as a measure of autonomic overreactivity, or what might be more broadly termed "emotional lability," and as a result, a lower score on H would be expected.

☐     OTHER TEST-RESPONSE PATTERNS

On the MCMI-II, the degree of elevation on A, D, and H may depend on the depth of the confrontation with the feared stimulus. Those whose prominent personality features are represented by scales 2, 8A, C, or S may be more likely to develop phobias in that they may connect their anxieties to many aspects of life, increasing the chance that a formerly innocuous situation will become phobic.

☐     TREATMENT OPTIONS

The classic treatment for simple phobia is systematic desensitization, and it is effective throughout the range of phobias usually seen by clinicians (Kleinknecht, 1991). The clinician can actuate this approach either in imagination or in vivo.

The therapist can vary the desensitization procedure by including a modeling phase. In this approach, the therapist first models the desirable behavioral pattern and then physically guides the person through the performance of the desired behavior (e.g., actually helping the person pick up the feared object). This can be combined with verbal support as one goes through the procedure, as well as with covert conditioning techniques.

For those clients who are not responsive to SDT, implosive therapy, or other cognitive-behavioral interventions, the controversial technique of aversion relief, pioneered by L. Solyom, can be effective. Simple phobics who have obsessive or hysteric trends benefit more from this procedure. An application of aversion relief would be to ask the client to tape record organized narratives of past and potential phobic experiences in the first person, present tense. The tape is then played back to the client through earphones, and lapses of silence, approximately twenty seconds in duration, interrupt the narrative of the appropriate juncture and are followed by electric shock. The tape then resumes immediately after the cessation of the electric shock (see Solyom, in Goldstein and Stein, 1976).

As noted in the prior section on social phobia, propranolol can reduce some of the accompanying anxious mood, though it does not cure the phobia. Propranolol is contraindicated where there is any evidence of asthma or congestive heart failure.

■ ## Panic Disorder

The panic disorder, suffered by about one in seventy-five adults, is primarily denoted by recurrent anxiety attacks and nervousness that the individual recognizes as panic. The person experiences anticipatory anxiety, an initial period of often intense apprehension, and the thrust of anxiety that is accompanied by autonomic symptoms and discharge. On occasion, these attacks may last for a period of hours, although attacks are typically for a period of about fifteen minutes during which the person literally experiences terror (Hoehn-Saric and McLeod, 1988). They present a high suicide risk (Fawcett, 1992). Up to one-third of such individuals develop agoraphobic patterns.

The disorder is recurrent and episodic; in at least 50 percent of these cases the course is chronic (Keller and Baker, 1992). The panic attacks are clearly separate incidents, and the anxiety experience is not a response to a phobic stimulus or to any event that is very dangerous in reality. Also, unlike the avoidance patterns noted in the phobias, panic disorder focuses more on the experience of terror and the temporary physiological discharge symptoms, such as cold sweats or hyperventilation. The terror experiences are not unlike "free-floating anxiety," an experience of anxiety with the inability to specify any source or reason for the anxiety, combined with "discomfort anxiety," the fear of being overwhelmed by the experience of anxiety (Walker et al., 1991).

☐ ### DSM-III-R

The DSM-III-R offers the specific diagnoses of Panic Disorder with Agoraphobia (300.21) or without Agoraphobia (300.01). To diagnose a panic disorder, the DSM-III-R requires that there be either one or more attacks with a month of persistent fear of another attack or at least four panic attacks within a month and that these not be in response to a naturally anxiety-arousing stimulus, heavy physical exertion, a phobic stimulus, or a situation in which the person was the focus of others' attention. It also requires the presence of at least four of the following symptoms during most of the attacks: dyspnea, palpitations, chest discomfort, choking or smothering sensations, dizziness, feelings of unreality, paresthesia, hot or cold flashes, sweating, faintness, trembling, nausea or abdominal distress, or fears of going crazy, losing control, or dying. During the attack, at least four of these symptoms develop suddenly and increase in intensity within ten minutes of the appearance of the first symptom.

To cope with these panic attacks, some individuals respond to this anticipatory fear of helplessness by becoming increasingly reluctant to leave the comfort and familiarity of home. If this fear increases, the diagnosis will likely change to agoraphobia with a panic attack. With this disorder, it is important to rule out physical disorders such as hypoglycemia, hyperthyroidism, withdrawal from certain drugs, or any other disorders that could engender such psychopathology.

☐      MMPI-2

A common MMPI-2 pattern for the anxiety neurosis—particularly where the emphasis is on anxiety, such as in the panic disorder and the generalized anxiety disorder—is a 2-8 code, with high scores on 7, 3, 1, and 4, in that order (Johnson et al., 1980). As such individuals move toward chronicity, they show profiles similar to agoraphobics (see the preceding section). One fairly rare MMPI-2 profile, the 3-9/9-3 pattern, has been characterized as typical of free-floating anxiety. As such, it would predict this disorder, as well as the disorder to be discussed next: generalized anxiety disorder.

The 1-3-7 profile has been characterized as showing high anxiety, passive dependency, and proneness to develop psychophysiological disturbance. Hence, it is possible for this profile to show up in a panic disorder. Scale 7 is likely to be consistently elevated in this profile, as well as scales 1 and 3, whether or not there is a primary elevation on other scales. In some individuals, an accompanying high scale 2 reflects a feeling of loss of control and a sense of hopelessness. As these feelings increase, 2-3/3-2 or 1-3/3-1 profiles are likely. They tend to be high on the A and ANX anxiety scales.

☐      16 PF

The 16 PF profile of the panic disorder is similar to the standard profile for the anxiety disorders: high scores on I, L, M, O, and $Q_4$; a moderately high $Q_2$; and low scores on C, E, F, G, H, and $Q_3$. Since the $Q_4$ score is the measure par excellence of anxiety, it should be particularly elevated here, and in that regard $Q_4$ shows a consistently high correlation with scale 7 on the MMPI-2. Other differences from the standard anxiety disorder profile are scale L is not quite as high, $Q_2$ may be moderately low rather than moderately high, and scale G is not as low.

☐  OTHER TEST-RESPONSE PATTERNS

High scores on A and D are expected on the MCMI-II. The autonomic arousal that occurs may produce substantial elevation on H. If these individuals become increasingly withdrawn and begin to confine themselves to avoid the possibility of panic, they may become more dependent, producing increasing elevation on 3.

☐  TREATMENT OPTIONS

Understand that panic attack clients are especially prone to suicide attempts (Fawcett, 1992), so consider the issues discussed in Chapter 14 on suicide potential. Since the hallmark of the panic disorder is episodic anxiety reaction accompanied by a high level of psychological tension, the development of a sense of mastery over anxiety and a controlled relaxation response is one priority (Keller and Baker, 1992). Progressive relaxation, autogenic training, or any other form of systematized relaxation training is helpful. Also, inhalation therapy using carbon dioxide can be very effective in some cases (Wolpe, 1987). These approaches can be amplified by encouraging the client to take up ancillary interests, such as meditation or yoga. In the initial treatment stage, it may be helpful to give the client a small prescription of tranquilizing medication to be used as needed. This helps avoid problematic side effects, only moderately intrudes on the person's sense of being able to handle it alone, and gives the person a sense that control is immediate and available (Foa and Kozak, 1986). If more long-term medication is needed, alprazolam has been effective here (Hecker and Thorpe, 1992), as has phenelzine, fluoxetine, and imipramine.

Treatment can be amplified by having clients work on the relaxation training in a group setting. Not only does this give them the awareness that others share this problem, but it also easily sets up a discussion of problems in a quasi-therapy setting. Later, they are more amenable to entering actual group therapy and thus may come into greater touch with the sources of their anxieties. As they do so, techniques more appropriate for the phobias, noted in prior subsections, can be brought into play so that they can confront and stay with the feared stimuli, a critical variable in obtaining a significant cure (Wickramasekera, 1988).

# ■ Generalized Anxiety Disorder (300.02)

Although the next consecutive listing in the DSM-III-R is the Obsessive Compulsive Disorder (300.30), the Generalized Anxiety Disorder (300.02) will be discussed first because it is functionally a chronic and less cyclical version of the panic disorder. Again, as in the panic disorder, there is autonomic disturbance, although this is now evident in more chronic manifestations. Some free-floating anxiety may be present in the generalized anxiety disorder, but the essential feature is chronic autonomic hyperactivity (Rapee, 1991). Thus it is similar to the general physiological-stress syndrome originally described by Hans Selye (1956).

Because it is a chronic disorder, persons have more apprehensive rumination and muscular tension than would be expected in a panic disorder. Emerging patterns of hypervigilance and self-checking will crystallize into the variety of patterns that are subsumed under the diagnosis of obsessive-compulsive disorder, which will be described next.

## □ DSM-III-R

The DSM-III-R requires evidence of persistent and generalized anxiety and worry about two or more life circumstances, as manifested in at least six symptoms out of a possible eighteen within the following three categories: (1) motor tension (high fatigue, muscular aches, twitches, or easy-startle responses); (2) autonomic hyperactivity (dry mouth, gastrointestinal distress, heart racing or pounding, or sweating disturbance); and (3) vigilance and scanning (hyperalertness, irritability, or related sleep difficulties). The DSM-III-R also requires that this anxiety occur more days than not during a six-month period and that it not be caused by an organic factor or be a part of a mood or psychotic disorder.

## □ MMPI-2

The profile of this disorder parallels the general profile for the anxiety disorders. Similar to the panic disorder, the profile will show high 2, 3, and 7 scores. The chronic autonomic hyperactivity is reflected in a relatively high 9 score, and if the person is beginning to fear loss of control about these behaviors, a rise on scale 8 is likely. A high F scale is also expected.

## □ 16 PF

As with the MMPI-2, the profile should resemble the modal anxiety disorder profile, with the extremes accentuated, as in the panic disorder. O and $Q_4$ should be very high, and H should be low.

□          OTHER TEST-RESPONSE PATTERNS

The impairment and tension resulting from high anxiety should lower the digit-span and arithmetic scores within the WAIS-R verbal scale scores. In general, the performance scores should be lower than the verbal scores, particularly object assembly. The rest of the notations in this section about overall anxiety disorders are also applicable.

High scores on A are expected on the MCMI-II, along with H representing the considerable physiological symptoms that occur. For the most part, the scores here should be similar to those of anxiety disorders. Elevation on scale 2 indicates the individual's feared cognitive failure, low self-esteem, and helplessness. Scale 8A would also be high, stemming from the impatient, irritable factors usually present in the anxious individual. Among the pathologic personality scales, an elevated S may occur if the individual is withdrawing from other people and social situations because they cannot handle the ensuing pressure. The interrupted sleep patterns, moodiness, and anxious worry typified by the borderline predisposes to this disorder. Combinations of elevations on A, D, and H may be expected, depending on the individual pattern of disturbance.

□          TREATMENT OPTIONS

The focus in the generalized anxiety disorder is on chronic states of autonomic arousal, which to some degree is genetically based, accompanied by apprehension (Rapee, 1991). Biofeedback is particularly helpful in the treatment of autonomic tension, and the clinician is advised to use a variety of modalities sequentially, such as electromyography (EMG), EEG, or the various measures of skin change (Schwartz, 1987). Concomitantly, teaching the client a controlled relaxation response is helpful (see prior section on panic disorder). Some form of meditation training may be useful, as is inhalation therapy using carbon dioxide (Wolpe, 1987).

It may be necessary to administer tranquilizing medication as needed in the initial stages, then to move quickly toward treatments that emphasize the client's increasing ability to control the response. As a client begins to gain more control over the anxiety, a treatment technique such as client-centered therapy, as originally advocated by Carl Rogers (1951), may become the primary treatment mode. The focus on empathy and warmth, combined with the initial low demand for specific discussion material, proves helpful here.

■          ## Obsessive-Compulsive Disorder (300.30)

Although the obsessive-compulsive disorder is listed as one of the anxiety disorders in the DSM-III-R, the direct experience of the anxiety is not as evident as in the other anxiety disorders (Kozak et al., 1988).

Obsessive-compulsive patterns are seen by the person performing them as irrational and ego-alien, yet there are usually no panic experiences or sudden upsurges of anxiety on encountering the anxiety-arousing stimuli or mental images. At least initially, the person attempts to resist the obsession or compulsion (Pato et al., 1991).

The obsessive-compulsive disorder is an excellent transition category to the somatoform disorders. These latter disorders were traditionally included in the term "neurosis," but anxiety is often not apparent in them, just as it is also not so obvious in the obsessive-compulsive disorder. The ego-alien quality is what discriminates the obsessive-compulsive disorder from the obsessive-compulsive personality disorder (Kozak et al., 1988). In the personality disorder, the compulsions are ego-syntonic (that is, they are not viewed by the person as in conflict with the essential qualities of the personality).

The usual age of onset for the obsessive-compulsive disorder is late adolescence or early adulthood. By the age of twenty-five, more than half of the treated obsessive-compulsives have already shown clear symptoms. This syndrome occurs proportionately more often in middle- and upper-class individuals. This should not be surprising, especially in a society that so highly values achievement, since those with compulsive patterns are often quite efficient and productive. Obsessive-compulsives are brighter on the average than individuals with the other anxiety disorders—obsessions are intellectual coping strategies for anxiety (Kozak et al., 1988).

The obsessive-compulsive disorder has traditionally been thought to be relatively rare, at least as compared to the other anxiety disorders, at a rate of around 3 percent of all "neurotics" and a rate of a bit less than 1 percent of the general population. This could be a function of the embarrassment that many of these individuals experience, which would result in a lower reported incidence (Kozak et al., 1988). Many who might be willing to report phobic anxiety would be more distressed to disclose that they think and act in ways they cannot control.

The most common obsessions seen by clinicians are repetitive thoughts of contamination or of violence, doubts about religion and one's duties, and self-doubts. The most common compulsion include checking behaviors, repetitive acts, and handwashing. The obsessive-compulsive disorder does not include compulsions to perform behaviors that are inherently pleasurable, such as alcohol indulgence or overeating. A person may not be able to control these latter behavior patterns, but they are not ego-alien. While they do not want the detrimental effects of their behavior (i.e., alcoholism or obesity) they do not experience inherent discomfort about eating or drinking behaviors.

□    DSM-III-R

The DSM-III-R requires evidence of obsessions (recurrent and persistent ego-alien impulses and ideas) and/or compulsions (repetitive behaviors

viewed not as a product of one's own initiative, accompanied by a sense
of subjective compulsion and a desire to withstand the compulsion). In
addition, the person must be distressed and recognize the irrationality
of the behaviors, which need to occupy at least an hour of the day or
significantly disrupt one's life. Also the clinician must rule out such syndromes as schizophrenia, organic mental disorder, or a major depressive
disorder, since all of these may be accompanied by obsessions or compulsions. The obsessive-compulsive disorder is often chronic and accompanied by some disruption in personal functioning.

☐          MMPI-2

The two common profile combinations related to the obsessive-
compulsive disorder are the 7-8/8-7 and 2-7/7-2 (Lachar, 1974). The 7-8/8-7
commonly includes an intense preoccupation with inner mental processes. Inspection of relative scores on the Harris-Lingoes subscales is
often very useful with these clients, both as a diagnostic tool and as
fodder for the therapy hour. If a person obtains an 8-7 profile, the clinician is more likely to encounter a combination of deteriorating personality function and depression, whereas a 7-8 profile indicates some continuing struggle and in that sense is more benign. In the 2-7/7-2 profile,
depression about one's functioning is a major component, and the person may have begun to show signs of social withdrawal.

It has been noted that the 2-7-8 high-point combination is a common
profile in patients but rare in normals. It reflects people who are self-
analytic and inclined toward catastrophic expectations and a sense of
hopelessness. They require goal-directed therapy combined with emphasis on reinforcement for any achievements, with a concomitant de-
emphasis of their tendency toward introspection and extensive
self-analysis.

The spike 7 profile is rare but suggests an obsessive-compulsive
diagnosis. Such individuals show a high number of phobias and obsessions, which should be reflected on those content scales, and are close
to breaking down and deteriorating into a psychotic condition. It should
be noted that the scores on the 7 scale predict obsessiveness more than
the compulsive aspects of the disorder. If health concerns are a central
focus, they should score high on the HEA content scale.

☐          16 PF

The modal 16 PF profile obtained by persons with an obsessive-
compulsive disorder (IPAT Staff, 1963) shows high scores on I, O, and
$Q_4$ and moderately high scores on L and M. They obtain a moderately
low score on C and low scores on E, F, H, and $Q_3$. A comparison with
the modal profile for the anxiety disorder shows that obsessive-
compulsives are only moderately low on C and only moderately high
on L and M, whereas persons with the anxiety disorders are high on C,

L, and M. Also, persons with anxiety disorders show a low score on G and a moderately high score on $Q_2$, whereas obsessive-compulsives perform in the average range on these variables. This is surprising; I would expect the obsessive-compulsive to score high on $Q_2$, relative to anxiety neurotics. Also, I would expect obsessive-compulsives to score high on scale B because they tend to be brighter than most individuals with a diagnosis of psychopathology. Clinicians should be aware of the possibility that the IPAT sample did not tape these variables. It also is probable that obsessive-compulsives—particularly if they are still gaining a sense of control from the patterns and thus are not yet deteriorating—should score higher on $Q_3$ than those with most other disorders, with the possible exception of the paranoid disorders. Furthermore, one should consider the possibility that the G score will be higher than average in obsessive-compulsives.

□     ## OTHER TEST-RESPONSE PATTERNS

On the MCMI-II, extreme elevations of D and H are more prominent than A. Indeed, overt expression of anxiety may not be present at all. Yet, obsessive-compulsives are very likely to express dismay regarding the ego-alien quality of their disorder and to express their anxiety through somatic channels. Unlike the personality profiles typically associated with anxiety, elevations on C, S, 2, and 8A are not as likely to be present in the obsessive-compulsive disorder. Rather, the controlled, conforming type is more likely to react to anxiety in an obsessive-compulsive way, very likely indicated by an elevated 7.

On the WAIS-R, there is an overall higher IQ than in other disorders, reflecting the obsessive-compulsive's average to above-average intelligence (Kozak et al., 1988). Those who are primarily obsessive score higher on the overall IQ score and also have a higher verbal- than performance-IQ score. Self-deprecation and questioning of one's performance, along with rather detailed verbalizations, are common. A meticulous approach to the block design and object assembly subtests is probable, occasionally leading to a loss of speed-bonus points but seldom resulting in inaccurate responses. Obsessive-compulsives usually do very well on vocabulary, similarities, and comprehension because of their meticulousness. At the same time, however, their inability to change "set" can sometimes penalize them on similarities. They also do well on both arithmetic and digit span (Rapaport et al., 1968). The intellectualization characteristic of the obsessive-compulsive disorder can result in a decrease in picture arrangement performance. A rather precise approach can again be expected on the Bender-Gestalt figures. The figures may be placed in a linear path, and a counting of the dots in appropriate cards is common.

On the Rorschach, expressions of doubt are expected, along with pedantic and esoteric verbalizations. Additionally, one expects a high number of responses overall, a high number of W and/or Dd, a high F+ percentage, edge details, and the likelihood of space responses. There are generally few color responses, and if color responses of poor form occur, they are thought to indicate decompensation (Shafer, 1954).

Obsessive-compulsives like to criticize the blots as well as their own responses and may express concern about the symmetry of the cards. Some surprising combinations or imagined responses (e.g., "two earthworms coming out of a rabbit's eyes" on card X) may occur. Similarly, pedantic wording ambivalence over themes and an emphasis on details rather than story content are common on the TAT, especially if the individual is orientated toward paranoia as well. Idealistic stories and esoteric, although nonemotional, fantasies may occur.

There are several questionnaires and inventories that have been specifically devised to further elucidate the obsessive-compulsive patterns, e.g., the Leyton Obsessional Inventory and the Maudsley Obsessional-Compulsive Inventory (Wetzler, 1989).

□     TREATMENT OPTIONS

Most experts recommend a combination of treatments for the obsessive-compulsive disorder (Kozak et al., 1988). A clear and consistent program of response prevention (e.g., taking all soap and towels away from a handwasher) combined with constant exposure to the eliciting stimuli to promote extinction provided in the context of a firmly and consistently demanding, yet supportive, therapy relationship is the core of an effective treatment program for the compulsive aspects of the disorder.

A dramatic example of this regimen is provided by Lazarus (1987):

We had him under 24-hour surveilance. He was not to do the circles. We even put mittens on his hands. Second, in terms of the germ phobia and the flooding, we got him to handle all of the dirty laundry in the hospital and he was not allowed to wash his hands for a week. He had to eat his food everyday without even washing his hands once. I was terrified that, with my luck, he would come down with the flu or a cold, and that would be the end of the therapy. Luck does play a great part. However, he was fine and of course he was flooded with anxiety. As for the obesity, we got everybody who was fat to sit on him, to roll him, to touch him; this was the flooding technique. Some people said to me, I hope you get a good EKG before you start these things. But the point is that sometimes these heroic methods are essential or else you are not going to get anywhere with these kinds of encrusted problems. However, if this is all you do, if breaking the web of obsessive-compulsive rituals is all you do, my prediction is that relapse will be pretty rapid. But having broken through with response prevention and participant modeling and flooding, in my approach you proceed to work on the other residual problems; sensation, imagery, cognition, and personal

**and biological malfunctions have to be looked at as well. That is the muiltimodal concept (p. 262).**

As is evident, level of motivation is a critical predictor of success in such a program, so a degree of both courage and confidence are necessary.

The anxiety discomfort component can be handled by SDT techniques and in vivo exposure supplemented by self-instructional training and cognitive reframing (Hecker and Thorpe, 1992). This approach is effective to the degree that the individual becomes more adequate in focusing on the sources of anxiety. It is also very helpful to first reduce any depressive components before administering any full-blown treatment directed at the obsessive aspects. Thought-stopping or paradoxical-intention techniques can also work to eliminate the ritualistic behaviors and to counter the specific automatic thoughts that are unique to that individual client. Although thought stopping is especially efficient in dealing with the obsessive component, paradoxical intention (discussed in the subsection on the compulsive personality disorder) is most efficient in controlling the compulsive aspects (Seltzer, 1986). As progress occurs on these fronts, standard group therapy and/or psychotherapy can be used, as these help obsessive-compulsives get in touch with their high level of repression and suppression and at the same time help them become willing to self-disclose more easily. Of the possible adjunct chemotherapies, chlorimipramine has been the most effective.

The standard thought-stopping procedure for the obsessions asks clients to let the obsessions flow as in free association. Clients are then told that on a cue (e.g., a raised hand by the therapist), they should shout "Stop!" Generalization is introduced by having clients practice this at home and to vary randomly the amount of time before vocalizing.

Thought stopping can be amplified by having clients visualize a pleasant scene immediately after saying "stop," thus furthering the relaxation and the control of the interruption sequence. In addition, moderately painful although harmless shocks can be administered by the therapist as the word "stop" is stated; this significantly reinforces the effect. The clinician can add biofeedback training to increase the percentage of alpha brain rhythms, since they are antagonistic to problem solving or ruminative thought sequences (Schwartz, 1987). However, remember that obsessives are so perfectionistic, particularly early in therapy, that they fight the process, which hinders progress and results in their viewing themselves as failing.

In those cases that do not show some reasonably immediate response to psychological techniques, especially where depression is interfering with motivation, a regimen of chemotherapy, traditionally imipramine, has been found to facilitate progress. In recent years, clomipramine has been found to be effective, as well as buspirone (Pato et al., 1991). Psychosurgery has had some traditional acceptance as a treatment for severe obsessive-compulsive patterns, but this has not received any consistent research support. Ironic anecdotal support comes from the report about a young Canadian (*The New York Times,* 2/25/88) whose severe phobia of germs and obsession with washing his hands disappeared after a .22-caliber slug lodged in his frontal lobe during an unsuccessful suicide attempt. The left frontal lobe is the usual target for psychosurgery for obsessive-compulsive patterns.

# ■  Post-Traumatic Stress Disorder and Adjustment Disorder

The essence of the post-traumatic stress disorder (PTSD) is a delayed distress response pattern to an atypical and severe traumatic event, an event such that most people would have very negative and disturbed responses. Such clients generally reexperience the stressor in intrusive thoughts and dreams, and depression and anxiety are common. Delayed disturbances in combat veterans—as from the Vietnam conflict, which was a spur to the conceptualization of this disorder—are often appropriately diagnosed here (Watson, 1990; Wolf and Mosnaim, 1990).

If the stressor is more within the normal range, with little in the way of a vivid reexperience of the trauma, the appropriate diagnosis is the traditional one of adjustment disorder. The diagnosis is appropriately qualified by the following terms:

with depressed mood

with anxious mood

with mixed emotional features

with disturbance of conduct

mixed disturbance of emotions and conduct

with work or academic inhibition

with withdrawal

☐          DSM-III-R

To apply the diagnosis of post-traumatic stress disorder, there must be evidence of a substantial stressor that would seriously disturb most people, such as being raped or being in an airplane crash. Reexperiencing of the stressful event is indicated by at least one of the following: (1) direct evidence of persistent reexperiencing of the event, as in recurrent related dreams, déjà vu about the event, or persistent memories of the event; (2) persistent avoidance of the event or general numbness of response, as in lessened affect, lowered intererst in at least one usual interest or activity, or detachment from others, etc.; and (3) persistent indications of increased arousal in two of the following behaviors that are existent, but not present before the stress; sleep disruption, hyperalertness, guilt over survival, memory or attention disruption, or exaggerated startle responses.

The post-traumatic stress disorder is sublabeled "delayed" if onset of symptoms is at least six months after the stressor.

□ DIAGNOSTIC CONSIDERATIONS

These disorders closely resemble the patterns seen in individuals with a panic disorder. The only major difference is that the person with a post-traumatic stress disorder or adjustment disorder may show fewer evident signs of disruption in overall personality functioning (Hammarberg, 1992).

For example, MMPI-2 scales 8 and F will probably be a bit lower. Interestingly, F scores were significantly lower among persons suffering from PTSD than those who were *faking* suffering from PTSD. Yet, the F-2-8 code type appears to be the most common code type in those actively suffering from PTSD (Litz et al., 1991). The 7-2 code type is also particularly likely, as it incorporates the emotional distancing and the distress that are characteristic of this disorder. Graham (1987) suggests that a 1-9/9-1 code is indicative of this disorder. Burke and Mayer (1985) found that PTSD patients in a VA hospital showed an 8-2-7 profile, as opposed to an 8-2-6 profile shown by random psychiatric VA patients, with the PTSD patients being noticeably lower in F, 6, 9, and the Goldberg Index. They tend to be high on the PK and PS supplementary MMPI-2 scales.

On the 16 PF, scales C, G, and $Q_3$ should not be as low as in the panic disorder. Scores on O and $Q_4$ are especially likely to be high. Clues to methods of crying come especially from selected TAT plates, e.g., cards 4, 6BM, 7BM, and 8GF (Swiercinsky, 1985). Otherwise, the diagnostic comments on panic disorders, the generalized anxiety disorder, and the anxiety disorders generally apply. In addition to the indicators of the panic disorder, 2, 6, and 8 may become more elevated on the MCMI-II as the disorder becomes more chronic, reflecting the lessened affect and detachment that occur.

There are a number of specific scales that have been designed to measure PTSD, a couple of which are embedded in MMPI-2. Most use face-valid responses, and the reader is referred to Watson (1990) for an extended discussion of these scales and their usefulness. The Penn Inventory appears to be especially useful (Hammarberg, 1992).

□ TREATMENT OPTIONS

Based on a comparison of psychodynamic, behavioral, and biochemical treatments for PTSD, it appears that direct therapeutic exposure to the trauma (e.g., via systematic desensitization or flooding or even focused group discussion) and cognitive reframing have emerged as the most important factors in treatment (Hecker and Thorpe, 1992; Wolfe and Mosnaim, 1990). A working-through process in which the client's world-beliefs, i.e., an overall cognitive schemata, are modified in accord with the traumatic memory is often necessary for a successful treatment.

In treating post-traumatic stress disorders and adjustment disorders, the clinician is also advised to keep in mind the principles of crisis intervention—immediacy, proximity, and expectancy—that were developed in World War II to decrease the consequent problems of the severe distress of combat. Immediacy emphasizes early awareness and detection by others close to the person, treatment as quickly as possible, and an emphasis on returning clients to their typical life situations as quickly as possible. Proximity emphasizes the need to treat clients in their own worlds—not distancing them from their upset by hospitalization. Lastly, the clinician must communicate a clear expectancy that although fear and anxiety are normal processes here, they do not excuse clients from functioning adequately; the sick role is not reinforced, and there is an emphasis on experiences that demonstrate that they are regaining control of their worlds (Wolf and Mosnaim, 1990).

These principles can be specifically amplified by the treatment techniques used for the panic disorder and the generalized anxiety disorder (the reader is referred to those sections). As the fears begin to focus more on specific concerns, SDT or implosive therapy is appropriate. Mild tranquilizers to be used as needed can also be a helpful adjunct treatment. Sessions with family and/or friends that help clients implement the principles of crisis intervention in his or her immediate world also facilitate a return to adequate functioning (Wolf and Mosnaim, 1990).

## ■ Anxiety Disorder NOS (300.00)

This category is a catch-all applied to apparent anxiety disorders that do not exactly fit the previous categories. For example, where all the criteria for the generalized anxiety disorder are met, but the anxious mood has not lasted for up to six months, an anxiety disorder NOS diagnosis would be appropriate. Any other such mixtures of symptomatology where anxiety and its control are still the primary features can be placed in this category.

# CHAPTER 6

# Somatoform and Pain Disorders

Persons with somatoform disorders, like those with the factitious disorder, manifest complaints and symptoms of apparent physical illness for which there are no demonstrable organic findings to support a physical diagnosis. However, the symptoms of the somatoform disorders are not under voluntary control, as are those of the factitious disorders. Thus, the diagnosis of somatoform disorder is made when there is good reason to believe that the person has little or no control over the production of symptoms. Disorder and/or dominance problems in the non-dominant hemisphere of the brain should be ruled out, because symptoms occur statistically more often on the left side. While factitious disorders are more common in men, somatoform disorders occur more frequently in women (Kellner, 1986).

There are five major subcategories of the somatoform disorders: somatization disorder, conversion disorder, somatoform pain disorder, body dysmorphic disorder, and hypochondriasis. There is also a catch-all category, somatoform disorder NOS, in which individuals are placed if they fit the general criteria for somatoform disorder but not the specific criteria of the other five major categories.

The somatization disorder is chronic with multiple symptoms and complaints, usually presented in a vague fashion. The conversion disorder usually focuses on one or two specific symptoms suggestive of a physical disorder, which on closer examination reflect primarily a psychological issue, either as a reflection of symbolic conflict or from the attainment of secondary gain. Somatoform pain disorder is functionally a conversion disorder that refers specifically to psychologically induced pain states. Hypochondriasis is the consistent overresponse to and concern about normal and/or insignificant bodily changes, in spite of expert reassurance that there is no reason for concern. Body dysmorphic disorder (dysmorphophobia) refers to rumination and preoccupation with some imagined defect in what is actually a normal-appearing person; in one sense, it is a variation of hypochondriasis.

## ■ Treatment Options

Even though conscious deception is not a factor with somatoform disorders, reality therapy (Glasser, 1980) can be appropriate, particularly to the degree the person becomes aware of the unrealness of the physical symptoms. The therapist can facilitate that awareness through such methods as consciousness raising, hypnosis, amytal interviews, or other methods of getting in touch with the repressed facets of the personality. In this regard, biofeedback may not be directly appropriate since there is no strictly physical damage, but it can be helpful in modifying some of the symptomatology. Also, it may give the person some insight that the disorder is not primarily physiological (Schwartz, 1987).

Rehabilitative medical-physical therapies can also be useful here because they (a) can deal with some of the secondary actual physical problems that are common, (b) reassure such clients that their condition is not being dealt with lightly, and (c) allow them a "face-saving" way of dropping the somatoform system.

## ■ Somatization Disorder (300.81)

The chronic although cyclic multiple somatic complaints that mark this subcategory of the somatoform disorders are not primarily due to any physical illness. They may be mixed with other symptoms derived from an actual disease, so arriving at this diagnosis is initially difficult. It is not uncommon for this disorder to be an exaggeration of symptoms associated with a previously cured physical disease (Katon et al., 1991).

The diagnosis of somatization disorder is difficult because a self-report of symptoms combined with apparent prior history is convincing to most physicians. Family physicians or general practitioners are more often than not the target of these complaints and are not inclined to see the somatization disorder as real. Physicians often believe such people are only malingering or that, at the very lest, there is a degree of faking involved. Hence, they are inclined to put them in the too-commonly used category of "crank" and attempt in various ways to avoid spending any time with them.

Since it is the supportive atmosphere of the physician's manner and/or the hospital structure that is at least one of the needs of persons with a somatization disorder (and to a degree the conversion disorders), such evident rejections begin to lay bare the underlying inadequacy of these persons to cope effectively with their worlds (Kellner, 1986). Depression then becomes an emergent and eventually paramount symptom, and the person may develop methods (e.g., alcohol) to deal with the depression. Alternately, the person with a somatization disorder may develop a new symptom picture and generate new systems of hospitals and physicians to work through. Restrictions of time and money, however, often bring the person full circle.

Symptoms are often presented in a vague but exaggerated fashion. Incidentally, this dramatic component was the linkage between the traditional diagnostic terms "hysterical neurosis" and "hysterical personality." Fortunately, the DSM-III-R terminology does away with some of the confusion inherent in these labels. Hysterical personalities are now referred to as having a histrionic personality disorder. Hysteria is typically subsumed under one of the somatoform disorders, usually as a conversion disorder that is still sublabeled the hysterical neurosis, conversion type.

One disorder occasionally misinterpreted as a somatization disorder, hypochondriasis, a conversion disorder, or even depression is myasthenia gravis, an immune-mediated polyclonal antibody disorder of receptors in the postsynaptic membrane. Referral to a neurologist for further consideration is advisable when the client shows the following symptoms: (1) significant somatic weakness, occasionally resulting in collapse after use of any particular muscle group, (2) visual disturbances, including the dropping of one or both eyelids (more likely to occur in the evening), and (3) difficulty inspeaking and swallowing (Sneddon, 1980).

☐ ## DSM-III-R

The DSM-III-R requires evidence of a vague yet dramatic and complicated medical history, focused on a belief that one is sickly, with evidence that the physical symptoms began before the age of thirty. A person's own report of personal physical history is considered enough to substantiate the diagnosis. In addition, there must be evidence of at least thirteen reported symptoms out of the thirty-five symptoms listed in DSM-III-R under the following five subgroups: gastrointestinal, cardiopulmonary, pain conversion, female reproductive system, or psychosexual.

Confirmation that the symptom has physically occurred is not required, but there should be indications of symptoms severe enough to require the individual to seek medical help or to alter the life situation in some way in response to the belief that it occurred.

Depression may accompany this pattern, but it is not diagnosed unless it is severe enough to warrant the diagnosis of depressive episode. In a schizophrenic with somatic delusions, the schizophrenic diagnosis takes precedence. The somatization disorder is thought to be diagnosed rarely in males, but approximately 1 percent of females are alleged to have this disorder at some point in their lives.

Systems of health care based on the group practice model make restriction and detection of this disorder easier, since this model facilitates higher levels of interspecialist communication. Also, these practices are more likely to include psychological services and be more sophisticated in implementation than an individual physician. Inclusion of psychological services actually reduces the cost of health care in most physical disorders, mainly by a reduction of repeated visits and unnecessary surgery.

☐                    MMPI-2

Scales 1, 2, and 3, and to a lesser degree 7, are elevated in most of the somatization patterns (Dahlstrom et al., 1986), and they are typically close to the HEA (health concerns) content scale. Combinations of 1, 2, and 8 accompany the more bizarre somatic complaints. As has been noted, some depression naturally accompanies this syndrome and is reflected in the moderate elevation on scale 2. If scale 2 is high, it is possible that the person is beginning to feel that he or she is losing control. Scale 1 is elevated in most of these profiles, and the 1-2/2-1 profile is best thought of as somatization disorder with underlying depression. In this instance, one might also consider alcohol abuse as a compounding variable.

Elevations on scale 7 point to the degree of passivity and complaining that can be expected (Greene, 1991). The 1-7/7-1 client expresses chronic tension-related complaints and demands physical care and responsiveness from physicians, but is resistant to following orders and is difficult to change. A 3-8/8-3 profile has also been associated with this disorder, although the chronic worry, dependency, and schizoid tendencies of these individuals should warrant consideration of a psychotic diagnosis.

The 1-4/4-1 profile reflects a high level of physical complaints, as well as excessive narcissism and egocentricity. If 6 is elevated, anger or rage in the face of rejection by the physician is to be expected. The 3-6/6-3 profile is similar—there is anger as well as rigidity and lack of cooperation. This anger is more often directed toward family members; clients are not quite as manipulative toward physicians.

When actual physical disorder is an accumulation of chronic psychological stress and accompanied by an equally high level of psychological repression, the 3-7/7-3 profile is common. A circumscribed physical disorder to which the person has responded with a reactive depression is more likely to produce a spike scale 2 profile.

The 3-9/9-3 profile is on the border between actual physical disorder and somatization disorder. A common complaint is acute upset accompanied by chest pain and anxiety. These individuals in particular respond well to superficial assurance and to continuing therapist contact.

A small subgroup of clients with a somatization disorder show virtually psychotic profiles. They are remarkably elevated on scale 4, sometimes above the 100-T level, and are also high on scales 6, 8, 2, 3, and 1, in that order. In fact, all scales except 0 and 5 may be well above the 70-T level (Propkop et al., 1980).

<br>

□          ## 16 PF

Characteristics of the 16 PF commonly noted throughout all somatoform disorders, but particularly in the somatization disorder, are at least moderately high scores on I, N, and $Q_4$, moderately low scores on H and $Q_1$, and a low score on S. Karson (1959) suggests that individuals who are lower on A and M are also inclined toward this disorder. The B and M scores reflect the client's degree of sophistication and in that sense correlate with different somatization patterns. The less-sophisticated symbolic conversion patterns, which were seen more commonly in Freud's era, are more typical of naive and less-educated individuals.

Men who have high E and I scores have conflicts between the need to be sensitive in interpersonal relationships and yet to dominate relationships. Ambivalence about assertion and aggression is common and may surface in a somatization pattern. It has been hypothesized that women will encounter the same conflict as they move away from traditional female roles.

Clinicians have noted that persons with a somatization disorder also tend to be more average on C and $Q_4$ than do those with the anxiety disorders. They vary markedly on scales I and $Q_3$, depending on the degree of depression. Although a pattern with a combination of a low E and a high $Q_1$ score is relatively rare, it predisposes that person to the somatization disorders.

<br>

□          ## OTHER TEST-RESPONSE PATTERNS

Performance scale scores on the WAIS-R are usually higher than verbal scale scores. In particular, the performance subtests that depend on motor coordination and speed are relatively high, with an occasionally surprising exception in object assembly. Within the verbal scale scores, lower information and digit-span scores are expected, relative to higher comprehension scores. In females, where the somatization disorder incorporates histrionic components, the arithmetic score is low.

The typically salient feature of the MCMI-II profile here is elevation of 85 or higher on H. Somatically channeled anxieties are often the source of somatization disorders, and this is indicated by considerable elevation on A. Four and 7 are often also high (Choca, et al., 1992). Somatization also occurs as a result of motoric dysfunction present in psychotic depression, so an elevation of 75 or higher on CC may occur. Personality types most prone to developing somatization disorders are the avoidant, the negativistic, the schizoid, and the cycloid, so elevations of 75 or higher may be predictive of the development of this disorder as a coping mechanism or during periods of stress.

Persons with a somatization disorder typically do not provide a high number of responses on the Rorschach and occasionally "fail" to give a response, and the percentage of W or complex M responses is usually low. They are more likely to give simple, Popular responses, using only the easily discerned details. A high number of M responses is rare, and when they are provided, they often have a more static quality than do normal M responses. Responses involving color as a determinant are uncommon. Responses focusing on bony-anatomy content and occasionally pure C responses, such as "blood," do occur (Wagner and Wagner, 1981).

☐    TREATMENT OPTIONS

The comments in the section on somatoform disorders are also applicable to the somatization disorders. The symptomatology here is more similar to actual physiological disorder than it is in several of the other somatoform disorders. Hence, biofeedback can be useful in turning around some of the surface physiological symptomatology and at the same time can give clients concrete feedback that may convince them, along with supportive therapy, to look at psychological vulnerability as the source of their disorders. Most persons with this disorder are defensive about it, and as a result, the comments about the paranoid disorders are applicable. At some point, a shift into an existential orientation may be necessary to confront clients fully with their escape mechanisms.

## Conversion Disorder (300.11)

The conversion disorder is similar in many respects to the somatization disorder. The difference is that in the conversion disorder there is a specific symptom or a related set of symptoms used for the attainment of some secondary gain or to express a psychological conflict. Conversion symptoms are not under voluntary control. Somatoform pain disorder, discussed in the next section of this chapter, can be considered a subcategory of conversion disorder where the specific symptom is simply pain (Rachman and Arntz, 1991).

With some of the psychosexual dysfunctions (discussed in Chapter 8), it may be difficult to decide whether the problem directly expresses a psychological issue and is thus technically a conversion disorder or whether it is a physiological response to anxiety. In actuality, it may be a mixture of both. For this reason, as well as for convenience, these cases are included among the psychosexual disorders. Some clinicians might also consider anorexia nervosa to be a conversion disorder, yet most consider the syndrome different enough to warrant separate discussions, but there are parallels.

A conversion disorder is still referred to as a "hysterical neurosis, conversion type," and an individual with one is said to manifest *la belle indifference,* an attitude in which there is little concern about the apparent serious implications of the disorder. Persons with a conversion disorder appear to be aware at some level that their complaints do not predict the further dire consequences that others might infer from them. Although indifferent to their presenting symptoms, emotional lability in response to other stimuli is commonly noted (Kellner, 1986).

The attitude of *la belle indifference* is not found in all conversion disorders: Some people develop their symptoms under extreme stress and manifest that stress quite directly. Even in *these* individuals, however, anxiety seems to dissipate over the duration of the disorder in favor of a focus on physical symptoms.

A dependent or histrionic personality predisposes individuals to the development of conversion symptoms. Another important predisposing factor is a history of actual physical disorder during which excessive caretaking behaviors or other secondary gains occurred.

## DSM-III-R

The DSM-III-R requires evidence of a disturbance that implies a physical disorder, with symptoms that are not under voluntary control and in which psychological factors are seen as a primary cause. This is supported by evidence of a temporal relationship and is usually accompanied by avoidance or secondary-gain patterns. It cannot be explained by a known physical disorder or a culturally sanctioned response. It is not limited to pain or sexual problems.

## MMPI-2

Most of the comments made about diagnostic observations on somatization disorders are relevant here. It has been traditional to expect that in most cases of conversion disorder there is a classic conversion V, wherein scales 1 and 3 are both high and 2 is relatively low. Note that conversion Vs do show up in a number of people with actual physical disorder, so it should not be used as any per se diagnostic indicator. When actual physical disorder is not supported, the conversion V is especially indicative of a conversion reaction in which the individual takes a naive and Pollyannaish attitude and manifests *la belle indifference.* However, Johnson et al. (1980) found that the 2-1-7 pattern, with a high score on 3, is more common in this disorder. If scale 3 is very high, scale 4 is low, and scale 1 is around 60–70 T, histrionic characteristics are emphasized. In persons where *la belle indifference* is lacking, a higher scale 4 is likely.

Another profile occasionally seen in conversion disorders is the 3-9/9-3. These people experience conversion reactions in acute form, accompanied by at least moderately high anxiety levels. Over time, they are likely to show more histrionic characteristics, and the 9 scale should be somewhat lower.

☐     ## 16 PF

The observations on the 16 PF relevant to somatization disorders are applicable here as well. However, if there is *la belle indifference,* N and $Q_3$ are higher and there is a relatively lower score on L. A high F score is also probable. Since these individuals are usually not as sophisticated as others in the overall group of somatoform disorders, a lower B scale is noted. Also, the concrete quality of their thinking predicts a lower M score.

☐     ## OTHER TEST-RESPONSE PATTERNS

Although the overall group of conversion disorders is similar to the somatization disorders, those with *la belle indifference* in particular show higher scores on digit symbol and digit span on the WAIS-R. In addition, they seldom show bright-normal or superior intelligence and do poorly on tests that measure more subtle intellectual discriminations, such as comprehension, similarities, and picture arrangement. Emotional distancing from the Rorschach cards—through such comments as "they are weird" or "they are ugly"—is common. They are prone to deny depressive or aggressive feelings in the content of the Rorschach and the TAT.

Because physical symptoms in conversion disorder are usually specific, elevated H is not highly likely on the MCMI-II. The submissive personality (scale 3) and the gregarious personality (scale 4) are most likely to develop conversion disorders as a way to achieve secondary gain. The submissive personality is especially likely to exhibit *la belle indifference.* High scores indicating the presence of these personality patterns may be predictive of the development of conversion disorders. The ambivalence and psychological conflicts of those with elevated scores on scale 8A may be predisposed toward developing this disorder.

☐     ## TREATMENT OPTIONS

Since the time of Freud, hypnosis as a means of directly suggesting a cure or as a means of exploring unconscious conflicts has been effective in the treatment of conversion disorders (Meyer, 1992b). Also, it is worthwhile to include several placebo and/or physical techniques with a client with conversion disorder, particularly one who focuses on the dramatic.

Physical therapies in conjunction with psychotherapy are the standard intervention mode.

Hendrix et al. (1978) successfully used behavioral techniques to cure the conversion disorder symptom of a clenched fist. In general, aversion relief and variations of the time-out technique (removing the person from the situation and not responding to his or her disturbed behaviors) can be useful here. In the cognitive behavioral technique of covert extension, the conversion disorder client would be asked to imagine the general conversion pattern while at the same time imagining that the reinforcing events that usually occur with this behavior in the real world do not occur in imagination. The effectiveness of the technique depends on already having attained some awareness as to the source of the conversion disorder. Thus, it is best used as a subsequent procedure to such techniques as hypnosis, psychotherapy, or free association, which are used to first explore these unconscious ties.

## ■ Somatoform Pain Disorder (307.80)

Somatoform pain disorder is a conversion disorder that specifically involves pain not due to a physical cause. Yet, as with the other somatoform disorders, a history of physical disorder involving the actual symptom is common (Katon et al., 1991). The emergence of a somatoform pain disorder is facilitated by developmental-stage transitions and by specific stressful events. Somatoform pain disorder differs from the other conversion disorders in tht the commonly associated histrionic features of sexual ambivalence, *la belle indifference,* and dependency are not usually observed. The pain seldom follows known anatomic or neurological patterns, and extensive diagnostic work reveals no evidence of organic pathology. In the more sophisticated patient, it may mimic well-known diseases, such as angina or arthritis. There are indications that people with certain life styles or family backgrounds are more likely to use pain as a manipulator:

1. People who have a history of extensive medical treatment and multiple surgical procedures
2. People with a history of hypochondriasis or of factitious disorders
3. People who have a history of taking significant dosages of pain medicine
4. People who are highly suggestible
5. People who had stressful childhoods and/or are from large families
6. People who began working full-time and/or had children at an early age
7. People who complain of too little pain for their injuries as well as those who complain too much

As with the other conversion disorders, somatoform pain disorder may reflect a psychological conflict and/or exert a controlling influence on the person's interactions with other people, resulting in some secondary gain and/or allowance for avoidance.

Benedikt and Kolb (1986) found in a study of those presenting themselves at a chronic pain center of a VA hospital that a large subgroup had undiagnosed post-traumatic stress disorder. They postulated that since the pain was usually focused in areas of injury related to the disorder, such as shrapnel wounds, the reexperiencing of the events had precipitated in this form. Many in this subgroup had been previously treated for the chronic pain with medications, surgery, or electric stimulation—it seems the psychological nature of their pain had been unrealized. The finding that chronic pain may be associated with post-traumatic stress syndrome should alert the clinician to alternative treatment strategies.

☐     DSM-III-R

The DSM-III-R requires evidence of nonorganic severe pain in which psychological factors are seen as a primary cause, as shown by an absence of support for any organic pathology, or excessive response to actual organic pathology. There is often a maintenance of the pain by reinforcement of avoidance pattern or by secondary gain. The symptoms are of at least six months duration and are not under voluntary control.

☐     MMPI-2

Although somatoform pain disorder can be considered a conversion disorder, the classic conversion V is not always found (Love and Peck, 1987; Strassberg et al., 1981). Because depression is evident in many cases, the 2 scale and the DEP (depression) content scale may be elevated, and the HEA (health concerns) content scales are usually elevated. Elevations (in order of degree) in the 1-2-3 scales are common (Love and Peck, 1987). Interestingly enough, clients with a single pain complaint tend to score higher on these scales than do clients with multiple pain complaints (Strassberg et al., 1981). Clients who are using their illness to obtain compensation are more likely to score higher on scale 4 and, to a lesser degree, on scale 9, and other cues for malingering should be considered.

As symptoms become more chronic and patients are more often rejected by diagnosticians and treaters, a rise in scale 7 is probable. When pain is focused in the extremities or is manifested in headaches or back problems (a pattern in which repression and denial are common), a 1-3/3-1 profile is likely.

One group of patients with multiple pain complaints shows high scores on 1, 3, 7, and 8, in that order. This group is characterized by somatic preoccupation, obsessive thinking, isolation, and denial of psychological problems. Another subgroup is denoted by high scores on scale K and scale 1 and a low score on scale 6. This group is particularly inclined to deny their psychological difficulties, almost in a naive fashion, and is interpersonally insensitive (Propkop et al., 1980).

Clients with actual chronic pain do not often show much elevation immediately after the injury. However, if they are tested several months after it occurs, elevations on scales 1 and 3 are likely. Also, an elevated conversion V along with an elevated scale 4 predict poor recovery from pain or from surgery in general (Love and Peck, 1987).

Patients with chronic pain are also likely to become increasingly depressed, so elevations on the 2 and DEP scales are even more common. Many patients with chronic pain become addicted to toxic levels of pain-killing drugs and as a result begin to show cognitive slippage and other indications of brain damage. A 2-9, with an 8 that is high and greater than 7, or other indicators of disinhibition, such as a high 4, accompanied by indications of distress are potential indicators of this addiction and toxicity.

Certain patients with chronic pain appear to reflect a one-trial learning process associated with the originating trauma (Rachman and Arntz, 1991). As a result, they emit indications of phobiclike behavior on the MMPI-2. They are often suggestible and thus manifest high K and L scores, with a high scale 3 and a relatively high scale 1, often accompanied by a 7 scale that is elevated at least ten points over scale 8.

## 16 PF

The comments regarding conversion disorders are appropriate here, except those that focus on the symptoms of *la belle indifference*, since this is not typical for the somatoform pain disorder.

## OTHER DIAGNOSTIC CONSIDERATIONS

Extreme elevation on H on the MCMI-II is not likely here, although some specific patterns of pain may be indicated by elevations between 75 and 85. Some elevations on A and D is also likely. Those with elevations of 75 or higher on 2 may utilize psychogenic pain as a way to avoid interpersonal interactions, while the psychological conflict and ambivalence of the 8 and C patterns predispose them to the development of psychogenic pain. The personality patterns indicated by elevated scores on 2 and 8A are more likely to be present here, in contrast to conversion disorder, where the most likely patterns are indicated by elevations on 3 and 4.

Beyond the standard means (psychological tests, hypnosis, "truth serums") for differentiating a conversion disorder from an organic condition, there are other methods specifically helpful in discriminating psychogenic from organic pain (or from malingering; see Chapter 16). Cortical evoked potentials have shown promise as a diagnostic instrument in this area, as well as in many other diagnostic situations. Also, certain EEG patterns appear more consistently in organic than in psychogenic pain, and assessment of blood plasma cortisol can be a helpful discriminator. Unfortunately, most people with somatoform disorders, particularly conversion disorders, are seldom seen by a psychologist or psychiatrist, and such specific and more sophisticated assessments are never made.

## ☐ TREATMENT OPTIONS

The major goal in a pain management approach is to work to help patients through social-skills training, assertiveness training, vocational rehabilitation, and the like to a more independent, active life style (Love and Peck, 1987). Also, since somatoform pain disorder is a specific form of the conversion disorder, the comments in that section are appropriate. As noted, hypnosis is appropriate in conversion disorders. David Cheek (1965) has pioneered in the use of hypnosis to find the subconscious causes for chronic psychogenic pain. While his clients are under hypnosis, Cheek asks them to gradually release this symptom, often having them point to a date on the calendar designating when they might be willing to give up the symptom. He then makes an appointment for that day and gradually ties the insights under hypnosis into conscious awareness. With chronic pain, the musculature has often conformed over time to a bodily posture that continues the pain. Hence, even psychogenic pain may have an overlay of real pain (Rachman and Arntz, 1991). Biofeedback to release this tense muscle posture can be helpful. Other clinicians would argue that techniques derived from chiropractic, such as Rolfing, are useful here as well.

Secondary gain is particularly important in the conversion disorders, especially when these occur in adolescents and young adults. Therefore, the clinician should look at family and marital situations for possible reinforcement patterns, as well as for possible sites for intervention.

## ■ Hypochondriasis (300.70)

Hypochondriacs unreasonably interpret normal or relatively unimportant bodily and physical changes as indicative of serious physical disorder. They are constantly alert to an upsurge of new symptomatology, and since the body is constantly in physiological flux, they are bound to find signs that they can interpret as suggestive of disorder. In many hypochondriacs, their distorted coping strategy is an attempt to avoid a feeling of loss of control and, in that sense, parallels the panic disorder.

In one sense, hypochondriacs do not fear being sick; they are certain they already are. Hypochondriasis is as relatively common pattern from adolescence to old age. It is seen most frequently in the age range thirty to forty for men and forty to fifty for women (Meister, 1990). Meister also believes that there are many "closet hypochondriacs," those who do not constantly go to physicians, yet are heavily involved in health fads, checking of body behaviors, and discussion of their concerns with close friends (who may relish this quasi-therapist role). These closet hypochondriacs would not earn a formal DSM-III-R diagnosis because they do not fit some of the specific requirements, such as seeking out medical reassurance and going through physical examinations. Nonetheless, they manifest the disorder.

A number of common factors have been observed in the development of hypochondriasis (Kellner, 1986; Meister, 1980):

1. For most hypochondriacs, there has been a background marked by substantial experience in an atmosphere of illness. This could include identification with a significant other who was hypochondriacal or early exposure to a family member who was an invalid.

2. Hypochondriacs often have had a strong dependency relationship with a family member who could express love and affection in a normal or intense fashion during periods when the hypochondriac had been ill, yet was distant or nonexpressive at other times.

3. Hypochondriacs often channel their psychological conflicts and their needs for existential reassurance into this pattern. As a result, the hypochondriac pattern of behavior may mask a mid-life crisis or some other challenge that is not being met effectively.

4. A certain subgroup of hypochondriacs is postulated as having a predispositional sensitivity to pain and body sensations. This could be stimulated by prior physical disorder in systems in which the hypochondriacal pattern is now manifest.

All of these factors are facilitated by reinforcement of the hypochondriasis in the client's world, and avoidance of tasks or demands because of being sick is often noted here.

☐                    DSM-III-R
_____

There is not so great a focus on actual physical symptoms in hypochondriasis as in the somatization disorder. Rather, such people interpret physical sensations and natural changes in their bodies as indicative of significant physical disorder—although not at a delusional level and not in the midst of a panic attack—in spite of expert assurance that there is little danger. The duration of disorder is at least six months, and some area of social or vocational functioning is often disrupted. Persons with a cardiac neurosis or cancer phobia may be placed in this category.

□    DIAGNOSTIC CONSIDERATIONS

Hypochondriacs function similarly to individuals with the somatization disorder, except that hypochondriasis is more focused and intellectualized. As a result, the MMPI-2 profile will be somewhat tempered, being lower on scales 7 and 8 in particular. Scale 1 is at least moderately elevated, and a common code type here is the 3-1/1-3 profile, as is the 1-2/2-1 when there is evident distress. Since there is at least a moderate amount of defensiveness associated with this disorder, scales K, 6, and 7 are usually moderately high. If the person is relatively naive in response to personal conflicts, the L scale is also somewhat elevated. Hypochondriacs who are inclined to discuss their problems with others should score lower on scale 0, indicating the extroverted aspect of their pattern.

As with the MMPI-2, the 16 PF is tempered from the profile usually noted with the somatization disorder. Specifically, C is usually not as low nor is $Q_4$ as high. However, E, I, and $Q_3$ are usually higher, reflecting the even more controlled psychological world of hypochondriacs in comparison to that of persons with a somatization disorder.

Preoccupation with matters of health will serve to moderately elevate H on the MCMI-II, so that scores of 75 or higher might be expected. A and D scores of 75 or higher are likely because hypochondriacal symptoms often occur in response to underlying anxiety and/or depression relevant to external situations. Those personality patterns that are likely to develop hypochondriacal disorders are those presenting a great deal of anxiety and compulsive behavior. Prominent patterns indicated by elevated 7, 8A, and C scores are particularly likely.

Due to the mild obsessive component usually found in this disorder (Kozak et al., 1988), hypochondriacs overelaborate their responses on the WAIS-R and thus tend to do better on comprehension, similarities, and vocabulary. These are people who cope with words; as a result, the verbal scale is often higher than the performance scale. Blatt et al. (1970) found that a low score on object assembly was predictive of high bodily concern, including hypochondriacal patterns.

This same mild obsessive factor should result in longer latencies to the Rorschach cards, as well as a number of the other response patterns manifest in the obsessive-compulsive disorder. Anatomic responses to the cards are expected, and there is some indication that this anatomy content increases as they proceed through the cards. CF is usually greater than FC, and there is a relatively low production of M responses.

□    TREATMENT OPTIONS

Direct reassurance on medical symptoms is usually not a curative factor, although it is important that some reassurance be given so that the therapy can focus on consideration of psychological concerns. The development of trust is critical in this disorder; in that regard, the reader is referred to the discussion of trust development in the section on the paranoid disorders (Chapter 3).

Another approach can be helpful with specific hypochondriacs: Therapists can suddenly state that they feel a hypochondriac client is "dead right" about his or her concerns. The shock from this unexpected agreement, with the apparent verification of their dreaded suspicions, can often elicit the underlying psychological concerns. This technique must be carried out with care, as it can backfire and solidify the hypochondriacal concerns.

Family therapy is also helpful with certain hypochondriacs (Brown, 1991). Many of them have evolved a response system in which significant others consistently reinforce their pattern; with the supervision of the therapist, this pattern can be broken. Family members can be taught to give the person psychological reassurance and caring responses, while at the same time ignoring or otherwise avoiding the reinforcement of the concerns about physical disorder.

Such a technique takes into account the importance of underlying existential issues in the treatment of subcategories of hypochondriasis, such as cancer phobia and cardiac neurosis. Several clients appear to use specific concerns in these areas as a distraction from more anxiety-arousing issues, such as a basic realization of mortality or facing the potential to fail. Existential confrontation, in a context of supportive psychotherapy, allows the hypochondriacal concerns to cease so that clients may confront these deeper problems. Similarly, many of the techniques specific to the obsessive-compulsive disorder are applicable here.

Physicians who take the overall disorder as a serious problem and who do not write these patients off as "crocks" can go a long way toward breaking the hypochondriacal pattern. Once such patients begin to trust the physician, they can open up more about their total problems and then, under the umbrella of trust, possibly accept referral for psychological treatment.

## ■ Body Dysmorphic Disorder (300.70)

Body dysmorphic disorder (BDD) has been traditionally referred to as dysmorphophobia. BDD is characterized by a preoccupation with some imagined imperfection in physical appearance or an exaggerated reaction to some minor defect (not exclusively occurring during trans-sexualism or anorexia nervosa). It is not held so firmly as to be delusional in nature. Victims may, if pressed, admit to the possibility that their concerns are excessive, but they persist in their concerns and in behaviors related to those concerns (Kellner, 1986). For example, they may make repeated visits to plastic surgeons or dermatologists in order to have their concerns confirmed and to get some relief from the imagined defects. Unfortunately, there are a number of cases of such individuals undergoing extensive plastic surgery at the hands of careless or unscrupulous surgeons.

As is no doubt evident, BDD is a variation of hypochondriasis. Hence, the comments on diagnostic indicators and therapeutic considerations for hypochondriasis apply to BDD as well, although there is usually a greater degree of narcissism and a general concern with controlling interpersonal relationships in BDD. Thus on the MMPI-2, BDDs tend to be higher on scales 4 and 0 and lower on scales 1 and 3 than classic hypochondriacs. Also, the BDDs tend to score higher on A on the 16 PF and generally show more of the indicators of narcissism on the MCMI-II.

## ■ Undifferentiated Somatoform Disorder (300.70) and Somatoform Disorder NOS (300.70)

These catch-all categories include any pattern that generally fits the requirements for somatoform disorder but does not fit the specifics of the individual patterns just covered. In actual practice, many individuals do not fit a specific somatoform disorder — not fulfilling the requirement of evidence in four or five symptom groups — and hence are included here. In general, the "undifferentiated" label is used when the pattern persists for more than six months, "somatoform disorder NOS" if it is less than six months.

# CHAPTER 7

# Dissociative and Sleep Disorders

The dissociative disorders, traditionally referred to as the hysterical neuroses, dissociative type, are characterized by a sudden disruption or alteration of the normally integrated functions of consciousness. This disturbance is almost always temporary, although it may wax and wane, particularly in amnesia and fugue.

The various subcategories are psychogenic amnesia, an acute disturbance of memory function; psychogenic fugue, a sudden disruption of one's sense of identity, usually accompanied by travel away from home; multiple personality, the domination of the person's consciousness by two or more separate personalities; and depersonalization disorder, a disturbance in the experience of the self in which the sense of reality is temporarily distorted.

There is also a category referred to as dissociative disorder (NOS), simply a residual category. The patterns most commonly included in this diagnosis are those of persons who experience a sense of unrealness that is not accompanied by depersonalization and who also show some trancelike states.

It can be argued that the depersonalization disorder, also referred to as the depersonalization neurosis, is not appropriately included in this general category, as there is no substantial memory disturbance. Yet there is a significant disturbance, albeit temporary, of the sense of reality, and thus the identity is certainly affected.

## ■ Diagnostic Considerations

With the exception of the depersonalization disorder, the dissociative disorders are not especially common (Dunn, 1992). As a result, there is not much significant literature on discrimination of these states by psychological tests. This is not as unfortunate as it might seem. In the dissociative disorders, the symptoms are usually reasonably clear indicators of the particular subcategory, even though other disorders have to be screened out. For example, many of these disorders have to be initially differentiated from schizophrenia. However, people with a dissociative disorder do not show the confusion and deteriorated functioning in most personality areas that are indicative of schizophrenia. A history of sexual or physical abuse (with derealization as a common later sequelae of sexual abuse) occurs more often than not in the dissociative's history. These disorders may also need to be distinguished from those in which the behavior mimics an organic condition, such as a head trauma, tumor, epilepsy (Iacono, 1991; Gass and Russell, 1991). Indeed, when the clinician is confronted with the symptomatology noted here, a medical consultation is usually warranted.

## ■ Psychogenic Amnesia (300.12)

This is a category where the commonly understood use of the term "amnesia" almost directly reflects the diagnostic implications. Psychogenic amnesia is a temporary loss of ability to recall personal information. It can be information about a specific topic or memories of the immediate or distant past. Although media portrayals lead people to believe that the memory for *all* past events is lost in amnesia, this is rare (Schachter, 1986). Recovery of memory is usually rapid, whereas the recovery is gradual in organic conditions, if it takes place at all. The alcohol amnestic disorder differs from psychogenic amnesia. In the former, the person is able to recall information for only a few minutes after it is obtained, since that ability to transfer information from short-term to long-term memory has been lost. This condition is also observed in some individuals who have had significant ECT treatments. Those with a history of traumatic sexual abuse are predisposed to psychogenic amnesia.

☐     DSM-III-R

The DSM-III-R requires evidence of sudden memory failure for important personal information that has been previously stored in memory. The memory failure is too significant to be explained by ordinary forgetfulness, and it is not explained by alcohol-related "blackouts," by other organic conditions, or by such disorders as catatonia and stupor or multiple personality. It also needs to be discriminated from malingering, but such discrimination is often quite difficult (Wiggins and Brandt, 1988; Schachter, 1986). The findings of faking scales on psychological tests are helpful here, as are interviews with the use of amytal or hypnosis.

This disorder is typically observed in adult and adolescent females who are undergoing significant stress and in young males experiencing the distress of wartime. A subjectively intolerable life experience, such as an unexpected loss, is a common catalyst for amnesia, as well as for the related category, psychogenic fugue, which will be discussed next.

There are four common subgroupings of psychogenic amnesia. The first and most common type, localized, refers to the loss of memory for events during a circumscribed period of time (following a severe stressor, such as an accident). Selective amnesia is a loss of memory for only certain types of events during the circumscribed period of time. Generalized amnesia, a failure to recall all events in one's life, and continuous amnesia, a loss of memory from one time to another, are both rare.

□ MMPI-2

A high 3-4/4-3 pattern on the MMPI-2, particularly the 3-4 profile, means fertile ground for the development of dissociative experiences. This pattern is marked by immaturity and significant difficulty in coping directly and maturely with disturbances in one's psychological world. It implies the use of denial, either psychologically (as in amnesia) or physically and psychologically (as in the fugue state). While scale 4 usually means sociopathy, it is also a measure of lack of social poise, naiveté, and immaturity and so may be high here.

Scale 1 is occasionally raised in this profile, as is scale 8, depending on whether the person is gravitating toward somatic concerns as an expression of disorder or into a general loss of integrated decision making. The F scale is low compared to other groups of pathology. If anger and hostility are being denied and avoided, an elevation on scales K and L is likely. The naiveté of the amnestic is especially reflected in a higher L score than would usually be obtained in an individual of similar social and intellectual levels.

□ 16 PF

A modal profile for this type of disorder has not been determined. However, most clinicians agree that low scores on H, C, and N are to be expected. Suppressed anxiety should result in at least a moderate elevation on $Q_4$, and although $Q_3$ may be initially high, any increasing loss of integration of self-concept should lower $Q_3$. Higher scores on O and I, reflecting oversensitivity and apprehension, can be expected, particularly in the young-adult and adolescent females who are manifesting this pattern. Also, E is usually high. The suggestibility and sense of inadequacy often found in such individuals also reflect the contrast between their rigid problem-solving skills and their desire to place trust in an authority figure.

☐           TREATMENT OPTIONS

Hypnotic techniques to gain access to subconscious material have been a traditional treatment for amnesia, and they are generally effective (Meyer, 1992b). Psychotherapy, with an emphasis on interpretation of possible conflicts before adequate realization of them, is also useful, particularly if a supportive atmosphere both in and out of the therapy hour can be generated (Storr, 1990). This gives clients the sense of safety and potential for reintegration that they so desperately look for. Since this disorder is so often a response to a significant stressor, the techniques discussed in the treatment of the post-traumatic stress disorder are also applicable here.

■           ## Psychogenic Fugue (300.13)

Psychogenic fugue is a specific form of amnesia in which people are unable to recall the essentials of their previous personality. In addition, they are likely to wander away from their home environment and assume an entirely new identity. Although they are seldom able to recall the behaviors that they carried out while in the fugue state, the recovery is usually complete.

The syndrome often occurs as a reaction to a severe psychosocial stressor, such as the unexpected breakup of a marriage or loss of a job without warning. It is facilitated by previous heavy alcohol or drug use, which points to the dissociative quality inherent in states of consciousness engendered by drug abuse.

Somnambulism, traditionally considered a dissociative reaction, is now listed in DSM-III-R as a sleep disorder. This is reasonable since it is usually not associated with organic disorder, as is true in most cases, it is best considered a simple learned behavior that was not suppressed in the early stages of development (Hauri, 1991).

☐           DSM-III-R

To diagnose psychogenic fugue, the DSM-III-R requires evidence that the individual suddenly assumed at least some elements of a wholly or partially new identity, left the normal home or workplace, and could not recall his or her previous life. This is not due to organic conditions or multiple personality.

This relatively rare disorder bears some similarity to the multiple personality, since the new identity is often in sharp contrast to the previous one. As previously noted, the pattern usually occurs in response to a significant loss of some sort and is catalyzed in some individuals by the shock of a natural disaster or a war.

□ TESTING CONSIDERATIONS

These individuals are seldom tested while they are in the midst of the fugue state. As they are brought back into their natural environment, the recovery of memory begins to occur. When they are tested, they show patterns similar to psychogenic amnesia.

□ TREATMENT OPTIONS

Since psychogenic fugue is analogous to psychogenic amnesia, the techniques described for the treatment of the post-traumatic stress disorder are also applicable; a subjectively disturbing stressor is almost always a critical catalyst here. As a follow-up, it would be useful to deal with the subjective reasons for the severity of this trauma through humanistic and existential techniques, for example, through gestalt therapy, since its emphasis is on reintegration of the person's wholeness. Hypnosis is also used for this purpose, but care has to be taken because what appears to be a reintegration of true memories may in actuality be virtually new memories.

# ■ Multiple Personality (300.14)

The multiple personality receives a great deal of attention in the media, in part because it is often confused with schizophrenia. From this attention, it could be concluded that it is a common disorder. However, Winer noted in 1978 that there have been only about two-hundred reasonably well documented cases at that time. Although no doubt an underestimate even then, this skepticism can be a good antidote to those mental health professionals who are far too quick to conclude a client is a "multiple" (Dunn, 1992).

Multiple personalities come into treatment because they note some peculiarities in their worlds: forgetting of certain interactions with people, general confusion, and loss of memories. A different personality is then discovered through psychotherapy, which is often supplemented by hypnosis. In some cases, personalities continue to be produced, first by the indirect suggestion of the therapist's interest and reinforcement, then by the reinforcement of the therapist's reinvigorated concern for the person's problems.

Amnesia is a pathognomonic sign of a future multiple personality, and it is critical to reliable diagnosis (Dunn, 1992; Spiegel and Cardena, 1991). A history of physical or sexual abuse (especially incest) is a common precursor, and stress is an important precipitating factor in the genesis of this disorder. Stressors in a person's psychological world often trigger the sudden transitions in personality noted here (Clum, 1989).

☐    DSM-III-R

According to DSM-III-R, the multiple personality is a person who is consecutively dominated by at least two separate and distinct personalities that determine separate behavior patterns, and at least two of these personalities alternately take full control of the person's behavior. The personalities are complex and reasonably well integrated, often starkly contrasting, and the transition from one to another is sudden. The disorder is most commonly observed in young-adult and adolescent females. The latter personalities are usually a crystallization into a personality of opposite facets from the original one.

☐    TESTING CONSIDERATIONS

Because the personalities of a multiple personality will vary markedly (Spiegel and Cardena, 1991), depending on what facets of that individual they are expressing, no particular patterns can be expected, although a 3-8/8-3 MMPI-2 pattern is commonly noted in dissociative reactions. A high L scale is also occasionally noted. Fowler (1981) suggests that a 1-3/3-1 code type is also probable here. Histrionic and dependent personality components are often found in the separate personalities, and there is a greater likelihood of an acting-out of aggressive and sexual impulses. The sections on the histrionic and the dependent personality disorders deal with this. The confusion and peculiarities initially presented by the multiple personality may be present as an elevated S or SS on the MCMI-II. However, because of the nature of the disorder, no single prediction can be made; profiles should vary as personalities do.

Osgood et al. (1976) demonstrated an ingenious application of the semantic differential to the assessment of the contrasting features of a multiple personality. Clinicians who happen to see this rare disorder could apply this method to monitor changes in the individual as he or she goes through various personalities and then begins to integrate again into a single personality. Also, in a few cases, EEG indicators of amplitude (attention) and latency have discriminated various personalities over time. Chapter 16 is useful here since some people are inclined to feign this disorder for the sake of media attention.

☐    TREATMENT OPTIONS

The classic treatment for the multiple personality has been hypnosis, which is used to get in touch with the dissociated subpersonalities (Meyer, 1992). In the few cases that have been available to clinicians for study, this has generally been reasonably successful, but the cost in time has been high. Also, it is arguable that since hypnosis itself may involve a dissociative experience, it may iatrogenically increase the tendency to produce multiple personalities, particularly in the short run.

One could also argue that transactional analysis (Berne, 1964) could further the dissociative process, since it so clearly emphasizes separate ego states. However, it could be useful in getting the person in touch with the message that all of us play different roles and when these roles become crystallized, the potential for dissociative experience is heightened. This would at least place this experience closer to a normal experience and thus foster reintegration. Psychoanalysis has been used effectively with the multiple personality (Osgood et al., 1976), although the therapist may have to deal with the unique problem of multiple transferences.

## ■ Depersonalization Disorder (300.60)

As noted earlier, the depersonalization disorder is dissimilar to other dissociative reactions, since consciousness is never truly segmented and significant memory loss is not a factor in the depersonalization disorder. Because there is no better place for depersonalization disorder in the DSM-III-R and because it includes dissociation from the usual sense of reality, it is listed here.

In the depersonalization disorder, individuals experience a sense of separation from normal consciousness and may report feeling as if they are a separate observer of the self. The typical reality of the usual world seems as if it has been altered. This is an experience that many people have on occasion—the issue is whether it is a consistent pattern. (It is interesting to note that if one follows certain modern gurus, the ability to constantly perceive one's functioning as a separate observer is the mark of progress toward enlightenment.)

Since depersonalization is experienced by many people at times, the definition of disorder is appropriate on the basis of either frequency or a feeling of lack of control. Many people are not really bothered by such experiences, whereas others feel as if they are going crazy. In the latter situation, the sense of depersonalization can be conditioned to anticipatory anxiety, leading to a vicious cycle: reinforcing the belief that they might indeed be going crazy (Spiegel and Cardena, 1991).

Because this disorder focuses on an experience of a changing identity, it is not surprising that it occurs most frequently during adolescence. There is little impairment from the experience itself, but when it is accentuated by a conditioned anxiety response, it becomes troublesome. In that sense, it is similar to the conditioned anxiety response that many argue is the cause of the flashbacks during certain drug experiences. Abuse of alcohol or drugs facilitates the development of this disorder.

☐          DSM-III-R

Referred to as the depersonalization neurosis, the present category retains some of the DSM-II characteristics. There is usually more anxiety here than in the other dissociative disorders; however, the dissociative aspect is the essential feature.

DSM-III-R requires substantive indication of an episode of depersonalization occurred potent enough to cause significant distress, although reality testing remains intact, and there must be a persistent experience of either being outside of and/or detached from one's body, or feeling as if one were an automaton or in a dream. The possibilities of minor organic dysfunction, anxiety disorders, or even a developing depressive episode must be ruled out. For example, people with anxiety disorders, especially if there is a panic component, will sometimes report depersonalization-type experiences. These are primarily offshoots of their constant self-monitoring rather than a true depersonalization.

☐          MMPI-2

This disorder was included in the DSM-II as the depersonalization neurosis, and the modal profile reflects this. Elevations on scales 3, 7, and F are likely, as these tap both the anxiety and hysteric components. The anxiety and identity confusion also lead to an elevated 8 scale, and since identity is threatened, changes in scale 5 away from stereotypical sexual-role scores are expected. Since these individuals are usually young, active in their response to their distress, but inclined to denial accompanied by somatic concerns, elevations on scales 1 and 9 may also occur. The various possible scale 4 elevations reflect the degrees of hostility and anger and the lack of social sophistication that vary within individuals with this disorder. In rare cases, a spike 0 profile may be noted early in its development (Kelley and King, 1979c).

☐          16 PF

Instability and loss of a sense of reality are reflected in moderately low C and $Q_3$ scores. O and M are likely to be high, while the low score on N reflects naiveté and a relative lack of sophistication. Individuals who manifest a depersonalization disorder are usually of higher intelligence, so scale B should be average or above.

☐          TREATMENT OPTIONS

In some respects the depersonalization disorder is as much an identity development disorder as it is a dissociative experience, so any techniques useful for getting in touch with the less-integrated aspects of the personality might be useful here. This could range from Rogers' (1951) client-centered therapy through gestalt therapy, supplemented by an emphasis on the problems of self-labeling, as detailed by Meichenbaum (1985). In this approach, clients are trained to label experiences viewed as alien as actually an integral part of their personality, to be dealt with in a confrontational and honest manner.

Psychodrama could also be useful here. In this vein, Yablonsky (1976, p. 4) states, "In psychodrama a person is encountering his conflicts and psychic pain in a setting that will more closely approximate his real life situation than in most other therapeutic approaches. A young man in conflict with a parent talks directly to a person as an auxiliary ego playing his parent. His fantasy (or reality) of his hostility or love can be acted out on the spot."

The acting-out of such fantasies about one's own reality, or the experiencing of that reality, can ultimately lead to a positive, integrative experience.

## Sleep Disorders

The humorist and movie star W. C. Fields once quipped that "the best way to get a good night's sleep is to go to bed." Unfortunately, it is not that simple for many people. In fact, sleep disorder plagues everyone at one time or another. While estimates range widely, it is reasonable to assume that up to 15 percent of all adults will suffer a period of chronic insomnia at some point in their lives (Hauri, 1991; Montplaisir and Godbout, 1991).

There is a wide variety of sleep disorders, even though such disorders were not clearly recognized in the DSM until DSM-III-R, which included sleepwalking and sleep terror disorder (referred to as parasomnias) and sleep–wake schedule disorder, primary hypersomnia, primary insomnia, and insomnia disorder (referred to as dyssomnias).

An alternative and very well respected diagnostic classification system for sleep disorders is that of the Association of Sleep Disorder Centers (ASDC), published in their booklet "Diagnostic Classifications of Sleep and Arousal Disorders." It includes, for example, the subcategories for insomnia by etiology:

1. *Psychophysiological:* Insomnia is based on chronic tension and anxiety. It is unrelated to medical disease or psychiatric problems.

2. Insomnia due to *psychiatric disturbance* is the most commonly diagnosed insomnia. Insomnia is a symptom of psychopathology.

3. The use of *drugs and alcohol* can often lead to insomnia. Hypnotics described for insomnia may pose a special problem. The individual gains a high tolerance for the drug and takes more, resulting in an eventual rebound problem.

4. Some insomnias are caused by *sleep-induced respiratory impairment.*

5. Insomnia associated with *sleep-related mycoclamus and "restless legs"* is characterized by periodic episodes of repetitive leg muscle jerks.

6. Insomnia may be associated with other *medical, toxic, and environmental conditions.*

7. *Childhood onset* of insomnia is characterized by a history of complaints well before puberty.

8. Insomnia *associated with other conditions* includes such things as repeated awakenings and intrusion of alpha waves into REM sleep.

9. Insomnia due to no abnormality includes those insomniacs who do not have psychopathology or medical problems. They experience difficulty sleeping only during conventional sleeping hours.

☐          DIAGNOSTIC CONSIDERATIONS

The first diagnostic recommendation is that any apparently serious sleep disorder should be evaluated at a sleep disorder center; a thorough evaluation should include some observation and physiological monitoring, ideally of at least a couple of nights of sleep.

As regards standard psychological tests, Keles (1983) found that chronic insomniacs show a significant level of pathology on the MMPI-2. The highest three-scale code was 2-7-3. Fifty-six percent of the insomniacs tended to have a pathologic elevation on scale 2, while 42 percent had a pathologic elevation on scale 7 and 38 percent a pathologic elevation on scale 3. The 2-7-3 code reflects the chronic anxiety, difficulty expressing feelings, denial, and feelings of depression common to the insomniac. Interestingly, Keles found that 30 percent of his subjects had pathologic elevation on scale 8, which reflects self-image problems and difficulty integrating emotions. Scale 1 was significantly elevated in 20 percent of his subjects. Keles also found significant differences between age groups in their MMPI-2 scores. The most common three-scale code in those younger than thirty was 2-7-8; in ages thirty to forty-nine, 2-7-3 was the most common.

On the 16 PF, it is hypothesized that the insomniacs would have high scores on scales I, L, O, and $Q_4$, while scores on scales E, F, and H would be low and C relatively low. A high $Q_4$ would tap the high anxiety level that is common to most insomniacs. A high score on O would reflect the insecure and oversensitive nature of the insomniac. Introspection, rumination, and inability to deal with conflict would be reflected by a high scale I and at least a mildly elevated M.

On the ten basic personality pattern scales of the MCMI-II, an elevated scale 2 and moderately elevated 8A may be expected. A high scale 2 (avoidant) would tap two common personality characteristics of the insomniacs: mild cognitive intrusions and perceptual hyperactivity.

Since many insomniacs have problems expressing their emotions, this may be reflected on scale 1. On the pathologic personality disorders (scales C, P, and S), little elevations are expected.

☐        TREATMENT OPTIONS

Many insomniacs have significant anxiety, depression, and/or obsessive-compulsive features that contribute to the insomnia, as well as to other aspects of functioning. If these exist, the reader is referred to those chapters for relevant treatment recommendations.

Chemotherapy is commonly used for insomnia, sometimes with a very specific focus, e.g., oxycodone for restless-leg syndrome. However, chemotherapy directed toward the sleep disorder as a whole must be administered with caution (Montplaisir and Godbout, 1991). It can be especially useful in breaking the insomnia cycle, but if prescribed for any length of time loses its effectiveness, brings on the risk of drug dependence and/or addiction, and can generate a rebound effect of even greater insomnia.

Various behavioral techniques have been found to be effective (Hauri, 1991; Montplaisir and Godbout, 1991), but the most efficient techniques are probably relaxation training and biofeedback, especially where the emphasis is on muscle tension release. Ancillary techniques include (1) initiating a regular program of vigorous exercise—but it is best to avoid vigorous exercise late in the evening; (2) avoiding large or late meals or, conversely, going to bed very hungry—a high carbohydrate snack is helpful; (3) avoiding long or late naps during the day; (4) cutting down on caffeine or heavy smoking or alcohol use, especially just before bedtime; (5) don't fret over inconsistencies in your sleep pattern—give yourself some "quiet time" before going to bed, and tell yourself as you prepare for bed that you will sleep well; (6) keep your bedroom as quiet, dark, and comfortable as possible—most find a temperature of 65 degrees to be optimal; and (7) relearning a more appropriate bedtime routine by (a) going to bed only when feeling tired, (b) awakening at the same time each morning, (c) avoiding all nonsleep-related activities (within reason) in the bedroom, and (d) leaving the bedroom in twenty minutes if sleep has not occurred, i.e., as the philosopher Friedrich Nietzsche said in *Thus Spake Zarathustra,* "It is no small art to sleep: to achieve it one must stay awake."

Sleepwalkers often present management-control issues, and any therapist who works with such problems is advised to present the client with the following recommendations, as adapted from Gilmore (1991):

1. Use no drugs, alcohol, or caffeine, and use no psychotropic medications unless prescribed by a physician who is aware of the potential of such medications to exacerbate sleepwalking. Avoid any over-the-counter cold remedies or diet pills that contain stimulants.

2. Remove, to the degree feasible, any lethal weapons from access by the sleepwalker.

3. Take special precautions, such as placing locks on doors and windows, tying one's ankle to the bedpost, and placing a "kiddie fence" by the bedroom door.

4. Sleep on the ground floor.

5. Get psychiatric help for depression and/or other concurrent emotional problems.

6. Learn stress management skills and obtain skills and reassurance to lower anxiety, and consider marital counseling for related stress.

7. Maintain a regular sleep-wake cycle and get adequate sleep at regular intervals.

8. Get a complete assessment by an expert in sleep disorders who can monitor physiological measurements.

# CHAPTER 8

# The Sexual Disorders

This category in the DSM-III-R is used for those disorders in which a psychological variable is a significant factor in a sexual disturbance or disorder. If the disorder is caused by a physical factor, such as impotence from arteriosclerosis, it would be coded as an organic mental disorder.

In DSM-III-R, there are two divisions: the gender identity disorders and the sexual disorders. The sexual disorders are then subdivided into the paraphilias (the DSM-III-R term for the traditional "sexual deviations") and the sexual dysfunctions. There is also a residual category: paraphilia NOS. Gender identity disorder is differentiated from transsexualism only in that there is no persisting preoccupation with changing (via medication or surgery) into the sexual characteristics of the opposite sex. Thus, the following discussion will focus on transsexualism with the understanding that most of this discussion applies equally well to the gender identity disorder. Although the DSM-III-R does not directly provide for a diagnosis of sexual compulsion, it is a factor in many of the following diagnoses, and there is evidence that it may even be a recognizable pattern occasionally found apart from these other diagnoses (Masters et al., 1991).

## ■ Transsexualism (302.50)

The DSM-III-R category of gender identity disorders is hardly a category, as it comprises only Transsexualism (302.50; usually considered the major subcategory), the parallel category for children called Gender Identity Disorder of Childhood (302.60), Gender Identity Disorders of Adolescence or Adulthood, Nontranssexual Type (GIDAANT) (302.85), and a residual category called Gender Identity Disorder NOS (302.85).

Transsexuals are persons who strongly identify with the opposite sex, as manifested in cross-dressing and a persistent desire for a physical change to the opposite sex. This strong desire to change gender and the feeling of having an underlying opposite-sex identity are what primarily differentiate the transsexual from the transvestite (Francoeur, 1991). Transsexualism is a chronic disorder, and it is almost always preceded by gender identity problems in childhood. A disturbed parent–child relationship, particularly the absence of a model of the same sex, predisposes a child to this disorder. Also, any other characteristics, either physical or psychological, that cause identification of a child by others as one of the opposite sex (such as long hair and soft features in males) also facilitate transsexualism.

The first sex-change operation occurred in Europe in 1930. Most changes are made from male to female, in large part because there is a greater initial demand for this type of change, but also, just as importantly, because the surgery for the reverse procedure, female to male, is much more difficult and has a higher likelihood of failure.

Clinicians have an important role not only in diagnosing transsexualism in standard clinical settings but also in the psychological screening of such persons as appropriate for sex-change surgery. It is controversial whether this surgery is necessary. However, because such surgery is likely to continue, it is most important that people be thoroughly screened. Most reputable surgeons who deal with these problems mandate a team assessment by a psychologist, psychiatrist, and an endocrinologist. The early success rate of this surgery, about 90 percent in male or female sex reassignments (Pauly, 1968), undoubtedly reflects the thorough psychological screening techniques that have been done. As this procedure becomes even more commonplace, screening will probably become more lax and individuals who are inappropriate candidates will have an increasing chance of being operated on. For example, certain schizophrenics have a delusional belief that they are of the opposite sex, and some disturbed homosexuals and transvestites who cannot deal with the demands of their perceived role conflicts may unconsciously view a sex change as an escape from these conflicts. The clinician involved in such procedures should especially consider indicators for schizophrenia, paranoia, transvestism, and homosexuality when dealing with potential transsexual candidates (Money, 1987).

☐           DSM-III-R

There should be evidence of continuous (at least 2 years) and pervasive feelings that one is the wrong sex, with a consequent desire to change genital structure to the other sex and then to live in the life style of the opposite sex. There should be no evidence of directly related genetic abnormality, such as hermaphroditism. To warrant a diagnosis of transsexualism, individuals should first be screened for such conditions as schizophrenia, as well as for a primary or ancillary diagnosis of transvestism.

The disorder is subcoded as "heterosexual," "homosexual," or "asexual," with the label determined solely by the dominant sexual preference in the history of the individual.

☐         MMPI-2

One would expect the GF score to be elevated in male-to-female transsexuals and the GM scale elevated for the reverse pattern (Gentry and Meyer, 1991). Tsushima and Wedding (1979), in a study that looked at the MMPI profiles of transsexuals, found them to be surprisingly within normal limits. Of course, scale 5 is high in males due to nonidentification with the traditional male role, along with the conflicts about sexual identity. While presurgical males-to-females were found by Fleming et al. (1981) to be high on 5, 6, and 8, presurgical females were high on 5 and relatively high on 6, 7, and 8. Postsurgical females (those who had been male) were high on 5 and relatively high on 6 and K. Postsurgical males were high on 5 and relatively high on 6. Fleming et al. note that the tendency to peak on 5 and 6 is consistent with the early research literature about MMPI profiles of transsexuals.

On occasion, scale 1 and, to a lesser degree, 3 may be slightly elevated, reflecting preoccupation with body structure. In accordance with the preceding, scale F may be elevated. On the other hand, if transsexuals perceive the need to present themselves as healthy to pass the screening, scale K would be quite high and signs of pathology would be suppressed. If they are anxious and ambivalent about the identity issue, scales 4 and 8 may be slightly elevated, and if this has generated depression, scale 2 is raised.

☐         16 PF

As with the MMPI-2, the pattern is generally within reasonable normal limits. However, the mode of sexual adjustment results in slightly higher I scores and slightly lower E, H, and N scores in most males, with the converse being true in most females. Scale B should reflect the average or above-average intelligence in most transsexuals, and since they endorse attitudes that differ from the average, they are likely to be higher on M and $Q_1$ and moderately low on G.

☐         OTHER TEST-RESPONSE PATTERNS

On the Rorschach test, transsexuals (compared to normals) displayed significantly more intense levels of aggression, a lower level of object relations, poorer reality testing, and impaired boundary definition, being in this way similar to a borderline personality. Certain TAT cards, e.g., 1, 5, 13 MF, 17 BM, and 18 BM, often elicit themes relevant to sexual identity (Bellak, 1993).

On the MCMI-II, the distress and confusion about gender identity may cause elevations on A and D to 75 or higher, and very likely on C as well. Although no clear-cut pathological indicators are typically present, some generalizations may be possible. Males who seek to be females may be more likely to have personality types that are more commonly characteristic of females, so the prominent scale indicator may be 3 or 4. Conversely, females wishing to be males may have personality characteristics traditionally thought of as male, so scale 6A may be prominent.

□          TREATMENT OPTIONS

A classic option for the transsexual has been surgery to change the genitalia to that of the opposite sex. There is good evidence (Pauly, 1968) that in certain individuals this is an effective procedure, although psychotherapy for the social adjustment to the new sex is also an important adjunct. Also, covert modeling to retrain more appropriate sex-typed mannerisms and behaviors is helpful for all clients. In general, the surgical success is higher when the change is from male to female. In large part, this reflects the much more complex surgery required when the change is from female to male, as well as the accompanying higher probability of problematic side effects and outright failure.

In some cases, surgery is an unnecessary intervention, as psychotherapy and the passage of time can deal effectively with these identity concerns. This is particularly true when therapy is combined with aversive sexual-reorientation training and other techniques of psychosocial conditioning (Abel et al., 1986; Money, 1987). The clinician might also take note that well-known attorney Melvin Belli (1979) once argued persuasively that therapists can come under tort liability for taking a person through transsexual surgery, and it can possibly be considered under "criminal mayhem" statutes if there is any lack of clarity about the person's consent or ability to consent. Belli argues that adequate consent is problematic in most cases because the "compulsive" quality of the need to change sex is contradictory to the law's requirement that consent be "an affirmative act of an unconstrained and undeceived will" (p. 498). However, could not this concept of being compelled into treatment be applied to almost any disorder?

■          ## Paraphilias

"Paraphilia" is the DSM-III-R term for the sexual deviations, and both terms will be used interchangeably. The authors of the DSM-III-R assert, not totally convincingly, that the term "paraphilia" is superior to "sexual deviation" or "variation" because in paraphilia it is correctly indicated that the deviation *(para)* is in that to which the individual is attracted *(philia).*

Paraphilias consist of sexually arousing fantasy behavior associated with nonhuman sexual targets or nonconsenting humans and/or sexual activity with humans that involves either simulated or actual pain or humiliation or nonconsenting partners. As with most of the DSM-III-R categories, the paraphilias are classified as (1) mild–marked distress but no acting-out, (2) moderate–occasional acting-out, and (3) severe–repeated acting-out.

The essential disorder is in the lack of capacity for mature and participating affectionate sexual behavior with adult partners. Traditionally, these disorders have been far more common in males, but this discrepancy has decreased in recent years. Occasionally engaging in such fantasy or behavior does not usually qualify one as a paraphiliac. Exclusivity, persistency (even compulsivity), and pervasiveness are the hallmarks of the disorder (Hollin and Howells, 1991).

The specific paraphilia categories included in DSM-III-R are (1) Fetishism, (2) Transvestic Fetishism, (3) Pedophilia, (4) Exhibitionism, (5) Voyeurism, (6) Frotteurism, (7) Sexual Masochism, and (8) Sexual Sadism. There is also a residual category, Paraphilia NOS (302.90), that could be used often when making a diagnosis, since the range of potential sexual deviations is restricted only by the limits of the imagination. The variations included in the DSM III R are those that have traditionally been labeled as deviant and/or that have involved a legal issue. Thus "variation" is an even more appropriate term than "deviance," since "variation" more clearly implies this wide range of potential behaviors and the fact that many of these patterns may in certain circumstances be acceptable and adaptive and that the "deviance" of the disorder is often only in the eye of the beholder.

☐          DIAGNOSTIC CONSIDERATIONS

In general, the paraphilias, unless they are confounded by the presence of other psychopathology, do not present modal abnormal patterns on either the MMPI-2 or the 16 PF, although convicted sex offenders tend to obtain 4-5/5-4 or 4-8/8-4 profiles (Erickson et al., 1987). Because they are obtained in a clinical setting, some pathology is suggested, or else society, through a legal or social agent (e.g., a marital therapist) is concerned about the pattern. Certain scales may then be markedly elevated.

Measuring sexual responses to suggested imagery or to actual pictures of various stimuli is helpful in specifying the focus of the sexually deviant fantasies that are a key to behavior. Direct measures of penile tumescence (Freund and Watson, 1991) (usually via changes in a rubber tube encircling the penis, as in a pneumograph) are the most precise, although in some cases thermography has distinct advantages of ease of access and less embarrassment.

☐     TREATMENT OPTIONS

Since the paraphilias range from disorders that involve passivity (sexual masochism) to those that involve coercive aggression and legal sanctions (pedophilia), treatments will differ as well (Woody, 1992). Indeed, a clinician working in this area is constantly challenged by the creative diversity found in sexual preferences. For example, antisex crusader John Harvey Kellogg originated Kellogg's breakfast cereals to calm sexual lust and promote a generally healthy life style in the general population. Yet, Kellogg avoided sex with his wife and obtained gratification from enemas—a pattern known as klismaphilia.

In general, all of the paraphilias are difficult to treat, and success is often negligible and/or short-term. Within that perspective, the behavioral (and often, more specifically, aversive) conditioning techniques have been useful, e.g., using electric shock or inhalation of valeric acid, much as they are throughout the habit disorders (Hollin and Howells, 1991). Since fears of intimacy and self-esteem issues are often involved, psychotherapy is a useful adjunct, and if fears become specifically focused and take on a phobic quality, systematic desensitization and the implosive therapies can be used. Cognitive behavioral approaches, such as covert sensitization, as well as the existential therapies, are useful adjuncts to deal with the issues of sociolegal guilt and lack of responsibility.

The following are potential components of a typical sex-offender treatment program:

**1.** Assessment of the offender. This includes nature of specific offense, victim characteristics, antecedents of the offender's crime, previous offenses, level of psychopathology, developmental history, educational history, social history, sexual history-knowledge-experience, religious beliefs, occupational history, level of anger, level of ability to empathize, awareness of emotions, cognitive distortions about men, women, and children, and sexual arousal. Techniques to assess and to evaluate the offender include clinical interviews, self-reporting, psychological tests, questionnaires, rating scales, and physiological measures.

**2.** Group and individual therapy. This is necessary to clarify the individual's range of deviancy, level of disorder, level of commitment to change, and ability to tolerate confrontation. It provides a context for retraining more prosocial sexual patterns (Woody, 1992).

**3.** Operate and interpret an adequate system of phallometric measurement e.g., penile plethysmography (Fedora, Reddon, Morrison, Fedora et al. (1992). Self-report of offenders is faulty due to their tendencies to minimize involvement and their wishes to conceal information, and some suffer from disorders that affect their thought process to such an extent that self-reported information is invalid. Plethysmography is defined as the use of an instrument for determining and registering variations in the size of an organ or limb. Typically, an electronic device, called a penile transducer, is attached to the penis by the client. It detects changes in the size of the penis when sexual stimuli of both deviant and nondeviant content are presented. The associated degree of erection provide an indication of his sexual interests, preferences, and inhibitions. Therapists are trained to utilize the plethysmograph to condition the offender to appropriate sexual stimuli as well as to counter-condition him to inappropriate stimuli.

**4.** Covert sensitization is an imagery-based counter-conditioning procedure in which a client is instructed to imagine the relevant deviant sexual act or stimulus followed by the imagining of some negative reaction, usually either severe anxiety, terror, or nausea.

**5.** Assisted covert sensitization employs a strongly noxious odor to aid in the development of a nausea response.

**6.** Olfactory conditioning is when inappropriate sexual stimuli are presented to a client via slides, audio-tapes, or videotapes, followed by the presentation of the noxious odor.

**7.** Satiation therapy involves having the offender masturbate to an appropriate sexual fantasy while verbalizing it aloud. Following this, the offender is required to continue to masturbate for a period ranging from fifty minutes to two hours (or try, in some cases) while verbalizing deviant sexual fantasies.

**8.** Aversive behavioral rehearsal attempts to decrease sexually deviant behaviors and arousal by making the behavior publicly observable. The offender describes in detail the types of offense committed and then by use of mannequins, clothing, apparatus, etc., reenacts the offense. The tape is narrated by the offender while discussing his plans, actions, feelings, and thoughts. Having victims, friends, and/or family members as an audience heightens the aversive effect.

**9.** Relapse prevention emphasizes that sex offenses are not impulsive criminal acts, but more commonly are planned. Offense precursors, a common sequence of risk factors that cumulate in sexual violence, form chain-like processes. Offense precursors are emotion, fantasy, cognitive distortion, plan, and act. The two models of relapse are the internal, self-management dimension and the external, supervisory dimension. The first model increases the client's awareness and range of choices concerning his behavior, in developing specific coping skills and self-control capacities, and in creating a general sense of mastery over life. The second model imposes external controls through a team which involves the parole officer, the therapist, the parole board, the family, and friends.

Of course, first and foremost, the offender has to admit guilt before he can be accepted into sex offender programming. He has to participate in the assessment process by taking tests, by relating his life's history, and by cooperating to the fullest extent. Most programs require the offender to sign a contract outlining his responsibilities and the results that can occur if he does not meet these responsibilities. The goals and responsibilities agreed to are developed by the treatment team. Appropriate goals of treatment include, but are not limited to, the following:

1. To actively participate in and follow all treatment requirements
2. To learn to control his deviant arousal pattern
3. To place obstacles in the path of converting nonsexual problems into sexual behavior
4. To learn to solve nonsexual problems in nonsexual ways
5. To take responsibility for his behavior without minimizing, externalizing, or projecting blame onto others
6. To make some form of restitution to the victim

# ■ Fetishism (302.81)

The DSM-III-R defines fetishism as a condition where, for a period of at least six months, intense sexual fantasies, urges, and arousal were generated from an attraction to nonliving objects and the person acted on these or is markedly distressed by them. The traditional use of this term included an attraction to isolated though still-attached body parts, but this does not fit with the DSM-III-R definition. If the fetish is simply an article of clothing used in cross-dressing, the diagnosis could be transvestic fetishism. Also, if the arousal value is inherent in the object, such as a vibrator, the diagnosis of fetishism would be inappropriate.

Sexual stimulation from fetishes is typically obtained by tasting, fondling, kissing, or smelling the objects. Bras, panties, and shoes are the most common objects. The objects may be used while masturbating alone or, in some cases, as a necessary preliminary to intercourse. A degree of fetishism is associated with any sexual experience. Normal foreplay includes attention to sexually arousing objects or parts of the body, with consequent sexual arousal and progression toward coitus. In fetishism, however, the fetish takes primacy as a necessary means for developing arousal and allows avoidance of intimacy (Levin and Stava, 1987).

A confounding variable in fetishism, as well as in a number of other paraphilias, is the potential legal issue. Acts of breaking and entering are occasionally committed by the fetishist who is seeking a supply of women's used bras or panties. New articles of clothing are seldom arousing, in part because they are not identified with any individual person and also because they do not have the odors that are often arousing to the fetishist. In many cases, the illegal behavior itself increases the excitation and consequently increases the sexual arousal.

Although fetishism tends to crystallize as a behavior pattern in adolescence, it often has precursors in childhood. It is chronic, and most fetishists are men.

☐      ## DSM-III-R

To diagnose a person as a fetishist, it is required that the fetish, a nonliving object, be a preferred mode of arousal while the client is alone or is a necessary factor when used with a partner. It may occur in either actual behavior or fantasy. Transvestism or objects that are inherently sexually stimulating as the only evidence of fetishistic behavior would not warrant this diagnosis.

☐      ## MMPI-2

Fetishists seldom show a markedly elevated MMPI-2 profile. If the fetishism reflects some insecurity with the male sex role or some disguised homoerotic trends, an elevation on scale 5 is expected (Graham, 1977). In fetishists who indulge alone, a fear of the opposite sex may exist, which would elevate scales 4 and 7 to a degree. When the fetishism is embedded in heterosexual relationship, such elevations are less probable. When there is a legal problem involving fetishism, the reader should consult the section on malingering.

☐      ## 16 PF

The fetishist who indulges while alone is more likely to be low on factor. Those who accept their fetishistic behavior should have a reasonably high $Q_1$, whereas if they do not accept it, $Q_1$ may be at an average level or even lower. These clients are also likely to be relatively low on scale G and moderately high on M. If distressed by their pattern, high scores on O and $Q_4$ are likely. If they are being legally or socially coerced because of their behavior, such defensive patterns as malingering may be expected, with a higher score on L.

☐      ## TREATMENT OPTIONS

The aversive conditioning therapies are especially appropriate with fetishism, since specific behavior patterns are the central focus. Mild electric shock, inhalation of valeric acid, and nausea-inducing drugs have been successfully used in aversive conditioning procedures in which the object of the fetish, or fantasy of it, is paired with the aversive stimulus. In general, mild electric shock is preferable to such nausea-producing drugs as apomorphine because the contiguity between the avoidance stimulus and the deviant response is more easily controlled when shock is used. The aversion therapy procedures of both fear conditioning and aversion relief have also been used. Once the person has decreased the arousal value contingent on the fetishistic object, training in more normal sexual patterns is possible (Lo Piccolo and Stock, 1986).

## ■ Transvestic Fetishism (302.30)

Transvestism, or transvestic fetishism (the DSM-III-R term), is the dressing in clothes of the opposite sex for a period of at least six months, accompanied by intense sexual urges and fantasies that result in acting-out and/or distress. It also includes any other voluntary manifestations of those behaviors traditionally thought of as specific to the opposite sex. DSM-III-R limits this concept even more by asserting that it is only diagnosed in males, a perversely chauvinistic position for which there is no clear supportive rationale.

Beyond simple cross-dressing, the behavior must be sexually arousing. In most transvestites, the cross-dressing behavior was initiated in childhood and, in some, was significantly reinforced by parents, sometimes by "petticoat punishment," the humiliation of a boy by dressing him in girl's clothes. It typically becomes paired with masturbation and eventuates in the classic transvestite pattern.

Transvestic fetishism (TF) is considered to be a rare disorder; an even smaller subgroup eventually goes from TF to transsexualism, where the diagnosis of transsexualism takes precedence. TF is obviously related to fetishism. Just as in fetishism, an inanimate object is the stimulating variable, and there is often little or no dependence on human relationships for sexual gratification. When the transvestite has a partner, there may be masochistic fantasies that progress into behavior (Hollin and Howells, 1991). This then adds a secondary diagnosis of sexual masochism.

### ☐ DIAGNOSTIC CONSIDERATIONS

Transvestites do not show particularly pathologic MMPI-2 or 16 PF profiles. A high GF scale score for male transvestites is highly likely, as is a high GM scale score for female transvestites (Gentry and Meyer, 1991). The clinician can expect a high scale 5 whether this is a male or female transvestite (although DSM-III-R limits this disorder to males dressing as females). There is also a moderate rise in scale 3, which indicates some histrionic components, and possibly mild elevations in scales 4 and 6, reflecting concern about being discovered in a secret life style and hostility toward standard social mores.

On the 16 PF, moderately elevated L and $Q_1$ scales and moderately low scores on G and $Q_3$ occur. A higher score on N is also probable, and if anxiety is a reason for this clinical situation, elevation on $Q_4$ in particular, and possibly on O, could be expected.

Anxiety and depression may occur if dressing is inhibited, producing significant elevations on A and/or D on the MCMI-II. As in other psychosexual disorders, 1 and/or 2 may occur as the most prevalent personality syndrome. C is also likely to be high. Additionally, the indifference to social expectations may also be reflected by elevation on 5.

□     TREATMENT OPTIONS

Since TF is easily considered a subcategory of fetishism, the procedures noted in that section are equally applicable here. In addition to using aversive procedures, the therapist could use thought stopping to control the initial impulse to cross-dress. TF may have certain compulsive features, so the reader is referred to the section on the obsessive-compulsive disorder. Both the aversion therapy and the thought stopping can be amplified by the use of a portable, self-administered shock unit. The person can wear this unit discreetly under clothing, and when the impulse arises, a shock can be administered in conjunction with the aversion or thought-stopping procedure.

Covert sensitization (Cautela and Wall, 1980) is particularly helpful in the habit disorders and can easily be dovetailed with the aversive conditioning procedures in the therapist's office. In the covert sensitization procedure, some highly aversive contingency is imagined immediately on the occurrence of the fantasy of the undesired behavior. In this case, it is the transvestite pattern. As a result, the undesired impulse toward TF is weakened.

## ■     Pedophilia (302.20)

Pedophilia literally—and ironically—means "love of children," and a pedophiliac is one who consistently seeks out sexual experiences with children. Pedophilia is extremely rare in females, and although it is not a particularly common behavior in *any* demographic group, it has traditionally been viewed as a disorder of middle-aged males—"dirty old men." Recent research (Abel et al., 1986; Levin and Stava, 1987) has shown, however, that while the offender is almost always male, the molestation typically started by age fifteen; most early victims are known to the pedophile; boys are more likely to be victims than girls; girls are more likely to be victims of "hands-off" crimes like exhibitionism; most pedophiles over time commit a wide range of crimes, including exhibitionism, voyeurism, and rape; and pedophiles who molest boys do it a great deal (an average of over 200 incidents), whereas female-oriented pedophiles average approximately twenty-five incidents and rapists of adults five to ten incidents. Not surprisingly, few sex offenders will admit to such numbers unless given complete anonymity.

There are significant differences between those pedophiliac men who are exclusively inclined toward sexual experiences with male children and those who primarily seek out females. Heterosexual pedophiles are more likely to be married and prefer a younger target—females aged eight to ten—as opposed to the homosexual pedophile's preference for boys aged twelve to fourteen. Homosexual pedophiles show a poor prognosis for change, are less likely to know their victim, and are more interested in proceeding to orgasm rather than focusing on the touching and looking behavior often preferred by heterosexual pedophiles. Many heterosexual male pedophiles have problems with potency and are likely to prefer ejaculation achieved through voyeuristic-exhibitionistic masturbation. When they do attempt intercourse with a child, they are more likely to generate trauma and pain and in that way raise their chances of being reported and eventually apprehended (Rice et al., 1991).

Pedophiles, whether homosexual or heterosexual, often feel inadequate about their sexuality, and the contact and/or comparison with the sexually immature target may alleviate this anxiety and allow a nonthreatening release for sexual tension.

Alcohol abuse is a common catalyst for this behavior, as are marital problems among married pedophiles. Another catalyst (which does not detract in any way from the pedophile's responsibility for the act) is victim behavior. Finkelhor (1985) points to interesting data showing that an unusually high percentage of sexually victimized children had lived without their mothers for a significant length of time prior to the age of sixteen. It is possible that they may have missed a subtle training in behaviors conducive to fending off this type of sexual coercion. Evidence shows that when the pedophile is mentally retarded or schizophrenic, the victim sometimes initiated the contact (Friedrich, 1991).

A subcategory of pedophilia is incest. While incest occurs in any potential family structure relationship, father–daughter incest is by far the most common target of societal concern. Three psychological subpatterns occur in this specific form of incest (Finkelhor, 1985; Smith and Meyer, 1987). The first pattern is the inadequate and psychosexually immature father who is functionally a pedophile and who often has sexual contact with his daughters, sons, and other children. Such individuals show a combination of pedophiliac and psychopathic diagnostic indications. The second is a true "primary psychopath." This person relates to virtually all people as objects, is promiscuous in all directions, and shows little remorse over any behavior patterns.

Family-generated incest is the third pattern, and it is usually marked by a passive and inadequate father and an emotionally disturbed mother. Persons engaging in this type of incest show characteristics of the pedophile plus aspects of the passive-aggressive and dependent personality disorders.

☐            DSM-III-R

To warrant a diagnosis of pedophilia, the person must over a six-month period experience strong urges and fantasies for sexual contact with a prepubescent child (13 or younger), resulting in marked distress or acting-out. The DSM-III-R arbitrarily defines the required difference between the ages of the persons as five years, with the perpetrator being at least sixteen years old. The diagnosis should be further specified as to whether it is (1) same sex, opposite sex, or same *and* opposite sex, (2) limited to incest, and (3) exclusive or nonexclusive.

☐            MMPI-2

As might be expected from society's repugnance for this type of behavior, pedophiles are far more defensive than persons with most other paraphilias. As a result, elevated K and L scales are common, and elevations on 4 and 8 are most common in the clinical scales (Hall et al., 1986). Denial, along with an avoidance of intrapsychic concern, is reflected in an elevated 3 scale.

    Erickson et al. (1987) found that offenders against children were more likely to obtain 4-2/2-4 profiles, whereas offenders against adult women tended to obtain 4-9/9-4 profiles. While the most common MMPI-2 profile in child molesters is a 2-4/4-2, the particularly inadequate pedophile who has significant difficulties in dealing interpersonally with the opposite sex often presents a 1-8/8-1 profile. Likewise, incestuous pedophiles score higher on 0 than nonincestuous pedophiles, who in turn are higher than normals (Levin and Stava, 1987). Those who show a consistent immaturity throughout many of their behavior patterns and who have problems in controlling impulse behavior may show a 3-8/8-3 code. Where the pedophiliac behavior is a classic counterphobic mechanism to deny feelings of inadequacy about masculinity, the 4-8/8-4, with a surprisingly low scale 5 score (considering the person's general behavior patterns), is obtained. Where the person is more aware of the disturbance in sexual identity, an elevation on scale 5 is seen.

☐            16 PF

On the 16 PF, the emotional disturbance, impulsivity, and deviant mores are reflected in low scores on A, C, G, and $Q_3$. Anxiety and insecurity, possibly induced by the potential for being apprehended, elevate scores on O and $Q_4$. The deviant fantasy and the isolation from society because of the repulsiveness of the acts result in high scores on L and M. Homosexual pedophiles are moderately high on E and H and moderately low on I; the reverse is true for heterosexual pedophiles. Scores on scale B vary markedly, although they are usually moderately low.

☐ OTHER TESTS

In human-figure drawings, Johnson and Johnson (1986) found pedophiles, when compared to normals, to show poorer overall quality in the drawings, poorer gender differentiation, the female figure often larger than the male figure, and a number of male figures with blank or missing eyes.

Except for possible elevation on B, the clinical-symptom syndromes do not usually show much disturbance on the MCMI-II. The interpersonal indifference and behavioral apathy indicated by elevated 1 are less likely here than elevated scores on 2, 5, and 6A. Although high scores on 2 indicate a detached style, pedophiles may seek less threatening children as a source of sexual satisfaction to deal with their interpersonal inadequacy. A and D are likely to be high if the behavior is egodystonic, and 6 may be high if the person has become embroiled in legal troubles.

☐ TREATMENT OPTIONS

Because of the disgust with which most people respond to this disorder, it is not surprising that the typical treatment approaches are somewhat coercive. Pedophiles rarely bring themselves into treatment and are typically coerced by sociolegal pressure (Abel et al., 1986). Castration is still a favored response in some cultures, and in our society, chemocastration is still considered to be a reasonable option. Anti-androgens such as cyproterone acetate (in Europe) or medroxy-progesterone acetate (in the United States) suppress the sexual libidos of male pedophiles; these drugs also have been used with rapists and exhibitionists (Abel et al., 1986). They function by reducing serum testosterone levels to a level at which sexual arousal is diminished or absent, and they have moderate success when combined with psychotherapy. The aversion therapies have also been used with moderate success.

Covert sensitization can be helpful. Aversive mental images are immediately associated with images and impulses for initiating and continuing pedophiliac behaviors. Forgione (1976) presented an interesting variation on this approach. He filmed pedophiles while they reenacted their pedophiliac behaviors in response to a childlike manikin; simply watching the playback proved aversive and reduced the pedophiliac behavior. The clinician could vary this proceed by making slides from the tape and pairing electric shock with them to further the aversive response.

Since inadequacy in social interactions is a major factor in most pedophiles, assertiveness training, particularly directed toward adults of the opposite sex, is helpful here. It can be complemented by general social retraining toward an ability to attain mature heterosexual partners.

In one of the better studies on recidivism from treatment, in this case a maximum security psychiatric institution, Rice et al. (1991) found that the recidivism of 136 such extrafamilial child molesters who had received phallometric assessment and treatment from 1982 to 1983 was determined over an average 6.3-year follow-up. Fifty had participated in behavioral treatment to alter inappropriate sexual age preferences. Thirty-one percent of the subjects were convicted of a new sex offense, 43 percent committed a violent or sexual offense, and 58 percent were arrested for some offense or returned to the institution for a parole violation. Those convicted of a new sex offense had previously committed more sex offenses, had been admitted to correctional institutions more frequently, were more likely to have been diagnosed as personality disordered, were more likely to have never married, and had shown more inappropriate sexual preferences in initial phallometric assessment than those who had not. Unfortunately, behavioral treatment did not significantly affect recidivism.

## ■ Exhibitionism (302.40)

The term "exhibitionism" was first introduced into psychopathology by Lasegue in 1877, although the act itself was described as early as 4 B.C. (Cox, 1980). Exhibitionism is the act of exposing one's genitals to a stranger in order to obtain sexual arousal. Certain rare individuals do expose themselves without ever having been aroused, but they usually turn out to be psychotic, senile, or at least moderately mentally retarded.

The DMSs traditionally argued that the condition was found only in males, but this proviso is dropped in DSM-III-R. There are few reports to police of females who exhibit themselves, but to assert that the behavior *never* occurs in females is unsubstantiated (Masters et al., 1991). Although it is treatable, exhibitionism, along with voyeurism, has had the highest recidivism rate of all the sexual disorders (Cox, 1980, Marshall et al., 1991).

□ DSM-III-R

The DSM-III-R requires, for at least six months, recurrent sexual urges and sexually arousing fantasies involving the exposure of one's genitals to an unsuspecting stranger. The person has either acted on these urges or is markedly distressed by them.

□ DIAGNOSTIC CONSIDERATIONS

From the legal perspective, exhibitionism is probably the most commonly reported paraphilia, but the cost to victims and society is lower than that of some of the other disorders, such as pedophilia. It is estimated to account for about one-third of all sexual offenses reported to authorities, and only a small percentage of exposure acts are ever reported to the police (Abel et al., 1986; Hendrix and Meyer, 1976). Indications are that there is a bimodal distribution of the mean age of onset of first exposure, with peaks in the age ranges eleven to fifteen and twenty-one to twenty-five. The mean age of first arrest is approximately twenty-five. Exhibitionists seldom gravitate toward more serious sexual offenses (Cox, 1980).

The high overall recidivism rate is partially explained by a markedly increasing recidivism rate for those who are convicted more than once. Even though there is a conviction rate of only 10 percent for first offenders, the rate is almost 60 percent for those with more than one previous sexual offense and 70 percent for those with previous sexual and nonsexual offenses. If intervention can keep the exhibitionist from exposing himself for at least eighteen months after treatment, there is a low likelihood of future exposures (Cox, 1980).

There is a high incidence of disrupted father–son relationships in the background of exhibitionists—indeed, this is true to a degree for most of the paraphilias (Levin and Stava, 1987). Exhibitionists show poor interpersonal relationships during adolescence, and masturbation is always of unusual importance to them as a sexual outlet, even when other partners are available.

Of the personality types that eventuate in exhibitionism (Smith and Meyer, 1987), the "characterological type," a small group, is the only one that shows any significant danger to the victim. They have profiles similar to rapists, with the same elements of anger and hostility. The shock response of the victim is a major reinforcement, and there is little guilt or remorse.

A second subtype is the "unaware group," where the act is an outgrowth of extreme alcohol intoxication, organic brain disorder, or severe mental retardation. A third type is the "inadequate group." These individuals are similar to those with the avoidant personality disorder, although they have a few more obsessional features and more anger. The reader is referred to the section on the avoidant personality disorder, with the notation that scales 4 and 6 on the MMPI-2 and the correlated scales on the 16 PF should be a bit more elevated here.

The fourth group, the "impulsive-compulsive type," is obsessional, tense, anxious, and both sexually compelled and confused. Their behavior is an impulsive response to intrapsychic conflict and distress. It is this last group, the largest group of exhibitionists, that we will focus on in the following discussion of diagnostic parameters.

☐          MMPI-2

A summary of MMPI-2 data collected on exhibitionists shows them to be moderately nonconforming individuals who have a history of mild violations of social norms, but with no extensive allied psychopathology (Cox, 1980). Throughout most studies the standard elevations are on scales 4, 5, and 8, but these are often below 70 T. The elevations on scales 4 and 8 reflect the mild antisocial nature of the behavior, the lack of impulse control, and a degree of hostility toward the general environment. The elevation on 5 reflects sexual confusion, but there are "macho" exhibitionists who are low on 5. Exhibitionists are usually very low on scale 0 and moderately low on scales 1 and 9. To the degree scale 8 is elevated in relation to other scales, these persons are likely to be self-defeating and their exposure patterns more likely to be discovered. For example, the author is aware of numerous exhibitionists who have admitted exhibiting themselves over five hundred times without ever being apprehended. Similar cases have shown a low 8 scale, with a high 4 scale and moderately high 5 and K scales. Exhibitionists are generally lower than rapists on 4, 8, 6, 3, 2, and F, in order of magnitude (Levin and Stava, 1987).

## 16 PF

Exhibitionists score moderately high on O and $Q_4$, however their scales may revert to average if they are not under some kind of legal scrutiny. Similar to obsessives, they are only moderately low on C and moderately high on L and M. To the degree they have been self-defeating in their exposure patterns, they are likely to show a low score on N and $Q_3$ and a high score on H. Other scales are usually not remarkable.

## TREATMENT OPTIONS

Exhibitionism, like pedophilia, has a high rate of recidivism. For that reason, some therapists eventually resort to chemocastration through the use of such antiandrogen drugs as medroxyprogesterone acetate. However, the major treatment for exhibitionism is some form of aversion therapy, and cognitive therapy and relationship skills training appear to be necessary to produce any long-term change (Marshall et al., 1991). Some retraining in social skills and orgasmic reconditioning are also usually necessary. Covert sensitization can be used, amplified by adding noxious odors and shocks at the time the exhibitionist is presenting the aversive images to himself.

Hendrix and Meyer (1976) demonstrated that exhibitionism can be controlled through a multifaceted treatment approach that includes no aversive techniques. They used progressive relaxation to lower a client's tension-anger pattern and cassette tapes and autogenic training to further the relaxation response. Psychotherapy uncovered the suppressed anger and fear of interacting with females, and assertiveness training was used to control these situations. This was combined with increased self-verbalizations designed to heighten self-esteem and confidence. At that point, standard sexual counseling helped in the attainment of adequate heterosexual relationships. Also included was systematic desensitization, which was used to dissipate a phobic fear of being rebuffed by females. In addition, Dr. Hendrix accompanied the exhibitionist to in vivo situations, such as the campus snack shop (being introduced as his friend, if necessary). Dr. Hendrix monitored the situation and then later counseled the client on his socialization patterns.

Wickramasekera (1976) proposed a then unique treatment. He required the patient to undress and dress several times before a mixed-sex audience of therapists who had the subject explore associated affect, bodily sensations, and fantasy during exposure. The patient was asked such questions as "What do you think we see (feel/think) as we look at you right now?" in an objective, noncritical yet unempathic manner. During the second part of the session, the patient was again required to undress and dress several times (at his therapist's direction) and was asked questions to facilitate comparison of present feelings with antecedents, moods prior to and during exposure, and consequent moods and events. Videotaping (to be reviewed later by patient and therapist) and having the patient observe himself in a mirror are also part of this procedure. The treatment induces a high degree of anxiety in patients for whom it is appropriate (those who are nonpsychotic, nonpsychopathic, and somewhat anxious), which appears critical to the success of the treatment.

In persons who do not experience the required level of anxiety, it could be increased by bringing into the audience either victims or people close to the exhibitionist (wife, mother, daughter) or even by chemically increasing anxiety, e.g., by injections of sodium lactate prior to the sessions (Liebowitz et al., 1985).

Wickramasekera offers several explanations for the treatment's effectiveness: (1) it involves extinction of the exhibitionist's private fantasies, since the female or mixed-sex audience does not react with shock or fear, (2) punishment by the connection of aversive visceral consequences (profuse sweating, headache, rapid heartbeat) to other internal cues or self-disclosure, and (3) cognitive dissonance, which predicts maximum attitude and behavior change with voluntary participation, minimal reward, and maximal effort (all of which are involved in the treatment).

No matter what technique is used or how effective it appears to be, periodic "booster" sessions are worthwhile because of the high level of recidivism.

# ■ Voyeurism (302.82)

Voyeurs continually search for situations in which they may view individuals or groups of individuals in the nude or in some form of sexual activity in order to obtain sexual arousal. Like pedophiles and exhibitionists, voyeurs have a high recidivism rate (Levin and Stava, 1987). Virtually all cases of voyeurism reported to the authorities are males, but there is no evidence that this behavior never occurs in females. Our society is organized to respond differently to exhibitionistic and voyeuristic behavior by females.

Approximately one-third of voyeurs are married. Even though the age of the voyeur at the time of the first voyeuristic act is the middle to late twenties, there has usually been a significant history of sexual and other offenses throughout adolescence. As with exhibitionists, there is a large history of broken homes and marital distress. Voyeurs seldom maintained close relationships with sisters or other girls when they were young.

Most voyeurs are not markedly disturbed, and the simple act of obtaining arousal from looking is of course a normal part of many sexual experiences. Triolism, or the sharing of a sexual partner while one observes, is a major reinforcement in group sex experiences and is not classified as voyeurism.

Only a small proportion of voyeurs pose a serious physical danger to their victims (Hollin and Howells, 1991). They are psychopathic in personality and show the following specific behavior patterns: They are most likely to enter a building in order to carry out their voyeuristic behaviors, and in some way, they draw attention to themselves while they are in the act.

## DSM-III-R

To make the DSM-III-R diagnosis of voyeurism, the clinician must establish that the behavior occurs over a six-month period; the person experiences strong urges and fantasies to observe an unsuspecting person disrobe, be in the nude, or engage in a sexual act; and acts-out or is distressed by these urges. The DSMs traditionally limited the diagnosis to males, but this has been dropped in DSM-III-R.

## DIAGNOSTIC CONSIDERATIONS

Like the exhibitionist, the voyeur does not show extensive psychopathology on psychological tests and has similar personality test patterns. Lachar (1974) suggests that the prototypical MMPI-2 pattern for a voyeur shows elevated scores on 3, 4, and 5, with the elevation on 3 or 4 being the highest, and with a T score seldom being above 70. On the average, the score on scale 9 tends to be lower for the voyeur than for the exhibitionist. That very small subgroup of voyeurs who pose a danger to others has diagnostic patterns parallel to those of primary psychopaths, although they show more elevation on scale 5.

On the 16 PF, voyeurs are relatively close to the pattern of exhibitionists, but voyeurs average a bit higher on scales L and $Q_3$. This reflects their more circumspect patterns of pathology, which is usually accompanied by feelings that they would like to retain control of events in their worlds. Those with the detached personality characteristics indicated by elevations on 1 and/or 2 on the MCMI-II may be more predisposed to engage in this behavior.

☐        TREATMENT OPTIONS

All of the techniques noted for the treatment of exhibitionists are equally appropriate to the treatment of the voyeur. In particular, the aversion therapies have often been used. However, the treatment of one voyeur by a colleague of the author brought home the point that it is critical to be accurate regarding which stimuli are to be eliminated by the shock. This client had been administered shock on presentation of the hypothesized arousal stimuli: a clear view of the nude bodies of a couple through a window. This treatment was ineffective until the shock was eventually paired with slides of open windows as they would appear from a distance of about thirty feet. This unique scene had become the initial discriminative stimulus for the arousal pattern, and the voyeurism decreased markedly when these slides were paired with shock in an aversive therapy procedure.

## Frotteurism (302.89)

Frotteurism is generally defined as the act of rubbing up against the body of a stranger, usually the stranger's buttocks, in order to achieve sexual arousal or even orgasm, if feasible. The act is usually carried out in a crowded public place, like a subway, swimming pool, or dance floor. In the traditional literature, frotteurism was often not distinguished from fetishism or partialism, although there are fundamental differences. The fetishist becomes aroused by and attached to a particular nonliving object that symbolizes the desired love object, and unlike frotteurs who make attempts at heterosexual life and fail, the fetishist rarely attempts. Partialism is differentiated from frotteurism in that the partialist is attracted to and can only achieve arousal from a specific part of the body, whereas the arousal for frotteurs is generated in a more generalized manner and is not tied to a specific body part.

Not unlike many voyeurs and exhibitionists, the frotteur usually has evolved a series of cover-up plans to avoid the embarrassment of being caught and publicly humiliated. The violation of the taboo of sexual behavior in a public place is arousing, but the humiliation one could experience if caught is aversive enough to generate these cover-up behaviors.

☐              DSM-III-R

In order to apply this diagnosis, the DSM-III-R requires that over a period
of at least six months the person has experienced recurrent intense urges
and fantasies of rubbing against or touching a nonconsenting person
(but the touching, not the coercive nature of the act, provides the primary
arousal) and that the person is significantly distressed by these urges
or has acted on them.

☐              DIAGNOSTIC CONSIDERATIONS

Freund et al. (1983) note that the great majority of frotteurs also show
other deviant behaviors, e.g., voyeurism and exhibitionism, rather than
a pattern marked by frotteurism alone. Hence, many of the diagnostic
responses and therapeutic considerations noted for voyeurism and exhibitionism also apply here. Like exhibitionists, elevations on MMPI-2
scales 4, 5, and 8 can be expected, although frotteurs could be expected
to be higher on scales 9 and 0.

On the 16 PF, 0 and $Q_4$ are likely to be elevated to the degree the
frotteur labels his (virtually all frotteurs studied have been male)
behavior as ego-alien. Scales A, G, H, and $Q_3$ are likely to be moderately depressed—especially G and $Q_3$, because they indicate a disregard for social norms and a lack of control over impulsive behavior.
On the MCMI-II, scales 1 and 8A should be moderately elevated, 2 moderately to significantly elevated, and scales 4 and 7 likely lower, the
latter reflecting the usual introverted personality style and the impulsive behavior pattern, respectively. With frotteurs who have sought
therapy, scales A and D on the MCMI-II are often elevated.

On the Rorschach, one would expect a number of texture responses
denoting a passively expressed need for affection, a higher incidence
of shading and achromatic responses, a higher E-B ratio reflecting any
introverted personality characteristics, and a high number of flexion-
movement responses (toward the center) (Exner, 1986).

☐              TREATMENT OPTIONS

The techniques applicable to voyeurs, exhibitionists, and fetishists are
all applicable here, depending on which components are paramount in
the individual case. Shame aversion therapy (Wicksramasekera, 1988,
1976) would be especially useful here. For example, the frotteur would
be required to perform his frotteurism on a woman in front of an audience of several women who were particularly selected for similarity
in appearance to the type of woman the frotteur normally seeks out.
During the act, the frotteur would be required to conduct a dialogue
with himself discussing what he is thinking, describing physical sensations, predicting how the observers and the victim are perceiving him,

and what their opinions of him may be. The observers and victim could be instructed to show no emotion and to stare at the frotteur for the duration or to spontaneously generate aversive emotions, such as laughter. As with exhibitionist, periodic "booster" sessions will likely be required to maintain any therapeutic effect, and social-skills training will be necessary in most cases.

# ■ Sexual Masochism (302.83)

Sexual masochism has traditionally been considered as a need to engage in fantasy or actual behavior in which the experience of having pain inflicted on oneself is necessary to gain sexual arousal. The DSM-III-R emphasizes that this be *actual* behavior rather than simply fantasy.

The term "masochism" was coined in 1896 by Richard von Krafft-Ebing and was taken from the works of Leopold von Sacher-Masoch (1836–1895), whose novels focused on the theme of men being dominated by women. Sacher-Masoch actually obtained excitement from the fantasy that his wife might be unfaithful to him and flaunt the fact to him.

Sexual masochism predominantly occurs in males and has its beginnings in childhood experience where the infliction of pain in some way becomes tied to sexual arousal (Holin and Howells, 1991). Crystallized behavior patterns are usually evident by late adolescence. In some cases, there is an increased need for pain over a period of time. In extreme cases, a bizarre form of sexual masochism originally referred to as "terminal sex" occurs. A male (typically) hangs himself by the neck with a noose while masturbating, in order to increase sexual pleasure. Releasing the noose just before the loss of consciousness theoretically increases the pleasure. This practice has increased in recent years and occurs most commonly among fourteen- to twenty-five-year-olds. Miscalculation is thought to cause as many as two hundred deaths in the United States every year.

☐     DSM-III-R

A diagnosis of sexual masochism is applied if over a six-month period the person experiences an act (not simulated) of being humiliated, beaten, bound, or otherwise made to suffer and is distressed or acts out.

☐     DIAGNOSTIC CONSIDERATIONS

Masochists seldom come to the attention of legal authorities, or even therapists, unless they have been a victim of extreme sadism that requires medical treatment, and this is uncommon. In many respects, they have the personality characteristics of the dependent personality disorder, except with a greater emphasis on a disordered sexual identification and a higher level of intrapsychic distress. Hence, higher elevations on scales 5 and 7 occur. Scores on scales 6A and 9 are substantially lower than would occur in sadism, which reflects the masochist's passivity and apathy, as well as the subtle defensive quality that may be hidden from others.

Again, the 16 PF profiles should be similar to those of a person with the dependent personality disorder, with some specific exceptions. I would hypothesize that scale N should be significantly higher, as should scores on $Q_1$ and, to a lesser degree, $Q_2$. L is not usually as low as one might expect, since the submissiveness and adaptation to another is balanced by a subtle paranoid element, usually resulting in scores that are not extreme on this variable. A lower G score also reflects the unconventionality of this behavior, and in those individuals with guilt and a punitive conscience, a high O score is obtained. Scale B is relatively low. An elevated 3 on the MCMI-II, represented by dependent submissiveness, is likely. The self-condemnatory and dependency aspects of the borderline (scale C) may predispose toward masochistic behavior. Some components of the avoidant personality may be present, indicated by elevation on 2. The masochist may well give Rorschach responses that clearly indicate a submissive control behavior, such as being "yoked" or "chained." Small or passive animal responses may also be noted.

□        ## TREATMENT OPTIONS

Sexual masochism, to the degree that it is motivated by a need for sexual arousal, can be treated with the aversion therapies (see the section on exhibitionism). In most cases, this deviant arousal pattern involves interpersonal inadequacy, and both compulsion and pathologic dependency pervades the relationship (Coleman, 1987). In that regard, the reader is referred to the next chapter on treatment options for the obsessive-compulsive and dependent personality disorders.

The therapist can help the masochist focus on the quality of the relationship by a neoanalytic technique used by Kirman (1980) in which he has the client write letters to the significant other. This helps to focus the feelings and bring to consciousness the many aspects of the relationship that often remain out of awareness. One might also use the "empty chair" technique made famous by Fritz Perls. Rather than writing out his feelings, the client addresses the fantasized other in the empty chair in an oral dialogue; this is aided by its being done in a group. In either case, these feelings are used as a stimulus for new behavior patterns.

Covert extension can also be employed. Here, the client is asked to imagine the masochistic behavior pattern and then immediately imagine that the reinforcement that is expected to follow does not occur. Assertiveness training or psychotherapy with an Adlerian focus (since

Adlerian therapy so directly focuses on inferiority issues) could comple-
ment and aid the development of a repertoire of more-positive behaviors.

## ■ Sexual Sadism (302.84)

Sexual sadism is a condition wherein a person obtains sexual excitement from inflicting pain, injury, or humiliation on another (Fedora et
al., 1992). It differs from the sadistic personality disorder, described in
Chapter 9, which is an optional category in the DSM-III-R. The term
"sadism" is taken from the writings of the Marquis de Sade, whose works
focused on sexual pleasure gained from inflicting pain and even death
on others.

Most sadists show evidence of this pattern by early adolescence. The
condition is chronic and is seen far more frequently in males than
females. Sadism overlaps the concept of rape (Calhoun and Atkeson,
1991), although not all rapists are sadists, and vice versa. However, the
reader is referred to the section on rape (Chapter 14) since there are
parallel diagnostic considerations.

☐    DSM-III-R

A DSM-III-R diagnosis of sexual sadism is appropriate if over a period
of six months occur recurrent intense sexual fantasies and urges toward
acts (real, not simulated) in which another person is hurt (physically
or psychologically) or humiliated and the person is not distressed by or
acts on these urges.

☐    MMPI-2

Unlike the sexual masochist, the sadist shows significantly disturbed
patterns on the MMPI-2, with one or more scores above 70 T. This
usually indicates a lack of impulse control, specifically on scales 4 and
8A (Hall et al., 1986); scale 9 is also usually elevated. The high scores
on 8A and 8B show the unusual attitudes and thought patterns, hostility,
and aggression inherent in this disorder.

Most male sadists present a macho image, with stereotypical male
behaviors. Physical prowess and aggressive thrill-seeking behaviors are
often evident. This can result in a low score on scale 5, except that the
confused sexual identification may counterbalance this, particularly if
the person is oriented toward homosexual sadism. Females involved in
sadistic behaviors tend to score high on scale 5.

☐    16 PF

Sadists are likely to show high scores on scales E and H, emphasizing
the dominant and aggressive components of this disorder. In addition,

their distance from standard moral systems results in a low score on G and high scores on M and $Q_1$. Scores for L and $Q_3$ are also likely to be moderately high. A is usually low, reflecting the lack of any true interest in interpersonal relationships.

☐ OTHER TEST-RESPONSE PATTERNS

A score of 85 or higher on the MCMI-II scale 6B is common here, with elevation on 6A and 5 likely. Some paranoid qualities may be present, causing relative elevation on P. The impulsivity present in these persons may cause some elevation on N, while traits represented by elevated A, D, and H are not present. In addition to Rorschach Content responses that directly portray a sadistic element, such as hammers, explosions, and needles, figures that symbolize controlling authority, such as eagles, are occasionally noted. Mutilation content is also thought to be indicative of sadistic fantasy and possible sadistic behavior (Shafer, 1954).

☐ TREATMENT OPTIONS

Since sexual sadism more often focuses on deviant sexual arousal than does sexual masochism, the aversive therapy techniques are appropriate (Fedora et al., 1992) (see the section on exhibitionism). This approach could be aided by some of the cognitive approaches, such as covert sensitization. The person should also somehow be made aware of the psychological effect on the "victim," and "couple" therapy with the victim could be instituted. Other techniques for teaching more-apropriate interpersonal behaviors, such as those noted in the section on exhibitionism, would also be helpful because sadism is often a reaction to inadequacy and/or modeling from early training where physical abuse was common.

# ■ Zoophilia

Although this disorder was included in DSM-III, it has since been dropped as a formal diagnostic category in DSM-III-R, probably because of the rarity of its occurrence. The essential variable in zoophilia is the use of animals as the means of producing sexual arousal. This label is most appropriate when such behavior or fantasy is consistently preferred even though there are other outlets reasonably available. Zoophilia, which occurs primarily in males, is very rare. It may occasionally be a sign of schizophrenia.

The traditional term, "bestiality," referred primarily to having sexual intercourse with animals, whereas "zoophilia" refers to *any* type of sexual contact with animals. The preferred animal is usually one with which the person had contact during childhood, such as a pet or farm animal. Zoophilia is a moderately common theme in pornography and usually involves a female having a sexual experience with a pony or a dog. This theme is common because the usual consumer of pornography is male, and this appears to be an exciting theme for males. In actuality, the data of Kinsey et al. (1948, 1953) suggest that such patterns are extremely rare in females and only a bit more common in males, at least where the pattern has clinical significance.

□     DIAGNOSTIC CONSIDERATIONS

In the typical person who shows clinical zoophilia, the major features are significant depression, problems in interpersonal skills, and anxiety. Hence, I would expect MMPI-2 elevations on scales 2, 7 and 0, respectively. Also, the disordered sexual life could cause at least a mild elevation on scale 5.

In the 16 PF, the shame, anxiety, lack of interpersonal skills, and social isolation mean to this author that there should be high O and $Q_4$ scores and relatively low A, C, and F scores. Scale B is low in these individuals, and similarly, N is expected to be low and $Q_2$ moderately low. One may, again, expect 1 and/or 2 as a prominent feature of the MCMI-II profile, although the behavioral apathy of the asocial type may make a prominent score on 1 less likely here. Any depression and anxiety will be indicated by elevations of at least 75 on scales A and D.

□     TREATMENT OPTIONS

There are few reports in the literature concerning the treatment of zoophilia. Aversive conditioning procedures would be helpful regarding any fetishistic components. Since immaturity and inability to make adequate heterosexual contacts are often a factor, social retraining and the techniques of rational-emotive therapy (Ellis and Dryden, 1987) might also be applied.

■     ## Male Psychosexual Dysfunction

There are three major subcategories of male psychosexual dysfunction. First, Hypoactive Sexual Desire (302.71) refers to a condition, psychologically generated, where a person consistently experiences few fantasies about or little interest in proceeding into a sexual act. This occurs rarely as a separate disorder, and organic dysfunction should always be ruled out. It is often a reflection of disorder in a marital relationship rather than evidence of significant individual pathology. A more extreme variation is the Sexual Aversion Disorder (302.79). This refers to extreme aversion to and avoidance of virtually all genital sexual contact with a partner.

The third category is Premature Ejaculation (302.75). This disorder is an inability to exert voluntary control over ejaculation accompanied by persistent or recurrent ejaculation with minimal stimulation and before the person wishes it; it occurs in the absence of other significant pathology and is not an organic condition. It is difficult to define exactly what an "absence of voluntary control" means, and the DSM-III-R does not directly deal with this. Masters and Johnson (1970) define premature ejaculation as a clinical problem if the orgasm occurs involuntarily more than half the time before the partner's orgasm. Males may also now be diagnosed as suffering from Dyspareunia (302.76).

Premature ejaculation can be further subdivided into primary premature ejaculation (related to inexperience in the sexual area): a chronic, high state of arousal, possibly accompanied by fear of dealing with intimacy. As might be expected, it is most often a disorder of the young, and it does not correlate with any significant pathology. In secondary premature ejaculation, it is common that a disturbance in the relationship with a partner results in conflict expressed through premature ejaculation. The trouble is in the relationship, although individual personality factors of the partners may contribute (Masters et al., 1991).

Other major DSM-III-R categories in this area are Male Erectile Disorder (302.72) and Inhibited Male Orgasm (302.74), which refer to a disruption (at different points) of attempts to attain orgasm. The major organic factors to be ruled out are spinal cord disorders, nondominant-hemisphere parietal-lobe dysfunction, significant circulatory problems (often found in severe diabetics, but also not that uncommon in otherwise normals), and consistent alcohol or drug use (Schnarch, 1992; Masters et al., 1991).

The research literature refers to male erectile disorder as "erectile dysfunction," and most people simply term it "impotence." The latter term is undesirable for several reasons, primarily because it connotes general personality inadequacy and weakness of character. It is interesting to note that weakness in the male and coldness in the female, as connoted by the terms "impotence" and "frigidity," respectively, are opposites of the characteristics most commonly prescribed for sexual roles in our society: power and competence for males and sensitivity and warmth for females. Most erectile dysfunction is partial, that is, a man can attain erection but either cannot reach orgasm or does not maintain the erection for very long. Total erectile dysfunction over a significant period of time is not that common in young to middle-age males and suggests a biological cause. It is noteworthy that at least 25 percent of erectile dysfunction cases include both a significant organic and psychogenic component (Mohr and Beutler, 1990).

□          DIAGNOSTIC CONSIDERATIONS

The following cues are suggestive of erectile dysfunction in which organic factors play a major part:

Gradual onset

Sequentially deteriorating erections

Normal libido

Can initiate but not maintain erection

Loss of nocturnal and masturbatory erection

while the following are generally indicative of psychogenic erectile dysfunction:

Episodic

Sudden onset

Acute, brought on by life stresses

Normal morning and nocturnal erections

Loss of libido

Most researchers agree that persons with psychosexual dysfunction do not show markedly deviant profiles on standard psychological tests. There are some trends and differences, depending on whether the dysfunction is psychologically or biologically generated. Beutler et al. (1975) report a 90 percent success rate in using the MMPI to differentiate psychogenic versus biogenic erectile dysfunction, by two rules: (1) In psychogenic erectile dysfunction, scale 5 is typically higher, i.e., above 60, than if it is biogenic. (2) There is no consistency in the scores that are above 70 (65 in MMPI-2), but those scales that are, are usually the ones that reflect the sexual role problems (i.e., scale 5, a histrionic denial of problems as in scale 3, or depression on scale 2).

Another factor that often effectively differentiates psychologically generated dysfunction from biogenic cases is the occurrence of nocturnal penile tumescence (NPT), or erections that occur during sleep. Just as most females show clitoral arousal while sleeping, most (but not all) sexually normal males experience a number of NPTs every night during sleep. Almost all NPTs occur during REM sleep, and NPTs decrease, slowly, in frequency and duration with age. Although rigidity slowly decreases with age, circumferential increases during the tumescence period typically do not (Mohr and Beutler, 1990). Those individuals whose biogenic erectile dysfunction is psychogenic show a number of NPTs—although the "hit rate" of diagnostic accuracy with this technique can be as low as 65 percent (Mohr and Beutler, 1990). For example, various medications and clinical depression can suppress NPTs. The initial problem with this diagnostic cue was getting someone to stay awake all night to watch. The solution is to put a measurement device around the penis during sleep. Two widely used methods are the potentest (perforated gummed stamps placed around the penis) and the snap gauge. The snap gauge, which consists of three plastic bands, each of which breaks at different degrees of expansion of the penis, thus has the advantage of measuring both rigidity and circumferential expansion.

The urologist's traditional technique in this area, the Doppler ultrasound, provides the Penile Brachial Index (PBI), a contrast of blood pressure in the arm and the penis. Unfortunately, this is not always a reliable measure, in part because it is administered when the penis is flaccid and also because it cannot consistently distinguish between the deep arteries (those most critical to erection) and the superficial arteries. A much more reliable measure is obtained with the Rigi-Scan. The Rigi-Scan is a portable device that stores more information, e.g., duration of erection and rigidity at both the base and on the shaft. Measurements need to be taken for more than one night, ideally with a device, such as the Rigi-Scan, that measures strength and persistence of erection in addition to simple occurrence (Lo Piccolo and Stock, 1986). Several methods (e.g., covernography, a radiologic procedure) can assess vascular involvement, and vascular factors have been increasingly recognized as implicated in "gray area" cases (Mohr and Beutler, 1990).

On the 16 PF, persons with erectile dysfunction are likely to show higher than average scores on $Q_4$ and O, reflecting anxiety and insecurity. Their scores on E and $Q_3$ will vary depending on whether they have coped with the dysfunction by resorting to even more stereotypical masculine behaviors (resulting in high E and $Q_3$ scores) or have become more submissive in relationships and see themselves as unable to control their worlds (low scores). If they experience guilt over failing in their relationships, scores on O are likely to be raised. A high level of performance anxiety is likely to correlate with at least an average or moderately elevated M score. They show more reproductive anatomy responses on the Rorschach, as well as more emphasis on pelvic anatomy and more use of the internal white space.

No particular personality syndrome is commonly associated with male psychosexual dysfunction, although a scale 4 score of 85 or higher on the MCMI-II may predispose one toward this disorder. To the extent that performance anxiety, guilt, and depression are present, elevations of 75 or higher on A and D should occur. Scale 3 may also be elevated. High scores on B and/or T should alert the clinician that the dysfunction may be caused by organic factors.

The Derogatis Sexual Functioning Inventory is the most sophisticated and useful self-report instrument available for providing information about sexual functioning (Mohr and Beutler, 1990).

## ☐     TREATMENT OPTIONS

A number of physical, chemical, and psychological techniques have been developed to treat erectile and orgasmic dysfunctions (Lo Piccolo and Stock, 1986; Mohr and Beutler, 1990; Masters et al., 1991; Woody, 1992). Penile artery bypass surgery can be used where a specific circulatory problem is the issue, and other forms of revascularization can also be useful. Certain prosthetic devices can be used for organically based cases and occasionally for severe psychogenic cases as well. One is a rod that is implanted in the corpora cavernosa, the parts of the penis that engorge with blood in an erection. The consequent permanent erection can be an embarrassment, and it interferes with urological diagnostic procedures. An alternative is a hydraulic system. For example, erection is attained when a rubber bulb implanted in the abdomen or scrotum is pressed. It has the disadvantages of any implanted mechanical device, especially postsurgical complications, and is also expensive. But it does appear that patients are more satisfied with, and show higher sexual activity levels with, the inflatable devices (Mohr and Beutler, 1990).

It is noteworthy that the idea of a prosthesis is not necessarily a product of our modern, high-tech culture, as is documented in this true anecdote reported by R. O'Hanlon in his book *Into the Heart of Borneo* (1984).

"But Leon, when do you have it done? When do you have the hole bored through your dick?"

"When you twenty-five. When you no good any more. When you too old. When your wife she feds up with you. Then you go down to the river very early in the mornings and you sit in it until your spear is smalls. The tattoo man he comes and pushes a nail through your spear, round and round. And then you put a pin there, a pin from the outboard motor. Sometimes you get a big spots, very painfuls, a boil. And then you die."

"Jesus!"

"My best friend—you must be very careful. You must go down to the river and sit in it once a month until your spear so cold you can't feel it; and then you loosen the pin and push it in and out; or it will stick in your spear and you never move it and it makes a pebble with your water and you die."

"But Leon," I said, holding my knees together and holding my shock with my right hand, "do you have one?"

"I far too young!" said Leon, much annoyed; and then, grinning his broad Iban grin as a thought discharged itself: "But you need one Redmon! And Jams—he so old and serious, he need two!"
(p. 82–83)

Testosterone derivatives have been helpful in some cases (although these seem to inflate interest more than erections), but a hormone deficiency is seldom the critical issue. An oral drug, Gingko biloba, derived from the leaves of the Gingko tree, available in the United States as an herb in health food stores, has shown promise in improving erections as a secondary result of its positive effect on periploral circulation. Injections into the penis, at the time sex is desired, of a vasodilator such as papaverine, along with the alpha blocker phentolamine, is effective in providing erections in 65 to 80 percent of cases; those who don't respond are usually the very old, the very ill, and those with vascular impairment (so these can have a diagnostic function as well). A small proportion of normal men do not respond to these injections when they are administered while lying down, but do respond if they are standing. Aside from the requirement of self-injection, other drawbacks are the high costs and, in some cases, accumulated scarring, priapism, decrease of effectiveness over time, and even abnormal liver functioning.

The vacuum construction device (VCD) is a promising, noninvasive technique. The VCD is a cylinder which is placed over the penis and pressed against the body to produce an airtight seal. A vacuum is created, which engorges the penis, and rubber bands are slipped off of the end of the device, retaining the erection for up to thirty minutes. VCD-produced erections are less rigid although slightly larger than normal and are especially helpful with erectile dysfunction where vascular insufficiency is a critical factor (Mohr and Beutler, 1990).

However, the safest and generally most effective treatments are the psychological technique pioneered by Masters and Johnson (1970)— "sensate focusing"—and the more-sophisticated cognitive therapies, which are both used to help the client stop spectatoring (becoming too distanced from the act). These are particularly effective if carried out with a stable partner from the client's natural world. Sensate focusing is not a totally modern development: Sir John Hunter, a physician practicing around 1750, would advise his clients to go home and lie in bed "a fortnight and caress and fondle." His only reported difficulty was that "no one ever completed the treatment" (Lo Piccolo, 1985). Cognitive therapy and sensate focusing can be aided by systematic desensitization for specific phobias that might hinder erection, such as vaginal odor. In many cases, problems in the interpersonal situation are major contributors to the erectile and orgasmic dysfunction, so marital (or couple) therapy, including an emphasis on improving both social and communication skills in the primary client, is necessary to eliminate these precursors to the dysfunction sequence (Schnarch, 1992; Francoeur, 1991).

Treatment for inhibited sexuality components (whether with males or females) is difficult, first and foremost, because a low desire for sex predicts a low desire for sex therapy. Also, a low sex drive, in an otherwise healthy adult, is a paradoxical disorder in that people are "hardwired" rather than "programmed" for sex and a low interest in sexuality runs so counter to society's cultural values. In addition to couple therapy and sensate focusing, therapy here usually needs to focus on helping the person become more aware of both general affect and body states and also to include some sexual-drive induction techniques (Woody, 1992). The latter could include training the person to use sexual fantasies (have the client write them out, but make it clear you only want to know that the task was carried out; you are not going to cause embarrassment by checking the content). Very likely, this will need to be amplified by the use of erotica and instruction in masturbatory techniques and the control of masturbatory fantasy.

Most individuals (male or female, or couples) who have any of these types of problems need to be challenged on underlying, yet common, problematic cognitive assumptions, such as (a) sex should be "perfect," "special," "ecstatic," "novel," "routine," etc.; (b) sex should occur "in bed," "in the dark," "somewhere exciting," "after a show of romance," "with all our clothes off," etc.; (c) without intercourse, it's not "real" sex; (d) without both of us having an orgasm, it's not "real" sex.

Relapse among men treated for erectile dysfunction or inhibited sexuality is commonly reported. Success is much better where specific coping strategies for relapse have been taught and monitored. Such skills include role playing a discussion with a partner subsequent to an erectile dysfunction occurrence; articulating and then replaying specific behaviors learned in therapy; using specific cognitive "mantras" such as "I was told this would happen, but I know it will pass," "I'm loved and accepted whether these episodes occur or not," etc. (recovering heart attack victims may need to add mantras such as "It's absurd to think I'd die because of intercourse, I'll feel better"); reading positive information books or pamphlets; generating a sensual, romantic, and/or erotic mind-set (Schnarch, 1992); and undergoing "booster" sessions.

Another major problem in males, premature ejaculation, is usually treated by the "squeeze technique." The couple is admonished to engage in sensate focusing without attempting intercourse. As ejaculation appears imminent, the partner squeezes hard just below the rim of the head of the penis, interrupting the cycle of pre-ejaculatory muscle spasms, and then the couple continues in the sensate focusing until control is gained (Masters et al., 1991). In many cases of premature ejaculation, a very high sexual-drive level is operating, so counseling about increased frequency of masturbation can help alleviate it.

## Female Psychosexual Dysfunction

Some of the same issues, as well as most of the diagnostic considerations, noted about male psychosexual dysfunction apply equally well to the problems of female psychosexual dysfunction. The categories entitled Hypoactive Sexual Desire (302.71) and Sexual Aversion Disorder (302.79) mean exactly the same for women as they do for men; obviously there is no category similar to premature ejaculation. Other female categories include Dyspareunia (302.76) or Vaginismus (306.51). Dyspareunia refers to significant pain during intercourse. It is most common in females, but can be diagnosed in males as well. Vaginismus refers to the correlated muscular spasms that prevents intercourse, or at least makes it extremely painful. There is no significant personality pathology correlated with these patterns, although scales reflecting depression and immediate anxiety are likely to be raised, just as they are in premature ejaculation and in erectile dysfunction.

The category of Inhibited Female Orgasm (302.73) is also similar to that for males. Female Sexual Arousal Disorder (302.72) specifically refers to the woman's inability to attain or maintain the swelling and lubrication responses of sexual excitement for a long period of time to allow the completion of sexual intercourse—even though the person engages in sexual activity of sufficient preparation and duration—accompanied by a persistent lack of a subjective sense of sexual excitement.

□ DIAGNOSTIC CONSIDERATIONS

It is generally agreed that female sexual dysfunctions are less likely to reflect allied pathology, either generic or situational, than male sexual problems (Masters et al., 1991). In part, this is because the female can perform adequately in spite of inhibited responses in different phases or activities of sexual arousal.

The 2-3/3-2 MMPI-2 code is often found in these cases, but the elevations are not usually above 70 T. This reflects an overcontrolled individual, one who is denying responsibility for problems and yet is experiencing depression from them. An anxious and introverted woman with psychosexual dysfunction is more likely to have a 1-2/2-1 profile, again without the scales being markedly elevated.

To the degree that anxiety and guilt are a result of the psychosexual problems, high I and $Q_4$ scores are likely on the 16 PF. The other scales do not vary in any consistent manner. In that small subgroup of females with psychosexual dysfunction who have been traditionally labeled as hostile and castrating, high scores on E, L, $Q_1$ and, to a moderate degree, on H and $Q_3$ are found.

Scale 4 on the MCMI-II is likely to be high. The superficial flirtatiousness and seductiveness of the histrionic may be a predisposing factor toward psychosexual dysfunction. As psychosexual problems serve a psychological function, scale N will be elevated. As with male psychosexual dysfunction, elevations on A and D may indicate anxiety, depression, and guilt concerning dysfunction.

Elevations on the MCMI-II scales A, H, D, 8A, and C correlate most highly with coexisting conditions. Elevations of A, H, or D indicate conditions especially likely to foster or coexist with sexual dysfunction. Those with personality patterns represented by scales 1, D, and CC may be more likely to experience inhibited sexual desire.

□ TREATMENT OPTIONS

Just as with the male, the sensate focusing techniques pioneered by Masters and Johnson (1970) is particularly effective and can be similarly aided by systematic densensitization of specific fears and phobias. Masturbatory training is emphasized more in the treatment of female dysfunction than in male dysfunction (Masters et al., 1991). The woman is advised to masturbate regularly (and the use of a vibrator is often helpful here) with fantasies of intercourse, with the male gradually taking his place in the masturbatory experience and then literally in the vagina while masturbation still takes place to facilitate orgasm.

Some nonorgasmic women, or those who are weakly orgasmic, have improved their ability to experience orgasm through exercise of the pubococcygeal muscle. To perform these exercises, referred to as the "Kegal exercises," the woman contracts the pubococcygeal muscle as though she were trying to keep from urinating. This is performed in sets of ten, several times a day. Various companies market electronic devices that act to stimulate the muscles of this area through electrotherapy. These devices are purported to tone and condition, involuntarily and quickly, the pelvic muscles and thus to facilitate orgasm, although it is clear they are not effective with all women (Chambless et al., 1984).

The other major female psychosexual dysfunctions, vaginismus and dyspareunia, are usually the result of involuntary spasms of the vaginal musculature. Vaginismus has been most effectively treated by the insertion of graduated catheters into the vagina. The first one used may be as thin as a pen, and only when it can be tolerated comfortably for a period of time is one of somewhat larger dimension inserted. Eventually, a catheter the size of an erect penis is used. The technique is most efficient when the partner participates in the insertion of the catheters. It is also advised (Masters and Johnson, 1970) that the partner witness a pelvic examination, since this helps to dispel any irrational fears that may have developed. Possibly more important, it reassures the partner that the physical responses are not specific to his overtures for intercourse. Cox and Meyer (1978), as well as others, have found that various forms of relaxation training and general sexual counseling have also been helpful with dyspareunia. (Although psychological factors can be causal, the primary causes are usually painful childbirthing, abrasion by pubic hair, and inadequate lubrication for intercourse.)

# The Personality Disorders

Personality disorders are probably the most common pattern of disorder, yet they seldom have been given the attention they deserve. In addition to the many clients who receive only a personality disorder diagnosis, the great majority of clients with an axis I diagnosis, no matter what it is, also gets an axis II diagnosis. And if we count the subclinical patterns (see Table 9.1), which often are a critical focus in the therapeutic enterprise, a great majority of the population could be included.

The personality disorders are chronic, pervasive, and inflexible patterns of perceiving and responding to the environment that are sufficiently maladaptive to cause disruption in functioning and environmentally generated subjective distress. In DSM-III-R, the personality disorders are listed on axis II. Even if a prominent personality pattern does not warrant a formal diagnosis of personality disorder, it can still be listed on axis II, but without the relevant code number that formally designates it as a disorder.

Most individuals in need of a personality disorder diagnosis do not originally think there is any compelling reason for changing themselves (Turkat, 1990; Beck et al., 1990). Any such realization only comes when they move into situations that require higher levels of intimacy or more flexible behavioral adaptations. The fact that they cannot meet these requirements results in coercion from the environment, or at least feedback that they cannot ignore, resulting in referral for therapy.

The clinician needs to decide whether the personality disorder pattern is an outgrowth of another disorder, such as a major depressive disorder. For that reason, the clinician needs to assess carefully the issues of chronicity and pervasiveness of behavior. The DSM-III-R does

# TABLE 9.1     Personality Types and Correlated Traits and Disorders

### PERSONALITY TYPES

| CORRELATES | CONTROLLING | AGGRESSIVE | CONFIDENT | SOCIABLE | COOPERATIVE | SENSITIVE | RESPECTFUL | INHIBITED | INTROVERTED | EMOTIONAL |
|---|---|---|---|---|---|---|---|---|---|---|
| **Typical Behaviors** | Manipulative | Bold Initiating | Poised | Animated Engaging | Docile | Erratic | Organized | Watchful | Passive | Energetic |
| **Interpersonal Patterns** | Authoritarian | Intimidating | Unempathic | Demonstrative | Compliant | Unpredictable | Polite | Shy | Withdrawn | Flamboyant |
| **Thinking Styles** | Calculating | Dogmatic | Imaginative | Superficial | Open | Divergent | Respectful | Preoccupied | Vague | Distracted |
| **Mood-Affect Expression** | Disappointment | Anger | Calm | Dramatic | Tender | Pessimistic | Restrained | Uneasy | Bland | Intense |
| **View of Self** | Unappreciated | Assertive | Self-assured | Charming | Weak | Misunderstood | Reliable | Lonely | Placid | Interesting |
| **Probable Personality Disorders** | Paranoid Antisocial Sadistic | Passive-aggressive Antisocial Sadistic | Narcissistic Paranoid Antisocial | Histrionic Borderline Narcissistic | Dependent Compulsive Avoidant | Passive-aggressive Borderline Avoidant | Compulsive Paranoid Passive-aggressive | Avoidant Schizotypal Self-defeating | Schizoid Schizotypal Compulsive | Borderline Schizotypal Histrionic |

Adapted in part from Millon, T. (1981) *Disorders of Personality, DSM-III: Axis II:* New York. John Wiley.

not list a specific time or duration necessary to warrant a personality disorder diagnosis, except when a personality disorder is diagnosed in children. In that instance, duration of at least one year is required, and even then, the DSM-III-R still forbids the application of the term "antisocial personality disorder" before the age of eighteen.

The DSM-III-R personality disorders have traditionally been grouped into three clusters in the DSMs. The first includes the paranoid, schizoid, and schizotypal personality disorders, as these are denoted by peculiar or eccentric behavior. The second cluster focuses on dramatic and emotionally labile behavior: It includes the histrionic, narcissistic, antisocial, and borderline personality disorders. The last cluster, which emphasizes chronic fearfulness and/or avoidance behaviors, includes the avoidant, dependent, obsessive-compulsive, and passive-aggressive personality disorders. There is of course a catch-all category termed Personality Disorder NOS (301.90), used for individuals who do not fit any of the criteria for a specific category, yet clearly fall within the overall patterns of the personality disorders.

## ■ Treatment Options

By definition, individuals with the personality disorders are not likely to seek therapy out of a perception of intrapsychic deficit or conflict. Their presence in therapy has usually been stimulated by some social or legal coercion (Beck et al., 1990). For the clinician in private practice, this is most likely in the form of distress generated among the client's intimate others. When forced by dire circumstances, for example, possible loss of a needed relationship or their freedom in society, they may pledge to change. But, they will usually say something like "I will try really hard to . . ." rather than "I will do it." At such times, keep in mind the adage "trying is lying."

Some form of marital therapy or family therapy is often required. A variety of family therapy options are available. A frequent approach, in which the nuclear-family members are seen together or in various combinations by two or more therapists during the sessions, is termed "conjoint family therapy." It is the type most likely to be effective with the personality disorders, as it provides the multiple perspective, duration, and intensified focus that are important here. Kin network therapy brings close friends, neighbors, and more-distant family members into therapy. It is particularly useful in the schizophrenic disorders or allied disorders where the person has deteriorated socially, but it can also be useful in the schizoid, avoidant, and dependent personality disorders.

### □ TRANSFERENCE AND THE PERSONALITY DISORDERS

Modern psychodynamic theorists point out that treating the personality disorders, particularly those with antisocial, narcissistic, or borderline components, requires a rethinking of the transference issues (Stevenson and Meares, 1992). They note that such individuals often elicit an "objective counter-transference." This is usually a response of anger and frustration, even hate, but in some cases can be a type of protective affection.

The important point is to recognize that these emotional reactions of the therapist are reasonable and based on good data; this is in contrast to the traditional conception of the therapist's reactions to neurotics. In the latter instance, such feelings would be seen as indicative of emotional blocks in the therapist, which would signal a need for more analysis for the therapist and/or a transfer of the patient to another therapist.

However, in the "objective counter-transference" to the personality disordered client, the therapist needs (a) to recognize and "metabolize" such feelings, i.e., not act out toward the client in response to such feelings, (b) gradually let the client know that such reactions are occurring, (c) relate them to the eliciting behaviors, and (d) thus let the client know they can and are being controlled. Therefore, rather than allowing the client to project "onto" the therapist, as with a neurotic type, this type of client is allowed to project "into" the therapist. Most such clients seem to use this as a means of communication, as well as control, almost as if it is the only way another can ever know the level of pain they went through.

## ■ Paranoid Personality Disorder (301.00)

The paranoid personality disorder can be thought of as anchoring the other end of the continuum of paranoid disorders from the most disturbed and fragmented pattern, paranoid schizophrenia (Oltmanns and Maher, 1988). However, since there is neither thought disorder nor even a well-formed minor delusional system in the paranoid personality disorder, it is not listed under the paranoid disorders and is not a psychotic condition. Like the other personality disorders, it is a chronic, pervasive, and inflexible pattern of behavior that typically has been in evolution since childhood and is already recognizable in adolescence. Modeling of parental or other significant others is possibly even more important in this disorder than the psychotic paranoid conditions.

Paranoid personalities manifest hyperalertness toward the environment and have a chronic mistrust of most people. They see themselves as morally correct, yet vulnerable and envied, and see others as morally inferior and/or malicious. As a result, their information base is continuously distorted and their affect is constricted. Consequently, they find it difficult to adapt adequately to new situations or relationships, which is paradoxical because of their hyperalertness to their environment. As Turkat (1990) has pointed out, they will frequently be correct in assuming that other people are against them. Yet the paranoia is usually a disabling overreaction to a low initial level of scrutiny by others.

Unless these individuals have almost absolute trust in another person, they cannot develop intimacy and are continually seeking various ways to be self-sufficient. They avoid the emotional complexities of working out a meaningful relationship and tend to be litigious. For example, they may write negative letters to public figures or bring lawsuits on minimal grounds. It is rare for them to come into therapy without significant coercion from others. The disorder is more common in men.

☐          DSM-III-R

The DSM-III-R's desire for an operational definition for paranoid personality disorders results in clumsy criteria. The DSM-III-R requires evidence of chronic, pervasive, and unreasonable mistrust of others, beginning by early adulthood as indicated by at least four of the following behaviors: (1) expects harm or exploitation, (2) reads hidden threatening or demeaning messages where unwarranted, (3) is unforgiving and bears grudges, (4) fears confiding in others, thinking the information will be used against him or her, (5) is easily slighted or angered, (6) questions sexual fidelity of partner without warrant, or (7) questions loyalty of others without warrant. Finally, the occurrence must not be exclusively during the course of schizophrenia or a delusional disorder.

☐          MMPI-2

As with the paranoid disorders, it might be expected that the paranoid personality will be high on scale 6. However, this is not always the case, as such individuals are hyperalert about being perceived as paranoid and may guard against this (Turkat, 1990). Hence, there is a wide range of scores for the paranoid personality disorders on scale 6, although on the average it is well above the mean. Blacks score higher on scale 6 throughout the range of both normal and paranoid patterns.

The paranoid personality will occasionally use some kind of random or devious answering scheme with the MMPI-2, so the reader is referred to the section on malingering in Chapter 16. They are easily irritated at the forced-choice format, especially since they are only allowed a binary decision. They also become irritated at the significant self-disclosure required in many of the MMPI-2 items.

The scales that tend to be highest in the paranoid personality disorders are 3, 6, 1, and K. This reflects the use of denial and projection, the inclination to focus on physiological concerns when in treatment, and the need to present a facade of adequacy. Since the clinician is not likely to see paranoid personality disorders unless persons have somehow been coerced into treatment (as in marital therapy), there may also be a mild elevation on scale 8, reflecting immediate distress and the dawning awareness that the personality system is maladaptive. A moderately elevated scale 4 is also expected, but it is typically not as high as in many other disorders.

☐ ## 16 PF

Just as on the MMPI-2 scale 6, a person with the paranoid personality disorder does not always score as high as might be expected on the L scale. This is another disorder where it is particularly worthwhile to score for faking-bad on the 16 PF (Winder et al., 1975; Krug, 1981) to assess the extremity of the response patterns.

The suspiciousness, guardedness, and lack of a disintegrating delusional system suggest that $Q_3$ will be high and scales $Q_1$ and N will be low. $Q_4$ can be expected to be low, although if persons are seen for testing in a mental health situation, that score is raised.

The moralistic nature of the paranoid personality attitude system (Turkat, 1990) predicts a higher G score. The need for dominance combined with a fear of vulnerability suggests high E, low I, high N, and high H scores. Scale A is likely to be lower than might be expected from overt behavior, reflecting an inner reluctance to be self-disclosing and to exchange intimacy. These people are usually higher on scale B than are most other psychopathology groups.

☐ ## OTHER TEST-RESPONSE PATTERNS

The most typical features of the MCMI-II profile are an elevation on scale 6B and P (Choca et al., 1992). Because paranoid personalities often sense themselves incapable of judging safe from unsafe, experiences of apprehension may be present and reflected in an elevated A scale. Paranoid personality styles are more likely to occur with the antisocial personality (elevations on 6A and P), the narcissistic personality (elevations on 5 and P), and the passive-aggressive personality (elevations on 8A and P).

The paranoid personality responds to the WAIS-R with the same argumentativeness and even condescension that are consistently seen in the other tests (Allison et al., 1988). Their meticulous approach results in many details, which aids their score in such tests as comprehension and similarities. At the same time, their rigidity, suspiciousness, and peculiar information systems can detract slightly from the comprehension score, so the highest score in the profile is on similarities. These factors can result in good scores on both arithmetic and picture completion, as well as some peculiar picture arrangement sequences. If they become too meticulous and detailed, they do poorly on digit symbol.

On the Rorschach, they are prone to resent the ambiguous stimuli and hence respond with condescending criticism, occasional rejection, flipping of the cards, and a focus on detail responses. F% and F+% are high, and there are relatively few M responses (particularly in light of their intellectual level) and few Color responses. The more grandiose they are, the more likely they are to have W responses. Animal and Popular responses are common, and the record is generally constricted. Suspiciousness on certain TAT cards, e.g., 9 GF, 11, and 16 (Bellak, 1993), is likely.

## □ TREATMENT OPTIONS

The reader is referred to the earlier section on the paranoid disorders (Chapter 3), since most of the comments there relate to this disorder as well. As with other disorders in which there is a paranoid issue, it is essential to gain the trust of the client through empathy, but not through participation in the disorder patterns. It is especially necessary to empathize with and articulate the consequences of the client's behavior, such as the sense of being isolated and not understood or the interpersonal rejection that appears unfair to the client. If there is any positive change because of these approaches, catharsis techniques may be helpful to get at the conflicts that are causing the avoidance patterns. Then the therapist can begin to build in more appropriate socialization patterns.

Overall, the following guidelines are usually helpful with paranoid personalities:

1. Openly accept the client's mistrust as a "reasonable first strategy" (sometimes), and be careful not to violate that trust.

2. Focus on the least sensitive issues at first, acknowledging that self-disclosure and/or self-critique is painful and a bit risky.

3. Understand that a basic horror of feeling inadequate underlies the paranoid system. This is often combined with the fact that emotions (especially positive, complex emotions such as love) are difficult, or sometimes virtually incomprehensible to such individuals. Emphasize real personality strengths and work to bolster accessible but less competent patterns, e.g., appropriate assertiveness, stress management, etc. Model and reward any glimmers of humor, especially any self-deprecating humor.

4. Be willing to collaborate on issues, such as time of sessions or number of sessions per month. While this behavior would feed the pathology of the histrionic, it bolsters the sense of adequacy of the paranoid. Avoid techniques, such as hypnosis that emphasize a client's vulnerability.

5. Help the paranoid develop "tests" of his hypotheses that others are generally malevolent, e.g., in small tasks and commitments. Follow up with any exercises that build empathy toward others' feelings.

6. Realize paranoids often have spouses and significant others that have a covert investment in their partner's paranoia, i.e., consider referral or ancillary family sessions.

7. Challenge the underlying beliefs that (a) I am unique and others are jealous, (b) Others will exploit my mistakes, (c) It always pays to be wary, accusatory, and adversarial (some paranoids do make good trial lawyers), (d) People who are trusting or content are fools, i.e., I can't be that way, or (e) Negative events are generated purposefully by others.

## ■ Schizoid Personality Disorder (301.20)

The essential feature of this disorder is impairment in the ability to form adequate social relationships. As a result, schizoid personalities are shy and socially withdrawn or, as Joan Didion states in *The White Album* (p. 121), "only marginally engaged in the dailiness of life." They have difficulty expressing hostility and have withdrawn from most social contacts. But, unlike that of agoraphobia, the behavior is ego-syntonic.

If, in addition to inadequate interpersonal skills, the person shows peculiarities and difficulties in communication, the appropriate diagnosis is the next disorder to be considered: the schizotypal personality disorder. Schizotypals are more likely to have a family history of schizophrenia. Thus, that category predicts more consistently the eventual emergence of a schizophrenic disorder than does the schizoid personality disorder (Widiger et al., 1986).

The temperament of schizoids is such that they gravitate into jobs that require solitude, such as work as a night watchman. As they age or become vocationally dysfunctional, they are likely to move into a "skid row," particularly if they are males. Even though they excessively fantasize and also communicate in peculiar ways, they show no loss of contact with reality.

☐     DSM-III-R

According to the DSM-III-R, although schizoids have few if any friends, they show no communication disturbance. The disorder—which is marked by social-relationship deficiencies, introverted behavior, and constricted affect—causes vocational or social disruption. It is noted specifically in a pervasive pattern of indifference to emotions and social relationships as indicated by at least four of the following: (1) typically chooses solitary activities, (2) does not appear to or claim to have strong emotions, (3) neither enjoys nor desires close friendships, (4) shows little interest in sexual experience with another, (5) is indifferent to criticism or praise, (6) has no close friends or confidants (other than first-degree relatives, or (7) shows constricted affect. Before the age of eighteen, the appropriate diagnosis would be Schizoid Disorder of Childhood or Adolescence, which would be coded on axis I. If the person is under the age of eighteen and only avoids relationships with strangers, not with family or close friends, the diagnosis of Avoid Disorder of Childhood or Adolescence (313.21) would be appropriate.

□ MMPI-2

When the schizoid is reasonably well integrated and is not disturbed by pressures from the environment to change, a predominantly normal MMPI-2 profile is attained. As Lachar (1974) points out, a high score on the O scale is obtained, but the other scores are not usually consistently elevated. If schizoids become more disturbed by the environment and begin to question the appropriateness of their functioning, a raised scale 2 occurs. As upset increases, a rise on scales F and 8 is likely, with a lesser rise on scale 9.

The 1-8 profile has been labeled as that of a nomadic individual in whom there is little clear evidence of emotional lability. Attempts at interpersonal interaction are sporadic, and significant problems occur in dealing with persons of the opposite sex.

□ 16 PF

The social isolation of schizoids is evident in low scores on scales A, E, F, and H. They are high on $Q_2$ and, to a lesser degree, on $Q_3$. To the degree that they fit the characteristics of the classic schizoid personality, they are lower on M, O, and I and higher on C, whereas these scores move in the opposite direction as the criteria fit the schizotypal personality disorder more closely.

□ OTHER TEST-RESPONSE PATTERNS

The most salient indicator in the MCMI-II profile is elevation on scale 1. Low scores on scales 4, 5, and N are likely. To the degree this pattern is closer to the schizotypal, elevations should be higher on 2, 7, and 8A (Edell, 1987). Depersonalization can occur, which may cause elevation on S. When decompensation occurs or during periods of great stress, elevation on SS may occur, although SS is more typically in the low range of scores.

The schizoid personality, as is true of most of the character disorders, shows somewhat higher WAIS-R performance scale scores than verbal scale scores. The interpersonal problems of both the schizoid and the schizotypal affect the verbal scales more directly. Within the verbal subtests, higher arithmetic and digit-span scores are characteristic of this and other groups that tend toward an interpersonal-detachment syndrome (Keiser and Lowy, 1980). Within the performance subtests, lower picture arrangement and picture completion scores occur. Golden (1979) states that such individuals demonstrate a constricted use of space on the Bender-Gestalt test.

Both the schizoid and the schizotypal, particularly the former, provide a constricted response record on the Rorschach, as well as some rejections. A high percentage of animal content responses and few color-based responses are expected. Few H responses or poor quality H responses can be expected. Occasionally, there is a vague response that cannot be pinned down, or even an occasional oddly supported FC response. Exner (1978, 1986) asserts that similar individuals are likely to have a higher Experience Potential than Experience Actual and that their M production is usually high relative to the overall quality of the protocol. They are also likely to show slow reaction times tc many of the cards. A constricted response along with a blandness of theme and character portrayal is a common performance on the TAT.

□               TREATMENT OPTIONS

Like the person with an avoidant personality disorder (discussed later in this chapter), the schizoid has inadequate interpersonal relations. But unlike one with an avoidant personality disorder, the schizoid does not care, so therapy is quite difficult. In fact, these clients are not likely even to enter into therapy because such a relationship is the magnification of what is usually avoided. If for some reason they do become involved in therapy, the therapist must help them develop trust in that relationship and yet not overwhelm them with initial confrontations.

Thus, the therapy process is analogous to gaining the trust of the paranoid personality. If that trust *is* obtained, the source of avoidance can possibly be located and dealt with via systematic desensitization, client-centered therapy, or some other means to dissipate withdrawal patterns.

Covert extension may even be useful here. Schizoids would be asked to imagine their distancing patterns vividly and then immediately complete the image by envisioning that the usually occurring reinforcing events do not occur. Since in many ways the schizoid is trying to develop a completely new response pattern, covert modeling may also be used. In this, the client repetitively imagines the desired behavior, probably an interpersonal pattern, and reinforces it by imagined positive outcomes.

Overall, the following strategies may be helpful with a schizoid personality:

1. Understand that schizoids show a significant reluctance to use their therapists as a coping resource, as they have never learned to use other people for social support, so it is unwise to stress the schizoid in this dimension, especially if early in therapy.

2. Understand that your relationship with the client may be their most in-depth social connection. But, they still won't value you very much, on a relative basis to other clients, and will tax your empathy and warmth.

3. If a comfort level is reached, consider "bridging" (i.e., continue your individual sessions) the client into a therapy group that you are sure will be supportive and not too demanding initially.

4. Help the client toward "collecting" pleasurable memories and events that involve others.

5. Role play social skills and verbalize "emotional responses" one might expect to emerge over time in someone having such adventures. Remember that a social relationship of any duration is as much an adventure for a schizoid as is Mt. Everest for a novice climber.

6. Conversely, help the client tie negative emotions, e.g., depression, to the schizoid pattern. It's amazing how well schizoids can dissociate the two.

7. Contract for periodic (actually, reasonably often for schizoids) "booster" sessions to help them avoid a relapse.

8. Challenge underlying assumptions such as (a) Any disruption of my emotional routine (however minimal the emotions are) is scary and messy—in that sense they are analogous to the obsessive-compulsive's fear of disruption of external routines, (b) People don't really mean anything to me, (c) I can survive alone (maybe not optimally, but at least predictably) and need space to do that, or (d) It's necessary to be free and independent—other people are like Brer Rabbit's "Tar Baby," if you relate to them, you get stuck to them.

■        ## Schizotypal Pesonality Disorder (301.22)

The reader is referred to the previous category, the schizoid personality disorder, since many of the features of that disorder are found here. The essential difference is that in addition to the disturbances in social functioning, the schizotypal personality manifests peculiarities in the communication process. Schizotypal individuals are much more likely than the schizoid to show dysphoria and anxiety, and because of their odd thinking patterns, they are more likely to have developed eccentric belief systems and become involved in fringe religious groups. The schizotypal personality is also more likely to be emotionally labile, overtly suspicious, and hostile of others than is the schizoid (Widiger et al., 1986). Many schizotypal individuals also meet the criteria for the borderline personality disorder, to be discussed in a subsequent section. In that case, both diagnoses should be given.

☐      DSM-III-R

A diagnosis of schizotypal personality disorder can be supported by establishing at least four of the following: (1) evidence of magical thinking or odd beliefs, (2) ideas of reference, (3) high social anxiety, (4) presence of occasional illusions (rather than delusions) or odd perceptual experiences, (5) peculiar communications (metaphorical, vague, digressive), (6) inappropriate or constricted affect, (7) suspiciousness, (8) no close friends or confidants (other than first-degree relatives), or (9) odd or eccentric behavior or appearance.

It is not rare to find some evidence of schizophrenia in family members. If blatant schizophrenic symptoms begin to occur, the schizophrenic diagnosis takes precedence and the schizotypal label is not used.

☐      MMPI-2

Edell (1987) finds the 2-7-8 code to be especially likely to be manifest in the schizotypal personality disorder. As with the schizoid, scale O is typically raised. Because of the more pervasive disorder reflected in communiction problems and labile emotionality, scales F and 4 also are relatively high, in addition to 2, 7, and 8. If depression is not a major factor, 2 and 7 will be lower. If the person is more inclined to be nomadic and to have flat affect and somatization in addition to the communication problems, a pattern with a moderately elevated F and higher scores (in order) on 8, 1, 2, and 3 can be expected.

☐      16 PF

To the degree the schizotypal shows aspects similar to the schizoid, the profile will resemble that discussed in the prior subsection. However, as is more likely, emotional lability, confusion, and suspiciousness are present, so scores on B, C, and $Q_3$ would be lower, and scores on $Q_4$, E, A, and L will be somewhat higher. Also, the score on O is typically higher than in the classic schizoid personality disorder.

☐      OTHER TEST-RESPONSE PATTERNS

As is evident, there are some similarities to the test patterns of schizoids. However, in many respects the schizotypals are closer to the schizophrenic and the borderline personality disorder, particularly in their performance on such tests as the WAIS-R and Rorschach (Swiercinsky, 1985). The patterns noted previously for the acute or less disturbed schizophrenic are applicable here.

☐      TREATMENT OPTIONS

Since, phenomenologically, this is a somewhat polyglot diagnosis, and individual schizotypals will show differing primary and secondary patterns, the comments noted in the subsections on the schizoid, paranoid, and borderline personality disorders apply to a degree to the schizotypal personality disorder. The section on schizophrenic disorders is also useful because the schizotypal individual is seen as predictive of later schizophrenic functioning. Hence, the therapist's attention must be directed not only toward the interpersonal withdrawal processes but also to the emergent disturbances in affect and thinking that are common. Family therapy may be useful in preventing the emergence of a full-blown schizophrenic disorder. These individuals have great difficulty in group therapy because they are quickly perceived as "weird" and may be "scapegoated" or even directly attacked by the group.

## ■ Histrionic Personality Disorder (301.50)

The histrionic personality disorder is commonly encountered in clinical practice (Kernberg, 1984). The disorder is marked by dramatic and intense behavior, problematic interpersonal relationships that others perceive as superficial and shallow, and problematic sexual adjustment. These persons seek attention and are overreactive, with responses being expressed more dramatically and intensely than is appropriate—hence, the term "histrionic." This category has traditionally been labeled the "hysterical personality." However, as noted earlier, "hysteric" wrongly suggests a disorder that parallels the causes and symptoms of what has been previously labeled "hysterical neurosis."

Histrionic personalities may elicit new relationships with relative ease, as they appear to be empathic and socially able. However, they turn out to be temperamentally and emotionally insensitive and have little depth of insight into their own responsibilities in a relationship. They quickly avoid blame for any difficulties in interpersonal relationships and, in that sense, show a degree of the projection that is characteristic of paranoid disorders. Even though they may be flirtatious and seductive sexually, there is little mature response or true sensuality. If one accepts the apparent sexual overture in the behavior, the histrionic individual may act as if insulted or even attacked.

There has been a continuing controversy as to whether this disorder occurs with any frequency in males. This is not surprising, since the meaning of the Greek root term *"hysteria"* is "uterus." Ancient explanations for this disorder blamed an unfruitful womb, which became distraught and wandered about the body. Hippocrates thought marriage would cure hysteria by anchoring the womb. Even Freud suggested marriage as a cure. Since conflict over expressing sexual needs may be a factor, such "medicine" might even work at times. But just as often, this "medicine" brings on iatrogenic problems that are worse than the "disease."

It is clear that this disorder is found in males (Turkat, 1990), but because the symptoms are a caricature of the traditional role expectations for women, it is more common in women (Millon, 1981). The DSM-III-R suggests that it is uncommon in males and that when it does occur, it is likely to be associated with homosexuality, an assertion that is best regarded as a theoretical speculation. There is evidence that the same developmental patterns in females that eventuate in histrionic behavior lead to more antisocial behavior patterns in males, and this would fit with the role expectation theory.

☐ DSM-III-R

In general, histrionic personalities show attention-seeking and overly emotional and dramatic behaviors and are seen by others as shallow and insincere. DSM-III-R requires dramatic and intensely manifested behavior, beginning by early adulthood, as evidenced by at least four of the following: (1) constantly seeks or demands reassurance, (2) is inappropriately sexually seductive, (3) is overly concerned with physical attractiveness, (4) expresses emotion with inappropriate exaggeration, (5) is uncomfortable at not being the center of attention, (6) has rapidly shifting and shallow emotions, (7) is self-centered and has no tolerance for frustration, or (8) has a style of speech that is excessively impressionistic and lacking in detail.

☐ MMPI-2

The 2-3/3-2 profile is the one most commonly encountered in the histrionic personality disorder. When the histrionic personality is seen in the clinical situation, there are usually distress and upset, possibly accompanied by manipulative suicide gestures. Thus, an elevation on scale 2 of greater than 70 T can be expected. When distress is not so marked, the expected elevation on scale 3 takes precedence. The elevation on scale 3 often signals the histrionic's monstrous lack of insight. The rare 3-9/9-3 profile is also indicative of histrionic functioning (Kelley and King, 1979c), as is the more common 3-4/4-3 and 4-9/9-4 patterns (Graham, 1990).

Scales 4, 7, and 8 are also likely to be moderately elevated. Scale 4 reflects the histrionic's tendency toward egocentricity, overdramatization, and shallow interpersonal relationships. The underlying self-doubt and anxiety raise the 7 score, and the tendency toward impulsive emotionality and self-dramatization elevates scale 8.

Scales L, F, and K usually fall within normal limits. If the individual has begun a defense by focusing on somatic complaints, scale 1 may be elevated. Scale 5 is likely to be elevated in males, reflecting the association of hysteria with traditional feminine role behaviors; it is usually quite low in females. Scale O is not usually markedly elevated; *any* elevation, however, is surprising because these people make a first impression on the unsophisticated that they are highly sociable. If controls are breaking down and the histrionic feels that he or she is losing control, a higher score on scale 9 is expected, although it is usually within normal limits.

## OTHER TEST-RESPONSE PATTERNS

Elevation on scale 4 would be expected on the MCMI-II. Because histrionics are often seeking attention and validation from others, scales 1 and 2 should be relatively low. The somatization factor may be used as an attention-getting device, in which case one would expect an elevation on scale H. Other scales that may be periodically elevated because they serve as methods for dramatic attention-getting devices include N and S. Anxiety may be experienced when needs for dependence are not being met, resulting in elevated A, although typically the histrionic's style is quite ego-syntonic.

The WAIS-R verbal score is typically less than the performance score for histrionics. Within the verbal scales, the information subscale is usually low, as is the arithmetic subscale (particularly in females). Histrionic females are prone to make complaints about the arithmetic test or to make comments like "I've never been able to do math at all." Digit span is expected to be moderately high, and comprehension is often the highest subscale. The histrionic is occasionally inclined to moralize in response to some of the items, particularly in the comprehension subtest.

Within the performance subtests, those that tap speed and visual-motor coordination (such as digit symbol) are high, as is picture completion. Block design is sometimes surprisingly low compared to the other tests of similar skill requirements.

On the Rorschach, histrionics often provide what may be an initially surprisingly low number of responses and blocked responses and/or a low number of Color shading responses, considering their apparent intensity and involvement. But, this relates directly to their lack of introspection and insight. There is a low W%, and there is an emphasis on easy, obvious details. They may portray some of the cards as scary or ugly. They may see monstrous or frightening animals and give responses involving sexual innuendo. At the same time, they deny dysphoric content in the cards. There are a relatively low number of W and M responses, relative to intelligence. Occasionally, the histrionic will make "blood" responses to the color cards.

TAT stories often contain dependency and control themes, and they may even become personalized and generate some affective display.

Blocking occasionally occurs to "sexual" or "aggressive" pictures, and some cards may be called "ugly," "sickening," or the like. As with borderlines, "primitive splitting," presenting characters as all good or all bad, or in an incongruous juxtaposition, are occasionally seen (Bellak, 1993).

☐     ## TREATMENT OPTIONS

Histrionics, being prone to dramatic and exaggerated patterns, are most responsive, at least initially, to a dramatic therapy approach. Hypnosis, some of the consciousness-raising techniques, and even dramatic placebos can be useful here. Low-key or nonintense therapy approaches may be seen as invalid by such clients simply because of the lack of intensity.

Once there is an engagement in the therapy process, a shift has to be made to an approach that deals with the disturbed interpersonal relationships and avoidance of responsibility. Group therapy can eventually be helpful because it provides the consensual data so important to convince histrionics of their disorder. However, unless there has been some trust and dependency generated in the group and/or with the therapist, the group will quickly perceive the histrionic as shallow and deceptive. Denial and flight from therapy will be quick, and the critical necessary confrontation with the fear and anxiety that have been kept out of consciousness is avoided.

Over time, the following guidelines for therapy with a histrionic are usually helpful:

1.  Reward their product, not their presentation—the opposite of their behavioral history.
2.  Reward any attention to reflective thoughts or efforts toward systematization or routine behaviors—again a real change.
3.  Emphasize appropriate assertiveness and mastery behaviors as therapy goals.
4.  Avoid the role of rescuer, understanding that you will be guided toward that role and toward feeling frustrated and/or responsible for any of the client's failures.
5.  Avoid the demands that the client be treated as "special," e.g., an unwarranted break on fees or seeing them for longer periods or at hours you don't normally see clients.
6.  Consider an up-front financial fee-contract that gives greater rewards for staying in therapy to at least an agreed-on point, e.g., a high up-front fee that can be credited to later (or more productive) sessions.
7.  Use writing assignments to develop analytic and problem-solving thought patterns (usually sorely lacking) and attention to detail.

**8.** Challenge such common underlying beliefs as (a) Unless my emotions at least appear intense, they won't mean anything to others (and eventually, even to me), (b) Being responsible or attending to details means the loss of "zest for life," (c) Rejection is disastrous, (d) People won't love me for what I do but will for what I pretend to be or what I present to entertain/entice them, or (e) Being "special" means never having to say "I'm sorry" (or at least I don't have to feel it or mean it).

## ■ Narcissistic Personality Disorder (301.81)

This category, new in the DSM-III-R, centers on individuals who are to a degree products of our modern social-value systems. They are "flattery-operated"; more specifically, they manifest arrogant, haughty behaviors and/or attitudes, an unrealistic sense of self-importance, exhibitionistic attention-seeking, an inability to take criticism, interpersonal manipulation, a lack of empathy, and a sense of "entitlement" that allows them to break the rules (Raskin and Novachk, 1991) resulting in substantial problems in interpersonal relationships.

No doubt, such people have always existed, but it appears that this pattern has become more common in recent years. It is not a surprising development when there are advertisements about "The Arrogance of Excellence" and self-help seminars unequivocally urging people to live out the axion "I'm number one" (with little evidence that there is much room for a number two or three close behind).

The pattern is usually evident in adolescence, and the disorder is chronic. As with other personality disorders, narcissistic personalities only come to the attention of a clinician when coerced by circumstances (Kernberg, 1984). The prognosis for major change is moderate at best. Narcissistic personalities are similar to antisocial personalities, except that they are not so aggressive or hostile and their value systems are more asocial and hedonic than antisocial.

☐ DSM-III-R

According to DSM-III-R, the essential diagnostic features of the narcissistic personality disorder—which is a pervasive pattern of grandiosity, hypersensitivity, and lack of empathy, beginning in early adulthood—must include five of the following: (1) grandiose self-evaluation with related fantasies, (2) consistent need for attention, (3) emotional lability after criticism or defeat (which they share with borderlines and paranoids), (4) little ability to empathize, (5) an assumption that they will receive special treatment from others without any need for reciprocal behavior—entitlement, (6) exploitative interpersonal behaviors, (7) belief that his or her problems are unique, (8) preoccupation with feelings of envy. Arrogant grandiosity appears to be the most important differentiating symptom.

Such people naturally have a rather fragile personality integration and may on occasion manifest brief psychotic episodes. As a character in Peter de Vries's novel *Consenting Adults* (1980, p. 183) so aptly puts it, "I have this crush on myself—but the feeling is not returned." They also may show characteristics of the histrionic and/or antisocial personality disorder, and if so, an additional diagnosis can be used.

☐     ## MMPI-2

Lachar (1974) finds that individuals who can develop only superficial relationships score low on scale O. Since the narcissistic personality disorder is so interpersonally exploitative (Raskin and Novachk, 1991), an elevation on scale 4 is also expected. They often fit a stereotypical sexual role, so males are usually low on scale 5.

If their patterns are ineffective in coping with the environment, they show situation-generated depression, so a rise on scales 2 and 9 can be expected. If instead, they become suspicious and irritable, a rise on scale 6 occurs. If they begin to descend emotionally into a brief psychotic disorder, scale 8 should reflect this.

The 4-9 narcissist is not uncommon—they blame their problems on the world and want quick-fix solutions in therapy. They will be impatient for therapy results, and this can quickly generate interpersonal and counter-transference therapy issues.

☐     ## 16 PF

Their inflated sense of worth and extroverted assertiveness are expressed in high scores on A, E, and H, while the asocial value system is evident in a low score on G. They also score moderately high on $Q_1$, and they also tend to be high on $Q_3$. They are variable on scales C, O, and L, depending on the degree of personality integration and whether or not they are moving toward a brief psychotic episode, suspiciousness, or depression.

☐     ## OTHER TEST-RESPONSE PATTERNS

The most prominent indicator on the MCMI-II is elevation on scale 5. Scales 4, 6A, and 6B may also be elevated. Because these persons do not like to admit personal weaknesses or admit psychic distress, elevations on scales A, D, and S are rare, although when they do occur, they may be used as rationalizations for being unable to live up to their inflated self-image. During periods of stress, elevations on P and PP may occur (Choca et al., 1992).

Throughout the testing situation, narcissistic personalities are prone to avoid tasks that demand introspection and/or persistent problem solving, particularly if they can use wit or charm to distract the clinician. If the charm does not work effectively, they occasionally feign inadequacy to avoid a task. They are also likely to produce some pedantic, almost condescending responses. They occasionally will assert that they only guessed when they sense that they have missed an arithmetic solution, even when the evidence shows that they did not guess.

As a result of these tendencies, they do more poorly on WAIS-R tasks that demand persistence and detailed responses, such as object assembly, arithmetic, vocabulary, comprehension, and block design. The picture arrangement subtest occasionally elicits personalized comments that reflect the narcissism. Overall, they do a bit better on the performance scales than on the verbal scales.

On the Rorschach, such personalities are inclined to give "to me" responses. If they feel the clinician is positively attending to them, they provide more responses than do histrionic individuals, yet seldom in accurate detail, particularly in the M and W responses. As a result, these responses show poor quality. In a related fashion, the $F+\%$ is not high. If they are at all distressed, they produce constricted records that focus on Popular and Animal responses and may provide "pair" or reflection responses.

They have a higher number of C responses than individuals with the obsessive-compulsive disorder, and those that occur in the obsessive record are better integrated into the overall response pattern. The narcissistic personality seldom responds directly to shading, but often makes texture responses that are apparently suggested by form or outline. If the narcissism is channeled into direct body expression, responses such as "people exercising" may be noted. Responses that have an ornate or flashy quality are found. Responses focusing on fancy food or clothing, particularly exotic forms of clothing, or gem or perfume responses are also thought to be indicative of the narcissistic personality disorder (Shafer, 1954). Also, an emphasis on both CF and pure C responses is indicative of narcissism.

TAT stories are often void of meaningful content, and the narcissist may detract from the essence of the story by a "cute" ending or a related joke. Cards that demand a response to potentially anxiety-inducing fantasy, such as 13 MF, may result in either a superficially avoidant story or one with blatantly lewd or shocking content, again reflecting an avoidance of the essential features of the cards (Bellak, 1993).

□          TREATMENT OPTIONS

The narcissistic personality may be even more difficult than the antisocial personality to engage in therapy, in large part because the therapist seldom has as much coercive control. For example, one of the few times narcissistic personalities enter therapy is when they fear the loss of a dependency role, as in a marital situation. It also may occur when there is a marked discrepancy between expectations (usually fueled by fantasy) (Raskin and Novachk, 1991) and reality. Psychoanalytic therapy appears well suited to confront the pathology of narcissism, and transactional analysis within marital therapy (Berne, 1964) may be of help because it can give both spouse and client a way of more positively conceptualizing the narcissism, that is, the "child" in the personality. Groups can be initially "seduced" by the narcissist, but with time such clients are viewed as exploitative and self-centered, often resulting in anger and rejection from the group.

To the extent the pattern can be more easily accepted, feedback should be followed by some modeling of new behaviors (first, by channeling the psychopathology into "productive narcissism"), either in role playing with the therapist, in a multiple marital-group setting, or in imagination. Role playing and *quid pro quo* behavioral contracting are useful adjuncts in attempting to change these behaviors, although they require helping the narcissistic personalities to articulate needs, a difficult step.

Overall, the following guidelines may help:

**1.** Set clear therapy relationship limits, e.g., schedules of visits and payments, amount of fees, behavior with staff and people in waiting room, smoking rules, or any other indications of "elite" status. When the rules are broken, and they will be, use it as fodder for the therapy hour.

**2.** In this same vein, occasionally expect your counter-transference reaction to be very negative at times (track your thoughts in response to this response) and bring it into the therapy session. The critical point is communicating how these negative thoughts were generated, without kicking off such clients' easily elicited humiliation or rejection fantasies.

**3.** Expect to have these clients occasionally make you feel very good. When this happens, realize you have just succumbed to one of their most powerful manipulations and use that in the session. Conversely, a therapist may sometimes "go the extra mile" to get this type of approval. Ultimately, maintain a stable, objective response to attempts to either devalue or flatter your work.

**4.** Be cognizant that such clients are often involved in allied hidden patterns such as drug abuse (especially high-status drugs), abusive patterns (after all, the victims are lesser mortals), or financial and vocational irresponsibility. Allied psychopathic and/or histrionic patterns are common.

**5.** Eventually challenge such underlying beliefs as (a) I am special (unique, elite); (b) I like to challenge or compete with others, but because of both (a) and the fact it is psychologically necessary for me to prevail,

I may play by other rules (usually known only to me); (c) Any defects I have come from my bad parents and/or background; (d) Recognition, admiration, and respect are necessary, and others exist to provide it and, indeed, promote it; or (e) Sharing, serving others, or selfless behaviors are signs of weakness and signal disintegration of self.

# ■ Antisocial Personality Disorder (301.70)

The essential characteristic of the antisocial personality disorder is the chronic manifestation of antisocial behavior patterns in amoral and impulsive persons. They are usually unable to delay gratification or to deal effectively with authority, and they show narcissism in interpersonal relationships. The pattern (see Table 9.2) is apparent by the age of fifteen (usually earlier) and continues into adult life with consistency across a wide performance spectrum, including school, vocational, and interpersonal behaviors (Loeber, 1990; Hare, 1986; Hare et al., 1991). Hare et al. (1991) point out that this category has too many criteria and includes too many diverse personalities, and this will likely be changed in DSM-IV.

Although the DSM-III-R discusses only the overall category of antisocial personality, there is good evidence that it can be further subdivided into categories of primary psychopath and secondary psychopath (Lykken, 1957; Zuckerman et al., 1980; Quay, 1987). The primary psychopath is distinguished by the following characteristics: (1) they have a very low level of anxiety and little avoidance learning, (2) they are significantly refractory to standard social-control procedures, and (3) they are high in stimulation-seeking behaviors, particularly the "disinhibition" factor that refers to extroverted, hedonistic pleasure-seeking. It is advisable to delineate the consequent ramifications of the differences in a primary and secondary psychopath in a clinical report, since such discriminations are glossed over by the use of the overall term "antisocial personality disorder."

☐ DSM-III-R

The DSM-III-R term "antisocial personality disorder" has evolved through a variety of terms and now supersedes the terms "psychopathic" and "sociopathic," at least in formal diagnostic labeling. Pritchard's 1835 term "moral insanity" is considered by many to be the first clear forerunner to the present "antisocial personality disorder" label. "Psychopath" first emerged in the label "psychopathic inferiority," introduced by Koch late in the nineteenth century (Cleckley, 1964).

Terms incorporating "psychopath" were common until the DSM-I, published in 1952, used "sociopathic personality." The DSM-II, in 1968, introduced the term "antisocial personality," which is used in the DSM-III-R.

In spite of this evolution (or possibly because of it), there have been significant data indicating that this diagnostic grouping is a meaningful concept to clinicians (Hare, 1986). In an early study on the diagnostic reliability of the standard categories, Spitzer et al. (1967) found the highest level of agreement (r = .88) when clinicians assigned persons to the "antisocial personality" category, with the lowest index of agreement (r = .42) found with psychoneurotic reactions.

To apply the diagnosis of antisocial personality disorder, the DSM-III-R requires that the individual be eighteen years old. There should also be evidence that the behavior has been relatively persistent. Incidentally, if the individual is younger than eighteen, the appropriate diagnosis is conduct disorder (Quay, 1987).

Onset before the age of fifteen is supported by evidence of three or more types of acting-out behavior. At least four of the following must have occurred since the age of fifteen: (1) problematic occupational performance, (2) repetitive, easily elicited fighting, (3) repetitive avoidance of financial responsibility, (4) failure to plan ahead, as indicated by transient traveling without a goal or a lack of a fixed address for a month or more, (5) recklessness, (6) failure to accept social norms, (7) no regard for the truth, as indicated in repetitive deception of others, (8) indication of inability to function as a responsible parent, (9) inability to sustain a monogamous relationship for a year, or (10) lack of remorse.

A more recent conceptualization views psychopathy as composed of two main factors (1 = Affective-Cognitive Instability, 2 = Behavioral-Social Deviance) (Hare, Hart, and Forth, 1992; Hare et al., 1991). This view has helped generate, and, in turn has been facilitated by Hare's PCL-R (Psychopathy Checklist-Revised), a 20-item assessment technique that uses self-report and interview observation data, which is then cross-checked with collateral information. A score of 30 or higher (out of a potential 40) is considered as a good cut-off for indicating psychopathy. There is a newer 12-item "screening" version, which has less validation data, but which has an "r" of approximately .80 with the full PCL-R, and which is more applicable to non-forensic populations. A score of 18 or more (out of a possible 24) on the shorter version is considered as a good cut-off for indicating psychopathy.

The following components contribute to the Affective-Cognitive Instability factor (#1): glibness, a grandiose sense of self, pathological lying, conning-manipulative behaviors, lack of remorse, shallow affect, callousness and lack of empathy, and failure to accept responsibility. Components of the Behavioral-Social Deviance factor (#2) are a higher need for stimulation, a parasitic lifestyle, poor behavioral controls, early behavior problems, lack of realistic goals, impulsivity, irresponsibility, having been adjudicated delinquent, and a history of violating supervision or probation. Factors 1 and 2 show an average "r" of about .50.

In general, recent research on the psychopath (much of which includes use of the PCL) indicates:

**1.** While there is a dropoff in criminal activity for psychopaths at about age 40–45, this effect holds primarily for non-violent crimes. There is only a slight dropoff for violent crimes, so "Life does not begin at 40" for psychopaths.

**2.** Concomitantly, while the Behavioral Deviance factor starts to drop off at age 40–45, the Affective-Cognitive Instability factor only lessens slightly with age.

**3.** Similarly, while the Behavioral Deviance factor (#2) is a good predictor of general criminality and recidivism, is highly correlated with criminality, and is negatively correlated with SES and to a lesser degree, I.Q., factor 1 is a better predictor of violence, but is virtually uncorrelated with SES and I.Q.

**4.** Factor 1 is negatively correlated with neuroticism and trait anxiety, and is positively correlated with narcissism and dominance. Conversely, factor 2 is positively correlated with trait anxiety, psychoticism, and a higher Pa–Ma index from the MMPI.

**5.** While treatment may effect a positive change in the average criminal, it does not with psychopaths, especially to the degree they are strong on factor 1. Indeed, there is evidence that psychopaths who are high on factor 1 may get worse with treatment, i.e., group and individual psychotherapy can be a "finishing school" for psychopaths. True to their nature, they seem to learn little about themselves in therapy, but learn more about others, and then more boldly use such information. At least, in part, this is because they are language-disordered in the sense that the affective components of language are weak or missing, voiding the likelihood of empathy or remorse.

**6.** In general, while socio-economic and family background variables are good predictors of general criminal behavior, they are relatively non-predictive for psychopathy, especially where it is loaded on the Affective-Cognitive Instability factor. However, since psychopaths are good learners of violence, positive family and socioeconomic factors somewhat lessen the probability of violence in psychopaths.

□                    MMPI-2

The 4-9/9-4 profile has been considered the clasic profile of the antisocial personality. The "9" component can be conceptualized as the activator/ energizer into behavioral acting-out of the more basic cognitive components of the psychopathy. As Megargee and Bohn (1979) show, distinct bimodality indicates an amoral psychopath who fits most of the classic descriptors of the antisocial personality, yet is not particularly hostile.

When the profile contains a definite spike 4 profile with only a secondary moderate elevation on scale 2, it is more likely to be a primary psychopath who in addition is easily provoked to violence. The primary psychopath who is prone to violent behavior commonly scores high on scales 8, 6, and 4. Such individuals appear to be especially dangerous if they have a high scale 9 score in addition to high scores on scales 8, 6, and 4. Within a psychopathic population, the level of scale 6 is an indicator of whether hostility is overt or suppressed.

The bimodal 4-9/9-4 profile, noted earlier, is more indicative of secondary psychopathy, as is another common code, the 2-4/4-2 profile with moderate elevations on the other scales. In the 4-9/9-4 group, to the degree that 9 is greater than 4, one is likely to observe a higher level of tension and more somatic concerns. The rare spike 9 profile (when not under treatment because of a spouse's complaint of marital difficulties) is indicative of a primary psychopath who has also abused drugs heavily.

A high F scale is more characteristic of the secondary psychopath and/or the younger psychopath than the primary psychopath and/or the older psychopath. When one obtains a 4-8/8-4 profile and most other scales are low, a hostile, cold, and punitive psychopath who borders on schizophrenia should be considered (Lachar, 1974). If the 4-8/8-4 elevation is accompanied by elevations on the Bizarre Mentation and Family Problems content scales, consider psychosis; but if elevations are on the Cynicism and Anger content scales, consider a diagnosis of aggressive psychopathy. The expression of aggression in the psychopath appears to be inhibited to the degree that scales 2 and 3 (and 5 for males) are high. Aggression is much more likely, as noted earlier, when scales 6, 8, and 9 are high. When psychopathic individuals are seen in a hospital setting rather than as outpatients, they are more likely to score higher on scales F, 1, 2, 3, and 7, reflecting their greater situational distress.

## 16 PF

The modal 16 PF profile for primary psychopaths finds high scores on scales O, L, and M, with average high scores on $Q_4$ and A. They obtain low scores on $Q_3$ and G, with moderately low scores on C and B. They generally score high on E, although this fluctuates rather wildly, with some primary psychopaths scoring very low. Since low I predicts to roughness and insensitivity, this is likely, especially in more aggressive psychopaths.

Golden (1979) also suggests that a high N score is typical of the psychopath, and this appears to be logical because shrewdness and manipulation of others are characteristic of this pattern. Those psychopaths who are particularly high on the stimulation-seeking variable should score low on G and $Q_3$ and high on $Q_2$ and L. Within all subgroups of the antisocial personality disorder category, a high M score is thought to predict recidivism.

The modal profile for secondary psychopaths shows high scores on scales $Q_4$, O, and A, with low scores on C, $Q_3$, and H. They are also moderately low on G and $Q_1$ and tend to be average or below on N (in contrast to the primary psychopath), although again they also vary widely on N. On the average, they are not as low on scale B as the primary psychopath.

□ ## OTHER TEST-RESPONSE PATTERNS

The highest MCMI-II elevations are expected on 5 and 6A. When the 5-6A code is highest, B, T, and PP also tend to be somewhat elevated, and P, S+P, and C+P are high as well. Because the antisocial personality is generally not highly distressed, marked elevations on A, D, and H are not likely; however, elevations on A may occur, especially just prior to acting-out. Because alcohol and drug abuse are common here, elevations on B and/or T are likely.

On the WAIS-R, antisocial personalities, especially those more inclined toward primary psychopathy, generally have a performance IQ higher than the verbal IQ, sometimes by ten points or more. If they have had school-related problems, as is almost always the case, their low scores in the verbal subtests are on information, arithmetic, and vocabulary, reflecting their lack of adequate achievement in academic subjects. On the comprehensive subtest, the "marriage," "bad company," and "laws" items can bring out relevant content. Also, some explanations of the picture arrangement subtest elicit similar material. Picture completion and block design usually give two of the higher scores, and these persons usually do reasonably well on object assembly. Digit symbol and digit span are also often quite high (Keiser and Lowy, 1980).

In certain older individuals (with a mean age of forty-four), probably best viewed as secondary psychopaths, Heinrich and Amolsch (1978) found an unusual WAIS-R pattern consistently associated with persons who have poor work and marital histories, show drinking problems, are assaultive while drinking, and are inclined toward somatic concerns and situational depressions. They show a verbal IQ greater than a performance IQ by six to twenty-one points; high vocabulary and comprehension scores; low digit-symbol, block-design, and object assembly scores; and an average picture completion score.

On the Rorschach, antisocial personalities usually present casual yet alert facades (Hare, 1986), which is in contrast to their at least moderately constricted, and they may reject cards that they can clearly handle cognitively. Otherwise, a low to average number of responses is provided. Vague percepts may be seen at first and then developed in a flashy and flamboyant manner, possibly accompanied by "cute" although hostile comments. There may be guarded rejections of cards, and there is usually a delayed response to the color cards. They do respond to color (particularly the primary psychopath), although often in fairly primitive and impulsive manners, with pure C responses. While there is a low number of M and W responses, an absence of shading, and a low F+%, there is a high number of Popular responses. There is a high number of Animal responses, rather than human responses, and weapons are occasionally noted (Wagner and Wagner, 1981; Shafer, 1954).

The TAT stories are often somewhat juvenile in theme, and although the protagonist may be caught in a negative act, there is little mention of deserved punishment. If, on the other hand, they perceive the social demand of the situation as requiring some commentary on punishment, they will so comment, yet with superficial shallowness (Karon, 1981).

As noted, one of the better measures of psychopathy is the Hare PCL-R (Hare et al., 1991; Serin et al., 1990). Iacono (1991) points to a number of physiological markers for psychopathy that could be built into specialized evaluations, e.g., they show relatively attenuated electrodermal responses to a "countdown" threat of predictable but noxious stimuli—smaller anticipatory skin conductance increases but high anticipatory heart rate changes.

□    TREATMENT OPTIONS

The treatment problem with all the personality disorders—getting the client into therapy and meaningfully involved—is acute in the antisocial personality disorder. To the degree the person shows primary psychopathy, the chances become poorer for any meaningful change, no matter what treatment is used. Most effective are controlled settings, with personnel who are firm and caring and sophisticated in controlling manipulations, in which the antisocial client resides for a significant period of time. Confrontive therapies can be also effective (Quay, 1987), but they require some form of coercion, such as institutionalization, to keep the person in therapy.

Any inpatient treatment program should include four major components: (1) supervision, manipulation of the environment, and provision of education by the staff to facilitate change; (2) a token economy system that requires successful participation for one to receive *anything* beyond the basic necessities; (3) medical and psychiatric treatments to deal with ancillary psychopathology, e.g., neurological disorders and depression; and (4) a system of necessary social cooperation to maximize conformity and encourage development of the group ethic. This last component is seldom a consideration. In such a program, every task that can be found that can reasonably be performed by another and which is not essential to health, will be *required* to be performed only by one inmate *for* another. For instance, no inmate will be allowed to go to the soda machine for himself; he must get someone else to do so for him. Again, this encourages cooperation and reciprocation and may help inmates to internalize some mores. If some inmates are left out by others, it may become necessary to assign "partners" who will fulfill these functions for one another.

Aside from institutional settings, the chief time a therapist is likely to see an antisocial personality disorder is in a disturbed family situation. Marital and family therapies that work on a *quid pro quo* rather than on a good-faith contracting approach are of most help.

Various medications can be of help with certain components of the antisocial personality. For example, antipsychotics can be helpful with various paranoid components, especially when there are additional indications of seizures. Antipsychotics, lithium, carbamazepine, or beta-blockers can be helpful for various dimensions of lack of control or violent tendencies, but benzodiazepinies (e.g., Valium or Xanox) may be counterproductive.

Attention should also be paid to the stimulation-seeking nature of these clients (Quay, 1987; Zuckerman et al., 1980). This need can be interpreted to one with an antisocial personality disorder as similar to that of the alcoholic, in that the person needs somehow to fulfill this drive or be inclined to indulge in deviant patterns. Therapists can work with psychopaths to develop means of gaining stimulation in less self-destructive ways. A consistent pattern of engagement in sports and other strenuous and/or exciting activities and jobs that provide for a high level of activity and stimulation are helpful. The paradoxical effect of stimulant drugs (as with hyperactives) can be helpful with a small subgroup of the more manic psychopaths, but much care must be taken in management.

Overall, the therapist generally needs to

**1.** Expect resistance to entering therapy, and then to staying in therapy. Since these clients are easily bored and, as noted above, are highly stimulation-seeking, this must be considered in planning for general rehabilitation as well as specifically for the therapy hour.

**2.** Expect such clients to be deceptive about their history and present status. To the degree feasible, independently corroborate any critical questions about history or present behaviors. Contract ahead of time that if you feel it necessary, you will obtain such data from significant others, or other appropriate persons.

**3.** In line with this, clearly confront the individual's psychopathy and any record of deviant behavior. The presentation of "objective" profiles from tests like the MMPI-2 or 16 PF can be effective here. Confront the psychopathology as a life-style disorder that will require treatment of significant duration (and cost)—thus, one might contract for some financial penalty for early withdrawal. At the same time, avoid the role of judge and stay as much as possible in the role of collaborator. Maintaining a degree of adequate rapport is critical. Any exercises that help to develop empathy or social sensitivity are useful.

**4.** Challenge the following underlying beliefs as delineated by Beck et al. (1990): (a) rationalization—My desiring something justifies whatever actions I need to take; (b) the devaluing of others—The attitudes and needs of others don't effect me, unless responding to them will provide me an advantage, and if they are hurt by me, I need not feel responsible for what happens to them; (c) low-impact consequences—My choices are inherently good. As such, I won't experience undesirable consequences or, if they occur, they won't really matter to me; (d) I have to think of myself first. I'm entitled to what I want or feel I need and, if necessary, can use force or deception to obtain those goals; (e) Rules constrict me from fulfilling my needs.

## ■ Conduct Disorder

According to the DSM-III-R, this conduct disorder is the precursor to the antisocial personality, but unlike it, the disorder is broken down into three subcategories (group, solitary-aggressive, and undifferentiated) and thus may actually predict some other disorders as well.

The conduct disorders are marked by a persistent pattern of behavior that violates major age-appropriate social norms and the rights of others. To earn the basic diagnosis of conduct disorder, at least three of the following factors—in descending order of discriminating power—should be in evidence: (1) more than one occasion of stealing without confrontation, (2) at least twice running away from home, (3) frequent lying, (4) an incident of deliberate fire setting, (5) frequent truancy, (6) breaking into a car, building, or house, (7) deliberate property destruction (other than fire starting), (8) physical cruelty to animals, (9) an incident of coercive sexual activity, (10) use of a weapon in more than one fight, (11) frequent initiation of physical fights, (12) theft while confronting the victim, or (13) physical cruelty to people.

If the predominate pattern is aggression toward others and it is initiated individually, the diagnosis is the Solitary-Aggressive type (312.00); if most of the problem behaviors occur as a group activity with peers, the diagnosis is the Group type (312.20); otherwise, the diagnosis is Undifferentiated (312.90).

The diagnosis of conduct disorder requires evidence of the pattern for at least six months. If the person is eighteen or older, there should be evidence that the criteria for the antisocial personality disorder have not been met. A full evaluation of the family is essential for adequate diagnosis of the conduct-disordered child (see Figure 9.1). Young children who show evidence of an oppositional defiant disorder are at clear risk for a later conduct disorder diagnosis to the degree they show aggression and lying and there is associated family pathology.

The breakdown of the conduct disorder categories in many ways reflects a refinement of the concept of the primary versus the secondary psychopath discussed previously (Kernberg and Chazan, 1991). The Solitary-Aggressive type (312.00) comes closest to the violent acting-out of the primary psychopath, and the Undifferentiated type (312.90) at least includes the secondary (or neurotic) psychopath who is engaged in passive acting-out behaviors. The Group type is close to the classic concept of the "gang-oriented" juvenile delinquent. The categories are also reflected in some of the differences noted in Megargee's research on the criminal personality (Megargee and Bohn, 1979).

□          MMPI-2

Overall, scales 4, 8, and 9 have been "excitatory" in regard to acting-out in adolescence, whereas scales 0, 2, and 5 have been seen as "suppressor" scales. A moderately elevated 4-9 code, with most of the other scales not particularly high, is typical of the group-type conduct disorder, but it is also occasionally seen in the other types. A combination of the 4-8-9 scales with generally elevated scales throughout would be more consistently found in the solitary-aggressive conduct disorder. A caret-shaped profile on the validity scales (low L, high F, and low K) typifies the most severely emotionally disturbed subgroup of this disorder.

The 8-4 profile, with an elevation on 6 as well, is likely to be found in the solitary-aggressive who also has a paranoid component. They often show an incredible amount of alienation from self and others, usually directed in the Harris-Lingoes subscales. But the 8-4 profile without a high 6 would be more likely with an individual who is acting-out aggressively but is at least somewhat more socialized. The 2-4/4-2 profile, with a distinctive slope to the right and possibly a mild elevation on scale 6, is characteristic of those who are more likely to be undersocialized and nonaggressive—they are usually placed in the undifferentiated category. In general though, scales 0, 2, and 5, if high, predict lower rates of delinquency.

□          16 PF

On the 16 PF, the group type should score somewhat higher than the solitary-aggressive on scales A, B, G, and, to a moderate degree, N and $Q_3$. They are likely to be lower on L and $Q_1$ and, to a moderate degree, on E. The aggressive continuum is reflected in several scores: likely higher on E, H, and L, lower on B, C, G, I, and M, and moderately lower on N and $Q_3$. $Q_4$ particularly reflects the anxiety experienced in the evaluation situation, as well as other environmental conditions. The more socialized the individual, the more situational anxiety and thus a higher score on $Q_4$.

**TABLE 9.2**     Paths to Various Antisocial Patterns

| AGGRESSIVE/VERSATILE PATH, LEADING TO "CAFETERIA-STYLE" OFFENDING, INCLUDING VIOLENT, PROPERTY, AND/OR DRUG OFFENSES/ABUSES | NONAGGRESSIVE ANTISOCIAL PATH, LEADING TO MORE SPECIALIZED OFFENDING, INCLUDING PROPERTY, AND DRUG OFFENSES/ABUSES |
|---|---|
| Characteristics of the Aggressive/ Versatile Path | Characteristics of the Nonaggressive Path |
| Higher rate of genetic, prenatal, and birth disorders | Lower rate of genetic, prenatal, and birth disorders |
| Onset of conduct problems in preschool years | Onset of conduct problems in late childhood or early to middle adolescence |
| Aggressive and concealing problem behaviors | Mostly nonaggressive conduct problems |
| More hyperactive/impulsive/ attention problems as children | No appreciable hyperactive/ impulsive/attention problems |
| Poor social skills | Capable of social skills |
| Poor peer relationships | Association with deviant peers |
| Academic problems | Sporadic or minimal academic problems |
| High rate of instigation of offenses | Low rate of instigation of offenses |
| Low remission rate | Higher remission rate, at least for delinquency |
| More males than females | Higher proportion of females than in the aggressive/versatile path |
| Higher rate of drug abuse | Lower rate of drug abuse |
| Higher rate of stimulation-seeking | Lower rate of stimulation-seeking |

**EXCLUSIVE SUBSTANCE ABUSE PATH LEADING TO DRUG OFFENSES/ABUSES**

Characteristics of the Exclusive Substance Abuse Path in the Juvenile Years

Standard progression in substance abuse

Beer or wine → Cigarettes and/or hard liquor → Marijuana → Other illicit drugs

Onset of illicit drug use in middle to late adolescence

No appreciable prior conduct problems

Adapted in part from Loeber (1990).

□          OTHER TEST-RESPONSE PATTERNS

To the degree that the client is socialized and more likely to be the group type, WAIS-R and WISC-R scores will be more even between and within the verbal and performance tests, and the differences are more pronounced with the WISC-R than the WAIS-R (Grace and Sweeney, 1986). To the degree that the client is more aggressive and undersocialized, performance scores are likely to be higher than verbal scores. To the degree that avoidance of school is a factor, scores would be lower on information, arithmetic, and vocabulary than on other subtests. The ability to abstract has been hypothesized as important in curbing physical aggression; hence, aggressive individuals may be lower on similarities, all other variables being equal.

The solitary-aggressive individual is more likely to be resistant to the testing process itself and to show negativism throughout both this test and the Rorschach. To the degree the person is undersocialized, he or she should do somewhat less well on comprehension and picture arrangement than clients who are more aware and attuned to social norms. From a general perspective, individuals with conduct disorders who are more involved with passive or status offenses are more likely to have higher intelligence overall than those who are involved in more aggressive acting-out behaviors (Quay, 1987).

On the MCMI-II, the group type may experience more distress related to associated behaviors, producing more frequent elevations on A and D, where the solitary-aggressive type may show relatively higher elevations on 1, 2, 5, and 6A. To the degree the person is undersocialized yet nonaggressive, elevations on 1, 2, 6A, 8A, S, B, and T and low scores on 4, 7, and N can be expected.

On the Rorschach, solitary-aggressive individuals are likely to reject cards, to avoid the task in a variety of ways, to give more personalized (PER) responses, and to show more direct manifestations of violent and bizarre content than are more socialized and/or less aggressive clients. Those tending to be undersocialized, solitary, and aggressive are also likely to show the following characteristics: lower F percentage, lower W percentage, lower M percentage, more pure C, CF greater than FC, more Animal responses, higher white-space responses, more emphasis on D and Popular responses in an overall protocol with a low number of responses (Quevillon et al., 1986).

On the TAT (Quevillon et al., 1986), conduct-disordered male youths typically make more mention of parents, give more aggressive stories, and give responses that involve materialistic objects and a need for achievement. Aggressive youths in general give stories in which the hero was aggressive but received little punishment for his actions, as well as themes that include vivid and instructive stories about murder, burglaries, and hold-ups. These youths tend to ramble on without any clear themes and often have difficulty describing card 2. Stories that are superficial and have an absence of empathy or sympathy are common. Some youths give stories that are evasive, and they frequently mention that the stories are not autobiographical. Human figure drawings can be useful with this group, as it is a task they are more receptive to (at least in one-on-one testing), and some norms have been developed for them (Marsh et al., 1991).

**FIGURE 9.1**    Evolution of Aggressive Delinquency

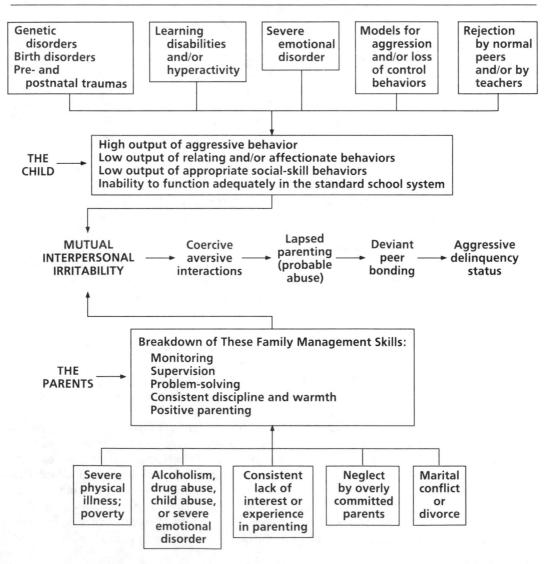

Early intervention is critical, and indeed, children first arrested at a young age are more likely to commit a greater number of and more-serious crimes (Kernberg and Chazan, 1991). If the individual is more solitary, undersocialized, and aggressive, there is a need for a highly controlled living system that includes all aspects of functioning. Token economy programs, combined with an emphasis on basic academic and vocational skills, will likely be necessary, along with a focus on the control of behavior. The more subtle strategies designed for the primary psychopath and the paranoid may also be appropriate. In response to the group type, especially when nonaggressive, the requirement of a highly structured and supervised residential program is lessened. An emphasis on a group-living model comes to the fore, and in some cases, outpatient treatment with such approaches as reality therapy, support groups, and the more traditional psychotherapies can be useful (Lyons and Woods, 1991; Brigham, 1988). A focus on parent training and classroom control using time-out procedures, contracting, and reinforcement structuring would also then be appropriate. Family therapy is usually necessary, and community-based interventions (e.g., setting up sports activities, scouting programs, and other positive group experiences) can also be effective (Loeber, 1990).

## Borderline Personality Disorder (301.83)

This disorder was a confusing entity in the original DSM-III-R drafts, but now it seems to be more clearly defined (Widiger et al., 1986). At first glance, it may seem to overlap with the schizotypal personality disorder, as both imply an easy transition into a schizophrenic adjustment. However, individuals with borderline personality disorder are neither as withdrawn socially nor as bizarre in symptomatology as are schizophrenics. Although the DSM-III-R does not specifically mention it, this category seems to be a resurrection of an old term at one time much favored by clinicians: "emotionally unstable personality." Persons in the borderline personality disorder category show significant emotional instability, are impulsive and unpredictable in behavior, are often antisocial, are irritable and anxious, often show "soft" neurological signs, and avoid being alone or experiencing the psychological emptiness or boredom to which they are prone (Stone, 1990). There is some evidence that as these individuals improve, they show more predictable behavior patterns, yet this is combined with increasingly evident narcissism. Ironically, a number of borderlines who appear to be very disturbed in their twenties look much better in their thirties, although much of the underlying psychopathology is still there (Stone, 1990).

An additional feature of this disorder is pseudologia phantastica.

Snyder (1986) reports several case studies in which pathologic lying is a cardinal feature. This lying may reflect an attempt to control or to enhance self-esteem. Some borderline individuals may be aware of their lying, while others may not be. In clinical cases where the individuals were confronted with their inaccuracies, they quickly dropped or changed the stories.

□ DSM-III-R

To diagnose borderline personality disorder—a pervasive pattern of mood, self-image, and interpersonal instability beginning by early adulthood—at least five of the following are required: (1) unpredictable impulsivity in two areas, such as sex and drug or alcohol use; (2) physically self-damaging behaviors; (3) uncontrolled, inappropriate anger responses; (4) unstable and intense interpersonal relationships; (5) unstable mood; (6) unstable identity; (7) persistent boredom experiences; or (8) avoidance of being or feeling alone or abandoned.

This disorder is thought to be relatively common, and it is one of the most consistently diagnosed personality disorders. Yet, it may be a confusing diagnostic category for clinicians. This category would probably be less commonly used if the older term "emotionally unstable personality disorder" were reinstituted. A multiple diagnosis with schizotypal and histrionic components is not improbable (Widiger et al., 1986). If the person is under the age of eighteen, a diagnosis of identity disorder takes precedence.

□ MMPI-2

In many respects, the syndrome of borderline personality disorder parallels that of schizophrenia, without the distinct emphasis on delusions or hallucinations, but with a higher level of responsiveness toward other persons. Elevations on scales 2, 4, and 8 should be expected (Trull, 1991; Edell, 1987). While the F scale should be lower, scales O and K should be higher than in schizophrenia. Scale 6 should show elevation if problems in management of anger are involved, although manipulative borderlines, especially young adults, will sometimes exaggerate responses contributing to this scale. The rare 2-6/6-2 type is likely to receive a diagnosis of borderline personality disorder or a similar one (Kelley and King, 1979c). If mood instability is involved and the person is in a manic phase, a rise on scale 9 and a drop on scale 2 are likely, with the opposite expected in the converse mood situation.

□ 16 PF

If these persons avoid being alone, even though there is instability in interpersonal relationships, A should be high and $Q_2$ should be low.

Overall, scales C, H, and $Q_3$ should be low, with high scores on $Q_4$, O, and I. Mood at the time of the testing will determine the score on F, and the degree of suspiciousness will be reflected in the height of the L scale. On the average, moderately low scores on M and N can be expected, but these can fluctuate markedly.

The variable self-assertion and avoidance exhibited in borderline personality disorders emerge on scale E, although such individuals can be docile and passive in order to fulfill their dependency needs. At other times, they are aggressive, paranoid, and manipulative, particularly when they are rejected. Also, since their social instability and irritability disrupt their social functioning, probable rejection results in their occasionally appearing at the more assertive end of the E continuum.

OTHER TEST-RESPONSE PATTERNS

From an overall perspective, the inadequate insulation of intellectual abilities from the intrusion of emotion can be observed in the connotations of the borderline client's language (Stevenson and Meares, 1992). It often becomes colored by personal concerns, although it usually stays within the bounds of appropriateness. For example, an explosive borderline client, when asked to define "terminate," replied, "To murder or kill someone—say, for revenge" (Swiercinsky, 1985). While some of these impairments may suggest organic dysfunction, borderline clients do not usually show such features as perplexity, concreteness, perceptual failure, constriction, oversimplification, or psychomotor retardation.

The most likely elevation of the borderline's profile on the MCMI-II is elevation on scale C. These individuals are subject to most of the clinical-symptom syndromes at some time or another, so periodic and variable elevations on A, H, N, and D are to be expected. Elevations on scale 8A may be present, in that the moodiness and behavioral unpredictability that characterize the passive-aggressive are often present in a more extreme form in the borderline. Those with high scores on 3, 4, and 7 and/or 8A are at risk with respect to this pattern in that these types are more prone to borderline functioning as they deteriorate.

On the performance subtests of the WAIS-R, in particular object assembly and block design, the increasing difficulty of the tasks often elicits haphazard trial-and-error efforts that are laced with noticeable displays of frustration and impatience. Their inclination to resort to abitrary solutions is often evident in the arithmetic subtest, especially when these clients are requested to reveal the manner by which they came to the incorrect responses. Requests as to how they arrived at their responses on other subtests can often be similarly useful. On the Rorschach, illogical and fabulized combinations occur, but when actual contaminations occur, it more likely bodes a schizophrenic disorder (Swiercinsky, 1985). On tests like the TAT, "primitive splitting," an oft-cited characteristic of the borderline, is seen in characters that are all bad, e.g., angels or devils, in characters in which only one side of the personality is portrayed or even admitted to, or good-bad characteristics are juxtaposed incongruously. Inappropriately extreme affect portrayals, separation anxiety themes, and acting-out rather than delayed gratification themes are common (Bellak, 1993).

## TREATMENT OPTIONS

This category is truly a polyglot syndrome and will therefore require equally variable treatment responses (Stevenson and Meares, 1992; Stone, 1990). The impulsivity demonstrated in this disorder suggests that the reader should refer to comments regarding the antisocial and narcissistic personality disorders, as well as those regarding substance abuse or possibly one of the sexual deviations. The comments on the antisocial personality regarding stimulation-seeking are also particularly relevant, since boredom is common in the borderline personality. Also, borderlines show a high rate of suicide attempts and "successes"; Stone (1990) reports a 9 percent rate of eventual suicide. Schizotypal and histrionic components are also not uncommon and require the treatment responses noted in those categories (Widiger et al., 1986).

Medication may be necessary, e.g., for any depressive components, and fluoxetine has been useful to generally calm and stabilize extreme response patterns. Since there is usually some disordered autonomic-emotional functioning, biofeedback and relaxation training may be appropriate. If there are a number of neurological "soft" signs, treatment will have to take probable CNS involvement (see Chapter 11) into account. Group therapy can be helpful if the person will allow the development of trust in the group, but such clients are often unwilling to share the attention of the therapist and are so emotionally unpredictable that they are difficult to work with. They can exert such a high cost on the progress of the group that they make it unwise to include them.

From an overall perspective, the therapist needs to

1. Help them establish a clearer sense of identity. Realize that borderlines have extreme but poorly organized views of relationships with caretakers and thus bring odd and unrealistic expectancies into interpersonal relationships.

2. Borderlines are intense and labile emotionally and are draining to significant others (and therapists). Yet, paradoxically, they need to understand that they avoid facing any intense negative emotions, so find it hard to grieve the many relationship losses they generate. They maintain a facade of competence and independence, yet desperately want various types of help, then react negatively when it is not forthcoming. They need to role play expressing their emotions as they develop and also how to ask for types of help in more appropriate ways.

**3.** Borderlines need to be helped to understand that they are prone to "dichotomous thinking," i.e., they perceive issues, persons, etc. in extremes, or in black-and-white terms. When people fail them somewhat they perceive the failures as total.

**4.** Give the client a sense of control over the emotional aspects of the therapy relationship. In contrast to therapy with narcissists, allow borderlines as much input as feasible over such issues as therapy schedules, seating arrangements, topics to be discussed, whether to use homework assignments and what types, etc.

**5.** Understand that borderlines consistently generate "crises," so clear guidelines for responding need to be formulated early on and communicated to the client.

**6.** Challenge, although more subtly than with other personality disorders, the following beliefs: (a) I'm afraid I'll be alone forever, as no one who really gets to know me will want to love me; (b) If I ignore my own needs, I can entrap some people into relationships, but, since I can't control my feelings and I need the relationships, I'll be very unhappy; (c) Although I need people, they will eventually hurt or reject me, so I must protect myself; (d) People and/or relationships are usually all good or all bad; (e) I deserve any bad things that happen to me; or (f) My misery (and/or "badness") is how people recognize me as a unique self.

■ ## Identity Disorder (313.82)

The identity disorder has occasionally been related to the borderline personality disorder, yet they are not highly similar (Widiger et al., 1986). To diagnose an identity disorder, the DSM-III-R requires evidence of disturbance for at least three months, impairment in social or occupational functioning, and uncertainty about identity in three of the following areas: career choice, sexual patterns, friendship choices and behavior, moral values, religious identification, peer group loyalties, and long-term goals. This disorder naturally occurs most commonly in late adolescence, when people are forced by society to make choices and face changes in these areas. Most people who face these choices experience some distress; a clinical diagnosis is indicated when this distress persists and is so severe that it results in significant disruption of coping with life challenges (Clum, 1989).

□ ### DIAGNOSTIC CONSIDERATIONS

The depression and anxiety consistently found in this syndrome predict elevations on MMPI-2 scales 2 and 7, and there is some elevation on scale 8, reflecting a sense of alienation and isolation from others with a consequent feeling of self-doubt. Scores on scale 5 are usually at either extreme, depending on which way the person's identification is swinging. People of higher intelligence and socioeconomic status tend to move to the upper extreme of scale 5, particularly males. Where this disorder has resulted in impulsive behaviors and/or feelings of alienation from others, elevations on scales 4 and 6 are probable.

As a reflection of high anxiety, $Q_4$ is typically elevated on the 16 PF, and the concern about values is manifested in a high O and F, as well as a low $Q_2$. There is a degree of guilt, which differentiates this pattern from that of a psychopathic personality, and this is seen in the elevations on G and O.

High scores on scales A and/or D of the MCMI-II would be expected; anxiety may also be represented by high scores on H, N, B, and T. The alienated quality experienced by these persons may be reflected in moderate elevation on 1 or 2.

Performance on the WAIS-R is similar to that of the depersonalization disorder and the anxiety and depressive disorders. The thrust of the person's identity disorder will determine the patterns here. The most probable marker of an identity disorder on the WAIS-R is the comparison of obtained IQ scores to academic or work achievements, as it is likely that the IQ score will be above the level of achievement.

The depression and anxiety usually evident in an identity disorder are reflected in the standard Rorschach patterns for this disorder. The responses are usually filled with figures that are more passive and inadequate than normal, and occasionally there is an allusion to young humans or animals, which suggests an attempt to hold on to an earlier period of a more integrated identity. If the identity disorder is focused on the sexual area, responses similar to those noted in ego-dystonic homosexuality can be expected.

## TREATMENT OPTIONS

Therapies that are effective here are similar to those usually applied to the depersonalization disorder and to some of the more neurotic disorders. In some of these clients, a low dose of antidepressants—e.g., 25–50 mg of imipramine or its equivalent—may be of significant help. The client-centered therapy of Carl Rogers is especially appropriate, since he initially developed this while working with young ministerial and graduate psychology students who were going through various identity conflicts.

If the client has moved too far in avoidance of choices, the reality therapy of William Glasser may be more appropriate. An existential perspective is important in whatever therapy takes place. Clients need to face the choices that they are avoiding and to envision and accept the consequences. An adolescent therapy or support group is often useful here because it gives such clients awareness that others are moving through the same choices and it provides feedback about new choices and initiatives (Brigham, 1988).

■          # Avoidant Personality Disorder (301.82)

These individuals are shy and inhibited interpersonally, yet at the same time desire to have interpersonal relationships, which distinguishes them from those with the schizotypal or schizoid personality disorders. They also do not show the degree of irritability and emotional instability seen in the borderline personality disorder.

A major feature of this chronic disorder is an unwillingness to tolerate risks in deepening interpersonal relationships (Millon, 1981). They resonate, negatively, to this refrain from the poetry of W. B. Yeats:

**Only God, my dear**
**Can love you for yourself alone**
**and not for your yellow hair**

These persons are extremely sensitive to rejection and seem to need guarantees ahead of time that relationships will work out. Naturally, such guarantees are seldom available in healthy relationships. Thus, the friends they manage to make often show a degree of instability or are quite passive.

In many ways, this disorder is close to the anxiety disorders, since there is a degree of anxiety and distress, and low self-esteem is common (Eysenck, 1985). However, the behaviors that produce the distress are reltively ego-syntonic. Their depression and anxiety are more related to their perceived rejection and criticism by others.

This common disorder is seen more often in women. Any disorder in childhood that focuses on shyness predisposes one to the avoidant personality disorder.

□          ## DSM-III-R

To diagnose an avoidant personality disorder, the clinician must observe the following as consistent and chronic behaviors: a persistent pattern of timidity, social discomfort, and fear of rejection, beginning by early adulthood, and at least four of the following: (1) an unwillingness to be involved with people unless sure of acceptance, (2) no confidants or close friends (except first-degree relatives), (3) avoidance of occupational or social activities high in social contact, (4) reticence in social situations, (5) embarrassment easily shown by anxiety or blushing, (6) exaggeration of risks and strong need for routine, or (7) strong fear and sensitivity to criticism or rejection. If they are under age eighteen, the appropriate diagnosis would be Avoidant Disorder of Childhood or Adolescence (313.21).

☐          MMPI-2

A 2-7/7-2 profile is common, reflecting depression about assumed rejection and apprehension and self-doubt about the ability to deal with others. To the degree that this has resulted in social withdrawal, a high score on scale O is expected, as well as a moderate decrease on scale 9. Since this disorder often appears in females who are strongly identified with the traditional feminine role, a low score on scale 5 occurs. If the individual still has energy that is being channeled into anger, a 3-4 profile can be expected, with allied mild elevations on 2, 7, and 6. Indeed, a 6-7/7-6 profile is indicative of this disorder (Graham, 1987). If functioning is beginning to go to pieces as a result of the rejection and social withdrawal, an elevation on scale 8 occurs.

☐          16 PF

Low scores on scales E, C, and H are consistent with this syndrome, reflecting shyness, threat sensitivity, passivity, and emotional upset. High scores on $Q_4$ and O are evidence of the expected tension and insecurity, and a moderately high score on I reflects fear of rejection and sensitivity. Social clumsiness is balanced by a hyperalertness in social situations, hence particularly deviant scores on N are not too common. The self-perception by avoidant personalities that they should automatically be accepted interpersonally may result in a higher than average A score. However, actual experience, of which they are somewhat aware, keeps this from being very high and will even temper it to average or below in some profiles. These people tend to be moderately low on $Q_3$ and M, although this is highly variable. The L score, usually low, will depend on whether they have begun to channel their rejection into anger and suspiciousness of others.

☐          OTHER TEST-RESPONSE PATTERNS

To the degree avoidant personalities feel accepted by the examiner, they do better on the verbal subscales of the WAIS-R than on the performance subscales. Since they are often females with strong traditional role identities, low scores on arithmetic are common. Dependency may be reflected in some of the content of the comprehension items, as well as in the picture arrangement subtest, which is low in introverted clients. Blocked or relatively inactive M responses on the Rorschach are common. A high number of Popular responses occurs, and content may focus on more-passive animals, such as rabbits and deer (occasionally being hurt or killed), or on passive interactions in the M responses.

The most prominent characteristic on the MCMI-II is an elevation of 85 or higher on scale 2, with depressed scores on scales 4 and 7. Generalized anxiety, a common symptom in this pattern, is evidenced by elevation on A. The ego-dystonic detached style of the avoidant personality causes elevation on D. Moderate elevations (75–85) may occur on scales 8B and C, in that characteristics of these disorders are likely to occur concurrently. The higher the elevation on S, the more decompensation has occurred.

□          TREATMENT OPTIONS

Training in social skills is critical here. Also, the need for assertiveness training is often as great in this disorder as it is in the dependent personality (see the following subsection for suggestions equally applicable here). In addition, since the avoidant personality is more concerned with the risk in relationships, existential and confrontive therapy approaches are useful adjuncts. Rational-emotive therapy (Ellis and Dryden, 1987) is especially useful because it was worked out on a population that had these kinds of concerns. Since the Adlerian therapies focus on issues of inferiority, there may be special applicability here. Also, since there is a neuroticlike component to this pattern (Eysenck, 1985), paradoxical-intention approaches may be useful. Avoidant personalities may elicit "protective responses" within a group therapy setting, but an unwillingness to self-disclose may eventually lead to rejection by the group.

Another helpful treatment for dependent and avoidant personality disorders is covert negative reinforcement; this technique is most useful when the client cannot easily envision the desired behavior and would not be highly responsive to covert positive reinforcement. In covert negative reinforcement, the client imagines a highly aversive event and then imagines this event is terminated by the performance of a new set of desired behaviors. It is critical that there be as little time lapse as possible during the switch-over in images.

# ■          Dependent Personality Disorder (301.60)

People with the dependent personality disorder have a pervasive need to cling to stronger personalities who are allowed to make a wide range of decisions for them. They are naive and show little initiative. There is some suspiciousness of possible rejection, but not to the degree found in the avoidant personality disorder.

In one way, dependent personality disorders can be seen as successful avoidant personality disorders. They have achieved a style that elicits the desired relationships, but at the cost of any consistent expression of their own personality. They show elements of agoraphobia, not crystallized, and they lack any real self-confidence.

Since this is an exaggeration of the traditional feminine role, it is not surprising that it is far more common in women (Kernberg, 1984). If the individual is not in a dependent relationship, anxiety and upset are common. Even if enmeshed in a dependent relationship, and many dependent personality disorders also carry a borderline personality disorder diagnosis as well, there is still residual anxiety over the possibility of being abandoned. The borderline is more likely to show rage at the prospect of abandonment.

☐ DSM-III-R

To make a formal diagnosis of dependent personality disorder, five of the following should be noted with some regularity over a significant period of time: (1) unable to make everyday decisions alone, (2) allows others to make most decisions, (3) overly agreeable, (4) lacks initiative, (5) volunteers in order to gain approval, (6) uncomfortable or helpless when alone, (7) devastated by losses, (8) preoccupied with abandonment, or (9) easily hurt by criticism.

☐ MMPI-2

The 2-7/7-2 profile is characteristic of an individual who is experiencing anxiety and depression, who is passive-dependent and docile, and who presents a picture of severe dependency. A high 3 scale and a mildly elevated K scale are common. Naiveté and passivity are reflected in a surprisingly elevated L scale, but the F scale is usually in the average range. Some dependents (and avoidants) elevate the "naive" Harris-Lingoes subscales, e.g., on Hy and Pa. These people are afraid to acknowledge any faults in others for fear that they may be rejected.

The acceptance of the stereotypical feminine role shows up on a low scale 5, and the lack of resistance to coercion from authority is reflected in a low 4 scale. There is a subgroup of dependent personalities who are a bit more aggressive and manipulative, and they tend to show the 2-4/4-2 profile (Anderson and Bauer, 1985). Scale 9 is also low, reflecting passivity and lack of initiative, Scale O tends to be elevated, although this is variable, depending on emerging concern about their own behavior and their sense of comfort about the permanence of their dependency relationships. If anger is beginning to develop as a result of any consistent rejection of the dependency, some elevation on scale 6 occurs. Otherwise, this is rare.

In young men, an interesting and rather rare profile, the 1-9/9-1 type, with both T scores greater than 70, has been found to indicate passivity and dependency. However, there is a hostile component directed toward females that is associated with this profile, so the dependency relationship would probably be directed toward males. Thus, one would look to the 5 scale for elaboration on the issue of sexual identity and possible preference.

☐          16 PF

The dependent personality disorder should result in scores quite low on the classic 16 PF dependency factors: scales E, L, M, $Q_1$, and $Q_2$ (Karson and O'Dell, 1976, p. 90). In addition, the I score should be high in females. In males, moderately low scores on $Q_4$ may be noted and A is high.

There are probably low scores on $Q_3$ and N and a high score on O. Surprisingly, there is not a particularly low H score—it may even be above average.

It is also noteworthy that a low score on L is not consistently found in this disorder, which may reflect not only a high threshold for jealousy but also the unconscious anger alleged to be a result of the submergence of one's personality to another.

☐          OTHER TEST-RESPONSE PATTERNS

A high score on scale 3 of the MCMI-II would be expected, along with an elevation on A when any insecurity about having placed their welfare in the hands of others occurs. Dependents often adopt physical problems to further the pattern of requiring help and care, resulting in an elevation on H. An elevated D may appear during periods when the individual is not getting needed nurturance and security. Because elements of the avoidant and histrionic personality disorders are often present, elevations on scales 2 and 4 may occur.

On the WAIS-R, the performance scale score may be higher, although this is not as consistent as in some of the other personality disorders. Arithmetic and information seem to be consistently low, relative to other scores, reflecting a withdrawal from a problem-solving approach to the world. Within the performance subtests, lower scores on object assembly occur and odd responses indicating a need for support are occasionally found in picture completion.

A constricted use of space is a common feature in the drawing of the Bender-Gestalt figures.

The Rorschach record is highly reflective of the attitude of the examiner. If the dependent personality feels accepted in the testing situation and believes that the examiner desires a high number of responses, she will produce an extensive record. Otherwise, a record with a less than average number of responses can be expected. As with the avoidant personality, passive Animal and passive M responses are found, as well as a high number of Popular responses. There is also a tendency toward use of color rather than form in determining responses, relative to other personality disorders, and there is a likelihood of perceiving small-detail responses. Dependency and compliance themes are often elicited in card 2 of the TAT (Bellak, 1993).

☐    TREATMENT OPTIONS

Assertiveness training is a standard feature in the treatment of the dependent personality disorder. It may need to be preceded by methods that help clients gain a greater awareness and articulation of their dependency, via consensual feedback from a group, from catharsis, or from other consciousness-raising techniques.

In the response acquisition stage of assertiveness training, modeling is carried out with audio- or videotaped demonstrations by same-status, -age, and -sex models. Covert modeling is particularly helpful where persons are trying to develop a whole new behavior style. Clients imagine another person performing the assertive behaviors that they wish to have in their repertoire. After response acquisition, there is response reproduction, in which behavior rehearsal, role playing, and even directed practice are useful. After this, response consolidation is effected through clear feedback, again possibly using audio- or videotape. Changes are crystallized into the ongoing personality through cognitive self-reinforcement and by requests and contracting for increasingly widening the range and targets of the assertive behavioral responses. Since this disorder often occurs in the context of family or marital difficulties, attention will have to be paid to the partner, who may view any change as threatening.

Overall, the therapist needs to

**1.** Present the goal of therapy as "controlled freedom," since the dependent personality has a strong underlying fear of "independence"; independence signifying isolation and loss of self.

**2.** A totally nondirective approach, especially at first, is too threatening for these clients. Move as soon as feasible into a Socratic type of "guided discovery," when the dependent personality requests what to do, as they inevitably will. Guided imagery can help nurture embryonic independence behaviors.

**3.** Be careful to avoid the authoritarian or "benevolent guru" role. It is tempting to do with dependent clients as they will quickly reward you, and understand they have finely-honed skills in eliciting such patterns and intuiting what will be rewarding to each individual in that role. While "rescuing" can be frustrating with borderline personality disorders, it feels good with dependent personalities.

**4.** Set clear limits in areas where dependency can emerge. These clients easily "fall in love" with therapists, making the therapist vulnerable to a variety of dual-relationship behaviors, including sexual intimacies.

**5.** Remember that dependent personalities may be getting many rewards for their behaviors, in the midst of the negatives that have led them into therapy, e.g., abusive relationships. Very often significant others only want very circumscribed changes, so once changes begin, they and their partners will likely subvert things. At the same time, the eventual termination of therapy is always threatening with these clients. Group therapy can sometimes help as a sort of weaning process.

**6.** Challenge such underlying belief systems as (a) I am perpetually at risk of being alone in a cold and dangerous world, (b) I'm not able to cope with and/or enjoy life without a supportive other, (c) A loss of self is a fair price to pay in order to obtain a relationship with a supportive other, even if they periodically abuse me in some fashion, or (d) I need constant access to this other, with as much intimacy as I can elicit, so I'll be as subservient and inoffensive as I need to be.

## ■ Obsessive-Compulsive Personality Disorder (301.40)

This disorder is occasionally confused with the obsessive-compulsive disorder, but there are significant differences between the two syndromes. First, the obsessive-compulsive personality seldom becomes obsessed about issues. Second, the term "obsessive-compulsive" here refers to a life style in which obsessive-compulsive features are pervasive and chronic; it does not refer to a specific behavior. Third, the obsessive-compulsive life style is ego-syntonic, and for the most part, persons only come to treatment when coerced in some fashion.

Obsessive-compulsive personalities are preoccupied with rules and duties, are unable to express warmth and caring except in limited situations, are highly oriented toward a life style marked by productivity and efficiency, are temperamentally and emotionally insensitive, and are generally distant from other individuals. They can be described as workaholics without warmth. One associate of the author commented that this is the type of person who can obtain a complete physical exam from a proctologist.

It is true that a degree of compulsivity is effective, particularly in our society. It becomes a problem when it overwhelms the rest of the personality. Paradoxically, obsessive-compulsives are often indecisive and poor planners of their time, a result of their narrow focus and concern with precision, even when precision may be irrelevant. They are inclined to be excessively moralistic, litigious, and hyperalert to criticism and perceived slights from others (Kernberg, 1984).

□ DSM-III-R

To diagnose an obsessive-compulsive personality disorder, the DSM-III-R requires a clear pattern of rigidity and perfectionism, as indicated by at least five of the following: (1) overemphasis on details, to the exclusion of an overall perspective (they see the trees rather than the forest, and not even all of the trees), (2) perfectionism that interferes with tasks, (3) constriction of affection and emotionality, (4) excessive devotion to vocation and productivity, (5) need for dominance in personal relationships, (6) indecisiveness, (7) hoarding behavior (even where there is no sentimental value), (8) lack of personal generosity where no personal gain accrues, and (9) overconscientiousness or inflexibility in matters of ethics or morality.

☐     MMPI-2

Obsessive-compulsives attain a moderately high K scale and seldom have highly elevated MMPI-2 profiles because they are not inclined toward self-disclosure. They often attain elevations on scales 3 and 1, the latter particularly so if physical complaints have become a focus for their distress. They find it more comfortable to see themselves as having a physical rather than a psychological disturbance. The 9 scale is also elevated; in large part, this elevation reflects how autocratic and dominant these individuals are in personal relationships. Litigiousness and developing paranoid concerns are reflected on scale 6. A moderately high 7 score may occur if there is a querulous and complaining attitude, although scale 7 usually reflects obsessionalism rather than compulsive factors.

☐     16 PF

Obsessive-compulsives also present a reasonably normal profile here. It is recommended that if there is a suspicion of compulsivity, the protocol should be scored for faking-good. Since there is denial of anxiety, $Q_4$ is low, and the need for control of intrapsychic processes leads to a high $Q_3$. Isolation from other people results in a high $Q_2$ score, and the rigidity and possibly developing paranoia lead to a high L score. Scale A is also lowered for the same reasons. Scores are not particularly low on C or high on O. They tend to be high on E, the degree depending on the orientation toward dominance in interpersonal relationships. Scores are moderately high on G or N and moderately low on I and F. Since the coping systems of obsessive-compulsives result in better academic performances and intellectual achievements, they attain one of the higher scale B scores.

☐     OTHER TEST-RESPONSE PATTERNS

On the MCMI-II, a high score on scale 7 is expected. Elevation on A is rare, as anxieties are usually controlled. Occasionally, anxieties are expressed as psychosomatic or physical complaints, represented by elevation on H. Characteristics of the dependent or paranoid personalities may be present, causing elevations on scales 3 or P, respectively.

As a result of an emphasis on achievement and productivity, persons with an obsessive-compulsive personality disorder score at least in the average range—usually above—on the WAIS-R. They will give overly precise and detailed answers, which helps on comprehensive and similarities. But in tests based on speed, such as digit symbol, block design, object assembly, and picture arrangement, the same traits can lower the scores. Their interpersonal and problem-solving rigidity causes difficulties with the more complex puzzles in picture arrangement. Generally, they attain a higher verbal IQ than performance IQ.

On the Bender-Gestalt test, they are inclined to count the dots or small circles in the cards, may orient all the figures in a precise arrangement, and generally approach the task in a systematic and methodical fashion.

On the Rorschach, there is an emphasis on Dd and D responses, with a high F+% and fewer W and color-based responses. Some responses are described in overly specific detail, and they make criticisms of the blots. Relative to those with the other personality disorders, they provide a high number of responses overall. TAT stories are often lengthy, with varied themes offered. Occasionally, the primary theme is lost in a focus on details, especially as elicited by certain cards, e.g. card 2 and 13 MF (Bellak, 1986).

## TREATMENT OPTIONS

Cautela and Wall (1980) suggest the use of covert conditioning procedures to counteract the compulsivity; in particular, they recommend the use of the covert sensitization technique. This technique involves the imagination of a highly aversive event or contingency immediately after developing the imagery of the undesired behavior—in this case, the compulsive pattern to be eliminated. The technique is effective not only for this pattern but for a number of the habit disorders.

In another useful technique, paradoxical intention, clients are simply instructed to do the very acts they have been resisting (Seltzer, 1986). As this proceeds, clients are told, by a number of apparently absurd instructions, to vary the circumstances and quantity of the behaviors produced. As this occurs over time, they develop a greater sense of control over their behaviors and may then choose to give them up. Group therapy is a helpful follow-up because these clients are likely to regress into their cold and distancing compulsive behaviors if the changes are not thoroughly incorporated into their life styles for some length of time. However, the group can be impatient with the judgmental behaviors and condescension of this type of clients.

In general, therapists should consider the following when working with an obsessive-compulsive personality:

**1.** Developing rapport can be difficult, as such clients usually lack emotionality and a sense of humor. Usually they only allow rapport after a base of competence-based behaviors have been "produced" by the therapist. Since therapists are often subclinical MMPI-2 4-9s, and want to "get on with it," they easily become impatient with the details and periodic tediums such clients engender. So, appropriate monitoring and constructive use of counter-transference responses are important.

**2.** Humor is a natural antagonist to obsessive-compulsive patterns. Model humor for them or consider showing and discussing humorous tapes or books ("Saturday Night Live's" classic vignettes of The Anal-Retentive Gardener, Fisherman, etc.) are excellent.

**3.** Consider bibliotherapy assignments (an assignment they usually take to easily), not only in books with humor, but those that describe and thus model a more relaxed life style, e.g., Thoreau's *Walden,* Zen, Taoist, and other Eastern religion literature, mystery books about "laid-back" detectives such as John MacDonald's Travic McGee series, etc. Participation in classes on meditation or yoga or tai chi can also be beneficial. Relaxation training is also helpful.

**4.** Monitor for ancillary patterns often found in obsessive-compulsive clients, i.e., depression, psychosomatic disorders, sexual inhibition, substance abuse (occasionally rationalized as self-prescribed medication), etc. They are more inclined to hide these "defects" than some other clients.

**5.** Obsessive-compulsive personalities tend to set higher expectations for themselves than others—which may be only at the overt level, as they usually harbor much anger (the expression of which they fear) toward others for not working as hard as they do. Consider having them develop written comparison charts of themselves with specific others, and use the contrasts as access to the anger, and as a means of helping them toward concretely lowering their standards.

**6.** Challenge common underlying beliefs such as (a) To err, or worse, to fail, is anxiety provoking, will allow others to criticize me, and makes me feel less than a whole person; (b) To lose control or to face uncertainty is anxiety provoking; (c) My obsessiveness and/or compulsivity are powerful enough to avoid errors, failure, or finding myself with nothing to do, yet, (d) as regards meaningful decisions, rather than "Better to have tried and failed than to never have tried at all," my motto is "Better to have not tried at all, than to have tried and failed"; (e) Details are important, i.e., if you can see trees, no need to look for the forest; (f) Feelings or emotions interfere with thinking, and I must depend on logic; (g) I am responsible for myself and others; or (h) I hate others when they don't follow "the rules," i.e., my rules, and especially if they get by with it.

■ ## Passive-Aggressive Personality Disorder (301.84)

The essential behavior pattern in the passive-aggressive personality disorder is indirectly expressed resistance to social and occupational performance expectations that results in chronic ineffectiveness. The core disorder is hostility that is not directly expressed, so "double messages" to others result. The underlying hostility affects significant others, yet the passive-aggressive denies, often as if insulted, any aggressive or hostile motivation. The actual behavior expressed may be either passive or aggressive, but physical aggression seldom occurs.

Most parents have had the experience of a child pushing them to the limit of their control and then backing off. Like that child, the passive-aggressive becomes acutely sensitive to such limits and is consistently able to go so far but no further. When this pattern becomes an integral part of a social and vocational life style, a passive-aggressive personality disorder exists. Although these patterns are commonly modeled and learned in childhood, such a family usually reaches a state of mutual détente. The pattern then causes severe problems when it is transferred into any new intimate, consistent contact relationship, such as marriage.

The passive-aggressive personality takes the standards and belief systems of significant others and turns them around to immobilize the others effectively. The strategy (which is not thought to be a conscious behavior) is to present the "enemy" (often a person depended on) with a choice that forces one either to capitulate or to violate an individual belief system. That person is thus immobilized, with no adequate reason to justify retaliation.

☐ ### DSM-III-R

Since the authors of DSM-III-R were initially concerned about the rationale for continuing this diagnostic category, surprising in light of the consistent use it receives, they emphasize that it is only used when behavior does not first meet the criteria for other personality disorders. To warrant the diagnosis, there has to be evidence in social or vocational areas that there has been indirect resistance to performance demands resulting in chronic problems in these areas. At least five of the following behaviors are required to substantiate this resistance: (1) dawdling, (2) sulkiness, irritability, or argumentativeness when asked to do something he or she does not want to do, (3) procrastination, (4) purposeful inefficiency, (5) convenient forgetfulness, (6) unjustified protests that others are unreasonably demanding, (7) resentment of productive suggestions from others, (8) unreasonable criticism or scorn of authority figures, or (9) belief that he or she is doing a much better job that others think. If the client is under the age of eighteen, the appropriate diagnosis would usually be oppositional defiant disorder.

☐          MMPI-2

The 3-4/4-3 combination is commonly seen in the passive-aggressive personality disorder (Graham, 1987). Where scale 3 is greater than 4 and both scales are relatively high, the individual is oriented toward the passive mode. When scale 4 is higher than 3, accompanied by a moderate to high elevation on scale 6, the aggressive mode is predominate. If both scales 3 and 4 are high together, there is a tendency toward dissociative responses (Lachar, 1974).

Elevation on scale K is also probable since passive-aggressives will downplay their faults and show a lack of insight about intrapsychic dynamics. An avoidance of responsibility, possibly through somatic complaints, produces mild to moderate elevations on scales 1 and 7. Scale 9 is average to low in this pattern, except when hostility is a counterphobic defense against dependency, when the rare 3-9 profile may be given. Also, when a man is being seen as a result of his wife's complaint of marital problems, a spike 9 profile has been found to be indicative of passive-aggressive functioning (King and Kelley, 1977). Graham (1987) also notes that a 1-2/2-1 profile may be indicative of this disorder.

The "Scarlett O'Hara" Von scales 4-5-6 for women is a marker for significant and often very destructive (though passively) personality traits. The passive-aggressive personality who is closest to actual loss of control of aggression shows a 4-6/6-4 profile, with high F and 8 scales, as well as a low scale 2 score. Persons with this profile have much cross-sex hostility. If the scores here are very high, consider an emerging paranoid schizophrenic adjustment.

☐          16 PF

The 16 PF profile of the passive-aggressive personality disorder is generally not remarkable. The E score fluctuates, depending on whether the passive (low E score) or aggressive mode is operative. The apparent dependency of many passive-aggressives would suggest a low $Q_2$ score. However, this is balanced by underlying hostility and resistance, which raises the score into the average range and occasionally to an above-average score. Passive-aggressives are usually moderately low on G, although not markedly low on C. The interpersonal manipulation inherent in this pattern results in a high N score and at least an average L score. The L and H scores are higher in the aggressive mode, with the I score being lower.

☐          OTHER TEST-RESPONSE PATTERNS

An MCMI-II scale 8A score of 85 or higher suggests a passive-aggressive personality disorder, and 6B is also likely to be elevated. During stressful periods, elevations on A and D are likely to occur. Psychosomatic complaints may occur, causing a raised H score. Moderate to high elevations on scales 4 and especially C are possible since these disorders occur relatively frequently in conjunction with 8A.

Golden (1979) found passive-aggressive individuals to be high on the comprehension scale of the WAIS, but in general, the performance scale score is slightly higher than the verbal scale score. They do well on visual-motor tasks, such as digit symbol, block design, and object assembly. They also do well on digit span but are only average on arithmetic. Elaboration of responses on picture arrangement and comprehension may cue the passive-aggressive orientation.

On the Rorschach, a long response latency as well as a high percentage of FC and Space responses are noted, as well as a relatively high number of Texture and Popular responses. Occasional odd combinations of aggressive and passive content may occur, such as children and guns, or there may be rather arbitrary assignments of color or content to a space (Wagner and Wagner, 1981). Passive-aggressive personalities may produce responses that directly suggest their pattern of relating, such as people passively manipulating others or arguing or animals sneaking around.

Many authors have asserted that the use of white space suggests the negativistic tendencies that are characteristic of a passive-aggressive personality. An aggressive-content response, such as bombs, fire, scissors, or volcanoes, is more likely to be evident in the passive-aggressive personality who is inclined to actually threaten aggression on occasion. Phillips and Smith (1953) assert that a rough-texture response is also characteristic of this pattern.

## TREATMENT OPTIONS

The critical task for the clinician treating a passive-aggressive personality disorder is to set up feedback situations so that the person can no longer effect their interpersonal controlling patterns and yet cannot deny their existence. Some form of family or marital therapy that confronts the underlying belief system is often indicated (Baucom and Epstein, 1990).

Also, any form of effective data presentation about personality patterns is helpful, especially if it can be stored for future use (Cattell, 1986). For that reason, audio- or videotapes of different sessions are useful in confronting passive-aggressives with their patterns. Consensual feedback from a group is also useful in overcoming avoidance mechanisms, although some passive-aggressives may be too sophisticated for some groups and, as a result, will absorb too much of the therapist's psychic energy. Since inadequacies are often at the core of this pattern, assertiveness training may be appropriate. If anger is the focus, it is still helpful, but it may need to be embellished with methods that focus on catharsis.

From an overall perspective, a therapist working with a passive-aggressive client should

**1.** Remember that since the most common reason passive-aggressives enter therapy is because of complaints they are not meeting expectations, e.g., in job or relationships, you can assume they will act in a similar fashion with you. They can be deceptive, but of course not directly so; rather, they often give partial or misleading information, or just don't bring forth relevant facts.

**2.** The automatic thought "I don't have to get there on time—nobody can tell me what to do" is common to passive-aggressives. Thus, they are inclined to be late for payments, sessions, etc., so clear contracts with detailed consequences are necessary.

**3.** Passive-aggressives are also often late within a much longer perspective—the developmental tasks of life, e.g., establishing a career or getting married or having children. This stems not only from their "You (in this case, society) can't make me do it" attitude but also from an impaired inability to tie responsibilities to time and the fact that responsibility per se is often aversive because it is interpreted as a "society should." This is an area that most therapists usually ignore but one which is critical to any long-term change (Oates, 1987).

**4.** Analogously, there is often passive refusal to accept the disciplines and sacrifices needed to develop either vocational or interpersonal "careers." Attaining the required credentials and "putting in time" in order to attain the payoff of an accrual process is seen as too restricting and demanding. Asking them to sketch past histories of "critical choices," to keep diaries of present choices, and to project desired life goals (followed by means to attain them) may open up this area for discussions and possible changes.

**5.** These clients quickly test a therapist's "unconditional positive regard," as they tend to whine and project blame onto others, or as one colleague put it, "They don't quite have the guts to be truly paranoid."

**6.** The whining behaviors can be addressed by talking to them about the "Help me . . . yes, but" syndrome in which they implicitly ask for help (by whining) then passively refuse intervention.

**7.** Getting them to take responsibility for their life circumstances is difficult. One book that deals effectively with this general issue is *Rapid Relief from Emotional Distress* (actually a somewhat misleading title) by Gary Emery and James Campbell (New York: Rawson Associates). The discussions and exercises therein are very useful for such clients.

In addition to challenging the beliefs embedded in the prior points, the therapist must look at these central beliefs of the passive-aggressive:

(a) I know I can really be self-sufficient, but I apparently do need others, at least now, and I resent that; (b) Any control by others is aversive; (c) Straightforward confrontation or resistance is dangerous and doesn't work; (d) While I apparently have to accept some subjugation of my desires and/or loss of control, they'll pay a price for making me do so; (e) If the conditions were right (and/or I really tried), I would be outstanding; (f) Following rules, expectations, deadlines, etc., makes me less of a whole person; and (g) No one, including me, really deserves to have authority.

## Oppositional-Defiant Disorder (313.81)

The oppositional-defiant disorder is commonly considered to be a precursor to the passive-aggressive disorder. Many of the same behaviors are noted, although there is a more direct expression of hostility and negativism in the oppositional-defiant disorder. The DSM-III-R requires that the pattern last for at least six months and that there be evidence of at least five of the following symptoms: (1) defies adult rules or requests, (2) argues with adults, (3) swears or uses obscene language, (4) deliberately irritates others, (5) projects blame on others, (6) has temper outbursts, (7) is easily irritable, (8) easily angers, or (9) is spiteful or vindictive. DSM-III-R also requires that there be no evidence that the behavior goes so far as to violate or aggress against the rights of another, such as is found in the conduct disorder. It is subcategorized into mild (a few symptoms), moderate, or severe. This behavior is typically carried out toward significant others, such as teachers and parents, and it may persist into various self-destructive social interactions. Such children and adolescents show a degree of conformity and usually resist any interpretation that they are oppositional, just as passive-aggressives do.

### DIAGNOSTIC CONSIDERATIONS

In general, the diagnostic considerations here are analogous to those in the passive-aggressive personality. There are some differences, however, since aggression may be more overtly expressed, rebelliousness is more commonly a factor, and the client is younger. As a result, scales 4 and 6 on the MMPI-2 are more likely to be high. On the 16 PF, scale E would typically be somewhat higher, reflecting stubborn aggressiveness, and G would be quite low, reflecting rebelliousness. Since the oppositional-defiant individual is likely to be more naive socially, N would be lower than in the passive-aggressive personality, and $Q_1$ and $Q_2$ would probably be a bit higher. A more overt anti-establishment attitude is probable, so persons would be more resistant to taking the tests. An MCMI-II profile similar to that of the passive-aggressive is likely, with some elements of scale 6A present, as minor acting-out is more likely to be present here. On the Rorschach, more pure C and fewer Popular responses can be expected than in the passive-aggressive personality disorder. They express both avoidance and negativism on both the Rorschach and TAT (Quevillon et al., 1986).

☐    TREATMENTS OPTIONS

Behavioral interventions are often helpful here (Bellack et al., 1990), and family therapy and/or parent support-group participation may be necessary to strengthen the parent's resolve to stick to a behavioral plan. Overall, treatment is similar in many respects to that for the passive-aggressive personality disorder. Considerations expressed in the section on the paranoid disorders regarding the development of trust are also relevant here. Since the oppositional-defiant disorder is often evidence of a systemic family disorder, family therapy should be considered for that reason as well.

## Sadistic Personality Disorder

As noted in Chapter 1, the term "sadistic personality disorder" does not officially appear in the DSM-III-R, although it is made available in an appendix as an optional diagnosis for clinicians to add when they find it helpful. In any case, the concept has a long history (Kernberg, 1984). He terms the sadistic personality the "malignant narcissistic" and places it between the antisocial and the narcissistic personalities on this continuum. The personality might also be thought of as an antisocial pattern, but with better socialization and a more prominent quality of revenge.

To make this diagnosis, the DSM-III-R requires that a pervasive pattern of cruel, aggressive, and demeaning behavior, starting at least by early childhood, be established by the repeated occurrence of at least four of the following: (1) uses violence or cruelty to establish a dominance relationship, (2) demeans or humiliates people in the presence of others, (3) takes pleasure in physical or psychological suffering of other humans or animals, (4) has, with unusual harshness, disciplined someone under his or her control, (5) has lied with the goal of inflicting pain or harm, (6) uses intimidation, or even terror, to get others to do what he or she wants, (7) restricts the autonomy of someone with whom he or she has a close relationship, or (8) is fascinated by weapons, martial arts, injury, torture, or violence in general.

The dominant trend is a love of cruelty and an absence of remorse (Kernberg, 1984). Extreme cases are described in the literature, including the torture and murder of innocent victims with knives, garroting, or flagellation. The motive for these actions is described as an irresistible urge, the fulfillment of which produces strong satisfaction for the sadist. The sadist is most often male and his behavior is described as being both coercive and yet seductive, frequently promising children amusement, candy, or gifts and attracting women by posing in some fashion, e.g., as a scout for a modeling agency.

There is a noteworthy distinction between sadism, which is a paraphilia and thus appears on axis I of a DSM-III-R diagnosis, and the sadistic personality disorder, which is an axis II diagnosis. While sadistic sexual patterns are common in the sadistic personality disorder, it is not a necessary part of the pattern. In essence, the sadistic personality disorder is marked by a very assertive life style based on power motives, commonly accompanied by gender dominance, the inflicting of pain for pleasure, and extreme aggression with or without sexual motivation. Yet, the sadistic behavior is well rationalized, and the individual may even present a very self-righteous air. Two childhood patterns of behavior are often noted (Kernberg, 1984). One is similar to that of the antisocial personality, that is, inordinate lying, gross disrespect for authority, impulsive anger, temper tantrums, and excessive truancy. The other involves a shy, introverted child who shows few or only subtle early signs of aggression, with sadism later used as a method for covering feelings of inferiority.

☐            ## MMPI-2

The primary elevation in the sadistic personality disoprder is commonly on scale 4, reflecting the aggressive hostility, interpersonal exploitiveness, and lack of respect for social norms found in such individuals. Scale 6 should be at least moderately elevated, reflecting the paranoia mentioned earlier. Scale 3 may also be elevated due to the narcissistic elements of the disorder. Scale 9 is often above average, although not usually as high as in the antisocial personality. The 9-3 or 9-4 profile, which is found in the narcissistic and aggressively competitive person who inflates his or her own self-esteem by the devaluation of others, would apply here. This pattern of sadistic behavior is occasionally found in athletes, who may receive significant reinforcement for such attitudes.

Scale K is commonly higher than F. Low scores should be expected on scales 2, 0, and 7 because these individuals are generally socially adept, if somewhat superficial, and because the sadistic behaviors and attitudes are typically ego-syntonic. In males, scale 5 is usually low, just as this scale is generally low in narcissistic and antisocial individuals. As noted earlier in this book, a punitive or interpersonally destructive person who goes about in the guise of a helpful role often shows elevations on 4 and 8 and could fit this pattern.

☐                    16 PF

Sadistic personalities should score quite high on E, reflecting their aggressive dominance, on N because of their manipulativeness, and on
H because of their usual interpersonal boldness (Golden, 1979). Scales
A and F should also be moderately high, reflecting the extroversion and
level of socialization that would be high, yet usually not so clearly pronounced as in narcissistic individuals. Their lack of respect for social
norms is usually reflected in a low score on G and a high score on $Q_1$.
The lack of remorse and guilt and the inflated self-esteem of such individuals should show up in higher scores on C and $Q_3$ and lower scores
on I, O, and $Q_4$. L should be at least moderately high, reflecting their
lack of trust in the world in general.

☐                    MCMI-II

On the MCMI-II, persons with sadistic personality disorder are most
likely to score high on scale 6B, as well as on 6A antisocial (aggressive),
and on scale 5, narcissistic, because of the similarities they share with
these patterns. A high score on scale P, paranoid, is also likely. Drug
and alcohol abuse are frequent complications of this pattern, so there
should be elevations in scales B and T as well. Low scores should occur
on scales 3, dependent; 7, compulsive (conforming); A, anxiety; and D,
dysthymia. These scales reflect anxiety and a low sense of self-efficacy
and self-esteem, seldom problems for sadistic personalities. Scale H,
hypomania, is elevated in some sadistic individuals, although usually
not to the extent that one would find with antisocial persons.

☐                    OTHER TEST-RESPONSE PATTERNS

Sadistic personalities usually give constricted and guarded responses
to the Rorschach. Like antisocial and narcissistic individuals, F+% can
be expected to be low, but not quite as low as the antisocial because of
often greater sophistication and integration (although a distorted form)
of the personality (Hare, 1986). The number of W responses is indicative
of the grandiose rationalizations and sense of entitlement (Exner, 1986).
M should be low, as it is in the case with the antisocial personality. But,
when it *is* present, it is likely to be active and, quite frequently, aggressive. Animal and Popular responses should be common as well,
reflecting guardedness. An analysis of the content of responses may show
some ostentatious and flamboyant responses, reflecting grandiosity.

  Responses to the TAT are not likely to manifest much overtly aggressive content in more socialized and sophisticated subjects. Since
many sadistic personalities rationalized their behaviors, they are often
quite frank about their violent proclivities. Many statements they make
will be interpreted by others as jokes when they are actually quite

earnest. Some of this ideation may appear in responses to the TAT. Sexually aggressive stories would not be surprising in many of the cards representing male–female interactions, and perhaps in other cards, depending on the sexual orientation of the sadist or the degree to which he reduces others to external objects (Kernberg, 1984). Intimidation through shocking stories would not be surprising in such persons. Sadists are likely to denigrate the task here, as well as in other projective tests. Answers are also likely to be short and constricted, reflecting the more suspicious orientation of some of these individuals, especially if they feel unable to gain a sense of control over the task.

Many of the comments regarding the Rorschach and the TAT apply as well to the production of drawings. The sadistic personality will either try to shock the clinician with an overtly grotesque drawing or will draw overly simple pictures to avoid disclosure of any intrapsychic content. In either case, the sadistic personality is likely to approach the task with contempt. The human figure he identifies with is likely to be complete and to seem powerful and confident, reflecting the feelings of superiority. When he draws others, they are likely to be smaller and less detailed and to have a generally inferior aspect about them. Drawings of trees and houses are also likely to be large, powerful, and indicative of a well-defended self.

## TREATMENT OPTIONS

As with any disorder of personality, and especially with a sadistic personality disorder, the problem is to bring the client into therapy in the first place and then to get him to participate in a meaningful way. In addition, his behavior and threats of violence represent a significant danger to the clinician and others. Direct financial or other exploitation is to be expected. As one clinician facetiously (I think) commented, "This is the type of client you refer to a colleague you never liked."

Kernberg (1984) offers some helpful suggestions: Eliminate the possibilities and potential implements of harm to the client or therapist, establish honesty, confront the inability of the client to depend on the therapist, and confront the client's desire to destroy the therapist because he or she represents an autonomous nurturing person and generates resentment. Any confrontations should be calculated to cause the sadistic personality to project dishonesty and attempts at sadistic control onto the therapist, a process Kernberg calls "paranoid regression in transference." Yet there is an emphasis on maintaining a consistent affirmation of reality. The core belief "Inflicting pain brings me control, and/or sexual arousal, and/or escape from boredom" has to be at least nullified if any success is to be had.

When the syndrome is accompanied by a paraphilia or a disorder of impulse control, behavioral therapies could prove helpful. Risky and/or competitive sports or strenuous physical activity can be useful as socially acceptable outlets for the client's aggressive impulses (Zuckerman et al., 1980). Marital counseling is in order when the individual is involved in a long-term dominance-submission relationship. Overall, a strong emphasis on the concrete consequences of destructive behaviors is important, and although long-term therapy is almost always required, it is not often effective.

# ■ Self-Defeating Personality Disorder

Self-defeating behaviors can be defined as any behavior one employs to achieve a desired consequence or goal that paradoxically inhibits the attainment of that desired goal. Self-defeating behaviors can be observed in all persons to some degree. Such behaviors may be recognized by some persons even though they are continued. In other cases, individuals may be unaware that their actions are self-defeating, similar to "oppositional" children who may long for closeness with their parents but distance themselves through hostile and rebellious behaviors. In all instances, self-defeating behaviors are dysfunctional and bring dissatisfaction and discomfort to the individual. These behaviors are paradoxical in that they are at one and the same time self-perpetuating and self-defeating—thus, the traditional term "neurotic paradox" (Kernberg, 1984). Indeed, the self-defeating personality disorder seems as much akin to some of the more "neurotic" diagnoses as it does to the personality disorder diagnoses. However, it is likely to be listed as a personality disorder, if and when it is officially included in a future DSM.

In order to diagnose a self-defeating personality disorder, the DSM-III-R requires a pervasive pattern of self-defeating behaviors, starting at least by early adulthood, manifested in a variety of contexts and indicated by at least five of the following: (1) chooses situations and/or people, even when better options are evident and available, that lead to disappointment, failure, or mistreatment; (2) rejects or subverts the efforts of others to help him or her; (3) responds with guilt, depression, and/or pain-producing behavior (e.g., accident-proneness) to positive personal events; (4) incites rejecting or anger responses from others, then feels devastated; (5) rejects opportunities for pleasure or has difficulty acknowledging that he or she is enjoying him- or herself; (6) subverts or fails to accomplish tasks critical to personal objectives; (7) engages in excessive self-sacrifice that is unsolicited by the intended recipient; or (8) rejects or is uninterested in people who consistently treat him or her well. It is also required that these behaviors do not occur only when the person is depressed and do not occur exclusively in response to, or anticipation of, some form of abuse.

Unlike the other new, optional diagnoses offered by DSM-III-R—late luteal phase dysphoric disorder and sadistic personality disorder—the self-defeating personality disorder does not as neatly fit into either traditional or consensually agreed-on parameters. Thus, it would be premature to assert, or even speculate about, the test results that might be expected. Treatment approaches will depend on whether the primary component in an individual case is closer to the characterological disorders or to the anxiety disorders.

# CHAPTER 10

# Disorders of Impulse Control

This section in DSM-III-R is primarily a catch-all grouping for those patterns that are not efficiently classified elsewhere. The essential features of a disorder of impulse control are a buildup of tension prior to the act, failure to resist the impulse, an experience of pleasure or release on carrying out the act, and consequent harm to others and/or oneself. Even though there may be some guilt after the act, it is essentially ego-syntonic, and there may be little in the way of conscious resistance to the impulse.

The subcategories in this section of DSM-III-R are pathological gambling, kleptomania, trichotillomania, pyromania, and intermittent-explosive disorder. There is also a residual category: other-impulse disorder. Anorexia nervosa and bulimia nervosa are not disorders of impulse control in the classic sense; however, they will also be discussed here, as they don't fit neatly into any other grouping of disorders.

■ ## Overall Test-Response Patterns

On the MMPI-2, a lack of impulse control is generally reflected in elevations on scales 4, 6, 8, and 9. The MAC score is likely to be elevated. On the 16 PF, high scores are usually obtained on F and $Q_1$ and often on A, whereas low scores on $Q_3$ and G are typical. Performance scale scores are higher than verbal scale scores on the WAIS-R. Within the verbal scale, arithmetic and information are usually two of the lower scores. Response times to the Rorschach are short, and the record may often have a lower than average number of responses. F and F+% are lower than normal, and there is a greater use of color than in most disorders.

Oas (1984) found that certain variables in drawing tasks, particularly the Draw-A-Person and Bender-Gestalt tests, predicted to a general trait of impulsivity. Oas studied samples of adolescents, but the experience of a number of clinicians suggests many of these variables apply equally well to adults. The variables that Oas found to discriminate impulsive from nonimpulsive individuals are as follows: (1) quick completion time, (2) obvious aggressive content, (3) poor overall quality, (4) discontinuity, (5) obvious omissions, and (6) lack of proportion. Nonimpulsivity is indicated by the (1) degree of overall detail, (2) amount of sketching, (3) eye emphasis, (4) mouth detail, (5) amount of shading, and (6) absence of omissions and discontinuities.

## ■ Pathological Gambling (312.31)

The characteristics of this category are a progressive and chronic preoccupation with the need to gamble and a consequent disruption in some area of the individual's world (Jacobs, 1987). Because more states have moved toward legalized gambling, at least in the form of lotteries, thus making it increasingly accessible to people, the number of pathological gamblers continues to rise. Realize that during the 1980s nationwide lottery sales increased fivefold to over 20 billion dollars. Sales are still rising, although at a slower pace. In 1991, *per capita* spending was about $5.00 *per week* in Massachusetts and the District of Columbia, the two highest spending areas. There's a lot of impulse-addiction in those figures.

Compulsive gamblers, like antisocial personalities, are stimulation-seeking, and both specifically show "disinhibition," or the inability to control impulses (Zuckerman et al., 1980). The initial streak of compulsive gambling is usually set off by a first big win.

Many compulsive gamblers report that they only feel alive when they are gambling and may refer to the rest of their lives as boring. They are generally nonconformists and are narcissistic and aggressive (Walker, 1985). A number of compulsive gamblers work only to make enough money to gamble heavily when they get to a spot like Las Vegas. Others have a more normal outward appearance, especially those who gamble in more legitimate outlets like stock and commodities markets.

Most gamblers are extroverted and competitive individuals. They are brighter than average, yet surprisingly they often experienced learning difficulties as they grew up. Many had placed their first bet by the age of fifteen. Other factors that predispose to pathological gambling are an overemphasis in early family life on marital symbols, with little value placed on financial planning and savings; an absent parent before the age of sixteen; and availability in the family of a gambler as a model (Meyer, 1992a; Walker, 1985).

☐         ## DSM-III-R

To diagnose pathological gambling, the DSM-III-R requires that an individual show progressive preoccupation with gambling, which consequently disrupts his or her world in at least four of the following ways: (1) preoccupation with gambling or with obtaining money to gamble, (2) gambling larger and larger amounts, (3) a need to increase both size and frequency of bets, (4) restless need to gamble, (5) repeated loss of money and attempts to win it back, (6) repeated efforts to stop, (7) interference with important social obligations, (8) social or occupational sacrifice to gamble, or (9) gambling despite inability to pay debts.

☐         ## MMPI-2

There are few data on the modal test patterns for this group, although the variables noted above correlate with the personality descriptors associated with the bimodal, moderately elevated 4-9 profile. Another type of pathological gambler shows scores more consistent with major depression. Also, when pathological gamblers are seen by a clinician, however, they have already begun to experience substantial distress and hence are likely to score higher on scale 2. The stimulation-seeking quality is reflected on scale 9 and the MAC scale, and the extroversion characteristic of this pattern is seen in a low scale 0. At the point of referral, they would also probably be agitated and distressed, which in combination with their impulsiveness should result in an elevation on scale 7. A moderate elevation on scale 3 can also be expected since the tendency to reject responsibility for changes and forces in their worlds is reflected here. F or K scale elevations will depend on the situation in which the gamblers are being tested. If for some reason they are defensive about gambling, the K scale would be elevated. On the other hand, there are situations in which being labeled "disturbed" would help them avoid some of the consequences of their behaviors. As a result, a high F scale would occur, which in turn would also elevate a number of the other scales.

☐         ## 16 PF

On the 16 PF, the extroversion, stimulation-seeking, and lack of self-control that characterize this pattern are reflected in high A and H scores and a low $Q_3$ score. $Q_1$ and, to a slightly lesser degree, C and O will be dependent on the characteristics of the testing situation, that is, on whether the subjects have reasons to be defensive or open about the pathological gambling.

They are also likely to be higher on E in particular, as well as on B, F, N, and L. A lower score is obtained on I.

☐     OTHER TEST-RESPONSE PATTERNS

The nonconforming, narcissistic, and aggressive components present in the personality of the pathological gambler are likely to be evidenced by MCMI-II elevations of 75 or higher on 5 and 6A, with low scores on 7. Elevations on A and D are likely when the life style of the pathological gambler begins to create significant problems within the family or with financial status. Alcohol abuse may coincide with this disorder, producing an elevated B.

☐     TREATMENT OPTIONS

Since the disorder of pathological gambling is very likely to surface first in family problems, family or couples therapy is often necessary. Also, many pathological gamblers need to be treated for an underlying depression. In addition, the following phases of intervention, similar to those used in the treatment of other addictions, are useful here (Walker, 1985).

1. Elimination of immediate opportunity to gamble by way of inpatient hospitalization.
2. Immediate initiation of an educational process about pathological gambling and the insidious role it takes in every individual's life.
3. Individual and group psychotherapy to help the individual explore attitudes and beliefs that have supported his or her gambling behavior over a period of years.
4. Economic counseling for living within a set income.
5. Possibly preventive periodic inpatient hospitalization as a preventive measure once every six to eighteen months.
6. Regular attendance at Gambler's Anonymous.
7. Confront the pathological gambler's underlying cognitive distortions such as (a) the credo "If at first you don't succeed, try, try again" applies to my life only when I'm gambling, and it always does there, and (b) "I really deserve a better break from life than I've received," along with their memory distortion of more easily recalling wins than losses. Normals remember each equally well.

Since stimulation-seeking (with concomitant disrupted norepinephrine levels) is often a critical variable in the reinforcement pattern for pathological gambling, the comments regarding fulfilling the need for stimulation-seeking detailed in the section on the antisocial personality disorder are relevant here.

For the over-aroused, the anxious and harried type, the following additional treatment procedures would appear indicated (Jacobs, 1987):

1. Relaxation training—particularly important is the use of this procedure as a self-control device to combat symptoms of nervousness and related discomforts.
2. Various forms of meditation and stretching techniques for achieving relaxing, mind-altering states.
3. The regular use of exercise—particularly helpful in this regard would appear to be walking, jogging, and swimming.
4. The short-term use of tranquilizing medications to help the client through a particularly stressful period, such as dealing with the legal/financial consequences of past excessive gambling. Great care has to be exercised here because of the potential for addiction-dependency.
5. Employing the old truism to "take a vacation" should not be dismissed out of hand. Time away does allow a temporary escape from impending stressors, which in turn short-circuits a buildup of stress to an unbearable level.

Managing a case involving hypo- or under-arousal is more problematic. In general, the strategy is one of helping the client to find some source of stimulation and challenge which does not involve gambling. Some possibilities to consider are

1. Hobbies or sports which would seem to give the gambler the needed amount of excitement. Gamblers, like alcoholics, tend to be deficient in recreational skills, and the counselor may find referral to a university physical education department or a YMCA helpful.
2. A challenging activity like taking a course or undertaking a project such as building a boat.
3. Vocational assessment and guidance should be considered in an effort to help the pathological gambler find a job in which more of his or her needs are met. It's possible that an assembly-line worker would find gambling no longer necessary after switching to work as a private investigator.

Participation in Gamblers Anonymous (213-386-8789; P.O. Box 17173, Los Angeles, CA 90017) is helpful for many such clients. Spouses can get information about the support group Gamanon at P.O. Box 157, Whitestone, NY 11357.

## ■ Kleptomania (312.32)

Most authorities agree that thievery in various forms has been on the rise in our society. For example, statistics annually compiled by the U.S.

Department of Commerce suggest that about 150 million instances of shoplifting occur every year, and that almost 25 percent of business losses are accounted for in this fashion. They suggest that about one in every twelve shoppers is a shoplifter, although no more than one in thirty-five shoplifters is ever apprehended.

Certainly, many people steal simply because it seems so easy to get something free, for a lark, or to be one of their crowd (Meyer, 1992a). However, a small proportion of these individuals show actual kleptomania. They are distinguished from typical thieves in that kleptomaniacs seldom have any real need for the objects they steal and may even throw them away. They usually prefer to steal while alone, and there is a quality of "irresistible impulse" in their behaviors.

Kleptomania often begins in childhood, primarily through stealing small items or sums of money from parents or friends. Stealing, as a means of being accepted into an adolescent peer group is another common feature in the backgrounds of kleptomanicas. There is usually evidence of depressive features (McElroy et al., 1991), reflecting an inability to control the behavior, as well as some problems in interpersonal relationships. For example, many older women who show a kleptomaniac pattern are widowed or emotionally neglected by their husbands; the behavior gives them a thrill, sometimes sexually tinged, although they often pay for it with remorse. In fact, many show a clear sense of relief when apprehended. Some kleptomaniacs are not significantly disturbed psychologically in areas other than this lack of specific behavioral control. Yet, the condition is often chronic and is commonly associated with significant depression, anxiety, and/or eating disorder problems (McElroy et al., 1991).

☐ DSM-III-R

The DSM-III-R offers the following diagnostic criteria for this pattern: an irresistible impulse accompanied by rising tension before the act; the actual stealing behavior accompanied by a sense of release or even pleasure, sexual arousal, or euphoria; no apparent need for the item or important monetary profit; and no need to commit the act to express anger or vengeance. There is usually a lack of planning and little involvement with others in the pattern.

☐ DIAGNOSTIC CONSIDERATIONS

Consistent with the comment that some kleptomaniacs are not often significantly disturbed psychologically, their MMPI-2 and 16 PF protocols are also usually unremarkable. If persons are being seen in the criminal justice system rather than the mental health system, they are likely to show a higher K score on the MMPI-2 and, to the degree they are unsophisticated, a higher L score. If they are being seen in the mental health system or if they are viewing psychopathology as a means to avoid criminal sanctions, F will be higher. However, since many are significantly depressed, scale 2 is typically raised, reflecting the situationally generated depression, as well as an ongoing underlying depressive component. In that regard, scale 7 is also likely to be raised. Scale 9 is average or low, and scale 0 is usually a bit elevated, reflecting their propensity for being alone with their conflicts.

Similarly, on the 16 PF they tend to show elevations on scales C, $Q_4$, and O and are usually not high on scale A. Scale $Q_3$ will vary depending on whether it directly reflects their inability to control impulses, which would result in a low score, or they are counterphobically trying to control their impulses, which would raise $Q_3$.

## ☐ TREATMENT OPTIONS

Since schizoid behaviors and/or depression are common precursors to kleptomaniac behavior, treatment approaches for those patterns are often important here. Thymoleptic medication is often useful (McElroy et al., 1991). For the specific behaviors of kleptomania, the aversive therapies are often used (Bellak et al., 1990). Kellam (1969) employed a particularly ingenious aversive procedure to control shoplifting in a chronic kleptomaniac. Kellam required this person to simulate his entire shoplifting sequence, which was filmed. As the film was played back, the client was asked to participate with internal imagery in what was going on, and a painful shock was administered at crucial points. Such a technique could be amplified by having a person take a portable shock unit and self-administer shock whenever the impulse arose. If the shock unit is clumsy, the person could be instructed to hold his or her breath until discomfort ensues, since this acts as an aversive cue.

The alternative aversive technique is to have such clients go into a store and when their impulses become so severe that they feel they will not be able to resist, they are to take an expensive and fragile object and drop it on the floor. Embarrassment, the need for a coping response with store employees, and the need for restitution all act to create a very aversive moment.

Other clinicians have treated kleptomania by systematic desensitization, hypothesizing that the behavior will subside if one can decrease the tension in the sequence of anxiety arousal-completion-release. As anxiety then lessens, better coping behaviors for dealing with anxiety are developed. Cognitive behavioral techniques and/or existential approaches that deal with the loss of interests and meaning evident in some kleptomaniacs, particularly older females, may also be necessary.

## ■ Pyromania (312.33)

As with thievery, deliberate fire-setting behavior appears to have increased substantially in modern society. Of course, most cases of arson are not really indicative of pyromania. It is now estimated that as much as 80 percent of business property fires are caused by arson. In these cases, the perpetrator is far more likely to be an antisocial personality who is doing it for hire—a "paid torch." Cases of arson in which there is no clear reward for the individual who started the fire could indicate pyromania, but mental retardation should also be considered.

Pyromaniacs, like kleptomaniacs, experience a buildup of tension prior to the behavior and a release of tension after performing the fire-setting. The behavior is often first seen in childhood or adolescence, and it is seldom the only antisocial behavior displayed. Hyperactivity, problems in school, poor peer relationships, and stealing are commonly associated behaviors. It has been found that fire-setting in childhood, when combined with enuresis and/or cruelty to animals, is predictive of assaultive crimes in adulthood, although these crimes may not include fire-setting (Meyer, 1992a).

Pyromania is much more common in males than in females and is often found in an individual who has had trouble in making transitions through developmental stages. There are analogous data showing that peaks in the incidence rate of arson occur around the ages of seventeen, twenty-six, forty, and sixty in males. If there is a problem with alcohol, pyromaniacs show patterns of alcohol abuse rather than addiction, and they often show an inordinate interest in fire-fighting paraphernalia. Pyromaniacs may be indifferent to a fire's destruction or stimulated by it.

□     DSM-III-R

Similar to kleptomania, the DSM-III-R requires evidence of at least one deliberate fire-setting, with a buildup of an irresistible impulse before the setting of the fire, continuing inability to resist the impulse, and a release of tension after setting the fire. There should also be an indication that neither profit nor some sociopolitical belief system is the basic motive for the fire-setting.

□     DIAGNOSTIC CONSIDERATIONS

Also like kleptomania, there is not much consensual clinical literature nor are there hard data to indicate the patterns one can expect here. However, on the average, pyromaniacs are more disturbed than kleptomaniacs. They are likely to score high on scales 4 and 8 of the MMPI-2, but not usually at a psychotic level. They will probably also score higher on scales 6 and 9, and to the degree the impulses are denied, scale 3 is elevated. The F and the 4 scores are elevated to the degree there is an antiauthority component. Moodiness, a sense of alienation from others, and inability to control impulses are also reflected in any elevations on scales 8, 0, and 6.

On the 16 PF, pyromaniacs show more evidence of disorder than kleptomaniacs. Pyromaniacs will likely be low on scales C, G, and $Q_3$ and higher on scales L and $Q_4$. They are also likely to show some elevation on scales E and H, reflecting their destructive and controlling orientations toward the environment. Analogously, this latter component as well as the distancing from others may raise scale $Q_1$ and lower scale A. Scale B on the average is low, reflecting their usual less-than-average intelligence.

Pyromaniacs may show labile and impulsive affect responses, as indicated by a number of uncontrolled reactions to the color cards of the Rorschach. In fact, it is suggested that when children with borderline psychosis provide "blood," "fire," or other similarly destructive associations to the Rorschach color areas, potential dangerousness in general, and possible fire-setting behavior in particular, should be suspected (Armentrout and Hauer, 1978). MCMI-II elevations of 75 or higher on scales 5 and especially 6A are probable. Hypomania (elevated N) is more likely to be present in this disorder, although—as with anxiety—it may vacillate, depending on whether testing is done before or after pyromanic activity occurs.

☐    ## TREATMENT OPTIONS

The significant disturbance, often characterological in nature, that usually accompanies pyromania suggests that a wide variety of treatment options may have to be considered, depending on the trend of the overall pathology (Kernberg, 1984). Since these individuals are often adolescents or young adults, family therapy is especially warranted (Brown, 1991), and since schizoid patterns are typical, the reader is referred to that section of this book. A low level of serotonin is occasionally noted, so chemotherapy may be of help.

Two specific behavioral techniques are appropriate for the fire-setting behaviors. Overcorrection requires the individual to make a new, positive response in the area of specific disorder. For example, public confession and a restitution of damages through working for the individual who is offended would be one application for pyromania. Negative practice has also been used, wherein the pyromaniac is required to perform a behavior *ad nauseam* until it takes on aversive qualities. For example, the client is required to strike thousands of matches in a row, over several sessions. These techniques would be embedded in an overall treatment program.

■    # Trichotillomania (312.39)

The term "trichotillomania" was first introduced into the clinical literature in 1889 by Hallopean (Krishnan et al., 1985). However, it was not until the DSM-III-R that it was designated as a DSM diagnostic category. Trichotillomania is defined as recurrent irresistible impulses to pull one's own hair. It is more common in females and usually first starts in childhood or early adolescence, although it can occasionally erupt in a mature adult.

This behavior can persist for many years, often recurs after spontaneous remission, and is marked by efforts at concealment (Christenson et al., 1991). Bald spots (alopecia) often appear, in some cases leading to total baldness, so wigs are frequently used.

☐     DSM-III-R

To warrant a diagnosis of trichotillomania, the DSM-III-R requires that there be noticeable hair loss resulting from the recurrent inability to resist impulses to pull out one's hair. There is an increasing tension experienced before giving in to the impulse to pull out the hair, with a sense of relief experienced afterward. The diagnosis is not made when this is a secondary response to a hallucination or delusion or to a pre-existing skin disorder.

☐     DIAGNOSTIC CONSIDERATIONS

Since the literature suggests that there is a connection between trichotillomania and obsessive-compulsive disorders, and in some cases is a mask for depression (Krishnan et al., 1985), a 2-7/7-2 profile or a 7-8/8-7 profile with some elevation on 2 is to be expected on the MMPI-2. In those cases with a strong hypochondriacal element, scales 1 and 3 should be effected, and to the degree denial and secretiveness are involved, K and 6 should be elevated.

On the MCMI-II, the commonly reported dependency-family conflict (Krishnan et al., 1985) should generate a high scale 3, with the compulsive components raising scale 7. In those clients that are closer to the borderline personality disorder, scale C should be high. On the 16 PF, scales C and $Q_3$ should be low, and the dependency issues should generate low scores on $Q_2$, L, and E. Similar parallels to obsessive-compulsive, depressive, and dependency-oriented profiles should be noted on the Rorschach and TAT.

☐     TREATMENT OPTIONS

For child and adolescent trichotillomaniacs, a central focus for the therapist will be the dependency issue within a standard psychotherapy format, as well as efforts at response prevention (Christenson et al., 1991). Chemotherapy (especially clomipramine) can be useful, not only to quell secondary itching and skin problems, but—in older children and adults—to deal with obsessive-compulsive and depressive components.

Hypnosis and certain behavioral techniques (e.g., thought stopping and aversion therapy) have proven useful as well.

■           ## Intermittent-Explosive Disorder (312.34)

The distinguishing feature of the explosive disorder is a sudden eruption of aggressive impulses and the loss of control of these impulses in an individual who normally inhibits or does not experience them (Goldstein and Keller, 1987). Regret and guilt are common, and the behavior is disproportionate to any environmental stressors. Because occasionally both prodromal physiological or mood symptoms and consequent partial amnesia for the behavior are reported, the pattern was traditionally referred to as "epileptoid." A concomitant clear diagnosis of organic epilepsy is not common. However, in a number of these cases, there are some nonspecific EEG abnormalities or minor neurological signs. The presence of such signs is not so rare, even in a sample of apparently normal individuals, but clear evidence for a physiological contribution should be thoroughly considered.

□           ### DSM-III-R

The DSM-III-R diagnosis for intermittent-explosive disorder requires (1) several discrete episodes of loss of control, as in property destruction or assaultive acts, (2) that the aggressiveness is clearly out of proportion to any precipitating event, and (3) that there be no signs of generalized impulsiveness between the episodes or that the episodes do not occur in conjunction with a diagnosis of any psychotic disorder. The disorder appears most commonly in late adolescence or early adulthood.

□           ### MMPI-2

As noted in the section on aggression potential, persons who are continually assaultive and without guilt tend to score high on scales F, 4, and 9, with secondary elevation on 8 or 6. However, although the continuity factor does not fit with the descriptors of the intermittent-explosive disorder, Fowler (1981) notes that high 4 and 6 scores can be expected here. The degree of guilt and rumination over this behavior is reflected in the elevation on scale 7.

The 4-3 profile, as described by Davis and Sines (1971), would be more likely to call for the explosive disorder diagnosis. In this profile, there is a peak on 4, a secondary peak on 3, and little significant elevation elsewhere. This profile, mainly seen in males, is particularly characteristic of individuals who maintain a quiet ongoing adjustment but are likely to demonstrate occasional hostile-aggressive outbursts.

Such behavior may or may not warrant the diagnosis of intermittent-explosive disorder, depending on the characteristics described above. This profile is applicable to females and occurs quite generally.

To the degree that both 4 and 3 are highly elevated, the likelihood of aggressive episodes increases. In general, when scale 3 is greater than 4, the potential for control and inhibition of the aggression is increased, whereas to the degree that 4 is greater than 3, control dissipates.

Lachar (1974) suggests that the rare 3-9 code is indicative of persons who are emotionally labile and show recurrent hostility and irritability. Since they naturally suppress the hostility in clinical assessment, they could be diagnosed as an explosive disorder. However, it is more likely that they are a passive-aggressive personality disorder, a histrionic personality disorder, or both.

There is a derived scale on the MMPI-2, termed the Over-Controlled Hostility Scale (Megargee et al., 1967), composed of thirty-one MMPI-2 items. Although a few studies have not been positive, a number of them have supported the validity of this scale in predicting persons who show outbursts of aggression (Greene, 1991). Hence, they could easily fit the DSM-III-R diagnosis of explosive personality. The scale has been an accurate predictor in incarcerated adult populations, but it has sometimes been weak in the normal population. Nevertheless, it is one of the most well-researched scales and is worthy of consideration.

□      ## 16 PF

Since these individuals generally show regret over their behaviors and see them as ego-alien to a degree, a low score on G is not likely, as it would be in most cases of aggressive behavior. Also, C is not usually low nor are $Q_4$ and N high, as would be common in the psychopath. $Q_3$ is usually high, reflecting the attempts at control that are characteristic of this person, and $Q_1$ is usually moderately low. In spite of their passivity, they do not score markedly low on E or H, but neither are they very high. Scores are average or lower on M and N, reflecting the general denial of the aggression and the lack of introspection about motives and conflicts.

□      ## OTHER TEST-RESPONSE PATTERNS

There is some evidence that quiet but potentially explosive persons attain lower picture arrangement scores on the WAIS-R than do more extroverted and consistently aggressive types. Comprehension and similarities subtests are usually relatively lower here. Rorschach patterns are quite constricted, and there is less abstraction content. M responses are not that uncommon, and when they do occur, they tend to be more passive. Responses with content like "blood" or "explosions" or responses indicating inner tension and turmoil occur in a number of explosive disorders. Responses with a color component tend to have poorer form than otherwise expected. Minor neuropsychological signs on a variety of tests are often associated with this disorder, and it is a reasonable axiom that there is some impaired brain functioning, although seldom any gross brain damage.

☐         TREATMENT OPTIONS

It is critical in treating this disorder to get the clients in touch with their ongoing anger responses, usually suppressed, and at the same time to teach them more effective ways either to abort the anger or to deal with it productively (Storr, 1990). Awareness techniques, such as those found in Gestalt therapy, can put them in touch with the anger that is typically not evident in their usual functioning. Group therapy can provide the feedback essential to breaking down their defenses against seeing themselves as having chronic anger (Ellis, 1992). The keeping of a diary or the writing of (undelivered) letters to significant others who may be a factor in generating the anger (Kirman, 1980) also aids clients to get in better touch with their anger.

Once this is accomplished, the therapist could attempt to use the development of a controlled relaxation response to abort the anger. Similarly, biofeedback training to develop an overall relaxation response could be useful to mute or abort the anger. Assertiveness training or analogous procedures could then be used to structure more-effective ways to cope with the ongoing frustration and anger. Lithium treatment has been found effective with that subgroup of persons with intermittent-explosive disorders who show evidence of a latent or cyclical manic component. Clients in this category also occasionally respond well to ethosuximide, and those with a CNS lesion causing the rage have been helped by propranolol (Yudofsky et al., 1981).

## Anorexia Nervosa (307.10) and Bulimia Nervosa (307.51)

Anorexia nervosa is not a classic impulse disorder wherein the impulse overcomes the individual. Rather, there is an overcontrol of the impulse to eat. There is also occasional accompanying binge-eating (bulimia), so it is included in the impulse disorder section.

The essential features of anorexia nervosa, according to DSM-III-R, are an intense concern about becoming overweight and a persistent feeling of being fat, even when weight loss has begun or has even been substantial. This is combined with a refusal to regain or continue body weight at 15 percent of the minimally appropriate level, considering age and height; evidence of a weight loss of at least 15 percent from the original weight; and, in females, absence of three consecutive menstrual cycles when otherwise expected to occur.

This apparently voluntary self-starvation is seen primarily in middle and upper socioeconomic classes of women (Bruch et al., 1988; Agras, 1987). It typically occurs first during puberty as a young woman becomes more conscious of her self-image. Sexuality may be channeled into the eating area, as these women usually avoid sexual acting-out. After the "sin" of eating, they may resort to self-induced vomiting and laxatives to "cleanse" the body of food. Although anorexia nervosa is rare in males, when it does occur, there are systematic differences from female anorectics. Males are less likely to use laxatives, are often less conscientious about school, are less likely to have had large appetites premorbidly, are more likely to have had enjoyable sexual experiences, and are less likely to die from the condition.

Anorectics who also show episodes of bulimia (binge-eating), in general are more disturbed than anorectics who do not (Bruch et al., 1988). Approximately 1 in every 250 females between the ages of twelve and eighteen develops this disorder, and follow-up studies estimate mortality rates at between 5 and 15 percent.

The parents of the anorectic are typically very controlling, yet caring, individuals. As a result, the anorectic appears to use the disorder as a statement of independence from the family in the narrow area that she can control. The salient personality characteristics are excessive dependency and sensitivity, introversion, perfectionism, and a subtle but persistent selfishness and stubbornness (Bruch et al., 1988).

The converse pattern is bulimia nervosa, a chronic pattern of binge-eating. Bulimia (from the Greek words for ox and hunger) is known as the gorge-purge syndrome. The essential features, according to DSM-III-R, are recurrent binge-eating, a sense of lack of control, a minimum of two binge episodes a week for at least three months, and persistent overconcern about body shape and weight. It is associated with attempts to control weight by diets or vomiting and also by eating high-calorie foods in an inconspicuous manner.

Blouin, Blouin, Aubin, Carter et al. (1992) found significant seasonal variations in bulimia. They found a high correlation of binge behaviors, but not purging behaviors or severity of depression, with number and occurrence of dark hours within the month, and an overall much higher rate of binging and purging in the winter months.

Although anorectics are typically shy, they are passively controlling and stubborn. Those bulimorectics who are also anorectic are more likely to be extroverted perfectionists who attempt to control their peers in direct ways (Agras, 1987). Many bulimorectics weigh in at normal levels, while others are obese; anorectics are almost always cadaverously thin. Both groups come from families in which food is a focus, as in socialization or recognition. Anorectics will often cook exotic meals for others, although they may eat only a small portion themselves. Bulimorectics do not usually like to cook because they are afraid they will eat all the food before the guests show up.

There is increasing support for a diagnostic category such as "binge-eating," which refers to the compulsive overeater who does not engage in such self-destructive behaviors as purging (Wilson and Walsh, 1991). Many of the treatment recommendations at the end of this section will apply to them as well.

☐                    DIAGNOSTIC CONSIDERATIONS

Where the anorectic pattern is similar to other adolescent patterns that emphasize rebelliousness, distress, and family discord, a 2-4-8 MMPI-2 pattern can be expected. In the more classic anorectic patterns, the combined dependency and perfectionism of the anorectic are likely to elevate scale 7, while the general psychopathology should elevate scales 6 and 8 (Small et al., 1981). The subtle selfishness, self-centeredness, and stubbornness should elevate scales 1 and 3 somewhat. The interpersonal avoidance and sensitivity would tend to elevate scale 0. At the same time, all of the patterns are influenced by the denial of pathology, so scales L and K tend to be elevated while F is depressed, although less so to the degree she is an adolescent rather than an adult. The anorectic who also shows episodes of bulimia is more likely to score higher on scales 2, 3, 4, 6, and 7 than the anorectic who does not also manifest bulimia, and scale 7 is most often elevated in bulimorectics (Kirkley and Janick, 1987).

Bulimorectics are more likely to be extroverted and should therefore show a low 0 scale, as well as a higher scale 8, reflecting the sense of loss of control. Since they are more overtly self-disclosing, all scales should be more highly elevated, on the average, particularly scales 2 and 4.

On the 16 PF, the anorectic tends to score low on scales A, F, H, and $Q_1$ and moderately low on M, while the bulimorectic tends to score high on these scales, particularly A, H, M, and $Q_1$. The anorectic is higher on $Q_3$ and $Q_2$; the bulimorectic tends to be in the middle on these scales. The anorectic also scores quite high on G, whereas the bulimorectic scores toward the middle. Surprisingly, the anorectic is toward the middle on scales I and L, reflecting the subtle stubbornness and selfishness that are not apparent in initial interactions (Yager et al., 1991). Both usually score quite high on scale B, reflecting their tendency to be in the upper range in intelligence and socioeconomic status. Both also tend to be reasonably high on O.

Personality patterns most likely to develop anorexia or bulimia nervosa include those patterns represented by MCMI-II elevations on scales 3, 7, 8A, 1, E, and C. Passive-aggressive controlling tendencies are evidenced by elevation on 8A, while high scores on 3 indicate shyness and dependency and high scores on 7 point to compulsivity and perfectionism. Elevated scores ond 1 and E are more likely in the anorexic than in the bulimic.

Higher intelligence and socioeconomic status predict overall high scores on the WAIS-R, with verbal scores usually being a bit higher than performance scores. The perfectionism and compulsivity evident in anorectics, combined with their conservative and production orientation to school situations, usually result in elevations of information and vocabulary scores. Their stubborn perfectionism usually slows them down somewhat on the digit-symbol, block-design, and object assembly tests, yet they seldom make the errors of impulse that are more often noted in the bulimorectic.

There has been little in the way of research on Rorschach patterning in anorexia nervosa (Wagner and Wagner, 1978), although there are some detected commonalities. Reflecting the perfectionism and denial of pathology, the total number of responses is low, there is a low proportion of movement (M) to detail (D) responses (reflecting an individual who is making economical use of constricted or limited resources), and response latencies are slow. There is a high F and F+%, with closely integrated color responses and subtle sexual and anatomical responses occasionally included. Not surprisingly, responses that focus on food are common. Wagner and Wagner (1978) conclude that in most other respects they resemble the conversion disorder.

The bulimorectic is believed by this author to have a higher number of responses and a more adequate W:M ratio, although content that focuses on food is similarly present. If W:M is high, then they are striving beyond their resources. There is much greater use of integrated color, although the F+% is lower, and overall there is less use of form.

The Bulimia Test (BULIT) (Smith and Thelan, 1984) is a thirty-two-item, self-report multiple-choice scale that has been found to be a reasonably valid and reliable predictor of bulimia in a nonclinical population. A revised version with improved items and validity is available (Thelan et al., 1991). The Eating Attitudes Test is an effective measure of general attitudes toward eating (Koslowsky, Scheinberg, Bleich, Mark et al., 1992).

☐     TREATMENT OPTIONS

In all cases, a complete physical is recommended (Yager et al., 1991), including thyroid and other glandular tests to rule out such primary physical causes as Simmonds' disease. General goals include weight restoration, treatment of physical complications, and "a change in the relentless pursuit of thinness." Since anorexia nervosa often results in a very severe—even life-threatening—weight loss, hospitalization combined with forced and/or intravenous feeding may be necessary. Nutritional counseling may be helpful, but one has to be careful to avoid moving back into the anorectic's favorite battleground—food. Noradrenergic-blocking medications, such as chlorpromazine, are effective with those anorectics who have high anxiety, peripheral vasospasms, and little appetite. Those who seem to show early satiety, rather than little appetite, may respond to low dosages of dopamine blockers. At this stage, a behavior modification program to develop feeding behaviors may be helpful, although the critical issue is in deriving the reinforcements that can build up the feeding behavior (Agras, 1987).

A more psychodynamic approach has been found to be useful as a person moves into more-normal functioning, with a focus on the ambivalence over dependency, the high need for perfectionism, and, as trust develops, the subtle selfishness and narcissism that emerge. Family therapy is also likely to be necessary since so much of this pattern is related to the interactions over dependency and control in the family.

The bulimorectic can respond to many of the same therapy techniques noted for the anorectic (Freeman, 1991; Agras, 1987). Those with an electrolyte imbalance from intense vomiting will need medical intervention, e.g., for a depletion of potassium. Antidepressants may be indicated in some cases of bulimia (Blouin, 1992). In addition, group therapy and/or a support group may be helpful (Ettin, 1982). This provides both a sense of control and a source of feedback. Adolescent group therapy can be useful for anorectics, too, but only after they have made substantial improvements through other techniques. The bulimorectic may also need counseling regarding diet facts and simple control of eating behaviors, counseling of the type used with the more common problems of binge-eating without purging, general obesity, and persistent-eating disorders (Ruderman, 1986), such as the following. These facts could be presented via a handout and supplemented by an oral amplification that is modified to the specific eating disorder involved.

1. There is a biological drive toward high-fat and very sweet foods, so control should be directed toward "what" as much as "when" and "how much."

2. Weight loss is not hard to attain; keeping it off is.

3. It is more difficult to lose weight during the second diet than the first.

4. For women, food cravings often increase in the days before their menstrual periods, so they are more vulnerable to lapses during those times.

5. Most diets are broken in the late afternoon.

6. Persons trying to lose weight must keep fluid intakes high. The body needs a LOT more water and other fluids when undergoing weight loss.

7. If activity level remains the same and there is a cessation of smoking, there will be a weight gain.

8. Changing exercise amounts and patterns is usually more effective in generating weight loss than changing diet amounts and patterns.

Also, it is highly recommended that any person with an eating disorder implement and monitor, via a diary, a day-to-day program based on general diet tips such as the following:

1. Eat a high carbohydrate breakfast and avoid eating anything at least two hours before going to bed.

2. Eat a salad or have a cup of soup before a meal, then delay eating any main meal for an extra five minutes.

3. Slow down while you eat, chew longer, and savor flavors.

4. Don't eat standing up, in front of the television, while talking on the phone, in the car, or on the run. Try not to eat alone.

5. Try to eat two or three main meals, and two small snacks every day, at predetermined times so that you develop a feasible routine.

6. Avoid drinks with alcohol or sugar.

7. Be creative. For example, visualize yourself eating slowly before you even sit down for dinner.

8. Use thought control. About to binge? Yell, "STOP," although, admittedly, this may not be practical in a public place.

9. Avoid keeping food, other than planned food, in the house.

10. Brush your teeth after every meal; you'll be less likely to snack.

11. Identify times when you are prone to binge or overeat and plan alternative activities that are not compatible with eating.

12. Avoid weighing yourself unless it is specifically prescribed. Don't look for weight loss when you are learning normal eating patterns.

13. Develop an exercise program that is effective and that you can comfortably integrate into your life. Make a decision to walk rather than drive whenever possible.

14. If you find yourself thinking too much about food or body image, this may be because you have a conflict you haven't dealt with and/or you are anxious or depressed. Try to identify what's going on and take some positive, coping measures.

15. Drink six to eight glasses of water each day, at least.

16. Plan ahead as to how you will handle "tough" situations like being in a supermarket, at a party, etc. Drink a lot of water and a high fiber snack one-half to one hour before you go.

17. Set aside some time each day to reflect on how you are doing in this area and in life in general. Decide what you are doing well, affirm yourself for that, and visualize how you can improve in areas where you are not doing as well.

18. Recruit help from family and friends and any other source of help that has meaning or usefulness to you. Be open about your decision

to lose weight, ask them to help you, and then spell out how they can help.

As noted, a diary is part of an effective therapeutic regimen for persons with virtually any type of eating disorder. In addition, the daily report form in Figure 10.1 (adapted from Freeman, 1991) (specific to bulimia nervosa, but which can be easily modified to be useful with any eating disorder) is useful as part of the diary and is an efficient reporting device to give you a better feel for what is happening with your client.

**TABLE 10.1**    Daily Report Form for Eating Disorder Clients

NAME . . . . . . . . . . . . . .

Your next appointment is on:

at:

Please call          extension
if you cannot keep your
appointment

Please record daily everything
that you eat and drink, the
number of binges that you have,
and the number of times that
you vomit and the number
of laxatives you take.

NUMBER OF BINGES _____
PLEASE BRACKET ALL BINGES

| Date | Day | | |
|---|---|---|---|
| | Vomit | Lax | Other |
| Breakfast | | | |
| | | | |
| Lunch | | | |
| | | | |
| Evening meal | | | |
| | | | |
| Totals | | | |

Comments:

The desire to not eat today has been:

|———————————————|
Not                    As strong as it
there                  possibly could be
at all

Today's urge to overeat has been:

|———————————————|
Not                    As strong as it
there                  possibly could be
at all

Today in general I have felt:

|———————————————|
Not                    Extremely
emotionally            emotionally
upset at all           upset

# Central Nervous System Impairment, Attention-Deficit Hyperactivity Disorder, and Retardation

■ ## Central Nervous System Impairment

Clinicians often face the issue of whether or not there may be central nervous system impairment (CNSI) in a client (Orsini et al., 1988; Gass, 1991b; Margolin, 1992). Earlier in this book, I used the traditional and less accurate terms "organic dysfunction" and "organic brain damage" because they are so commonly used by clinicians; throughout this chapter, I'll simply refer to it as CNSI. The intricacies of a broad, thorough CNSI evaluation will not be discussed here because this would require more material than is appropriate for this book. If there is reason to think there is CNSI and there is a request or need for a more certain and/or localized diagnosis, it is important to have a full evaluation carried out by a clinical neuropsychologist and/or a neurologist with specific, supervised speciality training, who, preferably, is board certified.

The types and the range of information needed for a full neuropsychological assessment are embedded in the model report format in Chapter 16. It is evident from that format that a good history is always critical. Sudden onset of symptoms, whatever their nature, should alert the clinician to possible CNSI. Changes in functioning of any sort are important data, so information from family and friends is helpful.

Close observation of speech quality and problems, dress, grooming, gait and coordination while walking to and from the office, and affect can all provide clinical signs to help the clinician. For example, the number of hesitations of two seconds or longer in an ordinary sentence is a useful cue in picking up on the possibility of Alzheimer's disease. Whereas normals seldom make more than one such hesitation every thirty seconds, persons with Alzheimer's will make about four in a thirty-second period. Any signs of asymmetry should particularly be noted. For example, one client with visual-field deficits neatly shaved one side of his face, but only roughly and sloppily shaved the other side. Obtaining some subject-as-own-control data is also useful, such as grip strength, finger-tapping tasks, or having the person touch various body parts with either hand with the eyes closed. Deficits may be especially meaningful if a short-form measure of IQ, such as the Shipley Institute of Living Scale (Jacobsen and Tomkin, 1988), indicates average-or-better general intelligence. In addition to these specific performance tasks, there are also normative or test data, the focus of this section. Test-retest data— say, at six-month intervals—can also be useful.

Dementia, the central feature of many organic brain dysfunctions, may sometimes be confused with dementia masquerading as depression (referred to as pseudodementia). The following, adapted from C. Wells and G. Duncan (1977) *Neurology for Psychiatrists,* Philadelphia: FA Davis, presents clinical features that help to differentiate the two:

| DEMENTIA | PSEUDODEMENTIA |
|---|---|
| 1. More disruption of recent memory | 1. Long- and short-term memory equally disrupted |
| 2. Memory gaps for specific events is unusual | 2. Memory gaps occur for specific periods and events |
| 3. Symptoms are of long duration | 3. Symptoms are of short duration |
| 4. Infrequent complaints of cognitive loss | 4. Frequent complaints of cognitive loss |
| 5. Complaints of cognitive dysfunction usually imprecise | 5. Complaints of cognitive dysfunction usually detailed |
| 6. Clients often appear unconcerned | 6. Clients usually communicate distress |
| 7. Attention and concentration usually faulty | 7. Attention and concentration often well preserved |
| 8. "Near miss" answers frequent | 8. "Don't know" answers typical |
| 9. Clients conceal disability | 9. Clients emphasize disability |
| 10. Clients struggle to perform tasks | 10. Clients make little effort to perform even simple tasks |

| | |
|---|---|
| 11. Clients delight in accomplishments, however trivial | 11. Clients highlight failures |
| 12. Clients rely on notes, calendars, etc., to keep up | 12. Clients do not try to keep up |
| 13. Consistently poor performance on tasks of similar difficulty | 13. Significant variability in performing tasks of similar difficulty |
| 14. Affect labile and shallow | 14. Affective change often pervasive |
| 15. Clients often retain social skills | 15. Loss of social skills, often early and prominent |
| 16. On tests of orientation, clients mistake unusual for usual | 16. On tests of orientation, clients often give "don't know" answers |
| 17. Behavior usually compatible with severity of cognitive dysfunction | 17. Behavior often incongruent with severity of cognitive dysfunction |
| 18. Nocturnal accentuation of dysfunction common | 18. Nocturnal accentuation of dysfunction uncommon |
| 19. History of previous psychiatric dysfunction uncommon | 19. History of previous psychiatric dysfunction common |

If the clinician is to carry out a substantial neuropsychological assessment, extensive methods of obtaining normative data, such as the Halstead-Reitan, Luria-Nebraska, or Smith-Michigan batteries, are appropriate here. It is worth noting that for many years the Halstead-Reitan battery which includes a WAIS-R or WISC-R and requires four to five hours test time, was seen as the "benchmark" battery by clinicians. In recent years, however, much more diversity has emerged. Such batteries are prognostic as well as diagnostic and can be extremely useful in other applications, such as evaluating the effects of drug trials. A good intermediate-level screening battery for CNSI might include a WAIS-R (or a validated short form such as the Satz-Mogel), MMPI-2, specific tests for lateralization (such as grip strength), the Purdue Pegboard and/or tapping tests, tests for sensory response, and at least some of the other tests that help cover the required variety of modalities and functional domains (e.g., Reitan Aphasia Screening Test, Word Finding Test, Indented-Paragraph Reading Test, Benton Visual-Retention Test, Wechsler Memory Test, Trail-Making Test Part B, Boston Naming Test, Rey Auditory Verbal Learning Test, Symbol Digit Modalities Test) (Margolin, 1992; Orsini et al., 1988).

The Trail-Making Test Part B is one of the most sensitive indicators of CNSI in the Halstead-Reitan Battery. For young to middle-age adults, a time of 0–26 seconds is considered normal, 27–39 seconds is in the mild range, 88–120 seconds is moderate, and over 120 seconds is in the severe range. On Trails B, age is a factor in performance. Respective borderline deficit and critical deficit performance in seconds, for the following ages, are: age 40 (+95, +125); 40–49 (+100, +150); 50–59 (+135, +175); 60–69 (+170, +280); and 70+ (+250, +375), although an important confounding variable is IQ and responsiveness to the test situation (see Table 11.1). The Indented-Paragraph Reading Test (Caplan, 1987), a test with an uneven left border, has proven effective in helping pinpoint right-hemisphere damage.

A major issue of concern has to do with how emotional ("functional") status affects performance on these tests. To the degree that psychiatric problems impede performance on these tests, they may lose their value as "indicators" of CNSI. The WAIS-R is more problematic in this respect than many other neuropsychological tests, even when controlled for education. For example, two of the most sensitive tests to organicity on the WAIS-R—arithmetic and digit symbol—are also commonly affected by psychiatric disturbance. On the other hand, Trails B and many of the Halstead-Reitan tests tend to be fairly resilient to the affects of emotional disturbance (Gass, 1991a). Also, pattern analysis is important in diagnosing CNSI using neuropsychological tests, since it is common for psychiatric patients to have a few scores within the impaired range in a battery of tests. In fact, experts often accept the guideline that even normals are "allowed" to "blow" one test.

The CNSI literature often discusses the value of fixed versus flexible batteries. In many ways, this is a false issue because one can simply use one of the fixed batteries, e.g., the Halstead-Reitan, and then supplement it with whatever other specific tests are viewed as helpful in a particular case. In clinical situations, it is certainly arguable that an individualized battery might be optimal, as it is more directly tailored to the referral question, and should be more flexible and cost-efficient. However, one minor advantage of the fixed battery, i.e., norms for the battery as a whole, is not available for a flexible battery, and this cost has to be factored into the decision. In forensic situations, some clinicians may feel the defensibility and protection of fixed-battery norms may tip the scales in this decision.

More importantly, any diagnostician must be aware of the common signs of CNSI in the standard tests and in behavior, particularly in the event that no one has yet asserted the possibility of CNSI. For example, the interaction of type of symptoms with rapid-versus-gradual onset can distinguish between cerebral impairment and such psychopathology as the affective disorders. When a syndrome with a gradual onset of a wide range of affective symptomatology is accompanied by neurological and cognitive deficits, along with aphasia and agnosia and/or a loss of sphincter control, irreversible CNSI is probable, although reversible conditions such as normal-pressure hydrocephalus could cause this. If the

affective symptomatology is unaccompanied by the latter symptomatology and the depression and/or mania are severe and possibly
accompanied by persistent delusions, an affective or bipolar disorder is
more probable, although CNSI later in life can produce such symptoms.

If instead, there is a rapid onset of symptoms focusing on confusion,
agitation, attention problems, and disrupted sleep patterns, along with
problems in self-care (including impaired sphincter control), and a focus
primarily on visual hallucinations, there is a high probability of acute
CNSI, such as delirium. If death does not occur, recovery is often
reasonably rapid. But if symptoms do not include such evident self-care
problems and instead include delusions or auditory hallucinations, then
an affective or schizoaffective disorder is probable.

The discrimination between right- and left-cerebral-hemisphere impairment has fascinated clinicians for a long time. As an overall rule,
specific deficits in spatial orientation and perceptual and/or organiza-
tional functions point to right-hemisphere disorder, whereas specific
problems in language, motor, and executive functions suggest left-
hemisphere or frontal impairment. Right-hemisphere impairment is
more likely to be manifest in a disruption of emotion-laden knowledge
and a disruption of the nuances of speech.

Difficulties in right-left spatial-orientation problems have traditionally been seen as suggestive of disorder in the right hemisphere. But
language is a critical factor in such discriminations, and so attention
to the quality of a client's difficulty may lead to a hypothesis that there
is left-hemisphere disorder instead.

Benton (1980) has commented on the ability to make facial recogni-
tions as a diagnostic sign. His data, as well as those of others, suggest
that specific facial agnosia, that is, the loss of ability to recognize familiar
friends and family, is a good indicator of a bilateral lesion that has
damaged a small number of cells in the lower rear portion of both sides
of the brain. Damage to only one side appears to result in only partial
prosopagnosia: The patient is able to identify familiar faces in photos,
but not in real life, and makes "close mistakes" in identification. Consistent problems in facial discrimination, such as in identifying new ac-
quaintances, usually indicate right-hemisphere impairment, and again,
if the lesion turns out to be even more localized, it is probably posterior
rather than anterior.

A clinician might consider including a test like the Reitan Aphasia
Screening Test, a shortened version of Halstead and Wepman's Aphasia
Screening Test (Reitan and Wolfson, 1986), in a routine test battery.
It takes only about ten minutes to administer and is a rough assessment of spatial and verbal factors, as well as aphasia. It is a good gross
screening measure for significant cerebral impairment, as normals
seldom make errors and perform effortlessly. It is very important to elicit
the best possible performance the person can honestly give, to the point
of allowing extra trials, and never immediately accept "I don't know"

responses. If a client then makes even two or three errors, it is worthwhile to take a deeper look for more signs of cerebral impairment. An excellent item on the Reitan Aphasia Screening Test is the request for the client to produce a Maltese cross. Clinicians could add some version of the Maltese cross in conjunction with a few other figures, perhaps similar to cards A and 7 of the Bender-Gestalt, to the routine self-administered battery in Appendix A. Some specific measure of memory is also useful.

The clinician can also include a finger-tapping test, using a simple event counter. The general assumption is that performance will be about 10 percent better with the dominant hand (thus the opposite hemisphere), so any substantial deviation from this pattern can be suggestive of disorder in one hemisphere. A test of grip strength is also advised. In these tests, a result wherein the left hand is 20 percent or more deficient in comparison with the right hand in right-handed clients or the left hand is no better than the right in a left-handed client is suggestive of right-cerebral damage. If performance on these tests has the reverse results, this is suggestive of left-cerebral damage. With syndromes in which dementia is suspected, especially in older individuals, the Boston Naming Test is useful, as language-naming deficits are often an early sign. Van Gorp et al. (1986) provide normative data on this test for individuals over 59 years of age. When testing older individuals, the data on normal, healthy older adults, provided in Table 11.1, should be of help.

## MMPI-2

There is no modal MMPI-2 profile for CNSI, and for good reason: There is no modal CNSI pattern of deficit, and the following needs to be read in light of that caution. In this area, the dominant axiom should be that individual differences are determinative (Gass and Russell, 1986, 1991). Yet there are a number of patterns that should alert the clinician to pursue a consideration of possible CNSI. An obvious first sign is not a code type but an examination of how the person completed the form. For example, persons with visual-field deficits may neglect portions of the answer form, thus invalidating the profile. Extremely erratic profiles will show up in the validity scale elevations; confusion or dementia may be casual, although the reader should also consult the section on malingering for relevant information.

An alternate approach is to identify the most common (approximately 25% of patients) and discriminating MMPI-2 items in samples with specific CNSI patterns such as closed head injury and stroke (Gass, 1991b, 1992). In closed head injury, the affected scales are scale 8 (10 items), scale 7 (6 items), and scales 1, 2, and 3 (5 items each). The pattern is fairly different with stroke and probably with other focal lesions (e.g., hematoma, tumor, infection, etc.) as well. In Gass's sample, the

**TABLE 11.1**  Normative Data on Neuropsychological Tests for 156 Healthy, Well-Educated ($\bar{X} = 14$–$15$ Years), Elderly People

| | VERBAL IQ | PERFOR- MANCE IQ | WMS* LOGIC PROSE IMMED. | WMS VISUAL REPROD. | WMS LOGIC PROSE DELAY (45 MIN.) | VISUAL REPROD. DELAY (45 MIN.) | TRAILS A | TRAILS B | BOSTON NAMING TEST |
|---|---|---|---|---|---|---|---|---|---|
| **58–85 (N = 156)** Mean | 117.650 | 110.617 | 8.925 | 7.633 | 6.233 | 4.733 | 48.700 | 107.550 | 54.017 |
| STD DEV | 13.527 | 13.493 | 2.752 | 3.498 | 2.733 | 3.741 | 14.468 | 45.631 | 5.391 |
| **58–65 (N = 28)** Mean | 117.200 | 109.200 | 9.750 | 9.600 | 7.800 | 6.600 | 41.500 | 84.400 | 55.500 |
| STD DEV | 11.331 | 11.555 | 2.395 | 2.757 | 2.163 | 2.459 | 7.832 | 24.600 | 4.528 |
| **66–70 (N = 45)** Mean | 114.800 | 111.467 | 8.467 | 8.667 | 5.733 | 6.333 | 43.200 | 105.200 | 55.467 |
| STD DEV | 17.034 | 16.831 | 2.649 | 3.811 | 2.235 | 3.830 | 14.982 | 43.432 | 3.944 |
| **71–75 (N = 156)** Mean | 122.875 | 115.083 | 9.271 | 7.792 | 6.313 | 4.375 | 50.083 | 97.791 | 53.875 |
| STD DEV | 11.380 | 11.938 | 3.148 | 2.992 | 3.158 | 3.932 | 12.884 | 30.404 | 5.728 |
| **76–85 (N = 26)** Mean | 110.545 | 101.000 | 8.045 | 4.091 | 5.318 | 1.636 | 59.727 | 153.090 | 51.000 |
| STD DEV | 11.246 | 8.775 | 2.185 | 2.256 | 2.483 | 1.690 | 15.950 | 62.603 | 6.356 |

*Wechsler Memory Scale
Table adapted from data provided by Wilfred Van Gorp., Ph.D., of the West Los Angeles VA Medical Center.

affected scales are scale 3 (13 items), scale 1 (12 items), scales 2 and 8 (7 items each), scale 9 (4 items), and scale 7 (3 items). As a result, in stroke the "conversion V" is a common artifact arising out of bona fide physical symptoms of stroke. For that reason, a correction factor can be helpful in analyzing the MMPI-2 where a specific CNSI diagnosis is at issue (Gass, 1991b).

A number of individuals with a left-hemisphere dysfunction (especially to the degree that this is the dominant hemisphere) will show a "catastrophic response" pattern on the MMPI-2 (although numerous individuals with a right-frontal trauma also show the same pattern); those with right-hemisphere dysfunction are more likely to appear "indifferent" or depressed. Lachar (1974) notes that the relatively rare 1-9/9-1 code, with a low scale 2, is found in a number of persons with acute CNSI. This most commonly occurs where there is a dawning awareness in clients that they have suffered a loss of function and where they are dealing with it in a counterphobic manner. As they lose the will to fight in response to the loss and depression emerges, a 2-9/9-2 code is relatively common. When their personality functions begin to fall apart, accompanied by activity levels raised against their phobia, the 9-8/8-9 profile may occur (Gynther et al., 1973a). While scale 8 is often the highest scale in epileptic patients, scales 1, 2, and 3 are more likely to be elevated in clients with multiple sclerosis. Scale 8 is also often elevated as aphasic clients begin to withdraw.

Persons with CNSI from a toxic substance are likely to show a generally elevated MMPI-2 profile with a particularly high score on scale 8 and scores on most other scales (excluding the 5 scale) at about 70 T. Scales that tend to be higher in this profile are 1 and 2. When CNSI occurs as a result of senility or a neurological degenerative process, elevations are more likely on scales 2 and 8, both around the 70 T mark. The senile group tends to have a slightly higher elevation overall in the other scores, with scale 1 being particularly higher than in the neurological degenerative group (Pennington et al., 1979).

According to Lachar (1974), the chronic CNSI patients are more likely to have scores elevated above 65 T on scales 8, 6, 4, and 2. Scales 1 and 3 are usually lower, except with those who have multiple sclerosis and similar disorders. In one sample of neurological clients, scales 1, 2, and then 4 were the highest (Dahlstrom et al., 1986). Watson et al. (1978) find that the scale-1:scale-7 ratio is much higher for CNSI clients than for other groups with psychopathology. Also, the F scale is high, particularly if damage is severe. In chronic CNSI, the 9 scale is often a barometer of the person's reaction to it; a lower 9 score indicates either acceptance or a lack of reaction to it, while a high 9 suggests an attempt to cope, although poorly at times. When scales 8 and 6 are very high and there are other solid indications of CNSI, the CNSI disorder is possibly accompanied by schizophrenia.

When dealing with possible CNSI cases, particularly in the aged, the

MMPI-2 may have to be administered over several sessions because of fatigue and/or attention problems, or it may only be possible to use a short form.

☐                          16 PF

Because of the variety of reactions subsumed under the term "central nervous system impairment," a modal 16 PF profile for CNSI is not available. However, persons with CNSI are generally high on scales O and $Q_4$, reflecting their sense of insecurity and anxiety. Those individuals who have moved into depression would probably not score so high. $Q_3$ is low, reflecting the degree of personality disintegration, and scale B is lowered, indicating the correlated loss of intellectual functioning. Moderately low scores on $Q_2$, F, and H are also standard. The scores on scale E vary markedly, depending on the reaction to the awareness of loss. If persons have become depressed and submissive to a hospital environment, E is low, whereas if they are attempting counterphobic mechanisms, it is elevated. G tends to vary markedly as well, but usually is at least moderately high.

☐                          OTHER TEST-RESPONSE PATTERNS

Before looking at possible cues from specific WAIS-R subtests, several overall perspectives that can aid the clinician in this type of assessment must be stated.

**1.** On the WAIS-R, the general rule has been that low verbal scales relative to performance scales indicate left-hemisphere lesions (if it has been determined that the left hemisphere is the dominant one), and with a lesser degree of applicability, low performance scores relative to verbal scores indicate a right hemisphere lesion, especially to the degree that this discrepancy is determined by low scores on picture arrangement and block design. Unfortunately, these discrepancies are not always clear-cut or perfectly correlated. Indeed, a number of normals show a significant VIQ–PIQ split, and patients with acute right-hemisphere damage and diffuse bilateral degenerative conditions (e.g., Alzheimers) show a low VIQ to PIQ ratio. Chronic hemisphere lesions often fail to show any pattern unless they are large enough and strategically located. Nevertheless, these are good first rules of thumb. Left-hemisphere damage may produce a very low profile, and such clients may be difficult to differentiate from those with mental retardation. Persons with right-hemisphere damage do better on comprehension, similarities, and vocabulary than on other verbal tests, and better on picture completion within the performance tests. Those clients with relatively acute but diffuse CNSI do somewhat better on verbal tests than performance tests, particularly on vocabulary and information, but they also do well on picture completion in the performance tests. They do particularly poorly on digit symbol, as do most CNSI groups, as well as on arithmetic, and usually on block design.

Overall, it is reasonable to assert that a low-performance/high-verbal pattern is more suggestive of overall CNSI than is the high-performance/low-verbal pattern. Also, it is worthwhile to remember that traumatic head injuries clearly to one side produce patterns more similar to diffuse CNSI than one would find in unilateral CNSI produced by processes other than acute trauma.

**2.** In general, marked verbal–performance splits are likely to indicate intracerebral tumors or cerebrovascular accidents. Clients with cerebrovascular accidents are then more likely to show disrupted differential performance on grip strength and tapping tests than do clients with tumors.

**3.** In verbal subtests that require a high level of verbal precision and identification (the vocabulary scale), expressive-speech problems are suggested by hesitating and circuitous speech – the patient cannot find the precise word.

**4.** The picture completion subtest can also be helpful in assessing the difficulties in expressive speech. It is important that the clinician create very specific demands. If the clinician's style is to accept approximate answers easily, or pointing rather than naming, for example, the client is not adequately pressed to make the precise designation.

**5.** The similarities subtest and the proverbs on the comprehension subtest test general intellectual and abstracting abilities, and thus identify more diffuse cerebral impairment or at least cerebral trauma that leads to a wide range of impairment.

**6.** The overall range between lowest and highest WAIS-R subscales is a good indicator of general impairment. When the range between scale scores is greater than five in persons without another handicap (such as lack of education), the clinician should consider the possibility of CNSI.

**7.** The highest WAIS-R subscale scores provide a reasonably good index of premorbid intellectual functioning in cases of cerebral impairment, but only when they are scales that correlate reasonably well with the full-scale WAIS-R, as in the vocabulary subtest. When digit span is the highest postmorbid scale, it would not be an especially efficient predictor.

**8.** Within-subtest scatter (consistently missing easy items while answering hard ones accurately) is an important indicator of the ability to maintain set. Clients with certain cerebral impairments find it hard to keep the program in mind and to process the data at the same time. For example, they may keep in mind the general problem on the arithmetic subtest but forget the exact numbers in the process – or the reverse.

Digit symbol is commonly low in all brain-injured persons. Arithmetic is almost as consistently low, especially in those with left-hemisphere injuries. In combination with digit span, arithmetic is an excellent measure of the degree of transient anxiety and depression, although the CNSI can affect digit span as much as or more than depression can. Information may be low in persons who are suffering early CNSI in the left hemisphere, but it remains reasonably high in most CNSI cases, as do comprehension and similarities. Picture arrangement most often reflects right-hemisphere disorder (often the right anterior temporal lobe—the frontal lobe is also a strong possibility as well), as do object assembly and block design. The diagnostician may see unusual placements in block design and object assembly, placements that the client finds difficult to explain. Picture completion and similarities are rarely affected, except in chronic CNSI. Most schizophrenics do better on information than on similarities; this can be one cue to distinguish between them.

Block design also helps in the discrimination between CNSI and schizophrenia. It usually remains relatively high in schizophrenia, whereas it is virtually always affected to some degree in CNSI. It is consistently low in diffuse brain injuries and in injuries involving the right temporal and parietal lobes. In another important discrimination, object assembly is often one of the higher scores in mentally retarded persons, whereas both CNSI and schizophrenics, as well as depressives, are prone to do poorly (Golden, 1979).

Fuld (1984) has provided further validation data of a marker of dementia of the Alzheimer type that was occasionally noted earlier in the literature. This WAIS-R–subtest profile marker, indicating the probable presence of this dementia, is defined by the following formula:

$$A > B > C < D, A > D$$

in which $A$ is the mean of the information and vocabulary subtest scores, $B$ is the mean of the similarities and digit-span scores, $C$ is the mean of the digit-symbol and block-design scores, and $D$ is the object assembly score. All subtest scores are age-corrected. This marker was positive in approximately 50 percent of actual Alzheimer-dementia cases, but in only 11 percent of non-Alzheimer-dementia cases, in two separate studies (Fuld, 1984). A further validation by Paul Satz and his colleagues (Satz, 1987) found the marker gives an equally effective discrimination between Alzheimer-dementia cases and the normal elderly.

On the Wide-Range Achievement Test-Revised (WRAT-R), disorders in reading ability should cue the clinician toward the possibility of temporal-occipital left-hemisphere disturbance or long-standing learning disability in the presence of average or above average IQ. A significant loss of spelling ability should suggest the possibility of parietal and/or occipital dysfunction (Cantwell and Baker, 1987).

The classic signs of CNSI on the Bender-Gestalt are perplexity, impotency, distortions, perseveration, significant rotation of designs, and peculiar sequencing. Impotency, or statements indicating dissatisfaction with one's performance, is common throughout all the tests when such a client runs into difficulty. Also common is the element of perplexity, wherein a person overtly indicates confusion and uncertainty about handling the task given.

On the Benton Visual-Retention Test, signs similar to that on the Bender-Gestalt are evidence of CNSI. More specifically, Golden (1979) states that persons with CNSI are most likely to make three types of errors here: the omission of a peripheral figure, rotation, or size error (a loss of the size relationship between the major and peripheral figures). It is important to note that even though rotations do occur in normals, they are more likely to be stabilizing errors: when a figure that is presented as at an angle is then rotated so that it sits flat. Alexias or aphasias may be involved if the client has difficulty recognizing previously learned configurations (e.g., circle or square) (Bender, 1938).

As with the other drawing tests, distortions, perplexity, impotency, and perservation in response to the Draw-A-Person Test are classic signs of cerebral impairment. The clinician might find it useful to have clients routinely write their name as well as a novel sentence (e.g., "The shed is next to the house") on the same page with the person they have drawn. In general, clients with left-hemisphere impairment can often do the overlearned task—that is, write their names—reasonably well. But at the same time, they have marked difficulties with the novel sentences. Also, as a general rule, if the drawing is adequate but the writing is bad, the left hemisphere may be impaired, whereas if the drawing is poor and the writing is acceptable, the localization, if any, may be in the right hemisphere. Differences in the general style of drawings between those with right-hemisphere CNSI and left-hemisphere CNSI are reflected in the following contrasts:

| RIGHT-HEMISPHERE CNSI | LEFT-HEMISPHERE CNSI |
|---|---|
| Loss of adequate gestalt relationships | Sequential relationship is impaired |
| Scattered and fragmented individual responses | Simple and coherent individual responses |
| Loss of adequate spatial relationships | Spatial relationships are adequately retained |
| Corrective lines are added | Gross lack of detail |
| Drawings are made energetically, almost driven | Drawings are made slowly and laboriously, haltingly at times |
| Orientation to the general task is faulty or lost | Orientation to the general-task structure is reasonably accurate |

It is important to look for perseveration in the drawing tests, as well as in a wide range of performance areas. One cerebrally impaired client kept doing an infinite division problem almost to a point of exhaustion, at which time he simply said, "There's too much of this."

On the Rorschach, perplexity, repetition, and impotency are also common, which is not surprising in light of the ambiguity of the stimuli. There is often a delayed reaction time to the cards, and persons may turn the cards in a confused manner, indicating an attempt to cope with a task in which they lack confidence (Exner, 1986).

Overall, there are a low number of responses, with the average time per response quite high, and a deterioration of the response quality as clients proceed through the cards. Constriction, being bound to stimuli (e.g., "This is where some ink has been splashed"), fragmented responses, and a high need for more structure are common. Positional responses are more common than normal. Occasional perseveration of content occurs, sometimes even to the point where there is a repetition of automatic phrases. In particular, there may be a perseveration of CF responses in the last three cards. "Color naming" and crude CF and C responses are given, in contrast to a low number of M responses and a low F+%. Vague W responses, with good form Dd responses, may be found. Responses about anatomy content and those in which humans or animals are mutilated reflect the client's concerns about his own deterioration.

Bellak (1993) points to the following consistent features found in the TAT stories of persons with CNSI (some of these apply equally well to other tests, such as the Rorschach):

1. Use of fewer ideas and words
2. Longer response times, often with punctuating pauses
3. Concrete, simple descriptions; occasionally a listing of items in the picture
4. Trite stories with little action
5. Confusions and misinterpretations
6. Proportionately fewer common themes
7. Perseveration of themes; repetition of words and phrases
8. Difficulties in providing adequate responses (especially to more complex or vague cards) or in changing adequate responses
9. Expressions of self-doubt
10. Missing the most salient objects in a card, e.g., the violin in card 1 of the TAT
11. Stereotypical stories from TV or popular stories
12. Inability to focus on one central character throughout

13. Problems in developing any parallel plot or bringing the story to a reasonable conclusion

14. Lack of coordinated plot or action sequences

15. Themes of problems in learning, dependency on others in everyday behaviors, being isolated from peer situations, or of impulsive unplanned actions

Before moving on to the next section, take note of several "uniformity myths" that have unfortunately been pervasive in the traditions of CNSI assessment.

### UNIFORMITY MYTHS

The term "brain damage" is an accurate description of the effects of central nervous system impairment.

Individual differences do not significantly affect the manifestation, course, or outcome of CNS impairments.

Lesions of CNS tissues constitute a homogeneous class of phenomena.

Brain injuries are relatively static events and are comparatively insensitive to the effects of time.

The clinician's role in neuropsychological investigations is confined primarily to diagnostic activities.

The rehabilitation of CNSI must be concerned with building on remaining strengths rather than rebuilding deficits (or vice versa).

## ■ Attention-Deficit Hyperactivity Disorder

Attention-deficit disorder (ADD) refers to a condition that involves the persisting inability to keep one's attention focused. Children and adolescents with attention-deficit disorder are presumed to possess adequate basic cognitive capabilities, but these capacities are periodically disrupted and they are typically unable to focus themselves effectively enough to get things done (DuPaul et al., 1991). DSM-III-R recognizes two forms of ADD: with or without hyperactivity. The latter is termed Undifferentiated Attention-Deficit Disorder (314.00). Attention-Deficit Hyperactivity Disorder (ADHD) (314.01) involves behavioral manifestations of attentional problems, including persistent symptoms of restlessness, fidgeting, and constant activity. ADHD occurs at an incidence rate of about 6 to 8 percent with about a 5:1 ratio of males to females and an even higher ratio for the more active and aggressive forms (Silver, 1992; Gillberg and Gillberg, 1988; Robe, 1987).

DSM-III-R requires disturbances of at least six months, with onset before age seven, during which at least eight of the following are observed: (1) fidgets or squirms, (2) has difficulty in remaining seated, (3) is easily distracted, (4) has difficulty awaiting one's turn, (5) blurts out responses, (6) has difficulty completing tasks, (7) has difficulty sustaining attention, (8) often shifts to other activities, (9) seldom plays quietly, (10) interrupts or intrudes, (11) talks excessively, (12) does not pay attention, (13) often loses things essential to tasks, or (14) takes risks or seeks thrills.

Current recognition of ADHD in the DSM-III-R reflects the belief of physicians, teachers, and psychologists over the years that persisting problems in regulating both attentional processes and motor behavior comprise a distinct syndrome frequently seen in clinical settings. Originally, terms such as "hyperactivity," "hyperkinesis," and "minimal brain dysfunction" were used to characterize the condition, which was believed to involve various forms of mild central nervous system impairment. So strong was the association between excessive activity and underlying brain impairment that the corresponding diagnostic terms were used interchangeably for years. In practice, the nature of this deficit was seldom specified, owing to the wide range of disorders and conditions that may have hyperactivity as an associated symptom. This caused endless confusion among professionals and considerable anxiety on the part of parents whose children were labeled as having "minimal brain damage" or the "hyperkinetic syndrome."

Recent research, however, strongly suggests that neither attentional problems nor hyperactivity should *necessarily* be assumed to involve CNS damage (Silver, 1992). Because of these findings, the popularity of the term "hyperactive" has declined. Its inclusion in the DSM-III-R as an auxiliary condition used only in conjunction with ADHD is consistent with its diminished status from a distinct diagnostic entity. Current research has amply documented the fact that genetic, physiological dysfunction, nutritional, motivational, social, and environmental factors all may play important roles in the regulation and allocation of attentional capabilities.

☐ ## INDIVIDUAL HISTORY VARIABLES OFTEN NOTED IN HYPERACTIVE CHILDREN

Family history of hyperactivity or learning disability

Mother's trauma or illness during pregnancy

Mother's substance abuse

Oxygen disruption during delivery

Poor coordination

Difficulties with speech, writing, reading, spelling

Conduct problems in general, especially if little evidence of guilt or remorse

Preference for very bland or overly spiced foods

Disturbed by loud noises

Mirror writing

Letter reversals

Visual disturbances

Severe headaches

Fainting

Impulsivity

Aversive to peers and/or caretakers

Problems or trauma during delivery

Perceived from early on as "overactive"

Slow development

High fevers

Head banging, knee–elbow rocking

Hyperkinesis

Reduced attention

Tendency toward food "addictions" and/or allergies

Transfixed by high-action TV or movies

Behavior problems in school

Left-handedness

Easily distracted

Disturbed by bright lights

Migraines

Convulsions

Epilepsy

EEG abnormality, or if "normal" some nonspecific abnormalities

☐ DIAGNOSTIC CONSIDERATIONS

In many ADHD cases, a neuropsychological evaluation (see preceding section) and/or an evaluation for possible retardation (see upcoming section) are indicated. In any case, a thorough assessment for ADHD includes an evaluation of the following factors: (1) the client's overall behavioral repertoire and patterns of interactions with the environment, (2) patterns of motor activity, and (3) how the person typically approaches and works through tasks. Evaluations should include a multimethod assessment that includes structured and unstructured interviews with parents and the adolescent, direct observation in the natural setting, self-report measures, completion of behavior rating scales by parents and teachers, intelligence and achievement tests, and specific assessments such as the Continuous Performance Test (CPT), the Child Behavior Checklist (CBCL), the Connors Parent-Rating Scale-Revised (CPRS-R), etc. (DuPaul et al., 1991). By the time an evaluation has been completed, a person with ADHD may well have been assessed by pediatricians, teachers, psychologists, and parents. Each of these individuals has relevant information to the overall decision.

☐ TYPES OF HYPERACTIVITY

Of course, some cases will not fit neatly into any category, but a helpful conceptualization is that there are four major types of hyperactivity (Gillberg and Gillberg, 1988; Robe, 1987; Silver, 1992). The least common is environmentally generated hyperactivity, about 5 to 10 percent of all hyperactive children. This type may even be labeled "pseudohyperactivity," as it has no significant biologic component, unlike the three other forms of hyperactivity.

The two major causes of environmentally generated hyperactivity are a severe stress, such as loss of a parent or child abuse, and the child who has been spoiled in such a way that he or she has never learned to deal with limits on activity. Not surprisingly, the parents of the latter type of hyperactive child do not see the behavior as nearly the problem that teachers and day-care workers do.

A common characteristic of such children is an absence of hyperactivity before the trauma or hyperactive behavior only in certain situations, e.g., where limits are not clear or are not enforced. Treatment for such children includes anxiety reduction techniques if stress is involved and school consultations and family therapy to teach the teachers and parents how to more effectively set limits.

A second pattern is stimulant- or food-incuded hyperactivity. Some people have argued that certain foods or food additives cause the great majority of hyperactive cases. It soon became apparent to most experts that this was erroneous, but many experts do agree that these factors are the major cause in about 10 to 15 percent of hyperactive cases. Such children often manifested food allergies as early as infancy and may show standard allergy patterns.

Such children also show more unpredictable outbursts of hyperactivity than do the other forms of hyperactivity, although they are especially likely to increase their hyperactivity after certain meals. Commonly suspected culprits here are foods high in simple sugars, foods high in additives and preservatives, chocolate, and milk, egg, or wheat products. It's important to note that the range of foods that could be the cause of such behavior is wider than originally imagined.

Naturally, the focus of treatment is to eliminate those foods that generate the hyperactivity. However, this should only be done after an exhaustive survey of food intake and related behaviors. For example, for a minimum of two weeks, and often longer, parents should keep a log of all foods the child eats, including the lists of ingredients. An hourly behavior chart is also kept. These are very time-consuming tasks, but if they are not diligently carried out, the problem substance will escape discovery. All of this should be done in consultation with the child's pediatrician.

If the hyperactivity is food-generated, certain consistent patterns should become clear. Those foods can then be systematically eliminated, and the hyperactivity should diminish. If the hyperactivity does not lessen, one of the more common hyperactivity patterns should be considered—overstimulated (overactive) hyperactivity, about 30 percent of all cases of hyperactivity, or understimulated (underactive) hyperactivity, which accounts for approximately half of all cases of hyperactivity.

In spite of the opposite labels, children in both of these patterns show high levels of activity and distractibility. Also, unlike environmentally generated hyperactivity, both patterns start becoming evident even in early childhood. The following chart highlights the characteristics and differences between these two major hyperactive patterns.

## OVERACTIVE (OVERSTIMULATED) HYPERACTIVITY (30%)

Child carries a high level of neurophysiological arousal, so is highly "stimulation-respondent."

Responds reasonably well to "quiet time" or stimulus reduction methods; responds to standard "time-out" wherein stimuli are highly restricted.

Becomes somewhat calmer as evening progresses; will usually fall asleep easily enough, but is a restless sleeper, and hard to awaken.

Likes TV, but can be easily overstimulated by it. Often has to do other things while watching TV.

Is overstimulated and has difficulty "coming down" from periods of physical activity.

Is finicky eater. Doesn't like green vegetables or strong-flavored foods, like broccoli, curry, etc. Favorite foods are bland, like macaroni and cheese, meat, potatoes; often will use cheese or sauces to mask flavors.

Often shows hyperactive response in new situations or to changes in routine. The more consistent, structured, and calm the home and school environment, the better the child behaves.

## UNDERACTIVE (UNDERSTIMULATED) HYPERACTIVITY (50%)

Child carries a low level of neurophysiological arousal, relative to psychological needs, so is highly "stimulation-seeking."

Has difficulty calming down at "quiet time"; needs some structured activity even during "time-out" or will quickly be disruptive or destructive; liable to be excessively spanked, as they show little response to it.

Has difficulty going to bed and to sleep—"the tireder they get, the worse they are"—but usually sleeps soundly. Often awakens early and is ready to go right away.

Likes TV, especially highly stimulating programs, but can sit for hours in front of such programs, as if hypnotized.

Can be calmed by long periods of intense physical activity.

Usually enjoys a number of strong-flavored foods; will quickly overseason and over-sugar foods. Loves colorful, oversweetened, novelty breakfast cereals. (These children are the perfect target for the Saturday morning cartoon advertisement.)

Often is well behaved in new situations, but gets progressively worse as newness wears off (so clinicians may need to schedule several sessions in order to see the problem behavior emerge). Constantly seeks more-stimulating environments.

☐          OTHER TEST-RESPONSE PATTERNS

For a young adult who is still diagnosable as ADHD, elevations on the MMPI-2 scales 4, 6, 8, and 9 are probable. The expectations for those in the population that would come to clinical detection would be that about half would fit in the category of conduct disorder. If there is a lack of reported violent behaviors, expect a 4-9/9-4 profile. A 2-4/4-2 profile would also be a possibility. The high 9 should be especially prominent in those patients who are still experiencing an active episode.

Scale 4 often covaries with the degree of resentment over constraints on overactivity, and this score also indicates how the person will react to later constraints and rules. As 2 rises, indicating a whining, dissatisfied component over constraints, a lack of activity/emotion outlets is more likely.

On the 16 PF (or more likely the HSPQ, since this type of referral question is more likely to occur in adolescents), low scores on $Q_3$ and B are most probable, with high scores on O, L, and M also being likely. On the MCMI-II, scale N is most likely to be high, with V high to the degree the attention span is actually limited. To the degree an antisocial component has developed, scale 6 would be high.

On both the Rorschach and TAT, ADHD clients are likely to show the general affects of impulsivity and distraction (see Chapter 10). They may end out with long response times, show a confused sequential analysis of the blot or picture, and tend to stay with Popular responses or stories. Boundary/containment response issues are common. Parts may be missed: For example, Bellak (1993) noted that the failure to even identify the violin in TAT card 1 has been observed in numerous ADHD cases. On the Rorschach, a higher number of Animal responses and delayed responses to the color cards are expected.

In performance drawings, the ADHD adolescent is likely to attempt them in a brusque and rapid manner (Oster and Gould, 1987). Where there is an associated spatial dyslexia, drawings of a face tend to be "neolithic," (there is no separation of the nose from the forehead and no suggestion of a nose bridge). To the degree he is also emotionally disturbed, he is likely to show a confused order of drawings, overly large drawings, and boxed figures (Rossini and Kaspar, 1987). Watching him attempt the drawings may be at least as instructive as what the drawings actually produce. He may be distracted easily and may make this apparent by glancing around the room, investigating distracting objects, fidgeting, or drawing objects that are different from those requested. Because ADHD tends to result in a lower school performance, related concerns may lead such individuals to draw figures that reflect strong feelings of inadequacy and guilt, and they sometimes describe their drawings as stupid or crazy.

☐ TREATMENT OPTIONS

Therapy of some sort is critical for these cases as the long-term effects of hyperactivity on both academic and social adjustment are negative. Hyperactivity is, of course, a precursor to academic failure, but it can also be a precursor to a wide variety of other patterns, such as schizophrenia and criminality (Gillberg and Gillberg, 1988). Both family therapy and parent-training techniques are necessary for most cases (Dangel and Polster, 1986). Part of the family therapy should be directed toward helping parents and siblings reduce the stress, guilt, and wear-and-tear these children generate in their families. The parents of such a child are apt to heartily agree with the following classic quip: "Life begins when the children leave home and the dog dies."

Chemotherapy with methylphenidate (Ritalin) and related substances (e.g., Cylert) is a common approach (Silver, 1992). Clonidine, an alpha-adrenergic stimulating agent whose action consists of inhibiting noradrenergic activity, has been increasing in popularity. All of these medications have significant side effects, including inhibition of growth in height and weight, if used for any significant length of time. Yet, they do lead to improvement in many ADHD children and adolescents, which leads to some difficult cost–benefit clinical questions. Imipramine is now often used in ADHD cases where there is evidence of a depressive component.

A variety of behavioral and cognitive-behavioral techniques have proven helpful for ADHD (Silver, 1992; DuPaul et al., 1991). The drawbacks with these techniques are the high cost in personnel time and the problems of generalization of effects. If there is a neuro-psychological problem, specific rehabilitative efforts are usually required. For older children and adolescents with ADHD, a support therapy group can be helpful.

■ ## Mental Retardation

Mental retardation is another common referral problem for the clinician; it is generally agreed that about 1 percent of the population falls into this category (Berk, 1989). The DSM-III-R requires indication of subaverage intellectual functioning (an IQ of 70 or below) in an individually administered test, correlated problems in adaptive coping behaviors, and onset before the age of eighteen. If onset is later than age eighteen, the term "dementia," subcoded as an organic mental disorder, is appropriate. The criteria for severity are noted in the following four subcategorizations.

Mild Mental Retardation (317.0x) is designated by IQ scores of 50–55 to approximately 70. This is the largest group of retarded individuals, comprising about 85 of the overall retarded population; such persons are commonly referred to as "educable." Many of these individuals develop sixth- or seventh-grade academic skills by the time they are in their middle adolescence.

Moderate Mental Retardation (318.0x), approximately 10 percent of the retarded population, is classified by an IQ score of 35–40 to 50–55. This group usually requires at least moderate supervision, particularly in financial matters and/or when under stress. They seldom progress beyond the third-grade achievement level, but they can often communicate adequately.

Severe Mental Retardation (318.1x), classified by an IQ score of 20–25 to 35–40 comprises about 3 to 4 percent of the retarded population. This group is not likely to profit from any vocational training, although they can usually learn elementary self-care skills through behavioral interventions (Matson and Gardner, 1991).

Profound Mental Retardation (318.2x), 1 to 2 percent of the retarded population, is designated by an IQ score of 20–25 or less.

If there is good reason to believe that significant intellectual retardation is present with functioning at least below an approximate IQ of 70, and for some reason the individual is untestable, the term Unspecified Mental Retardation (319.00) is used. The diagnosis of Borderline Intellectual Functioning (V40.00) requires evidence of problems in adaptive coping and an IQ of 71 to 84.

Since the MMPI-2 requires approximately an eighth-grade reading level, it is seldom administered to most mentally retarded persons, although the taped version can be used effectively, or it can be read to the client (the reader is referred to the initial portion of Chapter 12 on the clinical correlates of the MMPI-2. Regardless of which method of administration is used, such clients sometimes respond with a random response pattern (Sabine and Meyer, 1992) (see the section on malingering).

Aside from the overall scores obtained on the WAIS-R, there are certain trends in the subtest patterns of mentally retarded individuals. First, they score relatively high on object assembly, whereas persons with CNSI score low. Performance subtests may exceed the verbal subtests, but this is not always the case. Academically oriented tests, such as information and arithmetic, are usually low. Also, the similarities test is relatively low, while comprehension, picture completion, and digit span are higher.

On the Rorschach, a low number of overall responses is usually obtained, containing a low F+%, a high F%, few or poor M responses, and a high percentage of Animal responses. When W responses are made, they are of poor quality. Repetitive and perseverative content occurs, and apparently impulsive inferences to content from the stimuli of the blots are common. On the Bender-Gestalt, changes in angulation, closure difficulty, irregular use of space and sequence, a probability of rotations, and collision tendencies are noted. Simplistic drawings, such as attachment of the appendages to the head, are seen on the Draw-A-Person Test in more severely retarded persons (Newmark, 1985).

A wide variety of interventions are necessary to effectively deal with mental retardation and its associated problems. Those with less impairment profit most from psycho-educational and social skills interventions, and the greater the degree of impairment, the more necessary are the various behavioral interventions (Matson and Gardner, 1991).

# CHAPTER 12

# Clinical Correlates of the MMPI-2

The task of collecting the classical descriptors and correlates of the MMPI-2 and 16 PF scales has been carried out by numerous authors throughout the years, mainly through an accrual process. Those authors and I owe much to many other clinicians and researchers who have contributed their ideas and data. In this section on the MMPI-2, I have taken material from my own experience and integrated it with both the classical and recent sources of clinical interpretation of the MMPI-2, primarily those noted earlier (see Table 1.1 in Chapter 1).

## ■ MMPI-2

The Minnesota Multiphasic Personality Inventory, with the revision into a second edition that was first published in 1989 (MMPI-2), is composed of 567 (as opposed to 556 in the original form) self-reference statements that cover topics from physical condition through social history, emotional states, social attitudes, and moral belief systems. Clients are encouraged to answer every question, although they often skip a few, and their only option is a true or false answer.

The MMPI test was originated by Starke Hathaway, a medical psychologist, and Jovian McKinley, a neuropsychiatrist, who, at the time, were working at the University of Minnesota Hospitals. Hathaway and McKinley accumulated a large collection of self-reference statements from textbooks, psychological reports, and other tests. They eventually limited their pool of statements to the 504 they thought were relatively independent of one another. They hoped that they could develop a test that would substantially aid in the routine psychological examinations given there. Indeed, Hathaway has stated that he only expected it to be used locally. However, their efforts eventually culminated in the publication of the original form in 1943 by the Psychological Corporation.

Hathaway and McKinley first administered the test to groups of normals and to patients in the following clinical groups: Hypochondriasis, Depression, Hysteria, Psychopathic Deviant, Paranoia, Psychasthenia, Schizophrenia, and Hypomania. They performed an item analysis in order to detect which items significantly differentiated these groups. In the second stage, the scales derived from that item analysis were administered to groups of normals and patients who had those specific clinical diagnoses already assigned, and after adequate cross-validation, the scales were accepted into the test. It was only later that the Masculinity-Femininity (MF) scale was added, with the original purpose of differentiating heterosexual males from homosexual males. The final addition to the basic scales, the Social Introversion (Si) scale, was initially used to distinguish female college students who were socially retiring from those who were active in a number of extracurricular activities. Only later was this scale generalized to males.

Although the original MMPI was the most widely used personality test in the world, as is MMPI-2 now, it was clear to most clinicians and researchers that changes were needed in the original form. Efforts, orchestrated primarily by James Butcher, John Graham, and Grant Dahlstrom, culminated in MMPI-2, published in 1989.

To make it more "user-friendly," items that were dated, e.g., "I like to play 'drop-the-handkerchief,'" were eliminated, and dated, difficult, and sexist vocabulary items and language were rewritten. Religious items, sixteen repeated items (originally included only to facilitate machine scoring), and approximately fifty items found to be useless were eliminated.

Yet, overall, only relatively small changes occurred in the items that contribute to the three Validity scales and the ten basic Clinical scales, which can be scored if the client completes the first 370 items. For example, four items in F and Mf and three in D were eliminated; otherwise only one or zero items were eliminated in the other scales. This was fortunate, as it left the essence and great bulk of all the research concerning these scales directly applicable to MMPI-2 (Ben-Porath & Butcher, 1989; Graham, 1990).

In the latter part of MMPI-2, items 371–567, substantial changes were made (Graham et al., 1991a; Butcher et al., 1990; Ben-Porath & Butcher, 1989). This allowed the development of new scales and provided information in areas not directly tapped by the original form, e.g., suicide, orientation to therapy, attitudes toward work, mental and eating disorder items, etc.

The most significant early criticism of the MMPI-2 normative group (2600 individuals) was that it was more highly educated than the general population. The criticism was technically correct, except that it was made in comparison to 1980 census data. Census data in 1990 revealed a marked increase in the educational level of the populace, and that trend is predicted to continue. So, the original difference in 1989 was much smaller than critics were apparently aware, and possible inadvertently, the MMPI-2 is well designed in this dimension for the long run.

Also, in the MMPI-2 normative sample, the highly educated and blacks do not score significantly differently than the general population, so separate norms are not needed. Differences by sex are found, but these are incorporated into the scoring and then in the clinical interpretations.

The MMPI-2 can be administered individually or in a group and can be hand or machine scored. There are a number of short versions of the MMPI-2, but they have many drawbacks in regards to reliability and validity. National Computer Systems (NCS), by agreement with the University of Minnesota, has the copyright to the MMPI. Only they, or their lessors, have a legal right to sell a program to score the MMPI. There is some indication that computerized administration may produce lower overall profiles, yet using T scores, anyone may develop their own computerized *interpretation* program. However, it is clear the clinician using such a program is ultimately responsible for its use—its report should be used as a guideline, and the clinician is responsible to know how adequate the program is that he or she is using and, outside of NCS's service, that is hard to know.

NCS, although it says it does not desire to do so, is required by state laws to market to nonpsychiatric physicians. Unfortunately, virtually all of them (and numerous mental health practitioners, for that matter) have little or no training beyond a few weekend workshops, if that. Use by such an individual without a consult by someone more expert is unethical. The only recourse to control such use is through a civil liability suit or a complaint to the appropriate state licensing agency or professional association.

A number of clinicians use a computer terminal. The client may take the test at the terminal or the answer sheet can be directly fed into the terminal; in either case, the results are quickly provided to the clinician. No significant differences have been found between taking it by hand or at a computer terminal. (See also the comments on computer-generated reports in Chapter 18.) Any computerized interpretation of an MMPI-2 protocol should always be first routed through a clinician who has had *substantial* training in MMPI-2 interpretation, since that clinician can consider the profile in light of the many and often subtle particulars of an individual case that are not fed into the computer.

The raw data from the MMPI-2 are translated into T scores. These are the scores that are eventually coded onto the profile sheet. Separate norms are available for males and females. After any initial scoring, a

K correction is added to the raw scores obtained for scales Hs (1), Pd (4), Pt (7), Sc (8), and Ma (9), although there is some evidence that this can lead to more false-positives and fewer false-negatives in diagnosis (Hsu, 1986).

There are several methods by which the whole profile can be coded. Using this book does not depend on knowing how to fully code an MMPI-2, although such codes are occasionally found in the literature. There are two major coding systems for use with the MMPI-2. Hathaway's (1947) was the original system, although the more complete system developed by Welsh (1948) is far more commonly used. The reader is referred to Graham (1987, 1990) for a detailed discussion of his adaptation of this method. As an example of his adapted Welsh code, the following profile has been coded from the T scores:

7* 2" 1' 8- 46/ /:<u>35#</u> 0 to the right of #9

What this actually says is that:

7*    Scale 7 is 90 T to 99 T
2"    Scale 2 is between 80 and 89
1'    Scale 1 is between 70 and 79
8-    Scale 8 is between 60 and 69
46/   Scales 4 and 6 are between 50 and 59

/:    The juxtaposition of two break symbols (/ and :) indicates no score was in the T range of the one to the right—in this case, 40–49 range

<u>35#</u>   # indicates scales 3 and 5 are between 30 and 39 T; the underlining states that they are within one T score point of each other

To the right of 9 indicates that scale 9 is 29 T or less

If a scale(s) was in the 100–109 range, those scale numbers would be preceded by **; if in the 110–119 range, by !; if above 120, by !!.

While there is no inherent upper age-level limit for the MMPI-2, only individuals with at least an eighth-grade reading level and eighteen years of age can validly complete the MMPI-2 (Paolo et al., 1991). Those with less than an eighth-grade reading level can take the test by having someone read the items to them or by listening to an audiotape.

One might ask why a sixth- to seventh-grade reading level was deemed appropriate for the original form, but an eighth-grade level is the rule-of-thumb for MMPI-2, especially when an attempt was made to reduce problematic language and concepts. Quite simply, it reflects an overall drop in reading skill in the populace. Hence, an eighth-grade reading level today is about the same level of skill as a sixth- to seventh-grade reading level twenty-five years ago.

Average reading difficulty was computed for the 567 items and 61 sub/special scales of the MMPI-2 (Paolo et al., 1991). The mean for all items was 600.02 (SD = 304.57), which essentially corresponds to a fifth-grade reading level. Approximately 90 percent of the items require less than a ninth-grade reading level; three items require a high-school education or more. The Amorality (Mal) subscale has the highest requirement, an average reading level greater than eighth grade. The scale 9 subscales were the most demanding. For persons with low reading ability, interpretation of the nine subscales should be made cautiously, and use of the taped version is recommended (Sabine and Meyer, 1992).

Both the normal and abnormal profiles of adolescents differ from those of adults, and when dealing with adolescents, the adolescent form of the test should be used. That test is for use with adolescents in the 14 to 18 age range, whereas MMPI-2 is appropriate for 18-year-olds and up. With an 18-year-old, consider whether that person has started to drop an adolescent life style and is beginning to accept some primary responsibility for taking care of adult-level needs.

Clinicians have often used "critical items" on the MMPI-2, and the best set, the Koss-Butcher items, is scored by NCS. Critical items are usually single items whose content is used to cue the clinician to further inquiry in that area or to indicate a problem because of the face validity of the item. A number of sets of these critical items have been used historically, but most have not consistently predicted the behavior they seem to reflect. Additionally, most of them are loaded with items to which the deviant response is "true," which leaves them open to a "yes-saying" bias. In addition, many of them overlap too highly with the F scale and may reflect a tendency to "fake-bad."

If the clinician uses them, a perusal of critical items marked by the client is worthwhile. For one thing, clients who admit to these face-valid items usually feel that they have communicated directly to the clinician and may be quite surprised if the later content of a clinical contact indicates a lack of awareness about these issues. An extremely high level of endorsement of critical items may be indicative of malingering.

Readers who need more familiarity with the administration and scoring of the MMPI-2 are referred to the books of Graham (1990) or Dahlstrom and Welsh (1980), which contain detailed discussions. In proceeding through the individual scales of the MMPI-2 here, there will be descriptions of each scale, along with overall behavior correlates, correlates of high and low scores on each scale, some patterns the clinician can expect from the scale interrelationships, and guidelines for developing and using code types.

In the traditional clinical-interpretation approach to the MMPI-2, authors referred to the basic clinical scale name rather than its number. As the years passed, however, it became clear that the actual behavioral correlates of a scale have not always matched the originally applied scale name. Therefore, the scale numbers, rather than names, will be used throughout this text. The traditional names are listed here for the sake of convenience.

| SCALE NUMBER | TRADITIONAL SCALE NAME |
|:---:|:---|
| 1 | Hypochondriasis (Hs) |
| 2 | Depression (D) |
| 3 | Hysteria (Hy) |
| 4 | Psychopathic Deviant (Pd) |
| 5 | Masculinity-Feminity (Mf) |
| 6 | Paranoia (Pa) |
| 7 | Psychasthenia (Pt) |
| 8 | Schizophrenia (Sc) |
| 9 | Hypomania (Ma) |
| 0 | Social Introversion (Si) |

It is common to hear persons experienced in the use of MMPI-2 referring to individuals as, say, "a high 4" or "4-8." These shorthand descriptors are helpful as an abbreviated communication of various behavioral descriptions. In general, a high score on the MMPI-2 is one above 65 T, moderately high is a score of from 58 to 65 T, moderately low is from 40 to 45 T, and low is below 40 T (see p. 293).

A more precise understanding is gained by periodically referring to Table 12.1. While MMPI-1 was plotted in linear T scores, in MMPI-2 the basic clinical scales, with the exception of the validity scales (L, F, and K) and scales 5 (Mf) and O (Si), are plotted in uniform T scores. Also, the MMPI-2 Content scores are in uniform T scores. Thus, a T score of 65, whether it is on scale 2 (D) or 4 (Pa) or one of the content scales like

**TABLE 12.1**  Percentile Equivalents for K-Corrected T Scores
(Applies to the basic clinical scales, except L, F, K, 5 (Mf) and 0 (Si), and also to the content scales)

| UNIFORM T SCORE | PERCENTILE EQUIVALENT |
|:---:|:---:|
| 30 | < 1 |
| 35 | 4 |
| 40 | 15 |
| 45 | 34 |
| 50 | 55 |
| 55 | 73 |
| 60 | 85 |
| 65 | 92 |
| 70 | 96 |
| 75 | 98 |
| 80 | 90 |

*Source:* Auke Tellegen, Department of Psychology, University of Minnesota, Minneapolis, MN 55455, data from MMPI Restandardization Project.

ANX (Anxiety) or BIZ (Bizarre Mentation), indicates that approximately 8 percent of the MMPI-2 normative group scored at this point or higher. With a T score of 40, no matter which of these scales it is on, you know that approximately 15 percent of the normative group scored lower than this. Note that the Supplemental scale, e.g., Anxiety (A), Repression (R), Ego Strength (Es), etc., and the Harris-Lingoes subscales are *not* in uniform T scores. Thus, a T score of 65 will tell you nothing about the percentage of persons in the normative sample scoring above or below this point on that scale; *however,* whatever the distribution, the concept of the T score, i.e., that this is clinically high or low or whatever, does apply.

There was good evidence that various groups (blacks or Hispanics, males or females, younger or older persons) differed in their average scores on some of the original MMPI-1 test scales. Yet, it had also occasionally been asserted that this was not evidence of bias, but simply reflected actual differences or response-set differences in those persons being tested that can be accounted for in interpretation (Montgomery and Orozco, 1985; Pritchard and Rosenblatt, 1980; Graham, 1977). In any case, a major virtue of the MMPI-2 is that the normative data shows that education level has been virtually eliminated as a variable in the interpretation of the basic scales. Post-graduate males average about five points higher on scale 5 (they averaged much higher on the original scales), and more-educated individuals certainly score lower on L. But these are the only major differences. Also, on MMPI-2, race is much less of an interpretive variable than it was on the original form. Even with the original form, Pritchard and Rosenblatt (1980) presented impressive data to support their assertion that there is no significant evidence the original form was racially biased, although they and others note that blacks tended to score higher on F, 4, 8, and 9 (Butcher and Graham, 1988; Dahlstrom et al., 1986). These differences are even less in MMPI-2, and this appears to reflect actual (although socioeconomic rather than true racial) differences rather than artifact. Similarly, females are a bit more likely to show peaks on 3 and 6, and males on 1, 4, and 7.

The following traditional conceptualization of the MMPI-2 scales (shown in Figure 12.1) gives a schema that many clinicians find useful. It should never be applied in a hard-and-fast manner, but rather used as a guideline.

## ■ Individual Scale Interpretations

This section gives the correlates of 1-point codes, followed by a section that delineates 2-point codes, as well as the rarer data available on 3-point codes, and information on how these codes are affected by scores on the other basic scales.

**FIGURE 12.1**

| Social Dependency | | Hostility; Acting-Out |
|---|---|---|

| | | |
|---|---|---|
| Self-Blame (Neuroticism) | D(2) ◄─── Activity Level ───► Ma(9) | Self-Aggrandizement (Psychopathy) |
| | Pt(7) ◄─── Behavioral Control ───► Pd(4) | |
| Somatic and/or Self-Pity (Psycho-physiological) | Hs(1) ◄─── Compliance Trust ───► Pa(6) | Reality Contact (Psychosis) |
| | Hy(3) ◄─── Attachment, Thought Clarity ───► Sc(8) | |

Several guidelines for interpretation are suggested in the following paragraphs.

**1.** Use a well-defined breakpoint to establish a code type, i.e., at least a difference of five points or more between the two scales. The greater the difference, the more confidence you have in making a code type interpretation.

**2.** For your primary interpretation, use the most complex well defined code type for which data are available. For example, presume there is at least a five-point T-score difference between the highest and the second highest T scores (which gives you a well-defined 1-point code, i.e., the top score). Presume also a five-point T-score difference between the second and third highest scores (which gives you a well-defined 2-point code, i.e., the top score and then the second highest). If there are interpretive data available for the 2-point code, which is likely, make your primary interpretation from that information base and then supplement it with data from the well-defined 1-point code, i.e., the top score. If there was also a well-defined break between the third and fourth highest T scores, and data was available on that 3-point code, that would provide your primary interpretive base.

**3.** If there is a well-defined break between the third and fourth highest scores, i.e., a 3-point code, but no data are available for interpreting that 3-point code, use the code type of the two highest scores for your primary interpretation, whether or not there is a five-point break between these two top scores.

**4.** If there is no well-defined code type with an available interpretation information base, go to the most clearly defined (as close to five T-score points as feasible) 1-, 2-, or 3-point code type(s) and integrate these to the degree feasible, realizing you have to place less confidence in the available interpretations.

**5.** Within some clinical scales (i.e., 2, 3, 4, 6, 8, and 9), the Harris-Lingoes subscales can be used to analyze which components most contributed to an elevated score. These scales derive from a systematic analysis of subgroups of related construct and content items within those clinical scales. This analysis was refined during the development of MMPI-2. The Harris-Lingoes scales (discussed at greater length later in this chapter) help provide a general analysis of relative weights of factors contributing to any elevated score. They are especially useful (a) to analyze why a client received an elevation on a score that was not expected from history or observation data and (b) to help interpret scores that are marginally elevated (T = 60–65).

**6.** Use the following table when reading the individual scale interpretations.

|            | MMPI-2 T SCORE |
| ---------- | -------------- |
| Very low   | 38 and below   |
| Low        | 44 and below   |
| Normal     | 45–57          |
| Moderate   | 58–64          |
| High       | 65 and above   |
| Very high  | 75 and above   |

□     THE ? SCALE

On the ?, or "cannot say," scale, it is generally considered that within the first 370 items, a raw score of 30 or more renders the profile invalid, and a score of 20–30 within the first 370 items suggests the profile be interpreted with considerable caution (Butcher, 1990). This is not actually a true scale, because it accounts only for the number of items to which the individual has not responded. If a client obtains a high ? score, a reading difficulty should first be considered. If this can be ruled out, gross impairment in the decision making required to give an answer should be considered. If this is not the problem, then obsessive, paranoid, or blatant avoidance issues should be considered. Obsessive clients may feel constrained by the either-or dichotomy allowed in the MMPI-2, rather than commit themselves, they may skip the item. Paranoids naturally fear the self-disclosure involved in a number of items and may avoid them.

Obviously an ounce of prevention is the most logical cure for this problem. The client should be clearly instructed ahead of time to fill out *all* the items or leave, at most, only a few blank. One has several options in the face of a high ? score. In most instances where many items have been skipped, the client can be persuaded to answer more questions, which leads to a valid profile. Some clinicians score the items that have been skipped in the direction they feel the client would have answered them, while other clinicians score them in the significant direction. Such scoring reflects the finding that a nonresponse can refer to either controversial content or decisional ambiguity (Fulkerson and Willage, 1980). In either case, the profile should be compared with that obtained by the original scoring.

## THE L SCALE

The L scale is composed of fifteen items—such as, "I do not always tell the truth"—that are scored only if they are answered "false." High L scales are seen as more important as a validity indicator in MMPI-2 than on MMPI-1, especially for men (Graham et al., 1991a). These face-valid items identify people who, in a naive and open fashion, present an overly idealistic and perfectionistic portrayal of themselves. Interestingly, high L scores do not totally negate the validity of the profile since they are generally independent of elevations on most other scales. L scales do tend to be a bit higher among the elderly. Sophisticated, psychologically minded, or well-educated people seldom score high on this scale, as the items are quite transparent. When well-educated clients do score high, they are likely to be repressed and rigid in their personality structure, tense and introspective, and conforming in behavior. Oddly enough, high scores actually seem to predict to underachievement.

A clinician should naturally consider possible deception any time a high score is obtained, although this is usually true only when the person is not well educated. After considering demographics, people with high scores, generally, are naive and defensive about their conflicts, are often unable to perceive the effects of their behaviors on others, are inflexible in problem solving, and have a low tolerance for stress. Persons in occupations where there is a strong demand to present a "good person" image (e.g., a minister) score higher on this scale, whatever their educational level. A high L score is also associated with a denial of any need for help and with an unwillingness to be honest about deficiencies, admit guilt about behavior, or admit to alcohol abuse (Hedlund, 1977). Thus, the groups most likely to score high on this scale are saints, priests, ministers, rabbis, and some prisoners—the prisoners because they are trying to present themselves as "normals." Prisoners, however, have a poor feel for what normal is since neither they nor their associates are in that range.

Highly sophisticated individuals who are manipulative and defensive may score low on the L scale, although a low score usually indicates a fairly relaxed and independent individual who has responded openly to the items. A very low score (0–1 raw score) may occasionally be associated with wariness and cynicism, but a moderately low score (2–4) primarily reflects a person who is not particularly defensive, is willing to admit some deficiencies in the self, and is able to communicate reasonably well with others. Finally, a very high score suggests a pathologic confusion that may be either organic or functional in nature.

## THE F SCALE

The F scale consists of sixty items chosen because they were answered as true by fewer than 10 percent of a normal adult population. High to very high T scores suggest either marked confusion, significant errors in scoring, inability of the client either to read the items or to understand the directions, random responding, a false claim of negative symptoms, hostility toward the examiner, or, for other reasons, a clearly invalid profile (Butcher, 1990). If a reading problem is suspected, simply having the client read the first ten items out loud may give a clue in this regard. If a reading problem is noted, the use of a tape-recorded version (one available from the Psychological Corporation) is suggested. Extremely high T scores (above 90) may indicate that item response was random or that the client either answered true to all questions, was faking-bad, or, if an inpatient, was psychotic. The clinician should rule out organic brain dysfunction in these clients. Gynther et al. (1973a) have shown that high F scores in an adult inpatient population may warrant the term "confused psychotic." If the F is high and K is low, the F score has been pulled up by the Schizophrenia scale items (8). In an outpatient population, it is more likely to indicate some form of an invalid profile. Responding with clearer instructions or a confrontation and acceptance of any hostility in an apparently intact client who produces a high F profile usually results in a subsequent valid test. Since the F scale is highly correlated with scales 6 and 8 (reflecting item overlap), a 6-8/8-6 profile with a high F score may be directly interpreted, although with some caution.

Moderate T scores (in the range of 58–64) are associated with mild confusion, some significant emotional problems marked by moodiness or agitation, and unconventional and sometimes very deviant religious, social, or political views. Antisocial (acting-out) and withdrawn behaviors are commonly, and paradoxically, associated with these moderate scores in adolescents. But psychotics and those labeled as severe neurotics often have F-scale scores in this range, so severe psychopathology must be ruled out. If there are other indications of anxiety, a score in this range may be a plea for help.

Normal to low scores on the F scale are associated with normal response sets, a calm demeanor, and conventional behavior patterns. If the score becomes very low, a denial of psychopathology and even more rigid and conforming personality patterns are likely. Faking-good should also be considered.

In general, if one can rule out an invalid profile (Berry et al., 1991), the F scale is a good indication of overall psychopathology. The higher it is, the more likely it is that there is general psychopathology. Conversely, the lower the F scale, the more likely it is that any existing problems are focused and under control.

## THE K SCALE

The K scale consists of thirty items obtained by comparing the responses of disturbed individuals who had normal profiles with normals who also had normal profiles, and it is now generally used to identify faking-good cases, although this should be done with caution (Graham et al., 1991b). These items correlate well with social-desirability scales, by measuring more subtle defensiveness than the L scale. In that sense, they function as a suppressor variable in the other scales (Meehl and Hathaway, 1980). The amount of K contributing to the T scores of other scales should always be considered. K scores are inversely related to elevations on scales 8, 7, and 0.

There is usually a negative correlation between scores on F and K, but certain clients, especially inpatients, may score moderate to high on both. These persons are likely to have a reason for avoiding responsibility for psychopathology, such as in a criminal case. At the same time, they feel the need to be honest, possibly from the urging of an attorney or from a need to use an admission of specific psychopathology to excuse behavior. Well-educated and/or sophisticated individuals score higher on this scale, although the positive deviation from the mean is usually not as marked as it is in the opposite direction on L.

High K scores are generally associated with attempts to deny vulnerability and psychopathology. Such persons are unwilling to admit to psychological or physiological deficits, are inclined to blame others for their problems, and as a result are not likely to cooperate in intervention attempts. They have little insight into their own patterns and are intolerant toward deviant or disturbed behavior in others. A high K indicates resistance to intervention, whereas a normal to moderate elevation (50–60) indicates a good prognosis for treatment change. In fact, a rise in K is often found with improvement through treatment. A high K score generally contraindicates delinquency in adolescents, especially in females, and indeed, contraindicates antisocial acting-out in general. A generally "false-responding" set will elevate K as twenty-nine of the thirty items are scored by marking "false."

Low K scores indicate weak emotional-behavioral controls and that the person is hurting and/or is feeling vulnerable. Such individuals have low self-esteems, are surprisingly harsh or clumsy in dealing with others, and thus usually have marked interpersonal problems. Low scores may also represent an exaggeration of problems as a plea for help, excessive opening up, masochistically confessing, or faking-bad, and to the degree scores are very low, indicate a confused state that may be either organic or functional.

The F-K index, long a popular indicator with clinicians (Woychyshyn, et al., 1992) is discussed later with regard to several of the ensuing diagnostic categories. In particular, the reader is referred to the section on malingering for qualifications of the interpretation of this index. It has been traditionally asserted that when the index (in terms of raw scores) is negative and is greater than 12, it indicates a deliberate effort by the client to be seen as emotionally healthy and without vulnerability, and when F-K is positive and more than 11, faking-bad should be considered. Most clinicians now feel that wider differences should be allowed, and that the index is more effective in assessing faking-bad than faking-good (Graham et al., 1991b).

☐  ## TREATMENT PREDICTIONS WITH L, F, AND K COMBINATIONS

In general, if L and K are high and F is low, these persons are poor candidates for psychotherapy. Both conscious and unconscious denial are usually present—their problems are perceived as the faults of others or fate. There may be some acceptance of a strictly biologic explanation of disorder. If F is very high and L and K are below average, these clients are saying they are overwhelmed and not sure they can continue to "hang on." They need "first aid" and/or hospitalization. When F is about 65 and L and K are a bit below 50, these clients admit to having problems but are not in dire need, yet they are reasonably receptive toward therapy. If F is high and L and K are above 60, there is a significant degree of confusion in several directions, and the confusion can be functional, organic, or toxic in origin.

☐  ## THE BACK SIDE F SCALE [F(B)]

MMPI-2 includes an additional forty-item validity measure, F(B), the Back Side F scale, to detect deviant responding in scales that tap items after the first 370 items. If the F scale indicates an invalid profile then the F(B) is not needed because the whole profile is considered invalid. If the F is in the valid range and F(B) is below T = 89, then validity is established for the whole set of responses. But, if the T score for F is considered valid and F(B) is at a T score greater than 90, cautious interpretation of even the clinical and validity scales is indicated, and interpretation of scales based on back-side items can only be made with great caution, as so many of these scales are filled with face-valid items.

Like the F scale, the Back F consists of items, forty in this case, that no more than 10 percent of the population sample would endorse, and item 281 is the first item to appear in the test.

Most of the interpretive comments that apply to the F scale apply to the Back F as well. Extreme scores (raw score of 23 and above) suggest an invalid profile, psychosis, and/or an adolescent in the midst of an identity crisis. A raw score of 16–22 F is comparable to an interpretation of a high score on F, 8–15 to a moderate F score, 3–7 to a normal F, and 2 or less to a low F score.

□    SCALE 1 (Hs)

Scale 1, traditionally referred to as the Hypochondriasis scale, is comprised of thirty-two items that focus on bodily functions and disorders, although in a number of ways it is more of a characterological scale. This scale is relatively unidimensional, the items are reasonably obvious in content, and the complaints embedded in the items are not very specific. Symptoms, if specific, tend to be epigastric. Thus, persons with actual physical disorders are generally below 65 on this scale and are more likely with time to score higher on scale 2 as a reaction to the disorder. Scale 1 is a good indicator of overall pessimism—the higher the score, the more pessimistic the view of the world—and correlates particularly with the channeling of pessimism into somatic concerns and complaints. Higher scores seem to correlate negatively with intellectual ability, and those who score high on this scale are often described as dull, unambitious, unenthusiastic, and lacking ease in oral expression (Graham, 1987). Clients with high 1 scores (65 T and above) may be using physical symptoms to focus tension, to express hostility, or to control others. They are nonpsychologically minded. As a result, it is commonly a high score in persons consulting a physician, and these individuals are often very frustrating for a physician to deal with. High scores are also associated with clinical depression (usually exogenous rather than endogenous), although this correlation or "r" with depression does not usually hold for blacks. High scores on scale 1, unless found in the relatively rare 1-8/8-1 profile, are seldom correlated in a consistent fashion with extreme psychotic processes. T scores greater than 80, however, may indicate somatic delusions. Even moderate scores (T score 58–64) on this scale are likely to be associated with a degree of somatization (as well as actual physical handicap and illness), and since this is combined with the narcissism, immaturity, lack of ambition, and stubbornness that are also characteristic of this group, the clinician's patience is sorely tested. As might be expected, such individuals are demanding and critical regarding intervention attempts and are particularly resistant to psychological interpretations of their disorder. As a result, they seldom respond positively to psychotherapy, instead demanding support, attention, and concrete physical explanation for their disorders. Therapists may find it a helpful technique with such clients to contract for a set period of time in the therapy hour during which a focus on physical complaints is allowed (sort of an "organ recital"). This procedure can facilitate a later uninterrupted discussion of the other critical issues that are often avoided. Shorter sessions are also helpful with such clients (Fowler, 1981). Placebos can be useful; however, they are at risk for dependency if medicated.

If scales 1 and/or 3 are significantly elevated, especially if they are the only ones elevated, such clients are not usually tolerant of psychological intervention. If they feel the need for treatment, they expect it to be traditionally medical. They particularly do not want to make the connection between psychological factors and their overt symptoms. One approach is to overtly avoid the apparent connection at first, e.g., with interpretations such as "I can't tell you why your stomach distress occurs (although you may actually have a very good idea why), so let's talk a bit about what's going on with your life." Later, you may speculate on possible connections, but the client may only stay at the level of everyday problem solving and never be willing to make that connection.

Persons who are low (below 45 T) on scale 1 are usually adjusting adequately to their worlds and are usually cognitively insightful, although some may appear moralistic and may have problems with the warmth and sharing demands of intimate interpersonal relations. Persons who are very low (T score of 38 or below) on scale 1 have deinvested in their bodies and may act as if they don't care what happens to them, e.g., riding a motorcycle at high speed, which, along with the gun, is the neuropsychologist's most dependable referral source.

## SCALE 2 (D)

Scale 2, subtitled the Depression scale, consists of fifty-seven items. It is the most frequent peak scale in psychiatric clients, and it clearly measures what it purports to: the degree of contentment with the world, level of self-esteem, and one's view of the future. People who score high on scale 2 are clearly *distressed*. They usually are depressed and withdrawn and show psychomotor retardation; they may be schizoid. There is a good chance they may harbor suicidal ideations if 2 is elevated above the 80-T mark or if 2 is the only scale elevated above 65 T. Adolescents score somewhat lower than the general population, whereas the elderly score higher on the average, probably reflecting the different range of options available in these age groups, as well as their different sense of optimism about the future.

Unless they are attempting to fake-bad, persons with a very high score on scale 2 do consistently show a clinical level of depression, and they likely warrant the potentially psychotic-depressive diagnosis. If the elevation is moderate, it may reflect either a depressive episode, a neurotic-depressive component, a state of mild chronic dissatisfaction, or depression from an accompanying maladaptive personality style that cannot cope with changes in the world.

People with high scale-2 scores are at least moderately withdrawn and show low activity levels, whereas persons low on scale 2 are typically comfortable with their worlds and are reasonably gregarious, active, and alert. In some cases, a very low 2 score may reflect a lack of impulse control and possible conflict with societal mores, yet this has not usually brought the person into legal difficulties. Hedlund (1977) asserts that there is no strong correlation of scale 2 with psychotic symptomatology.

Persons high on scale 2 (and scale 7 as well) initially show a moderate to marked interest in therapy. However, this can be a direct result of their situational distress; when the crisis passes, they may terminate therapy, even though pathological patterns remain. If there is no elevation, it is probably difficult to do intrapsychic psychotherapy. Some elevation on 2 is a good prognostic sign for psychotherapy. Contracting for behaviors that increase activity level are helpful here.

Although there is no definitive suicidal profile on the MMPI-2, it appears that scale 2 is more indicative of suicidal ideation than of actual suicide attempts, and factors tapped by other scales, e.g., scale 9, appear to act as catalysts for actual behavior in this regard.

As noted, persons low on 2 are usually reasonably well adjusted, active, and alert; they are even enthusiastic, although they may be perceived by others as too flamboyant and uninhibited. Healthy adolescents often show low 2 scores. Very low scores here may reflect the manic phase of a cyclothymic process.

Using the Harris-Lingoes scales (especially helpful with a score between 60 to 80 T), high scorers on D1 (Subjective Depression) show classic depression commonly marked by agitation and nervousness, although they may complain of lack of energy. They lack the focus to cope with everyday tasks; they are inadequate and insecure and show low self-esteem. They also ruminate, cry, and show appetite and sleep disturbance. Low D1 scorers lack these symptoms and are usually happy, extroverted, and self-confident. High scorers on D2 (Psychomotor Retardation) are immobilized, socially nonparticipating and even avoidant, slowed motorically, and denying of hostility. Low D2s are active, initiating, and admit hostility when appropriate. High D3s (Physical Malfunctioning) are preoccupied with and report many physical symptoms; low D3s report good health. High D4s (Mental Dullness) communicate hopelessness, helplessness, energy depletion, and problems in memory and/or concentration; low D4s deny such symptoms and see life as interesting and within their mastery. High D5s (Brooding) ruminate, see themselves as unable to control their thought processes, are irritable and easily hurt by criticism, and feel life lacks meaning. Low D5s show opposite patterns.

☐        ## SCALE 3 (Hy)

Scale 3, termed the Hysteria scale, is comprised of sixty items that tap two overall constructs: (1) a denial of problems or vulnerabilities in one's emotional or interpersonal world and (2) complaints of reasonably specific somatic problems. Naiveté, narcissism, neurotic defensiveness, and a lack of awareness of intrapsychic issues are characteristic of persons high on scale 3. Like those with the avoidant personality disorder, they may be highly demanding of attention and caring responses, although they avoid committing themselves in this way.

Scale 3 is only moderately correlated with the development of conversion symptomatology, the initial construct that it was thought to tap, and it shows a low correlation with psychotic complaints. However, a T score above 80 is suggestive of a conversion reaction. Rather than evidencing the hypochondriasis so characteristic of scale 1, scale 3 is more likely to tap depression-generated somatic complaints as well as ego-alien anxiety and agitation. Thus, sophistication is a factor in the score obtained on scale 3. Those who are brighter or higher in socioeconomic class tend to score higher on scale 3; women are more likely than men to be high on scale 3. Persons with a spike on 3 often show problems with authority and feel unaccepted by their social groups. They often show their rebellion in passive ways or via somatic symptoms but, in some cases, will blatantly act out in a sexual or aggressive mode.

Persons high on scale 3 are usually still interpersonally adequate, although they may be rather manipulative. The naiveté, anxiety, and need for attention result in an initially high level of apparent interest in psychotherapy. In particular, they love advice; they simply do not follow it. When these persons realize that they cannot manipulate the therapist to feed their egos, they may stop in a huff or attempt to maneuver the therapist into a physical or medical interpretation of their difficulties—they consistently seek "medical" reassurance. Yet they are also quite suggestible and usually responsive to hypnosis. When 3 and K are both elevated and F and 8 are low, the person is often overly conventional and affiliative, with an exaggerated need to be liked. They have problems with assertion and avoid the exercise of power.

Persons with a moderate elevation on 3 tend to be optimistic, even Pollyannish at times. They are also likely to be cognitively and socially superficial and are extroverted, even exhibitionistic.

Persons low on scale 3 may be tough minded and cynical. They usually have a relatively low need for involvement with people, may even be misanthropic, and have a narrow range of interests. Generally, these people are conforming to social mores and show little affect.

Referring to the Harris-Lingoes scales, high Hy1s (Denial of Social Anxiety) are socially skilled and extroverted and accept criticism; low Hy1s are socially introverted and conforming. High Hy2s (Need for Affection) seek attention and affection, are trusting and nonconfrontational and avoid or deny unpleasant situations or feelings; low Hy2s are inclined to be self-absorbed and are suspicious and critical of others. High Hy3s (Lassitude-Malaise) report general weakness and fatigue rather than specific symptoms. They report sleep and concentration problems and seek reassurance and attention. Low Hy3s do not show such symptoms. Hy4s (Somatic Complaints) report multiple specific somatic symptoms, e.g., chest pains, dizziness, nausea. They deny affect and convert conflict into symptomatology. Low Hy4s do not show such patterns. High Hy5s (Inhibition of Aggression) say they are decisive and sensitive to others and deny hostility or depictions of crime or aggression; low Hy5s show opposite characteristics.

☐     SCALE 4 (Pd)

Scale 4, traditionally termed the Psychopathic Deviate, has fifty items that generally tap the following factors: (1) an angry rebelliousness against recognized rules and mores, (2) shallow and often hostile and manipulative interpersonal relationships, (3) inability to profit from experience or to plan effectively for long-term future contingencies, and (4) anger at family and a belief that one was victimized as a child.

Behaviorally, scale 4 shows a high correlation with antisocial behavior, moodiness, characterological patterns, substance abuse, and sexual immorality. A high scale 4 indicates potential for hostile and aggressive outbursts, particularly in whites (Hedlund, 1977), as well as depressive ideation (not necessarily accompanied by psychomotor retardation). Whether or not they act out their problems in some fashion depends on whether scales 8 and/or 9 are high and K is low. Normals who are high on 4, i.e., they are showing no demonstrable psychopathic behaviors, are unconventional, rebellious, immature, sometimes exhibitionistic, and are seldom popular persons. Blacks, adolescents, and males score higher on this scale, on the average, which can be adjusted for by subtracting up to ten T points when interpreting the scale. Indeed, a reasonably high scale is "normal" in many adolescents. High-scale-4 individuals are usually extroverted yet do not empathize well with others' needs; they are also impulsive and lack social poise. They do not usually have blatant psychotic symptoms or high intrapsychically generated anxiety.

Individuals who show a moderate score on 4 may be responding to social and/or authority conflicts (so the score should lessen as the conflict lessens, e.g., maybe they are college students—about 10% of college students will be above 65 T on 4, or they may show chronic but not extreme social conflicts or concerns.

Persons who are normal on scale 4 usually show adequate interpersonal relationships and are perceived by other people as sincere and concerned. If their scores are low, they are more likely to be conforming and even rigidly responsive to the dictates of authorities, to be manipulated by others, to tolerate boredom and mediocrity, and may lack enough energy to actuate plans. Males who score very low often have a lack of interest if not a deep-seated mistrust of females.

Whereas persons who are low on scale 4 can become dependent on the therapist's advice and recommendations and will even seek out a therapist who will give such direction, persons high on scale 4 are likely to be manipulative in any quest for or response to therapy. They may seem to be good candidates because they are usually articulate and socially sophisticated. However, at their best, they subtly project blame onto other persons or situations and are inclined to use therapy to avoid problems of the real world, such as coercion from legal authorities or from intimate others. They are likely to terminate therapy as soon as they have obtained the goal of their manipulations or if they perceive the therapist as either unresponsive toward that end or able to confront their manipulations effectively.

Using the Harris-Lingoes scales, a high score on Pd1 (Familial Discord) reflects an experience of present and/or family of origin as distressing, lacking in warmth or support, controlling, and possibly abusive. Low Pd1s see their families in opposite terms. If Pd1 is the clear major source of variance in an elevated scale 4 score, there may be little true psychopathy. High Pd2s (Authority Problems) are assertive, opinionated, resent and rebel against authority or social demands, and have often been in trouble in school or with the law. Low Pd2s are conforming, suggestible, and self-effacing. High Pd3s (Social Imperturbability) seek and are skilled in social interactions, sometimes to the point of trying to be the center of attention (or conversely, show managed blandness), deny dependency, and are assertive in their opinions. Low Pd3s are clumsy in and avoidant of social situations and are quiet and conformist. High Pd4s (Social Alienation) feel lonely and estranged socially, are self-centered and inconsiderate, and express regrets about life but externalize conflicts and project responsibility to others. Low Pd4s have a sense of "belongingness," like routine, like and trust others, but are not especially suggestible. High Pd5s (Self-Alienation) feel agitated and unhappy, have a sense of guilt and a lack of self-integration, have problems in concentration, and are inclined toward alcohol abuse. Low Pd5s see life as stimulating and enjoyable, seek predictability, and deny excessive use of alcohol.

## SCALE 5 (Mf)

Scale 5, the Masculinity-Feminity scale, is composed of fifty-six items that tap vocational preference, esthetic interests, sexual-role interests, and an activity-passivity dimension. In general, low scores indicate a person who fits closely with traditional role expectations of his or her sex, whereas high scores reflect a person who in some fashion has moved away from the traditional role. For both sexes, a T score above 80 suggests a serious sexual problem. Scale 5 is highly correlated with education and intelligence, with an "r" of up to .25 with intelligence often being reported.

Men who are low on scale 5 are usually perceived by others as bland, insouciant, and/or macho. They are not likely to be introspective; they are self-indulgent and overly independent (but actually rather conforming); they disdain intellectual and artistic pursuits in favor of active out-door interests; and they often delight in being coarse and adventurous, and may see themselves as "good-old boys." They avoid psychotherapy.

Men who are high on scale 5 may have a homosexual identification and/or show a lack of identification with activities associated with the traditional male role. However, a more precise understanding of sex-role orientation is gained by looking at the supplemental scales GM and GF (Gentry and Meyer, 1991). High-scale-5 males tend to be more passive, dependent, and submissive in interpersonal relationships. They are peace loving and usually avoid confrontations. They are usually sensitive, sophisticated, higher socioeconomically and intellectually, and likely to have interests in the humanities and arts. They usually do well in therapy, especially group therapy. Ambitious and intrapsychically introspective individuals also tend to score higher on scale 5. If combined with a low 4, it suggests a very passive man, a milquetoast. By contrast, low-5, high-4 males show an exhibitionistic, almost compulsive, masculinity, often as a counterphobic reaction to issues of tenderness or vulnerability. High-5 males in a psychiatric population are dependent and insecure, may show identity ambivalence, and are socially sensitive and passive. Depression, guilt, and anxiety are common.

Women who score low on scale 5 are likely to be passive and submissive, although sometimes petulant. They prefer to be involved in dependent interpersonal relationships, and if they exert any control in the relationship, it is through passivity and stubbornness. Low-score women who are well educated are more positive and assured about themselves and their sex roles. They may not be stereotypically feminine, but they often have many feminine characteristics. They may view themselves as plain (Graham, 1987). A very low 5 suggests some masochism, but they are also usually self-pitying, fault-finding, and appear (and may be) helpless. Women high on scale 5 have rejected many aspects of the traditional female role. They perceive themselves as extroverted and content with their worlds, but they can be emotionally insensitive, and others may see them as unfriendly or even aggressive. As a result, they easily elicit aggression in others, including therapists.

Women with a high 5 more often are interested in sports and other outdoor activities than women low on this scale. High scoring, normal females are independent but adventurous. In psychiatric populations, high-5 females are usually perceived as competitive, dominating, and irritating. A high scale-5 score in a hospitalized woman has in a number of cases been associated with underlying psychosis; such clients may exhibit hallucinations, delusions, and suspiciousness, although acting-out is uncommon (Graham, 1987).

## SCALE 6 (Pa)

Scale 6, termed Paranoia, includes forty items, and a high score comes from paranoid or unusual ideas or even delusions, feelings of being wronged, actual persecution, or complaints about others. At the same time, a low score does not rule out similar ideation. In fact, if the person is a sophisticated, integrated, and defensive paranoid individual, he or she may score quite low on this scale. In general, there are few false-positives, but true-positives may be missed. Very high scores are relatively uncommon, but to the extent that T is greater than 75, look for frank psychosis, clear paranoia, or paranoid schizophrenia as a possible diagnosis.

High scorers are seen as hostile, externalizing, overly sensitive, suspicious, and egocentrically self-righteous. As scores drop into the moderate-to-high range, more-integrated paranoid ideation and hypersensitivity is probable and sexual deviation or preoccupation is a significant possibility. Anger toward others for a deprived or punitive childhood or toward authority also elevates this scale into at least the moderate range. However, moderate scores are usually obtained by individuals who are perceived by others as cooperative and intelligent and without any psychological disturbance, although they may be overly sensitive interpersonally. As a result, it is worthwhile to examine responses to individual items on this scale. High scores here with female psychiatric patients are more likely to reflect suspiciousness and emotional withdrawal than they do in male psychiatric patients; the male's high score is more likely to reflect odd thought content.

As noted, a person with a low score on scale 6 may well be a very sophisticated and guarded paranoid, although it's more likely that he or she is a generally optimistic and productive individual. They are often interpersonally insensitive and usually underachieve. In a psychiatric population, a low scale 6 is associated with subtle defensiveness and stubbornness; when a score of less than 40 T is present, frank paranoid disorder is possible, and controlled anger and suspicion are likely.

Individuals high on scale 6 seldom become meaningfully involved in psychotherapy. They are much more concerned with "Who did that to me?" than "How could I have done that?" At best, they are intellectualized and rigid. Some success can be attained over time if the therapist is able to give adequate feedback, maintain integrity as a therapist, and gradually develop in them at least a modicum of trust.

Using the Harris-Lingoes scales, persons high on Pa1 (Persecutory Ideas) show classic paranoid symptoms, i.e., perceive threat from others, possibly at a delusional level, feel misunderstood, are suspicious, blame others, and project conflict and responsibility onto others. Low Pa1s do not show these patterns and generally trust others. High Pa2s (Poignancy) perceive themselves as more sensitive and more intense in their feelings than others, feel misunderstood and/or lonely, are subjective and "thin-skinned," and can be stimulation- and risk-seeking. Low Pa2s show the opposite characteristics. High Pa3s (Naiveté) are trusting toward others, deny hostility or negative motives in self and others, and see themselves as nonhostile, noble, and/or moral. Ironically, low Pa3s show some paranoid components as they are suspicious, self-centered, and hostile. They are untrustworthy, yet see others as dishonest.

☐    SCALE 7 (Pt)

Scale 7, called the Psychasthenia scale, consists of forty-eight items that include factors of (1) general discontent with one's world, (2) obsessional concerns, (3) anxiety, and (4) indecision, poor concentration, and self-devaluation. Scale 7 primarily taps the obsessional—rather than the compulsive—features of the obsessive-compulsive disorder. The primarily compulsive personality is not that consistently high on this scale, presumably because their rigidity and denial wards off feelings of insecurity or low self-esteem. People high on this scale anxiously ruminate about problems in their worlds and have perfectionistic standards of performance that they seldom feel they actually meet. As a result, they show feelings of inferiority in many areas and have negative self-images. A T score over 75 suggests excessive fear and apprehension, even panic. With high T scores, generalized physical complaints, such as fatigue, exhaustion, and insomnia, are commonly reported, as well as more specific complaints involving the heart or the gastrointestinal or genitourinary systems (Graham, 1987). They are described as being anxious and indecisive. These features, not surprisingly, lead them into psychotherapy, but the obsessiveness and perfectionism often cause initial problems. They are not likely to give in, so they continue to introspect and ruminate when changes in behavior would be more productive. They usually do best with structured therapies, at least in the initial stages, as they can think themselves to death in unstructured situations. If the therapist can be patient and keep such clients involved beyond this initial stage of resistance, the prognosis becomes more positive. An abrupt involvement in therapies that quickly knock out repression and denial, such as confrontational therapies and encounter groups, can be dangerous to high-7 clients, since they may be attempting to hold onto control of very high anxiety or self-destructive impulses.

Hedlund (1977) found the presence of phobias to be correlated with a high scale-7 score for white samples only. In female patients, there is a significant negative correlation of irritability and delusions with high scale-7 scores. In general, when a high 7 is found in a psychotic client, it points to a more acute onset. High-T scorers who are apparently normal are described as verbal and idealistic (if male, unemotional and responsible but sentimental; if female, emotional, "high strung," and having self-discontent).

Persons with a moderate score on 7 are conscientious, punctual, and not that anxious (unless faced with uncertainty or a disruption of schedule). Persons low on scale 7 are perceived by others as contented and satisfied with their lives, self-confident and emotionally stable, and yet also ambitious and status-seeking. They are generally content and are at least relaxed toward responsibilities.

☐                   SCALE 8 (Sc)

Scale 8, traditionally termed the Schizophrenia scale, is the longest subscale on the MMPI-2, comprising seventy-eight items that focus on factors of (1) confused thought processes, (2) hallucinations and other indications of formal thought disorder, (3) social and interpersonal alienation, and (4) depression and dissatisfaction. Scale 8 correlates most highly (approximately .75) with scale 7 and moderately (approximately .50 to .55) with F, 4, and 2. It is a difficult scale to interpret since a person who has an average K score need only endorse any subset of twenty items on scale 8 to gain a T score of 65.

Persons high on scale 8 are usually significantly disturbed, although a subsample of individuals may be faking-bad, especially when the T score is over 90. As noted, confusion, bizarre thought processes, and social alienation are characteristics of high-8 scorers. Most who have a high score feel as if they are out of phase with the world, as if they are "space cadets" in a new world. It is interesting that a score over 100 T here is not necessarily indicative of schizophrenia; it is more likely to reflect acute situational distress and/or an identity crisis. Agitated neurotics and people who are severely emotionally unstable, and yet only borderline with respect to psychosis, are also likely to score extremely high on scale 8. Schizophrenics are more likely to score between 70 to 90 on the T score. Persons in the high T-score range are likely to show problems in attention and staying with tasks, with accompanying agitation and anxiety, even if not schizophrenic. They often have high standards that they feel unable to meet, are inclined toward guilt, and have low self-esteems. When under stress, they are prone to become irritable and stubborn.

Persons very low on scale 8 are perceived as happy and reasonably productive individuals, accepting of authority and yielding in interpersonal relationships. Yet, they have rigid and conventional thought patterns and are unable to come up with abstract or creative solutions to interpersonal and vocational problems, particularly if scale M on the 16 PF is also low.

Persons with high scores on scale 8 are enigmatic for the therapist. They are often willing to discuss their problems openly, but it is hard to pin them down about concrete ways to change their behaviors. They are prone to discussions that distract from the focus on the problems and are unstable in their trust of the therapist. Nevertheless, they are likely to remain in some form of contact with the therapist over a long period of time, and if a degree of trust can be generated, modest and steady progress may occur.

Referring to the Harris-Lingoes scales, individuals high on Sc1 (Social Alienation) feel alienated, misunderstood, and mistreated. They have had few love relationships, are socially avoidant, feel their families have rejected and/or patronized them, and lack rapport with others. Low Sc1s show an absence of such responses and feel accepted by their families. Persons high on Sc2 (Emotional Alienation) lack self-rapport and show marked depression and despair and/or flat affect along with apathy; they may be masochistic and/or sadistic. Low Sc2s deny such patterns. High Sc3s (Lack of Ego Mastery, Cognitive) show a pattern expected in schizophrenia, i.e., thought disorder. They report odd and/or confused thoughts and feelings of unreality and/or depersonalization. Low Sc3s report an absence of such symptoms. High Sc4s (Lack of Ego Mastery, Cognative) see life as a strain and feel they can not cope. They show high levels of inhibition and "psychological weakness." They worry, withdraw, and show depression and despair. They may feel hopeless and wish they were dead. Low Sc4s do not show such symptoms and say they find life worthwhile. High Sc5s (Lack of Ego Mastery, Defective Inhibition) experience and are frightened by a sense of impending loss of control. Emotion and affect are ego-alien. They show hyperactivity, labile emotions and irritability, and may report amnesic episodes. Low Sc5s do not admit to such symptoms. High Sc6s (Bizarre Sensory Experiences) report a variety of unusual physical symptoms, experience depersonalization, and admit to unusual thoughts, delusions of influence, and hallucinations. Low Sc6s report an absence of such experiences.

## SCALE 9 (Ma)

This scale, termed the Mania scale, includes forty-six items that focus on a propensity for (1) high energy output, (2) distractibility and lack of persistence in tasks, (3) extroversion and stimulation-seeking, (4) grandiosity, and (5) amorality. Scale 9 can be thought of as a force that drives whatever else is there, sort of a behavioral and emotional amplifier. Persons very low on scale 9 show little energy and may be depressed; most are lacking in self-confidence and a reasonable degree of optimism about the future. A high 2 with a low 9 suggests severe depression. The clinician should note that even when scale 2 is not elevated, a very low score on scale 9 is a cue for underlying depression. As 9 moves up toward the average range, the client is more likely to be quietly productive, reliable in most job situations, and possibly perceived as quiet and withdrawn.

This scale is age-driven, and elderly individuals on the average score up to ten points lower on scale 9; adolescents average up to ten points higher than normal adults. Blacks also tend to score a bit higher here. In some females, a high 9 may result from counterphobic attempts to deny dependency and/or passivity.

In general, people very high on scale 9 are likely to be significantly disturbed psychologically and show grandiosity and a high level of distractibility. A T score of greater than 80 may suggest a manic or psychotic episode; in some individuals, a high 9 may reflect a counterphobic attempt to avoid an anticipated (at some level of consciousness) depression. As they move into the moderate to higher ranges, these tendencies are muted, although the person still has problems organizing tasks. They may be creative, but they need others to carry their plans to the point of actualization. They tend to be extroverted and perceived by others as gregarious, occasionally as pushy.

High-9s are difficult for the therapist to work with because they are hyperactive and distractible, not inclined to view themselves as vulnerable or responsible for problems in their worlds, and not able to persist introspectively to connect contingencies between their behaviors and the difficulties they are encountering. Also, high-9s often struggle over control issues with therapists and others. If confronted by the therapist, they are likely to intellectualize their problems, attempt to distract from the issue by acting-out, or simply terminate therapy. Lithium therapy should be considered here.

A high 9 score, associated with moderate elevations on scales 4 and 3 and a moderate or greater elevation on K, denotes narcissistic and aggressively competitive persons. They do not tolerate vulnerability or dependency, and they raise their self-esteems by denigrating others. If this pattern is bolstered by real-world support for the narcissism, such as a high level of physical attractiveness or athletic skill, the personality style is reinforced in a vicious cycle. When these people enter therapy, the therapist hears various fascinating anecdotes and may even be entertained by dramatic self-confrontations. However, marked change cannot be expected unless the cycle of narcissism is broken in some way, such as aging or trauma resulting in a forced loss of attractiveness.

Persons with T scores in the moderate range usually show the ability to balance their resources and productivity reasonably well. They tend to manifest a pleasant, outgoing temperament, but will respond with agitation to external restrictions. A low score on 9, especially when this scale is the lowest on the profile, usually suggests a somewhat lethargic individual. If 9 is very low, depression may be present, reflected in fatigue and physical exhaustion. Low-9 clients may occasionally be tense and anxious, yet are usually reliable, dependable, and responsible and may confront their problems with perseverance and practicality. Low-scoring males often have home and family interests and are willing to settle down. The prognosis is more favorable for hospitalized patients with low 9 scores.

Using the Harris-Lingoes scales, persons high on Ma1 (Amorality) use their perceptions of others as dishonest and self-centered to rationalize similar patterns in themselves and enjoy manipulating and exploiting others, often with a veneer of disarming frankness. Low Ma1s trust others and see them as caring. High Ma2s (Psychomotor Acceleration) report classic manic symptoms, i.e., accelerated motoric, thought, and speech patterns, labile affect, are highly stimulation-seeking and/or hyperactive, can revert to boredom if unsatisfied, and experience impulses to shock and/or harm others. Low Ma2s deny such patterns and are calm and risk-avoidant. High Ma3s (Imperturbability) deny social anxiety but feel impatient and irritable toward others and say they are seldom influenced by the arguments or opinions of others. Low Ma3s are suggestible yet uncomfortable with others. People high on Ma4 (Ego Inflation) can be grandiose, certainly have a streak of narcissism, and resent demands from others, especially if the others are somehow perceived as underlings. Low Ma4s accept most demands from others as reasonable and make reasonably objective self-appraisals.

□      ## SCALE O (Si)

Scale O, subtitled Social Introversion, containing sixty-nine items, was developed later than the other scales and as a result does not have as much consensual clinical experience or data supporting it. Subscales are now available for this scale. Si1—Shyness/Self-Consciousness, Si2—Social Avoidance, and Si3—Self/Other Alienation (Ben-Porath et al., 1989). These subscales can help considerably in the clinical interpretation of the Si scale. Persons high on Si1 show classic shyness and social discomfort and avoidance, both with individuals and groups. Si2s especially avoid group interactions. Si3s are more "neurotic," i.e., they have low self-esteem, lack self-confidence and are nervous and indecisive.

Scores on 9 are usually quite stable over time and may represent biologic and constitutional factors that contribute to an introversion-extroversion component and feelings of social discomfort.

This scale was designed to assess the propensity for avoidance of social responsibilities and contact with others. While it seems to assess this factor, it also may tap psychomotor depression, particularly when associated with social insecurity. Such individuals would score high on scale O and are usually perceived by others as oversensitive and touchy. Charles Manson, certainly a touchy person at best, had an O score above 80 T, along with scores over 80 T on 4, 8, and 9. A T score over 70 occasionally signifies a well-socialized and controlled but basically psychotic personality who has not been identified by the other scales. Individuals scoring low on scale O are likely to be seen as happy-go-lucky and extroverted, but also as opportunistic and manipulative, and they may occasionally manifest problems in impulse control. Yet, a low score on O often mutes the pathology suggested by elevated scores on other scales; it indicates the person may be able to vent pathology in socially acceptable ways or in a reasonably non-self-destructive manner. Very low scorers are very superficial, and often manipulative, in relationships.

Elderly individuals score a bit higher on this age-driven scale. Persons high on scale O are often initially resistant in therapy because they fear rejection in interpersonal relationships and are insecure about increased vulnerability. Yet, if they can deal with this issue in the initial stages of therapy, the prognosis is reasonably positive, for they are inclined to work productively in dealing with their symptoms. Social-skills training is useful here. Marital couples with a T-score difference of twenty or more are very likely to experience marital difficulties.

## ■  MMPI-2 Interrelationship Interpretations

The reader should use the guidelines for interpretation delineated at the front of the prior section on individual scale interpretations. Since there is a small number of MMPI-2 3-point codes with valid correlates, they are discussed within the first relevant 2-point code, e.g., the 2-4-7/2-7-4/4-7-2 code is discussed within the section on the 2-4/4-2 code.

Note that one of the most frequent code types in psychiatric settings is a WNL (Within Normal Limits). They describe themselves in a variety of positive terms. If this is not consistent with the data, consider the possibility you may have a person with a chronic, severe personality disorder or possibly a psychotic individual who can cover and/or deflect attention from his or her symptomatology.

Spike 1s have a long somatization history that they use to control others (even if they have some actual symptomatology). They are not at all psychologically minded and are refractory to intervention.

The 1-2/2-1 combination is consistently indicative of somatic disturbance, accompanied by a degree of irritability, agitation, and anxiety. These individuals do "hurt" in one way or another. Unfortunately, they have often learned to live with their complaints (and their complaining), so even when they change through intervention, a return of symptoms is probable. The 1-2 code is relatively infrequent and, without associated elevations, points to the somatoform disorders. If 7, 8, and F are also elevated, schizophrenia should be considered. The 2-1 code is a more frequent combination, particularly in males. Men here show somatic tension along with pessimism and depression, and there is usually little physical basis for their disorders. Women who score a 2-1 code show more classical hypochondriacal patterns, with an emphasis on restlessness and tension, while adolescents are tense and shy and often have academic problems, sometimes school-phobia. When the pattern is 2-1 rather than 1-2, there is a greater emphasis on tension-anxiety and depression.

When one is assessing an inpatient sample, particularly male, alcoholism and depression should be considered, particularly episodic forms of alcoholism accompanied by somatic concerns. Persons with the 1-2/2-1 code are generally passive-dependent in interpersonal relationships, are concrete in their thinking, and are not likely to take responsibility for their behaviors, especially if 3 and 4 are also elevated. This passivity, combined with a general avoidance of responsibility, makes them at best a moderate risk in therapy. They need very directive and structured therapy targeted at overt symptoms and do not do well in traditional psychotherapy. They can become medication-dependent, but an antidepressant like imipramine, can help restore disturbed sleep patterns (Lewak et al., 1990).

Scales 1, 2, and 3 are commonly referred to as the neurotic triad, and elevations on these scales are found in most neurotic disorders, although "chronically hypochondriacal" may be the most applicable term when all three scales are elevated. These clients often exhibit an exaggerated need for affection. When scales 1 and 3 are elevated, with a valley (10 T-score points or more) on scale 2 (the conversion V), these clients are prone to use somatic disorder as a projection channel for their personal difficulties. The function is hysteroid and/or hypochondriacal rather than classically psychophysiological in nature, and they strongly resist psychological interpretations of their disorders. Persons with an acute illness tend to have high scale-2 scores, often without remarkable elevations on other scales. Persons with a 1-2-3 code (in that order) are indeed on a downward slope, that is, their functioning is often deteriorating. Acute clinical distress, with possible neurologic involvement, and/or masking of depression is signaled by 1-2-9 and 2-1-9 codes. Persons with 1-2-3-4 or 2-1-3-4 codes are usually alcoholics, often with a strong hostility and/or acting-out component.

The 1-3/3-1 pattern is common in older people and in women, and when other scales are not particularly elevated, it reflects a combination of neurotic symptomatology and psychophysiological concerns. Consistent with the hysteric component, these persons have shallow interpersonal relationships, are narcissistic, and are either somewhat Pollyannaish or avoidant in reaction to their problems. They are resistant to psychological treatment; brief stress-innoculation treatment may be the most useful approach (Butcher, 1990). Males who show the 1-3/3-1 pattern may be feminine in orientation, particularly if this is accompanied by an elevation on scale 5. When elevations on 1 and 3 are accompanied by a high 7, a panic disorder is quite possible. In adolescents, this profile is often accompanied by somatic problems and attention-seeking behaviors, and they are often referred because of school problems.

The 1-3/3-1 codes are common, and if 1 is greater than 3, there is more irritability, whining, and pessimism. When 3 is higher, there is more optimism, so a more long-suffering martyrlike complex may be in evidence. To the degree that scale 1 is close to the height of scale 3 and scale 2 is somewhat lower, conversion reactions are more likely, although true medical conditions (even though "real" symptoms may be exaggerated here too) also show this pattern. Such complaints as hypertension, low-back pain, eating disorders (such as anorexia nervosa and obesity), and gastrointestinal disorders are common. These individuals are seldom truly incapacitated by their symptoms, and there is usually a neurotic component. They dissociate from anger, sadness, and/or grief. They fear being judged as "bad" by others. Persons who show a multiple personality are also likely to obtain a 1-3/3-1 code. The combination of passivity, resistance to responsibility in a psychological disorder, preference for medical explanations, and the suggestibility and high need for structure all predict problems in psychotherapy with 1-3/3-1 clients. They prefer powerful and magical cures and are inclined to terminate the therapy relationship prematurely if signs of concern by the therapist are not forthcoming. When a 1-3/3-1 is associated with a high K, and especially if F, 2, 7, and 8 are low, they are very defensive, almost "overly normal," helpful, and sympathetic. They cannot tolerate the role of "patient" and resist any interpretation of unconventionality or vulnerability (Butcher and Graham, 1988). They easily habituate to drugs.

When the 1-3/3-1 profile is accompanied by a marked elevation on scale 8 and an elevation on F, one must look for somatic delusions and/or psychotic paranoia. Types under the 1-3-8 code are commonly diagnosed as schizophrenic disorder, paranoid type, or paranoid personality disorder. They may appear as delusional, with bizarre symptomatology. Depression and suicidal ideation or behaviors may be present, and such individuals often are preoccupied with religion or sex. They are prone to substance abuse; are often loud, angry, anxious, restless, or bored; and aren't particularly interested in forming personal relationships. Types under the 1-3-9 code are occasionally diagnosed as having organic brain syndrome or, more likely, somatoform disorder (especially conversion reactions). They tend to be impulsive, and if the organic brain syndrome is present, they will likely show spells of aggressiveness (Graham, 1987).

The 1-4/4-1-code type is relatively infrequent with inpatient groups, yet it occurs at least moderately often in outpatient clinical settings. In either case, it occurs far more often in men; commonly indicates consistent problems in meeting the responsibilities of life, with resultant self-pitying and antiauthoritarian attitudes rather than classic psychopathy; is correlated with hypochondriasis; and is possibly focused on low-back pain or headaches. With inpatients, it is more often associated with a combination of somatization symptoms, narcissism, and alcohol problems, and there are correlated problems with the vocational and interpersonal areas, particularly with the opposite sex. The 1-4/4-1 adolescent is provocative, defiant, and pessimistic, with problems at both home and school, and may even make manipulative suicide attempts.

Persons of this type are most responsive to short-term symptomatic treatment, and even here, the response is up and down at best. There is often a high associated score in the L scale, and if so, such persons do poorly in psychotherapy because of their resistance, somatization, and possible problems with alcohol. A very low score on 1, combined with a high score on 4, suggests someone who has truly given up on his or her body and is likely to take high risks physically, possibly as a counterphobic reaction to early anxiety about bodily symptoms (Fowler, 1981).

The 1-6/6-1 code is also rare. It indicates somatic and hypochondriacal preoccupations, probably delusional in nature if 8 is also high. It may indicate an attempt to stave off an emerging psychotic process and has the associated projected hostility. Adolescents with this code are emotionally insecure, defensive, and evasive, with family problems in general and father-absence specifically occurring.

The 1-7/7-1 code, which occurs more often in males, generally reflects high somatic tension and many physical symptoms. Obsessive patterns, especially focused on somatic complaints and pain, and feelings of inferiority are typical. They may report sleep problems and depression.

The 1-8/8-1 code may be indicative of schizophrenia, especially acute schizophrenia, particularly if 8 is markedly elevated and F is also elevated. In general, such persons often have vague and even odd medical complaints, have trouble with expression of aggression, and may alternate behaviorally within a classic passive-aggressive pattern. Types under the 1-8/8-1 code may also feel socially inadequate (and often are) and lack trust in others. They become isolated and alienated from peers, which may lead to nomadic life styles and accompanying poor work histories. They may show sexual-deviate patterns. They usually have some dissociative or schizoid components, especially if scale O is also high.

The 1-9/9-1 profile is a rare code, marked by a high level of agitation, irritability, and distress, yet they may report themselves as carefree and independent. Masked depression should be considered. Gastrointestinal symptoms and headaches also occur. Types under the 1-9/9-1 code may appear to be ambitious, but they often lack direction and experience and may become frustrated when their goals are not met. Such persons may be passive-dependent in actual functioning, yet maintain gruff exteriors. If a number of other scales, including F, are moderately elevated, the possibility of brain damage should be considered. Although infrequent in adolescents, males with this code are aggressive and evasive, while females are extroverted and tense.

An extremely rare code, the 1-0/0-1 pattern indicates high social discomfort, passive-avoidant patterns, conventional behaviors (out of fear of being caught), and numerous somatic complaints.

Since a spike (a marked elevation relative to all other scales) on scale 2 particularly taps symptomatic or reactive depression, it is unstable on repeat testing, compared to other scales. The spike-2 type is seldom described in clinical literature, but when found, it is likely to be a depression in response to environmental stress. In some cases, it is related to an ongoing depressive process that develops out of an inability to deal effectively with aggression, with a concomitant history of rage reaction (Kelley and King, 1979a). They are usually introverted and reserved. If a person with a spike 2 denies depression, further evaluation for possible suicide risk is especially important (Butcher and Graham, 1988). They usually respond well to short-term therapy. If they don't, look for an emergence of elevations on 4, 7, and/or 8.

The 2-3/3-2 code is marked by apathetic depression, anxiety, and overcontrol, with depression predominating when 2 is higher than 3 and with anxiety and accompanying neurotic and somatic symptoms predominating when 3 is higher than 2. In both codes, there is evidence of passive dependency and shyness, particularly when 2 is high and 9 is low. The emphasis here is more on inadequacy than on somatization, the latter being primary in the 1-2/2-1 code. Clients with a 2-3/3-2 profile are more likely to have accepted their psychopathology, as opposed to the 2-7/7-2 types, who are usually still struggling to cope with it. The 2-3/3-2 in females has more emphasis on sexual dysfunction and depression (and their depression may reflect a failure of histrionic defenses), whereas in males there is a bit more of a dependent yet driven component. When scales 4, 7, and 8 are also moderately elevated in a 2-3/3-2 type, histrionic components are probable, although actual acting-out may be muted to the degree 7 is high. The 2-3/3-2s seem to seek responsibility in vocational and interpersonal situations but then are stressed by and dislike the responsibility associated with such commitments. They are achievement- and power-oriented and are overcontrolled, but they are sensitive to rejections, so they do not get into situations where actual competition could take place. In this sense, they are "homebodies" and prone to agoraphobic or avoidant personality disorder patterns.

To the degree that 2 is greater than 3, success in psychotherapy is more likely. In fact, some elevation on 2 is almost a prerequisite for success in psychotherapy because it suggests an allowance for vulnerability that the therapist can work with. When 3 is greater than 2, there is a greater tendency to avoid intrapsychic introspection and more likelihood of projection. Hence, response to psychotherapy is poorer and directive and dramatic therapies are more helpful. Medication can be helpful, although they are prone to quickly report "distressing" side effects (Lewak et al., 1990).

Moderate elevations on scales 2, 3, and 7 are characteristics of the phobic disorders and sexual dysfunctions. In addition to these types of problems, adolescents with this code types are clearly marked by poor peer relationships, especially with the opposite sex. They are loners, except for some subgroups in the school setting.

The 2-4/4-2 code is relatively common in inpatient populations, but not as likely to occur in outpatients. Since 2-4/4-2s are often both depressed and consumers of stimulation (Anderson and Bauer, 1985), alcoholism or other kinds of substance abuse are common. Other types of concomitant sociolegal problems (and some situational guilt) also occur; these people are often secondary psychopaths "in trouble." (After being apprehended for the assassination of Martin Luther King, Jr., James Earl Ray presented a clear 4 (T = 90)-2 (T = 82) pattern.) They are immature and egocentric and are ambivalent about whether to indulge in self-pity or projection. If scales 2, 4, 8, and 9 are all high, there may be evidence of schizophrenic disorder, and if 6 is also elevated, a possible paranoid component may be present.

Even though 2-4/4-2 types can often present a facade of confident behaviors, they easily move into manipulative and impulsive behaviors, including suicide. In that same vein, they are likely to manifest a "cry for help," possibly through manipulative suicide gestures. They verbalize a need for help, then when it is proffered, they terminate therapy before fully dealing with the more basic aspects of their problems. In general, male alcoholics with these patterns show a long history of alcohol abuse that is associated with secondary psychopathic patterns. Female alcoholics in this code type are more likely to have depressive components, situational stress, and physical complaints. A disturbed family background is common (Anderson and Bauer, 1985), so family and/or marital background is usually necessary. Working on a series of small, specific goals is a good strategy. Adolescents with this code usually also have very disturbed families, school problems, runaway behavior, and drug abuse patterns.

The 2-4/4-2 code, when accompanied by an elevation on 7, suggests a modal diagnosis of passive-aggressive personality disorder. Depression and anxiety may also be present. The 2-4-7/7-4-2/4-7-2 pattern is common among passive-aggressive personalities and male alcoholics, who tend to be fearful, worried, and high-strung. They avoid competitive situations and are conflicted about dependency, yet show anger, hostility, and immaturity. They tend toward phobic behaviors and may be ruminative or overideational. They may have problems with anxiety during treatment, but they seem to respond well to goal-oriented therapies (Graham, 1987).

The 2-5/5-2 code is very rare in females. Those few who do display it are usually from a lower social class, showing much interpersonal and social-role conflicts. Males with this code are passive, noncompetitive, sensitive, and idealistic and often manifest chronic but mild depression. Conflicts are handled via fantasy and self-awareness.

The profile type 2-6/6-2 is rare and is primarily seen in females. They are likely to complain of physical symptoms first; on further examination, they often report a recent interpersonal stress, such as breaking up with a lover or spouse (Kelley and King, 1979c). They tend to be more flat than depressed in affect, show paranoid ideation and anger, are often openly hostile, are likely to have had relatives who have had problems with alcohol, and are concerned about potential alcoholism in their own lives. They are inclined to be dependent (although they feel trapped and resentful), are preoccupied with thoughts of suicide, and have often made manipulative suicidal gestures in the past. They are significantly disturbed characterologically and thus may earn the diagnosis of borderline or paranoid personality disorder. Medications that do not threaten their vigilance set or tap their addiction potential can be useful in the short-run. To the degree 6 is high and is higher than an elevated 2, a psychotic paranoid pattern is possible. Therapy is difficult, although the elevated 2 makes it possible. Adolescents with a 2-6/6-2 are more inclined to be introverted and insecure, with strong conflicts over sexual feelings.

The 2-7/7-2 pattern is very common in outpatients, especially males. If both scores are very high, you can expect the presence of agitated depression, difficulty in concentration, somatic complaints, and a high probability of suicidal thoughts. When scales 4, 8, and 9 are also elevated and 1 is low, the probability of acting out suicidal thoughts is raised; the elevation on 8 in particular gives a cue as to the lack of control and/or presence of psychosis. If O is high, interpersonal avoidance and fear of rejection can also be expected. Males who show this overall pattern are more likely to have concomitant obsessive-compulsive patterns (especially when 7 is higher than 2), as well as vague somatic complaints and insomnia.

Persons with the 2-7/7-2 pattern are generally passive and dependent, yet are tense and often somewhat depressed, show little anger or hostility, and keep emotionally distant from most people. Further, 2-7/7-2 types may be rigid in their thinking and may be poor problem solvers. They may also be meticulous, perfectionistic, and present themselves as extremely moral and religious people (Graham, 1987). The scale-7 component points more to anhedonia than to classic depression; if it is high in the 2-7/7-2 combination, it points more to a lack of ability to experience pleasure than to psychomotor retardation (Gynther and Green, 1980). As a result, the clinician should explore possible suicide ideation. When scale 1 is also elevated, the agitated anxiety of the 2-7/7-2 profile is channeled into marked somatization. A neurotic diagnosis is probable, and assertive training can be helpful.

In general, the prognosis for 2-7/7-2 types in psychotherapy is positive, as they usually remain in therapy, especially to the degree 7 is elevated, since 7s persist in everything. If both 2 and 7 are very high, it is difficult to do therapy (especially if you are a 4-9 therapist and want to get on with things) as their problem-solving abilities are paralyzed. If 2 and 7 are below 50, it is difficult to do intrapsychic therapy. Anxilytic medications can be helpful, but should be administered on a time-contingent basis, e.g., 3 to 6 months, to avoid their proneness to habituation.

When scale 4 (rather than 1) is elevated (2-7-4), chronic alcoholism, family and marital problems, passive-aggressive patterns, and underachievement are probable. 2-7-4 individuals are self-deprecating, guilty, may be counterphobic to dependency, and show some chronic depression. They often show alcohol and family problems and are difficult to treat. When 2, 7, 4, and 5 are elevated (low 5 in females), these persons often appear weak and self-effacing and elicit deprecation from others. The person seen as the "clown" or "silly egghead-intellectual" is often found here.

When elevations on 2 and 7 are associated with an elevation on scale 3 (the 2-7-3), one finds both high aspirations and high standards. There is often success in achievement, yet with a high cost in stress; paradoxically, the tendency toward passive dependency is even more marked, and they elicit "rescuing" in others (including therapists). They need firm confrontation. Passive behaviors accompanied by underlying anger and hostility are more likely when the elevation on scale 2 is predominant, associated with high elevations on scales F, 8, and 4 and only a moderate elevation on scale 7 (Carson, 1969). Fowler (1981) notes than when a high 5 is combined with a high 2-7/7-2, there is a paradoxically high probability of sexual acting-out.

The 2-7-8/2-8-7 3-point code type shows features of both psychosis and neurosis. These clients are tense, phobic, depressed, and often suicidal, yet also may show brief psychotic episodes, somatic symptoms, and blunted emotional responses. They often need crisis intervention plus psychopharmacology. They set high standards for themselves, yet feel inadequate and inferior. They often are schizoid and show interest in obscure subjects. Males with some high point combinations of scales 2, 7, and 8 are more likely to be psychotic than females, who are more likely to be neurotic (Kelley and King, 1979b).

The 2-8/8-2 code occurs infrequently, particularly in outpatient groups. A sense of having been deprived or hurt as a child is typical, as if one had been raised by one of Harlow's "wire-mothers." Confusion, a sense of being "broken" or defective, concreteness, social awkwardness, a high level of tension, and depression are common. Individuals may also have blackouts, nausea, or vomiting. If scale 1 is also raised, then somatic delusions are probable. If 4 is high, too, acting-out and fears of loss of control are common. Another common diagnosis is bipolar disorder: When 2 is markedly high and greater than 8, psychotic depression is likely; but when 8 is greater than 2 and particularly high, a schizophrenic or schizoaffective adjustment is more likely. In either case, there is often suicidal ideation, and it is more likely to be associated with a specific plan than in the 2-7/7-2 profile. Even where the 2-8/8-2 code is associated with only mild elevations, inefficiency and problems in carrying out plans occur; they fear a (further) loss of control, and a sense of having been rejected by others, including therapists, is common. They need support and nurturance, but therapeutic relationships are stormy and not often successful. In general, this code type is more indicative of pathology in females, and with them particularly it should be a cue to look for substance abuse (Kelley and King, 1979a). In adolescents, these same patterns equally apply, although a history of nonspecific brain disorder and/or hyperactivity is not uncommon.

The 2-9/9-2 profile incorporates a true paradox, since it is the manifestation of simultaneous manic and depressive components; that is, it represents an attempt through manic defenses to cope with underlying depression, although such a coping pattern is not often successful. If both 2 and 9 are very high, a bipolar affective disorder is suggested, although possibility of a defense against depression caused by loss from organic brain damage should also be considered. Persons with this pattern often feel agitated, moody, and irritable. This pattern is occasionally found in male alcoholics who are agitated and also defending themselves against depression by increased alcohol abuse. Clients with the 2-9/9-2 profile may report anxiousness and somatic problems, particularly in the upper gastrointestinal tract. Medication is often necessary, but this requires a high level of monitoring as they are inclined to self-regulate their drug use. In adolescents, the 2-9/9-2 profile can reflect tension, narcissism, separation anxiety, and problems in developing a distinct identity.

When 2 is low, but K and 9 are elevated (the K-9 profile), the personality is organized around competitiveness and interpersonal power. These individuals are narcissistic and depend upon evidence of weakness in others for their self-enhancement—they like to "run up the score." In females, it may be evident in exhibitionistic attractiveness—the "Hollywood syndrome."

The 2-0/0-2 profile is obained by shy individuals who are insecure about their introversion and as a result have chronic, episodic depression. It is also particularly common in women and in adolescents who are having social difficulties. In all age ranges, it may manifest itself as a mild, chronic depression. Fowler (1981) reports that this pattern is notably common in parents (especially women) who bring their children to child-guidance clinics, and that 2-0/0-2s ultimately often beget 2-0/0-2s. Any training in social skills is helpful, as is psychotherapy to help these shy and socially inept people adjust to and accept the more stable components of the introverted pattern. Single doses of antidepressants at night can be helpful, as these clients often have sleep problems, do not like to take medications, and are sensitive to side effects (Lewak et al., 1990).

Spike 3s tend to be Pollyannaish and conventional, deny any disharmony with others, and can be phobic toward assertion or anger. They are non-psychologically-minded and easily develop physical symptoms that carry secondary gain. Although others are likely to see them as "spacey," they see themselves as rational and logical. They can be almost phobic toward experiencing physical or emotional pain. They may elicit exploratory surgeries (Lewak et al., 1990), looking for the "cause" of their inner pain. They are not likely to change much in therapy and usually quickly terminate therapy once the referral crisis is past.

The 3-4/4-3 profile, a common code in outpatients, especially females, is associated with problems in impulse control, usually focused on hostility. When 4 is greater than 3, there is a higher probability of acting-out behavior; this profile is often noted in female delinquents. The 4-3s are usually relatively passive, but show emotional or behavioral outbursts, as well as generally poor judgment. They are sensitive to, and project, any criticism. However, as Davis and Sines (1971) suggest, when 3 is greater than 4, the anger is more repressed and more likely to manifest itself in intermittent aggression. Diagnoses such as a dissociative reaction, intermittent explosive disorder, or passive-aggressive personality disorder are common, whereas a diagnosis that focuses on emotional instability and anger is more characteristic when 4 is greater than 3. Some 3-4/4-3 clients may exhibit sexual promiscuity. They may appear to be socially conforming, yet are inwardly rebellious. Suicidal ideation is likely following bouts of drinking and acting-out behaviors (Graham, 1987), reflecting an ongoing, unacknowledged depressive component (as a therapist, you must be aware of this or you will get nowhere). High conflict over dependency, denial, the antisocial aspects, and the tendency to avoid responsibility for behavior make high success in psychotherapy improbable. They also are prone to misuse prescription medications.

When this code type is found in females, it often reflects marital problems associated with sexual difficulties and, as already noted, problems in dealing effectively with anger. These persons are usually overcontrolled but occasionally fly into rages (Kelley and King, 1979c). As a 3-4 client changes to a 4-3, divorce becomes more probable (Fowler, 1981).

The 3-5/5-3 code, moderately common in males and uncommon in females, usually manifests itself in a man who *appears* to be competent and even charming. However, narcissism, denial, immaturity, and essential passivity mean there is little productivity, persistence, or ultimate responsibility. The code is frequent among fathers of child clients. Adolescents with a 3-5/5-3 are moderately depressed and withdrawn, are affectively shallow, often have weight problems, and lack skills with the opposite sex.

The 3-6/6-3 code is characterized by overt anxiety, tension, and rigidity that cover a strong fear of criticism and a blandly manifested but deeply suppressed hostility. There is a denial of this hostility, especially of any of its results as it emerges in a passive or episodic aggressive fashion. The hostility is often directed toward significant others, yet is denied or repressed, so marital, family, or social problems are common. But their hostility, egocentricity, and resistance to psychological causation make therapy difficult. Although adolescents with this code type often perform well academically, they often manifest drug abuse and/or suicide attempts and are oversensitive, evasive, and resentful.

People who score moderately high on these two scales are hypersensitive to criticism, suspicious, and hostile, yet they overtly promote themselves as naive and optimistic about the world. They were often, and sometimes still are, "model" children. They have significant difficulties in interpersonal relationships and perceive their problems as emanating from others. To the degree that these two scales are high, there is more likely to be a clear paranoid disorder. If there is distinct bimodality, paranoia is common, whereas a rise on scales F and 8 suggests paranoid schizophrenia as more likely.

The uncommon 3-7/7-3 person is an "anticipatory worrier." Although worrisome and prone to take (and seek identity in) responsibility, they are more denying and repressed (especially the 3-7) than their relatively high 7 would suggest is likely. They strongly fear the loss of control of anger in themselves or others, possibly reflecting abuse situations in childhood. They manifest various physical and psychosomatic disorders (often including insomnia), and especially if stressed. They may elicit elective surgeries, but are likely to respond negatively to the direct outcome or the side effects. Assertiveness training and anger management techniques are useful, as are behavioral procedures like thought stopping and relaxation training. They are prone to dependency on pain- or anxiety-reducing medications, but they respond well to them in the short run.

The 3-8/8-3 person (also an uncommon code) shows confusion, distress, and a high probability of anxiety attacks, which are occasionally then channeled into either phobias or acting-out (depending on scale 4). Histrionic, narcissistic, and dependency features are common. Obscure, intractable somatic symptoms are often reported. If both scales are very high and F is also high, consider possible cognitive dysfunction. When scores are more moderate, consider a diagnosis that includes dependency and dissociative and/or hysteroid defense mechanisms. This disturbed thinking may manifest itself in unclear thoughts, poor concentration, lapses of memory, unusual ideas, or loose and unclear ideational associations. Further, delusions and hallucinations, as well as incoherent speech, may be present. The most common diagnosis is schizophrenia, although somatoform disorder may also be present. If 2 is moderately elevated in this pattern, psychotherapy is usually effective. If it is low, a supportive and structured therapeutic orientation is more productive. When an elevation on scale 3 is accompanied by an elevation on K and concomitant low scores on scales F and 8, look for an individual who is conforming, constricted emotionally, and yet dependent on others without acknowledging his or her dependency because it signifies vulnerability.

The 3-9/9-3 profile is rare, usually found in women rather than men. These individuals are extroverted, often dramatic persons who quickly draw attention to themselves in social settings. They crave approval and dread failure, but then resent the control this need transfers to others. These persons usually manifest acute medical distress and/or depression as a referral complaint, often episodically, but on closer examination are likely to show evidence of a histrionic personality or, less frequently, an actual brain dysfunction or a conversion disorder. Alcoholism is common. They are verbally aggressive and inclined to distort their perceptions easily, and they have particular difficulty dealing effectively with sexual relationships, especially communication in the relationship. At a secondary level, they are likely to show headaches and a number of other somatic complaints (Kelley and King, 1979c). Adolescents show similar patterns and are often embroiled in family conflicts.

A spike-4 profile commonly suggests problems with the law. Spike 4s are often classic psychopaths (or college students, who are often high). They are egocentric and impulsive and have difficulty in any relationship of any depth, although they often relate well initially. As 0 approaches a T of 30, this is even more pathognomic; they easily show anger outbursts. They are emotional survivors who are unlikely to truly try again in a relationship. If both the IQ and K are high, calculated and more-clever criminal behavior can be expected, e.g., white-collar crime. They typically stay in therapy only because they have to, and medications are contradicted. The aging process is the most effective therapy.

The 4-5/5-4 code denotes an antiestablishment and antiauthoritarian personality, but the subtlety of expression of such attitudes is modulated by parental-cultural background, IQ, and level of education. Although a rare code in females, if present, it often includes a strong "masculine protest," as well as overt aggression. The model diagnosis for the 4-5/5-4 profile is passive-aggressive personality disorder (Graham, 1990).

Men with a 4-5/5-4 profile are often bohemian characters inclined toward various types of nonconformity. They are defensive, yet report themselves as emotionally stable, and are passively rebellious. Ambivalence over dependency and control is common, as well as regards sexual identity. They may be overtly homosexual and flaunt this in a passive-aggressive manner. Males with a high 4 and a low 5 show stereotyped macho masculinity. Females with low-5 and high-4 scores, on the other hand, lean toward social masochism. They adopt an overly feminine posture but carry a significant degree of underlying hostility. They often generate hostility and then use guilt and/or legal sanctions to punish the aggressor. To the degree 6 is also elevated, there is a transfer of blame onto others. Females with both a high 5 and a high 4 are those who have adopted behaviors that do not fit with the traditional female role. If these scores are not markedly elevated, they suggest a woman who has developed an independent and competent life style. Adolescents with this code type are more likely to directly rebel and act out. They are provocative, prone to abuse drugs, and often delinquent.

The 4-6/6-4 code is mildly similar to the 3-8/8-3 code, except that there are fewer anxiety and phobic components and the emphasis is on narcissism, suspiciousness, and anger. They report vague physical and psychological symptoms and often show very poor work and interpersonal histories. It occurs with some frequency in adolescents, where it does not signal the degree of pathology it does in adults, although they are likely to abuse drugs and have strong conflicts with parents and school. In both adolescents and adults, there is often a transfer-of-blame mechanism, and others view them as obnoxious. To the degree scale 3 is also elevated, the pattern is more one of immaturity than obnoxiousness.

A passive-aggressive diagnosis is common, although paranoid schizophrenia must be considered if scales 4 and 6 are very high and scales 8 and F are high. Women with this pattern who are also high on 5 are hostile and angry and are effective at eliciting rage reactions in others, especially males. Women with a 4-6/6-4 and a low 5 are overly identified with the traditional female role, but feel trapped as a wife or mother, and react with passive-aggressive patterns. Persons with a 4-6/6-4 pattern are usually bitter, obnoxious, and difficult to deal with. They expect others to change rather than themselves, and they quickly reject responsibility for any problems and may abuse alcohol. Intermittent aggression and a prepsychotic adjustment are also probable (Fowler, 1981). They may present somatizations in the forms of asthma, hay fever, hypertension, headaches, blackouts, and cardiac problems (Graham, 1987). They avoid being involved in any therapy, if at all possible, and seldom make any significant and lasting changes even when they are involved. Little progress can be made unless there is some resolution of the dependency that underlies the more overt anger patterns. Low doses of a nonsedating phenothiazine can be useful if the individual is very paranoid and angry, but addiction potential is possible.

In women, when 4 and 6 are high and 5 is low (the Scarlett O'Hara V), they are hostile and angry, but passive-aggressive in their expression. They bait others with their dependency and demands. Whereas a boat is a hole in the water you throw money into, this type of woman is a hole in a family you throw affection into. If 3 is also high, they are overtly social or warm. They still irritate, if not enrage others, but are blithely unaware of how or why this happens.

The 4-7/7-4 combination presents the paradox of the insensitivity and social alienation connoted by scale 4, combined with the moodiness and excessive concern about the effects of one's behavior connoted by scale 7. As a result, such individuals, both adolescents and adults, may be involved in cyclical emotional responses and acting-out behaviors in which damage to other people is followed by apparent regret—such as the alcoholic who goes on a spree and disrupts friends and family, then follows this with contrite pleas for forgiveness. They easily dissimulate, yet there is good reason to believe that they are truly insensitive to the feelings of others, and family situations are usually very dysfunctional. Certain sexual-deviate patterns that are a counterphobic response to a fear of the opposite sex attain a 4-7/7-4 profile. When the profile has high scores on 2-7 and 4-9, there is often a warring between these somewhat disparate elements. With age, both 4 and 9 tend to diminish, and the more obsessive and depressive elements of the 2-7 profile emerge.

Clients with a 4-7/7-4 do indicate a desire for change and will become involved in psychotherapy, especially to the degree 7 is higher than 4. Critical to success is their ability to see the link of their anxiety to consequent impulsive, self-destructive acting-out behaviors. At the same time, however, they are concrete in their thinking and not psychologically minded; thus, they are not easily responsive to most insight-oriented therapies and they prefer symptomatic support and structure.

The 4-8/8-4 code types are perceived by others as narcissistic, unpredictable, or weird, and these perceptions are accurate. They are inclined toward antisocial and schizoid behaviors, yet these are usually within a family structure and reflect some underlying dependency and a deteriorating loss of control. Very often, from an early age, they develop a set to perceive others as hostile and dangerous, and their consequent "striking-out" in turn reinforces their sense of alienation. In this vein, Scott and Stone (1986) found 4-8/8-4 profiles to predominate in a sample of adult and adolescent clients who had been victims of father–daughter incest as children.

They tend toward "black moods" and may have periods of obsessive suicidal ideations. And if both scales are very high, with 8 greater than 4, the likelihood of bizarre thinking, psychosis, and paranoid suspiciousness increases. In this case, the clinician should consider the diagnosis of paranoid schizophrenia. Usual diagnoses include schizophrenia (paranoid type), antisocial personality, schizoid personality, or paranoid personality. Persons with a 4-8/8-4 code, especially when there is also a high score on 6, usually had very destructive family backgrounds and appear to feel as if the "world is a jungle." As a result, they perceive their own acting-out as a matter of survival. Sirhan Sirhan, the assassin of Robert F. Kennedy, showed a clear 4-8-6 pattern, although his F was also almost as high (T = 80) (Fowler, 1981).

When 4 and 8 are high, such individuals may continually show antisocial behaviors (e.g., rape), they are prone to violence if cornered, and they prefer a nomadic and transient existence with few responsibilities. When elevations on 4 and 8 are accompanied by a high F and a low 2, one may find a punitive and interpersonally destructive person who yet goes about in the guise of a helpful person, such as a minister or guidance counselor. Punitive aggression, almost to the point of sadism, is directed into a good cause. In spite of apparently caring roles, they are often schizoid in their personal live. Adolescents of this type are extremely miserable and unhappy, show odd or even bizarre disorder patterns, and are immature and resentful. Therapy is difficult with 4-8s and includes constant "trust-testing," if it goes at all.

The 4-9/9-4 code is a very common one; when high, it is frequently found to indicate a characterological behavior disorder, most often an antisocial personality disorder, both in adults and adolescents. These individuals do not profit from experience, are seekers of a high degree of stimulation, may appear good-natured and charming—yet often get embroiled in sociolegal difficulties, and are self-centered; and show deficient functioning in the interpersonal and vocational areas. At the very least, they show an enduring propensity to subvert the potential "good" of self and family. They are narcissistic and impulsive, and even though they may manifest a certain degree of ambitiousness, they have many problems resulting from their transient life styles, narcissism, acting-out, and inability to follow through on plans. David Berkowitz, the notorious "Son of Sam" killer, presented a clear 9 (T = 78)-4 (T = 75) pattern.

Histories of alcohol abuse, notably episodic sprees, are common, especially if F is also high. On occasion, this pattern is indicative of a bipolar disorder (Graham, 1990). If the 4-9/9-4 profile is distinctly bimodal, these persons are not so consistently aggressive, but they are inclined toward deception. To the degree 8 and 6 are elevated, they are likely to be more directly aggressive. To the degree 0 is elevated, they are more likely to be slick and effective in their manipulations of others.

It is interesting that when women obtain a 4-9 profile that is not markedly high overall, they have been characterized as having high potential for a sales position. If 4 and 9 are only moderately elevated (in men or women) and there is an indication of psychological distress via scale 2, such persons can respond positively in psychotherapy, although initial sessions are generally replete with resistance and confrontation is often required. When 4 and 9 are quite high and 6 and/or 8 are elevated, success in psychotherapy is much less probable. When 4-9s appear in therapy (usually brought there somehow) they want you to fix their worlds, not them, and they also expect quick results.

Persons with a 4-0/0-4 code—usually females, as this is a rare code for males—carry much anger, but they are unable to directly express it because they are shy and evasive. They report little emotional distress and few health problems, but easily develop resentments and hold grudges and can be destructive to others if this does not entail any direct confrontations. One male who did show this pattern, Charles Manson, also had virtually equal elevations, all over 80 T, on 8 and 9 as well.

A spike-5 profile is often indicative of transient situational disturbance. If not, it is usually a person who reports they are self-confident and in good physical and psychological health. It is commonly high in normal, liberal college males and in avowed homosexuals.

The 5-6/6-5 code type is uncommon. These individuals are aloof, abrasive, and/or politically or morally self-righteous. They see themselves as positive on virtually all dimensions, including being liked by others. They are especially inaccurate on the last facet so, not surprisingly, have substantial interpersonal difficulties, especially heterosexually.

Males with a 5-7/7-5 pattern are introspective, excitable, interpersonally sensitive, and show episodes of anxiety and/or depression, along with schizoid components if 0 is also elevated. Females show many inter-personal problems, especially with males.

The 5-8/8-5 person is likely to have a personal and family history marked by physical or sexual abuse, substance abuse, and/or psychiatric disorder. Although not usually psychotic, they have odd or intrusive thoughts, are shy and reserved, and have substantial difficulties in sex-ual and family adjustment.

5-9/9-5 individuals are active stimulation-seekers and are easily bored; whether the consequent behaviors get them in trouble depends on 4, and also on 6, and 8. They like to be in control, and see themselves in a very positive light. They relate easily, although their heterosexual relationships are usually stormy.

Males with a 5-0/0-5 code are introspective but, unlike 5-7/7-5s, are more schizoid and anxious than they are depressed. Both females and males with a 5-0/0-5 code show problems in heterosexual relationships, are easily embarrassed, and see themselves as happy and well adjusted, but they are not. Females with this code often come from lower educa-tion and/or socioeconomic backgrounds and appear passive, yet they show many social-role conflicts.

Spike 6s are rare; when it occurs, the individual is openly distrustful and suspicious and probably clinically paranoid in some fashion. They need to develop trust, but this is a monumental therapeutic task.

The 6-7/7-6 code is uncommon, often associated with elevations on 2 or 8, and denotes anxious, tense, guilt-prone (especially to the degree 2 and/or 7 is high rather than 8), hypersensitive individuals. They typically use obsessive-compulsive defenses that are no longer effective in controlling anxiety and rumination. They misinterpret others, leading to distant or volatile relationships.

The 6-8/8-6 code type is closely associated with a prepsychotic or psychotic adjustment, especially if these scales are substantially elevated. There is much rebellion and anger and other persons are alienated, thereby creating a vicious cycle for their prophecy that they are persecuted. They can be episodically and inappropriately aggressive and, at best, appear unusual to others.

In general, 6-8/8-6s show underlying inferiority, fear-proneness, and low self-esteem, which seem to be counterphobically defended against by an irritable and hostile veneer. They demonstrate poor judgment in a number of areas and are emotionally unstable. They naturally do not respond well to psychotherapy and, if at all receptive, are inclined toward fad treatments. Significantly elevated 6-8/8-6 profiles, with high L and F scores and relatively low scores on scales 3 and 7, suggest markedly disturbed persons who show paranoid ideation, although organic brain syndrome should also be considered. The degree of available psychological energy, often reflected in the degree of accompanying elevation on scale 9, is the determining factor in whether the underly-ing hostility evidences itself.

If both the 6 and 8 scales are quite high (above 75 T) and 7 is relatively low (approximately 65 T), i.e., 6-7-8 — the "paranoid valley" — Gynther et al. (1973a) suggest looking for further evidence of paranoid schizophrenia associated with auditory hallucinations. This is especially true of psychiatric patients with this distinctive profile, as a diagnosis of schizophrenic, paranoid type, is common, but there should also be a thorough consideration of the validity of the profile. These individuals are likely to manifest psychotic behavior, autistic thinking, blunted affect, rapid and incoherent speech, and withdrawal into fantasy when stressed. Psychotropic medications should certainly be considered for this population. Scales 2 and 0 are often above a T-score of 60 in persons with 6-8 or 6-7-8 code types who have a thought disorder and below a 55 T-score in clients with a manic mood disorder (Greene, 1991). The 6-7-8 pattern occurs with adolescents, although learning disabilities and nonspecific brain damage are also commonly noted, as well as violent temper reactions.

The hallmark of the high 6-9/9-6 profile is hostile excitement, and a counterphobic response to emotional involvement, criticism, and dependency seems to underlie this hostile agitation. Referral is often precipitated by a perceived rejection or attack by a loved or trusted other. A diagnosis of paranoid schizophrenia is common. The clinician needs to consider the possibility of organic brain dysfunction where the manic and suspicious adjustment may be a reaction to loss of functioning in a personality that finds loss unacceptable. At more moderate levels, the 6-9/9-6 profile suggests strong dependency and affection needs that are usually not met. These individuals are overresponsive to emotional slights or threats, so often present as angry or hostile reactions. Medication is usually necessary, although they will be distrustful of it and especially of its side effects.

While shy and easily embarrassed, the 6-0/0-6 profiles, especially if 6 is not markedly elevated, are usually well-adjusted and have pleasant though sometimes distant relationships with others.

Spike 7s, an uncommon pattern, are quite shy and are fear-prone and uncertainty-phobic. They are tense and obsessive-compulsive, and phobic patterns are common. The pathology is commonly stable, and they are less successful in therapy than one might initially expect. Time-contingency medications, e.g., 3 months' prescription of antianxiety medication, are helpful.

The 7-8/8-7 pattern, in the moderate range, shows depressive and/or obsessive-compulsive features, although often with much inner turmoil (Butcher and Graham, 1988). If elevations are marked and accompanied by elevations on scales 0 and 2, severe depression, anxiety, and introverted behavior should be expected and deterioration into a more blatant schizophrenic adjustment is possible. If so, it is marked by the use of neologisms, bizarre speech, depersonalization, and possibly catatonic stupor. Even if the less extreme range, these individuals show a low level of social skills, and if they are not diagnosed as schizophrenic, they are likely to have borderline personality traits (Kelley and King, 1979b). When initially seen, 7-8/8-7 clients may be confused and panicked and are typically tense, anxious, insecure, and shy. They may feel chronically insecure, inferior, and inadequate and have a difficult time making decisions. They will usually report problems, especially sexual ones, in interpersonal relationships, and as a result may fantasize profusely (Graham, 1987). Suicide attempts are not infrequent, and to the degree that scale 8 is high, they may have a bizarre quality. To the degree that 7 is greater than 8, these individuals usually retain better control in behavior adjustment, are less likely to be blatantly psychotic, and are still fighting deterioration in functioning. Unfortunately, a high scale 7 is soluble in alcohol and other drugs; fortunately, closely-monitored medication can be of help.

If both scales 7 and 8 are elevated well above the 70-T mark and 8 is higher, schizophrenia is a strong probability, particularly so if scales 1, 2, and 3 are relatively low. This holds true even more for men than for women. Even if no psychosis exists, a significant and pervasive emotional disturbance of some sort is probable.

The 0-7/7-0 code is characterized by tension, insecurity, anxiety, and low self-confidence. This group is shy and has substantial difficulties in interpersonal relationships—especially adolescents with family members—and may be agoraphobic.

Spike 8s are odd, eccentric, and nonconformist, at best. Some are psychotic; most have odd sexual fantasies and often odd behaviors. They tend to be aloof, but unhappy in their aloofness. Their behaviors are often disorganized, and they show poor judgment. Occasionally an intelligent, self-confident and creative (but aloof) individual will present a spike 8. Spike 8s usually need medication, the type of medication often depending on the relative elevation of 2 and 7.

The 8-9/9-8 type identifies a person who is narcissistic and hostile, has difficulties relating effectively to others, and who may at times manifest inappropriate surges of anger or exuberance. It is a more common code in adolescents and young adults, where it is often associated with self-centeredness and hyperactivity. The fear of relating is handled by distractibility techniques, so psychotherapy is extremely difficult. It is very hard for them to focus on any issue for any significant period of time. Medication is often necessary. They are usually responsive to medication, but because of the high 9, may need high dosages of lithium. Even if the scores are only moderately high, there should be much concern about long-term adjustment. Multiple-drug abusers, particularly adolescents, may show this pattern. In adults, a high 8-9/9-8 is associated with a schizophrenic adjustment with a poor prognosis, odd or pressed speech patterns, and delusions and/or hallucinations and confusion. More likely than not, the pattern represents either a disorganized or agitated catatonic schizophrenic, depending on scales 6, 3, and K. If not psychotic, they are at least egocentric and dysfunctional in most life areas. There is often a history of delinquency or at least of behavioral problems. A high 8-9/9-8 associated with elevation on scales F, 2, and 7 may be a schizoaffective disorder, depressed type. Even moderately high 8-9/9-8 elevations are symptomatic of a significant psychopathological process (Butcher and Graham, 1988).

The 8-0/0-8 code is a relatively uncommon one, especially in males and young adults. They are significantly socially avoidant, nonverbal, indecisive, and isolated. Often diagnosed as schizoid, they are not very comfortable with their adjustment and show some anxiety as well as a propensity to become lost in fantasies.

A spike-9 profile is likely to indicate drug abuse and/or antisocial personality disorder; in males, it is also associated with aggressive acting-out (King and Kelley, 1977). In general, spike 9s are extroverted and sociable, but without intimacy. They have high energy levels and occasionally show manic or grandiose episodes. They are usually impulsive and rebellious, with scale 4 being an important modifier. They need to learn to avoid their anxious striving–perceived failure–frustration cycle. Guiding them to be "laid back" or live in the "here and now" is a therapeutic challenge.

Although shy, 9-0/0-9s (a very uncommon code type) usually have adequate social skills and high energy, but can be a bit manic. They are self-confident, occasionally to the point of grandiosity, and usually present themselves as happy and well adjusted.

A spike 0 on the MMPI-2 is suggestive of situational-adjustment difficulties, such as marital problems and/or a schizoid adjustment, or mild but chronic emotional distress that may indicate religiously oriented distress, perhaps an abrupt loss of faith in God (Kelley and King, 1979c). Spike 0s are shy and easily embarrassed, so are prone to phobias and fears, although usually not of major proportions. Their "affect starvation" and the need to positively cope with their characterological shyness will be foci in therapy.

# ■ Diagnosis Code Type Relationships

To facilitate the reader's use of the 2-point codes, a list of first-consideration (not exclusive) diagnoses associated with specific two-point codes is presented in Table 12.2. This table is coordinated with the material in the previous section, as well as with that discussed in the later sections on the various clinical syndromes.

**TABLE 12.2**    First-Consideration Diagnoses and Two-Point Codes

| CODE | FIRST-CONSIDERATION DIAGNOSES |
|---|---|
| 1-2 | Chronic Alcohol Intoxication, Anxiety Disorder, Female Psychosexual Dysfunction, Schizophrenia (rare), Somatization, Hypochondriasis, Depression, Passive-Aggressive Personality Disorder |

**TABLE 12.2**    Continued

| CODE | FIRST-CONSIDERATION DIAGNOSES |
|------|-------------------------------|
| 1-3 | Conversion Disorder, Hypochondriasis, Malingering, Faking-Good, Panic Disorder, Psychogenic Pain Disorder, Eating Disorders, Multiple Personality |
| 1-4 | Hypochondriasis, Social Phobia, Chronic Alcohol Intoxication, Substance Abuse, Somatization, Affective Disorder |
| 1-6 | Somatization, Paranoid Schizophrenia |
| 1-7 | Somatization, Obsessive-Compulsive Disorder, Eating Disorders |
| 1-8 | Pedophilia, Schizoid Personality Disorder, Acute Schizophrenia (relatively rare), Affective Disorder, Borderline Personality Disorder |
| 1-9 | Masked Depression, Post-Traumatic Stress Disorder, Central Nervous System Impairment (rare), Dependent Personality Disorder (rare), Sexual Masochism (rare) |
| 2-1 | Anxiety Disorder, Conversion Disorder, Chronic Alcohol Intoxication, Female Psychosexual Dysfunction, Somatization |
| 2-3 | Female Psychosexual Dysfunction, Depression (especially for females), Generalized Anxiety Disorder, Histrionic Personality Disorder, Panic Disorder, Affective Disorder |
| 2-4 | Acute Alcohol Intoxication, Schizophrenia, Secondary Psychopathy, Antisocial Personality Disorder, Suicide Potential, Unsocialized Nonaggressive Conduct Disorder, Adjustment Disorder |
| 2-5 | Passive-Aggressive Personality Disorder, Dependent Personality Disorder |
| 2-6 | Paranoid Personality Disorder, Major Depression, Paranoid Schizophrenia, Histrionic Personality Disorder, Borderline Personality Disorder (rare) |
| 2-7 | Agoraphobia Avoidant Personality Disorder, Dependent Personality Disorder, Major Depression, Bipolar Disorder, Depressive Episode, Dysthymic Disorder, Chronic Alcohol Intoxication, Factitious Disorder, Generalized Anxiety Disorder, Identity Disorder, Obsessive-Compulsive Disorder, Psychogenic Pain Disorder, Possible Toxic Addiction to Pain Killers, Schizotypal Personality Disorder, Sexual Masochism, Stuporous Catatonic Schizophrenia, Suicide Potential, Zoophilia |
| 2-8 | Depressive Episode, Possible Bipolar or Cyclothymic Disorder, Suicidal, Central Nervous System Impairment, Post-Traumatic Stress Disorder, Generalized Anxiety Disorder, Panic Disorder, Explosive Disorder, Schizoaffective Disorder |
| 2-9 | Bipolar Affective Disorder, Central Nervous System Impairment |
| 2-0 | Depressive Episode, Possible Bipolar or Cyclothymic Disorder, Schizoid Personality Disorder, Avoidant Disorder |

3-1     Compulsive Personality Disorder, Conversion Disorder, Hypochondriasis, Malingering, Faking-Good

3-2     Depressive Episode, Possible Bipolar or Cyclothymic Disorder, Female Psychosexual Dysfunction, Histrionic Personality Disorder

3-4     Histrionic, Borderline, Passive-Aggressive, and Avoidant Personality Disorders, Dissociative Disorder, Intermittent Explosive Disorder, Manic Episode (rare), Pedophilia, Psychogenic Amnesia, Voyeurism, Substance Abuse

3-6     Paranoia, Paranoid Personality Disorder, Paranoid Schizophrenia, Somatization, Affective Disorder

3-7     Depersonalization Disorder, Somatization, Anxiety Disorder

3-8     Multiple Personality, Pedophilia, Schizophrenia (rare), Somatization, Possible Psychosis, Affective Disorder

3-9     Somatization, Bipolar Disorder, Conversion Disorder, Explosive Personality Disorder (rare), Possible Psychosis, Histrionic Personality Disorder (rare), Panic Disorder, Passive-Aggressive Personality Disorder (rare), Somatization

4-1     Hypochondriasis, Social Phobia, Chronic Alcohol Intoxication, Somatization

4-2     Acute Alcohol Intoxication, Primary Psychopath, Antisocial Personality, Schizophrenia, Secondary Psychopath, Suicide Potential, Unsocialized Nonaggressive Conduct Disorder

4-3     Aggression Potential, Explosive Disorder of Impulse Control, Passive-Aggressive Personality Disorder, Pedophilia, Rape, Voyeurism

4-5     Narcissistic and Passive-Aggressive Personality Disorders, Exhibitionism, Homosexuality, Opiate Abuse, Aggression (in females)

4-6     Substance Abuse (especially Amphetamine Disorder), Oppositional Personality Disorder, Chronic Alcohol Intoxication, Paranoid Schizophrenia, Passive-Aggressive Personality Disorder, Somatization (rare), Intermittent Explosive Disorder, Depression

4-7     Chronic Alcohol Intoxication, Bipolar and Cyclothymic Disorder, Substance Abuse

4-8     Exhibitionism, Pedophilia, Primary Psychopathy, Schizoid Personality, Antisocial Personality, Borderline Personality, Pyromania, Rape, Schizophrenia, Sexual Sadism, Unsocialized Aggressive Conduct Disorder

4-9     Amphetamine Disorder, Chronic Alcohol Intoxication, Pathological Gambling, Rape, Secondary Psychopathy, Antisocial Personality, Histrionic Personality, Narcissistic Personality, Sexual Sadism, Socialized Nonaggressive Conduct Disorder

5-1     Transsexualism

5-3     Transvestism

**TABLE 12.2**     Continued

| CODE | FIRST-CONSIDERATION DIAGNOSES |
|---|---|
| 5-7 | Schizoid, Passive-Aggressive Personality Disorder, Anxiety Reactions |
| 6-1 | Paranoid Schizophrenia |
| 6-2 | Borderline Personality Disorder, Shared Paranoid Disorder |
| 6-3 | Paranoia, Paranoid Schizophrenia, Paranoid Personality Disorder, Somatization |
| 6-4 | Chronic Alcohol Intoxication, Paranoia, Paranoid Schizophrenia, Passive-Aggressive Personality Disorder, Shared Paranoid Disorder |
| 6-7 | Obsessive-Compulsive Disorder, Multiple Phobias, Anxiety Reactions, Affective Disorder, Avoidant Disorder |
| 6-8 | Aggressive Acting-Out, Polydrug Abuse, Paranoid Schizophrenia, Central Nervous System Impairment, Borderline Personality Disorder, Schizoaffective Disorder |
| 6-9 | Central Nervous System Impairment, Paranoid Schizophrenia |
| 7-1 | Somatization |
| 7-2 | Agoraphobia, Avoidant Personality Disorder, Dependent Personality Disorder, Depressive Episode, Bipolar or Cyclothymic Disorder, Dysthymic Disorder, Chronic Alcohol Intoxication, Obsessive-Compulsive Disorder, Post-Traumatic Stress and Adjustment Disorder, Sexual Masochism, Suicide Potential |
| 7-3 | Somatization |
| 7-4 | Chronic Alcohol Intoxication |
| 7-8 | Borderline Personality Disorder, Substance Abuse, Brief Reactive Disorder, Depression, Suicide Attempts, Obsessive-Compulsive Disorder, Schizophrenia, Schizophreniform Disorder |
| 7-0 | Anxiety Disorders, Agoraphobia, Avoidant Personality Disorder |
| 8-1 | Pedophilia, Schizophrenia, Schizotypal Personality Disorder |
| 8-2 | Depression, Schizoaffective Disorder |
| 8-3 | Multiple Personality, Pedophilia, Somatization |
| 8-4 | Paranoid Schizophrenia, Pedophilia, Primary Psychopathy, Anti-social Personality, Rape, Unsocialized or Socialized Aggressive Conduct Disorder |
| 8-6 | Central Nervous System Impairment, Schizophrenia, Paranoid Schizophrenia, Primary Psychopathy, Antisocial Personality |
| 8-7 | Borderline Personality Disorder, Brief Reactive Psychosis, Depression, Obsessive-Compulsive Disorder, Schizophreniform Disorder |
| 8-9 | Acting-Out in General, Polydrug Abuse, Agitated Catatonic Schizophrenia, Central Nervous System Impairment, Depression, Schizoaffective Disorder, Disoganized Schizophrenia, Mania, Paranoid Schizophrenia |

| 8-0 | Schizoid and Avoidant Personality Disorders, Schizophrenia |
|---|---|
| 9-1 | Central Nervous System Impairment (rare), Dependent Personality Disorder (rare), Sexual Masochism (rare) |
| 9-2 | Central Nervous System Impairment, Bipolar Affective Disorder |
| 9-3 | Conversion Disorder, Histrionic Personality Disorder (rare), Panic Disorder, Somatization (rare) |
| 9-4 | Chronic Alcohol Intoxication, Secondary Psychopathy, Antisocial Personality |
| 9-6 | Central Nervous System Impairment, Manic Episode, Bipolar or Dysthymic Disorder, Paranoid Schizophrenia |
| 9-8 | Central Nervous System Impairment, Depression, Schizoaffective Disorder, Disorganized Schizophrenia, Mania, Schizoaffective Disorder, Bipolar or Dysthymic Disorder, Paranoid Schizophrenia |
| 0-2 | Depression |
| 0-7 | Agoraphobia |

# ■ Additional Scales

Besides the traditional validity and clinical scales, the most widely us-ed scales are the Content scales, the Supplementary scales, the Harris-Lingoes scales, and the Subtle-Obvious scales, scoring for which has been provided by NCS ever since MMPI-2 came out.

# ■ Content Scales

Most agree the Content scales have been very useful. As noted earlier, in addition to the original clinical scales, they are the only scales plotted from the normative sample into uniform T scores. They are psycho-metrically sound (Butcher et al., 1990; Graham, 1990), but have vary-ing degrees of external validity. The major drawback is that they are easily faked, so a reasonably cooperative subject is required in order to assume that the following interpretations are accurate. At the same time, since they are face-valid, they can give you a sense of what your clients are trying to tell you about themselves or how they want you to see them. As with the clinical scales, a T score of 65 or above is high and a score of 40 or below is low.

**1.** Anxiety (ANX)—A high score suggests standard anxiety related symptoms like difficulty in concentration, low self-confidence, apprehen-sion, nervousness, sleep problems, and distractibility. Such individuals are likely to be pessimistic and feel stressed and/or depressed. Females are a bit more likely to show hostility and irritability. Low scorers are likely to be self-confident and show a low rate of these symptoms.

**2.** Fears (FRS)—A high score indicates multiple fears and/or phobias; a low score, the absence of same.

**3.** Obsessiveness (OBS)—High OBS scorers are rigid, ruminative, indecisive, worry a lot, lack self-confidence, and show various compulsive behaviors like hoarding unimportant things or counting behaviors. Low OBS scorers are adaptable, self-confident, and show an absence of obsessive-compulsive patterns.

**4.** Depression (DEP)—A purer measure of depression even than scale 2, high scorers report depressive thoughts, are indecisive and uninterested in life, and are sad and blue. They report feeling pessimistic, guilty, lonely, have health concerns, and may be suicidal. Low scorers do not report such symptoms and usually have adequate energy and self-confidence.

**5.** Health Concerns (HEA)—High scorers are preoccupied with bodily functions, report a variety of physical symptoms, and say they have little energy. True neurological disorder may be involved, e.g., clients with multiple sclerosis will report a wide variety of physical symptomatology. Low scorers report generally positive physical health.

**6.** Bizarre Mentation (BIZ)—High scores here reflect reports of psychotic symptoms, i.e., thought disorder, hallucinations, delusions, or depersonalization. Low scores reflect an absence of these symptoms.

**7.** Anger (ANG)—High scorers are openly admitting feelings of anger, hostility, and irritability. They feel they may lose control of their feelings in a physical or verbal manner. Low scorers claim to not experience these feelings or the sense that they might lose control of their feelings.

**8.** Cynicism (CYN)—High scorers are classic misanthropes. They expect the worst from others, even from those close to them, and from fate. They resent any demands from others, although they may set high demands for themselves. Low scorers report trusting, liking, and helping others and are generally not seen as pushy or hostile.

**9.** Antisocial Practices (ASP)—Those high on this scale also tend to be somewhat misanthropic, but use that as a basis to rationalize antisocial patterns. They have problems in school or with the law, resent authority, and vicariously enjoy others' criminal antics. Males are especially likely to swear, curse aggressively, posture, and/or exhibit temper tantrums when irritated. Low scorers report an absence of trouble with or distrust of others and can accept authority.

**10.** Type A (TEA)—This scale was included because it was a "hot" topic when MMPI-2 was being developed. High scorers reflect the refrain from *Alice in Wonderland* "I'm late, I'm late for a very important date." They are often direct but insensitive in interpersonal relationships.

Low scorers don't usually feel competitive, pressed for time, or easily irritated and are usually seen by others as easy-going.

**11.** Low Self Esteem (LSE)—A high score here reflects feelings of unattractiveness, incompetence, guilt, and failure. They are passive, sensitive to criticism, and tend to worry and be indecisive. Low scorers report self-confidence, can accept criticism, report few fears, and are usually decisive.

**12.** Social Discomfort (SOD)—High scorers are shy and introverted. They are interpersonally avoidant. Low scorers report being comfortable in initiating interpersonal contact, like being in social groups, and are extroverted.

**13.** Family Problems (FAM)—Persons with high scores report a high level of discord in their present and/or past families, perceive and resent intrusion from family members, and have a pessimistic view of marriage. They may have been physically abused as children. Low scorers value family life and see their own experiences in that realm as positive.

**14.** Work Interference (WRK)—High scorers have attitudes that predict to poor work performance. Such behaviors include questioning their career choices and the value of work to their lives, as well as obsessiveness, indecisiveness, low self-confidence, or tension and pressure relevant to work performance. Low scorers report an absence of work-disruptive attitudes and behaviors and are likely to be self-confident and at least reasonably ambitious.

**15.** Negative Treatment Indicators (TRT)—This is probably best construed as a measure of compliance in treatment, rather than probable success. Persons who score high here believe they cannot be helped, both as a result of the magnitude of their problems and their sense of inadequacy, as well as hostile and/or avoidant attitudes toward treatment personnel. They tend to show poor judgment and poor problem-solving abilities. Low scorers believe they can be helped, are willing to cooperate in that process, and show good judgment and problem-solving skills.

■          ## Supplemental Scales

There have been many scales constructed out of the MMPI-2 item pool, and no doubt more will be constructed in the future. All are scored in linear T scores rather than uniform T scores. They have varying levels of reliability and validity. Of the scales recognized by the architects of MMPI-2 from the time of its revision, the following scales have both consistent relevance to clinicians and sufficient reliability and validity.

**1.** Anxiety (A)—This scale is a less pure measure of anxiety than the previously described Anxiety (ANX) Content scale. High A clients are anxious, socially inhibited and awkward, compliant and conforming, cautious and cool, defensive, prefer a slow life pace, and function poorly under stress. Low A individuals are not anxious, are confident, resourceful, vigorous, interpersonally friendly and assertive—sometimes dominant, can be inclined toward status and/or power, are sometimes unable to delay gratification or impulse, and prefer actioon to thought.

**2.** Repression (R)—High R people are conventional and conforming but usually clear-thinking. They internalize conflict and can be slow and even compulsive in productive work. They resonate to formality and manners. Low Rs are emotional, enthusiastic, and occasionally eccentric. They eschew detail or decorum, can be impulsive, daring, and generous, but also at times selfish, shrewd, sly, and sarcastic.

**3.** Ego-Strength (Es)—This scale was originally designed to predict the response of "neurotics" to one-on-one psychotherapy. High scores still predict a good response to the degree those conditions hold. Otherwise, a good rule-of-thumb is that a high Es score in a person who is admitting problems and asking for help predicts a good response. If the person is not admitting problems and/or indicating an interest in help, a high Es doesn't predict that well in either direction. High Es's basically have better psychological resources and are reasonably well adjusted. Although admitting they have problems, they report fewer stressors. They are generally reliable, sociable, and not prejudiced toward opinions or people (except possibly authority figures). They can be manipulative, pushy, and even cynical. Low Es's lack self-confidence, do not persist psychologically or vocationally, feel (and usually are) inadequate, may be confused, and are inclined toward chronic physical or psychological disorder.

**4.** MacAndrews Alcoholism-Revised Scale (MAC-R)—See Chapter 2 for a discussion of this scale.

**5.** Overcontrolled-Hostility Scale (O-H)—See Chapter 14 for a discussion of this scale.

## Subtle-Obvious Scales

Scoring for subtle-obvious items has been available since the inception of MMPI on scales 2, 3, 4, 6, and 9, reflecting the development of these scales by Wiener in the mid-forties. John Graham articulates one clear perspective on the value of the Subtle-Obvious scales, occasionally saying, "They suck real bad and you shouldn't use them." He speaks only slightly better of them in his writings, while others see them as having more value (Greene, 1991). There are two foci in the research literature. The first is to assess whether subtle or obvious items predict to external correlates, e.g., depression. Yet, it really shouldn't surprise people that obvious items predict better to such external correlates as admitted depression. The real issue is the second research trend, i.e., to assess whether people who are instructed to (or actually do) fake one way or another can be detected. The evidence is mixed (Graham, 1990; Greene, 1991). But, certainly many clinicians report it is a useful approach to point to possible faking when there are only a few prior indicators. Also, in some instances, where an overall faking set is apparently not present, a major discrepancy between subtle and obvious items on one scale, e.g., scale 4, may point to an important area for further scrutiny.

# CHAPTER 13

# Clinical Correlates of Cattell's 16 Personality Factor Test (16 PF Test)

As noted in Chapter 1, it is recognized that the 16 PF is certainly not as widely used as the MMPI-2. However, it is recommended for consideration as a complementary test to the MMPI-2 because (a) the 16 PF for the most part measures ongoing personality traits, a number of which are important but are not measured in MMPI-2, and (b) it has motivational distortion scores that aid in the interpretation of this test and in the battery as a whole. Also, the 16 PF is well designed, has good validity and reliability data, has comparable tests available across the age span, and has accrued substantial clinical and research data. We'll first examine individual scale correlates and then turn to data based on scores of related factors.

## ■ The Cattell 16 PF Test

The Sixteen Personality Factor Questionnaire, developed primarily by Raymond Cattell and Herbert Eber and referred to here as the 16 PF, was devised to tap a wide range of a client's ongoing personality functioning. It is designed more for personality traits and conflicts than is the MMPI-2 (Cattell, 1989), which is oriented primarily toward categories of psychopathology. The 16 PF gives scores on sixteen dimensions that Cattell derived through a factor analysis of a huge number of personality descriptors; they were then validated on a wide variety of abnormal and normal client groups.

There are six forms of the 16 PF. The first five forms are designated by the letters A through E. The sixth is a short form (128 items), which is Part 1 of the original form of the Clinical Analysis Questionnaire (Krug, 1980). As a result, it is not quite as reliable as forms A or B. Form A is the one most commonly used. It is composed of 187 items, which means there are approximately ten to thirteen items for each of the sixteen scales. The client's response to an item affects only one scale on the 16 PF, whereas in the MMPI-2 a single response may affect more than one scale. The Institute of Personnel and Ability Testing (IPAT) (the present owners of the test) recommend that both forms A and B, which are similar in length, be administered to allow for greater validity. In practice, however, most clinicians usually administer only form A.

Forms C and D are much shorter than A and B and are useful in situations that require quick screening. It takes the average client about thirty minutes to complete forms C and D, whereas it takes about fifty minutes to complete either A or B. Form E is intended for those clients who read below the sixth-grade level. Unfortunately, the reliability and validity data on form E are not as strong as for forms A and B.

The 16 PF allows three response choices, with "undecided" commonly available as an option. This, along with the fact that it is much shorter and does not ask questions that are so personal, makes the 16 PF more acceptable to most clients than the MMPI-2. As with the MMPI-2, it is helpful to encourage the testees to give the most accurate responses they can and to answer every question, if possible. They should also be warned against spending extensive time mulling over an answer and be asked to give their first clear response.

The 16 PF can be either machine- or hand-scored, and IPAT now provides a service that gives a computer-scored and -interpreted report on the 16 PF. To score the 16 PF by hand, the examiner uses two templates provided by IPAT. If the client's mark appears in the hole on the template, the appropriate number of that hole, either two or one, is added to give a sum that is the raw score for that subscale. These raw data are converted into standard scores, termed "stens," a shortening of the phrase "standard ten." These stens, or standard scores, range from 1 to 10 on the answer sheet, have a mean of 5.5 (the middle of the answer sheet), and a standard deviation of 2. Thus, a sten score of 1 or 10 is considered quite extreme; scores 2, 3, 8, or 9 are significantly deviant; a score of 4 or 7 is mildly deviant from the norm; and a sten score of 5 or 6 is average. A sten score of 8, 9, or 10 is labeled "high" in this book, whereas a score of 1, 2, or 3 is "low." "Moderately high" generally refers to a score of 7 or 8, and scores of 3 or 4 are termed "moderately low." If the phrase "higher on scale" is used, it simply designates a sten score of 6 or above; "lower on scale" designates a score of 5 or lower. To convert raw data into sten scores, it is necessary to use the appropriate Tabular Supplement, based on the demographics of the client. IPAT provides tabular supplements on such groups as college students, the general population, and high school juniors and seniors. Along with the subscales, the 16 PF can be scored for faking-good or faking-bad (the reader is referred to the section on malingering in Chapter 16 for more details).

# ■ 16 PF Factors

## □ SCALE A

Scale A—formerly referred to as Sizothymia versus Affectothymia—is considered the major factor, by variance scores, in personality prediction, and generally differentiates between people who are reserved and aloof (low on scale A) and those who are sociable and warm. This is considered to be a relatively fixed trait, and women score a bit higher here than men. High As are more gregarious, adaptable, and trusting, sometimes to the point of being Pollyannaish, less prone to cyclical moodiness, and less vulnerable to criticism. However, very high A scores may be associated with mania and/or difficulties in impulse control. Also, they are gullible and avoid, sometimes at the cost of compulsive and/or self-defeating behaviors, being alone. They are successful in arenas that require social contact, e.g., families or organizations, but underachieve where working alone is a critical task component. Their clinical conditions reflect their potential flaws of gullibility, need for approval, and emotional dependency.

Most of the adjectives associated with low As are fairly negative, although such persons are often more compulsive and precise and therefore more productive in certain areas. They easily find the negative in people or situations. They are often more effective in tasks that require working alone and/or generating their own structure, especially if they are also high on B (intelligence). They are only self-disclosing and generate rapport if they feel comfortable in a particular relationship and, even then, are inclined to withdraw from requests for intimacy. Very low As tend to remain flat in their emotional lives and aloof in relationships, and Heather Cattell (1989) sums it up well, saying "Communicating a desire for intimacy to an A-person is often like describing color to the congenitally blind" (p. 24). Persons who score very low are more likely to earn adjectives like "schizoid" and "introverted," as well as "obnoxious," and frequently display the "burnt-child" syndrome (especially if scale E is also low) regarding interpersonal relationships (Karson and O'Dell, 1976).

## □ SCALE B

Scale B, the second largest 16 PF factor by variance, was originally labeled as High General Intelligence (appropriately enough, the high end of the scale) versus Mental Defectiveness. It is probably best thought of as the ability to discern relationships in terms of how things stand relative to one another—to classify events and form typologies. In actuality, low scores do not necessarily indicate low mental ability. For one thing, there are only thirteen items on this scale, and the scoring is binary rather than the "2, 1, or 0" scoring applied in the other scales, so any precise assertions of validity of predicting intellectual level are unrealistic.

Low scores may be associated with random or distorted answering sets, attentional difficulties, impulsiveness, or a lack of ability to persist on a task. Low scores should only be a major concern if there is good reason to believe the person was trying to do well. High scores (8–10) generally indicate at least average—probably higher—intellectual ability.

□     SCALE C

Scale C is considered to reflect dissatisfied and labile emotionality (the low end of the continuum), as opposed to emotional stability or ego strength. It taps emotional stability, maturity, and a low threshold for irritability and upset and consequent neurotic fatigue. Overall, scale C is probably the single most important predictor in the 16 PF for emotional stability, for the ability to cope with, adapt to, and/or solve the broad range of life's problems. Most neurotics show low C scores; criminals are only relatively higher here. Persons low on C may be faking-bad, while those scoring high may have a high motivation distortion or a faking-good score (Winder et al., 1975; Krug, 1978).

High-C persons have a somewhat stoic (although not necessarily passive) philosophy, are able to formulate problems in a concrete and specific manner, face problems without procrastination, are usually good time managers, are seldom perfectionistic, and accept limitations in self and life. They are good colleague-companions, although they can sometimes seem too invulnerable, like Mr. Spock. They tend to prepare effectively for anticipated stressful events and are usually reliable in emergencies. Often, they learned these skills in difficult childhoods, but in difficulties they were able to cope with. However, Cattell (1989) suggests that a person with a high C score, who also reports a difficult childhood, is prone to "burn-out," i.e., less ego strength later in life.

Low Cs tend to react to challenges or crises with more rigid emotional responses and cognitive solutions, may discount information and other persons' feelings, may respond too slowly or too impulsively, and are more likely to have emotional distresses produced by these situations. They are often disruptive interpersonally and are likely to report physical problems, anxiety, depression, and/or on rarer occasion, psychosis.

Low-C scorers need to have their self-esteems improved and some control over their emotional lability generated before they can make any strides with insight therapy. If there is no distortion, a higher C score offers a good prognosis for psychotherapy. There is some evidence that C will rise following a successful therapeutic intervention. In general, high Cs have learned to channel their emotionality into productive and integrated behaviors, as opposed to impulsively dissipating it.

## □          SCALE E

(The reader might wonder why there is no scale D in the 16 PF. In Cattell's original list of factors, D was referred to as Excitability, and it was not thought to be a major differentiating issue in adults, so it is only found on the Cattell tests for children.)

Scale E primarily assesses a dominance factor, as well as lesser contributions from assertiveness and a willingness to conform to authority. Scores on E decrease with age, and, reflecting both hormones and society, males tend to be higher on E. Scores on E increase with situationally positive events and decrease with negative ones (e.g., chronic illness).

A high score on E would indicate a dominant and tough individual who has strong needs to be independent (which may mask real feelings of inferiority), yet wishes to gain status and control over others (possibly as a form of self-protection). However, probably because of the conflicts over role expectations, high scores in females have extra factor-loadings from attention-getting, social poise, and possible hypochondriacal aspects. A high E score connotes an assertive (sometimes "abrasive" if it is very high—although a high E score does not inherently connote aggression) personality style, and, although it is not always associated with leadership ability, established leaders do tend to be higher on this score. Indeed, the more technologically advanced the society, the more intelligence is correlated with dominance. Yet, thought patterns can be rigid in high Es—these people not only know what's good for them, they know what's good for you as well. They feel little discomfort about their behaviors, but at an organismic level, these behaviors exert a cost in higher stress levels. They cope poorly with loss, especially irrevocable loss, such as death, so grief is very difficult for them. Also, if they are ever forced to confront their own powerlessness, they are often devastated. Interpersonally, high Es can be vigorous and forceful, but just as likely are to be conceited, sarcastic, quarrelsome, and/or opinionated.

Low Es tend to be submissive, acquiescent, and dependent. Over the long-run, they tend to be perceived as a bit boring. Persons who are shy are low on E, whereas those who are narcissistic, chronically angry, or inappropriately assertive are higher on E. Low Es are prone to be neurotic and self-defeating and often feel vulnerable to and frustrated by the control of others. They often react with resentful depression and/or passive-aggression. Alcoholics tend to be low on E.

Scale F, which is highly loaded on genetic factors, is denoted as Surgency versus Desurgency. This may be better described as an alert, enthusiastic, and even happy-go-lucky style versus sober, introspective seriousness (the low end of the scale). Along with scale A, scale F is an important predictor of extroversion-introversion. Persons who show bipolar affective disorders may swing markedly on this factor. Success in psychotherapy raises F, as does the initial effect of substance abuse. Hysteric individuals and those with sexual, personality, and impulsivity disorders usually score higher on this scale, whereas persons with depression, phobias, and introverted patterns score lower. A low score on F, along with a high 0, suggests depression.

The F score drops rather markedly between the ages of eighteen and thirty-five years, and there is some indication that F rises slightly with an increased metabolic rate. Although there is a slight correlation of an above-average F score with the holding of a leadership position, this does not necessarily connote *effective* leadership because the higher the F score, the more impulsivity is found. Persons in leadership positions who are high on F often need associates who can take the plans they generate and bring them to fruition.

High Fs resonate to the poet Walt Whitman's phrase "I celebrate myself," they "do what comes naturally" and enjoy novelty and variety. They enjoy social and sexual expression, so they may be overly attracted to the opposite sex. They are true "party animals." They are socially and physically mobile and are prone to dilettantism and narcissism (although it's a rather benign narcissism as it is not a retreat from the full self); hence, relationships are volatile when they persist for any duration. They are not likely to be effective in enterprises that require persistence. Unlike low C persons, where such failures are due to weak egos, such failures by high Fs reflect the foddish, associative style of their interests. High Fs can be flighty, even manic at times.

Low Fs are often "dour Scots," with dry senses of humor, if there is any sense of humor. They behave and think ponderously, but if they are highly intelligent, they can be both creative and productive. Their sober demeanors, however, seldom lend to popularity. Although not inherently shy, they avoid "high-energy" social gatherings. Their responsible, conventional patterns reflect inhibitions rather than weak superegos. Low Fs are prone to depressive episodes, and their periodic gloomy, "wet-blanket" attitudes don't support much marital happiness (although they may have marital status).

☐    SCALE G

Scale G denotes a person who is demanding, casual in moral standards, and potentially undependable (the low end of the continuum) versus a conscientious and responsible individual. HIgh-G individuals are guardians of the moral order, group-conforming, cautious in decisions, and set in their thinking and biases. High Gs are conscientious. They are responsible workers and usually high achievers. They do have difficulties in "understanding" the irresponsible person; hence, they are especially stressed when parenting teenagers. "Women who love too much" are often high on G, but have elicited a series of relationships with low G-men. Very high G scores are often obtained by professional moralists, i.e., priests, ministers, etc. The triad of high G and $Q_3$ and low $Q_1$ is the solid, stable citizen who can be a "stick-in-the-mud."

Heather Cattell (1989) sees four major variants in low-G persons: (1) faking-bad; (2) amorality, not necessarily psychopathy which has additional components of inability to profit from experience and a lack of response to standard punishment stimuli, but more of a primitive egocentricity; (3) moral immaturity—cued by a low C as well as other components such as low H and high L and $Q_4$—a morality based on concrete reciprocity and avoidance of punishment; and (4) nonconventional morality—often cued by high C and Q. Markedly low scores may suggest a self-disclosing psychopath, and even moderately low scores suggest a person who is likely to disregard obligations. However, since this measures adherence to subgroup standards as well, certain criminals do score high here. Rebellious adolescents particularly score low. Scale G measures the more-overt, standard, culturally accepted aspects of morality (rather than internalized guilt as tapped by O+), and other scores, such as on O, would further indicate whether this was a thoroughgoing personality trait. There is a definitive correlation with age and socioeconomic class; the older the person and the higher the socioeconomic status, the higher the score on scale G.

☐    SCALE H

Scale H, termed by Cattell as Threctia (sympathetic dominance) versus Parmia (parasympathetic dominance), denotes a person who is shy, constricted emotionally, and threat-sensitive (the low end of the continuum) versus one who is more adventurous, thick-skinned, and pushy but friendly. Cattell suggests that this is largely an innate (genetically determined) factor. High-H people imply social boldness, a high interest in the opposite sex, and a high need for environmental stimulation. They may enjoy feeling fear, e.g., love horror movies, roller coasters, and dangerous events and challenges. H+ delinquents respond far better to Outward Bound programs than psychotherapy. A higher-H person is more likely to be seen as intellectually and emotionally lazy, especially during the developmental years. You can easily contact them with an ad in *Soldier of Fortune* magazine. High Hs are prone to sociopathic patterns. They can be thick-skinned and inconsiderate in relationships and easily opt for "open" marriages, although they don't always communicate this choice to their partners.

A low H score indicates a person with an overresponsive sympathetic nervous system. Low Hs become self-absorbed, yet jealous when attending to others. They fear "doing the wrong thing" socially and can be friendly and polite so as not to draw attention to themselves, yet are basically shy. They live out the motto "Nothing risked, nothing lost." Their constricted worlds make for marital difficulties, and they do poorly outside of routinized jobs. Very low H scores are found in introverted personalities, and alcoholics who use alcohol either for disinhibition or "to steady my nerves" are low on H. This is one of the factors that predict a basic schizoid temperament as well as, on occasion, a chronic schizophrenic adjustment. Since H connotes threat sensitivity, it should be low in such disorders as agoraphobia, panic disorder, and PTSD. There is some evidence that low-H individuals are more likely to suffer ulcers.

☐            SCALE I

Although scale I was labeled by Cattell as Harria (hardness and realism) versus Premsia (protected emotional sensitivity), the more common connotations have to do with a person who takes a tough and realistic view of life, is inclined to be self-sufficient, and is not highly responsive to pain or conflict (the low end of the continuum), as opposed to a person on the high end (an I+) who is sensitive, dependent, and possibly effeminate or demanding.

Factor I is seen as one pole (i.e., two functions) in the set of four operations or functions (feeling, thinking, sensation, intuition) by which people respond to their environment and which form the basis of the "fad" test of recent years, the Myers-Briggs Inventory. I−, or low I, is seen as reflecting the feeling dimension, high I the thinking function. A low score on M, discussed later, apparently taps the sensation function, a high score taps the intuition. There is overlap, as high Is are often intuitive.

High Is are "intuiters" who make judgments on subjective and emotional responses, i.e., feelings as opposed to the objective logic and abstraction of the low I. High Is are more likely to be romantic, empathic, repulsed by crudity, occasionally indecisive, sentimental, and artistic. Unfortunately, like Felix of "The Odd Couple," they expect the same sensitivity and empathy in others, but when paired with a low I, i.e., Oscar, they are not likely to get it. They are prone to romantic fantasy and often have difficulty distancing themselves from their feelings. They can be prone to stress-based anxiety and psychosomatic disorders (especially if E is also high).

In general, this continuum reflects William James's traditional distinction between tough-minded and tender-minded people; those people in the tender-minded subgroup (high on I) generally wish to avoid conflict and have high esthetic interests. Being low on I does not necessarily help a person adapt to conflict, however, possibly because the tough-minded continuum is a more brittle adjustment and therefore less adaptive to certain types of stress.

Low Is lack such sensitivity, are inclined to be rough and crude, and not given to self-analysis or self-indulgence. They are not psychologically minded and usually have repressed rather than absent emotions. It is difficult for them to become aware of when they (or anyone else) are at the end of their emotional ropes, at which point they are emotionally brittle. Although scale I has not been found to be highly associated with psychopathology, psychotics, on the average, are slightly lower than normals on this factor. Low Is have repressed emotions and difficulties with intimacy. They are unable to accept their tender or vulnerable sides and are usually unprepared for any interpersonal crises that their distancing patterns don't take care of.

There is a high genetic loading here, and there are age and sex differences on I: Older people tend to score higher than the very young, and women consistently score higher than men. At the extreme high point, the clinician finds women who have stayed within the traditional female role, almost to a stereotypical degree. Macho men score very low on I.

□        SCALE L

Scale L, denoted by Cattell as Protension versus Alaxia (relaxed security) is often interpreted as suspicious jealousy and emotional distancing (an L+) as opposed to a relaxed trust and openness to the world (the lower end of the continuum). "Protension" is a term derived from the words "projection" and "(inner) tension," and, as is implied, paranoid concerns are often reflected here. Persons high on the scale tend to be cynical and defensively project their negativism and suspicions. Some take elitist views and arrogant postures and insist that their ideas be heard; in the latter sense, they reflect some of the dominance characteristics also attributed to scale E. Others with high L appear more furtive and frustrated, with low self-esteems and constricted life-views. Cattell (1989) sees the jealousy characteristic of high Ls as consistently including the sequence of a sense of deprivation, an unfavorable comparison between self and others, a sense of impotence and/or falling behind in any prospect of righting the perceived imbalance, and defensive projection to restore self-esteem, directed toward individuals or "fate." They are ever on the lookout to add more injustices and perceived deficits in others to their "collections." Persons high on L are not primarily schizoid, although their personalities easily result in rejection by others, so interpersonal isolation occurs and is a cause of distress marked by jealousy.

A major issue is how a person channels these traits into vocational and interpersonal interests. For example, eminent researchers often score higher on L because the characteristics of cynicism, isolation, and confidence in their intellectual superiority serve them well. But, the typical high-L person is at risk of being rejected, has too high a level of inner tension, has defenses that may be too brittle, and may not have enough access to other persons as emotional resources. Paranoid disorders commonly include a high L. Also, high scores predict general illness, especially coronary artery disease and psychosomatic concerns like low-back pain.

On the other hand, low-L persons in general are emotionally healthy, easily make others feel accepted as they feel at one with other people and the human race, and are usually noncompetitive, although they are subject to interpersonal manipulation and conning and can get heavily involved in dependency (from others) relationships. When the L score is not reflective of an individual's malingering or misperception, it is an indicator of good emotional health.

## SCALE M

Scale M, originally denoted as Praxernia (a neologism for practical concern) versus Autia, is now more commonly known as conventional practicality versus unconventional imagination (the high end of the scale) and is highly related to scale I. As noted earlier in discussing factor I, low M is seen as tapping the sensation pole of the Jungian sensation-intuition dimension, also a major component of the Myers-Briggs Inventory. In a slightly less direct manner, high M taps the intuition dimension. Whereas high Is are intuitive in the sense of suddenly apprehending a hitherto unrecognized insight without apparent effort, i.e., "out of the blue," high Ms are intuitive in the broader sense of the word, i.e., as "a habitual tendency to focus on the higher ratio of ideas, associations, and other internal mental processes, rather than to focus on external stimuli" (Cattell, 1989, p. 191).

Persons high on M have well-developed imaginations, tend toward narcissism, do poorly in detail work, and more easily dissociate than others. They easily consider unconventional options—when they act them out they may be labeled "ahead of their time," eccentric, or possibly criminal. One way of conceptualizing high Ms is to contrast them to factor traits they are commonly confused with. For example, high Ms may be thought of as socially withdrawn, like low As. But, rather than being truly schizoid, they are simply self-absorbed. It's also common to misinterpret high Ms' propensity to fail to make ordinary observations or forget important information as indicating lower intelligence than they do possess. Also, high Ms' inclination toward offbeat styles, naive projections, and obtuseness in the face of social cues move toward impulsive acting-out when G is low (expediency—lower superego strength). Clinically, Ms tend to be found in substance abusers, schizophrenics, and depressives and are prone to job dissatisfaction. There is some evidence that very-high-M persons alternate between outbursts of rumination-generated activity and rather placid periods when they seem to be totally wrapped up in themselves. In that sense, this scale is a measure of a type of introversion. High M is also significantly and somewhat paradoxically correlated with both creativity and accident-proneness (e.g., the absent-minded professor).

Whereas high Ms are prone to see a forest where there are only a few trees and shrubs, low Ms tend to see a lot of trees and miss the forest. From a philosophical perspective, Plato, with his view that perceptions can be misleading and have to be anchored to an internal theory, would be a high M, whereas Aristotle, who believed truth came directly through the senses, would be a low M. Low Ms are not psychologically minded and avoid introspection.They call a spade a spade, prefer the routine and familiar, have good memories and like details, seldom are able to innovate, and can be a bit boring and frustrating in relationships (including therapy or marriage). They often like to work with facts and things, rather than ideas or people. They are prone to obsessive and compulsive patterns. Persons with somatoform disorders are lower on M than are those with anxiety-based disorders. The assumed explanation for this difference is that persons with anxiety-based disorders are keeping their conflicts in higher levels of consciousness, thereby experiencing anxiety, whereas the somatoform disorders reflect a denial of inner conflict.

## SCALE N

Scale N is termed the Artlessness (lower end of the scale) versus Shrewdness continuum. Persons on the high end (N+) are socially alert, although a bit calculating and aloof, and may show sophisticated anxiety or concerns about success in relation to high internal standards. They do tend to present and/or value social facades. At very high levels, individuals are Machiavellian (or are faking-good), whereas if scores are too low, they manifest extreme naiveté—"I just let it all hang out. I'm ok, you're ok. could you do this for me?"). Generally, and a bit more so in males, moderately high scores on N indicate a good family upbringing and positive character integration. Clinically, high Ns are hard to read, and all other response distortion indices should be closely appraised. Clinicians need to be alert to cues that differentiate some high Ns who are "second-nature shrewd" (reflecting a long-term character) from those who are "second-thoughted shrewd" (who later in life adopted the pattern as a coping strategy) (Cattell, 1989).

Low Ns can be dominant, in a straightforward manner, interpersonally and tend to present a "transparent self." They are low in social ambition and can be conned or manipulated, but seem to recover relatively easily from disappointments. They also tend to be socially clumsy, overtrusting, and have rather simplistic interests. They tend to prefer animals, plants, young children, etc., over adults. Clinically, they are prone to immaturity, sometimes exhibit very poor judgment, and are usually a bit insensitive to others' feelings if they are not directly presented with them. Psychotics and neurotics on the average score lower on N.

□        ## SCALE O

Scale O is generally labeled placid confidence (the low end of the scale) versus an insecure proneness to guilt (primarily reflecting a sense of inadequacy rather than a violation of internalized moral standards). A high O score is probably best thought of as reflecting an absence of self-worth or low self-esteem, usually accompanied by feelings of shame and doubt. Persons high on this scale are avoidant of stimulation, oversensitive, show a strong sense of morality and duty, and are prone to anxiety-based disorders, e.g., phobias or hypochondriasis. A high O score occasionally reflects situational rather than trait low self-esteem and/or depression, especially if F is low. Whether characterological or situational, persons suffering from negative feelings about themselves are likely to score low on O. This makes them vulnerable to taking dependent and/or masochistic roles if they do enter relationships.

Moderately low O scores suggest self-confident, generally cheerful, relaxed, and resilient individuals. They can accept blame, but they don't appear to really "feel" sorry. On the other hand, scale O is quite low in individuals who are psychopathic, who are more likely to act out their conflicts, or who have well-ingrained defense mechanisms. Low Os may verbalize guilt, but there seem to be no true feelings of it nor any restitution efforts. They have trouble with intimacy because of their lack of empathy. Along with scale G, O taps what Freudians have referred to as "superego."

□        ## SCALE $Q_1$

Scale $Q_1$ denotes an orientation toward change, cautious conservatism (the low end of the scale) with a strong attachment to the past and present versus individuals who enjoy novelty and change from a purposeful perspective, with a free-thinking, future-oriented, and experimenting approach to life. Liberal (high $Q_1$) versus conservative political beliefs also affect this scale. Like the other Q scales, this factor has not been totally validated in all types of data collection, yet most clinicians find the Q scores to be extremely helpful. The interested reader is referred to Cattell (1973) for the subtle distinctions he used to discriminate the Q scales from the previously mentioned scales.

Persons high on the $Q_1$ scale are somewhat impatient and are rather critical of others but tend to be analytical and liberal in thought patterns, i.e., it represents an intellectualized form of anger. In males, high $Q_1$ is often correlated with anger toward authority. Depending on vocational and interpersonal situations, high-$Q_1$ persons can have difficulties with authority figures or establishment rules and hence can be disruptive in highly structured environments. High-$Q_1$ persons can be viewed as intellectualized aggressors, with an implicit potential for loss of impulse control. High $Q_1$s are future oriented and see change as good, but fear being controlled by others or archetypes of their past. They are often viewed as "troublemakers" in job settings. They manage adequately in marriage if control issues are settled, but quickly seek greener grass if dissatisfied.

Low $Q_1$s are cautious and uninvolved politically and anticipate changes with trepidation, but often adapt and resign themselves to negative circumstances. They are dependable and loyal and are often highly attached to their families of origin, but, unfortunately, in many instances because of dependency rather than affection. They want to stay with what they know. They are prone to conversion hysteria, psychosomatic disorders, obsessive-compulsive patterns, and adjustment disorders and are prone to being used or abused. People quite low on this scale are colorless individuals who, rather than being rejected by others, are often simply ignored. Very low Os endure situations that are distressing, even when it seems to others they could leave those situations. They are prone to stress-based disorders, obsessive-compulsive patterns, and of course to adjustment disorders.

## SCALE $Q_2$

Scale $Q_2$ taps basic dependency (the low end of the scale) as opposed to a self-sufficient resourcefulness. High $Q_2$s value privacy and freedom of choice. They are not schizoid per se or even shy but spend substantial amounts of time alone and rarely feel lonely. They are often rugged individualists and seldom seek advice or reassurance, which is probably why they have higher-than-average rates of coronary artery disease (which may be why the "Marlboro Man" is an archetypal high $Q_2$), hypertension, and peptic ulcers. As such, they are well advised to maintain at least one confidante, or even a beloved pet. A nondirective therapy approach (sometimes, paradoxically with bibliotherapy assignments) is the most effective approach with high $Q_2$. High-$Q_2$ males place a high value on sex, possibly because it allows a covert gratification of any unfulfilled intimacy needs.

Low $Q_2$s have a high need to "belong," often have strong family attachments, and in general show high rates of proximity-seeking behaviors. But, at times, they lack initiative or "character" and thus are prone to be exploited. They need much social approval, are chronic "joiners," and easily move into dependent roles in relationships. Very low $Q_2$s may have problems consequent on their lack of initiative, their tendency to be exploited, or the weakening of their sense of self. They often develop strong transference relationships, a la the movie *What About Bob?* In that sense, $Q_2$ reflects a more basic dependency factor than scale G, as G taps more of an adherence to group standards.

□    ## SCALE $Q_3$

Scale $Q_3$ is denoted as low self-concept integration (the low end of the scale) versus a controlled approach to life ($Q_3+$), with an emphasis on a strong, controlling will and a desire to retain the respect of self and others. High $Q_3$s constantly monitor the appropriateness of their behaviors in relation to standards or ideals (which are often set too high). They take pride in typically fulfilling (at least that's their perception) these goals, but they don't report high joy in life, and show little spontaneity. They actually have a deficit of unconditional self-acceptance, feel they are valued for what they do or will do, rather than for what they did do, or just the fact that they are, and thus show perfectionism. They are generally trustworthy and reliable, so are perceived as good co-workers but not as fun companions. People high on scale $Q_3$ are ambitious, persist in tasks, and keep their commitments, yet they are also inclined toward smugness toward others, toward suppression of anger, and toward obsessive and compulsive concerns. They are also predisposed to paranoid and narcissistic patterns and to schizophrenic and dissociative disorders. In clinical terms, high scores on $Q_3$ can reflect a great need to control conflict and anxiety that threaten to break through brittle modes of coping, i.e., they are wound too tight or, as Karson and O'Dell (1976) so aptly point out, there is a high need to bind anxiety into symptomatology or avoidance patterns.

On the other hand, a low score may reflect a lack of impulse control, a diffuse identity, or a lack of ability to structure one's psychological world effectively. Low $Q_3$s generally do as they feel and care little how they are perceived by others. They are fickle in relationships and are not the best employees, as they neither persist on tasks or take pride in their performances. Hence, they are high consumers of vocational and relationship counseling. They are prone to both antisocial patterns and the more "neurotic" personality and anxiety disorders. $Q_3+$ should cue to the issue of suicidal concern if there are other indicators of depression.

☐           SCALE $Q_4$

Scale $Q_4$ is generally termed low anxiety and tension (the low end of the scale) versus high tension and anxiety. $Q_4$ is the best 16 PF measure of situational anxiety; hence, there may be reasonable fluctuations over time. However, Cattell (1989) asserts that it "usually indicates that tension is a trait; therefore the examinee is characterologically a tense, volatile and easily upset individual" (p. 294). The client can often tell you whether it is a trait or a state. High $Q_4$s are behaviorally fidgety and "hyper," report feeling "pressured," "nervous," or "on the edge," and it can be easily manipulated so it can be an indication of faking-bad or a cry for help. High $Q_4$s are found in profiles of bipolars, alcoholics, psychopaths, and persons with impulsive, violent, or suicidal tendencies. If scale O is also high, it suggests an insecure and anxious quality that persists beyond the situational parameters. People quite high on $Q_4$ are likely to have experienced rejection by others, are oversensitive in various dimensions, and have a high level of frustrated sexuality. Once emotional disorder crystallizes into an obsessive or psychosomatic pattern, $Q_4$ is lower. Biofeedback, relaxation training, a program of vigorous exercise, and anti-anxiety medication are good antidotes for the high $Q_4$.

Very low $Q_4$s have a phlegmatic temperament, lack vigor and drive, and are tranquil, relaxed, and unfrustrated. They are seen as laid back (and they are) and do a good job living out the Zen admonition "sitting quietly, doing nothing." They show few strong passions or drives. To the degree $Q_4$ is more moderate, they are more relaxed but effective in most dimensions, although they are seldom mistaken for overachievers.

# 16 PF Scale Interrelationship Interpretations

The "second-order factors" on the 16 PF reflect those interactions of primary traits found to most clearly and consistently reflect a personality propensity. When using these second-order factors in a clinical analysis, it is of course important to consider the differential contribution of each individual component. I list scores in their order of importance in contributing to each second-order factor.

On the second-order factor of extroversion-introversion (QI), high scores on A, F, and H and a low score on $Q_2$ indicate extroversion. The opposite pattern points to shyness and, if extreme, to a schizoid orientation. On QII, Anxiety versus Dynamic Integration, a low score on C and on $Q_3$ and high scores on L and $Q_4$ suggest proneness to anxiety and personality disintegration, whereas opposite scores point to higher levels of personality integration. The second-order factor QIII, is termed Tough Poise Sentimentality. Low scores on A, I, and M predict to "sentimentality," persons who are easily disrupted by their emotions and who do poorly with details, either in work or relationships. Persons at the "tough poise" end are realistic and decisive, but may also be un-empathic (kind of like Mr. Spock from "Star Trek") and even cold or harsh. On QIV, Independence (Hostility) versus Subduedness, persons high on E, L, and $Q_2$ and low on M and $Q_1$ often show initiative and "stick-to-it-tiveness," but harbor excessive anger which impedes performance on many fronts. The opposite score pattern indicates someone who is passive, subdued, and usually dependent. On the last second-order factor, QV, Behavior Control versus Psychopathy, low scores on G, N, and O and high scores on $Q_3$, N, and F suggest problems in primary impulse emergence, with a concomitant lack of interest or ability in generating "brakes" on these impulses.

We'll now turn toward general interrelationships among the individual 16 PF factors.

If a person is high on scale A, it is important also to consider the score on $Q_2$; if that is low, the person has a particularly high need for interpersonal feedback and may be petulant and querulous if it is not provided. High scores on both A and F show a gregarious and friendly extrovert, whereas low scores on A and F point to a sober, serious personality, with a high score on L further indicating a hostile and suspicious introvert pattern. Low A and low H indicate a very shy and timid person, and low A and high $Q_2$ suggest a resourceful and independent person. When low A is combined with the sensitivity of a high I, expect a sensitive and reserved person, a la poet Emily Dickinson.

When a high scale B is combined with high scores on scales E and $Q_3$, there is likely to be much intellectualized hostility, with consequent rejection by others. It is also worthwhile to look at scale M in relation to scale B because this suggests to what degree intellectual competence is channeled into imaginative, creative activities rather than into more practical and immediate plans. High Bs who are low on A are very vulnerable to being conned and to being used by others.

C+ and $Q_3$+ point to a controlled, sometimes compulsive personality. C+O− individuals have very strong egos and are placid and serene, although sometimes frustratingly complacent. In contrast, C+H+ persons are "competent adventurers" in life. When C+ is combined with very low O and high L, distortions to protect a more fragile ego strength is suggested.

C−I− persons appear stoic, but it is a stoicism based on an absence of personal reflection and a suppression of feelings, rather than a functional philosophy of life. C−F− persons show constricted thinking, consequently cope poorly with novelty, and naturally hunger for routine. C−I+ persons vacillate in decisions and relationships, apparently in hopes of avoiding the harsher realities of life. C−$Q_3$− individuals cannot maintain behaviors that generate social approval and seldom carry through with whatever good intentions they can generate. C−E− persons tend to be masochistic. C−O+ individuals are insecure worrywarts,

$C-Q_4+s$ are tense and "stretched to the breaking point," and $C-L+s$ are usually quite paranoid in some dimension.

If a low scale C is found with a high H and lower G and $Q_3$ scores, a psychopathic quality is likely. When scales C, F, and A are low, particularly if associated with a moderately low H, look for a withdrawn, shy, and fearful individual. In general, a high O combined with a low C points to a deterioration in competency to adapt to environmental stressors, with $Q_4$ indicating the degree of concomitant anxiety.

As noted earlier, a high I score combined with a high E score predicts the development of stress-based disorders, especially if L and $Q_4$ are also high. A conflict arises in that the individual is both sensitive and dominant at the same time and is torn between the need to look assertive and yet to actuate a desire to reach out emotionally to other people. The competitiveness inherent in the high E blocks the needs of the high I. While $E-H+s$ are deferent out of a desire to be liked, $E-H-s$ are deferent to avoid attention. Cattell (1989) observes that high-E, along with $F+$, $C-$, $G-$, and $Q_3-$, persons are especially prone to violent responses when threatened with loss. Low E, along with $F-$, $Q_1-$, $O+$, and $Q_4+$, should raise concerns about possible suicide. She also reports on data that divides low-E individuals into five subgroups: (1) With low G = The Sufferer – Good Boy/Good Girl – Martyr. These individuals are willing to subordinate their self, but expect to be appreciated for it, and seldom are – they "keep count." (2) With low C = The Uninvolved (but emotionally labile and tense). These people are conciliators who "walk on egg shells" to avoid conflict, yet may have occasional uncontrolled outbursts of anger to "let off steam," and they usually carry a lot of steam. (3) With high L = The Passive-Aggressive or Saboteur. Persons here assume others will resent their self-expressions, then see themselves as compromised, thus become angry, but fear their anger will be detected, so express it covertly. (4) With low E, high C and high N = The Seducer or Shrewd Manipulator. This type "gets even, not angry." If such individuals also show high L (pattern 3), they are prone to violent discord in relationships, a la *Fatal Attraction*. (5) With low A and low F = The Wet Blanket, or whiny "sour grape". These individuals turn away from people and life, but take a piece of flesh on the turn.

High scores on E, L, and $Q_1$ particularly predict hostility, and the clinician should look to scores on scales B, M, and $Q_3$ to see whether this is likely to be intellectualized aggression or whether it is expected to manifest itself in controlled plans or actualized retribution.

A high F and low G combined with a high $Q_1$ and low $Q_2$ may indicate a young adult in severe conflict over identity development. When $F+$ is accompanied by $A-$ and $Q_2-$ scores, expect a detached, highly self-serving personality; here the $Q_2-$ is not an inherent attachment to others, but the using of others. When $F+$ is found with lower C, G, and/or $Q_3$, asocial behavior can be expected.

Low G combined with high O is found in persons who portray themselves as rebellious and free-thinking but who experience much guilt whenever they act out this behavior. This is different from the pattern of low G and low O, consistently found in psychopathic individuals who show little if any guilt. Low G and F accompanied by high O suggests possible depression.

When high H is not balanced by high A or I, look for an especially insensitive individual who is very likely to bore or irritate people. High H and low B predicts poor judgment and impulsive action, a bad combination. High H and low C predicts poor reality testing, some impulsivity, and low frustration tolerance. Very low H and E scores predict a "doormat personality," often showing masochism and/or dependency. Persons with high H in combination with high $Q_1$ are critical in interpersonal relationships, yet avoid the risks incumbent on taking responsibility for or acting on their criticism. When the isolated suspiciousness of the high L is combined with low scores on H and A, a paranoid-schizoid component is probable and warrants further scrutiny.

As noted, high I and high E are related to stress-based disorders. Conversely, low scores here predict an individual who appears passive, yet may be tough at the core and able to resist stress reasonably well. Very high I and F scores suggest narcissism and histrionic tendencies. High I, H, A, and F suggest an activist, personally and socially. High I with low F and H points to intense but bottled-up feeling states. Low I, high As are dangerous interpersonally as their extrovert components are perceived as sensitivity, but they never "come through" with that sensitivity and hurt others in the process.

When both L and O are high, a furtive, apprehensive, and very emotionally constricted individual is likely; when L is high and O is low, expect patterns of arrogance and grandiosity. When L and B are high, A low, and O at least a bit low, expect less projective defensiveness as these highly intelligent, high-self esteem individuals are basically indifferent to others. Their suspiciousness is channelled toward more abstract phenomena, so they can be productive in areas that require analytic thinking and skepticism, e.g., research. When L is low and other apparently contradictory scores occur, e.g., high N or E or low G, at least consider more subtle forms of faking. If L is low and I and M are high, look for a person who avoids interaction with the world by escaping into fantasy, whereas if I and M are low and L and N are high, look for a shrewd, cold, and pragmatically plotting individual. If a low L is accompanied by a low E, one may have an individual who is both very dependent and manipulative—a person who takes on a "poor me" role and yet manipulates other people in a passive-dependent fashion.

With high M, the more indicators of introversion, the more likely to have a deep thinker, but one who has trouble sharing ideas. The more indices of extroversion, the more likely to have a persuasive and effective doer. The more common combination of M+ and I+ predicts to a rich inner life, but a person who often lacks objectivity, whereas the combination of M+ and I− can be creative in the sphere of objective facts, e.g., the physical sciences. High M and C suggest withdrawal in the face of emotional distress; M+ and G− suggest a person with unorthodox views in many areas and with the potential to act them out. M−, I− persons are ultra-realists, while M−, I+ persons are practical, giving (although sometimes boring or obtuse) doers. M− and F− together suggest a very difficult therapeutic endeavor. Interestingly enough, a high M score generally predicts recidivism in criminal populations.

High Ns, particularly when they also score low on $Q_1$, are interpersonally provocative, and if scale B is also high, this provocativeness may be used in an intellectual manner. High scores on N along with a low score on G and high scores on E and H predict a con man, a person who manipulates others through a combination of assertiveness and shrewdness. The quality of the conning may be predicted by scores on M and B. Persons high on N, E, and $Q_1$ and low on G are particularly difficult to work with and cause a variety of troubles in interpersonal relationships. If they are also high on B and L, their disruption is more difficult to detect. When high N is found with high B (intelligence) and L, an apparently amicable demeanor may cover venomous jealousy and/or suspicion.

When low N is found with low B, a gullible "Simple Simon" is likely; if low N is with high I, high romantic expectations and sentimentality make them vulnerable to relationship manipulation. Low N and high M are seen as odd or "weird" and often elicit social rejection.

When both O and G are high, guilt embedded in low self-esteem is common, and the guilt is often neurotic rather than real. When the G is low (with high O), often found with young adults, there is guilt about not endorsing standard moral standards. High O and $Q_3$ reflect guilt from failing to meet a level of aspiration rather than guilt. When O is high and F is low, but other anxiety indicators are not marked, consider depression.

Persons high on $Q_1$ and F and low on C tend to be disorganized and impulsive in both thought and behavior. High $Q_1$ and $Q_3$ scores, along with a moderately high G score, predict compulsiveness; this is amplified into obsessive-compulsiveness to the degree that B is high and M is at either extreme (high-obsessive or low-compulsive).

When high $Q_2$ is combined with low B, expect a "closed (and ineffective) mind." If E and L are also high, the individual can be dangerous if "crossed." High $Q_2$, low A people have "given up" on others, often reflecting a disappointing loss. High $Q_2$ and L reflect severe mistrust and a tendency to project insecurities and conflicts. High $Q_2$ and O are individuals who have withdrawn out of a belief they would be rejected if others knew their "real" selves. Low $Q_2$ and high E create conflictual relationships as they both seek dominance and emotional reassurance.

Low $Q_2$ and high Ls have an analogous approach–avoidance conflict; they are suspicious, yet yearn for dependency.

High $Q_3$, E, and O predispose one to a very traumatic response to any perceived failure. High $Q_3$ and G and low C and/or H sets the stage for various dissociative disorders and responses. Low $Q_3$, C, and H with high L, O, and $Q_4$ are individuals who see themselves as stupid and inadequate (and often are at least the latter) and are highly prone to anxiety responses. Low $Q_3$, O, and $Q_4$, on the other hand, are relaxed and self-accepting persons, but appear sloppy and have a high level of "body hedonism." As noted, low $Q_3$ with low G and C are individuals highly prone to acting-out, have low impulse controls, and a propensity for characterological disorders; the problem is compounded if C is also low, but may be muted by the fear of punishment if F is also low. $Q_4$, the measure par excellence of present anxiety, takes on more ominous connotations if it is found along with high O and low C scores, as this predicts a more long-term disorder. When high $Q_4$ is associated with high M and I and low G and $Q_3$ scores, substance abuse is probable. When an individual is in a very difficult or stressful situation and is showing low $Q_4$ and O, look for someone who may be overly defensive to the point of distorting reality. When low $Q_4$ is in combination with high L, look for someone who is out of touch with his or her bodily sensations. When low $Q_4$ and high O are seen together, look for evidence of fatigue and depression.

Overall, profiles that clearly slope right (low A through a high $Q_4$) are more indicative of psychopathology. Those that clearly slope left (higher A, B, and C down through lower Q scores) are indicative of psychological health (Krug, 1981).

It should be noted that, on occasion, the 16 PF and MMPI-2 profiles on an individual client may appear to be somewhat contradictory. It is rare that any direct contradictions occur, as the two tests do not measure exactly the same areas. However, if there is an apparent contradiction, the validity scores for each test should be checked. If all is in order, the secondary adjective in the 16-PF-scale descriptors should be given more weight to see if that produces a better meld. If there is still no resolution, which is unlikely, greater weight should be given to the MMPI-2 because it has been more thoroughly researched and has more items per scale.

# CHAPTER 14

# Aggression Rape, Child Abuse, and Suicide Potential

One of the most difficult times for a clinician is dealing with a situation that involves a prediction of danger toward self or others. The Tarasoff (1976) decision and its spawn haven't made things easier. Before proceeding into the discussions of the specific patterns, consider the following assessment-management strategy for any client in which there is the possibility of any dangerous (to others or self) behavior:

1. Obtain a thorough history and directly question the client on thoughts about past behavior issues and about any present or recent thoughts of hurting oneself or others.

2. To resolve specific uncertainties, check with collateral sources (with appropriate permissions) such as family, friends, and co-workers, and review all prior relevant records. Deal with milieu issues that may encourage acting-out.

3. If you feel uncomfortable about the client's ability to control such behaviors, seriously consider hospitalization, including the possibility of involuntary civil commitment (see Chapter 9).

4. In those cases where the client would not qualify for involuntary commitment, but you are still concerned, strongly encourage a brief voluntary hospitalization. However, be careful how you word and record such episodes. For example, on September 14, 1989, Joseph Westbecker, upset over perceived grudges, went to a plant in Louisville where he had been employed, carrying five guns and

twelve-hundred rounds of ammunition. Using a semi-automatic AK-47 assault rifle, he went on a rampage, killing eight people and wounding twelve, then killed himself. Three days before, he had seen his psychiatrist who recorded his suggestion that Westbecker voluntarily check into a mental hospital; a behavior that would look reasonable under a routine peer review, but one this psychiatrist might reconsider in retrospect.

5. Develop a plan, in concert with a secondary monitor, e.g., a spouse, to keep guns and/or drugs away from the client.

6. Communicate your limits to the client, at the same time expressing a wish to help. In this vein, urge your client to refrain from using alcohol and/or nonprescribed drugs. Consider the use of a secondary monitor if risk warrants it.

7. Express your personal concern for and commitment to the client in a direct fashion; this may reduce feelings of violence to self or others.

8. Help them to recognize and label and the underlying emotions (commonly anger and/or depression) and help them to make the link to acting-out. Help the client to develop alternative means of catharsis, e.g., words and artistic expression.

9. Provide concrete avenues of access to you outside the therapy session, encourage their use, and/or increase the frequency of the therapy contact.

10. Consider the initiation or adjustment of a medication regimen to control symptoms such as depression or anxiety.

11. Periodically review your treatment plan and your client's mental status. Provide assurances about confidentiality, but in the context of a discussion of your special duty (under the law and/or ethics code, etc.) to design a plan that protects specific others and/or society as a whole if clinical interventions are unsuccessful. Consider putting some or all facets of this plan in a form of contractual agreement (see the related discussion of this approach in the section on suicide later in this chapter).

■     ## Aggression Potential

Given the low base rates of severe aggression behaviors (and suicide as well), making a highly accurate prediction to specific actual behavior is virtually impossible (Monahan, 1981, 1984). Monahan has pointed to the eight most critical demographic predictor variables for aggression. It is more common if the potential perpetrator (1) is young (this variable correlates strongly up until the thirty to thirty-five age range, after which the correlation is random), (2) is male, (3) is of a lower socioeconomic class, (4) is from a disadvantaged minority, (5) is less educated, (6) has a lower intellectual level, (7) has an unstable school and/or vocational history, and (8) has a history of juvenile violence and/or alcohol and/or drug abuse. Other demographic indicators of a potential for violence that have been noted throughout the literature are (1) a prior history of violent behaviors, (2) a prior history of suicide attempts, (3) a history of family violence, (4) soft neurological signs, (5) command hallucinations, (6) fascination with weapons, (7) histrionic personality traits, (8) a pattern of cruelty to animals as a child or adolescent, (9) a rejecting or depressed father, and (10) recent stress, especially if associated with low levels of serotonin (Bongar, 1991; Geen, 1990; Monahan, 1981, 1984). In addition to these predictors, assaultiveness on the ward by inpatient psychiatric patients is correlated with hallucinatory behavior, emotional lability, and a high level of activity.

There is even solid empirical evidence for specific imitative violence, for example, homicide rates increase consistently and significantly on the third day after a heavyweight championship fight, i.e., the most well-publicized type of prizefight (Miller et al., 1991). There is also increasing evidence of "bio-vio" indicators. For example, Virkkunen and Linnoila (1991) studied violent offenders and found that low cerebrospinal fluid 5-hydroxindoleacetic acid levels and a low blood glucose nadir in a glucose tolerance test predicted to aggressive acts, with the latter factor being the most predictive.

Additionally, there are test data that can help the clinician to make predictions at a higher level than that allowed by impressionistic data or chance.

☐ ## MMPI-2

There are several indicators of potential for aggression against others in the MMPI-2 (Kalichman, 1988). As in all areas of psychopathology, certain scales have been developed specifically to assess aggression potential. Ironically, in the general testing situation, the examiner would have to know the "answer" already, at least to a degree, to employ some of these scales. They are of help when there are prior cues, and it is worthwhile for the clinician to keep a range of specific tests available for such situations. A classic and useful scale, since it is embedded in a commonly used test, the MMPI-2, is the Overcontrolled-Hostility (O-H) scale, devised and refined by Megargee and his colleagues (Megargee and Cook, 1975). This scale is a subset of thirty-one MMPI-2 items and effectively identifies a subgroup of assaultive criminals who are generally overcontrolled in their responses to hostility but who sporadically are extremely assaultive. This scale can often be helpful, although it is less useful to the degree one strays from this population. It has been generally correlated with a reported lack of overt anxiety or depression, denial or repression of interpersonal conflict, and rigid control of emotional expression (Butcher, 1990). Blacks and females tend to score higher on this scale, so this should be accounted for in any interpretation.

The type of individual discovered in this scale is similar to the one with the 4-3 profile type described by Davis and Sines (1971). The profile peak is on scale 4, the second highest elevation is on scale 3, and there is little significant elevation elsewhere. This profile is characteristic of men who maintain an ongoing quiet adjustment, yet who are prone toward hostile, aggressive outbursts. They may or may not fit the aforementioned criteria for the intermittent-explosive disorder. Davis and Sines hypothesize that those with the 4-3 profile type are constitutionally predisposed to this behavior by some kind of a cyclical internal mechanism that occasionally causes acute emotional outbursts. Later research, for the most part, confirmed the validity of this profile as suggestive of aggression potential across a number of settings, and among females as well as males (Graham, 1990).

To the degree that both 4 and 3 are highly elevated in a typically nonaggressive person, the likelihood of an occasional aggressive outburst increases. In general, when scale 4 is greater than scale 3, control decreases. Conversely, as scale 3 increases over scale 4, potential for more ability to control and inhibit aggressive impulses increases. In females, the 4-3 pattern has also been commonly associated with promiscuity. This is probably true with males, but because of traditional sex role expectations, such behavior in males is not as commonly a focus in assessment.

Consistently assaultive individuals, whose overt interpersonal patterns are more consistent with this behavior, have high scores on scales F, 4, and 9, with secondary elevations on 6 and 8. All five of these scales have been classically regarded as scales that suggest a lack of impulse control. Persons with high scores on these scales combine social resentment and hostility, a lack of moral inhibitions, suspiciousness of and resentment toward authority and the world in general, and a lack of impulse control. Such a combination easily engenders hostility, even with minimal environmental stimulation. General problems in social adjustment also occur and combine with social resentment and envy of others to elevate the O scale. A high scale 5 score is generally indicative of ability to suppress aggression, although Graham (1987) notes that the 4-5/5-4 profile in women is correlated with aggression.

A specific criminal subgroup, Charlie, with elevations on these scores, is described by Megargee and Bohn (1979). Charlies—who are hostile, paranoid, and dangerous—showed characteristic elevations on scales 8, 6, and 4, in that order, with distinctly low scales on 1, 2, and 3. From an overall perspective, high scores on F, 6, 7, and 8 predict to violent incidents in a prison setting.

The subgroup How, also studied by Megargee and Bohn (1979), seeks interpersonal contact but is consistently rejected and builds up much anger, hostility, and anxiety. In that subgroup, scale 8 is usually highest, followed by scales 2, 4, and 1. The overall profile is distinctly elevated, with higher elevations on the above scales in a noteworthy jagged pattern.

The "double-M profile," with distinct elevations on 2, 4, 6, and 8, refers to individuals who are very unstable and dangerous to self or, more likely, to others. It is hard to bring them into a therapy situation, and if they appear, they are difficult to change.

## 16 PF

There has not been as much research on the prediction of aggression with the 16 PF as there has been with the MMPI-2. However, several scales considered together do modestly predict aggression. Scales that tap aggression potential per se are E, L, and $Q_1$, and in each a high scale is predictive. General impulsiveness is reflected in high scores on F and H. Low scores on G, O, and $Q_3$, along with a high score on F, are thought to be predictors of low ego control and thus to contribute to a prediction of acting-out.

## OTHER TEST-RESPONSE PATTERNS

Persons who are inclined toward easy aggression seem less able to deal with their concerns by articulating them verbally (Goldstein and Keller, 1987); this may be reflected in the WAIS-R, since they usually obtain a verbal score that is lower than the performance score. Clients who act out aggressively tend to score lower on the similarities, vocabulary, and block-design subtests.

Problems in aggression control are usually correlated with present or previous difficulties in adjusting to school. Hence, within the verbal section of the WAIS-R, scores tend to be lower on information, arithmetic, and vocabulary relative to the other three scales taken as a whole. Quiet but hostile and explosive individuals attain low picture arrangement scores, relative to the more extroverted and consistently aggressive type.

An elevation on MCMI-II scale 6 of 85 or higher should alert the clinician to aggression potential. The 5-6/6-5 codes also occur frequently in the context of the antisocial personality diagnosis and may therefore be predictive of aggression. The deficient social conscience and interpersonal exploitiveness of a high 5 (narcissistic), combined with the hostile affectivity and interpersonal vindictiveness of a high 6 (antisocial), would seem to be indicative of a potentially dangerous individual. To the extent that elevations on B and/or T occur, in conjunction with elevated 6, aggression potential increases. As P and PP become more elevated, aggression potential may increase.

Persons who exhibit patterns of intermittent-explosive behavior certainly have potential for aggression, though predicting these episodes may be considerably more difficult (Monahan, 1984). (The reader is referred to Chapter 10 for discussion of disorders of impulse control.)

On the Rorschach, individuals who are prone to aggressive behavior typically show short reaction times, do not provide extensive response records, and may give quick responses to card I and the color cards (Beck and Beck, 1978). They tend to be low in the number of FC responses and high in C, CF, and Popular responses (Phillips and Smith, 1953). Responses associated with fighting (swords, guns, blood) or aggressive animals (crabs, tigers) are expected in those individuals who consistently act out aggressively: assaultive psychopaths. The explosion-oriented response is more characteristic of the person who is making an attempt to control aggression: the explosive personality. Overall, elevated Rorschach special and content scales of Aggressive Movement (Ag), Explosion (Ex), and Morbid Responses (MOR) raise the probability of aggression. Conversely, the potential for assault is contraindicated by a high number of F+, D, and FC responses, a high amount of abstraction content, and/or a higher number of Popular and Original responses (Exner, 1986; Phillips and Smith, 1953).

A number of specific contents on the Rorschach are often considered signs of aggression. On card I, in reference to the central light-gray detail on the midline, the responses "tomahawk" or "hammerhead" are given mainly by aggressive psychopaths. A response on card II like "two bears fighting with blood splashed around" is significant for the type of psychopath who entertains aggressive fantasies and is hostile toward the outer world. When card III, lower central light-gray detail, elicits a response like "jaws closing" cojoined with "blood," there is a possibility of latent hostility and sadistic aggressivity.

Potential for aggression is occasionally seen in frank, unsublimated expressions of aggressive impulses (Geen, 1990). More-subtle clues are drawings that seem to press out against the edges of the page, heavy pencil pressure, short and/or jagged strokes, transparencies, unrelieved areas of white space, teeth, long spikelike fingers, and a same-sex person depicted in an explicitly aggressive posture (Oster and Gould, 1987).

The reader is referred to the previous sections on the antisocial personality disorder, conduct disorder, and the passive-aggressive personality disorder, since these disorders in particular contain the potential for ongoing aggression, and the criteria described there are applicable here as well. With regard to periodic aggression, the reader is referred to the sections on the explosive personality and on the paranoid disorders.

There are numerous potential causes of violent behavior. The following outline gives an overview of these causes, along with consensus intervention strategies.

A. Violence as an inherent part of human nature
  1. Traditional psychotherapy to modify basic personality patterns
  2. Medications to diminish anxiety and minimize inappropriate reactions
  3. Psychosurgery to change or interrupt patterns of brain functioning

B. Violence as a consequence of social learning
  1. Family therapy to change home environment or facilitate coping in the family setting
  2. Group therapy to enhance appropriate coping in social situation
  3. Assertiveness training and social-skills training to give concrete training in self-assertion without violence
  4. Systematic desensitization (SDT) to desensitize client to the precipitating stimuli, so as to diminish inappropriate or excessive reactions
  5. Token economy, time-out, and social isolation to extinguish violent behavior through removal of environmental reinforcers as well as to strengthen appropriate responses
  6. Classical conditioning to extinguish violent behavior, as in aversive conditioning
  7. Parent effectiveness training such as Parents Anonymous to enhance adequate coping skills and provide a supportive peer group

C. Violence as a consequence of frustration and other situational factors
  1. Traditional psychotherapy to release frustrations and to change coping patterns
  2. Family therapy, see B1
  3. Group therapy, see B2
  4. Assertiveness training, social-skills training, see B3
  5. Token economy-to provide opportunities for positively reinforcing experiences while extinguishing the violent behavior
  6. Parent effectiveness training, see B7

D. Violence as a means of communication
  1. Expressive therapies to substitute alternate means of expression of feelings underlying violent acting-out
  2. Assertiveness training, etc., see B3
  3. SDT, see B4
  4. Parent effectiveness training, see B7

E. Violence and aggression as protection of territorial integrity and body space
  1. SDT, see B4
  2. Assertiveness training, see B3

# ■ Rape

Rape does not appear directly as a diagnostic entity in DSM-III-R, but it is a most important syndrome, is often an impulsive behavior, and shows certain diagnostic correlates. A discussion is in order here.

There are a number of classification systems for rape, one of the most influential being the pioneering work of Cohen et al. (1969). The following discussion reflects their concepts.

Aside from the rapes that occur as an incidental result of such disorders as severe organic brain dysfunction or schizophrenia and those that are an impulsive and ritualistic gesture (the plunder of war), there is reasonable agreement that there are three major rape patterns. The first occurs where aggression is the major component and sexual satisfaction is somewhat irrelevant in the motivational system. These rapists are hostile toward females and in general carry a high level of aggression potential. The preceding section on aggression potential deals with the diagnostic considerations relevant to such persons.

The second type of rapist needs to administer pain to another person to obtain sexual satisfaction. The pain is requisite, so this type of rapist is classified under the psychosexual disorder of sexual sadism (see Chapter 8).

A third major category of rapists is that where the aggression is an avenue toward sexual contact and satisfaction, yet also in some ways to interpersonal contact, and most cases of date-rape fit here. This is the individual whose diagnostic correlates are presented here. This sexually motivated rapist fits the results of Barbaree et al. (1979), who found that, in most cases, forced sex for this person fails to inhibit arousal, although it does so in most normal individuals. Incidentally, Abel et al. (1986) found that some rapists (the aggression subtype) are especially aroused by stimuli that connote a woman who is aggressive or manipulative or by sexual images that include aggression.

☐     CHARACTERISTICS OF RAPE

Rape has traditionally been defined as the unlawful penetration of a female's vagina by a man's penis, reinforced by some form of coercion and without the consent of the victim. However, it is absurd to require penile penetration to define rape. Homosexual rape occurs, as does rape of men by women (although very rarely). Statutes have been rewritten in states to reflect this.

Rape is a common crime and is said to account for approximately 5 percent of all crimes of violence. Each year, about one in every two thousand women is a reported rape victim. However, it is estimated that only about 10 percent of victims of rape ever report it to the police. Also, only about two in twenty rapists are ever arrested, one in thirty rapes that take place is prosecuted, and one in fifty convicted. More than 50 percent of reported victims' homes, and in about 40 percent of the cases, the rapist is known to the victim (Calhoun and Atkeson, 1991; Abel et al., 1986).

☐  THE RAPIST

Most rapists are married, and a great percentage of married rapists have regular sexual relations with their wives. However, their sexual performance is often impaired during the rape. Like most other antisocial personalities and criminals, rapists are generally lower than average in intelligence.

A few researchers, e.g., Rada et al. (1976) have found elevated levels of plasma testosterone in some samples of the most violent rapists. In general, however, there is not much correlation between rape and physiological measures. An impossible problem is obtaining such measures at the critical predictive point, the time just before the rape, as many of these physiological variables differ markedly for any one individual depending on when they are assessed. However, measurements of penile response to sexual imagery may be useful here, as well as in making at least some tentative predictions about future behavior when that is important in disposition.

While any one rapist may show a combination of motivations, the following gives a list of identifiers pointing to the predominant emotional pattern.* Those who are sadistic rapists will show characteristics of sexual sadism, discussed in Chapter 8.

**ANGER RAPE**

1. Aggression: more physical force is used than is necessary to overpower the victim.
2. Offender's mood state is one of anger and depression.
3. Offenses are episodic and are generated more impulsively.
4. Language is abusive: cursing, swearing, obscenities.
5. Dynamics: retribution for perceived wrongs, injustices, or "put-downs" experienced by the offender.
6. Assault is of relatively short duration.
7. Victim suffers physical trauma to all areas of her body.

**POWER RAPE**

1. Aggression: uses whatever force or threat is necessary to gain control of victim and overcome her resistance.

*Adapted in part from Groth, W., and Birnbaum, J. (1979). *Men Who Rape: The Psychology of the Offender.* New York: Plenum.

2. Offender's mood state is one of anxiety-agitation.

3. Offenses are premeditated, are repetitive, and may show an increase in aggression over time.

4. Language is instructional and inquisitive: giving orders, asking personal questions, inquiring as to victim's responses.

5. Dynamics: compensation for deep-seated insecurities and feelings of inadequacy.

6. Assault may be of an extended duration with the victim held captive for a period of time.

7. Victim may be physically unharmed; bodily injury would be inadvertent rather than intentional.

### SADISTIC RAPE

1. Aggression: physical force (anger and power) is eroticized.

2. Offender's mood state is one of intense excitement.

3. Offenses are calculated and ritualistic, typically involving bondage, torture, or bizarre acts, and are interspersed with other, nonsadistic sexual assaults.

4. Language is commanding and degrading.

5. Dynamics: symbolic destruction and elimination.

6. Assault may be of an extended duration in which the victim is kidnapped, assaulted, and disposed of.

7. Victim suffers physical trauma to sexual areas of her body; in extreme cases she is murdered and mutilated.

□    MMPI-2

It has been generally found that rapists are more disturbed across the board on such tests as the MMPI-2 than are assaultists per se or exhibitionists (Levin and Stava, 1987). In many ways, rapists correlate with the dimensions of the antisocial personality (the reader is referred to that section). The 4-9/9-4 is the most common (Erickson et al., 1987). The 8-4/4-8 is also found, with the 8-4 being characteristic of rapists of adults, while the 4-8 is more characteristic of rapists of children (Armentrout and Hauer, 1978).

Kalichman et al. (1989) found five rather distinct MMPI-2 patterns in their sample of rapists. Those occurring most commonly were a subclinical 4-9 and a second group with a spike-4 profile. The next most common group showed elevations above 70 T on F, 4, 8, and 9, with moderate elevations on 5, 6, and 7. The last subgroup, a very disturbed group, showed elevations at about 100 T on 8, elevations above 80 on F, 4 (barely), 6, and 7, with elevations of 70 or above on most other scales except L, K, 5, and O.

Rapists may obtain a high K score, reflecting the fact that they are typically under scrutiny for a criminal offense (see the section on malingering). Scale 5 is usually low in these individuals if there is a strong identification with the stereotypical male role. Scale 0 is mildly elevated if there is general ineptitude in interpersonal skills. This type of behavior, along with an inclination to deny responsibility for it, is seen in an elevation of scale 3.

Rader (1977) has suggested that the 4-3 profile characterizes the more repressed rapist, who is inclined toward significant violence. In this case, scale 6 is also likely to be elevated, although this depends on the degree of hostility allowed into awareness. Scales F and 8 are elevated to the degree the individual is losing control of impulses and is degenerating into more-fragmented pathology, but faking-bad must also be considered.

## 16 PF

Rapists, if they are at all self-disclosing, score away from the average on a number of personality dimensions (Masters et al., 1991). The primarily sexually motivated rapist is more likely to score toward the average profile than is the aggression-motivated rapist. However, both types are likely to have a low score on C, reflecting their emotional instability; low scores on Q and G from their inability to control impulses and urges; and a high score on O from their insecurity. The sexual rapist who is more naive, suspicious, interpersonally open, and less aggressive is likely to score low on N, moderately low on H, and moderately high on $Q_4$ and I. Aggressively motivated rapists will score low on A and moderately low on I, but high on E, H, and $Q_2$. Both types are less than average on scale B.

## OTHER TEST-RESPONSE PATTERNS

The hostile affectivity and interpersonal vindictiveness typical of the rapist predict MCMI-II scores of 85 or higher on scale 6. To a lesser extent, the exploitiveness of the narcissist may predispose toward rape behavior, so an elevation of 75 or higher could occur on 5. Scale C is also high.

## TREATMENT OPTIONS

Castration has been a time-honored approach for dealing with the rapist, but it runs afoul of legal considerations and the beliefs of some liberals. Nonetheless, chemocastration, via drugs that lower the serum testosterone level, is still used (Abel et al., 1986). These drugs lower the likelihood of sexual arousal, but side effects are substantial and the drugs are not consistently effective. Suggestions for the legal disposition of the rapist even include some irony analogous to the above suggestions. Fersch (1980) states that in rape "the criminal act ought to be brought under assault and battery with a dangerous weapon. Then the attention could be focused on whether or not the accused possessed a dangerous weapon" (p. 14); albeit occasionally an impotent weapon.

The aversive therapies have been commonly used here and have shown moderate success (Calhoun and Atkeson, 1991). More-effective ways of coping with anger are also necessary, possibly introduced by modeling or role playing. Marital therapy may be specifically indicated, since for many rapists the initiation of the rape sequence immediately follows a marital battle. Refer to the program for sex offenders in Chapter 8.

## ■ Child Abuse

The physical and sexual abuse of children has been clearly documented throughout history across cultures (Friedrich, 1991; Nelson, 1984). Although such abuse is frequently abhorred, few actual preventive measures have been taken. It is ironic that the first formal legal intervention in a child abuse case, that of Mary Ellen in New York in 1975, had to be prosecuted through animal protection laws and with the efforts of the Society for the Prevention of Cruelty to Animals. However, in the spectacularly short time of about five years, child abuse in the United States went from being virtually a nonissue to being the focus of national political concern (Nelson, 1984). All fifty states, partly spurred by the federal Child Abuse Prevention and Treatment Act, have established legal routes to identify and intervene in abusive families. Yet, because of the private nature of abuse and the reluctance of both perpetrators and victims to reveal its occurrence, clearly identified cases of child abuse are generally believed to represent only a portion of the actual cases. The difficulty of legislating in this area is highlighted by the research of Berlin et al. (1991) that suggests that mandatory reporting statutes for mental health professionals may, in light of the emphasis on full informed consent, impair the probability of an abuser seeking or remaining in treatment.

### □ DIAGNOSTIC CONSIDERATIONS

In the vast majority of cases, the first diagnostic cue emanates from the child. There are a number of common physical signs of physical abuse. A way of remembering them are the "four Bs": unexplained or unusual bruises, burns, bald spots, or bleeding.

Look for bruises around the head or face or in easily protected areas, such as the abdomen; multiple bruises, especially if spread over the body; or bruises in the shape of an object, such as a hand or a belt. Likewise, burns of all types should cause concern, especially cigarette burns; burns with a specific shape, such as an iron; and burns that suggest that a hand has been immersed in liquid. Concern should be heightened if the child provides an explanation that does not fit the injury.

Behavioral signs of physical abuse include accident-proneness, problems with schoolwork and peers, shrinking from physical contact, and wearing clothes that seem designed more to cover the body than to keep one warm. Be especially on guard if any of these symptoms represent a change in the behavior pattern of a child. Over and above these signs, delinquency, drug abuse, anorexia nervosa, and excessive avoidance of parents may reflect an abuse situation in older children and adolescents.

Along with physical abuse, there has been increasing attention to the sexual abuse of children (Friedrich, 1991). The behavioral signs just noted also are found in cases of sexual abuse. Additional signs include extreme secrecy, excessive bathing, indications of low self-worth, provocative or promiscuous sexual patterns, appearing more worldly than friends, or suddenly possessing money or merchandise that could have been used to bribe the child to keep quiet.

Specific physical signs of sexual abuse are pain, rashes, itching or sores in the genital or anal areas, enuresis, frequent urinary infections, or frequent vomiting.

On the MMPI-2, women who are at risk for child abuse tend to show a 4-8-9 pattern (Engleland et al., 1991). The 4/8 code has been shown to be predominate in the victims of father–daughter incest, when they are either later-adolescent or adult clients (Scott and Stone, 1986). Adult victims may have significantly elevated 1, 2, and 5 scales, suggesting that depression is a feature. Adolescents show higher elevations on scale 9, suggesting acting-out behaviors.

One of the better measures for physical child abuse assessment is the Child Abuse Potential (CAP) Inventory, developed by Joel Milner (1991) (c/o Family Violence Research Program, Dept. of Psychology, No. Illinois University, DeKalb, IL 60015-2892). The CAP is a 160-item, self-administered, forced-choice questionnaire with a third-grade readability level, and it includes three validity scales. It shows classification rates, based on discriminant analysis, in the mid-80 percent to low 90 percent range, and unlike several other scales, produces more false negatives than false positives.

General diagnostic considerations flow from an understanding of the many factors that contribute to the ultimate emergence of an episode of physical and/or sexual child abuse (Finkelhor, 1985). These factors are found within three contributing systems: sociocultural, familial, and individual. To the degree these factors are present, the probability of an occurrence of child abuse is increased. At the most basic level are the following *sociocultural* factors that facilitate an increase in child abuse episodes:

**1.** Lack of affirmation and support of the family unit

2. Lack of emphasis on parent-training skills as a prerequisite to parenting

3. Acceptance of and high media visibility of violence

4. Acceptance of corporal punishment as a central child-rearing technique

5. Emphasis on competition rather than cooperation

6. Unequal status for women

7. Low economic support for schools and day-care facilities

These sociocultural factors heighten the probability of abuse in conjunction with the following *familial* factors:

1. Low socioeconomic and education levels

2. Little availability of friends and extended family for support

3. Single-parent or merged-parent family structure

4. Marital instability

5. Family violence as common and traditionally accepted

6. Low rate of family contact and information exchange

7. Significant periods of mother absence

8. High acceptance of family nudity

9. Low affirmation of family-member privacy

10. "Vulnerable" children (to the degree they are young, sick, disturbed, retarded, or emotionally isolated)

The probability of abuse in a specific instance is in turn increased by the following *individual* factors:

1. History of abuse as a child

2. Low emotional stability and/or self-esteem

3. Low ability to tolerate frustration and inhibit anger

4. High impulsivity

5. Lack of parenting skills

6. High emotional and interpersonal isolation

7. Problems in handling dependency needs of self or others

8. Low ability to express physical affection

9. Unrealistic expectations for child's performance

10. Acceptance of corporal punishment as a primary child-rearing technique

11. Presence of drug or alcohol abuse

In most cases, many (although not all) of these factors are found. Some predict more to physical abuse and some to sexual abuse, but most factors predict to either type. Other specific diagnostic considerations (including test correlates) and treatment considerations can be found in the prior section on aggression potential and in the sections on pedophilia and incest (see Chapter 8) and the personality disorders (see Chapter 9).

□        TREATMENT OPTIONS

In addition to individual psychotherapy, there are three core approaches that are potentially useful in almost all such cases (Friedrich, 1991; Marshall et al., 1991):

1. *Family therapy.* Since the family is virtually always disrupted, family therapy is necessary. Even where the family system eventually changes, family therapy can help to mute the damage to all concerned.

2. *Parent training.* When the abuse comes from a parent, parent training is necessary to deal not only with the problems that led to the abuse, but to those generated by the abuse as well. Parent training to deal with this latter factor is also important when the source of abuse is external to the family.

3. *Support systems.* Abuse often comes where there has been a sense of emotional isolation. In this vein, a community-based counseling and support group is available to abusing parents in Parents Anonymous. This organization works in the same manner as Alcoholics Anonymous or Gamblers Anonymous. A similar group is Parents United. Contact with other abusers and the opportunity to share problems with sympathetic and understanding others are helpful for parents for whom abusive behaviors are triggered by psychosocial stressors and a sense of emotional isolation. There are also support groups for the victims of child abuse, which are especially useful with older abuse victims.

These approaches can also be supplemented by other interventions, for instance, attempts to change the person's employment possibilities or social skills, cognitive-behavioral interventions (Marshall et al., 1991), etc. Where there is a couple involved, marital therapy is likely to be necessary if the marriage is to continue.

Children who have been sexually abused are more likely to show negative effects, both short-term and long-term, if (a) the abuse occurred over a substantial time span, (b) there were many episodes of abuse during that time span, (c) the child was abused by several, separate perpetrators, (d) the child was physically hurt, (e) the child was threatened or psychologically traumatized in or around these episodes, (f) the abuse was by the natural father or mother or by a loved parental figure, especially if that person is still loved and is separated from the child as a result of the abuse, (g) the child had to go through aversive confrontations in the legal process, especially if the perpetrator is found not guilty, (h) the child was old enough to experience some normal guilt and yet continued to participate, (i) the child does not have access to a loving, secure and stable family structure, or (j) the child was somehow made to feel responsible for whatever family disruption that did take place. A variety of treatment modalities will be needed, e.g., there is often a post-traumatic stress component to the abuse and its aftermath, so something like SDT to prepare for and/or recover from the court appearance may be needed.

While treatment may help in a specific case, the greatest changes will come with efforts at prevention (parent training *before* becoming parents, reduction of the percentage of very young and/or single parents without skills or resources, educational programs in schools) or cultural change (efforts to reduce the acceptance of physical discipline) (Nelson, 1984; Finkelhor, 1985). As recommended by the U.S. Advisory Board on Child Abuse and Neglect, programs should be designed to have health workers visit new parents in the home to discuss health care, make sure parents know how to care for the child, offer advice, and provide access to continuing support groups where needed.

## ■ Suicide Potential

As with aggression, the clinician is often called on to make predictions about suicide potential, and it is an equally difficult task (Bongar, 1991; Apter et al., 1991). Although suicide is still an issue of concern in legal areas, it is no longer considered a crime. Only in recent times has our legal predecessor, England, stopped responding to a suicide attempt with hanging. But hanging had superseded an even more flamboyant approach: driving a stake through the heart of one who attempted suicide. Edward Phillips claimed in his 1662 dictionary to have invented the word "suicide," but the British poetry critic Alfred Alvarez reported in 1971 that he had found the word used even earlier, in Sir Thomas Brown's *Religio Medici*, written in 1635 and published in 1642 (Schneidman, 1985).

The combined suicide rate in the United States during this century has remained at about 12 per 100,000 population. Many authorities believe that the suicide rate has been rising, but it is still not clear whether this is because of a greater willingness on the part of coroners and police officers to use the term or because there is a true increase in the incidence of suicide. The research of Murphy and Wetzel (1980) suggests that the suicide rate significantly increased throughout the years 1949–74; there is good reason to believe that this increase has not since abated (Bongar, 1991, especially in the 15–24 year age range). However, they point out that before these findings are used to authorize an expansion of traditional efforts to increase the number of suicide prevention centers, one should note that the rise in the suicide rate has coincided with a rise in the distribution and visibility of these centers in the United States. Interestingly, the opposite effect has been noted in England.

Suicide appears to be increasing among young adults; at present, it is the second highest cause of death for white males aged fifteen to nineteen (approximately 88 per 100,000). For many years, the reported rate of suicide in the United States has been approximately 10 to 12 per 100,000 population. In several European countries, notably Sweden and Switzerland, rates of approximately 25 per 100,000 have been reported. However, it is not clear whether this reflects truly differential rates.

More men than women actually kill themselves (at approximately a ratio of 3:1; in psychiatric patients it is only about a 1.5:1 ratio, although more women than men *attempt* suicide, again at approximately a 3:1 ratio (Schneidman, 1985). The majority of suicides, approximately 90 percent, are committed by whites (in both absolute numbers and per capita rate) as opposed to blacks, and most of the data about suicide is based on whites.

Suicidal individuals tend to give clues to those around them, and these areas should be the focus of any evaluation. Seriously suicidal individuals tend to perceive life in a negative manner and associate many attractive concepts with death; the reverse is true for those who are not so intent on self-destruction. Such measures as the semantic differential could be helpful in this regard. Approximately 80 percent of those who have made a suicide attempt discussed their intent to do so with persons around them, and they are usually open to discussing their suicidal concerns with clinicians.

In addition to being depressed, with feelings of hopelessness *and* helplessness, a loss of sense of continuity with the past and/or present, and loss of pleasure in typical interests and pursuits, suicidal persons are more likely to (1) have a personal history and/or family history of depression, especially if it is a major endogenous depression, or of psychosis, (2) have had a parent or other important identity figure who attempted or committed suicide, (3) have a history of family instability and/or parental rejection, (4) be socially isolated, (5) have a chronic physical illness, (6) have a history of self-damaging acts, often previous suicide attempts (in this context, the first axiom of psychology could well be "Behavior predicts behavior," and the second axiom could be "Behavior without intervention predicts behavior"), (7) show a preoccupation with death and/or make statements of a wish to die, especially statements of a wish to commit suicide, (8) manifest *consistent* life patterns of leaving crises rather than facing them (in relationships: "You can't walk out on me, 'I'm leaving you"; or in jobs: "You can't fire me, because I quit"), (9) show a family history of self-damaging acts, (10) show a personal or family history of addiction patterns, (11) live alone or are involved (married or similarly occupied) with a loved mate who is competitive and/or self-absorbed, (12) show sudden cheerfulness after a long depression, (13) are noted to be putting their affairs in order, e.g., giving away favorite possessions and revising wills, or (14) show some abrupt atypical behavior change, e.g., withdrawal from family or friends (Fawcett, 1992; Bongar, 1991; Schneidman, 1985).

At the biological level, depressions marked by low levels of 5-HIAA hydroxyindoleacetic acid—a metabolite of serotonin; a blunted thyroid-stimulating hormone (TSH) response to a thyrotropin-releasing hormone (TRH) stimulation; high levels of plasma cortisol (20 mcg % or higher); low platelet MAO, low platelet serotonin, high platelet serotonin-2 receptor responsibity; and a high ratio of adrenaline to noradrenaline have all been associated with an increased probability of suicide attempts. Also, suicide completers' brains show one-half to two-thirds the number of receptical, or "binding," sites for the chemical imipramine then do normal brains. The initiation of the suicidal event is especially likely to be triggered by a major life stress or, for example, the experience of a chronic debilitating illness or the loss of an important social support, such as a confidant (Schneidman, 1985).

The following factors can then increase this potential and increase the probability that an attempted suicide will be completed (there is about a 15% probability that a serious attempt will be successful, (Schneidman, 1985; Bongar, 1991):

1. A cognitive state of constriction, that is, an inability to perceive any options or way out of a situation that is generating intense psychological suffering.
2. The idea of death as a catalytic agent for the cessation of distress.
3. Acute perturbation-high distress/agitation/depression.
4. An increase in self-hatred or self-loathing.
5. Perception of self as a source of shame to significant others.
6. Fantasies of death as escape, especially if there are concrete plans for one's own demise.
7. Easy access to a lethal means, e.g., as in police officers and physicians, both of whom show high suicide rates.
8. Absence of an accessible support system (family and good friends).
9. Life stresses that connote irrevocable loss (whether of status or of persons), such as the relatively recent death of a favored parent, even something like retirement. This factor is particularly important if the person at risk is unable to mourn the loss overtly.
10. High physiologic responsiveness: cyclical moods, a propensity toward violence, and a high need for stimulation-seeking in spite of suicide thoughts. Ironically, in previously violent psychiatric patients, sadness showed a low correlation with suicide attempts, whereas it was consistently correlated with attempts by previously nonviolent patients (Apter et al., 1991).

11. Serious sleep disruption and/or abuse of alcohol or drugs.
12. Lack of a therapeutic alliance and/or constructively supportive friendship alliance.
13. Persistence of secondary depression after remission of primary disorder and/or recent discharge from psychiatric hospital (last 3 months).
14. A history of panic attacks, and even more importantly, recent panic attacks.

Fawcett (1992) finds that various factors are differentially predictive of suicide attempts, depending on whether the attempt is early (within one year) or later (one to five years). Although panic attacks, alcohol abuse, loss of interest, psychic anxiety, diminished concentration, and global insomnia are more predictive of early attempts, expressed suicidal ideation, a sense of hopelessness, and prior suicide attempts are more predictive of later attempts.

In general, most people who are severely depressed and suicidal are more dangerous to themselves when they begin an upswing out of the depths of depression. If successive testings by an MMPI-2 or specific depression scale reveal an initial upswing in a depressive who has discussed the possibility of suicide, precautions should be emphasized at that time. There are various types of suicide, as listed next, and type of intervention will depend on the motivation for the suicide in the individual case (Schneidman, 1985).

□　　TYPES OF SUICIDE

1. *Realistic.* These are suicides precipitated by such conditions as the prospect of great pain preceding a sure death.
2. *Altruistic.* The person's behavior is subservient to a group ethic that mandates or at least approves suicidal behavior, like kamikaze pilots in World War II.
3. *Inadvertent.* The person makes a suicide *gesture* in order to influence or manipulate someone else, but a misjudgment leads to an unexpected fatality.
4. *Spite.* Like the inadvertent suicide, the focus is on someone else, but the intention to kill oneself is genuine, with the idea that the other person will suffer greatly from consequent guilt.
5. *Bizarre.* The person commits suicide as a result of a hallucination (such as voices ordering the suicide) or delusions (such as a belief the suicide will change the world).
6. *Anomic.* An abrupt instability in economic or social conditions (such as sudden financial loss in the Great Depression) markedly changes a person's life situation. Unable to cope, the person commits suicide.

7. *Negative self.* Chronic depression and a sense of chronic failure or inadequacy combine to produce repetitive suicide attempts, eventually leading to death.

A dimension that is especially useful to most clinicians is the concept of manipulative versus "genuine" suicide (Schneidman, 1985). Both types will be discussed.

☐　　　　　MMPI-2

Greene (1991) notes that any time scale 2 is the only scale above 65 T, a careful evaluation of suicide risk is indicated, particularly if there are no overt signs of depression. However, the prototypical pattern for a suicidal individual is the 2-7/7-2 combination. This code particularly reflects suicidal ideation, and any time 2 is elevated above 70 T, the clinician should pursue the question of possible suicidal ideation. Reflecting the dictum that "If you want to know something specific about clients, you should ask them about it," the critical items concerning suicide (especially 150, 506, 520, and 524) should always be checked. The likelihood of this ideation's being actualized increases as scores on scales 4, 8, and 9 rise. Such a rise reflects an increasing loss of control over impulses, a rise in the energy available for behavior, and an increasing sense of isolation and resentment toward other people. A rise in scale 8 also reflects poor judgment; hence, suicidals who are not totally genuine in their suicide motivation may actually kill themselves whether they want to succeed or not, as the judgment may bring inadvertent "success."

Some people are suicidal for only short periods of time, usually when there is a severe loss in their psychological worlds that has not yet been integrated (Bongar, 1991). Such people are temporarily suicidal, and if they can be restricted during these periods and treated, they are likely to reintegrate and move away from the suicidal ideation. A high spike on scale 2 is characteristic here.

The 2-4/4-2 code is more likely to reflect a manipulative suicide. Where both scales 4 and 6 are elevated, in addition to at least a moderate elevation on scales 2 and 7, repressed anger and interpersonal hostility are basic to the suicide attempt as manipulation. It is an attempt to inflict punitive guilt and consequent behavior control on another.

Several observers have noted that an additional pattern, at least in women, has been associated with suicide attempts. The major features are a low K scale and a high 5 scale (both suggesting a strong, almost counterphobic rejection of femininity); a paradoxically high score on scale 3, indicating a histrionic component; and a high score on scale 0, reflecting a sense of social isolation and rejection. These women feel alienated and disturbed in their self-identities, yet they have no sense of possible alternatives to deal with their distress. Since they are impulsive as well, the potential for an acting-out behavior is heightened.

☐ 16 PF

On the 16 PF, attempters consistently show themselves to be more tense, expedient, shy, suspicious, emotionally unstable, apprehensive, self-sufficient, extremely anxious, and somewhat introverted. Translated into 16 PF scales, this means high scores on $Q_4$, 0, 1, $Q_2$ and lower scores on G, H, and C. Furthermore, repeated attempters typically score lower on scales $Q_3$ and C than do first-time attempters, indicating less stability and more impulsivity.

☐ OTHER TEST-RESPONSE PATTERNS

Exner (1978, 1986) has provided the most elegant and effective research on the use of Rorschach in the prediction of suicide. In 1978, he offered eleven variables that together form a prediction for suicide potential. The variables he first cited as important are as follows:*

1. FV + VF + V + FD is greater than 2.
2. An occurrence of a color-shading blend response.
3. Zd is greater than ± 3.5.
4. 3r + (2)/R is less than 0.30.
5. Experience Potential is greater than Experience Actual.
6. CF + C is greater than FC.
7. S is greater than 3.
8. X + % is less than 0.70.
9. Pure H is less than 2.
10. P is greater than 8 or less than 3.
11. R is less than 17.

In addition to the eleven criteria used in the original constellation, two new criteria have been established (Exner, 1986). By adding an upper range for the egocentricity scale (3r + (2)/R is greater than 0.45 or less than 0.30) and incorporating the Morbidity index (MOR is greater than 3) the accuracy of the index has significantly improved. The original criterion (eight of eleven variables) could accurately predict 75 percent of suicides, categorizing 20 percent of depressed inpatients and 12 percent of schizophrenics as false-positive errors. The new criterion (eight of thirteen variables) can predict 83 percent of suicides accurately, classifying only 12 percent of depressed inpatients and 6 percent of schizophrenics as false-positives. Neither of the two scales made false-positive

*J. Exner, *The Rorschach: A Comprehensive System*, Vol. 2: *Current Research and Advanced Interpretation.* New York: Wiley, 1978, p. 204. Used with permission of the publisher.

errors in classifying nonsuicidal controls as suicides. This change represents a significant increase in power.

Other authors have supported Exner's concepts that the number of responses is low in suicidals, especially when they are depressed, that less-integrated color responses are more common, and that the number of Popular responses is either very high or low (Swiercinsky, 1985). Also, there is some indication that transparency responses (such as light bulbs) or cross-sectional responses (such as X-rays) are found more commonly in potential suicides than in other persons, and the greater the number of vista and shading responses, the greater the depression-based suicide potential.

Phillips and Smith (1953) state that content suggesting decay or geographical depression (e.g., canyons) is indicative of suicidal ideation. Others have argued that landscape or serenity associations are indicative of suicides who have not yet communicated their intent. Responses that suggest hanging or drowning or other direct means of suicide should obviously alert the examiner to further consideration.

McCann and Suess (1988) examined 131 psychiatric inpatients to conclude that a 1-2-3-8 MCMI-II code type reflects an affect/mood disturbance, with prominent depressive features, and a blend of schizoid, avoidant, dependent, and passive-aggressive personality traits. One-fourth of their patients obtained this code type, which they see as offering a significant suicide risk.

As might be expected, elevations on the MCMI-II of 85 or higher on D and CC and a high score on the Desirability scale (Choca et al., 1992) would be indicative of suicide potential. If N begins to increase and a very high D begins to decrease on repeated testing, the patient may be acquiring the necessary resolve and energy to complete the act; thus, suicide potential may be high. Those personality patterns most likely to exhibit suicide potential are indicated by elevated scores on 2, 8A, 5, and/or C. These patterns represent the most inconsistent patterns and they are particularly susceptible to poorly developed support systems. High scores on scale 8A are particularly associated with manipulative suicide potential.

Since completed suicides are more often psychotic, while attempters are more often neurotic, greater elevations on the pathologic personality scales S, C, and P than on scales 1-8, along with greater elevations on SS, CC, and PP, are found in those who are more likely to complete bizarre suicide gestures.

Beck et al. (1983) found that a score of 10 or more on the Hopelessness Scale, devised by Beck, correctly identified 91 percent of later actual suicides. Also, the pessimism item of the Beck Depression Inventory was asserted to be predictive of later suicides.

Bongar (1991) discusses a number of scales specifically designed to assess suicide risk, e.g., Beck's Scale for Suicide Ideation (SSI) and Suicide Intent Scale (SIS), the Reason for Living Inventory, Suicide

Probability Scale (SPS), Index of Potential Suicide, etc. All have validity problems and are primarily research and/or minimal screening tools, but as such, can be useful in certain specific situations.

Extra data may be available if an individual has already attempted suicide but has been prevented from completing it: the suicide note. The work of Edwin Schneidman and Norman Farberow (Schneidman, 1985) over many years has found that people who attempt suicide and genuinely mean to kill themselves write notes that are matter-of-fact and practical in their content. They may ask the target of the note to pay back small debts, return small items, or otherwise show seemingly trivial concerns, and they do not show much emotional content. It is as if they have already integrated the idea that they will be dead, so emotion is no longer directly tied to living relationships. Those individuals who attempted suicide but apparently had no real intent to kill themselves left romantic, emotion-laden notes, thus attempting to institute guilt in others and pressure them to change their behaviors. Obviously, they believed they would be around to reap the fruits of those changes.

## PREVENTION

Suicide prevention techniques have been developed at both the societal and individual levels, but implementing them is not always easy. The following dialogue from the old television show "Mary Hartman, Mary Hartman" shows the difficulty most people have in responding effectively to a potential suicide's questions.

*Heather (Mary's twelve-year-old daughter):* I have nothing to live for.
*Mary:* Sure you do.
*Heather:* Like what?
*Mary:* Well . . . wait and see.

## INDIVIDUAL PREVENTION

Be aware and follow the general practice principles discussed in Chapter 16. The clinician should be especially and immediately alert to the person's access to lethal instruments and take direct steps to change that situation. Confrontation and exploration of any reported or inferred suicidal ideation is important. The presence and active involvement by pertinent significant others may be essential to such a process. The achievement of a time-limited no-suicide contract is a psychotherapeutic goal that many therapists choose to work toward. The client is asked if he or she will both agree to and verbalize a statement such as

I will not, for the next _____ days (up to at least the time of the next follow-up intervention) do anything to harm myself *or* anyone else, either on purpose *or* accidentally.

If, for any reason, I begin to feel that I might not be able to control thoughts or impulses to hurt or kill myself, I agree to immediately call

_____ at _____, (optional—or
                                  (phone number)

at _____.) If I am unable to reach _____
  (phone number)

(or _____), I agree to go immediately and directly

to _____ at _____.
  (hospital or agency)                      (address and phone number)

_____    _____
(Signature)                           (date)

_____    _____
(Therapist)                          (date)

_____    _____
(Witness)                           (date)

This "contract" is helpful if responded to in a reasonably sincere fashion. It may serve to relax the client, who then has the burden of the suicidal decision temporarily taken off his or her shoulders. At the same time, because the agreement is not a permanent one, it allows the person to retain some level of suicidal ideation (which the client may feel is necessary). Finally, it usually offers the family and also the therapist a greater level of comfort with the overall therapeutic plan. Such an agreement, however, should not be used (or at least is not considered as having any controlling impact) with an individual who either does not understand its nature or who is known to be unreliable or quite impulsive.

Clinicians can be effectively involved in suicide prevention education by promoting and emphasizing those precautions that can be taken at the individual level by laypersons, such as

1. Attending seriously to people who voice a desire to kill themselves or "just go to sleep and forget it all."
2. Attending especially to depressed individuals who speak of losing hope.
3. Attending especially to persons with panic disorder or a history of panic attacks.
4. To the degree possible, keeping lethal means (guns, large prescriptions of sedatives) away from suicidal individuals.

5. Generating a personal concern toward a suicidal person; a suicide attempt is most often a cry for help. Suicidal individuals need a temporary "champion" who can point them toward new resources, suggest new options, and at least in a small way can diminish their sense of hopelessness.

6. Trying to get the person to perform some of the following behaviors: (a) engage in regular physical exercise, (b) start a diary, (c) follow a normal routine, (d) do something in which he or she has already demonstrated competence, (e) confide inner feelings to someone, or (f) cry it out. Trying to get the person to avoid self-medication and other people inclined toward depression.

7. Making every effort to guarantee that a suicidal person reaches appropriate professional help. Making an appointment is a good first step; getting the person to the appointment (and helping them maintain that contact) is the crucial step.

☐          ## SOCIETAL PREVENTION

Several things can be done on a societal level to lower the incidence of suicide (Phillips, 1986; Schneidman, 1985). Educating the public on the myths and facts of suicide is an important first step. Second, there is evidence that suicide prevention centers and telephone hotlines can slightly decrease the suicide rate. A third step in suicide prevention (and analogously, in lowering the incidence of aggressive acts) may involve some restriction on media publicity about suicides (and violent aggression). Phillips (1986) documents the correlation between a rise and fall in suicide rates and the amount of newspaper publicity given to suicides in that locality. Such self-imposed restriction is a thorny ethical issue for newspapers and television, especially because rates of all externally directed violence (murder, rape) may also be increased by publicity about similar incidents (Miller et al., 1991).

# CHAPTER 15

# Psychopharmacology

Psychotropic medications can be a useful component in the treatment of numerous mental disorders (Lickey and Gordon, 1991; Poling et al., 1991). The introduction of the antipsychotic and antidepressant drugs in the 1960s revolutionized mental health treatment. Their use has resulted in decreased hospital stays, an increased emphasis on outpatient treatment, and an overall increase in the level of functioning for individuals with such disorders.

The term "psychotropic" broadly refers to medications that have an effect on the central nervous system to produce changes in aberrant behavior. These types of medications are divided into several groups based on their behavioral effects. However, psychotropic medications can have other uses, some of which will be discussed in this chapter, and there are drugs currently not classified as psychotropic medications that can also have behavioral effects. For example, Reserpine, developed as an antihypertensive in the 1950s, was routinely found to cause depression. In fact, Reserpine-induced depression in laboratory animals has often used as a model in the early development and testing of antidepressants. Cycloserine, currently undergoing clinical trials for use in the treatment of certain anxiety disorders, has been used for years, in higher dose ranges, for the treatment of tuberculosis. Other drugs currently used in neurology can also be used to treat psychiatric disorders. Some of these crossover drugs will be discussed where appropriate.

As in many aspects of medicine, the early psychotropics were found by serendipity or were related to drugs that were being used for other purposes and refined for use as psychopharmacologic agents. Imipramine, for example, was originally being studied as an antihistamine. MAO inhibitors had originally been used as antituberculin drugs. From observations that patients on these or similar compounds improved their moods, was born the field of psychopharmacology.

Familiarity with psychotropic medications is important for all mental health professionals in order to provide clients with the widest and most appropriate treatment range. It is important for all therapists to provide education to their clients about mental illness and possible treatment options.

## Pharmacokinetics

The term "pharmacokinetics" refers to how the body handles a drug that has been administered. In other words, what happens to the drug once a person takes it? There are four major components to the concept of pharmacokinetics: (1) absorption—where is the drug taken into the body, and how rapidly it is taken in? (2) distribution—how does the drug get to its intended site of action, and exactly what bodily systems does the drug affect? (3) metabolism—where is the drug broken down in the body, and how rapidly does this take place? and (4) excretion—how are the breakdown products from metabolism eliminated from the body? Let's now look at each of these four areas in more detail in order to understand how the psychotropic medications work.

Obviously, getting the drug into the body is the most important first step; this represents *absorption*. Most drugs are given orally. When taken by this route, the drug is swallowed and absorbed into the bloodstream somewhere in the gastrointestinal (GI) tract. Usually this occurs in either the stomach or the upper portion of the small intestine. A number of factors influence this process. The chemical composition of the drug, for example, will determine how rapidly it dissolves and also how quickly it passes through the gastrointestinal mucosa. The acid-base composition of the drug, referred to as its pH, will also affect rate of absorption, as will the pH of the GI tract. Drugs that are *lipid soluble* tend to be absorbed more rapidly; lipid solubility simply refers to whether or not a given drug is chemically similar or dissimilar to most fluids and molecules in the body. The more similar it is, the greater its degree of lipid solubility and the faster its rate of absorption. Two other routes of absorption exist for psychotropic medications. One is the intravenous route, where the drug is injected directly into the blood system. This is the fastest route of absorption, as you might imagine. Some psychotropic medications (such as the depot neuroleptics, described later in the chapter) are administered intramuscularly. They are injected directly into muscle tissue, where they bind with certain molecules and are released into the blood slowly over a period of days or weeks. This method has the advantage of eliminating the need for daily medication ingestion or injection. To summarize, absorption refers to how quickly a drug gets into the body. It is fairly obvious that the faster the absorption, the earlier the onset of therapeutic action.

*Distribution* refers to what happens to a drug after it gets into the bloodstream. In general, one of three things can happen: (1) the drug is freely dissolved in the blood, (2) it is bound to plasma proteins that circulate throughout the bloodstream, or (3) the drug is carried within the blood cells. How quickly the drug dissolves in the blood, binds to proteins, or gets absorbed and then released from the blood cells determines, in part, how quickly the therapeutic action of the drug begins. The psychotropic medications exert a large part of their actions on the brain. In order to reach the brain, however, these drugs must cross the *blood–brain barrier*. Not all of the blood vessels in the brain can release substances directly into brain tissue. In order for psychotropic medications to be effective in the brain, they must be able to gain access to those blood vessels that directly communicate with brain tissue. This requires that the drug molecules be of a certain size (i.e., very small), have a high degree of lipid solubility, and have affinity for certain neuroreceptors (more on these in the next section). If the drug has all of these characteristics, then it can pass through the blood–brain barrier. Once in the brain, the drug exerts its effects by acting on certain neurotransmitters and neuroreceptors, as described in the next section.

Once in the body, specifically in the brain, the drug begins to undergo a series of chemical changes which ultimately result in its degradation or breakdown; this process is referred to as *metabolism*. If metabolism does not take place, the drug would remain in its original form and exert its action indefinitely. In other words, there would be no way to control the action of the drug. The blood circulates throughout the body constantly, meaning that the drugs carried in the blood do the same thing. As a result, no psychotropic drug remains in the brain forever. One organ that the blood continually passes through is the liver, and it is here that most drug metabolism takes place. While some drugs are also metabolized by other organs, the liver is of primary importance. Metabolism simply involves a series of chemical reactions, facilitated by enzymes in the body, that transform the drug into a number of related compounds. Some of these compounds retain the actions of the original drug and are called "active metabolites." Others lose the therapeutic action of the drug and become inactive. It is the rate of metabolism and the number of active metabolites for each drug that determines how long the therapeutic effect lasts.

The metabolic products from the drug are then eliminated, or *excreted*, from the body. For most drugs this occurs via the kidney, with the drug metabolites being eliminted in the urine. Other routes of excretion include tears, saliva, sweat, feces, and breast milk. It is because of this latter route of excretion that many drugs are required to contain warnings against their use by women who are nursing. Excretion, then, is the final step in removing a drug from the body.

## ■ Classification

The psychotropic medications are typically divided into five groups based on their predominant behavioral effect: (1) antipsychotic agents,

(2) antidepressants, (3) antimanic drugs, (4) antianxiety agents, and (5) sedative-hypnotics. Many of these drugs have secondary actions such as the control of violent and agitated behavior, and some are utilized as "truth serums." These will also be discussed later in the chapter.

Each group of drugs is useful in the treatment of specific mental disorders. For example, the antipsychotic drugs, often referred to as neuroleptics, have their greatest application in the treatment of schizophrenia and other disorders accompanied by psychotic symptoms (e.g., psychotic depressions). Mood-altering agents such as the antimanic and antidepressant medications are useful in the treatment of severe depressions and bipolar (manic-depressive) illness. The antianxiety agents produce a generalized calming effect and are useful in any condition in which anxiety is a prominent symptom (e.g., panic disorder, phobias, or generalized anxiety). The sedative-hypnotics tend to induce drowsiness and alter consciousness and are used in the treatment of sleep disturbances such as insomnia.

There is a large number of specific drugs within each of the groups listed. The proper selection of an appropriate class of drug and then within a classification—the selection of the specific drug for the actions desired as well as those to be avoided if possible—depends on the clinician's skills in a number of areas. Most importantly, it depends on the ability to understand the specific etiology of the behavior to be treated, the ability to accurately define behavior in terms of target symptoms, the need to understand how specific drugs can be used to affect specific symptoms, the ability to understand delay of onset and length of action, and an understanding of drug interactions as well as possible side effects. Each drug has both a trade name, assigned by the manufacturer, and a generic, or chemical, name. In the sections that follow, both names will be listed for each specific agent.

Because of their potential to alter behavior, and because some of these drugs are addicting, a number of the psychotropic agents are classified as controlled according to their potential for abuse; the greater the potential, the more limitations are placed on their use. Only the antianxiety agents and the sedative-hypnotics are presently classified as controlled. Table 15.1 lists examples of controlled substances and the DEA classification system.

The clinician must be ever-mindful that dependency and abuse are also a function of personality factors as well as the substance itself. This is especially true for the anxiolytic drugs. For example, individuals who use increasing dosages of anxiolytics as a way of "feeling better," "taking off the edge," or "getting through a tough day" or who have a history of drug-seeking behavior with abuse or dependency in other areas are likely to abuse anxiolytics. Such individuals need to be carefully monitored by their prescribing physicians, therapists, and dispensing pharmacies.

I am reminded of a situation that occurred while leading a therapy

**TABLE 15.1**     Controlled Substances

| DEA CLASS | CHARACTERISTICS | EXAMPLES |
|---|---|---|
| I | High abuse potential; no accepted medical use | LSD, heroin, marijuana |
| II | High abuse potential with with severe physical and psychological dependence | Amphetamines, opium, morphine, codeine, barbiturates, cocaine |
| III | High abuse potential with low to moderate physical dependence and high psychological dependence | Compounds containing codeine, morphine, (i.e., narcotic analgesics) |
| IV | Low abuse potential with limited physical and psychological dependence | Benzodiazepines, certain barbiturates, other sedative-hypnotics |
| V | Lowest abuse potential | Narcotic preparations containing nonnarcotic active ingredients (e.g., cough medicines with codeine) |

group for substance abusers at the State Prison of Southern Michigan. One inmate had recently been returned to prison as a parole violator after it had been discovered that he had visited *every* emergency room in southern Michigan presenting with symptoms of panic attacks and a host of other disorders. A physician, who had just transferred hospitals, recognized the patient as having been at his prior hospital the previous month, presenting with symptoms of chronic low-back pain. A quick check of other emergency rooms turned up the fact that he had visited thirteen others within a two-month period!

A related concept is that of mind-altering versus mood-altering drugs. A mind-altering drug is a substance that will have a similar effect given to a general population of individuals. Stimulants, for instance, if given to one hundred people at large, will have a stimulating effect to virtually all. Antidepressants (which are mood-altering), as an example, when given to one hundred people selected at random, are likely to have a positive effect only on those individuals suffering from an affective disorder. Even then, it may take weeks, and the effect of the drug is not superimposed over the existing mood; rather, it re-establishes a normal range of appropriate mood. Mind-altering drugs, on the other hand, limit the range of mood and superimpose the effect in almost anyone taking that type of substance.

■          ## Antipsychotic Drugs

The antipsychotic medications are a large class of drugs that are useful in the treatment of psychotic disorders, such as schizophrenia. The characteristics of psychotic disorders are discussed in Chapters 3 and 4. A number of mental disorders, in addition to schizophrenia, may be accompanied by psychotic features. These include severe mood disorders such as psychotic depressions and mania. Transient psychoses may also be seen in certain of the personality disorders.

Antipsychotic medications are usually effective in correcting the thought disturbances, delusional thinking, and hallucinations seen in psychotic disorders. They are not directly effective with the apathy, social withdrawal, and blunted affects. A widely held theory asserts that many psychoses are caused by an overabundance of the neurotransmitter dopamine in the brain (Lickey and Gordon, 1991). Dopamine is believed to play an important regulatory role in thought and perception and is also important in coordinating fine motor movements. When imbalances in dopamine occur in the brain, the characteristic symptoms of psychosis (thought disorder, delusions, and hallucinations) are likely to occur. The antipsychotic agents appear to act by blocking dopamine receptors in the brain, thereby decreasing the functional availability of the neurotransmitter; this corrects the imbalance and thus restores thought and perception to their normal states.

In addition to their action on psychotic symptoms, most of the antipsychotic medications also cause some degree of sedation. This effect is useful in decreasing agitation that often accompanies a psychosis. As will be discussed later in the chapter, the sedating properties of these drugs also make them useful in the treatment of violent behavior. The phenothiazines (e.g., chlorpromazine and thioridazine), the largest group of antipsychotic drugs, tend to produce the most sedation.

In addition to their therapeutic properties, all medications have certain side effects and adverse reactions. As a group, the antipsychotics are noteworthy because of the large number of side effects that may occur. These are very potent drugs, and as such they affect a variety of systems in the body. One of the most common side effects is muscular stiffness and rigidity, referred to as dystonia. These drugs may also cause a vague feeling of restlessness and the inability to sit still, referred to as akathesia. The shuffling gait perceived by many as a hallmark behavior of the chronically ill patient who has been overmedicated is the result of akathesia. Some patients on high doses of these drugs for extended periods of time will develop involuntary movements of the face, mouth, and tongue; this syndrome is known as tardive dyskinesia. All of the neuromuscular side effects are described under the general heading of "extrapyramidal symptoms." This term derives from the areas of the brain and central nervous system that control movement, the extrapyramidal tracts. These symptoms are also often referred to as

Parkinsonian side effects because they clinically resemble the symptoms of Parkinson's disease.

The antipsychotic drugs exert an influence on other neurotransmitters in addition to dopamine. One of these is acetylcholine, a muscarinic transmitter that is involved in the regulation of many bodily functions. The antipsychotics block the action of acetylcholine, with the result that this group of side effects is often referred to as anticholinergic effects. Specific symptoms include dry mouth, intolerance to heat, constipation, and blurred vision. In extreme cases an anticholinergic delirium may occur, characterized by confusion, disorientation, and agitation. These drugs also may temporarily cause a drop in blood pressure, especially when arising from a sitting or supine position. This phenomenon, called postural hypotension, may lead to dizziness. These symptoms can serve to complicate the already complex clinical picture and often require the administration of medication to offset the effects.

Other side effects noted with the antipsychotic medications include photosensitivity to sunlight, liver damage, cardiotoxicity, a depression of blood cell production leading to anemia (agranulocytosis), and seizures. A very serious and potentially life-threatening side effect is the neuroleptic malignant syndrome, characterized by high fever, convulsions, muscular rigidity, and rapid progression to coma and death. With such side effects as these, it is not surprising that the antipsychotics have a low potential for abuse, dependence, or addiction.

**TABLE 15.2**     Antipsychotic Drugs

| NAME (GENERIC/TRADE) | DOSE RANGE * |
|---|---|
| **Phenothiazines** | |
| Chlorpromazine (Thorazine) | 50–1500 mg/day |
| Thioridazine (Mellaril) | 50–800 mg/day |
| Fluphenazine (Prolixin) | 5–40 mg/day |
| Fluphenazine decanoate (Prolixin D) | 25–100 mg IM Q1–4 weeks |
| Perphenazine (Trilafon) | 4–64 mg/day |
| Trifluoperazine (Stelazine) | 5–40 mg/day |
| **Butyrophenones** | |
| Haloperidol (Haldol) | 5–100 mg/day |
| Haloperidol decanoate (Haldol D) | 50–200 mg IM Q2–4 weeks |
| **Thioxanthenes** | |
| Thiothixine (Navane) | 5–60 mg/day |
| **Other Antipsychotic Drugs** | |
| Loxapine (Loxitane) | 20–250 mg/day |
| Molindone (Moban) | 20–225 mg/day |
| Clozapine (Clozaril) | 300–500 mg/day |

*Average therapeutic dose range.
IM = intramuscular administration.

A large number of specific drugs are available in this group and are listed in Table 15.2. Despite their numbers, virtually all of these agents are thought to primarily act by blocking dopamine receptors in the brain, and many of the specific agents are chemically related to each other. The main features that differentiate the individual medications are dose range, degree of sedation, duration of action, and intensity of side effects. All of these drugs are metabolized, or broken down, by the liver, so caution is required in persons with preexisting liver disease.

Three classes of antipsychotic drugs exist: (1) the phenothiazines, (2) the thioxanthenes, e.g., thiothixine (Navane), and (3) the butyrophenones, e.g., haloperidol (Haldol). Several other antipsychotics are also in clinical use that do not belong to any of these groups. The phenothiazines may be further subdivided into drugs with low potency that are used at relatively high doses (e.g., Thorazine and Mellaril) and those with high potency that are used at lower doses (e.g., Stelazine and Prolixin). As a general rule, the low potency–high dose drugs cause more sedation, whereas the high potency–low dose preparations have less sedation but more tendency to cause extrapyramidal reactions.

The two most commonly used antipsychotics are chlorpromazine (Thorazine) and haloperidol (Haldol). There is some evidence that haloperidol is typically prescribed at higher dosages than is necessary to gain the desired effect (Rifkin et al., 1991). Long-acting (decanoate) preparations are available for haloperidol (Haldol D) and fluphenazine (Prolixin D). Both of these are given intramuscularly by injection and have a duration of action of from two to four weeks. The duration of action for orally administered antipsychotics ranges from four to twelve hours, depending in part on how quickly the drug is metabolized.

The first therapeutic effect that occurs thirty to sixty minutes after ingestion is a generalizing calming effect, often accompanied by some degree of sedation. A person on antipsychotics is also likely to appear rather stiff and clumsy, due to the extrapyramidal effects mentioned previously. Although the person is fully alert while on these drugs, he or she may often appear emotionless and possess a rather blank stare, due also to the extrapyramidal effects. The full antipsychotic action on hallucinations and delusions may take from several days to several weeks to appear, depending on the severity and intensity of the symptoms. Unless the situation is acute, it is prudent to give low dosages in increasing frequency until one has titrated the dose of medication against behavior and side effects. Some psychotic patients do not respond significantly to these medications, for reasons that are not completely clear.

One of the newer antipsychotics, clozapine (Clozaril), seems to be effective with treatment-resistant patients (Green and Salzman, 1990) and also has much less potential for extrapyramidal side effects and tardive dyskinesia. Clozapine blocks a number of receptors in the brain: dopamine, serotonin, adrenergic, and muscarinic. Its specific mechanism of therapeutic action, however, is not known. Side effects include a potentially fatal agranulocytosis in 1 to 2 percent of patients receiving the drug (hence, consistent blood monitoring is necessary), as well as seizures, sedation, tachycardia, hypotension, hyperthermia, nausea, excessive salivation, and drooling. The dose range for clozapine is 300–500 mg/day (not to exceed 900 mg/day), but the risk of seizures increases dramatically at doses greater than 500–600 mg/day .

## ■ Antidepressants

Depression, described in Chapter 4, is one of the most frequently encountered psychiatric symptoms. Most depressions occur in response to some trauma or loss that the individual can identify. In many cases this type of depression is self-limiting and does not require treatment. In those cases that persist, psychological treatments are usually effective in alleviating the depression. Some people, however, experience severe depressions that are seemingly unrelated to any external event and apparently reflect abnormalities in the neurotransmitters that regulate mood.

Two different neurotransmitters that are known to consistently exert a major influence on mood are norepinephrine and serotonin (Poling et al., 1991). When levels of either of these neurotransmitters fall in the brain, a clinical depression may result. The traditional antidepressant medications consist of two broad groups of drugs: the tricyclic antidepressants (named for their three-ring chemical structure) and the monoamine oxidase inhibitors (MAOIs). The main differences between these two groups are how the drugs act on the neurotransmitters and their side-effect profiles. Although their mechanisms of action appear complicated, both groups ultimately and primarily act by facilitating the release of norepinephrine and serotin from neuronal cells, thus correcting the depression. These drugs also act by blocking re-uptake of the neurotransmitter, thus increasing their overall concentration in the brain. The newer antidepressants, such as fluoxetine (Prozac) and sertraline (Zoloft), are neither tricyclics nor MAOIs. Prozac acts on the neurotransmitter serotonin by an as yet unclear mechanism. Trazodone (Desyrel) acts specifically to block serotonin re-uptake. It is not anticholinergic, but can be quite sedating, and if taken on an empty stomach, can generate acute dizziness and fainting.

Another new antidepressant, a unicyclic, bupropion (Wellbutrin), has an unknown mechanism of action, but is thought to act by blocking norepinephrine re-uptake. It is not anticholinergic, but it can be too "activating" for some patients. Buproprion's release for use as an antidepressant was delayed when it was discovered, late in clinical trials, to have a higher seizure potential than the tricyclics to which it was being compared. Closer analysis of the data revealed that its increased seizuregenic potential was limited primarily to its use with a particular subgroup being studied—bulimic women. Because this increased the overall side-effect profile of the drug, Wellbutrin has only been approved for use in doses of approximately one-half that found to be effective for use in depression. Amoxapine (Asendin), with a four-ringed structure, can be helpful because of its rapid onset of effect, sometimes within four to seven days.

Most of the antidepressants require a period of from ten days to two weeks before they begin to exert their therapeutic action. This poses a problem when a client presents with a high risk of suicide. Control and monitoring must be exerted until the medications or other treatments apparently take effect. During this lag period, blood levels of the drug are rising into a therapeutic range. These levels can be measured and the dose adjusted accordingly to obtain an optimal clinical response. Monitoring of blood levels also decreases the likelihood of toxic reactions. As with the antipsychotics, these medications are metabolized by the liver.

Table 15.3 lists the antidepressant medications. The most commonly used tricyclics are amitriptyline (Elavil), imipramine (Tofranil), and desipramine (Norpramin). Predictors of postive response to tricyclics include high socioeconomic class, good treatment motivation, insidious onset, anorexia, weight loss, middle and late insomnia, and psychomotor

**TABLE 15.3**    Antidepressant Drugs

| NAME (GENERIC/TRADE) | DOSE RANGE* |
| --- | --- |
| **Tricyclic and Tetracyclic Antidepressants** | |
| Amitriptyline (Elavil) | 75–300  mg/day |
| Imipramine (Tofranil) | 75–300  mg/day |
| Desipramine (Norpramin) | 75–300  mg/day |
| Nortriptyline (Pamelor) | 30–100  mg/day |
| Protriptyline (Vivactil) | 15–40  mg/day |
| Doxepine (Sinequan) | 50–300  mg/day |
| Maprotiline (Ludiomil) | 75–150  mg/day |
| Amoxapine (Asendin) | 50–300  mg/day |
| Clomipramine (Anafranil)† | 150–250  mg/day |
| **MAOIs** | |
| Tranylcypromine (Parnate) | 20–60  mg/day |
| Phenelzine (Nardil) | 60–90  mg/day |
| **Other Antidepressants** | |
| Fluoxetine (Prozac) | 20–60  mg/day |
| Bupropion (Wellbutrin) | 200–450  mg/day |
| Trazodone (Desyrel) | 100–400  mg/day |
| Sertraline (Zoloft) | 50–200 mg/day |

*Average therapeutic dose range.
†Used also for treatment of the obsessive-compulsive disorder.

disturbance. Predictors of poor response to tricyclics include hypochondriasis, hysterical traits, multiple prior episodes, and delusions. The MAOIs, on the other hand, are used less often because of their side effects.

The initial effect experienced after taking an antidepressant is sedation. The severity of this effect varies with the drug; amitriptyline, for example, is very sedating whereas desipramine has relatively little sedation. Thus, a depressed patient with insomnia might benefit from amitriptyline. The drug would not be recommended, however, for a patient with prostate or bladder troubles because it can impede urination.

Antidepressants also can generate feelings of dizziness or lightheadedness. This occurs because norepinephrine exerts an effect not only on mood but on other organ systems, such as the cardiovascular system. Most clients will also experience a calming effect, related to either the sedative effect of the drugs or to the direct action on serotonin. Depending on the degree of sedation and calming, the person may appear either drowsy or detached and disinterested; it is unlikely, however, that the person would appear intoxicated. Once the antidepressant action of the drug takes effect, the person will probably not notice any major effect from the medication; their mood will simply appear to be normal. In some persons, however, the mood will become somewhat agitated resulting from too much stimulation of the norepinephrine system. In fact, persons with a bipolar disorder who take antidepressants may cycle into a manic episode.

The antidepressants have a number of side effects, many of which are potentially dangerous. Nearly all of the drugs in this class cause some degree of drowsiness and sedation. Like the antipsychotics, many also cause anticholinergic side effects. Other side effects include feelings of restlessness and agitation, sleep disturbances, nightmares, seizures, and exacerbation of psychosis in susceptible persons. The MAOIs may cause an interaction with certain foods and alcohol to produce a sudden rise in blood pressure (hypertensive crisis). Because of this effect, certain dietary restrictions (especially for foods containing tyramine such as beer, red wine, certain cheeses, liver, and pickled or smoked meats and fish) apply for MAOI use.

Several antidepressants, including maprotiline (Ludiomil) and bupropion (Wellbutrin), are associated with an increased risk of seizures, particularly when taken in high doses. The tricyclic antidepressants may cause a number of cardiac effects. At therapeutic doses these effects include tachycardia (rapid heart rate) and a decreased conduction time which causes electrocardiogram (ECG) changes. At very high doses, as seen in overdoses, these drugs cause cardiac arrhythmias, which may be potentially fatal, and slow the heart rate. This effect presents a significant risk for persons with preexisting heart disease or for those who overdose on these medications as part of a suicide attempt. Thus the tricyclics and tetracyclics should be prescribed in limited amounts to minimize the risk of overdose. Blood levels of the drugs should also be monitored to prevent toxicity. There is low potential for abuse or dependence in this group of drugs.

## ■ The Prozac Controversy

The most controversial newer-generation antidepressant is certainly fluoxetine (Prozac). This versatile compound was initially accepted with great hopes for the treatment of depressed patients, but quickly became highly controversial. Despite its demonstrated lack of toxic physiologic side effects, the drug was accused of creating some of the very conditions which it was supposed to treat. Reports surfaced of individuals on Prozac increasing their suicidal or homicidal ideations, sometimes going so far as to act on those impulses. As of the date of the writing of this chapter, many of these controversies continue despite the fact that there are only a few hundred reported cases of these kinds of behaviors in a population of almost five million people worldwide who have taken the drug.

So why the controversy? First, and foremost, were the actions of a very small group in the United States who, recognizing this compound as a major advance in psychopharmacology, targeted the drug for harassment. In addition, there are real problems and real issues that need to be addressed regarding this medication and others like it that will be coming to the marketplace in the near future. Prior to the release of fluoxetine, it was common practice to monitor antidepressants very carefully because of their potential for serious side effects. With the discovery and release of safer, less-toxic antidepressants, individuals in the medical profession began prescribing these newer drugs with the sense that they do not need the same close scrutiny which these types of medications were once given. Such individuals fail to recognize that it is not just the medication which needs monitoring, but the patient's overall progress.

By building a relationship with and educating a patient, while using the concept of target symptoms, clinician and patient can very rapidly identify the de novo appearance of new side effects from the medication or the heightening of symptoms which the drug was targeted to treat. By intervening early and directly with the patient when these types of impulses increase, one dramatically lessens the potential for greater consequences.

In point of fact, a similar controversy raged about desipramine in the 1960s when this stimulating antidepressant was released. One must be mindful that activation of a depressed suicidal patient may result in that individual now having the energy to act on the suicidal impulses before the underlying depression and suicidal ideation have been adequately treated by the medication and other interventions. Patients with a history of strong suicidal ideations, with or without impulsive behaviors, are probably best monitored in an inpatient setting until the dose of medication is stabilized and those impulses have subsided.

## ■ Antimanic Drugs

Manic episodes often cycle with recurrent depressions, forming what is referred to as a bipolar disorder (previously called manic-depressive illness). Lithium, a psychotropic medication that functions as a mood-stabilizing agent (Lickey and Gordon, 1991), remains the first line of treatment for the manic phase of a bipolar disorder. Certain schizophrenic individuals may also respond favorably to lithium used in combination with an antipsychotic medication.

The exact mechanism of action for lithium is not clear. It is generally thought that manic episodes result from an excess of the neurotransmit ter norepinephrine, just the opposite situation from depressive episodes. Lithium is believed to act by stabilizing the membranes of neuronal cells in the central nervous system, resulting in a decrease in the amount of norepinephrine released from the cells. There is also a probable increase in the re-uptake of norepinephrine by the cells, decreasing the overall concentration of the neurotransmitter. Lithium is metabolized and excreted by the kidney.

Because it is a salt that occurs naturally in the body, unlike many of the other psychotropic medications, lithium has a therapeutic dose range that can be measured in the blood. Dosage of the medication, beginning with divided doses of 300 mg two to three times per day, is increased until the blood levels reach a range of 0.5 to 1.5 mEq per liter. Within seven to ten days on a therapeutic dose, the manic patient should be observed to become calmer, less agitated, have a general slowing of speech and thought processes, and return to a normal, or euthymic, mood.

The monitoring of lithium blood levels is necessary to prevent toxicity, which is caused by doses of lithium that are too high. Lithium toxicity is characterized by nausea and vomiting, muscle cramps, diarrhea, excessive thirst, and incresed urination at blood levels between 1.5 and 2.0 mEq per liter. At levels above 2.0 mEq per liter, the individual experiences confusion, lethargy, tremor of the extremities, muscle spasms, ataxia (unsteady gait), slurred speech, convulsions, and ultimately coma. When maintained at therapeutic blood levels, however, lithium is notably free of day-to-day side effects. It is unlikely to cause sedation and has no potential for abuse or dependence. The most common side effects on therapeutic doses are fine tremor of the hand and skin rash. The long-term use of lithium virtually guarantees the eventual production of hyperthyroidism. Likewise, over time, there is a potentially reversible alteration of the basement membrane in the kidney, which requires careful scrutiny.

Lithium, when combined with certain other drugs, can have problematic effects. Many diuretics (drugs that remove water from the body) increase the level of lithium and can cause toxicity. Other diuretics, like coffee and tea, can lower the level of lithium. Problems may occur when lithium is combined with hydroxyzine (Atarax, Vistaril), antipsychotic drugs, or methyldopa (Aldomet and others). Patients who are taking lithium should tell all the doctors they see about all other medications they are taking.

The evolution of lithium as an effective treatment is a good example of the driving force of the profit motive in pharmacological research. Lithium is a chemical element that was first isolated in 1817 by John Arfwedson, a young Swedish chemistry student. He named it lithium because he found it in stone (*lithos* in greek). John Cade, an Australian psychiatrist, discovered the positive effect of lithium on mania by chance in the 1940s, while studying whether an excess of uric acid might be the cause of manic-depressive episodes. Cade injected humans with urea from the urine of guinea pigs. Expecting to learn that uric acid (a compound containing urea) increased the toxicity of urea, he added the most soluble salt of uric acid, lithium urate, and was surprised to find, instead, that the urea was less toxic as a result. Further experiments isolating lithium eventually indicated its curative properties.

However, it was a long time between initial discovery and the recent widespread marketing and use of lithium. In general, there had been surprisingly little research on lithium, while more exotic, less widely available compounds have received much attention. Two explanations for this seem plausible. First, there was warranted concern about the significant side effects of lithium. Second, since lithium is a naturally occurring element, it cannot be patented. Drug companies are much more interested in researching new synthetic compounds that they can patent, so that they can control the market and gain substantial profits.

Until ten to fifteen years ago, mania was often misdiagnosed and, to some degree, is still misdiagnosed as schizophrenia since in its most virulent form it can be accompanied by delusions, hallucinations, and other psychotic behaviors. Commonly, in the acute manic state, lithium is given with a neuroleptic until the manic storm has passed. If the psychotic component to the mania begins to clear, the neuroleptic can be withdrawn, and the patient maintained only on lithium. Because many people with mania and hypomania miss the energized nature of the "high," compliance with the use of lithium tends to be low. Also because it is a salt and is turned over fairly rapidly in the body, lithium has to be administered two to three times a day to maintain blood levels. There are some patients who are so precariously balanced with regard to their blood levels, that missing one or two doses can be enough to initiate hypomanic behavior and thinking.

Until the 1970s there were no alternatives to the use of lithium and/or neuroleptics for the treatment of mania. In the 1970s, Robert Post first described the possible application of carbamazepine (Tegretol), an anti-convulsant previously used to treat temporal lope epilepsy, for the treatment of mania.

While Tegretol does not produce the hypothyroidism common to lithium, it has significant side effects of its own; these include blood dyscrasias such as agranulocytosis and leukopenia and it can also disturb iron metabolism. Therefore, like lithium, Tegretol has a therapeutic dose level that needs to be carefully monitored.

Following the discovery of Tegretol's value in the treatment of mania, other anticonvulsants used to treat temporal lobe epilepsy have been tried and found to be useful as well. These include valporic acid (Depakote) and clonazepam (Klonopin). Depakote has been effective with some cases of refractory mania, while Klonopin has been effective with those bipolar patterns that have been resistant to other forms of treatment.

Klonopin resembles a benzodiazepine in structure and, like the benzodiazepines, it is quite sedating with a potential for abuse. It has little or no antipsychotic properties and, also like benzodiazepines, can mix poorly with alcohol by suppressing CNS and respiratory functions. Since alcohol is commonly abused by bipolar patients in the manic phase of the illness, caution needs to be given to the use of this medication.

Unfortunately, as noted, lithium is not always effective with mania. Some nonresponders to lithium have been found to respond to certain anticonvulsant drugs. Carbamazepine (Tegretol) is the anticonvulsant that has been most widely used. Bipolars who cycle rapidly—that is, they change from mania to depression and back again over the course of hours or days, rather than months—seem to respond particularly well to car-bamazepine. Valproic acid (Depakene) has been effective with some cases of refractory mania. Clonazepam (Klonopin) has also been effective with treatment-resistant bipolar patterns.

## ■ Antianxiety Drugs

Anxiety is one of the most frequent complaints among persons requir-ing mental health consultation. As a rule, anxiety is only considered to be pathological when it becomes excessive and begins to interfere with functioning (see Chapter 5). A complicating factor, however, is the fact that the ability to tolerate and deal with anxiety varies greatly from one person to another. As a result, levels of anxiety that may be handled effectively by one person may totally overwhelm another.

The antianxiety medications exert a calming and sedating effect to counteract the effects of anxiety. Originally, this class of drugs consisted primarily of the barbiturates, which had high potential for dependence and addiction as well as a variety of other side effects. Since the mid-1960s, however, a large number of drugs belonging to the benzodiazepine family have been introduced. For the treatment of anxiety, these drugs are more effective, safer, have less addiction potential, and generally produce less sedation than the barbiturates. Consequently, benzodiazepines have become some of the most frequently prescribed medications in the United States. In addition to their antianxiety effects, they are also useful as sedative-hypnotics. The introduction of chlordiazepoxide (Librium) and diazepam (Valium) heralded the benzodiazepine age. Both of these agents still have considerable clinical utility, but are also often drugs of abuse.

To understand the addictive nature or potential of these drugs, one must understand two important issues: the nature of anxiety and certain behavioral consequences of using the relatively short-acting benzodiazepines. Because anxious and fearful patients seek relief from very stressful feelings, any drug that brings about that relief has to be able to do so in a smooth, continuous fashion. Benzodiazepines, because of their varying half-lives, end up contributing to the problems they were prescribed to solve.

The term "half life" refers to the length of time it takes for one-half of a drug dose to be metabolized. Thus, half-life is a measure of how long a drug remains active in the body. the longer the half-life, the longer the overall duration of the drug's effect. The more recent benzodiazepines, such as alprazolam (Xanax), differ from those introduced earlier primarily in the length of their half-lives. Xanax has rapidly grown to be the most widely prescribed benzodiazepine and, consequently, the most widely abused. A sister compound, triazolam (Halcion), has recently been banned in Great Britain because of its reported production of amnestic states. There have been several reports of individuals committing serious crimes while in that state.

As a result of having such short half-lives, these shorter-acting benzodiazepines can create what is referred to as "breakthrough anxiety states," or mini-withdrawal states, as their serum level in the body falls. For this reason, a behavioral paradigm can be created whereby individuals who are feeling anxious develop drug-seeking behaviors in an attempt to ameliorate these feelings. This drug-seeking behavior reinforces the further use of the drug and begins the process of abuse by putting the patient in a constant state of anticipatory anxiety and, therefore, anticipating the next dose of relief (the drug). Longer-acting benzodiazepines, or timed-release medications of this class, should, theoretically, have less abuse potential, but may have no less potential for addiction since true physiological states of withdrawal are created when these drugs are used at therapeutic doses for extended periods of time. At the time of this writing, a sustained-release forms of Xanax is being planned for marketing as a once-daily treatment regimen for use with panic disorders. All of the benzodiazepines are metabolized by the liver. The currently used antianxiety agents are listed in Table 15.4.

**TABLE 15.4**      Antianxiety Drugs

| NAME (GENERIC/TRADE) | DOSE RANGE* |
|---|---|
| Benzodiazepines | |
| Diazepam (Valium) | 2–40 mg/day |
| Chlordiazepoxide (Librium) | 15–100 mg/day |
| Chlorazepate (Tranxene) | 15–60 mg/day |
| Prazepam (Centrax) | 20–60 mg/day |
| Halazepam (Paxipam) | 60–120 mg/day |
| Lorazepam (Activan) | 2–6 mg/day |
| Alprazolam (Xanax) | 0.5–6.0 mg/day |
| Oxazepam (Serax) | 30–120 mg/day |
| Non-benzodiazepine | |
| Buspirone (Buspar) | 5–20 mg/day |

*Average therapeutic dose range.

The benzodiazepines exert their antianxiety activity by facilitating the action of gamma-aminobutyric acid (GABA) in the brain, a neurotransmitter apparently responsible for modulating anxiety. The benzodiazepines bind to receptors in the brain and stimulate the release of GABA, which decreases anxiety. GABA, in turn, inhibits the firing of certain excitatory neurons that are responsible for many of the physiologic manifestations of anxiety.

In addition to their clinical action on anxiety and their sedative effects, the benzodiazepines also exert another effect: All members of this group are cross-tolerant with alcohol and other drugs such as the barbiturates. In other words, they may potentiate the effects of alcohol or other sedative drugs, making the concurrent use of antianxiety drugs and alcohol or other sedatives contraindicated. The clinical benefit derived from this finding, however, is that the benzodiazepines can be used to detoxify and withdraw individuals who are addicted to either alcohol or the barbiturates. Chlordiazepoxide (Librium), for example, is often used to withdraw persons from alcohol and to treat alcohol withdrawal delirium (delirium tremens, or the "DTs"). Of course, one has to be careful with this population that a secondary addiction to the benzodiazepines does not occur.

Because of the cross-tolerance with alcohol, a person who drinks while taking benzodiazepines will appear more intoxicated than a person using either drug alone. In fact, the sedating and tranquilizing effect of this class of drugs causes many persons taking them to appear drunk, even in the absence of alcohol consumption. Accompanying features sometimes seen with the benzodiazepines include slurred speech, ataxia (unsteady gait), impaired coordination, slowed reflexes, and impaired judgment. As a result of these effects, persons taking benzodiazepines should exercise considerable caution when driving or operating machinery. These drugs have a relatively rapid onset of action, usually within thirty minutes. Their duration of action ranges from four to six hours for the short-acting preparations (e.g., lorazepam) to more than twenty hours for the longer-acting drugs (e.g., diazepam).

A new-generation antianxiety drug of the non-benzodiazepine class, considered to be a partial serotonin agonist, was released in 1985. This drug, buspirone (Buspar), has generated a good deal of controversy regarding its usefulness in the treatment of anxiety. Because of its extended onset of action, requiring up to two to three weeks to become effective, anxious patients previously disposed to the faster-acting benzodiazepines may be less tolerant of waiting for the drug to take effect. As a result, patients often discontinue use of this drug or fail to comply with its thrice-daily dosing requirement. Although its antianxiety effects are not as potent as the benzodiazepines, it has the advantage of having a very low potential for addiction or abuse.

There is much research and investigation being put into testing non-benzodiazepine types of anxiolytics. A beta carboline (Abecarnil) is currently being studied in patients with anxiety disorders. This novel compound appears to have similar activity to the benzodiazepines when studied in animal models. These animal models have shown that the drug appears to have much less potential for addiction and abuse than the benzodiazepines.

The primary side effect of the benzodiazepines is excessive sedation, which is usually dose related. In other words, the higher the dose of the drug, the greater the degree of sedation produced. By themselves, however, the benzodiazepines are remarkably safe drugs. While overdoses of either the antipsychotics or the antidepressants are potentially life-threatening, this is not usually the case with the benzodiazepines. They may, however, interact with other drugs, such as the barbiturates, to depress respiration when taken at high doses. Tolerance, the need for progressively higher doses to achieve the same therapeutic effect, and addiction are potential risks. Because of this, these drugs are generally prescribed in the lowest effective doses for only brief periods of time. In general, tolerance and addiction are more likely at high doses taken over extended periods of time. Abrupt cessation of these drugs in an addicted person may cause seizures; thus, it is generally best to gradually reduce the doses over a period of several weeks before totally discontinuing these medications.

While the benzodiazepines and related compounds are used primarily in the treatment of anxiety disorders, other treatments such as biofeedback, relaxation training, and other forms of psychotherapy are also effective. Since these latter treatments are less intrusive and do not pose the problem of side effects, yet are still effective, they should be employed first.

A number of other drugs have been used to treat anxiety, although none are as effective as the ones previously described. Antihistamines, such as diphenhydramine (Benadryl) and hydroxyzine (Vistaril), have been used. Their antianxiety effect is largely a function of their sedating properties, and they are not thought to exert any direct effect on GABA. These drugs are also sometimes used to treat the extrapyramidal side effects associated with antipsychotic drug therapy. Propranolol (Inderal) acts to block receptors for beta-adrenergic neurotransmitters, a large group of transmitters that exert a number of effects throughout the body. Inderal has been reported to be effective in the treatment of such anxiety disorders as panic disorder.

Finally, clomipramine (Anafranil), a tricyclic antidepressant, has recently been introduced specifically for the treatment of obsessive-compulsive disorder. None of the other tricyclics have been found to be very effective in the treatment of this condition.

## Sedative-Hypnotic Medications

Sleep disturbances are common complaints and, in most cases, are transient and thus do not warrant treatment. These difficulties may also be related to some other disease process, such as a medical condition or depression. Many individuals, however, have chronic problems with sleep. This has led to the development of a group of medications, the sedative-hypnotic drugs, in which the primary action is the induction of sleep. Most of these agents act on serotonin and GABA in the brain, both of which exert a natural calming and sedating effect. Unlike other drugs whose sedating properties result from side effects (e.g., the antidepressants and antipsychotics), the sedative-hypnotics act primarily to induce sleep.

All of the commonly used, commercially available sedative-hypnotic agents are actually antianxiety drugs whose sedating properties are stronger than their antianxiety properties. Thus, any of the antianxiety agents can theoretically be used to promote sleep. Those drugs marketed solely as sedative-hypnotics are ones whose antianxiety effects are relatively weak. As a result, most of the sedative-hypnotics currently available are either benzodiazepines or barbiturates. As with the other members of these groups, there is a definite potential for abuse and dependence. These drugs also tend to lose their effectiveness when taken for extended periods of time, a process referred to as tolerance, or habituation. The result is that higher doses are required over time to exert the same therapeutic effect, a consequence that facilitates addiction and dependence. Table 15.5 lists the sedative-hypnotic drugs currently in clinical use.

The side effects for these drugs are similar to those for the benzodiazepines and barbiturates. The most common side effect is excessive

**TABLE 15.5**    Sedative-Hypnotic Drugs

| NAME (GENERIC/TRADE) | DOSE RANGE* |
|---|---|
| **Benzodiazepines** | |
| Flurazepam (Dalmane) | 15–30 mg/day |
| Temazepam (Restoril) | 15–30 mg/day |
| Triazolam (Halcion) | 0.25–0.5 mg/day |
| Estazolam (ProSom) | 1.0–2.0 mg/day |
| **Barbiturates** | |
| Secobarbital (Seconal) | 100–200 mg/day |
| **Other Sedative-Hypnotics** | |
| Chloral hydrate (Noctec) | 500–1000 mg/day |

*Average therapeutic dose range.

drowsiness on awakening. Persons taking these drugs will often complain of difficulty waking up and a "hangover" in the morning after drug use. In very high doses, respiratory depression may occur, particularly with the barbiturates. Tolerance and addiction, however, are the most serious long-term side effects for these drugs.

Specific drugs in this class have been perceived as especially problematic. In 1991, the British government banned triazolam (Halcion), at that time the world's most widely prescribed sleeping pill. It was alleged to be too highly correlated with amnestic states and depression.

There are several other drugs which have (1) a secondary sedative effect, (2) low addiction and abuse potential, and (3) a low ratio of side effects. One good example is the antihistamines, such as the over-the-counter medication Benadryl (diphenhydramine). Another is the group of drugs sometimes referred to as the ataraxics, such as Vistaril (hydroxyzine pamoate) and Atarax (hydroxyzine hydrochloride), which are primarily intended to reduce anxiety, especially where accompanied by physical conditions, e.g., dermatological and/or gastrointestinal distress.

It is good policy to first try to cure a sleep problem with something like Benadryl. Then, if that's unsuccessful, move to an ataraxic, especially if agitation from the stress of living is a factor. Then if these are unsuccessful, and manipulation or an addictive personality component are ruled out, one can move to the traditional sedatives.

## ■ Anti-Parkinsonian Medications

Earlier it was mentioned that the antipsychotic medications cause a variety of extrapyramidal side effects characterized by muscular stiffness and rigidity, feelings of restlessness (akathesia), involuntary movements (dystonias), and a general slowing of movements (Parkinsonian effects). These occur most frequently in young, adult males and in persons recently started on antipsychotic medications. These effects are naturally quite bothersome to clients and are frequently responsible for poor medication compliance. Since the apparent mechanism of action is the blocking of dopamine, the same action that leads to a diminishing of psychotic symptoms also leads to neuromuscular disturbances.

Fortunately, several medications exist that have the ability to lessen the degree of these extrapyramidal symptoms. Collectively, these drugs are often referred to as anti-Parkinsonian agents. The two most commonly used drugs in this group are trihexyphenidl (Artane) and benztropine (Cogentin). Both are administered orally in doses of 2 mg, up to three times a day. They may also be used either intravenously or intramuscularly. Both Artane and Cogentin have strong anticholinergic effects, so their doses should be kept to a minimum. Although neither Cogentin or Artane cause classic addiction, they are frequently abused because persons taking these medications often experience a temporary "high" immediately after ingesting the drug.

## Central Nervous System Stimulants

Certain central nervous system stimulants are effective in dealing with disorders such as hyperactivity and also in some forms of apathy-depression. For example, methylphenidate (Ritalin), one of the piperidyls, is commonly used to control hyperactive patterns, especially in children and adolescents. Other drugs that may be used to control these symptoms are diphenhydramine (Benadryl) or diazepam (Valium), both of which are used intravenously in acute situations.

## Medications for Control of Violent and Aggressive Behavior

Mental health professionals often deal with violent behavior when it occurs in association with mental illness. A variety of psychotropic medications have been found to be effective in controlling or diminishing this type of behavior. Such management is often complicated by the person's use of alcohol or drugs, which clearly facilitates violence for most individuals.

Violence and aggression are generally caused by complex interaction of biological, psychological, and environmental factors. The management of violent behavior with medication relies on an appreciation of the biological factors which underlie violence. As with other symptoms, the biological explanation of violence rests with the neurotransmitters. In general, violence is correlated with an interaction of three factors in the brain: (1) an overabundance of certain neurotransmitters (e.g., dopamine and norepinephrine), (2) a relative deficiency of other neurotransmitters (e.g., serotonin and GABA), and (3) excess electrical activity in the brain leading to seizures (Eichelman, 1988). Drugs that control violent behavior act by correcting the neurotransmitter imbalance or by decreasing the electrical activity in the brain.

It should be noted that violence occurring in mental health patients is not that common. Many clients with violent histories will also be found to have histories of drug or alcohol abuse. These substances promote violence by interfering with perception and judgment or by causing disinhibition of underlying aggressive tendencies. Clients who are intoxicated have much less control over aggressive impulses than nonintoxicated persons. When violence is associated with a mental health condition, it is generally related to a psychotic episode, personality disorder, or an organic mental disorder.

Table 15.6 lists the medications useful in controlling violent or aggressive behaviors. These drugs are members of several of the groups already described. When violent behavior is associated with a psychotic disorder, such as schizophrenia, the antipsychotic medications are clearly indicated. Violent tendencies in nonpsychotic persons may also be controlled by these medications because of their dopamine-blocking action. Antidepressants that increase the action of serotonin, such as trazodone

**TABLE 15.6**    Medications Used to Control Violent Behavior

| NAME (GENERIC/TRADE) | DOSE RANGE* |
| --- | --- |
| Benzodiazepines | |
| Lorazepam (Ativan) | 1–2 mg PO or IM Q2–4hr PRN |
| Oxazepam (Serax) | 15–120  mg/day |
| Mood-altering drugs | |
| Lithium carbonate | 300 mg in divided doses to attain a therapeutic blood level |
| Trazodone (Desyrel) | 100–400  mg/day |
| Adrenergic blocking agents | |
| Propranolol (Inderal) | 200–600  mg/day |
| Anticonvulsants | |
| Carbamazepine (Tegretol) | 200 mg in divided doses to attain a therapeutic blood level |
| Antipsychotics | |
| Haloperidol (Haldol) | 2–5 mg PO or IM Q2–4hr PRN |
| Chlorpromazine (Thorazine) | 50–100 mg PO or IM Q2–4hr PRN |

*Average therapeutic dose range.
PO = Oral administration.
IM = Intramuscular administration.

(Desyrel), may also be useful. One of the actions of serotonin in the brain is a calming influence on behavior. Those drugs that increase levels of norepinephrine, however, may actually facilitate violent or aggressive behaviors. Lithium, through its action to decrease norepinephrine activity, may be useful in controlling aggression in some clients. Norepinephrine-blocking agents such as propranolol (Inderal) have also been shown to be effective.

The benzodiazepines, by increasing levels of GABA in the brain, which exerts a calming effect similar to that of serotonin, may also decrease violence. These drugs must be used cautiously, not only because of their potential for abuse but also because they cause a paradoxical increase in violence in some individuals.

Finally, carbamazepine (Tegretol), an anticonvulsant medication, is useful when violence occurs in association with seizure activity. Carbamazepine is an interesting drug because it seems to exert other effects independent of its anticonvulsant activity. Some psychotic or manic patients who fail to respond to other treatments have been found to improve on carbamazepine. This drug also appears to cause a decrease in impulsivity, which is often associated with violent and aggressive behavior.

## ■ Drugs Used for Assessment

Certain psychotropic drugs are used to induce a light sleep or trancelike state during which the person remains conscious and able to talk. This state closely resembles the altered level of consciousness achieved during hypnosis. During this period, it is possible to interview the patient and obtain important diagnostic information. Previously repressed, or forgotten, memories may also be recalled. The drugs which promote such a state have often been referred to as "truth serums."

However, it is a common misconception that these drugs make people reveal information that they would otherwise withhold, but this does not occur with legitimate medications. It is also not possible to be sure that the information obtained from such an interview is entirely factual.

Currently, two drugs are most commonly used for this type of interview, often referred to as narcotherapy or narcoanalysis. One of these is the short-acting barbiturate sodium amobarbital (Amytal). The other is a short-acting benzodiazepine, lorazepam (Ativan). The primary use of these agents is for diagnostic purposes, although lorazepam is also a frequently prescribed antianxiety agent when taken orally. For example, interviews using these drugs are useful for clarifying the diagnosis of catatonic schizophrenia, in which patients are often mute, and with certain disorders characterized by dissociative symptoms (see Chapter 7).

For this type of interview, both sodium amytal and lorazepam are administered intravenously. Small doses are injected at one- to two-minute intervals until the patient becomes drowsy but not completely asleep. Blood pressure and respirations must be monitored throughout the interview. Injection of the medication too rapidly will produce sleep, and using doses that are too high may cause respiratory depression or arrest. Therefore, this type of interview should only be performed by a qualified physician who is familiar with the procedure. As the person becomes drowsy, a series of generalized questions are asked, proceeding then to more specific questions. If the person appears to resist questioning, additional medication is gradually infused until the person bcomes more open. Because the duration of action of these drugs is brief, additional medication must be infused periodically throughout the interview. At the close of the interview, medication is discontinued and the client is allowed to rest until fully alert and able to walk without difficulty. The client will be aware of information disclosed following the interview. How long this awareness remains depends on the underlying condition the client suffers from. Many neurotic individuals will remain aware of the contents of the interview, while catatonic patients are likely to lapse back into a psychotic state. As with all such procedures, this type of interview should only be conducted with the informed consent of the patient.

☐     OTHER DRUGS USED IN PSYCHIATRY

Many drugs, from a variety of classes, have been found to be effective for certain conditions where traditional drug therapy has been ineffective. One example of this is the calcium channel blocker verapamil (Calan, Isoptin). The calcium ion is an important intracellular messenger that exerts an effect on many neurons. An overactivity of this ion may result in signals being sent to neurons that are excessive brain activity. By blocking calcium in the brain, the neurons are restored to normal rates of firing. Verapamil has been found to be effective in the treatment of some types of bipolar disorder, tardive dyskinesia, and certain other movement disorders that are accompanied by psychiatric symptoms (e.g., Tourette's disorder).

Clonidine (Catapres) is an alpha-adrenergic receptor agonist (i.e., it facilitates the action of the alpha-adrenergic transmitters). This drug has been widely used to treat hypertension. The drug has also been found to be effective in treating Tourette's disorder and in helping patients to withdraw from opiods.

■     ## Legal Issues in the Use of Psychotropic Medications

Because the psychotropic medications exert powerful effects on behavior, mood, and thought, it is not surprising that a number of legal issues are associated with their use. Specific issues include informed consent, malpractice, right to refuse treatment, the right to treatment, and the role of medications in criminal proceedings.

One important legal concept involved in the use of psychotropic medications is informed consent. The basic principle underlying informed consent is that the patient has a right to determine what should be done to his or her body and cannot be forced to accept treatment that is not wanted. Informed consent requires that the client be apprised of the potential benefits and major risks of any proposed treatments, as well as all alternative treatments available. In order to give consent for treatment, the client must be competent, possess adequate information, and make the decision for treatment voluntarily. With respect to psychotropic medications, for example, the client must be informed about all potential major side effects and their relative risks, drug interactions, and any special precautions that should be taken. Common examples of risks that need to be explained thoroughly are tardive dyskinesia and the neuroleptic malignant syndrome associated with the antipsychotic drugs. It is often useful to start with low dosages of a medication to see if there is any negative response. If not, the dosage may be gradually "bumped up" until a therapeutic dose is reached.

Another related issue is malpractice, the negligent performance of a procedure. In order for malpractice to be proven, the following elements must be established: (1) the clinician owed a legal duty to the client, (2) the clinician breached that duty in the care rendered to the client, (3) the client suffered injury or damages, either physical or emotional, and (4) the damages resulted from the clinician's negligence (Wettstein, 1989). If a client suffers harm because of inadequate monitoring of medication, for example, the clinician may be held legally accountable. If a third party suffers harm as a result of a client's actions while under the influence of a psychotropic medication, the clinician may also be held accountable. Drug-induced reactions are responsible for about 20 percent of malpractice claims against psychiatrists (Wettstein, 1989). The major issues related to psychotropic medications include lack of informed consent, excessive dosage, lack of proper indications for medication, and tardive dyskinesia. A number of legal decisions have found psychiatrists and drug companies liable in cases of neuroleptic malignant syndrome. Suicide by overdosage of medication may also be grounds for a malpractice or wrongful death suit based on the argument that the clinician should have known of the potential for self-harm and taken proper steps to safeguard the client.

Related to the concept of informed consent is the right to refuse treatment. This concept basically says that a competent adult has the right to refuse treatment if the perceived risks or consequences are viewed as intolerable (Smith and Meyer, 1987). Even though the decision may be ill advised or have negative consequences for the person, the competent client retains the right of refusal. The question of competence, particularly in the psychotic client, becomes very important in this matter. It is interesting to note that almost all of these cases involving right to refuse treatment deal with the antipsychotic medications. Just as clients have a right to refuse treatment in most situations, they also (in varying degrees, depending on the situation) have a basic right to treatment. See Appendix B for a discussion of the relevant cases.

# CHAPTER 16

# Malingering and the Factitious Disorders

■　**Malingering (V65.20)**

The issues of malingering (in truth, an act, not primarily a mental disorder) and distorted response sets are often a part of any clinical evaluation, but they are especially important in considering the categories of factitious disorder, antisocial personality disorder, substance dependence, schizophrenia, and the dissociative disorders. It is often appropriate to broaden the concept of malingering to any type of response that distorts the production of an accurate record; this is the context in which the following discussion is placed.

The focus of the DSM-III-R criteria for malingering is the voluntary presentation of physical or psychological symptoms. Malingering is understandable by the evident incentives and circumstances of the situation, rather than from the person's individual psychology.

Malingering is likely to occur in job screening, military and criminal-justice situations, or wherever a psychological or physical disability has a payoff (Rogers, 1988). It occurs more commonly in early- to middle-adults, is more common in males than in females, and often follows an actual injury or illness. Problematic employment history, lower socioeconomic status, or an associated antisocial personality disorder are also common predictors of this disorder. The reader is advised to consult the section of Chapter 6 on the psychogenic pain disorder regarding the issue of chronic (actual) pain versus malingering.

□　OVERALL INDICATORS

Several overall patterns have been found to be characteristic or interview and test data from malingerers (Rogers, 1986, 1988; Ekman, 1985;

Woychyshyn, 1992). These characteristic patterns depend to some degree on the specific distorted response pattern that is being observed, i.e., whether it is the result of malingering, defensiveness, disinterest, etc.

First, it's important to use your experience with the various patterns of mental disorder to evaluate the validity of symptoms presented by suspected malingerers. Also, any symptom reports should be rigorously questioned, using open-ended questions such as "What are those voices telling you?" rather than "Do those voices tell you to do anything?"

Overall, malingerers more often report relatively rare symptoms, as well as a higher total number of symptoms, than do honest respondents. Malingerers are also more likely to be willing to discuss their disorder, especially how the negative effects of their disorder impact on rather narrow areas of functioning. They are more likely to report a sudden onset of the disorder; to report a more sudden cessation of symptoms if that has some functional value; and to endorse the more evident, flamboyant, and disabling symptoms. They are more likely to give vague or approximate responses when confronted, to make inconsistent symptom reports, to take a longer time to complete a test or an interview response, to repeat questions, to use qualifiers and vague responses, to miss easy items and then score accurately on hard IQ items, and to endorse the obvious rather than the subtle symptoms usually associated with a disorder. Because of the latter, obvious-subtle item discriminations on the MMPI-2 are quite helpful here.

Delusions or hallucinations are commonly reported by individuals trying to malinger psychological disorder. In general, the clues that lead one to believe that the reporting of a delusion or hallucination may be malingered are (Resnick, 1991)

1. An abrupt onset or cessation

2. If the person is eager to call attention to the delusion or hallucination or leads the discussion to this topic

3. If the person's conduct is not consistent with the delusion (if the person is not a burned-out schizophrenic)

4. If there is reported bizarre content without disordered thoughts or hallucinations

5. If the delusion or hallucination somehow specifically reduces the relevant responsibility of culpability

Auditory hallucinations are the most common in schizophrenia, but the examiner should be suspicious of a report of auditory hallucinations if

1. They are vague or if the person reports it is hard to hear them or to understand them

2. They are reported as continuous rather than sporadic or intermittent

3. The hallucination is reported as not being associated with a delusion
4. Stilted language is reported as the content of the hallucination
5. The content specifically exonerates the client from some blame or responsibility
6. The person reporting the voices can give no strategy to diminish the voices
7. The person says that he or she obeyed all command hallucinations

☐                    ## MMPI-2

On the MMPI-2, interest is naturally centered on the validity scales as predictors of distorted response sets (Woychyshyn, 1992). Nevertheless, it appears that a number of other measures may be useful here—in numerous instances, *more* valuable than a direct reading of the validity scales.

One effective method is to compare differences on those items originally designated by Weiner and Harmon (1946) as obvious and subtle (see Chapter 12). Hovanitz and Jordan-Brown (1986) found that when diagnostic or drug-outcome criteria were used, the exclusion of the subtle MMPI-2 items resulted in a statistically significant loss of predictive ability. The obvious items, however, were found to be related to many diagnostic constructs within the scales. Woychyshyn (1992) finds the subtle-obvious scales to be more effective in detecting faking good than faking bad.

The standard validity scales do, however, provide much valuable information in this regard, and there is support for the use of three validity scales excerpted from the test as a whole (Cassini and Workman, 1992). (The reader is referred to the discussion in Chapter 12 of the correlates of these scales.) The traditional rule-of-thumb has been that if the F-K ratio (the Gough Dissimulation Index) is +9, such people are trying to fake-bad; that is, to present a distorted picture of themselves that emphasizes pathology. If the score is −12 or less, the emphasis is on trying to look good and deny pathology. However, it is generally agreed that these axioms only hold if F and K are relatively low, and even then, there are a high number of false-positives and -negatives. For example, psychotic and other severely distressed individuals—e.g., those with a high level of anxiety—are likely to score in a T range of 65–80 on the F scale and so at first may appear to be malingering. It's also noteworthy that when there is evidence of a defensive profile—e.g., a high K—elevations in the T range above 65 are usually of high clinical significance (Butcher and Graham, 1988).

The most recent comprehensive data on faking-bad and -good on the MMPI-2 (Graham et al., 1991b) suggest the following guidelines. Remember, this is to gain maximum discrimination power in a statistical analysis; lower scores than those suggested may still suggest malingering, especially when combined with other MMPI-2 data or data from other sources.

**A.** For discriminating those consciously faking-bad within an essentially normal population (using raw scores)

1. Use a K cutoff score of 18 on F, with those faking-bad being higher
2. Use an F-K score of 17 for men and 12 for women; with higher scores indicating faking-bad
3. Use a raw score Fb (back side F) of 19 for men and 22 for women; again, higher scores indicating faking-bad

**B.** For discriminating those consciously faking-bad within a psychiatric population (again, using raw scores and assessing higher scores on all of these as suggesting faking-bad)

1. Use a K-cutoff of 27 for men and 29 for women
2. Use an F-K of 27 for men and 25 for women
3. Use an Fb of 23 for men and 24 for women

Using these scales to assess faking-good has always been a somewhat difficult discrimination, and Graham et al.'s (1991b) data echo that admonition. Also, those solid findings that were obtained are confounded by the issue of whether one is trying to identify faked profiles or honest ones. L proved to be the most effective scale for males: with an L score of 8 correctly classifying 93 percent of honest profiles, but only 67 percent of the fake-goods. To correctly classify 96 percent of the males faking-good, a cutoff of 4 on L was necessary. Scores of 8 and 5 produced similar respective discriminations in females, but did not work as effectively as L alone for males. The reader is referred to the extensive data and tables in Graham et al. (1991b) for information that will be useful in discriminations using a combination of variables in an individual case.

Gynther et al. (1973b) have shown that profiles with F scores that are in the T range above 90 are commonly associated with extremely disturbed individuals who manifest hallucinations, delusions, and general confusion. This is particularly so when one is dealing with an inpatient population. Also, individuals who have a T score of greater than 95 on the F scale have probably either responded to the MMPI-2 in a random fashion or have answered virtually all the items "true." If all or the great majority of items are answered "false," the T scores are typically in the 75–99 range. Graham et al. (1991b) note that, in addition to the high F, the highest scales, in order, are typically 8, 6, with lesser but substantial elevations (i.e., a T score of 80–90) on 7, 1, 4, and 9 (slightly less on 9 for females, but in this range on 2), with elevations above 70 on 3, 2, and 0. A "fake-good" profile tends to have all scores well within the normal range, most near 50, with mild elevations on 5 and 9 in females and 3 and 9 for men and occasionally on 2 in traditional females.

Malingering or other response distortion (or low comprehension or reading ability) may be reflected in an irrelevant (if not irreverent) and/or random response pattern. Since the Cannot Say scale is highly related to clinical profile stability and to item change measures, there is good reason for attempting to strongly limit the number of allowable missed responses.

The overall profile for a totally random response set is an L scale of approximately 60 T, an F scale of approximately 110, and K around 55, with an elevation on scale 8 being close to 95 T for females and approximately 110 for males. It is noteworthy that randomly generated MMPI-2s look very much like malingered fake-bad MMPI-2 protocols in many respects. Scale 6 is usually the lowest score. If there are all "true" responses, the F scale is practically off the top, the L scale is about 35, and the K scale is at 30 T. The profile peaks are on scale 8: 125 for males and around 105 for females, with a secondary peak on scale 6 of 90 T for both. It is worthwhile for the clinician at least to scan quickly the response sheet before turning it over for scoring. In cases where careless or random responding has occurred, it is often immediately evident, and the problem can be dealt with at that time.

By altering true and false responses, one obtains a T score of about 55 on L, 105 on F, and 65 on K, with a particularly strong peak on scale 8 (up to 120 T). Scores throughout the rest of the profile are high (Graham, 1977).

In general, when F and K are both high, look for deliberate faking. But, if L is high and F and K are well within acceptable limits, first consider faking-good, but also consider that the individual is either naive or unsophisticated (or both) and at the same time is trying to look good. If K is high and L and F are within the normal range, a more sophisticated defensive system is probable and the profile can be considered as an indication of subclinical trends.

Another relatively common pattern that results from a form of malingering is the 1-3/3-1 pattern, with a high K scale and very low scores on 2, 7, and 8. Such an individual is quite defensive and unwilling to admit any faults, therefore, will not tolerate the patient role and has a poor prognosis.

☐          TRIN AND VRIN

Two response inconsistency scales were developed for MMPI-2, TRIN (True Response Inconsistency) and VRIN (Variable Response Inconsistency), and there is good evidence that they are by far the best measures of random or inconsistent responding (Sabine and Meyer, 1992).

TRIN is based on twenty item pairs for which a combination of two true or two false responses is semantically inconsistent, e.g., the pair "I am happy most of the time" and "Most of the time I feel blue." In three pairs, the response of either true or false to both indicates inconsistency; in eleven pairs, inconsistency is indicated only by a true response, and in six pairs, only by a false response. By subtracting the number of inconsistent false pairs from inconsistent true pairs and then subtracting from 9 (total number of inconsistent false pairs), an index score of 0 to 20 is obtained. A high score indicates indiscriminate "true" responding; a low score points to indiscriminate "false" responding.

VRIN is composed of forty-nine item pairs that produce one or two, out of four, possible configurations (true-true, true-false, false-true, false-false), again, where responses would be semantically inconsistent. Scores occur in a range of 0 to 49, with high scores pointing to random responding and/or confusion.

☐     ## 16 PF

There are scales for faking-good or faking-bad on the 16 PF, derived by Winder et al. (1975). The faking-good scale, which they refer to as a "motivational-distortion" scale, is calculated by taking the sum of the responses that the individual gives to the following specific responses: 7-c, 24-c, 61-c, 62-a, 81-a, 97-a, 111-a, 114-c, 123-c, 130-a, 133-c, 149-c, 173-a, 174-c, and 184-a.

The faking-bad scale is calculated in the same manner, by totaling how many of the specific marker questions that an individual scores on the raw-data sheet. The responses that are used to calculate this score are 14-a, 38-a, 42-c, 51-b, 52-c, 55-c, 68-c, 80-a, 89-c, 117-a, 119-a, 123-a, 143-a, 176-c, and 182-c.

Winder et al. assert that a cutoff score of 6 is useful for determining both faking-good and -bad. However, Krug (1978) obtained data on a much broader and more representative sample, and he finds one major difference in the cutoff scores. Krug's sample included 2,579 men and 2,215 women. On the faking-good scale, scores ranged from 0 to 15, with a mean of 6.36 and a standard deviation of 2.87 for men, while women's scores ranged from 0 to 14, with a mean of 5.71 and a standard deviation of 2.72.

Krug's data suggest that the cutoff score of 6 for the faking-good scales, as suggested by Winder et al., is much too liberal, since in using this cutoff score, almost 55 percent of those people who are routinely screened would be labeled as faking-good, instead of the approximately 7 percent that Winder et al. report. Krug's data would suggest that a raw score of 10 on the faking-good scale would be a much more appropriate cutoff point. Only about 15 percent of people taking the test would attain a score this high.

On the faking-bad scale, men ranged from 0 to 12, with a mean of 2.45 and a standard deviation of 2.27, while women scored from 0 to 11, with a mean of 2.24 and a standard deviation of 2.04. Winder et al.'s suggestion of a cutoff score of 6 for the faking-bad scale is supported by Krug. Both report that fewer than 10 percent of those taking the test will score above 6 on this scale.

It should be noted that, in general, college students show lower average scores than the adult population on both of the faking scores, and high school students score even lower than the college students; hence, an age factor may be operating.

Those who are attempting to fake-good and deny anxiety score very low on O and $Q_4$, and in general, those who are faking-good score in the following directions: C+, H+, L−, O−, $Q_3$+, $Q_4$−, and G+. Those who are faking-bad tend to present a mirror image of these data.

Krug offers the following rules to be used for making the profile more accurately interpretable when scores range from 6 upward:*

### FOR FAKING-GOOD

1. If the score is 7, subtract 1 sten score point from C and add 1 point to $Q_4$.
2. If the score is 8, subtract 1 point from A, C, G, and $Q_3$ and add 1 point to L, O, and $Q_4$.
3. If the score is 9, subtract 1 point from A, C, G, and $Q_3$ and add 1 point to F, L, O, and $Q_4$.
4. If the score is 10, add 1 point to F, L, and O, add 2 points to $Q_4$, subtract 1 point from A, G, H, and $Q_3$, and subtract 2 points from C.

### FOR FAKING-BAD

1. If the score is 7, add 1 point to C.
2. If the score is 8, subtract 1 point from O and $Q_4$ and add 1 point to C.
3. If the score is 9, subtract 1 point from L, O, and $Q_4$ and add 1 point to C, H, I, and $Q_3$.
4. If the score is 10, subtract 1 point from L and $Q_4$, add 1 point to A, H, I, and $Q_3$, and add 2 points to C.

Individuals who randomly mark the 16 PF answer sheet show a very flat profile, with a low score on scale B.

☐     RORSCHACH TEST

A major problem with the use of the Rorschach (as well as other projective techniques) in the detection of deception—the apparent susceptibility

---

*S. Krug, "Further evidence on the 16 PF Distortion Scales," *Journal of Personality Assessment, 42,* 1978, 513–18. Printed with permission of the Society for Personality Assessment and the author.

to fake psychosis on the test—is evident in a classic study by Albert et al. (1980). Albert and his colleagues studied four different groups of Rorschach protocols. The first group, the Psychotic protocols, were obtained from actual mental hospital inpatients who were administered the Rorschach with standard instructions. The second group, labeled Uninformed Fakers, were obtained from college students who were given the instruction to malinger paranoid schizophrenia (that is, "You want the test result to show that you are a paranoid schizophrenic and not show that you are faking") with no other instructions. The third group, the Informed Fakers, were given the same instructions as the Uninformed Fakers, but additionally they heard a twenty-five-minute audiotape describing paranoid schizophrenia, which included actual examples of paranoid delusional thinking. However, at no point did the tape mention the Rorschach test or provide any specific suggestions as to how to fake psychosis. The fourth group, the Control group, consisted of college students on whom the protocols were obtained under standard instructions.

The protocols were sent for judging to clinicians experienced in the use of the Rorschach. Each judge was sent a randomly selected set of four Rorschach protocols and asked to provide a psychiatric diagnosis, to indicate certainty of the diagnosis, and to rate protocols on dimensions of psychopathology and malingering. Results suggested that these experts were unable to discriminate the fakers from the actual psychotic individuals, although they did discriminate all psychotic groups from the normal group. The group most often seen by these experts as psychotic was the Informed Fakers. This study suggests that while the Rorschach is effective in pointing to psychotic psychopathology, reliable cues for distinguishing malingering from other psychopathology have not been found. The relatively small N in the study is noted. However, other studies have supported the "fakeability" of both the Rorschach, TAT, most neuropsychological tests, and figure drawings, especially by sophisticated and/or prepared persons (Rogers, 1986, 1988).

With this in mind, it is generally agreed that malingering clients (especially if unsophisticated) will respond to the Rorschach with a reduced number of responses and will also show slow reaction times, even when they do not produce particularly well-integrated or complex responses. They take a cautious attitude and thereby produce few responses, primarily determined by color. There are high percentages of pure F and Popular responses. They easily feel distressed by the ambiguity of the stimuli and will subtly try to obtain feedback from the examiner as to the accuracy of their performances. Also, Seamons et al. (1981) note that if the F%, L, and X+% variables are in the normal range and there are a high number of texture, shading, blood, dramatic, nonhuman-movement, vista, or inappropriate-combination responses, malingering to cause a false appearance of a mentally disordered state should be considered.

☐     OTHER STANDARD TESTS

The MCMI-II contains four modifier indices, three of which are designed to assess various forms of malingering. These are the Disclosure Scale (DIS), the Desirability Gauge Scale (DES), and the Debasement Measure (DEB). The fourth modifier, the Validity Index (VI), consists of four items with an endorsement frequency of less than .01. The DIS was designed to detect the degree to which respondents are inclined to be self-revealing and frank and is thought to be neutral to psychopathology. The DES is thought to essentially measure "faking-good"; the DEB measuring "faking-bad." However, Bagby et al.'s (1991) data suggest that all three scales are bidirectional indicators of dissimulation, i.e., they tap both faking-bad and faking-good components; hence, they must be used with caution. When an individual is "faking-bad," the Thought Disorder scale of the MCMI-II is easily elevated, as it is quite susceptible to faking (Jackson et al., 1991). Also, as noted earlier, since the MCMI-II is more of an "in-house" test than the MMPI-2, it is still unclear how much of the research on the original version of the MCMI has any "carryover" to the MCMI-II, while it's quite clear there is a major if not virtually total carryover on the MMPI-2.

On intelligence and neuropsychological tests, there is an overall tendency for malingerers to perform too poorly and inconsistently in relation to observed behavior or abilities as assessed by indirect methods. They produce abnormal scatter; give illogical, inconsistent, or "approximate" answers; produce odd or surprising "near misses"; miss easy items while they pass hard ones; and also sometimes give bizarre responses where intellectually slow individuals might give concrete responses. Remember to look for consistency between two tests which look different but which measure the same ability.

David Schretlen and his colleagues (Schretlen, Wilkins, Van Gorp, and Bobholz, 1992) have provided interesting data to support the use of a recently developed Malingering Test (MgS), the Bender-Gestalt, and the MMPI in the detection of faked insanity. The MgS is a 90-item, paper-and-pencil test, composed of simple questions in both open-ended and forced-choice formats, that takes about 25 minutes to complete. On the basis of earlier research, the following scoring criteria (Schretlen et al., 1992, p. 78) for the Bender-Gestalt were found to be effective in detecting faked psychosis:

**(a) inhibited figure size, each figure that could be completely covered by a 3.2 cm square was scored +1; (b) changed position, each easily recognized figure whose position was rotated greater than 45 degrees was scored +1; (c) distorted relationship, each easily recognized figure with correctly drawn parts that were misplaced in relationship to one another was scored +1; (d) complex additions, each easily recognized figure that contained additional complex or bizarre details was scored +1; (e) gross simplification, each figure**

that showed a developmental level of 6 years or less was scored +1; and (f) inconsistent form quality, each protocol that contained at least one drawing with a developmental level of 6 years or less and at least one drawing with a developmental level of 9 years or more was scored +1. Scores for the first five of these features were then summed as a composite index of faking.

A more detailed scoring manual for this use of the Bender-Gestalt, and more information on the MgS is available from Dr. David Schretlen, Dept. of Psychiatry and Behavioral Science, Johns Hopkins School of Medicine, Meyer 218, 600 N. Wolfe St., Baltimore, MD 21205.

□          OTHER METHODS

It is ironic that, on a relative basis, clinicians have not carried out much research on the detection of deception, since it is a critical issue in many diagnostic decisions. In addition, most clinicians have not become sophisticated in methods other than psychological test measures of deception, and even here, testing has largely been restricted to the MMPI-2. Many people who use the 16 PF have been unaware of the deception scales that have been derived from it.

Only recently have clinicians shown an interest in adding physiological methods of deception assessment to their armamentarium (Iacono, 1991). At the same time, most states are passing laws that permit use of the titles "polygrapher" and "lie detection examiner" only by individuals who have training restricted to certain physiological tests. Unfortunately, some of the less efficient assessment modalities are often the ones used in the standard examination format and may even be mandated by state law.

Several consistent behavioral cues have been noted in individuals who present a dishonest portrayal of themselves (Ekman, 1985; Bull and Rumsey, 1988). For example, on the average, such individuals nod, grimace, and gesture more than honest interviewees do, and they have less frequent foot and leg movements. They also talk less and speak more slowly, although they make more speech errors and smile more often. In addition, the dishonest interviewees tend to take positions that are physically farther from the interviewer. High voice pitch and many face and hand movements, relative to the individual's standard behavior, are also indicative of deception.

There is no real support for the idea that people who are deceiving will necessarily avoid eye contact (Ekman, 1985). There is some evidence that females will look longer into the eyes of male examiners while lying but usually not into a female examiner's eyes. These same cross-sex results hold for males as well, but not as clearly.

Research by Michael Cody (1991) breaks down deceivers into those who tell "prepared" lies and those who tell "spontaneous" lies. Those who prepare ahead of time to deceive *tend* to (1) give the answer immediately after the question is asked, (2) provide very terse answers, (3) have speech microtremors, (4) nod their heads at the end of the lie, (5) rub some part of their bodies, and (6) lack enthusiasm and sound a bit as if they have rehearsed, which of course they have. On the other hand, people who tell spontaneous lies *tend* to (1) show odd grammatical errors, (2) provide brief but tentative answers, (3) show speech hesitations and silent pauses or pauses filled with "Ahhs," (4) use meaningless phrases such as "like that" and "you know," (5) employ "universal" words and phrases, e.g., "always," "never," "certainly," (6) completely freeze or scratch their heads or rub their hands together, and (7) fail to provide important or even obvious details.

Clinicians also do not make much use of systematized interview observations or techniques that change the set of the person taking the test in order to gain a more truthful response. With reference to the set in which the test is taken, Macciocchi and Meyer (1989) told people that the test that they were going to take had built-in scales to detect deception. These subjects provided more honest and less socially desirable response patterns than those who were told nothing except to be honest in their responses. Of even more importance, a group of subjects was told that if there was any hint in the psychological tests that they might have been deceptive, they would be given a lie detection examination. They were then even more honest and self-disclosing in their response patterns, compared to when the threat of detection was only by allegedly embedded psychological test scales designed to measure deception. More research in this area is needed to set test conditions more effectively so as to gain more honest responses.

Clinicians also need to look more to specific tests if there is any question of dishonesty (Schretlen et al., 1992). For example scales that tap a social-desirability response set, such as the Marlowe-Crowne Social Desirability Scale (Marlowe and Crowne, 1964), give an idea of the direction of a client's response set, and this test has shown good reliability and validity (Robinette, 1991). A validated short version of the Marlowe-Crowne (Zook and Sipps, 1985) can easily be included in a standard screening battery, such as the Meyer Information Battery which is found in Appendix A of this book. The Marlowe-Crowne scale and other scales of a similar nature—such as the M Test of Beaber et al. (1985) and the Structured Interview of Reported Symptoms, the SIRS, (Rogers, 1988)—are also helpful in conjunction with the other more standard detection scales built into such tests as the MMPI-2 and 16 PF. While Connell and Meyer (1992) found support for the use of the M Test and the SIRS in this respect, Gillis et al.'s (1991) data did not support the use of the M Test. The Personality Inventory for Children-Revised, Shortened Format, has been found to be effective in assessing deception in children (Daldin, 1985).

The Schedule for Affective Disorders and Schizophrenia (Spitzer and Endicott, 1978), a semistructured interview technique, is also of potential help here. A drawback of its use with malingerers is that it takes up to four hours to complete, although its length makes it easier to trip up a malingering client on inconsistent responses. Malingering is suggested if (1) sixteen or more of the "severe" symptoms are subscribed to, (2) forty or more symptoms are scored in the "clinical" range – a score of 3 or greater, or (3) four or more "rare" symptoms are subscribed to. These rare symptoms are each only found in 5 percent of a sample of 105 forensic patients, and only about 1 percent of this population showed five or more of these symptoms: (1) markedly elevated mood, (2) much less sleep in the previous week, (3) significantly increased activity level in the previous week, (4) thought withdrawal – something or someone is "pulling" thoughts from them, (5) delusions of guilt, (6) marked somatic delusions, (7) evident and recent loosening of associations, (8) incoherence at some point during the previous week, (9) poverty of speech, or (10) neologisms. These rare symptoms could probably be effectively included in a short screening procedure.

## ■ Amnesia

Amnesia (see Chapter 7) is a commonly malingered symptom, probably because (1) it is seemingly easy to carry off, (2) acts to void responsibility, yet (3) leaves the person fully functional in his or her world. True psychogenic amnesia is typically focused on personal memory, particularly those memories directly relevant to a traumatic event. Psychogenic amnesia can usually be differentiated from organic amnesia and faked amnesia by the sudden onset, shorter course, and sudden recovery, anterograde direction (continued ability to learn new information), recoverability under hypnosis, personal focus, and unimpaired ability to learn new information that are characteristic of psychogenic amnesia (Wiggins and Brandt, 1988; Rogers, 1986; Schachter, 1986).

It's worthwhile for clinicians to first remember that vigor and/or apparent sincerity of presentation are not indicators of true amnesia. Indeed, there seems to be no clear correlation here. It's also worthwhile to remember that there may be both true and malingered amnesia in the same case. However, there are cues that indicate malingered rather than true amnesia:

1. True amnesia for situation is seldom either total or very specific. The manifestation of such patterns should cue one to possible malingering.

2. True amnesiacs have shown lower scores on MMPI scales 1, 2, and 3 than malingering amnesiacs (Parwatikar et al., 1985).

3. Malingering amnesia often results in inconsistencies between reports, as well as with usual psychogenic or organic syndromes.

4. True amnesiacs rate themselves higher on the ability to recall information if they are told they will be given extra time or prompting, and indeed, they do function better if primed. Malingerers are more likely to indicate the improbability of change in their amnesia; they then do not show much change even if prompted.

5. Malingerers show amnesia "as characterized by recall performance better than, and recognition performance worse than, that of brain-damaged memory-disordered subjects" (Wiggins and Brandt, 1988, p. 74). In addition, malingerers' serial-position pattern resembles that of normals rather than that of amnesiacs.

## Factitious Disorders

Factitious means "not genuine" and refers to symptoms that are under voluntary control of the individual, a syndrome first clearly defined by Asher in 1951. At first, this syndrome may sound like malingering. The difference is that in a factitious disorder the goal or reinforcement sought is not obvious or inherent in the apparent facts of the situation. Instead, the motivation is understandable only within the person's individual psychology. These patterns have been traditionally confused with the conversion disorders, but in both the somatoform and conversion disorders of DSM-III-R, the symptoms are not under voluntary control. Also, in a conversion disorder, symptoms seldom follow a pattern that is true to the factitious disorders: Although the symptoms are not under voluntary control, they are usually associated with a degree of anxiety and have occurred more frequently in the person's history.

Factitious disorders are rare, and, according to Spitzer et al. (1979), they comprise the most difficult DSM category to diagnose, in part because the feigned symptoms are often accompanied by a more subtle, yet actual, physical disorder. When diagnosticians become aware of what they perceive as deception, they are inclined to make a diagnosis of an antisocial personality instead of a factitious disorder and then give the person little attention.

The factitious disorders are subdivided into (1) Factitious Disorder with Psychological Symptoms (300.16) and (2) Chronic Factitious Disorder with Physical Symptoms (301.51), the latter often referred to in the literature as Munchausen's syndrome. The general DSM-III-R requirements in each syndrome are the intentional production or feigning of symptoms and a psychological need to assume the sick role, with an absence of external incentives as primary. There have also been increasing reports of "Munchausen's by proxy"—e.g., where a mother has induced multiple hospitalizations in her child by administering laxatives. These mothers are preoccupied with medical terms and equipment and may even manifest some clear borderline personality disorder components. They also often initially present themselves as cooperative and then passively subvert or resist all interventions. In an also apparently increasing number of cases, a child is injured by the parent in order that the parent might gain the related attention. But this pattern is not yet specifically included in the DSM.

In the factitious psychological syndrome, the symptoms are mental rather than physical and therefore are often less well defined. These people usually talk around a point or give approximate although evasive answers to direct questions, a pattern referred to as *vorbereiten*. For example, if asked an arithmetic question (such as "How much is 35 minus 12?"), they may respond with only an approximate answer ("20 or 25"). In that sense, they are not unlike persons with Ganser's syndrome, although that pattern usually lasts no more than a few weeks, even if treatment is no more sophisticated than supportive therapy. The factitious disorders, on the other hand, are chronic.

The factitious disorders are thought to be more common in males. This may only reflect a more ready acceptance of verbalizations of sickness from females, so that the diagnostician would be less inclined to recognize a factitious disorder in females.

Munchausen's syndrome (Chronic Factitious Disorder with Physical Symptoms in DSM-III-R) was named after Baron Munchausen, an eighteenth-century German equivalent of our Paul Bunyan, both of whom are associated with tales of exaggeration.

The all-time champion victim of Munchausen's syndrome appears to be Stewart McIlroy, whose path through 68 hospitals (with at least 207 separate admissions) in England, Scotland, Ireland, and Wales was retraced by Pallis and Bamji (1979). Although McIlroy used false names and different complaints, he was eventually identified by scar patterns (i.e., the "gridiron stomach," a pattern seen in a number of these individuals) and other permanent medical characteristics.

McIlroy is an excellent example of one who suffered mightily to satisfy his addiction. Pallis and Bamji (1979) estimate that over the years of his disorder, he was subjected to thousands of blood tests and X-rays, his spine had been tapped at least forty-eight times, and his abdomen and body parts were crisscrossed with many scars from exploratory surgeries. It is probable that he cost the British Health Services the equivalent of several million dollars, although, given the "gridiron" scar pattern he carried, it's hard to be terribly sympathetic to their financial costs in this case.

The range of symptomatology is limited only by the client's imagination and degree of sophistication about medical information. Some experience with hospitals or medical situations, either through prior hospitalizations or through knowledge from family members involved in the medical profession, often contributes to this disorder. It is highly refractory to intervention, in part because the person can often find another cooperative physician. Ironically, the disorder can take a high physical toll on the person, as seen in the case of Mr. McIlroy.

□        TEST-RESPONSE PATTERNS

The functional performance of individuals with these disorders is that of malingering, although the psychology that generates the behaviors is somewhat different. However, the patterns and symptom picture described in the prior section on malingering is appropriate, especially as regards malingering used to gain admission to a hospital. It is unfortunate that clinicians have not paid more attention to the issue of the detection of deception, as it is relevant to so many disorders. The clinician is advised to depend on more than one test for indications of malingering. Also, the careful gathering and evaluation of past records, which is important in all disorders, is critical here (Rogers, 1988).

The factitious disorder with psychological symptoms generally parallels the classic signs of neurasthenia (Golden, 1979), in which the clinician can expect high 2, 7, 1, and 3 scales, in that order of elevation. The deception and sophistication found here would also suggest high 6 and 4 scales. A person with Munchausen's syndrome is more likely to show greater elevations on 1 and 3 than a person with psychological symptoms. The "Munchausen by proxy" mother often manifests a 1-3/3-1 pattern.

On the MCMI-II, elevations on 3 and C between 75 and 85 may occur. The submissive personality (elevation on 3) may use physical symptoms as a way to maintain nurturing and care-giving by others. Scale H may or may not be elevated, depending on the specific patterns of symptoms. It's important to note that the Rorschach and other projective tests are helpful because they present a situation in which it is hard to decipher the situational demands. Thus, such tests disrupt the sophistication and polish of deceptive clients in their presentation of symptoms. For that reason, it is advisable to use a projective test early in the battery; disturbing their sense of surety about performance may spill over into the tests that follow.

□        TREATMENT OPTIONS

Biofeedback and other allied techniques are useful for any physiological disorder, regardless of the source, even including a physiological disorder that is a direct result of psychological conflicts (Schwartz, 1987). The factitious disorder is a different story, though, because the essential aspect is deception. Not surprisingly, such persons are going to be openly hostile and avoidant of treatment. Thus, unless they are coerced by a significant other, they are not likely to become involved in treatment.

If they are coerced and are willing to participate, at least initially, many of the principles that hold for the paranoid disorders are applicable here.

Variations on reality therapy (Glasser, 1980) are also an appropriate therapeutic focus here. These emphasize that the person must accept responsibility for his or her behavior and, most importantly, for the consequences of that behavior. To the degree that reality therapy is effective, clients are more likely to come into contact with the conflicts central to their disorder. At that point, more traditional psychotherapeutic modes are appropriate.

# ■ Ruling Out Hypochondriasis, Factitious Disorder, or Malingering

There are three probable specific statuses that a clinician must invariable take into account where malingering or other distorted response sets are suspected. These three patterns are hypochondriasis (discussed in Chapter 6), factitious disorders, and true malingering. As noted, hypochondriases is one of the somatoform disorders (along with the somatization disorder, conversion disorder, and psychogenic pain disorder), all of which are denoted by complaints of physical symptoms that have no identifiable physiological base and are *not* under voluntary control.

Clinicians are often called on to determine if any of these three conditions exist. In order to facilitate this decision process, the following checklists for each of the three categories were developed by Elizabeth Salazar and me. In the great majority of cases, a high percentage (75% or more) of positive answers will occur on predominantly one checklist, indicating support for that pattern. If no condition clearly predominates, these three patterns can usually be ruled out. There are some cases in which two (or even, in very rare cases, all three) of these patterns will occur.

### HYPOCHONDRIASIS CHECKLIST

1. Is there a morbid preoccupation with the body, or a part of the body, that is felt to be diseased or functioning improperly?
2. Is there a long-term pattern of social or occupational impairment?
3. Are normal bodily functions/fluctuations exaggerated as indications of disease?
4. Are beliefs about the issue sustained in spite of consistent medical information to the contrary?
5. Is there a general indifference to the opinions of people in the client's environment?
6. Is the client anxious, worried, and concerned about this "illness"?

7. Does the client dwell excessively on the symptoms, turning interviews into monologues—an "organ recital"?

8. Does the speech content consist almost solely of symptoms, their effect on his or her life, and the difficult search for a cure?

9. During conversation, does the client frequently point out afflicted areas of the body?

10. Is there an expression of obsessive-compulsive traits such as defensiveness, obstinacy, miserliness, or conscientiousness?

11. Is there an indication of narcissistic traits, such as egocentrism or oversensitivity to criticism of slight?

12. Is there a lack of sense of inner worth, self-esteem, or adequacy?

13. Does the client appear to have a preference for being ill, showing positive emotions if any real sickness is found?

14. Are there indications of an affective disorder, such as significant depressive tendencies?

15. Is there a history of frequent doctor visits, with one physician or thorough "doctor shopping"?

16. Is there an unusual and wide-ranging familiarity with psychological or medical terms and jargon?

17. Is there an apparent addiction to reading medical journals, health magazines, and other related materials?

18. Does the client follow unusual health fads, diets, or exercise plans?

19. Has the client often made appeals for extensive tests, examinations, and prescriptions?

20. Do the symptoms commonly deal with the head, neck, abdomen, chest, gastrointestinal system, or generally the left side of the body?

21. Are there indications of a dependent relationship in which affection is not effectively displayed outside of sickness situations?

22. Do the symptoms seem to fulfill an ego-defensive purpose?

23. Do the symptoms ease an intolerable personal situation, avoid anxiety or personal responsibility, or gain needed attention?

24. Do the symptoms appear to be an attempt to control a situation that seems to be getting out of the client's control?

25. Did the pattern appear to have an early onset?

26. Did the client grow up in an "atmosphere of illness," e.g., with a bed-ridden, chronically ill, or terminally ill family member or a family member in the medical field who brought work home in some fashion?

27. Were the client's parents, especially the mother, overprotective, strict, or overly sanitary in health tendencies?

28. Did the client grow up without parents for a substantial period, or was there a pattern of self-mothering?

## FACTITIOUS DISORDER CHECKLIST

1. Is there an absence of evident or obvious gain that the client would achieve as a result of the presented disorder pattern?

2. Is there a gut-level sense that the client has been inducing the symptoms?

3. Could the problem fulfill a masochistic need, such as relieving guilt, or a need to identify with the "sadistic" doctor?

4. Does the client show any counterphobic responses to other disorder patterns or syndromes?

5. Are there indications that deceiving others acts as a defense mechanism, e.g., against low self-esteem or a sense of powerlessness?

6. Are there indications that the presented disorder provides distance from frustrating objects, internal conflicts, or anxieties or provides a temporary identity while ego-dysfunctions are reorganized?

7. Is there any evidence that dependency needs are being gratified in the pattern?

8. Was childhood marked with institutional placement or sadistic, abusive, or rejecting parents?

9. Did the patterns apparently start in adolescence or early adulthood?

10. Is there a history of multiple hospitalizations?

11. Is there any evidence of multiple surgeries?

12. Do the symptoms appear to have symbolic meaning or to have been derived from a previously suffered disorder?

13. Does the client have a background in the health professions or some other access to medical knowledge?

14. Did the client grow up in an "atmosphere of illness"?

15. Is there any indication of wandering to many different hospitals or clinics?

16. Has the client accumulated diagnostic labels, medical biographies, radiographs, or thick hospital folders?

17. Is the medical history inconsistent with known pathophysiological courses?

18. Have there been any inconsistent lab or test results?

19. Have there been any unusual recurrent infections?

20. Has the client failed to respond to therapy as expected?

21. Has the client falsified his or her history in any manner?

22. Does the client dramatically present one or more symptoms with elaborate stories, while interacting on a narcissistic level?

23. Is the client's attitude toward staff threatening, aggressive, hostile, and/or impatient?

24. Are there frequent requests for surgery, direct patient observation, or invasive procedures?

25. Does the client impassively or even eagerly submit to agonizing examinations and treatments, expressing high pain tolerance and/or exhibitionist traits?

26. Does the client show *pseudologia fantastica*, attention-seeking, or restlessness?

27. Has the client ever discharged himself or herself or retreated indignantly when confronted?

28. Are there indications of any underlying histrionic, antisocial, and/or narcissistic personality disorder patterns?

### MALINGERING CHECKLIST

1. Would the client obtain any obvious gain by being considered ill or disordered?

2. Does the client seem to perceive interviews as a challenge or threat?

3. Does the client appear to be annoyed at what he or she considers to be unusual tests?

4. Does the client appear suspicious, overly evasive, vague, or unusually lacking in comprehension of issues?

5. Are there seemingly exaggerated concerns for the symptoms?

6. Is there an easily expressed pessimism about recovery?

7. Is there a relative lack of concern about treatment for the presented disorder?

8. Is the client quickly or especially explicit in denying concern for financial (or other goal-oriented) matters?

9. Is there a focused rather than wide-ranging familiarity with medical or psychological terminology?

10. Does the client show an overly self-confident or assertive manner?

11. Are there any indications of antisocial or psychopathic personality traits?

12. Are there any indications that either of the parents showed manipulative or psychopathic patterns?

13. Do some symptoms seem to contradict symptomatology the client should have?

14. In cases that should supposedly show a long-term deficit or problem, is there an unusual lack of previous exams?

15. Are there other discrepancies, contradictions, omissions, or odd exaggerations?

16. Is there poor test-retest reliability in testing or interview patterns?

17. Whether or not there are discrepancies, exaggerations, etc., do some portions of the client's presentation just seem too "neat," as if coming out of a textbook?


■    ## Comments

It would be useful if graduate training programs in the mental health professions emphasized more the use of physiological measures in detecting deception. For example, the psychologist's extensive background in the study of human behavior and expertise in interviewing and psychological testing could easily be supplemented by this specific training. This not only would facilitate the accuracy of general psychological testing, it would also provide our court system with a much more expert and effective effort toward the detection of deception than is available from the usually minimally trained polygrapher (Smith and Meyer, 1987; Rogers, 1988).

# CHAPTER 17

# Criminal Responsibility (Insanity), Civil Commitment, Competency, and the Criminal Personality

Forensic issues are becoming increasingly important to mental health professionals (Meyer, 1992a). The clinician can be brought into the forensic arena in a number of ways, as is evident in the list on the following page.

However, most of these roles only come about if the clinician chooses to enter the forensic arena, e.g., helping to decide if parole should be granted, taking on child-custody or personal-injury cases, etc. Yet, any clinician, because of the status of one of his or her clients, can easily become involved in three of the broad and traditional areas on the interface of law and mental health: criminal responsibility, civil commitment, and competency. A discussion of the clinical assessment of the criminal personality is included in this chapter.

> **Reply to a plaintiff who claims his cabbages were eaten by your goat: "You had no cabbages. If you did they were not eaten. If they were eaten, it was not by a goat. If they**

**TABLE 17.1**   The Various Potential Roles of the Forensic Clinician as Fact-Finder in the Legal Arena

| CLIENT | ISSUE |
|---|---|
| Criminal Defendant (Client) | Criminally responsible or "insane"? |
| Witness to Event | Adequate enough in perceptual and information processing abilities? |
| Child Witness | Mature enough to testify? |
| Rape Victim | Credible or psychotic fantasy? |
| Offender | Dangerous to release? |
| Juvenile Offender | Emotionally and cognitively mature enough to stand trial as an adult? Dangerous to be released? |
| Parole Candidate | Rehabilitated? Dangerous to release? |
| Civil Commitment (Client) | Dangerous to community or to self? |
| Parent | Responsible enough to have custody of child? |
| Criminal Defendant | Competent to be executed? |
| Testator (Client) | Competent to make a valid will? |
| Contracting Party (Client) | Competent to make binding contract? |
| Guardianship/ Conservatorship (Client) | Able to make decisions on finances, etc.? |

Adapted from W. Curran and S. Pollack, "Mental Health and Justice." In W. Curran, A. L. McGarry, and S. Shah, Eds., *Forensic Psychiatry and Psychology*. Philadelphia: F. A. Davis, 1986.

> were eaten by a goat, it was not my goat. And, if it was
> my goat, he was insane." (Youngner, I.; quoted by
> McElhaney, J. W., *Trial Notebook, 2nd ed.* Chicago:
> American Bar Association, 1987, p. 49.)

# ■ Criminal Responsibility (Insanity)

The tests and standards used to assess insanity, or, more broadly, criminal responsibility, vary somewhat from state to state (Wettstein et al., 1991). The traditional formulation, referred to as the M'Naghten (1843) Test, is again influential in many states and is the basic concept in the Federal Rules of Evidence. This in large part reflects John Hinckley, Jr.'s acquittal by insanity subsequent to his attempted assassination of President Reagan (Low et al., 1986). The M'Naghten criterion is whether or not a person committed an unlawful act as a result of "defect of reason" arising out of "a disease of the mind" that results in not "knowing the nature of the act" or, if the individual was aware of it, not knowing that it was wrong. This is often referred to cryptically as the "knowing-right-from-wrong standard."

In 1954, the Durham Rule, whose primary author was Judge David Bazelon, focused chiefly on the issue of whether the unlawful behavior was "the product of mental disease or mental defect" (*Durham* v. *United States,* 1954). Although this rule received initial acclaim, it has seldom been followed since.

A legal definition of insanity that has been especially influential on legal theorists—although to a somewhat lesser degree on state laws—was formulated by the American Law Institute (ALI) and is included in the Model Penal Code. It is comprised of two major sections:

1. Persons are not responsible for criminal conduct if, at the time of such conduct, as a result of mental disease or defect they lack substantial capacity either to appreciate the criminality (wrongfulness) of their conduct or to conform their conduct to the requirements of law.

2. The terms ("mental disease" or "defect") do not include an abnormality manifested only by repeated criminal or otherwise antisocial conduct.

The rationale for the adoption of the ALI is well articulated in the case of *People* v. *Drew* (1978):

First, the ALI test adds a volitional element, the ability to conform to legal requirements, which is missing from the *M'Naghten* Test. Second, it avoids the all-or-nothing language of *M'Naghten* and permits a verdict based on lack of substantial capacity.... Third, the ALI test is broad enough to permit a psychiatrist to set before the trier of

facts a full picture of the defendant's mental impairments and flexible enough to adapt to future changes in psychiatric theory and
diagnosis. Fourth, by referring to the defendant's capacity to "appreciate" the wrongfulness of his conduct the test confirms our
holding ... that mere verbal knowledge of right and wrong does not
prove sanity. Finally, by establishing a broad text of nonresponsibil-
ity, including elements of volition as well as cognition, the test provides the foundation on which we can order and rationalize the con-
voluted and occasionally inconsistent law of diminished capacity
(p. 282).

Criticism of the ALI Rule focus on its alleged too-great-flexibility and
the difficulties in determining what is specifically meant by "appreciate"
and by "substantial capacity." Also, some jurisdictions used the phrase
"appreciate the criminality," while others used "appreciate the
wrongfulness," and they seem to communicate different concepts (Rogers,
1986). As the court noted, the ALI Rule has both a "cognitive" arm ("appreciate the wrongfulness") and a "volitional" arm ("capacity to conform
conduct to the requirements of the law"). The volitional arm is essentially an "irresistible impulse" test (discussed later); the question is
whether the defendant could have controlled himself. This question, of
course, presents the difficult problem of distinguishing between an irresistible impulse and an impulse that is not resisted. Many states have
dropped or ignored the "conform," or volitional, element, thus rendering the ALI Rule very similar to the M'Naghten Rule. This is consistent with the present Federal Rules of Evidence (the rules that apply
to federal rather than state courts) which offer what is basically a
cognitive test similar to the M'Naghten Rule.

Before proceeding, it should be remembered that the expert witness,
the clinician who offers an opinion in this area, does not make the
ultimate decision, as stated in *United States* v. *Freeman* (1966):

At bottom, the determination whether a man is or is not held responsible for his conduct is not a medical but a legal, social, or moral
judgment, ... it is a society as a whole, represented by a judge or
jury which decides whether a man with the characteristics described
should or should not be held accountable for his acts (pp. 619–620).

Inherent in all of this is the fact that insanity is not a
psychological/medical term, but is instead a legal term. Hence, the expert has the problem of transforming and explaining clinical data in
such a way as to facilitate the jury's opinion about whether the individual is insane. Although the judge and jury ultimately decide the
issue, it is not uncommon for the expert to be asked indirectly, and
sometimes directly, whether the individual is "insane." Also, even
though a subsequent term, "incompetency," refers to the person's mental status at the time of the examination, there is an extra difficulty

in that insanity requires an inference to mental status at the time of the alleged act (Szasz, 1987). This extra difficulty may be another reason why the insanity defense, in whatever form it is put forth, is not often effective as a defense (Roberts and Golding, 1991; Smith and Meyer, 1987).

Under the influence of the ALI standard, it seems reasonably clear that several conditions in DSM-III-R can be considered to fit with the concept of insanity. First, the presence of delusions, hallucinations, or other significant interference with cognitive functioning should be enough to warrant an assertion of insanity. Hence, most of schizophrenic disorders and those dissociative disorders in which the behavior is relevant to the criminal act would be considered appropriate. Also, in most instances, the delusional (paranoid) disorders and some of the severe affective disorders, such as manic episode and depressive episode, would fit these criteria. Some juries readily accept the idea that hallucinations and delusions void criminal responsibility. However, a true connection has to be made between these phenomena and the alleged offense. Appropriate sections in this text deal with the specific diagnostic criteria commonly associated with these categories.

Juries are also usually more willing to see organic conditions that are coincident with the alleged offense as both more "real" and more causal, even when there is little reason to argue cause rather than correlation (Smith and Meyer, 1987).

Wettstein et al. (1991) asked four forensic psychiatrists to indicate whether they thought 164 defendants met any or all of four major insanity tests (the ALI cognitive test, the ALI volitional component, the American Psychiatric Association Test, and the M'Naughten Rule). These raters decided that 97.5 percent of the defendants met the ALI volitional criterion, 73.9 percent met the APA criterion, 70.3 percent met the M'Naghten Rule, and 69.5 percent met the ALI cognitive criterion. Nearly two-thirds of the defendants met all four insanity tests, and 24.4 percent met only the ALI volitional test. Thus, elimination of the volitional test for insanity reduced the rate of psychiatric recommendations of acquittal by about 25 percent. The authors conclude that the primary logical division between volitional and cognitive standards appears to be powerful but that distinctions between types of cognitive standards are not very potent.

☐          IRRESISTIBLE IMPULSE

Because of the narrow cognitive focus of the M'Naghten Rule, there have been a variety of attempts to establish "irresistible impulse" as an additional rule, essentially beginning with *State v. Thompson* in 1834 (Rogers, 1986) and then evolving in the United States in *Parsons v. State* (1887) and its federal counterpart, *Davis v. United States* (1897). As noted, the central problem for both courts and clinicians has been to differentiate between an impulse that is irresistible and one that has not been resisted. In that regard, the reader is referred to Chapters 10 (Disorders of Impulse Control) and 16 (Malingering). In practice, this variation of criminal responsibility has not received strong support from either courts or clinicians, so it is recognized in only a few states. Federal courts have specifically curtailed its applicability to compulsive gambling (*United States v. Tonero*, 1984) and to the addictions (*United States v. Lions*, 1984), and when it has received any support, it is usually with "command hallucinations" in schizophrenia and in severe obsessive-compulsive disorder cases. Courts and legislatures have had great problems with the notion of irresistible impulse. On the one hand, it presents both conceptual and practical difficulties. On the other hand, it does provide an insanity defense for a small group who (at least at the extreme) are severely emotionally disturbed and for whom criminal responsibility is problematic. The political acceptability of the volitional test/ irresistible impulse has waxed and waned over the years, often depending on its use in some notable case. In recent years it has been at a low point.

## EXCEPTIONS TO INSANITY JUDGMENTS

There are two major exceptions to a judgment of insanity. The first is those conditions resulting from substance abuse, particularly if the substance was voluntarily ingested. As asserted in *Barrett v. United States* (1977):

**Temporary insanity created by voluntary use of alcohol or drugs will not relieve an accused criminal of responsibility even if that mental condition would otherwise meet the applicable legal definition of insanity (p. 62).**

However, there are occasions when this is not so clearly applicable. First, insanity may be argued if the substance abuse was *not* voluntary, i.e., when caused by another person without the victim's awareness, for example, where someone spikes the victim's drink. Second, when "insanity" continues well beyond the actual effect of the drug use that was a catalyst for it, as stated in *State of New Jersey v. Stasio* (1979):

**Insanity is available when the voluntary use of the intoxicant or drug results in a fixed state of insanity after the influence of the intoxicant or drug has spent itself (p. 467).**

The second exception to a judgment of insanity, under either the M'Naghten or ALI rules, is articulated in the secondary paragraph of the ALI Rule in stating there is no insanity defense available where there is an "abnormality manifested only by repeated criminal or otherwise antisocial contact." This would usually disallow the antisocial-personality syndrome (Wettstein et al., 1991).

Two of the other issues as regards criminal responsibility are guilty but mentally ill (GBMI) and diminished capacity. The relatively new GBMI, which essentially allows a finding of both insanity and guilt, has received much attention, probably because it gives the jury a way out of an especially difficult decision. Indeed, there is evidence that the availability of the GBMI defense substantially reduces the use of the Not Guilty By Reason of Insanity pleas and verdicts (Roberts and Golding, 1991). But the criteria and techniques for the insanity decision component of the GBMI are often the same as in other insanity formulations.

Diminished capacity is a potential, partial defense to a criminal charge. It permits a reduction of the level of offense on a showing that the defendant is actually incapable of forming the required intent. Ironically, of the many and varied referrals to the Center for Forensic Psychiatry in Ann Arbor, Michigan, for consideration of this defense, it has almost never been found to be viable in practice (Clark, 1988).

□ ASSESSMENT OF INSANITY

Kurlychek and Jordan (1980) presents an interesting study that compared the MMPI profiles of thirty male defendants who were found to be criminally responsible with those of twenty male defendants who were determined to be criminally not responsible. The modal code in the nonresponsible group was the 8-6 code. Six nonresponsibles obtained that code, and only two responsibles did. Three responsibles each obtained 2-3 and 2-7 codes, but no nonresponsibles scored in that pattern. The modal code for the responsible group was 8-7 (six subjects), although three nonresponsible subjects also obtained that pattern. The high incidence of the 8-6 code in the nonresponsible clients suggested to the authors that highly delusional thought processes are a prevalent factor in nonresponsible defendants. The common codes in the responsible group (8-7, 2-3, 2-7, and 2-0) indicate that more neurotic and inhibitory effects on any psychotic tendencies are found in responsible individuals.

Since faking-bad is particularly likely to be an issue in a decision about insanity, the reader is referred to Chapter 16. All reasonable precautions should be taken to prevent this. At the same time, clients should always be clearly told of the reason for the evaluation, what kind of decisions the information will be used for, and to whom it will be disseminated. To buttress the credibility of testimony, a number of clinicians argue that it is helpful to have protocols scored and interpreted by computer. Although this only offers part of the information a clinician needs to interpret the profile, they assert this lends support and apparent credence to testimony. On the other hand, introducing computer-generated reports into court easily leaves one "locked into" many of the comments in the report that the clinician may disagree with, as well as the potential ploy then available to a cross-examining attorney of asserting that the clinician has to rely on such a report because of a lack of expertise with that test.

As yet, effective "tests" specific to the assessment of insanity have not been developed, in contrast to those tests used to efficiently evaluate competency to stand trial (Meyer, 1992a). However, there is data to suggest that the Rogers Criminal Responsibility Assessment Scale (R-CRAS) is useful as a decision tree (Rogers et al., 1981; Rogers 1986, 1988). Twenty-three variables are rated to give scores on five discrete scales (the client's reliability, evidence of possible CNSI, psychopathology, cognitive control, and behavioral control). A hierarchical decision model, based on the ALI Rule, is then applied to these data.

Several studies have assessed the reliability and validity of the R-CRAS. Rogers (1986) reports that, overall, "reliability findings indicated a moderate degree of reliability for the individual variables (mean reliability coefficient was .58) and much higher reliability coefficients for the decision variables (average kappa coefficient was .81). Most important, clinical opinion regarding sanity was in almost perfect agreement, with a 97 percent concordance rate and a kappa coefficient of .94" (p. 168). Construct validity studies produced a .88 concordance rate, and a moderate degree of internal consistency (mean alpha of .60) was obtained. Grisso (1986) is generally positive about the value of the R-CRAS, only citing as negative the low reliability of several individual criteria and the absence of factor-analytic studies to statistically assess the structure of the R-CRAS.

Another scale, the MSE, devised by Slobogin et al. (1984), can be effective in one direction and, in that sense, is a good screening device. Those who are found on the MSE to have no significant mental abnormality almost uniformly are found in later court dispositions to be seen similarly. However, a finding of mental abnormality on the MSE has little predictive validity to subsequent court decisions.

## ■ Civil Commitment

Clinicians are becoming increasingly involved in assessments of dangerousness to self or others as this relates to civil commitment cases (Grisso, 1986). During the 1970s and early 1980s, the requirements for civil commitments were tightened considerably. Also, in the celebrated Donaldson case (*O'Connor v. Donaldson*, 1975), commitment without some form of treatment was held to be unconstitutional.

At present, the basic requirements in most states for civil commitment are presence of mental illness or disorder, leading to dangerousness. This dangerousness is usually further interpreted as being physically dangerous to others or unable to provide the basics of life for onself. In addition (particularly following the Donaldson case), most states require some form of effective treatment must be available where the client is to be committed, and a number of states require that the least restrictive alternative mode of dealing with the patient should be used. There is now a clear trend toward expanding the scope of civil commitment, usually under doctrines that sound very much like *parens patriae.* These new statutes are often patterned after a proposal endorsed by the American Psychiatric Association to permit commitment of the "gravely disabled," which is defined fairly broadly as those who may deteriorate mentally without hospitalization. One problematic consideration in commitment is that, according to *Buchanan v. Kentucky* (1987), evidence gathered by clinicians during involuntary civil commitment evaluations may in some circumstances be used against the person in a related criminal proceeding.

The prediction of dangerousness is one of the most difficult assessment questions a clinician must face (Monahan, 1981, 1984) (see Chapter 14). The decision has to focus on reasonably immediate dangerousness to self or others, and the clinician must come to a decision under the standard of "reasonable probability." On the first point, the clinician could act on the most accurate available prediction of dangerousness by simply collecting all persons who had been incarcerated for a severe assault just as they left a penitentiary and then commit them, since in the long run it is reasonably certain that a high proportion of these individuals will endanger others. Of course, most of them do not provide an immediate threat of dangerousness—the issue at hand.

With regard to the clinician's prediction of dangerousness in an individual client, the reader is referred to the sections on aggression and suicide potential in Chapter 14. Also, assessments for mental retardation are appropriate, since in some cases there is an inability to provide for one's basic life care. Consideration of organic dysfunction (or CNSI) may also be relevant, as in the senile individual who is a diabetic. Such persons would probably not be able to take medication as required and in that sense would endanger their own lives. The clinician must recall, however, that the ability to predict specific dangerousness in any reasonably circumscribed period of time is very low and, in most cases, probably not at a level to warrant the cost, that is, the restriction of a person's freedom and civil liberties.

## ■ Competency

Competency refers to a variety of legal doctrines—most notably, standing trial, managing one's own affairs (guardianship), and the contesting of a will—and the criteria differ for each of these (Smith and Meyer, 1987). There is even an increasing interest in "competency to be executed," evolving from the Supreme Court case of *Ford v. Wainwright*

(1986). With the exception of competency to stand trial, clinicians traditionally are not involved. However, some attorneys are now asking psychologists or other clinicians to assess their clients at the time they write a will if the attorney thinks there might be any future contesting of the will on the basis of competency. The clinician's report, made at the time of the writing of the will, is then filed with the will. This serves to make any later challenge rather absurd since the original assessment will be based on far more data than will be available following the individual's death. The procedure can be further strengthened by having the signing of the will and/or part of the evaluation videotaped as a record for later queries.

In general, competency to stand trial requires that a person has adequate mental ability to understand the charges and to participate in his or her own defense (Grisso, 1986). Insanity refers to the mental condition at the time the person allegedly committed the crime, whereas incompetency to stand trial refers to the person's mental condition at the time of the trial. In addition, and more specifically, the Supreme Court has stipulated that "the test must be whether he has sufficient present ability to consult with his lawyer with a reasonable degree of rational understanding—and whether he has a rational as well as a factual understanding of the proceedings against him" (*Dusky v. United States*, 1960). The individual has to understand the nature of the proceedings with which he or she is involved and the consequences of those proceedings and manifest an ability to cooperate with the attorney in defense preparation. Ironically, as held in *Colorado v. Connelly* (1986), severe mental illness (and apparently, incompetency to stand trial) does not necessarily make a confession involuntary and therefore inadmissible.

These are clearly different criteria from any of the notions relating to insanity. These are much more specific and more related to actual behavior than to inferred mental status. Yet, many clinicians who testify regarding incompetency do not realize this differentiation and as a result often confuse the issue of competency with that of either "psychosis" or "responsibility."

One of the major ways an individual can be incompetent is as a result of inadequate intellectual ability; the reader is referred to Chapter 11 on mental retardation. However, the clinician should not make a decision by using a strict transition from any particular IQ to an arbitrary cutoff point for competency. The IQ is a critical variable, but the final decision should also take into account other factors, such as history of adaptation, common sense (both in the client and in the clinician), and any already observed ability to cooperate with the attorney and discuss the issues of law. Most individuals with mild mental retardation can cooperate effectively, although not always. As one proceeds through the levels of moderate, severe, and profound mental retardation (see Chapter

11), the proportion of those persons who cannot competently assist in their trials rises quickly.

If clinicians do any significant number of competency screenings, it is strongly recommended that they become familiar with and use the various competency screening instruments that are available (Grisso, 1986). An excellent set was devised by the Laboratory of Community Psychiatry (1973) at Harvard, particularly the Competency Assessment Instrument (CAI) and the Competency Screening Test (CST). That group also attempted to develop a projective test for competency, similar in design to the TAT, but so far have not found adequate reliability and validity.

The CAI attempts to standardize and structure the interview procedure; unfortunately, instructions for its use are not at all detailed. It is formulated as a set of thirteen areas of ego awareness, covering virtually all of the legal grounds required of defendants if they are to cope effectively with such proceedings. Some of the areas assessed by the CAI are awareness of available legal defenses, understanding of court procedures, appreciation of charges, range and nature of possible penalties, appraisal of possible outcome, capacity to inform the attorney adequately, and capacity to testify. The client is then evaluated on a scoring system of one (total incompetency) to six (totally competent) on the degree of ability in each area, based on an extensive interview as well as the history data. For example, in the ego function of "quality of relating to attorney," some of the suggested questions are "Do you think your attorney is trying to do a good job for you?" or "Do you agree with his plans for handling your case?"

Interrater reliability on the scoring of responses to the items in the latest version of the CAI is .87, definitely an acceptable figure. The authors make the point that the efficacy and reliability of this instrument, as well as the CST (unfortunately, developed on an inpatient population and not originally standardized on an outpatient population), are directly correlated with experience with the instrument and with the competency process itself. Reliability increased dramatically from the point of the clinician's first experience with the CAI to its fourth or fifth use. Before using these instruments, a test use with some colleague consultation is advised. Persons can obtain a full report of this project, entitled *Competency to Stand Trial and Mental Illness*, from the National Institute of Mental Health, Center for Crime and Delinquency, 5600 Fishers Lane, Rockville, MD 20852, or can get in touch with the Laboratory of Community Psychiatry at Harvard University.

The Competency Screening Test is a sentence-completion technique that has been copyrighted by the project's psychologists, Paul Lipsitt and David Lelos. It consists of twenty-two sentence items, such as "When Phil was accused of the crime, he . . . ," and the like. A handbook in the appendix of the report gives differently scored answers for each item, as they are scaled as either 0, 1, or 2, with higher scores indicating higher levels of competency.

The five items that were found to be particularly predictive of competency are*

**9.** When the lawyer questioned his client in court, the client said . . .

**13.** When the witness testifying against Harry gave incorrect evidence, he . . .

**14.** When Bob disagreed with his lawyer on his defense . . .

**19.** When I think of being sent to prison . . .

**22.** If I had a chance to speak to the judge . . .

The scoring emphasizes degrees of legal understanding and psychological integration. For example, for number 9, answers such as "I am not guilty" or "I did not do anything" are assigned a 2, whereas an overspecific, vague, or hesitant response, such as "He had no knowledge of it" or "I don't know why—I guess I'm not guilty," brings the score down to 1. Irrelevant answers such as "He was too nervous to talk" or "The obvious thing" are scored zero. Similar scoring procedures are used with the other five items.

An impressive level of interrater reliability of .93 was obtained for the CST, using standard Z scores. Also, the overall predictive accuracy of the CST "in agreement with subsequent court determinations of competency," was 89.7 percent. By combining the CST predictive information with the validity scales of the MMPI-2 and the female and male Draw-A-Person test, an accuracy rate above .90 is obtained.

There is some evidence that the CST screening was more valid than the highly structured and practiced judgments made by their trained raters. For example, some persons who were eventually designated as incompetent by the raters, based on overall data, actually showed clear evidence of competence throughout all the tests. However, these particular individuals had a history of markedly aggressive behavior, and their crimes were repugnant to the community. Hence, the raters may have been swayed by those considerations.

Shatin (1979) found that a brief form of the CST (again, items 9, 13, 14, 19, 22) correlated .92 with the full-scale version in twenty-one female patients in a forensic psychiatric service examined for mental competency to stand trial, a result consistent with some data collected by the test's authors. This brief form also classified seventeen of the twenty-one patients in direct agreement with the results of a full clinical evaluation. Thus, there is good reason to believe that these five items will be

---

*P. Lipsitt and D. Lelos, *Competency Screening Test,* copyright 1970 by authors. Used with permission.

useful and applicable to preliminary competency evaluations, possibly by incorporation into the Meyer Information Battery found in Appendix A.

An alternative competency instrument has been presented by Golding et al. (1984). Based on their earlier work showing that elaborate live-in assessments for competency are not cost-effective, these authors developed the Interdisciplinary Fitness Interview (IFI). The manual and training procedures are more explicit than those for the CAI. There are three major sections: legal issues, psychopathological issues, and overall evaluation. The section on legal issues is divided into five areas. In a partial reversal of the trend started by the CAI, the authors have taken the position that psychopathological questions should be explicitly assessed in addition to purely legal questions and that both should contribute to the overall judgment of competency. The IFI can be used either as a screening device or as a full-scale assessment.

An excellent competency examination would include the CAI as a means of structuring the interview, the CST, a WAIS-R, an MMPI-2, and further assessments specific to potential malingering and personality functioning, such as the 16 PF and the Marlowe-Crowne Social Desirability Scale (Smith and Meyer, 1987; Grisso, 1986).

## The Criminal Personality

Although the DSM-III-R discusses the category of antisocial personality (see Chapter 9), it does little to distinguish the greater variety of individuals who are easily subsumed under the label "criminal personality" (Meyer, 1992a; Hare et al., 1991). There are a number of general characteristics of the criminal personality. The majority of offenses are caused by individuals aged twenty-one or younger, and approximately 80 percent of adult chronic offenders were chronic offenders before age eighteen. Overall, criminals are male by about a 5:1 ratio—up to 50:1 in the various categories of aggressive crime. With the rise in feminism, the ratio is increasingly closer to parity for "white-collar crime," but the high ratio of males persists for aggressive crimes. Both poor sociocultural conditions and heredity are major factors. Other more specific factors are low intelligence, especially verbal intelligence; mesomorphic body type; a history of hyperactivity; left-handedness; cold, harsh, and/or inconsistent parenting; psychopathy; and impulsivity.

By far the most exhaustive and elegant research on the psychological test discrimination of the criminal personality has been carried out by Edwin Megargee and his colleagues (Megargee and Bohn, 1979; Carbonell et al., 1984). Their typology, based on empirically derived and validated MMPI research, has been exhaustively studied by Megargee and his colleagues and students in a variety of settings, and it has received strong and independent verification from other researchers (Edinger, 1979; Hawk, 1983; Kalichman, 1988; Meyer, 1992a).

Megargee established ten reasonably discrete subcategories of the criminal personality, using incarcerated prisoners. These ten typologies and their associated MMPI-2 patterns are presented here; readers are strongly cautioned, however, to use Megargee's computer tapes if they are going to do any extensive diagnostic work in this area, as these tapes would provide a much more accurate assessment of those individuals who fall on the borderline of two or more patterns. Any reader who is regularly involved in diagnostic work with prisoners should be familiar with Megargee and Bohn (1979). The system is not generally applicable to short-form MMPI-2s. Even if one is not doing computer assessments, Megargee and Bohn provide more-extensive decision rules for the categories than are available here. Megargee can be reached at the Department of Psychology, Florida State University, Tallahassee, FL 32306.

Megargee's ten subtypes were given alphabetical names (e.g., Able, Baker) and in the early publication were listed in that order. In the later and more comprehensive publication (Megargee and Bohn, 1979), the subtypes were listed in order from the least pathological to the most pathological, and that system will be used here.

## ■ Megargee's Ten Criminal Subtypes*

☐ ITEM

Individuals in the Item classification show little or no psychopathology, which is fortunate since this is the largest group of the ten, comprising 19 percent of his prison sample. They are generally nonaggressive, friendly, and extroverted and are likely to have been incarcerated for victimless crimes. They come from stable and warm family backgrounds and have had the fewest problems when growing up. They seem able to make committed and lasting friendships.

They present an essentially normal MMPI-2 profile, with the major characteristic being an overall absence of elevations, although about 50 percent manifest one T score greater than 70. That high point is usually on the 5 or 9 scale. There is no consistent two-point code associated with this group; any elevation tends to be on scales 4, 5, or 9.

Although Items are inclined to pilfer things while on prison work assignments, they are at the same time rated as the most dependable workers by their supervisors. They show a low recidivism rate, and it

*This material, adapted from *Classifying Criminal Offenders* (Sage Library of Social Research, *82*, 118–35, 177–233), by E. Megargee and M. Bohn, copyright 1979, is reprinted by permission of the publisher, Sage Publications (Beverly Hills).

would probably be just as useful to them, and certainly far less expensive, if they were to be immediately placed on probation.

☐ ## EASY

The Easy group, like the Item group, has relatively benign psychopathology. They comprise 7 percent of Megargee's sample. They are brighter and appear to have had more natural advantages than the other groups. Coincidentally, they are well characterized by their randomly assigned label: Not only has life been easy, but they have also taken it easy—they are classic underachievers. Interestingly enough, they have had a high number of siblings who were behavior problems, but all indications are that the parental situation was good for Easy inmates themselves.

On the average, they show a "benign profile" on the MMPI-2, with all scores under the 70 T mark. A 4-3 profile is most common, and scale 2 is often relatively elevated. This group is occasionally confused with subsequent groups Baker and George, although these groups are more likely to show a spike on 2 than is the Easy group.

Easys show little upset or discomfort at being in prison They have the lowest recidivism rate of all groups, probably because they have the most in the way of natural assets on which to draw. Probation into academic and vocational training, with firm but kind limits, would appear to be a much more efficient option for this group than incarceration.

☐ ## BAKER

Bakers are a relatively small group, only 4 percent of the sample, and they are best labeled "neurotic delinquents." They are passive, anxious, and socially isolated individuals who are inclined to depend on alcohol to deal with everyday problems and upsets.

The most common MMPI-2 profile obtained is the 4-2, and the second most common is the 4-9. On the average, Bakers are moderately high on scale 4, with a secondary elevation of scale 2 and an interesting and consistent spike on 6 (athough this is not a high spike). They can be confused with Georges, but Georges show a higher elevation on the neurotic triad: scales 1, 2, and 3. Also, a mild elevation of 6 is more characteristic of Bakers than Georges.

Oddly, Bakers are surprisingly disruptive in institutions, although in a passive-aggressive fashion. The combination of supportive psychotherapy, vocational counseling, and an Alcoholics Anonymous program is the optimal treatment.

☐     ABLE

Ables are the second most common group in Megargee's population, comprising 17 percent of the overall group. Ables are sociopathic, opportunistic, self-assured, and immature. Rather than being hostile or antisocial, they are amoral and hedonistic.

The essential feature of the Able MMPI-2 profile is bimodality, with distinctive peaks on scales 4 and 9. The 4-9/9-4 two-point combination covers 83 percent of this sample. They are unlike the Delta group, where scale 4 is much greater than scale 9. Ables typically show little or no elevation on scales other than 4 and 9.

Although Ables move into subcultural delinquency at an early age, all indications are that they had a good family backgrounds. These backgrounds may explain why they perform well in prisons, at least when supervised. A controlled community-living situation is thought to be the best disposition for this group.

☐     GEORGE

The George group, 7 percent of the sample, closely resembles the Able group, except that Georges are brighter and come from more deviant family backgrounds. Georges "do their own time" and are characterized as quiet but not passive loners.

The 2-4/4-2 profile, with a distinctive slope to the right, is characteristic of this group. They are close to the Baker profile in some respects, but show higher elevations overall and a greater slope to the right in the profile. Also, there is no secondary spike on scale 6 in Georges. They can be confused with the Easy group, but the scale 3 score is less prominent in the profile of Georges.

☐     DELTA

Unlike previous groups, Deltas, who comprise 10 percent of the population, are a definite pathological group. These bright psychopaths are sociable, yet they are easily provoked to violence. Reflecting the classic descriptors of the primary psychopath, Deltas are impulsive, unable to delay gratification, amoral, do not profit from experience, are high in stimulation-seeking, are prone to violence, and seldom experience guilt or anxiety.

Deltas are likely to show a spike on scale 4, with an occasional secondary spike on scale 2. They are relatively low on scales 6, 8, and 9, so on occasion they can be confused with the Able group, one that is very different behaviorally. The best method of discrimination is the distinct bimodality on scales 4 and 9 that marks the Able group.

☐                    JUPITER

This rare group, 3 percent of the population, shows indication of making efforts toward a positive adjustment, but Jupiters are badly handicapped by very deprived family backgrounds. Unfortunately for this group, modeling is an enduring influence in teaching a person to deviate from the rules of society. As a result, Jupiters do not always make good adjustments in spite of their apparent motivation.

The Jupiter MMPI-2 profile is singularly marked by a climb to the right on the scales. Scale 8 is the most common peak scale, with scale 9 close behind, and then a high elevation of scale 7 further behind. Scale 6 is relatively high, reflecting their tendency toward paranoia. This group is defined by exclusion. If an MMPI-2 profile fits the concept of a climb to the right, and is excluded from other categories, it is labeled Jupiter.

Just the opposite of Easys, Jupiters do not have good family backgrounds, skills preparation, or even abilities, but they do have motivation. As a result, a heavy emphasis on developing basic academic skills, vocational training, and a supportive group experience at a halfway house are necessary ingredients for the rehabilitation of Jupiters.

☐                    FOXTROT

Foxtrots, 8 percent of the sample, have all the bad characteristics listed. They experienced poor family backgrounds, are poorly educated and not very intelligent, are antisocial, and are disturbed emotionally. They are evasive and easily provoke anger in others.

They are classically high on the 9, 4, and 8 scales. The elevation on the 8 scale is helpful in discriminating this group from the Ables, who appear more average on 8 and lower in general on the other scales.

Foxtrots do make friends with a few similarly deviant individuals, but by and large, they provoke hostility. They are readily aggressive toward the staff if there is much contact with them. Foxtrots can use help of any sort, but not surprisingly, they are quite unresponsive to any efforts to provide it. As a result, they have a very high recidivism rate.

☐                    CHARLIE

Charlies, comprising 9 percent of Megargee's population, are bitter and hostile antisocial personalities, with a definite paranoid element. In addition, they are usually intellectually, academically, and socially deficient. They are alienated and hostile loners who easily become violent.

Charlies show characteristic MMPI-2 elevations on 8, 6, and 4. The 8-6 and 8-4 profiles are the most common. Charles can be confused with

Foxtrots, but they have a high 6 score relative to Foxtrots. Charlies may also be confused with the How group, although Hows tend to be high on scales 1, 2, and 3.

From the perspective of violence in the prison or in the community and the high probability of recidivism, Charlie is one of the most disturbed criminal subgroups. Treatments useful for paranoid individuals are especially applicable here.

☐        HOW

The How group is large, comprising 13 percent of the sample. They are similar to Jupiters in that they are significantly handicapped by deprived early environments, but Hows are much more psychologically disturbed and less willing to change than are Jupiters. They are highly anxious individuals who also show some depression. Part of this depression stems from their roles as "reluctant loners," since they continually face rejection by others rather than withdraw from social contacts.

Like the Item group, their MMPI-2 profile is defined more by elevation than by specific subscale scores. Whereas Items are defined by low elevations across the scales, Hows show high elevations on most scales, especially elevations in a jagged pattern on scales 8, 2, 4, and 1. The profile is distinctive in its jagged elevation throughout the right and left sides of the profile. Scale 8 is the highest scale in more than 50 percent of the profiles obtained.

Like Foxtrots, Hows are prone to be aggressive toward staff if there is a high amount of interaction. Psychotherapy and chemotherapy, as well as any vocational and social-engineering programs available, are needed in rehabilitating them. Unfortunately, rehabilitation is seldom successful, and the recidivism rate is high.

# Summary

As noted, there is data from a number of researchers indicating that this system is relevant throughout most state and federal penal institutions. The system is applicable to women with almost the same accuracy and efficiency as it is for men, the sample from which it was derived. Race was considered throughout Megargee's research, so this does not seem to be a disqualifying factor in applying this MMPI-2 system. There are expected minor age differences among the subgroups, and an offender's subgroup type may change with age. Overall, Charlies and Jupiters tend to be younger, and Easys tend to be older. The reader is also directed toward the discussion of the antisocial personality disorder, as well as the juvenile delinquent or conduct disorder, in Chapter 9.

# CHAPTER 18

# Professional Case Preparation and Presentation: For Office or Courtroom

This chapter presents guidelines for more effective case preparation. By following these guidelines, the clinician will not only function more efficiently, but will significantly lessen the probability of being accused of malpractice. After the discussions on malpractice issues, is the set of guidelines concerned with case preparation in general; this is followed by a model case report format that can easily be adapted to most clinical, neuropsychological, or forensic case situations. After that, I present guidelines for entering into a case as an expert witness, preparing for a deposition, and preparing for the actual courtroom appearance, if that is actually required. The chapter concludes with an examination of some of the major role conflicts a clinician often encounters in the legal arenas. Some of the major legal cases are specifically cited and discussed in Appendix B.

Some of this material is more extensively developed in Smith and Meyer (1987) and Meyer et al. (1988). The author was influenced by the notable contributions of such experts in the area as Shapiro (1991, 1984), Brodsky (1991), Grisso (1986), Melton et al., (1987), Monahan and Walker (1990), and others, so they will not be repeatedly cited throughout the chapter.

## ■     Malpractice

Malpractice considerations have been increasing for all mental health professionals. Claims are much higher against psychiatrists, in large part because they prescribe medication and use a number of intrusive techniques, such as ECT and psychosurgery. However, claims are increasing in every mental health sector. For example, during the first ten years (1961–71) of the malpractice insurance program of the American Psychological Association, only a few malpractice claims were made, and none were paid. During the 1976–80 period, however, 122 claims were processed, with estimated payments totaling $435,642, and both claims and payouts have continued to markedly increase since then.

While some malpractice claims have been based on intentional torts (e.g., battery, false imprisonment, or intentional infliction of mental distress), most are based on the torts of negligence and/or contract liability, i.e., DDDD – Dereliction of Duty Directly causing Damage. Overall, claims commonly arise from concepts such as unfair advantage (e.g., sexual improprieties), incorrect or inadequate treatment or diagnosis, failure to obtain informed consent, breach of confidentiality, wrongful involuntary commitment, failure to prevent suicide, nonfulfillment of contract (implicit or explicit), defamation, or failure to refer and/or to avoid practicing in a specific area where competence is lacking. As regards actual claims, sexual-impropriety claims – and payouts – are the most common for mental health practitioners in general.

## ■     Dual Relationships

Dual relationships, especially involving sexual intimacies, can occur with any client (Boyer, 1990). They are the primary malpractice risk issues for mental health practitioners as a whole. You should be extra alert if the client (a) reports a history of sexual abuse, (b) reports "problems" with prior therapist, (c) has a history of being litigious even if "in the right," (d) specifically sought treatment because of your "reputation" or particular treatment approach, (e) reports sexual affairs, especially if with authority figures, (f) seeks out physical contact of some sort or reports particular pleasure in coming to therapy, (g) brings you gifts or sends cards, (h) dresses or behaves in a seductive manner, or (i) attempts to control time or place for therapy, becoming upset if you do not meet these demands.

If you sense a developing problem in this regard, consider the following actions, suggested by Boyer (1990):

1. Obtain permission from the client to consult regularly with a colleague, preferably one with hospital privileges. If the client needs hospitalization during the course of treatment, collaborate on the

case. A team approach can help to keep the client from overwhelming any single clinician.

2. Use a treatment plan that is rather traditional. Set clear limits on therapy sessions and phone calls as to place and time.

3. Avoid the appearance of a friendship by not giving cards or gifts to the patient. If small gifts or cards are given to you by the client, clarify that is not expected. Do not accept large gifts.

4. Avoid touching or behaving toward the client in any way that could be interpreted as sexual. Do not meet the client in places or at times that could be misconstrued. It is not a good idea to provide social services to the client.

5. Place responsibility for the solving of reality problems on the client. Avoid interceding on the patient's behalf with her or his employers, attorneys, friends, or family.

6. As always, clearly document the transference issues in the patient record. Records of any consultations on the patient should also be included in the record.

7. Refer the client to a colleague if you believe you may be vulnerable to dual relationship pressures. Sometimes even a competent clinician can fall into some form of dual relationship with such clients.

8. If, after all of the above precautions, the client complains about your actions to some authorized body, follow the suggestions offered shortly for responding to such actions.

As noted, the guidelines that are discussed throughout this chapter will help avoid the spector of malpractice, in addition to promoting their primary purpose: effective and efficient clinical functioning. Furthermore, several specific steps may be taken to lessen malpractice probabilities: (1) think of records as eventual legal documents; (2) remember that courts can be very concrete in the assumption that "if it wasn't written down, it didn't happen"; (3) get written releases; (4) as noted, unless necessary, avoid touching clients, especially of the opposite sex; (5) avoid dual relationships to the degree possible—especially avoid business relationships that involve clients because these easily lead to later lawsuits; (6) don't collect overdue bills from clients who you could reasonably expect to be litigious and/or who expressed disappointment with their treatment; (7) avoid, to the degree feasible, high-risk clients, e.g., paranoid, borderline, or narcissistic clients, chronic legal offenders, sexual problems in a fragmenting marriage, the seriously depressed and/or suicidals, et al.; (8) if you are supervising students or other clinicians, make sure communication and insurance-liability issues are covered and clear; (9) remember that courts judge the "standard of care" from hindsight and from the expert testimony of your colleagues, so maintain and document colleague counsel and supervision where necessary (or, better yet, whenever there is a controversial client or issue, or, still better, as a consistent part of your practice), e.g., if you feel a client is attracted to you and/or vice-versa; (10) use any other professional or community resources whenever indicated, and be aware of the confounding and/or exacerbating effects of any psychotropic medications the client is taking; (11) make an effective termination with any problematic client, i.e., (a) discuss fully the issues of why and when, transition, and financial arrangements, (b) if you feel further treatment is indicated, make that clear, provide some referral options, offer to do whatever would facilitate referral, and clearly state your perceived consequences of the client not seeking further treatment, (c) send a termination letter, with the relevant details just noted, in a form that requires a return receipt.

If you become aware that a malpractice, ethics, or licensing complaint has become active, take the following actions, as suggested by professional activity groups in the various mental health professional organizations:

1. Consider the merits of the complaint. If the complaint is of minor nuisance value, it is possible (although I don't recommend it) that you will not need legal assistance in responding to the complaint. If the complaint seems at all serious, you should most certainly seek the advice of an attorney in responding to the complaint.

2. Cooperate with the ethics committee or licensing board in their investigation of the complaint. Become familiar with their rules and procedures. Provide the ethics committee/licensing board with the documentation they request. Contact the chair of the ethics committee or licensing board if you have any questions regarding their investigation.

3. Gather all relevant documents and records, but do not show them to anyone except the ethics committee or licensing board and your attorney.

4. Do not destroy any documents.

5. Prepare additional documents, such as chronicles of events to refresh your memory.

6. Remember that professional case consultation with colleagues is not generally considered privileged information.

7. Be familiar with all the issues in your case.

8. Do not attempt to resolve or settle the case yourself.

9. Provide copies of your files, calendars, notes, etc., as advised by your attorney. Keep the originals.

10. Avoid any public comments and do not make self-incriminating statements. Remember, most professional liability policies do not

cover ethics committee or licensing board complaints, since malpractice coverage is usually restricted to lawsuits. But consider a consult with an attorney before responding to an ethics committee or licensing board complaint.

## Professional Liability Suits

If you become aware of the possibility that a suit may be filed against you, gather together all available information on the matter, meticulously follow all of the relevant steps noted previously, and, additionally, take the following steps:

1. Contact your insurance carrier.
2. Do not attempt to resolve or settle the case yourself or with the plaintiff's attorney while not working with your own attorney.
3. Provide the insurance carrier with all the written information you have regarding the allegations.
4. Contact the attorney assigned to handle your case by the insurance company. Follow his or her advice. Remember, though, that you may additionally retain your own attorney on certain issues, if you wish.
5. Do not panic or discuss the situation with anyone not directly representing your interests except for privileged conversations with your attorney.
6. Prepare any additional documents that could be useful in refreshing your memory.
7. Do not distribute any documents without your attorney's approval and refer all communications from the plaintiff or plaintiff's attorney to your attorney.

## Response to Public or Media Inquiries

These kinds of issues often bring inquiries from the public and/or media. A good rule-of-thumb is to say "No comment." If you fear that one or two of your comments will be taken out of context, and at the same time you do not want to be portrayed as avoiding making a comment, state that you would be wiling to comment as long as it is stipulated that the interview as a whole will be broadcast or published. You could then challenge, in whatever fashion seemed appropriate, a published statement suggesting or stating that you were unwilling to make any comment. But, if you do speak out (on this, or just in response to inquiries in general from the media), observe the following guidelines to minimize complications:

1. Try to make sure the reporter and the news organization are reputable.

2. Ask that quotes be read back to you as a condition of talking, if possible.

3. When reporters call, tell them you want to think over their questions and you will call them back.

4. Think about the context of your comments within the article and how controversial the topic is. Will your comments hurt anyone?

5. Ask the reporter what assurances can be given that he or she won't draw conclusions you are not making.

6. Ask yourself if you are violating anyone's confidentiality in speaking to the media and if you need a signed waiver.

In any case, using the specific steps already noted as well as the guidelines that follow should help you practice more effectively and avoid malpractice.

## ■ General Principles for Case Preparation

Clinicians can take a number of measures to insure that their procedures are ethical, appropriate, and expert. This set of suggestions concerns general issues with which most professionals in these areas would concern themselves; later, we will discuss the preparation of reports, the preparation for depositions, and the active courtroom appearance. The general suggestions for case preparation are as follows:

1. Don't take on a case in which you do not have a reasonable degree of expertise. There are numerous examples of mental health professionals taking on cases in which they only have a passing awareness of the issues or the requirements of practice. If you are trying to branch into a new area, make sure that you receive appropriate background education and supervision. After all, even the best and most experienced clinicians continue to use colleague consultation throughout their careers; indeed, such clinicians may be the best. It is also appropriate to inform the client, in a nonthreatening fashion, if this is a new area for you and to tell the client what the limits are that can be expected from your participation.

2. Establish a clear contract with your client. At the very least, make a thorough oral presentation in a contractual manner of what the client can expect from you and also of what you will expect from the client. It is usually advisable to put this in writing. The contract should clearly cover the issues of confidentiality (especially when seeing a child or adolescent) and compensation.

**3.** Keep meticulous notes on your encounter with the client and on related events, especially in diagnostic cases, because these often will have implications in the legal arena or in other decision-making agreements. Make sure that when you return after a lengthy period of absence from the case that you will be able to clearly reconstruct what occurred between you and the client and that you can report clearly what the client told you. Additionally, it is worthwhile to record your overall impressions at the time when you first summarized the data in your own mind.

**4.** Observe relevant guidelines in keeping records. The following are modeled on federal guidelines. A record should contain, at a minimum, identifying data, dates of services, and types of services and, where appropriate, may include a record of significant actions taken. Providers should make all reasonable efforts to record essential information within a reasonable time of their completion. If treatment is involved, a treatment plan must be included. The guidelines for retention of records are governed by state, federal, and professional regulations. From a conservative perspective, the full record should be maintained intact for three years after the completion of planned services or after the date of last contact with the user, whichever is later; the full record or a summary of the record should be maintained for an additional twelve years; the record should be disposed of no sooner than fifteen years after the completion of planned services or after the date of last contact, whichever is later. If those records are subsequently submitted to another professional or an agency, the records should be accompanied by an indication of whether or not the clinician considers the information (especially assessment data) to be obsolete.

**5.** Make sure your relevant history is a thorough one. Many cases have related issues that occur in the history of the client. The relevance of these issues may not be apparent at the time. Make sure that you have looked at all of the potential issues that are possibly relevant.

**6.** Use standard procedures and tests. Your results will be more acceptable to other professionals and to the courts. This does not preclude using some unusual techniques, but do so in a context of commonly accepted procedures and tests.

■      ## A Model Report Format

Whether the clinician is communicating with agencies, other professionals, attorneys, or the court, a formal report is often required. The following general outline has been found to be useful in such report writing. The clinician collects all relevant data and then goes through the sequence point by point as the report is dictated or written. Exclusion of subsections or inclusion of other information sections is easily accomplished to meet the requirements of an individual case and/or the court's request.

In order to be most effective here, the clinician should use a combination of information sources (Shapiro, 1991). These generally consist of (1) psychometric approaches, (2) observational approaches, (3) clinical interviews, (4) psychophysiological measures (possibly even polygraph examinations), and (5) peripheral methods, such as hypnosis and sodium amytal. Documentation of these sources that were used is especially important if the clinician must take this report into the legal arena. As noted in the last chapter, there are numerous ways the clinician can be brought into the legal system.

> **In a November 1989 interview, Jessica Hahn, the victim of a sexual assault by evangelist Jim Bakker, was quoted as saying, "If I weren't moving into show business right now, I would go to college and study law and psychology." (*Expert Opinion*, Vol. 3, No. 2, p. 10, 1990)**

Name of Client:

Name of Examiner:

Date of Examination:                Date of Report:

A.  Introductory Variables
    1. Age
    2. Sex
    3. Educational background
    4. Socioeconomic status
    5. Occupational status, responsibilities

B.  Referral Source and Related Information

C.  Circumstances of Examination
    1. Place of examination
    2. Length of exam
    3. Present medications and last time used
    4. Tests administered

D.  General Appearance
    1. Physical characteristics
    2. Dress and grooming
    3. Unusual behavior or mannerisms

E.  Level of Response
    1. Answers questions fully?
    2. Volunteers information?

3. Protocols adequate
4. Attitude toward testing and examiner

F. Presenting Problem and Dimensions of that Problem
1. Duration
2. Pervasiveness
3. Severity
4. Frequency

G. Consequences and Implications of Presenting Problem
1. Functional aspects of impairment regarding
   (a) job
   (b) family
   (c) school
   (d) social milieu
2. Legal status (e.g., pending litigation) of this incident or others
3. Necessary changes in habits, roles (especially if acute)
4. Adoption of coping skills or defense mechanisms, both healthy and unhealthy

H. Historical Setting
1. Was the onset of any symptoms acute or gradual?
2. Circumstances surrounding onset of symptoms
3. Evidence of data re premorbid functioning in these areas

I. Other Historical Factors
1. Level of adjustment as a child
2. Level of adjustment as an adolescent
3. Prior hospitalizations and diagnoses
4. Parental relationships, then and now.
5. Sibling relationships, then and now.

J. Other Present Situational Factors
1. Marital relationship
2. Children
3. Job or School
4. Other maintaining factors

K. Current Physical/Physiological Condition
1. Medication, types and dosages
2. Medical complications (e.g., removal of limb)
3. Other factors not directly related to presenting problem

L. Type of Affect and Level of Anxiety
1. Amount
2. Appropriateness
3. In-session versus ongoing functioning
4. General mood
5. Effects on testing and interview behavior

M.  IQ Level

1.  Subtest variability
2.  Preincident versus present level
3.  Educational preparation versus inherent ability
4.  Potential functioning
5.  Personality inferences

N.  Organic Involvement

1.  Any significant indicators
2.  Degree, if any
3.  Specific or global
4.  Cause: alcoholism, birth or prenatal factors, trauma
5.  Cause of or coincidental to other disorder

O.  Thought Processes

1.  Hallucinations or delusions
2.  Paranoid traits
3.  Degree of insight
4.  Adequate social judgments
5.  Adequate abstracting ability
6.  Orientation to environment

P.  Overall Integration and Statement of Personality Functioning—Diagnosis

Q.  Evaluation of Patient's Current Overall Attitudes Toward His/Her Situation

1.  Expectancies about recovery
2.  Attitude toward disorder
3.  Motivation for treatment
4 . Understanding of status/condition
5.  Coping skills, responses to stress and crisis

R.  Identification of Any Need for Further Referral or Consultation

S.  Identification of Targets for Modification, Intervention

T.  Treatment Recommendations

1.  Individual, family, and/or group therapy
2.  Chemotherapy
3.  Hospitalization
4.  Predictions of dangerousness to self or to others
5.  Interest in change
6.  Probability of maintenance in treatment

U.  Priority of Treatment Recommendations (Including Reevaluation and Follow-up), Based on Available Resources

V.  Judgment Regarding Prognosis, Based on

1.  Age at time of onset
2.  Phase of disease or disorder
3.  Known morbidity rates
4.  Severity of affliction
5.  Accessibility of family, other social-support systems

     6. Test results
     7. Patient's attitude

W.  Other Summary Formulations and Conclusions

# Expert Witness Case Preparation

While the suggestions and principles presented thus far are important for virtually any professional in the mental health area, there are several other suggestions that are important if you eventually become directly involved in the judicial process in a client's case.

**1.** Take some time to observe courtroom procedures in general and try to observe various mental health professionals in the role of an expert witness. This will allow you to become familiar and comfortable with courtroom process.

**2.** Even though mental health experts who are called by one party should be an advocate for their opinions and not for that party, they still must operate within the adversary legal system. Therefore, you should not discuss the case with anyone other than the court or the party for whom you have conducted an evaluation without the knowledge or permission of the court or that party.

**3.** Once the opinion has been formed, insist that the attorney who employs you provide the basic facts of the case, the relevant statutory and case law, and that he or she explains the theory under which the case is to be pursued. Understanding of these issues is crucial to your preparation for the case, and reports and testimony should specifically address these legal issues.

**4.** Prepare your case in language that will be meaningful to the court. Remember that jurors are going to be put off by jargon, or they will misunderstand and, thus, not give proper weight to your testimony.

**5.** Prepare yourself to give a thorough overview of all the examination devices that you will be referring to. In the courtroom, you may be asked about the reliability and validity of these devices, about how they were derived, or about what they are purported to measure. You should be ready to answer this in a crisp and efficient fashion, in a language that people will find understandable and useful.

**6.** Make sure you are current on the relevant literature.

**7.** Make sure ahead of time of the role you will take in the courtroom situation and communicate this to the attorney who has brought you into the case. It's especially helpful if you can get the attorney to role play all of the questions he expects to ask you, with your answers, so that you both know what to expect. It's also helpful if the attorney will role-play the questions he or she expects the opposing attorney to ask. Ask him or her to be a true "devil's advocate" in this process.

**8.** When you are close to actually presenting the case in deposition or in court, make sure you can be comfortable with your knowledge of the client. This may entail bringing the client in for visits shortly before the court testimony. In many court cases, the professional may do the evaluation years before actually going into court. In such a case, you really ought to see the client again, if at all possible, to check on prior data that was collected and to update your impressions and inferences.

■ ## Deposition Preparation and Presentation

In virtually every case that takes on a legal dimension, there is a strong likelihood that the clinician will be deposed. Indeed, in many cases there may be no courtroom appearance after a deposition, either because the case is settled out of court or the material that came to light in the deposition eliminated the need or desire to have the clinician testify in person.

Many of the suggestions already mentioned as critical in general and in expert witness case presentation—or that will be mentioned shortly as important in preparing for a courtroom presentation—are relevant to the deposition as well. However, the following are more specific to preparation for a deposition.

**1.** Organize and review all materials pertinent to the case and request a predeposition conference with the attorney.

**2.** Bring to the deposition only those records, notes, etc. that you are willing for all involved parties to be aware of or, in many cases, to gain access to.

**3.** Be aware that there are two types of subpoenas. The first, the *subpoena ad testicandum,* is what most people assume, a summons to appear at court at a specified date and time. The second, the *subpoena duces tecum,* requires the clinician to bring specific materials to the court.

**4.** Remember that just because a particular set of records has been requested, or even subpoenaed, does not mean it must be released. If in doubt, the clinician should (a) insist that the attorney requesting the information provide a valid authorization from the affected person, (b) request a court order before releasing the information (in some jurisdictions, even a court order is not sufficient), and (c) seek independent legal counsel before acting.

**5.** Bring an extra copy of your curriculum vitae, as it is likely it will be incorporated into the record at this time.

**6.** Be courteous and speak in a voice that is audible to everyone, especially the stenographic reporter.

**7.** Be honest in all responses, but do not provide information that is not requested. Avoid any elaboration.

**8.** Think before you respond. You can take as much time as you wish to think out your response since there is no issue of conveying a confused or tentative image to a jury, as there is in the courtroom.

**9.** If an attorney objects, stop talking. It is best to let the attorneys deal with the point in question.

**10.** Remember that the opposing attorney will be evaluating you as a witness and may try many things in deposition that won't be used in trial.

**11.** Thoroughly read and check the deposition when a copy is sent to you for your signature; do not waive your right to sign it. Correct any errors in it as your attorney instructs. Keep a copy of the deposition with your other records pertaining to that case.

**12.** Prior to going to court, review your copy of the deposition and take it with you to the witness stand.

## ■ Courtroom Presentation

While all cases in which the clinician is deposed do not result in a court appearance, many do. The following suggestions are useful when it actually comes to presenting testimony in the courtroom.

**1.** First and foremost, be honest in all of your testimony. If you do not know the answer, say so, and offer to give related information that may clarify the question. But do not try to answer questions when you really do not know the answer. Aside from the ethical issues involved, it is very likely that you will be tripped up later in the cross-examination.

**2.** Leave your ego at the courtroom door. Don't be overly reluctant to admit limitations in your expertise or in the data that you have available. If the cross-examining counsel presents a relevant and accurate piece of data, acknowledge this in a firm and clear fashion and do not put yourself into a defensive position.

**3.** Acknowledge, by eye contact, the person who has requested your statement, be it the judge or one of the attorneys. But at the same time, as much as possible, maintain eye contact with the jury.

**4.** Be aware of the classic errors of the expert witness: becoming (a) too technical, (b) too complex in discussion, (c) too simplistic, (d) too talkative and/or overdramatic, or (e) condescending and/or hostile. Any of these approaches is likely to lose the attention of the jurors and may also turn them against you and the content of your testimony.

**5.** Avoid long, repetitive explanations of your points. If at all possible, keep your responses to two or three statements, but occasionally vary the format of your presentation so that you do not come across as some sort of automaton. If you feel more is needed, try to point out that you cannot fully answer the question without elaborating.

**6.** Never answer questions that you do not really understand. If you are uncomfortable with the wording of the question, ask to have it restated and, if need be, describe your problems with the question as originally posed.

**7.** Similarly, listen carefully to what is asked in each question before you answer. If there is a tricky component to the question, acknowledge that and then try to deal with it in a concise fashion. Try to avoid "Yes, but . . ." answers. If the attorney has made an innuendo that is negative to the case or to you, respond, if you feel it is appropriate, without becoming adversarial. Keep your response unemotional. This *may* be a good time to bring in a bit of humor. However, the use of humor requires *great* caution, as it can easily communicate hostility, which is usually counterproductive.

**8.** If you feel the attorney has misstated what you have just said, when he or she asks a follow-up question, take the time to unemotionally clarify what you actually did say and then go on and answer the next question.

**9.** Speak clearly, fluently, and somewhat louder than you would normally speak. Make sure the jury hears you. Speak when spoken to and avoid smoking or chewing. Avoid weak or insipid speech patterns, commonly marked by (a) hesitation forms, such as "Uh," "You know," or "Well," (b) formal grammar, (c) hedges, such as "sort of," "I guess," or "I think," (d) overly polite speech, or (e) the use of a questioning form of sentence structure rather than straightforward sentences. Communicate a confident, straightforward attitude.

**10.** Avoid using any graphs, tables, or exhibits that are not easily visible, readable, and comprehensible by the average juror.

**11.** Be prepared for questions about journal articles, books, etc., relevant to issues in this particular case. This is more important now than it was at the deposition stage. You can't check up on all of the relevant literature, but by familiarizing yourself with some key recent articles, you can more easily blunt an attack.

**12.** Be prepared to be questioned about the issue of fees. Attorneys may ask questions like "How much are you being paid to testify for this client?" You need to correct that and state that you were asked to do an evaluation, then give your full and honest opinion to the best of your knowledge, and that it was then up to the attorney to decide whether he or she wanted to go ahead and use you in the courtroom. Also, make sure that you state that you are not being paid for your testimony, but that you are being paid for the time that you put into this trial, no matter what testimony would emerge from that time spent. For that reason, you probably will look better to the jury if you charge by the hour rather than charging a flat fee for a case. If you still feel there is any residual implication that you are being biased by the fee, confront that directly.

**13.** Be professional in both your dress and demeanor. Informal dress is seldom appropriate in a courtroom. Reasonably conservative attire makes a more positive impression on the jury. Similarly, your demeanor should be professional, and you should avoid becoming involved in any kind of tirade or acrimony.

**14.** Never personalize your interactions with an attorney who is attempting to disrupt you. At times, you may find it useful to call the attorney by name, but avoid any type of condescension. If you become emotional and make any kind of personal attack, you will likely taint the value of your testimony. There may be times when you do need to express some emotion in giving an opinion in order to emphasize that opinion. But, make sure the emotion is properly placed on the opinion and not as a defensive or attacking response toward the court, jury, or a cross-examining attorney.

**15.** Be prepared to go beyond a simple, linear presentation of data. Jurors look for a "Gestalt," a scenario that integrates and explains the data. Develop the scenario in your own mind, ahead of time, that makes your data meaningful, one that fits with the other facts of the case.

Just as the clinician is organizing to make an effective presentation to the court, the attorneys are preparing to devalue any or all parts of the clinician's testimony. The well-prepared clinician keeps in mind the strategies that he or she is likely to encounter.

## Anticipating the Cross-Examination

Cross-examination is designed to challenge or discredit those data and opinions that have been presented by the clinician that are inconsistent with that attorney's case. A harsh cross-examination, using the techniques and ploys described throughout this chapter, is most likely when the cross-examining attorney is working with a weak case. There are a variety of ways in which the cross-examining attorney will attempt to challenge your testimony.

**1.** A primary target for examination is the expert's qualifications. Two kinds of questions concerning qualifications are (a) whether a witness is sufficiently qualified to be permitted (by the judge) to testify as an expert and (b) the "weight" that should be given (by the judge or jury) to the expert's opinion. Presumably, the more highly qualified the expert, the greater the weight should be given that professional's opinion. The expert's experience in the area and the level of relevant education are common targets. More often, the critique is directed toward the specialization that is important in this particular case. For example, an expert clinical psychologist may have had little involvement in the area of neuropsychology, and yet the critical point in the case may involve a neuropsychological issue. This, of course, would appropriately reduce the credibility of the expert.

2. If you have strong credentials, ask the attorney who brought you into court to avoid the "stipulation" ploy by the opposing attorney, i.e., quickly stipulating that the expert is qualified in order to avoid having the jury hear about the relevant expertise and credentials.

3. Some attorneys like to use the "original source," "historic martyr," or "stupid experts" gambits. In the "original source" ploy, the expert is asked if they did the original work relevant to the issue, or if they ever did any research in this area. Conversely, in the "historic martyr" gambit, the witness is asked about those experts who went unrecognized in their own time for their brilliant findings in order to set a basis for criticizing your testimony. In the "stupid experts" approach, studies are brought forth that purport to show that experts are quite often wrong or do no better than laypersons. Have a spiel prepared to handle these issues in a direct, straightforward manner.

4. Another common way to challenge the expert witness is through contradictory testimony from other experts in the field. These experts may testify in the trial, or the challenge may be in the form of a book or article submitted as written authority. A favorite approach is to attempt to lead the witness down the garden path by asking if such-and-such a source is authoritative, etc., and then presenting the contradictory testimony from that source. So, when an expert is asked if this book or person is authoritative, it may be wise to make a disclaimer like, "Dr. _____ does write in this field. Other experts might agree with some of the things he says, but he's not my authority (or the only authority)."

If you are pushed to accept the results of an article, you can also reply to the effect that "There are many articles in this area; this is but one, and it would be inappropriate for me to comment on the findings you mention without looking at them in the context of the whole article. If the court wishes to grant a recess to allow me to do that, I'll be happy to comment on it." The court never likes to grant extra recesses.

5. Cross-examining attorneys often try to attack the procedures that are used by the expert witness. A classic instance is the discovery that the expert spent a very short period of time with the client. An expert who so cavalierly comes to such an important decision should be vulnerable in the cross-examination.

The particular tests used in an evaluation are also important. For this reason, most mental health expert witnesses prefer to use a variety of objective psychological tests in their examination. It is debatable whether having the tests scored and interpreted by computer adds something to the testimony. It can be argued that this adds a validation by an "apparently objective other." At the same time, sending off a test for scoring or interpretation can be construed, through the presentation of the cross-examining attorney, as dependency on outside opinions because of a lack of expertise. Also, one is prone to be "locked into" all of the statements made in the computer-generated report. Some may clearly not fit this individual case, and the clinician may disagree with a number of the statements.

Projective tests can, of course, be used in court, but they are much more vulnerable to cross-examination. A sophisticated attorney is likely here to pull out an ink blot and ask for the expert's response, or a typical response, and then try to get a statement from the expert as to what is the appropriate idea here or what can be made of a response the client made. This is one of those times when it is very critical for the expert witness to communicate that the opinions and inferences have been based on a variety of data and not from any individual piece of datum.

**6.** Another area in which the clinician can be impeached is through bias, for example, by attacking the expert witness as a "hired gun" and asking a variety of questions about how the individual has been paid. As noted earlier, it is probably wise for the expert to bill on an hourly basis, rather than through a flat fee, because this seems to communicate to jurors a more professional approach. Also, the expert should be prepared to note that it was his or her evaluation that was paid for, not any outcome or particular slant to the testimony, and that it was stated up front, "I will make my evaluation and give you my honest opinion."

**7.** Another possibility here is to attack the expert as a "professional witness," one who spends virtually his or her entire career going from courtroom to courtroom. People who do a lot of forensic work are vulnerable to this characterization, and they need to be ready to present a picture of how they become involved in court cases and why they appear frequently.

**8.** Another potential point of attack is any special relationship to the client. If there is any sense in which the expert is a friend of the client, is doing the client a "favor," or in turn is receiving "favors" for the testimony, the expert's testimony is likely to have little positive impact on the jury.

**9.** Expert witnesses are occasionally cross-examined on their personal vulnerabilities or deficiencies. Any general indications of instability or deviation in the history of the expert witness may be brought out if they can be discovered. Persons who have obvious vulnerabilities, possibly a history of alcoholism or hearing or vision problems (which may in some instances be relevant), should consider means of handling such an attack.

**10.** Just as the attorney will try to challenge the sources of an inference, they will also try to impeach the process of deriving the inference or opinion. They may try to introduce at least apparently contradictory data, or they may just simply ask "Isn't this alternate idea *possible?*" It is important for the expert witness not to become too defensive here. There may be a reasonable admission that other interpretations are possible. The expert witness needs to define that we live in a world of probabilities, possibly stating something to the effect that "Yes, almost anything is possible, for example, it's possible it will snow tomorrow, but it's really very improbable (this has more impact if you are testifying in Florida in summer than in Minnesota in winter). But I do want to emphasize that in my opinion the bulk of evidence supports the opinion I have rendered."

**11.** An excellent way to impeach an expert witness is to disclose prior reports or transcripts of court testimony given by the same expert that are contradictory to the present testimony. The expert should be aware of this possibility, and experts who publish a great deal are even more vulnerable. They need to be able to explain this situation reasonably, e.g., that opinions do change over time and that they may have made a statement some time before in a book with which they do not wholly agree now, or they need to point out why the earlier comments do not exactly apply here. Again, defensiveness is a bad strategy here. Openness can be the best method of handling this type of attack.

Clinicians should remember that at its root, cross-examination is a process of searching for the truth by challenging the ideas and conclusions of the expert. In this sense, it compresses into a short time the long process of challenge to publication and research. Cross-examination is not a perfect process of truth-finding. The presentation of information to a lay jury may, in a few instances, cause obfuscation through cross-examination. Some attorneys unfairly attack or even badger witnesses. The fact that some attorneys try these tactics, however, does not mean that they have succeeded; such tactics often backfire. Juries probably resent trickery on credible experts. If a mental health expert has drawn reasonable conclusions based on full examination and has avoided exaggerated statements and emotional responses to cross-examination, the expert will have succeeded in making his or her point to the jury. A dry run, a practice cross-examination, can be especially helpful, particularly for the expert who has not testified before. It may also be instructional to review Ziskin and Faust (1988) or similar materials so that the approaches any sophisticated attorney may take in a cross-examination can be anticipated.

## ■ The Clinician's Role in Court

As an increasing number of clinicians enter the forensic arenas, they encounter ethical situations and practical problems that are seldom found in other areas of practice. One of the most frequent dilemmas concerns being asked to take, in the same case, more than one of the following three roles: expert witness, consultant, advocate. Each has a different ultimate client focus: expert witness, court; consultant, client/attorney; and advocate, cause. Any one of these roles is proper for a clinician, but accepting more than one role in the same case, or even blurring the roles' boundaries, is inappropriate (Smith and Meyer, 1987).

Pressure to take more than one role in a single case may come from either the clinician or the attorney. Pressure from within the clinician often comes when there is a late call for help with the case. Demand characteristics of the situation, i.e., the "pull to affiliate," can readily couple with personal needs to put the clinician in the classical role of "rescuer." In the extreme, the unsuspecting clinician may soon be agreeing to testify as an expert witness, to suggest theories of defense, to offer advice on how to make the client more presentable to a jury, and to help select a jury.

A closer look at the three roles will make clear the reasons why the roles should not be combined or blurred. The expert is present to assist the jury with questions that it does not have the required special knowledge to address by itself. In that sense, the "client" is the court. The designation "expert witness" refers not only to the qualifications and expertise of the person in the role, but especially to the rules that will govern the person's testimony. Unlike other witnesses, the expert witness may render an opinion. Further, the expert witness may incorporate "hearsay evidence" that other witnesses may not use, and opinions may be based on this evidence. As Shapiro (1984) notes:

**Whenever one testifies in court, . . . one should not consider oneself an advocate for the patient, for the defense, or for the government. One is an advocate only for one's own opinion. When the expert witness allows himself or herself to be drawn into a particular position, because of a feeling that the patient needs treatment, that the patient should be incarcerated, or that society needs to be protected, the credibility and validity of one's testimony invariably suffers (pp. 77–98).**

It would be an abuse of process, as well as a way of diminishing the value of one's testimony, for the expert witness to use his or her unique role in order to advocate anything other than a professional opinion.

The role of consultant in forensic cases is also one that clinicians are occasionally called on to take. The "client," in this case, is the side that retained the consultant. Jury selection, preparation of direct- and cross-examination questions, review of treatment records, procurement of appropriate expert witnesses, recommendations for packaging and sequencing of evidence, courtroom jury monitoring, and other consultant functions may be performed. However, the forensic consultant must maintain some distance from the advocacy role taken by the attorneys.

Keeping professional distance from the advocacy process is one of the most challenging tasks faced by the consulting clinician. However, it is essential that this task be completed successfully. The consultant role, per se, requires that one "call it as one sees it" and not as the client wants it. It is possible that one's client will perceive such professional detachment as coldness and lack of care about the case, but that risk must be taken. Focus must be, instead, on the rendering of the best possible consulting opinion, regardless of what effect it might have on the advocate's behavior or case. The consultant cannot be accountable for the use that the client makes of the opinion that is given, nor is the consultant accountable if the advocate fails to use the opinion.

The role of advocate is seldom a legitimate role for clinicians. This is fortunate, since this role is fraught with ethical implications. As an advocate, the clinician is a member of the team and, like other team members, has the goal of winning. The sciences and arts of the mental health professions are here used to achieve an end that the advocate defines as worthy. This may include conviction, acquittal, or modification of sentences in criminal cases. It is possible, and perhaps likely, that an advocate in a case will have personal motives that are not necessarily related directly to the case. For example, advocates for or against capital punishment may be more concerned with the issue of execution than with presentation of the most complete or accurate possible case to a jury.

It is important for the clinician to make it clear when an advocate role has been taken. Otherwise, juries or the media may mistake statements intended only to advance a cause for a reasoned, responsible professional opinion. Use of such expertise to promote a particular view that is not scientifically supported generally would be considered unethical.

Thus, as an expert witness, the clinician will find a primary allegiance to the opinion rendered to the court; as a consultant, to the best information rendered to the client; and as an advocate, to service to a cause or point of view. Again, it can be appropriate to take the role of either expert, consultant, or advocate, but each of these roles has limits and one should neither take more than one role per case nor blur the role boundaries. In difficult cases of this sort, colleague consultation can be especially helpful. But if doubt still persists, the old adage "If in doubt, don't" is the wisest course.

# Appendix A:
# The Meyer Information Battery

Name _____ Age _____ Sex _____ Date _____

Please finish each of the sentences and say as much as you can about how you feel. Use your true feelings in your answers. Try to complete every one and say as much as possible about yourself. Thank you.

My favorite kind of job would be _____

_____

Men think I _____

_____

I could be a better worker if _____

_____

Women think I _____

_____

My school grades _____

_____

My father _____

_____

When adapting this battery, more-adequate space for responses should be included.

Failure _____

_____

Most bosses _____

_____

My blood boils when _____

_____

My biggest fear is _____

_____

The best way to control pain is _____

_____

The best way to control anxiety or depression is _____

_____

My mother _____

_____

I like best the kind of work that _____

_____

My proudest time is _____

_____

I wish I could forget _____

_____

If things go badly for you, do you get angry or depressed? _____

_____

What do you then do about it? _____

_____

Do you feel it would help to talk to anyone about your problems? _____

_____

Why or why not? _____

_____

What do you think the future holds for you and why? _____

_____

At what time in your life were you closest to panic? _____

_____

Why? _____

_____

When did you feel most guilty? _____

_____

Why? _____

_____

What does marriage mean to you? _____

_____

Explain in some detail what death means to you. _____

_____

_____

If I could be anything that I wished, I would choose to be _____

_____ because _____

_____

If I could have any three wishes in the world, I would wish

1. _____

2. _____

3. _____

If I could make any one change in other people, it would be _____

_____

because _____

The very earliest thing that I can remember as a child is _____

_____

_____

My most pleasant memory is _____

_____

_____

My most unpleasant memory is _____

_____

_____

Explain the four proverbs below. For example, the proverb *Large oaks from little acorns grow* means that great things may have small beginnings. Say as best you can what each of these proverbs means.

While the cat's away, the mice will play. _____

_____

_____

It never rains but it pours. _____

_____

_____

Don't cry over spilt milk. _____

_____

The burnt child dreads the fire. _____

_____

_____

If the following people were asked to describe you in one word, what word would each probably use?

Mother _____

Father _____

Brother(s) _____

Sister(s) _____

Your spouse or most intimate opposite-sex friend _____

Your best friend now _____

Your boss _____

Your son(s) _____

Your daughters(s) _____

I would most strongly wish to raise my child to be _____

_____

_____

If there is one thing that I could go back and change about my life, it would be

_____

_____

_____

_____

Briefly describe your history of arrests and convictions (either felonies or misdemeanors), including any moving violations while in an automobile.

_____

_____

_____

_____

Briefly describe any history of psychological or psychiatric treatment.

_____

_____

_____

_____

Has any blood relative ever had a problem controling their use of alcohol or ever been in significant trouble because of their use of alcohol?

Yes _____     No _____

Please describe your relationship to this relative(s) and give details.

_____

_____

_____

_____

Has any blood relative ever been *arrested* (not just convicted) for a felony?

Yes _____     No _____

Please describe your relationship to this relative(s) and give details.

_____

_____

_____

_____

■        # Draw-A-Group

Please draw a picture of any group scene that involves you and at least two other people. I know that many people are not artists and may seldom draw anything. However, simply go ahead and do your best. Use first names or role names (e.g., Jack, Sue, Amy, friend, father, sister, me, etc.) to label each of the figures in your drawing. Remember, I understand that not everyone draws well or even likes to draw. All I want is your best effort. Thank you.

## ■ Drawing Explanation

Use the space that follows to describe what is happening in the drawing you made. Describe what is going on, whether someone is talking to someone, what they are saying, or anything else that is important. Give all the details you can. Thank you.

What is your most serious physical problem at this time? _____

_____

What treatment are you receiving? _____

_____

What is your most serious emotional problem at this time? _____

_____

   Why? _____

_____

How could other people help you change for the better? _____

_____

Do you prefer to live in the city, the suburbs, or the country? _____

_____

   Why? _____

_____

Which man of the past or present do you most admire? _____

_____

   Why? _____

_____

Which woman of the past or present do you most admire? _____

_____

   Why? _____

_____

Who has been more meaningful to you, your father or your mother? _____

_____

Why? _____

_____

What is your favorite movie of all time? _____

Why? _____

_____

Who is your favorite male movie star? _____

Why? _____

Who is your favorite female movie star? _____

Why? _____

Do you believe in God? _____ Why or why not? _____

_____

Do you practice a religion? _____ Why and in what way? Or why not? _____

_____

Has your sexual history been good or bad? _____ Describe and say why it has

been good or bad for you. _____

_____

What has been the greatest injustice you have suffered? _____

_____ What did you do about it? _____

_____

Thank you for your cooperation

# Appendix B:
# Relevant Legal Cases

In addition to the cases that are cited and discussed in Chapter 17, there are numerous other cases that have some relevance to the practicing clinician. The following is a presentation of the major cases, important because they are either landmark cases, often older cases whose findings may now be modified to some degree, or they are more recent cases that have significant precedent value and/or present impact.

## CONSENT TO INTERVENTION

Schloendorff v. Society of New York Hospital—211 N.Y. 125, 105 N.E. 92 (1914)

- First clear statement that informed consent requires that a client be apprised of the potential benefits and major risks of proposed treatments, as well as available alternative treatments.

Canterbury v. Spence—464 F.2d 772 (D.C. Cir. 1972)

- Defined the elements of modern informed consent.

Rennie v. Klein—462 F. Supp. 1131 (D.N.J. 1976), eventually 720 F.2d 266 (3 Cir. 1983)

- First significant case to recognize that those who are civilly committed have a right to refuse medications, although this can be overridden by due process.

Addington v. Texas—441 U.S. 418 (1979)

- The level of proof in civil commitment is "clear and convincing" evidence.

Rivers v. Katz—67 N.Y. 2d 485, 495 N.E. 2d 337, 504 N.Y. 2d 74 (1986)

- Right to refuse treatment—state can only force treatment, e.g., medication, if not competent, or if dangerous in the hospital.

Washington v. Harper–494 U.S. 210 (1990)

- A prisoner may be forced to take antipsychotic drugs, with only an institution-based due process review, if (1) they suffer from "mental illness" and (2) are dangerous to self or others or are "gravely disabled."

Parham v. J. R.–442 U.S. 584 (1979)

- Juveniles may be civilly committed, on consent of their parents, without a hearing, but with a review at the hospital to which they are committed.

Zinermon v. Burch–494 U.S. 113 (1990)

- Patient may have a cause of action against those who hold that person in a hospital, under a voluntary admission, when it is clear the person is incompetent to make such decisions.

□    PRIVILEGED COMMUNICATION/CONFIDENTIALITY/
     DUTY TO WARN OR PROTEST

Caesar v. Mountanos–542 F.2d 1064 (9th Cir. 1976)

- Ninth Circuit recognizes a constitutional right to privacy that includes a limited psychotherapist–patient privilege, recognizes the client owns the privilege.

Tarasoff v. Regents of the University of California–17 Cal. 3d 425; 551 P.2d 334, 131 Cal. Rptr. 14 (1976)

- At first finds a "duty to warn" for clinicians; on appeal, amends it to a "duty to protect" third parties from dangerous clients.

In re Zuniga–714 F.2d 632 (6th Cir. 1983)

- Found a federal, limited common law psychotherapist–patient privilege.

Buchanan v. Kentucky–483 U.S. 402 (1987)

- The report prepared by a psychiatrist for a civil commitment hearing is allowed (against his wishes) into evidence when the defendant raised a defense of "extreme emotional disturbance" in a later criminal trial.

Pennsylvania v. Ritchie–480 U.S. 39 (1987)

- Judge was allowed to subpoena a state agency's confidential mental health file, over defense objections, to decide which material would be revealed in a criminal case.

□         PERSONAL INJURY

Dillon v. Legg–68 Cal. 2d 728, 60 Cal. Rptr. 72, 441 P.2d 912 (1968)
- Recognized "zone of danger" concept in personal injury cases, with three criteria: (1) a close relationship to the victim, (2) close proximity to the accident, and (3) the emotional shock is "sensory and contemporaneous" to the incident.

Molien v. Kaiser Foundation Hospital–27 Cal. 3d 916 (1980)
- Contrary to "zone of danger" concept, husband successfully sues physician who negligently misdiagnosed wife's condition as syphilis, leading to eventual divorce.

□         CHILD CUSTODY

Finlay v. Finlay–148 N.E. 624 (1925, 1926)
- Firmly established the principle that custody decisions should reflect the "best interests of the child."

Painter v. Bannister–358 Iowa 1390, 140 N.W. 2d 152 (1966)
- Although an odd set of circumstances, it helped establish the concept of "psychological parent"; court allowed grandparents to keep custody of child over the claim of the natural father.

Santosky v. Kramer–455 U.S. 745 (1982)
- "Clear and convincing" is the standard of proof required to terminate parental rights.

□         JUVENILE PROCEEDINGS

Kent v. U.S.–383 U.S. 541 (1966)
- Required due process in juvenile proceedings.

In re Gault–387 U.S. 1 (1967)
- Placed due process for juveniles within the 14th Amendment; requires (a) notice of charges, (b) right to have an attorney, (c) cross-examination and confrontation of witnesses, and (d) no self-incrimination.

McKeiver v. Pennsylvania–403 U.S. 528 (1970)
- Juvenile defendants have no constitutional right to a jury trial, although states may grant that right.

Parham v. J. R.–442 U.S. 584 (1979)
- As noted earlier, held that parents should be allowed to maintain a substantial, if not dominant, role in the decision to voluntarily

admit their child to a mental hospital, absent a finding of abuse or neglect.

Thompson v. Oklahoma—487 U.S. 815 (1988)

- States may not execute children who were under sixteen when they committed the crime.

Stanford v. Kentucky—492 U.S. 937 (1989)

- States may execute children who were over sixteen (i.e., in the disputed 16–18 year age range) when they committed the crime.

DeShaney v. Winnebago County—489 U.S. 189 (1989)

- There is no liability on a state for the failure of its child protective services agencies to protect a child and prevent the child's death at the hands of the child's parents, even when abuse has been repeatedly reported.

Maryland v. Craig—110 S.Ct. 3157 (1990)

- Closed-circuit televised testimony of child abuse victim (with defense attorney present, but alleged perpetrator only watching televised testimony) is held to be constitutional in some circumstances.

☐     ADDICTIONS

Robinson v. California—370 U.S. 660 (1962)

- It is unconstitutional to convict based on the "status" of being addicted.

Powell v. Texas—392 U.S. 514 (1968)

- May convict on behaviors stemming from addiction.

Traynor v. Turnage—485 U.S. 535 (1988)

- VA definition of primary alcoholism, i.e., defined as a type of alcoholism that is not the result of other psychological disorder, is "willful misconduct."

☐     PROFESSIONAL ISSUES

Barefoot v. Estelle—463 U.S. 880 (1983)

- Mental health professional is allowed to testify to the dangerousness of the defendant in a capital case, even though the professional has not examined the defendant.

Shapero v. Kentucky Bar Assoc.—486 U.S. 466 (1988)

- Supreme Court recognizes right of attorneys (and by implication, other professional groups) to aggressively advertise to specific groups.

West v. Atkins–467 U.S. 42 (1988)

- Contractual mental health professionals, who are not full-time employees of the state, can be sued, while full-time employees performing the same tasks may be protected from suit.

Blue Shield of Virginia v. McCready–457 U.S. 465 (1982)

- Antitrust laws are successfully employed by mental health professionals, in this case psychologists, against practices limiting reimbursement through physicians.

Patrick v. Burget–486 U.S. 94 (1988)

- Professional peer review committees are not exempt from antitrust laws, e.g., regarding hospital privileges.

Summit Health v. Pinhas–111 S.Ct. 1842 (1991)

- Expanded the availability of antitrust remedies in the health area by adopting a fairly broad definition of the "effect on interstate commerce" that is necessary to support health antitrust claims.

Supreme Court of Virginia v. Friedman–487 U.S. 59 (1988)

- A state may not require a professional to be a state resident to be admitted to practice by reciprocity.

Canton v. Harris–489 U.S. 378 (1989)

- Police departments may be liable for a failure to provide officers with adequate training to care for mentally ill "clients."

Peel v. Attorney Registration and Disciplinary Commission–110 S.Ct. 2281 (1990)

- State cannot prohibit professionals from advertising certification by a legitimate private organization, even if not the "best" or "highest" (or, in some cases, worth anything at all) certification available; permits lawyers and mental health professionals to claim to be "certified" or "boarded" by any "qualified" organization.

West Virginia University Hospital v. Casey–111 S.Ct. 1138 (1991)

- Held that the award of attorney fees does not include the cost of expert witness fees the prevailing party paid in pursuing its claim.

□         SUICIDE

Meier v. Ross General Hospital–69 Cal.2d 420; 71 Cal. Rptr. 903, 445 P.2d 519 (1968)

- Firmly established the basic duty of therapists to exercise adequate care and skill in diagnosing suicidality; it is a duty to protect the client from his or her own actions.

Dinnerstein v. State—486 F.2d 34 (Conn. 1973)

- Clearly establishes principle that clinician is held liable if treatment plan overlooks or neglects the patient's suicidal tendencies.

Bellah v. Greenson—146 Cal. Rptr. 535 (1978)

- There is no "Tarasoff duty to warn" significant others of possible suicidality of client, especially as this refers to an outpatient setting.

## HYPNOSIS

State v. Hurd—86 N.J. 525, 432 A.2d 86 (1981)

- Establishes the still influential "Hurd rules" or "Orne criteria" for reviewing hypnotically refreshed testimony.

People v. Shirley—31 Cal. 3d 18, 181 Cal. Rptr. 243, 641 P.2d 775 (1982)

- Applies a sweeping rule of inadmissability of hypnotically refreshed testimony in California.

Rock v. Arkansas—107 S.Ct. 2704 (1987)

- Supreme Court rules it is a violation of constitutional rights to arbitrarily exclude testimony about memories recalled during hypnosis in *criminal* cases.

## MISCELLANEOUS

Frye v. United States—295 F. 1013 (D.C. Cir. 1923)

- Procedure has to be generally accepted in the scientific community to be allowed into evidence.

Landeros v. Flood—17 Cal.3d 399, 551, P.2d 389, 131 Cal. Rptr. 69 (1976)

- Establishes basis for liability for failure to report child abuse.

Youngberg v. Romeo—457 U.S. 307 (1982)

- State has the obligation to provide the mentally retarded with "minimal services" that permit (1) the least restraint possible and (2) basic safety.

Rouse v. Cameron—373 F.2d 451 (D.C. Cir. 1960), *later app.,* 387 F.2d 241 (1967)

- "Habeas corpus" can be used if constitutional rights are not respected while committed in a mental hospital.

Wyatt v. Stickney—325 F.Supp. 781 (M.D. Ala. 1971), later decision 344 F.Supp. 387 (M.D. Ala. 1972) affd in part, 503 F.2d 1305 (5th Cir. 1974) (*sub mom* Wyatt v. Anderholt)

- The most significant effort to define the right to treatment.

Griggs v. Duke Power Co.–401 U.S. 424 (1971)

- Tests that have the effect of discriminating are illegal if they are not directly relevant to measurement of job capability.

Detroit Edison v. NLRB–440 U.S. 401 (1979)

- The Supreme Court rules that privacy interests of test takers is a sufficient privacy interest to bar the union's requested access to scores. But, the Court ignores the arguments that access to the test scores would ruin the validity of the tests, leading to the "truth in testing" movement on the legislative front.

Payne v. Tennessee–111 S.Ct. 2597 (1991)

- The Supreme Court reversed its earlier decisions and held that states may present victim impact statements to juries in death penalty cases.

# Bibliography

Abel, G., and Rouleau, J. (1990). "Male Sex Offenders." In M. Thase, B. Edelstein, and M. Herson, Eds. *Handbook of Outpatient Treatment of Adults.* New York: Plenum.

Abel, G., Rouleau, J., and Cunningham-Rathner, J. (1986). "Sexually Aggressive Behavior." In W. Curran, A. L. McGarry, and S. Shah, Eds. *Forensic Psychiatry and Psychology.* Philadelphia: F. A. Davis.

Adler, W. (1988). "Milieu therapy." In J. Lion, W. Adler, and W. Webb, Eds. *Modern Hospital Psychiatry.* New York: W. W. Norton.

Agras, W. (1987). *Eating Disorders.* New York: Pergamon.

Albert, S., Fox, H., and Kahn, M. (1980). "Faking Psychosis on the Rorschach: Can Expert Judges Detect Malingering?" *Journal of Personality Assessment, 44,* 115–119.

Allen, J., Faden, V., Miller, A., and Rawlings, R. (1991). "Personality Correlates of Chemically Dependent Patients Scoring High Versus Low on the MacAndrew Scale." *Psychological Assessment, 3,* 273–276.

Allgulander, C., and Lavon, P. (1991). "Excess Mortality Among 3302 Patients with 'Pure' Anxiety Neurosis." *Archives of General Psychiatry, 48,* 599–602.

Allison, J., Blatt, S., and Zimet, C. (1988). *The Interpretation of Psychological Tests.* New York: Hemisphere.

American Psychiatric Association (1952). *Diagnostic and Statistical Manual of Mental Disorders (DSM-I),* 1st ed. Washington, DC: APA.

_____ (1968). *Diagnostic and Statistical Manual of Mental Disorders (DSM-II),* 2nd ed. Washington, DC: APA.

_____ (1980). *Diagnostic and Statistical Manual of Mental Disorders (DSM-III),* 3rd ed. Washington, DC: APA.

_____ (1987). *Diagnostic and Statistical Manual of Mental Disorders (DSM-III-R),* 3rd ed., revised. Washington, DC: APA.

Anastasi, A. (1987). *Psychological testing,* 6th ed. New York: Macmillan.

Anderson, W., and Bauer, B. (1985). "Clients with MMPI High D-Pd." *Journal of Clinical Psychology, 41,* 181–188.

Apter, A., Kotler, M., Sevy, S., Plutchik, R., et al. (1991). "Correlates of Risk of Suicide in Violent and Nonviolent Psychiatric Patients." *The American Journal of Psychiatry, 148,* 883–887.

Archer,m R. (1987). *Using the MMPI with Adolescents.* Hillsdale, NJ: Lawrence Erlbaum Associates.

Armentrout, J., and Hauer, A. (1978). "MMPI's of Rapists of Adults, Rapists of Children and Non-rapist Sex Offenders." *Journal of Clinical Psychology, 34,* 330–332.

Aronow, E., and Reznikoff, M. (1976). *Rorschach Content Interpretation.* New York: Grune and Stratton.

Bagby, R., Gillis, J., Toner, B., and Goldberg, J. (1991). "Detecting Fake-Good and Fake-Bad Responding on the Millon Clinical Multiaxial Inventory-II." *Psychological Assessment, 3,* 496–498.

Barbaree, H., Marshall, W., and Lanthier, R. (1979). "Deviant Sexual Arousal in the Rapist." *Behavior Research and Therapy, 17,* 215–222.

Barnett, P., and Gotlib, I. (1988). "Psychological Functioning and Depression." *Psychological Bulletin, 104,* 97–126.

Barrett v. United States, 377 A.2d 62 (1977).

Barrett, C., and Meyer, R. (1992). "Cognitive Behavioral Therapy for Inpatient Alcoholics." In J. Wright, A. Beck, M. Thase and J. Ludgate, Eds. *Inpatient Cognitive Therapy.* New York: Guilford.

Baucom, D., and Epstein, N. (1990). *Cognitive-Behavioral Marital Therapy.* New York: Brunner/Mazel.

Beaber, R., Marston, A., Michelli, J., and Mills, M. (1985). "A Brief Test for Measuring Malingering in Schizophrenic Individuals." *The American Journal of Psychiatry, 142,* 1478–1481.

Beck, A. (1976). *Cognitive Therapy and the Emotional Disorders.* New York: International Universities Press.

Beck, A., Freeman, A., and Associates (1990). *Cognitive Therapy of Personality Disorders.* New York: Guilford.

Beck, A., Steer, R., Kovacs, M., and Garrison, B. (1983). "Hopelessness and Eventual Suicide: A 10-Year Prospective Study of Patients Hospitalized with Suicidal Ideation." *American Journal of Psychiatry, 142,* 559–563.

Beck, S., and Beck, A. (1978). *Rorschach's Test: II. 1 Gradients in Mental Disorder. Third Edition of II. A Variety of Personality Pictures.* New York: Grune and Stratton.

Beck, S., and Molish, H. (1952). *Rorschach's Test: Advances in Interpretation.* New York: Grune and Stratton.

Bellack, A., Hersen, M., and Kazdin, A., Eds. (1990). *International Handbook of Behavior Modification and Therapy,* 2nd Ed. New York: Plenum.

Bellak, J. (1993). *The T.A.T., C.A.T. and S.A.T. in Clinical Use,* 6th ed. Orlando, FL: Grune and Stratton.

Belli, M. (1979). "Transsexual Surgery: A New Tort." *Journal of Family Law, 17,* 487–504.

Bender, L. (1938). *A Visual Motor Gestalt Test and Its Clinical Use.* New York: American Orthopsychiatric Association.

Benedikt, R., and Kolb, L. (1986). "Preliminary Findings on Chronic Pain and Post-Traumatic Stress Disorder." *American Journal of Psychiatry, 143,* 908–910.

Ben-Porath, Y., and Butcher, J. (1989). "The Comparability of MMPI and MMPI-2 Scales and Profiles: Psychological Assessment." *A Journal of Consulting and Clinical Psychology, 1,* 345–347.

Ben-Porath, Y., Hostetler, K., Butcher, J., and Graham, J. (1989). "New Subscales for the MMPI-2 Social Introversion Scale." *Psychological Assessment, 1,* 169–174.

Benton, A. (1980). "The Neuropsychology of Facial Recognition." *American Psychologist, 35,* 176–186.

Berk, L. (1989). *Child Development: Theory, Research and Applications.* Needham Heights, MA: Allyn and Bacon.

Berlin, F., Malin, M., and Dean, S. (1991). "Effects of Statutes Requiring Psychiatrists to Report Suspected Sexual Abuse of Children." *American Journal of Psychiatry, 148,* 449–455.

Berne, E. (1964). *Games People Play.* New York: Grove.

Bernstein, A., Riedel, J., Graae, F., Seidman, D., et al. (1988). "Schizophrenia Is Associated with Altered Orienting Activity, Depression with Electrodermal (Cholinergic?) Deficit and Normal Orienting Response." *Journal of Abnormal Psychology, 97,* 3–12.

Berry, D., Wetter, M., Baer, R., Widiger, T., et al (1991). Detection of Random Responding on the MMPI-2: Utility of F, Back F, and VRIN Scales. *Psychological Assessment, 3,* 418–423.

Beutler, L., Karacan, I., Anch, M., Salis, P., Scott, F., Williams, R. (1975). "MMPI and MIT Discriminators of Biogenic and Psychogenic Impotence." *Journal of Consulting and Clinical Psychology, 43,* 899–908.

Blane, H., and Leonard, K. (1987). *Psychological Theories of Drinking and Alcoholism.* New York: Guilford.

Blatt, S., Baker, B., and Weiss, J. (1970). "Wechsler Object Assembly Subtest and Bodily Concern." *Journal of Consulting and Clinical Psychology, 34,* 269–274.

Bloom, B. (1992). *Planned Short-Term Psychotherapy.* Needham Heights, MA: Allyn and Bacon.

Bloom-Feshbach, J., and Bloom-Feshbach, S. (1987). *The Psychology of Separation and Loss.* San Francisco: Jossey-Bass.

Blouin, A., Blouin, J., Aubin, P., Carter, J., et al. (1992). "Seasonal Patterns of Bulimia Nervosa." *American Journal of Psychiatry, 149,* 73–81.

Blum, K., and Payne, J. (1991). *Alcohol and the Addictive Brain.* New York: The Free Press.

Bongar, B. (1991). *The Suicidal Patient.* Washington, DC: American Psychological Association.

Boyer, J. (1990). "Fatal Attraction: The Borderline Personality and Psychotherapy." *National Register Report, 16(2),* 5–7.

Breggin, P. (1979). *Electroshock: Its Brain-Disabling Effects.* New York: Springer.

Brigham, T. (1988). *Working with Troubled Adolescents.* New York: Guilford.

Brodsky, S. (1991). *Testifying in Court.* Washington, DC: American Psychological Association.

Brown, F., Ed. (1991). *Reweaving the Family Tapestry.* New York: W. W. Norton.

Bruch, H., Czyzewski, D., and Suhr, M. (1988). *Conversations with Anorexics.* New York: Basic Books.

Bryer, J., Martines, K., and Dignan, M. (1990). "MCMI Alcohol Abuse Scales and the Identification of Substance Abuse Patients." *Psychological Assessment, 2,* 438–441.

Buchanan v. Kentucky 483 U.S. 402 (1987).

Bull, R., and Rumsey, N. (1988). *The Social Psychology of Facial Appearance.* New York: Springer-Verlag.

Burger, G., and Kabacoff, R. (1982). "Personality Types as Measured by the 16 PF." *Journal of Personality Assessment, 46,* 175–180.

Burke, H., and Mayer, S. (1985). "The MMPI and the PTSD in Vietnam Era Veterans." *Journal of Clinical Psychology, 41,* 152–156.

Burrows, G. (1992). "Long-term Clinical Management of Depressive Disorders. *Journal of Clinical Psychiatry, 53* (Supplement), 32–35.

Burnstein, A., and Loucks, S. (1989). *Rorschach Test Scoring.* New York: Hemisphere.

Butcher, J. (1987). *Computerized Psychological Assessment.* New York: Basic Books.

Butcher, J., Ed. (1979). *New Developments in the Use of the MMPI.* Minneapolis: University of Minnesota Press.

Butcher, J. (1990). *MMPI-2 in Psychological Treatment.* New York: Oxford.

Butcher, J., and Graham, J. (1988). "Clinical Applications of the MMPI." Workshop. February 5–6, 1988, Cincinnati, OH.

Butcher, J., Graham, J., Williams, C., and Ben-Porath, Y. (1990). *Development and Use of the MMPI-2 Content Scales.* Minneapolis: University of Minnesota Press.

Calhoun, K., and Atkeson, B. (1991). *Treating Rape Victims.* Elmsford, NY: Pergamon.

Cantwell, D., and Baker, L. (1987). *Developmental Speech and Language Disorders.* New York: Guilford.

Caplan, B. (1987). "Assessment of Unilateral Neglect: A New Reading Test." *Journal of Clinical and Experimental Neuropsychology, 9,* 359–364.

Carbonell, J., Megargee, E., and Moorhead, K. (1984). "Predicting Prison Adjustment with Structured Personality Inventories." *Journal of Consulting and Clinical Psychology, 52,* 280–294.

Cargonello, J., and Gurekas, R. (1988). "The WAIS-SAM: A Comprehensive Administrative Model of Modified WAIS Procedures." *Journal of Clinical Psychology, 44,* 266–270.

Carson, R. (1969). "Interpretative Manual to the MMPI." In J. Butcher, Ed. *MMPI: Research Developments and Clinical Applications.* New York: McGraw-Hill.

Cassini, J. and Workman, D. (1992). "The Detection of Malingering and Deception with a Short Form of the MMPI-2 Based on L, F, and K Scales. *Journal of Clinical Psychology, 48,* 54–63.

Cattell, H. (1989). *The 16 PF: Personality in Depth.* Champaign, IL: IPAT.

Cattell, R. (1965). *The Scientific Analysis of Personality.* Chicago: Aldine.

⸻ (1973). *Personality and Mood by Questionnaire.* San Francisco, CA: Jossey-Bass.

_____ (1979). *Personality and Learning Theory*, Vol. 2: *The Structure of Personality in Its Environment.* New York: Springer.

_____ (1986). *Psychotherapy by Structural Learning.* New York: Springer.

Cattell, R., Eber, H., and Tatsuoka, M. (1970). *Handbook for the Sixteen Personality Factors Questionnaire.* Champaign, IL: IPAT.

Cattell, R., and Warburton, F. (1967). *Objective Personality and Motivation Tests.* Champaign: University of Illinois Press.

Cautela, J., and Wall, C. (1980). "Covert Conditioning in Clinical Practice." In A. Goldstein and E. Foa, Eds. *Handbook of Behavioral Interventions.* New York: John Wiley.

Chambless, D. (1985). "The Relationship of Severity of Agoraphobia to Associated Psychopathology." *Behavior Research and Therapy, 23,* 305–310.

Chambless, D., Sultan, F., Stern, T., O'Neill, C., et al. (1984). "Effect of Pubococcygeal Exercise on Coital Orgasm in Women." *Journal of Consulting and Clinical Psychology, 52,* 114–118.

Cheek, D. (1965). "Emotional Factors in Persistent Pain States." *The American Journal of Clinical Hypnosis, 9,* 100–101.

Choca, J., Shanley, L., and Denburg, E. (1992). *Interpretative Guide to the Millon Clinical Multiaxial Inventory.* Washington, DC: American Psychological Association.

Christenson, G., Mackenzie, T., and Mitchell, J. (1991). "Characteristics of 60 Adult Chronic Hair Pullers." *American Journal of Psychiatry, 148,* 365–370.

Ciraulo, D., and Shader, R. (1991). *Clinical Manual of Chemical Dependence.* Washington, DC: American Psychiatric Press.

Clark, C. (1988). "Diminished Capacity in Michigan: Factors Associated with Forensic Evaluation Referrals." Mid-Winter Meeting, American Psychology-Law Society, Miami Beach, FL.

Cleckley, H. (1964). *The Mask of Sanity,* 4th ed. St. Louis: Mosby.

Clum, G. (1989). *Coping with Panic.* Chicago: Dorsey.

Cody, M. (1991). Personal communication.

Cohen, M., Seghorn, T., and Calmas, W. (1969). "Sociometric Study of Sex Offenders." *Journal of Abnormal Psychology, 74,* 249–255.

Colligan, R., Osborne, D., Swenson, W., and Offord, K. (1983). *The MMPI: A Contemporary Normative Study.* New York: Praeger.

Colorado v. Connelly 479 U.S. 157 (1986).

Committee of the Institute of Medicine. (1990). *Broadening the Base of the Treatment for Alcohol Problems.* Washington, DC: National Academy Press.

Conley, J. (1981). "An MMPI Typology of Male Alcoholics: Admission, Discharge, and Outcome Data." *Journal of Personality Assessment, 45,* 33–39.

Connell, D., and Meyer, R. (1992). "Differential Validity of the SIRS and M Test." Unpublished paper.

Cooper, S., Perry, J. C., and Arnow, D. (1988). "An Empirical Approach to the Study of Defense Mechanisms: Reliability and Validity of Rorschach Defense Scales." *Journal of Personality Assessment, 52,* 187–203.

Corney, R., and Stanton, R. (1991). "A Survey of 658 Women Who Report Symptoms of PMS." *Journal of Psychosomatic Research, 35,* 471–482.

Costello, R. (1978). "Empirical Derivation of a Partial Personality Typology of Alcoholics." *Journal of Studies of Alcoholism, 39,* 1258–1266.

Cox, D. (1980). "Exhibitionism: An Overview." In D. Cox and R. Daitzman, Eds. *Exhibitionism.* New York: Garland.

Cox, D., and Meyer, R. (1978). "Behavioral Treatment Parameters with Primary Dysmenorrhea." *Journal of Behavioral Medicine, 1,* 297–310.

Craig, R., Verinis, J., Wexler, S. (1985). "Personality Characteristics of Drug Addicts and Alcoholics on the Millon Clinical Multiaxial Inventory." *Journal of Personality Assessment, 49,* 156–160.

Craigie, F., and Ross, S. (1980). "The Use of a Videotape Pre-Treatment Training Program to Encourage Treatment-Seeking among Alcoholic Detoxification Patients." *Behavior Therapy, 11,* 141–147.

Crisp, A., Burns, T., and Bhat, A. (1986). "Primary Anorexia Nervosa in the Male and Female." *British Journal of Medical Psychology, 59,* 123–132.

Dahlstrom, W., and Dahlstrom, L., Eds. (1980). *Basic Readings on the MMPI.* Minneapolis: University of Minnesota Press.

Dahlstrom, W., Lachar, D., and Dahlstrom, L. (1986). *MMPI Patterns of American Minorities.* Minneapolis: University of Minnesota Press.

Dahlstrom, W., and Welsh, G. (1980). *An MMPI Handbook: A Guide to Clinical Practice and Research.* Minneapolis: University of Minnesota Press.

Dahlstrom, W., Welsh, G., and Dahlstrom, L. E. (1972). *An MMPI Handbook,* Vol. 1: *Clinical Interpretation.* Minneapois: University of Minnesota Press.

Daldin, H. (1985). "Faking-Good and Faking Bad on the Personality Inventory for Children-Revised, Shortened Format." *Journal of Consulting and Clinical Psychology, 53,* 561–563.

Dangel, R., and Polster, R. (1986). *Teaching Child Management Skills.* New York: Pergamon.

Daniel M'Naghten's Case, 8 Eng. Rep. 718 (1843).

Davis, K., and Sines, J. (1971). "An Antisocial Behavior Pattern Associated with a Specific MMPI Profile." *Journal of Consulting and Clinical Psychology, 36,* 229–234.

Dawood, M. (1985). "Premenstrual Tension Syndrome." *Obstetrics and Gynecology Annual, 14,* 328–343.

Donnelly, E., Murphy, D., Waldaman, I., and Reynolds, T. (1976). "MMPI Differences Between Unipolar and Bipolar Depressed Subjects: A Replication." *Journal of Clinical Psychology, 32,* 610–612.

Dunn, G. (1992). "Multiple Personality Disorder." *Professional Psychology: Research and Practice, 23,* 18–23.

DuPaul, G., Guevremont, D., and Barkley, R. (1991). "Attention Deficit-Hyperactivity Disorder in Adolescence." *Clinical Psychology Review, 11,* 231–245.

Durham v. U.S., 214 F.2d 862 D.C. Cir (1954).

Dusky v. U.S. 362 U.S. 402 (1960).

Eber, H. (1975). Personal communication.

———— (1987). Personal communication.

Edell, W. (1987). "Relationship of Borderline Syndrome Disorders to Early Schizophrenia on the MMPI." *Journal of Clinical Psychology, 43,* 163–174.

Edinger, J. (1979). "Cross-Validation of the Mergargee MMPI Typology for Prisoners." *Journal of Consulting and Clinical Psychology, 47,* 234–342.

Eichelman, B. (1988). "Toward a Rational Pharmacotherapy for Aggressive and Violent Behavior." *Hospital and Community Psychiatry 39,* 31–39.

Ekman, P. (1985). *Telling Lies.* New York: W. W. Norton.

Ellis, A. (1992). "Group Rational-Emotive and Cognitive-Behavior Therapy." *International Journal of Group Psychotherapy, 42,* 63–80.

Ellis, A., and Dryden, W. (1987). *The Practice of Rational-Emotive Therapy.* New York: Springer.

Ellsworth, R., Collins, J., Casey, N., Schoonover, R., et al. (1979). "Some Characteristics of Effective Psychiatric Treatment Programs." *Journal of Consulting and Clinical Psychology, 47,* 799–817.

Engleland, B., Erickson, M., Butcher, J., and Ben-Porath, Y. (1991). "MMPI-2 Profiles of Women at Risk for Child Abuse." *Journal of Personality Assessment, 57,* 254–263.

Erickson, W., Luxemberg, M., Walbek, N., and Seely, N. (1987). "Frequency of MMPI Two-Point Code Types Among Sex Offenders." *Journal of Consulting and Clinical Psychology, 55,* 566–570.

Ekman, P., and O'Sullivan, M. (1991). "Who Can Catch a Liar?" *American Psychologist, 46,* 913–920.

Ettin, M. (1982). *Foundations and Applications of Group Psychotherapy.* Needham Heights, MA: Allyn and Bacon.

Exner, J. (1974). *The Rorschach: A Comprehensive System,* Vol. 2. New York: John Wiley.

_____ (1978). *The Rorschach: A Comprehensive System,* Vol. 2: *Current Research and Advanced Interpretation.* New York: John Wiley.

_____ (1986). *The Rorschach: A Comprehensive System,* Vol. 1, 2nd ed. New York: John Wiley.

_____ (1988). *Rorschach: A Comprehensive System: Assessment of Personality and Psychopathology,* 2nd Ed. New York: Wiley.

Eysenck, H. (1985). "Incubation Theory of Fear/Anxiety." In S. Riess and R. Bootzin, Eds. *Theoretical Issues in Behavior Therapy.* Orlando, FL: Academic Press.

Fabian, M., and Parsons, O. (1983). "Differential Improvement of Cognitive Functions in Recovering Alcoholic Women." *Journal of Abnormal Psychology, 92,* 87–95.

Fawcett, J. (1992). "Suicide Risk Factors in Depressive Disorders and in Panic Disorder." *Journal of Clinical Psychiatry, 53* (Supplement), 9–13.

Fedora, O., Reddon, J., Morrison, J., Fedora, S. et al. (1992). *Archives of Sexual Behavior, 21,* 1–16.

Feinberg, J., and McIlvried, E. (1991). "WAIS-R Intrasubtest Scatter in a Chronic Schizophrenic Population." *Journal of Clinical Psychology, 47,* 327–335.

Fenton, W. and McGlashan, T. (1991). "Natural History of Schizophrenia Subtypes." *Archives of General Psychiatry, 48,* 978–986.

Fersch, E. (1980). *Psychology and Psychiatry and Courts and Corrections.* New York: John Wiley.

Finkelhor, D. (1985). *Child Sexual Abuse.* New York: Free Press.

Fjordback, T. (1985). "Clinical Correlates of High Lie Scale Elevations Among Forensic Patients." *Journal of Personality Assessment, 49,* 252–255.

Fleming, M., Cohen, D., Salt, P., Jones, D., and Jenkins, S. (1981). "A Study of Pre- and Postsurgical Transsexuals: MMPI Characteristics." *Archives of Sexual Behavior, 10,* 161–170.

Foa, E., and Kozak, M. (1986). "Emotional Processing of Fear: Exposure to Corrective Information." *Psychological Bulletin, 99,* 20–35.

Ford v. Wainwright 477 U.S. 399 (1986).

Forgione, A. (1976). "Instrumentation and Techniques. The Use of Mannequins in the Behavioral Assessment of Child Molesters: Two Case Reports." *Behavior Therapy, 7,* 678–685.

Fowler, R. (1981). *Advanced Interpretation of the MMPI.* Guadaloupe, French W.I.: SEPA Workshops.

Francoeur, R. (1991). *Becoming a Sexual Person,* 2nd Ed. New York: MacMillan.

Freeman, C. (1991). "A Practical Guide to the Treatment of Bulimia Nervosa." *Journal of Psychosomatic Research, 35,* 41–49.

Freund, K., Scher, H., and Hucker, S. (1983). "The Courtship Disorders." *Archives of Sexual Behavior, 12,* 369–379.

Freund, K., and Watson, R. (1991). "Assessment of the Sensitivity and Specificity of a Phallometric Test. *Psychological Assessment, 3,* 254–260.

Friedrich, W., Ed. (1991). *Casebook of Sexual Abuse Treatment.* New York: W. W. Norton.

Fuld, P. (1984). "Test Profile of Cholinergic Dysfunction and of Alzheimer-type Dementia." *Journal of Clinical Neuropsychology, 6,* 388–392.

Fulkerson, S., and Willage, D. (1980). "Decisional Ambiguity as a Source of "Cannot Say" Responses on Personality Questionnaires." *Journal of Personality Assessment, 44,* 381–386.

Gass, C. (1991a). "Emotional Variables and Neuropsychological Test Performance." *Journal of Clinical Psychology, 47,* 153–157.

Gass, C. (1991b). "MMPI-2 Interpretation and Closed Head Injury: A Correction Factor." *Psychological Assessment, 3,* 27–31.

Gass, C. (1992). Personal communication.

Gass, C., and Russell, E. (1986). "MMPI Correlates of Lateralized Cerebral Lesions and Aphasic Deficits." *Journal of Consulting and Clinical Psychology, 54,* 359–363.

Gass, C., and Russell, E. (1991). "MMPI Profiles of Closed Head Trauma Patients: Impact of Neurologic Complaints." *Journal of Clinical Psychology, 47,* 253–260.

Geen, R. (1990). *Human Aggression.* Pacific Grove, CA: Brooks/Cole.

Gentry, S., and Meyer, R. (1991). "A Validation Study of the MMPI-2 Sex Role Scales: An Analysis of the GM, GF, and MF Scales." Presented to Annual Convention of American Psychological Association. San Francisco.

Gilberstadt, H., and Duker, J. (1965). *A Handbook for Clinical and Actuarial MMPI Interpretation.* Philadelphia: Saunders.

Gilbert, J. (1978). *Interpreting Psychological Test Data.* New York: Van Nostrand Reinhold.

_____ (1980). *Interpreting Psychological Test Data–II*. New York: Van Nostrand Reinhold.

Gillberg, I., and Gillberg, C. (1988). "Generalized Hyperkinesis: Follow-up Study from 7 to 13 Years." *Journal of the American Academy of Child and Adolescent Psychiatry, 27,* 55–59.

Gillis, J., Rogers, R., and Bagby, R. (1991). "Validity of the M Test." *Journal of Personality Assessment, 57,* 130–140.

Gilmore, J. (1991). "Murdering While Asleep." *Forensic Reports, 4,* 455–459.

Glasser, W. (1980). "Two Cases in Reality Therapy," in G. Belin, Ed. *Contemporary Psychotherapies*. Chicago: Rand McNally.

Goldberg, L. (1992). "The Development of Markers for the Big-Five Factor Structure." *Psychological Assessment, 4,* 26–42.

Golden, C. (1979). *Clinical Interpretation of Objective Psychological Tests*. New York: Grune and Stratton.

Golden, R., and Meehl, P. (1979). "Detection of the Schizoid Taxon with MMPI Indicators." *Journal of Abnormal Psychology, 88,* 217–233.

Goldfried, M., Stricker, G., and Weiner, I. (1971). *Rorschach Handbook of Clinical and Research Applications*. Englewood Cliffs, NJ: Prentice-Hall.

Golding, S., Roesch, R., and Schreiber, J. (1984). "Assessment and Conceptualization of Competency to Stand trial: Preliminary Data on the Interdisciplinary Fitness Interview." *Law and Human Behavior, 8,* 321–334.

Goldstein, A., and Keller, H. (1987). *Aggressive Behavior*. New York: Pergamon.

Goldstein, A., and Stein, N. (1976). *Prescriptive Psychotherapies*. New York: Pergamon.

Goodwin, F., and Jamison, D. (1990). *Manic-Depressive Illness*. New York: Oxford.

Gottesman, I. (1991). *Schizophrenia Genesis*. New York: Freeman.

Grace, W., and Sweeney, M. (1986). "Comparisons of the P > V Sign on the WISC-R and WAIS-R in Delinquent Males." *Journal of Clinical Psychology, 42,* 173–176.

Graham, J. (1977). *The MMPI: A Practical Guide*. New York: Oxford University Press.

_____. (1987). *The MMPI: A Practical Guide,* 2nd ed. New York: Oxford University Press.

_____. (1990). *MMPI-2: Assessing Personality and Psychopathology*. New York: Oxford.

Graham, J., Timbrook, R., Ben-Porath, Y., and Butcher, J. (1991a). "Code-type Congruence between MMPI-1 and MMPI-2: Separating Fact from Artifact." *Journal of Personality Assessment, 57,* 205–215.

Graham, J., Watts, D., and Timbrook, R. (1991b). "Detecting Fake-Good and Fake-Bad MMPI-2 Profiles." *Journal of Personality Assessment, 57,* 264–277.

Green, A., and Salzman, C. (1990). "Clozapine: Benefits and Risks." *Hospital and Community Psychiatry, 41,* 379–380.

Greene, R. (1980). *The MMPI: An Interpretive Manual*. New York: Grune and Stratton.

Greene, R. (1991). *The MMPI-2/MMPI: An Interpretive Manual,* 2nd Ed. Needham Heights, MA: Allyn and Bacon.

Grisso, T. (1986). *Evaluating Competencies: Forensic Assessments and Instruments.* New York: Plenum.

Gross, W., and Carpenter, L. (1971). "Alcoholic Personality: Reality or Fiction?" *Psychological Reports, 28,* 375–378.

Groth-Marmat, G. (1990). *Handbook of Psychological Assessment,* 2nd ed. New York: Wiley.

Guertin, W., Rabin, A., Frank, G., and Ladd, C. (1962). "Research with the WAIS: 1955–1960." *Psychological Bulletin, 59,* 1–26.

Gynther, M., Altman, H., and Slettin, I. (1973a). "Replicated Correlates of MMPI Two-Point Types: The Missouri Actuarial System." *Journal of Clinical Psychology.* Monograph Supplement 39.

Gynther, M., Altman, H., and Warbin, W. (1973b). "Interpretation of Uninterpretable Minnesota Multiphasic Personality Inventory Profiles." *Journal of Consulting and Clinical Psychololgy, 40,* 78–83.

Gynther, M., and Green, S. (1980). "Accuracy May Make a Difference, But Does a Difference Make for Accuracy? A Response to Pritchard and Rosenblatt." *Journal of Consulting and Clinical Psychology, 48,* 268–272.

Haaga, D., Dyck, M., and Ernst, D. (1991). "Empirical Status of Cognitive Theory of Depression." *Psychological Bulletin, 110,* 215–236.

Hall, G., Maiuro, R., Vitaliano, P., and Proctor, W. (1986). "The Utility of the MMPI with Men Who Have Sexually Assaulted Children." *Journal of Consulting and Clinical Psychology, 54,* 493–496.

Hammarberg, M. (1992). "Penn Inventory for Posttraumatic Stress Disorder: Psychometric Properties." *Psychological Assessment, 4,* 67–76.

Hare, R. (1986). "Twenty Years of Experience with the Cleckley Psychopath." In W. Reid, D. Dorr, J. Walker, and J. Bonner, Eds. *Unmasking the Psychopath.* New York: Norton.

Hare, R., Hart, S., and Forth, A. (1992). Workshop on the Assessment of Psychopathy. Biennial Meeting of the American Psychology-Law Society, San Diego, CA.

Hare, R., Hart, S., and Harpur, T. (1991). "Psychopathy and the DSM–IV Criteria for Antisocial Personality Disorder." *Journal of Abnormal Psychology, 100,* 391–398.

Hartmann, F., Poirier, M., Chantal-Bourdel, M., Loo, H., et al. (1991). "Comparison of Acetorphan with Clonidine for Opiate Withdrawal Symptoms." *American Journal of Psychiatry, 148,* 627–629.

Hathaway, S. (1947). "A Coding System for MMPI Profiles." *Journal of Consulting Psychology, 11,* 334–337.

Hathaway S., and McKinley, J. (1967). *The Minnesota Multiphasic Personality Inventory Manual.* New York: Psychological Corporation.

Hauri, P., Ed. (1991). *Case Studies in Insomnia.* New York: Plenum.

Hawk, G. (1983). "An Investigation of the Megargee MMPI Typology in a Forensic Setting." *Dissertation Abstracts International, 43* (11-B), 3732.

Hecker, J., and Thorpe, G. (1992). *Agoraphobia and Panic.* Needham Heights, MA: Allyn and Bacon.

Hedlund, J. (1977). "MMPI Clinical Scale Correlates." *Journal of Consulting and Clinical Psychology, 45,* 739–750.

Heilbrun, A., Blum, N., and Goldreyer, N. (1985). "Defensive Projection: An Investigation of Its Role in Paranoid Conditions." *Journal of Nervous and Mental Disease, 173,* 17–25.

Heinrich, T., and Amolsch, T. (1978). "A Note on the Situational Interpretation of WAIS Profile Patterns." *Journal of Personality Assessment, 42,* 418–420.

Heller, J. (1974). *Something Happened.* New York: Knopf.

Hendrix, E., Thompson, L., and Rau, B. (1978). "Behavioral Treatment of an "Hysterically" Clenched Fist." *Journal of Behavior Therapy and Experimental Psychiatry, 9,* 273–276.

Hendrix, M., and Meyer, R. (1976). "Toward More Comprehensive and Durable Client Changes: A Case Report." *Psychotherapy: Theory, Research, and Practice, 13,* 263–266.

Herbert, M. (1987). *Conduct Disorders of Childhood and Adolescence.* New York: John Wiley.

Hewett, B., and Martin, W. (1980). "Psychometric Comparisons of Sociopathic and Psychopathological Behaviors of Alcoholics and Drug Abusers Versus a Low Drug Use Control Population." *The International Journal of the Addictions, 15,* 77–105.

Hochn-Saric, R., and McLeod, D. (1988). "Panic and Generalized Anxiety Disorders." In C. Last and M. Hersen, Eds. *Handbook of Anxiety Disorders.* Elmsford, NY: Pergamon.

Holland, T., and Watson, C. (1980). "Multivariate Analysis of WAIS-MMPI Relationships among Brain-Damaged, Schizophrenic, Neurotic, and Alcoholic Patients." *Journal of Clinical Psychology, 36,* 352–359.

Hollin, C., and Howells, K., Eds. (1991). *Clinical Approaches to Sex Offenders and Their Victims.* New York: Wiley.

Hovanitz, C., and Jordan-Brown, C. (1986). "The Validity of MMPI Subtle and Obvious Items in Psychiatric Patients." *Journal of Clinical Psychology, 42,* 100–108.

Hsu, L. (1986). "Implications of Differences in Elevations of K-Corrected and Non-K-Corrected MMPI T Scores." *Journal of Consulting and Clinical Psychology, 54,* 552–557.

Iacono, W. (1991). "Psychophysiological Assessment of Psychopathology." *Psychological Assessment, 3,* 309–320.

IPAT Staff (1963). *Information Bulletin No. 8 to the 16 PF Handbook.* Champaign, IL: Institute for Personality and Ability Testing.

———— (1972). *Manal for the 16 PF.* Champaign, IL: Institute for Personality and Ability Testing.

Jackson, J., Greenblatt, R., Davis, W., Murphy, T., and Trimakas, K. (1991). "Assessment of Schizophrenic Inpatients with the MCMI." *Journal of Clinical Psychology, 47,* 505–510.

Jacobs, D. (1987). "A general theory of addictions." In T. Galski, Ed. *Handbook of Pathological Gambling.* Springfield, IL: Charles Thomas.

Jacobsen, R., and Tomkin, A. (1988). "Converting Shipley Institute of Living Scale Scores to IQ." *Journal of Clinical Psychology, 44,* 72–75.

Jarvik, M. (1967). "The Psychopharmacological Revolution." *Psychology Today, 1,* 51–59.

Johnson, F., and Johnson, S. (1986). "Differences Between Human Figure Drawings of Child Molesters and Control Groups." *Journal of Clinical Psychology, 42,* 638–647.

Johnson, J., Klinger, D., and Gianetti, R. (1980). "Band Width in Diagnostic Classification Using the MMPI as a Predictor." *Journal of Consulting and Clinical Psychology, 48,* 340–349.

Johnson, M. (1966). "Verbal Abstracting Ability and Schizophrenia." *Journal of Consulting Psychology, 30,* 275–277.

Johnson, R., Tobin, J., and Cellucci, T. (1992). "Personality Characteristics of Cocaine and Alcohol Abusers." *Addictive Behaviors, 17,* 159–166.

Kalichman, S. (1988). "Empirically Derived MMPI Profile Subgroups of Incarcerated Homicide Offenders." *Journal of Clinical Psychology, 44,* 733–738.

Kalichman, S., Syzmanowski, D., McKee, G., Taylor, J., and Craig, M. (1989). "Cluster Analytically Derived MMPI Profile Subgroups of Incarcerated Adult Rapists." *Journal of Clinical Psychology, 45,* 150–155.

Karon, B. (1976). "The Psychoanalysis of Schizophrenia." In P. Magero, Ed. *The Construction of Madness.* New York: Pergamon.

_____ (1981). "The Thematic Apperception Test." In A. Rabin, Ed. *Assessment with Projective Techniques.* New York: Springer.

Karson, S. (1959). "The Sixteen Personality Factor Test in Clinical Practice." *Journal of Clinical Psychology, 15,* 174–176.

_____ (1960). "Validating Clinical Judgments with the 16 PF Test." *Journal of Clinical Psychology, 16,* 394–397.

_____ (1989). "The 16 PF." In C. Newmark, Ed. *Major Psychological Assessment Instruments.* Vol 2. Boston: Allyn and Bacon.

Karson, S., and O'Dell, J. (1976). *Clinical Use of the 16 PF.* Champaign, IL: IPAT.

Katon, W., Lin, E., Von Korff, M., and Russo, J., et al. (1991). "Somatization: A Spectrum of Severity." *American Journal of Psychiatry, 148,* 34–40.

Kay, S., and Lindenmayer, J. (1987). "Outcome Predictors in Acute Schizophrenia." *Journal of Nervous and Mental Disease, 175,* 152–160.

Keiser, T., and Lowy, D. (1980). "Heroin Addiction and Wechsler Digit Span Test." *Journal of Clinical Psychology, 36,* 347–351.

Keles, A. (1983). "Biopsychobehavioral Correlates and the MMPI." *Psychosomatic Medicine, 45,* 341–347.

Kellam, A. (1969). "Shoplifting Treated by Aversion to a Film." *Behavior Research and Therapy, 7,* 125–127.

Keller, M., and Baker, L. (1992). "The Clinical Course of Panic Disorder and Depression." *Journal of Clinical Psychiatry, 53* (Supplement), 5–8.

Kelley, C., and King, G. (1979a). "Cross Validation of the 2-8/8-2 MMPI Code Type for Young Adult Psychiatric Outpatients." *Journal of Personality Assessment, 43,* 143–149.

_____ (1979b). "Behavioral Correlates of the 2-7-8 MMPI Profile Type in

Students at a University Mental Health Center." *Journal of Consulting and Clinical Psychology, 47,* 679–685.

_____ (1979c). "Behavioral Correlates of Infrequent 2-point MMPI Code Types at a University Mental Health Center." *Journal of Clinical Psychology, 35,* 576–585.

Kellner, R. (1986). *Somatization and Hypochondriasis.* London: Praeger.

Kernberg, O. (1984). *Severe Personality Disorders.* New Haven: Yale University Press.

Kernberg, P., and Chazan, S. (1991). *Children with Conduct Disorders.* New York: Basic.

King, G., and Kelley, C. (1977). "Behavioral Correlates for Spike-4, Spike-9, and 4-9/9-4 MMPI Profiles in Students at a University Mental Health Center." *Journal of Clinical Psychology, 33,* 718–724.

Kinsey, A., Pomeroy, W., and Martin, C. (1948). *Sexual Behavior in the Human Male.* Philadelphia: Saunders.

_____ (1953). *Sexual Behavior in the Human Female.* Philadelphia: Saunders.

Kirkley, B., and Janick, L. (1987). "Binge Eating in Obesity: Associated MMPI Characteristics." *Journal of Consulting and Clinical Psychology, 55,* 872–876.

Kirman, W. (1980). "The Modern Psychoanalytic Treatment of Depression." In G. Belkin, Ed. *Contemporary Psychotherapies.* Chicago: Rand McNally.

Kish, G., Hagen, J., Woody, M., and Harvey, H. (1980). "Alcoholics Recovery from Cerebral Impairment as a Function of Duration of Abstinence." *Journal of Clinical Psychology, 36,* 584–589.

Kleinknecht, R. (1991). *Mastering Anxiety: The Nature and Treatment of Anxious Conditions.* New York: Plenum.

Klingler, D., and Saunders, D. (1975). "A Factor-Analysis of the Items for Nine Subtests of the WAIS." *Multivariate Behavioral Research, 10,* 131–154.

Klopfer, B., and Davidson, H. (1962). *Rorschach's Technique: An Introductory Manual.* New York: Harcourt Brace.

Klopfer, W., and Taulbee, E. (1976). "Projective Tests." *Annual Review of Psychology, 27,* 543–576.

Koslowsky, M., Scheinberg, Z., Bleich, A., Mark, M., et al. (1992). "The Factor Structure and Criterion Validity of the Short Form of the Eating Attitudes Test." *Journal of Personality Assessment, 58,* 27–35.

Kozak, M., Foa, E., and McCarthy, P. (1988). "Obsessive-Compulsive Disorder." In C. Last and M. Hersen, Eds. *Handbook of Anxiety Disorders.* Elmsford, NY: Pergamon.

Kramer, J. (1990). "Guidelines for Interpreting WAIS-R Subtest Scores." *Psychological Assessment, 2,* 202–205.

Krishnan, R., Davidson, J., and Miller, R. (1985). "Trichotillomania: A Review." *Comprehensive Psychiatry, 26,* 123–128.

Krug, S. (1978). "Further Evidence on the 16 PF Distortion Scales." *Journal of Personality Assessment, 42,* 513–518.

_____ (1980). *Clinical Analysis Questionnaire Manual.* Champaign, IL: IPAT.

_____ (1981). *Interpreting 16 PF Profile Patterns.* Champaign, IL: IPAT.

Krug, S., and Johns, E. (1986). "A Large-Scale Cross-Validation of Second-Order Personality Structure Defined by the 16 PF." *Psychological Reports, 59,* 683–693.

Kurlychek, R., and Jordan, L. (1980). "MMPI Code Types of Responsible and Nonresponsible Criminal Defendants." *Journal of Clinical Psychology, 36,* 590–593.

L'Abate, L., Farrar, J., and Serritella, D., Eds. (1992). *Handbook of Differential Treatment Addictions.* Needham Heights, MA: Allyn and Bacon.

Laboratory of Community Psychology (1973). *Competency to Stand Trial and Mental Illness.* Rockville, MD: National Institutes of Mental Health.

Lachar, D. (1974). *The MMPI: Clinical Assessment and Automated Interpretation.* Los Angeles: Western Psychological Services.

Lambert, M., Hatch, D., Kingston, M., and Edwards, B. (1986). "Zung, Beck, and Hamilton Rating Scales as Measures of Treatment Outcome." *Journal of Consulting and Clinical Psychology, 54,* 54–59.

Landman, J., and Dawes, R. (1982). "Psychotherapy Outcome: Smith and Glass's Conclusions Stand Up under Scrutiny." *American Psychologist, 37,* 504–516.

Lane, J., and Lachar, D. (1979). "Correlates of Broad MMPI Categories." *Journal of Clinical Psychology, 35,* 560–566.

Lazar, B., and Harrow, M. (1985). "Paranoid and Nonparanoid Schizophrenia." *Journal of Clinical Psychology, 141,* 145–151.

Lazarus, A. (1971). *Behavior Therapy and Beyond.* New York: McGraw-Hill.

Lazarus, A. (1987). "Discussion." In J. Zeig, Ed. *The Evolution of Psychotherapy.* New York: Brunner/Mazel.

Levin, S., and Stava, L. (1987). "Personality Characteristics of Sex Offenders." *Archives of Sexual Behavior, 16,* 57–79.

Levitt, E. (1980). *Primer on the Rorschach Technique.* Springfield, IL: Charles C. Thomas.

Lewak, R., Marks, P., and Nelson, G. (1990). *Therapist Guide to the MMPI and MMPI-2.* Muncie, IN: Accelerated Development.

Lickey, M., and Gordon, B. (1991). *Medicine and Mental Illness.* New York: W. H. Freeman.

Liebowitz, M., Gorman, J., Fryer, A., Levitt, M., et al. (1985). "Lactate Provocation of Panic Attacks." *Archives of General Psychiatry, 42,* 709–714.

Litz, B., Penk, W., Walsh, S., Hyer, L., et al. (1991). "Similarities and Differences Between MMPI and MMPI-2 Applications to the Assessment of Posttraumatic Stress Disorder." *Journal of Personality Assessment, 57,* 238–253.

Loeber, R. (1990). "Development and Risk Factors of Juvenile Antisocial Behavior and Delinquency." *Clinical Psychology Review, 10,* 1–42.

Lo Piccolo, J. (1985). "Advances in the Diagnosis and Treatment of Sexual Dysfunction." Convention Workshop. Louisville: Kentucky Psychological Association.

Lo Piccolo, J., and Stock, W. (1986). "Treatment of Sexual Dysfunction." *Journal of Consulting and Clinical Psycholology, 54,* 158–167.

Lorr, M., and Suziedelis, A. (1985). "Profile Patterns in the 16 PF Questionnaire." *Journal of Clinical Psychology, 41,* 767–773.

Love, A., and Peck, C. (1987). "The MMPI and Psychological Factors in Chronic Low Back Pain: A Review." *Pain, 28,* 1–12.

Low, P., Jeffries, J., and Bonnie, R. (1986). *The Trial of John Hinckley, Jr.* Mineola, NY: Foundation Press.

Lykken, D. (1957). "A Study of Anxiety in the Sociopathic Personality." *Journal of Abnormal and Social Psychology, 55,* 6–10.

Lyons, L., and Woods, P. (1991). "The Efficacy of Rational-Emotive Therapy: A Quantitative Review of the Outcome Research." *Clinical Psychology Review, 11,* 357–370.

MacAndrew, C. (1965). "The Differentiation of Male Alcoholic Outpatients from Nonalcoholic Psychiatric Patients by Means of the MMPI." *Quarterly Journal of Studies on Alcohol, 26,* 238–46.

Macciocchi, S., and Meyer, R. (1989). "The Context of Self-Disclosure, the Polygraph and Deception." *Forensic Reports, 4,* 51–59.

Margolin, D., Ed. (1992). *Cognitive Neuroscience in Clinical Practice.* New York: Oxford.

Marlatt, A., Baer, J., Donovan, D., and Kiviahan, D. (1988). "Addictive Behaviors: Etiology and Treatment." In M. Rosenzweig and L. Porter, Eds. *Annual Review of Psychology,* Vol. 39. Palo Alto, CA: Annual Reviews.

Marlowe, D., and Crowne, D. (1964). *The Approval Motive.* New York: John Wiley.

Marsh, D., Linberg, L., and Smeltzer, J. (1991). "Human Figure Drawings of Adjudicated and Nonadjudicated Adolescents." *Journal of Personality Assessment, 57,* 77–86.

Marshall, W., Eccles, A., and Barbaree, H. (1991). "The Treatment of Exhibitionists." *Behavior Research and Therapy, 29,* 129–135.

Maser, J., Kaelber, C., and Weise, R. (1991). "International Use and Attitudes Toward DSM-III and DSM-III-R: Growing Consensus in Psychiatric Classification." *Journal of Abnormal Psychology, 100,* 271–279.

Mason, B., Cohen, J., and Exner, J. (1985). "Schizophrenic, Depressive, and Nonpatient Personality Organization Described Rorschach Factor Structure." *Journal of Personality Assessment, 49,* 295–303.

Masters, W., and Johnson, V. (1970). *Human Sexual Inadequacy.* Boston: Little, Brown.

Masters, W., Johnson, V., and Kolodny, R. (1991). *Human Sexuality,* 4th ed. Glenville, IL: Scott, Foresman, Little, Brown.

Matarazzo, J. (1972). *Wechsler's Measurement and Appraisal of Adult Intelligence.* Baltimore: Williams and Wilkins.

Matson, J., and Gardner, W. (1991). "Behavioral Learning Theory and Current Applications to Severe Behavior Problems in Persons with Severe Retardation." *Clinical Psychology Review, 11,* 175–183.

McCann, J., and Suess, J. (1988). "Clinical Applications of the MCMI: The 1-2-3-8 Codetype." *Journal of Clinical Psychology, 44,* 181–186.

McElroy, S., Pope, H., Hudson, J., Keck, P., and White, K. (1991). "Kleptomania: A Report of 20 Cases." *American Journal of Psychiatry, 148,* 652–655.

McGrath, E., Keita, G., Strickland, B., and Russo, N. (1990). *Women and Depression: Risk Factor and Treatment Issues.* Washington, DC: American Psychological Association.

McNiel, K., and Meyer, R. (1990). "Detection of Deception on the Millon Clinical Multiaxial Inventory (MCMI)." *Journal of Clinical Psychology, 46,* 755–764.

Meehl, P., and Hathaway, S. (1980). "The K Factor as a Suppressor Variable in the MMPI." In W. Dahlstrom and L. Dahlstrom, Eds. *Basic Readings on the MMPI.* Minneapolis: University of Minnesota Press.

Megargee, E., and Bohn, M. (1979). *Classifying Criminal Offenders.* Beverly Hills, CA: Sage.

Mergaree, E., and Cook, P. (1975). "Negative Response Bias and the MMPI O-H Scale: A Response to Deiker." *Journal of Consulting and Clinical Psychology, 43,* 725, 729.

Megargee, E., Cook, P., and Mendelsohn, G. (1967). "Development and Validation of an MMPI Scale of Assaultiveness in Overcontrolled Individuals." *Journal of Abnormal Psychology, 72,* 519–528.

Meichenbaum, D. (1985). "Cognitive Behavior Modification." In F. Kanfer and A. Goldstein, Eds. *Helping People Change.* New York: Plenum.

Meister, R. (1980). *Hypochondria.* New York: Taplinger.

Melton, G., Petrila, J., Poythress, N., and Slobogin, C. (1987). *Psychological Evaluations for the Courts.* New York: Guilford.

Mester, R. (1986). "The Psychotherapy of Mania." *The British Journal of Medical Psychology, 59,* 13–20.

Meyer, R. (1992a). *Abnormal Behavior and the Criminal Justice System.* Lexington, MA: Lexington Books.

Meyer, R. (1992b). *Practical Clinical Hypnosis.* Lexington, MA: Lexington Books.

Meyer, R., Landis, E. R., and Hays, J. R. (1988). *Law for the Psychotherapist.* New York: W. W. Norton.

Meyer, R., and Salmon, P. (1988). *Abnormal Psychology.* Boston: Allyn and Bacon.

Miller, T., Heath, L., Molcan, J., and Dugoni, B. (1991). "Imitative Violence in the Real World: A Reanalysis of Homicide Rates Following Championship Prize Fights." *Aggressive Behavior, 17,* 121–134.

Millon, T. (1981). *Disorders of Personality, DSM-III: Axis II.* New York: John Wiley.

Millon, T. (1985). "The MCMI Provides a Good Assessment of DSM-III Disorders: The MCMI-II Will Prove Even Better." *Journal of Personality Assessment, 49,* 379–391.

Millon, T. (1986). "The MCMI and DSM-III: Further Commentaries." *Journal of Personality Assessment, 50,* 205–207.

Milner, J. (1991). "Physical Child Abuse Perpetrator Screening and Evaluation." *Criminal Justice and Behavior, 18,* 47–63.

Mlatt, S., and Vale, W. (1986). "Performance of Agoraphobic Families Versus Nonagoraphobic Families on the 16 PF Questionnaire." *Journal of Clinical Psychology, 41,* 244–250.

Mohr, D., and Beutler, L. (1990). "Erectile Dysfunction: A Review of Diagnostic and Treatment Procedures." *Clinical Psychology Review, 10,* 123–150.

Moldin, S., Gottesman, I., and Erlenmeyer-Kimling, L. (1987). "Searching for the Psychometric Boundaries of Schizophrenia." *Journal of Abnormal Psychology, 96,* 354–363.

Monahan, J. (1981). *Predicting Violent Behavior.* Beverly Hills, CA: Sage.

Monahan, J. (1984). "The Prediction of Violent Behavior: Toward a Second Generation of Theory and Policy." *American Journal of Psychiatry, 141,* 10–15.

Monahan, J., and Walker, L., Eds. (1990). *Social Science in Law: Cases and Materials,* 2nd ed. Westbury, NJ: Foundation Press.

Money, J. (1987). "Sin, Sickness, or Status: Homosexual Gender Identity and Psychoneuroendocrinology." *American Psychologist, 42,* 384–399.

Montgomery, G., and Orozco, S. (1985). "Mexican Americans' Performance on the MMPI as a Function of Level of Acculturation." *Journal of Clinical Psychology, 41,* 203–212.

Montplaisir, J., and Godbout, R. (1991). *Sleep and Biological Rhythms: Basic Mechanisms and Applications to Psychiatry.* New York: Oxford.

Murphy, G., and Wetzel, R. (1980). "Suicide Risk by Birth Cohort in U.S., 1949–1974." *Archives of General Psychiatry, 37,* 519–525.

Myers, J., Weissman, M., Tischler, G., Holzer, c., et al. (1984). "Six-Month Prevalence of Psychiatric Disorders in Three Communities." *Archives of General Psychiatry, 41,* 959–970.

Nelson, B. (1984). *Making Child Abuse an Issue.* Chicago: University of Chicago Press.

Nelson, L., and Cicchetti, D. (1991). "Validity of the MMPI Depression Scale for Outpatients." *Psychological Assessment, 3,* 55–59.

Newmark, C., Ed. (1985). *Major Psychological Assessment Instruments.* Boston: Allyn and Bacon.

Newmark, C., Ed. (1989). *Major Psychological Assessment Instruments,* Vol. II. Needham Heights, MA: Allyn and Bacon.

Newmark, C., and Hutchins, T. (1980). "Age and MMPI Indices of Schizophrenia." *Journal of Clinical Psychology, 36,* 768–769.

Oas, P. (1984). "Validity of the Draw-A-Person and Bender-Gestalt Tests as Measures of Impulsivity with Adolescents." *Journal of Consulting and Clinical Psychology, 52,* 1011–1019.

Oates, W. (1987). *Behind the Masks: Personality Disorders in Religious Behaviors.* Philadelphia: Westminster Press.

O'Connor v. Donaldson 422 U.S. 563 (1975).

Ogdon, D. (1977). *Psychodiagnostics and Personality Assessment: A Handbook.* Los Angeles: Western Psychological Services.

Oltmanns, T., and Maher, B. (1988). *Delusional Beliefs.* New York: John Wiley.

Oren, D., Brainard, G., Johnston, S., Joseph-Vanderpool, J., et al. (1991). "Treatment of Seasonal Affective Disorder with Green Light and Red Light," *American Journal of Psychiatry, 148,* 509–511.

Orsini, D., Van Gorp, W., and Boone, K. (1988). *The Neuropsychology Casebook.* New York: Springer-Verlag.

Osgood, C., Luria, Z., Jeans, R., and Smith, A. (1976). "The Three Faces of Evelyn: A Case Report." *Journal of Abnormal Psychology, 85,* 247–286.

Oster, G., and Gould, P. (1987). *Using Drawings in Assessment and Therapy.* New York: Brunner/Mazel.

Pallis, C., and Bamji, A. (1979). "McIlroy Was Here. Or Was He?" *British Medical Journal, 6169,* 973–975.

Paolo, A., Ryan, J., and Smith, A. (1991). "Reading Difficulty of MMPI-2 Subscales." *Journal of Clinical Psychology, 47,* 529–532.

Parsons v. State, 81 Ala. 577, 2 So. 854 (1887).

Parwatikar, S., Holcomb, W., and Menninger, K. (1985). "Detection of Malingered Amnesia in Accused Murderers." *Bulletin of the American Academy of Psychiatry and the Law, 13,* 97–103.

Patalano, F. (1980). "Comparison of MMPI Scores of Drug Abusers and Mayo Clinic Normative Groups." *Journal of Clinical Psychology, 36,* 576–579.

Pato, M., Pigott, T., Hill, J., Grover, G., et al. (1991). "Controlled Comparison of Busiprone and Clomipramine in OCD." *American Journal of Psychiatry, 148,* 127–129.

Patrick, J. (1988). "Concordance of the MCMI and MMPI in the Diagnosis of Three DSM-III Axis I Disorders." *Journal of Clinical Psychology, 44,* 186–190.

Pauly, I. (1968). "The Current Status of the Change of Sex Operation." *Journal of Nervous and Mental Disease, 147,* 460–471.

Penk, W., Woodward, W., Robinowitz, R., and Parr, W. (1980). "An MMPI Comparison of Polydrug and Heroin Abusers." *Journal of Abnormal Psychology, 89,* 299–302.

Pennington, B., Peterson, L., and Barker, H. (1979). "The Diagnostic Use of the MMPI in Organic Brain Dysfunction." *Journal of Clinical Psychology, 35,* 484–492.

People v. Drew, Sub., 149 Cal. Rptr. 275 (1978).

Phillips, D. (1986). "The Effects of Mass Media Violence on Suicide and Homicide." *Newsletter of the American Academy of Psychiatry and Law, 11,* 29–31.

Phillips, L. and Smith, J. (1953). *Rorschach Interpretation: Advanced Technique.* New York: Grune and Stratton.

Piotrowski, C., Sherry, D., and Keller, J. (1985). "Psychodiagnostic Test Usage." *Journal of Personality Assessment, 49,* 115–120.

Piotrowski, Z. (1979). *Perceptanalysis.* Philadelphia: Ex Libris.

Poling, A., Gadow, K., and Cleary, J. (1991). *Drug Therapy for Behavior Disorders.* Elmsford, NY: Pergamon.

Prien, R., and Klupfer, D. (1986). "Continuation Drug Therapy for Major Depressive Episodes: How Long Should It Be Maintained?" *American Journal of Psychiatry, 143,* 18–23.

Pritchard, D., and Rosenblatt, A. (1980). "Racial Bias in the MMPI: A Methodological Review." *Journal of Consulting and Clinical Psychology, 48,* 263–267.

Propkop, C., Bradley, L., Margolis, R., and Gentry, W. (1980). "Multivariate Analysis of the MMPI Profiles of Patients with Pain Complaints." *Journal of Personality Assessment, 44,* 246–252.

Quay, H., Ed. (1987). *Handbook of Juvenile Delinquency.* New York: John Wiley.

Quevillon, R., Landau, S., Apple, W., and Petretic-Jackson, P. (1986). "Assessing

Adolescent Conduct Disorders and Oppositional Behaviors." In R. Harrington, Ed. *Testing Adolescents.* Kansas city, MO: Test Corporation of America.

Rabin, A. (1964). Lectures and personal communication.

_____, Ed. (1968). *Projective Techniques in Personality Assessment.* New York: Springer.

_____ (1981). "Projective Methods: A Historical Introduction." In A. Rabin, Ed. *Assessment with Projective Techniques.* New York: Springer.

Rachman, S., and Arntz, A. (1991). "The Overprediction and Underprediction of Pain." *Clinical Psychology Review, 11,* 339–356.

Rada, R., Laws, D., and Kellner, R. (1976). "Plasma Testosterone Levels in the Rapist." *Psychomatic Medicine, 38,* 257–268.

Rader, C. (1977). "MMPI Profile Types of Exposers, Rapists and Assaulters in a Court Services Population." *Journal of Consulting and Clinical Psychology, 45,* 61–69.

Rapaport, D., Gill, M., and Schafer, R. (1968). *Diagnostic Psychological Testing.* New York: International Universities Press.

Rapee, R. (1991). "Generalized Anxiety Disorder: A Review of Clinical Features and Theoretical Concepts." *Clinical Psychology Review, 11,* 419–440.

Raskin, R., and Novachk, J. (1991). "Narcissism and the Use of Fantasy." *Journal of Clinical Psychology, 47,* 490–499.

Reitan, R., and Wolfson, D. (1986). *Traumatic Brain Injury: Recovery and Rehabilitation.* Tucson: Neuropsychology Press.

Rennie v. Klein, 462 F. Supp. 1131 (D.N.J. 1978), later proceeding 476 F. Supp. 1294 (D.N.J. 1979), modified, 653 F.20 836 (3d Cir. 1981), vacated, 458 U.S. 1119 (1982), on remand, 720 F.2d 266 (3d Cir. 1983).

Resnick, R. (1991). Personal communication.

Retzlaff, P., and Gibertini, M. (1987). "Factor Structure of the MCMI Basic Personality Scales and Common-Item Artifact." *Journal of Personality Assessment, 51,* 588–594.

Reuter, E., Wallbrown, F., and Wallbrown, J. (1985). "16 PF Profiles and Four-Point Codes Seen in a Private Practice." *Multivariate Experimental Clinical Research, 7,* 123–147.

Rice, M., Quinsey, V., and Harris, G. (1991). "Sexual Recidivism Among Child Molesters Released From a Maximum Security Psychiatric Institution." *Journal of Consulting and Clinical Psychology, 59,* 381–386.

Rickers-Ovsiankina, M., Ed. (1960). *Rorschach Psychology.* New York: John Wiley.

Rifkin, A., Doddi, S., Karajgi, B., Borenstein, M., and Wachspress, M. (1991). "Dosage of Haloperidol for Schizophrenics." *Archives of General Psychiatry, 48,* 166–170.

Robe, H. (1987). Personal communication.

Roberts, C., and Golding, S. (1991). "The Social Construction of Criminal Responsibility and Insanity." *Law and Human Behavior, 15,* 349–376.

Robinette, R. (1991). "The Relationship Between the Marlowe-Crowne Form C and the Validity Scales of the MMPI." *Journal of Clinical Psychology, 47,* 396–400.

Rogers, C. (1951). *Client-Centered Therapy*. Boston: Houghton Mifflin.

Rogers, R. (1986). *Conducting Insanity Evaluations*. New York: Van Nostrand Reinhold.

———, Ed. (1988). *Clinical Assessment of Malingering and Deception*. New York: Guilford.

Rogers, R., Dolmetsch, R., and Cavanaugh, J. (1981). "An Empirical Approach to Insanity Evaluations." *Journal of Clinical Psychology, 37,* 683–687.

Rorschach, H. (1953). *Psychodiagnostics*, 5th ed., New York: Grune and Stratton.

Rossini, E., and Kaspar, J. (1987). "The Validity of the Bender-Gestalt Emotional Indicators." *Journal of Personality Assessment, 51,* 254–261.

Ruderman, A. (1986). "Dietary Restraint: A Theoretical and Empirical Review." *Psychological Bulletin, 99,* 247–262.

Sabine, D., and Meyer, R. (1992). "The Utility of the MMPI-2 Taped Version in a Low Socioeconomic Group." Unpublished paper.

Satz, P. (1987). Personal communication.

Schachter, D. (1986). "Amnesia and Crime: How Much Do We Really Know?" *American Psychologist, 43,* 286–295.

Schnarch, D. (1992). *Constructing the Sexual Crucible*. New York: W. W. Norton.

Schneidman, E. (1985). *Definition of Suicide*. New York: John Wiley.

Schretlen, D., Wilkins, S., Van Gorp, W., and Bobholz, J. (1992). "Cross-Validation of a Psychological Test Battery to Detect Faked Insanity." *Psychological Assessment, 4,* 77–83.

Schuyler, D. (1991). *A Practical Guide to Cognitive Therapy*. New York: W. W. Norton.

Schwartz, M. (1987). *Biofeedback*. New York: Guilford.

Scott, R., and Stone, D. (1986). "MMPI Measures of Psychological Disturbance in Adolescent and Adult Victims of Father-Daughter Incest." *Journal of Clinical Psychology, 42,* 251–259.

Seamons, D., Howell, R., Carlisle, A., and Roe, A. (1981). "Rorschach Simulation of Mental Illness and Normality by Psychotic and Nonpsychotic Legal Offenders." *Journal of Personality Assessment, 45,* 130–135.

Seltzer, L. (1986). *Paradoxical Strategies in Psychotherapy*. New York: John Wiley.

Selye, H. (1956). *The Stress of Life*. New York: McGraw-Hill.

Serin, R., Peters, R., and Barbaree, H. (1990). "Predictors of Psychopathy and Release Outcome in a Criminal Population." *Psychological Assessment, 2,* 419–423.

Shafer, R. (1948). *Clinical Application of Psychological Tests*. New York: International Universities Press.

——— (1954). *Psychoanalytic Interpretation in Rorschach Testing*. New York: Grune and Stratton.

Shapiro, D. (1984). *Psychological Evaluation and Expert Testimony*. New York: Van Nostrand Reinhold.

Shapiro, D. (1991). *Forensic Psychological Assessment*. Needham Heights, MA: Allyn and Bacon.

Shatin, L. (1979). "Brief Form of the Competency Screening Test for Mental Competence to Stand Trial." *Journal of Clinical Psychology, 35,* 464–467.

Siegel, M. (1987). *Psychological Testing from Early Childhood Through Adolescence.* Madison, CT: International Universities Press.

Silver, L. (1992). *Attention-Deficit Hyperactivity Disorder: A Clinical Guide to Diagnosis and Treatment.* Washington, DC: American Psychiatric Press.

Silver, R., Isaacs, K., and Mansky, P. (1981). "MMPI Correlates of Affective Disorders." *Journal of Clinical Psychology, 37,* 836–839.

Silverman, L. (1976). "Psychoanalytic Theory: The Reports of My Death Are Greatly Exaggerated." *American Psychologist, 31,* 621–637.

Slobogin, C., Melton, G., and Showalter, C. (1984). "The Feasibility of a Brief Evaluation of Mental State at the Time of the Offense." *Law and Human Behavior, 8,* 305–320.

Small, A., Madero, J., Gross, H., Teagno, L., et al. (1981). "A Comparative Analysis of Primary Anorexics and Schizophrenics on the MMPI." *Journal of Clinical Psychology, 37,* 773–736.

Smith, M., and Glass, G. (1977). "Meta-analysis of Psychotherapy Outcome Studies." *American Psychologist, 32,* 955–1008.

Smith, M., and Thelen, M. (1984). "Development and Validation of a Test for Bulimia." *Journal of Consulting and Clinical Psychology, 52,* 863–872.

Smith, S., and Meyer, R. (1980). "Working Between the Legal System and the Therapist." In D. Cox and R. Daitzman, Eds. *Exhibitionism.* New York: Garland.

_____ (1987). *Law, Behavior and Mental Health: Policy and Practice.* New York: New York University Press.

Sneddon, J. (1980). "Myasthenia Gravis–The Difficult Diagnosis." *British Journal of Psychiatry, 136,* 92–93.

Snyder, S. (1986). "Pseudologia Fantastica in the Borderline Patient." *American Journal of Psychiatry, 143,* 1287–1290.

Solovay, M., Shenton, M., and Holzman, P. (1987). "Comparative Studies of Thought Disorders: 1. Mania: 2. Schizoaffective Disorder." *Archives of General Psychiatry, 44,* 13–30.

Spicgcl, D., and Cardeña, E. (1991). "Disintegrated Experience: The Dissociative Disorders Revisited." *Journal of Abnormal Psychology, 100,* 366–378.

Spitzer, R. (1992). Personal communication.

Spitzer, R., Cohen, J., Fliess, J., and Endicott, J. (1967). "Quantification of Agreement in Psychiatric Diagnosis: A New Approach." *Archives of General Psychiatry, 17,* 83–87.

Spitzer, R., and Endicott, J. (1978). *Schedule of Affective Disorders and Schizophrenia.* New York: Biometrics Research.

Spitzer, R., Forman, J., and Nee, J. (1979). "DSM-III Field Trials: Initial Interrater Diagnostic Reliability." *American Journal of Psychiatry, 136,* 815–817.

Spotts, J., and Schontz, F. (1984). "Drug-Induced Ego States." *The International Journal of the Addictions, 19,* 119–151.

State of New Jersey v. Stasio, 78 N.J. 467 (1979).

Stevenson, J., and Meares, R. (1992). "An Outcome Study of Psychotherapy for Patients with Borderline Personality Disorder." *American Journal of Psychiatry, 149,* 358–362.

Stone, M. (1990). *The Fate of Borderlines.* New York: Guilford.

Storr, A. (1990). *The Art of Psychotherapy,* 2nd Ed. New York: Routledge.

Stout, A., and Steege, J. (1985). "Psychological Assessment of Women Seeking Treatment for Premenstrual Syndrome." *Journal of Psychosomatic Research, 92,* 621–629.

Strassberg, D., Reimherr, F., Ward, M., Russell, S., and Cole, A. (1981). "The MMPI and Chronic Pain." *Journal of Consulting and Clinical Psychology, 49,* 220–226.

Swann, A., Secunda, S., Koslow, S., Katz, M., et al. (1991). "Mania: Sympathoadrenal Function and Clinical State." *Psychiatry Research, 37,* 195–205.

Swiercinsky, D., Ed. (1985). *Testing Adults.* Kansas City: Test Corporation of America.

Szasz, T. (1987). *Insanity: The Idea and Its Consequences.* New York: John Wiley.

Tamminga, C., and Schulz, C., Eds. (1991). *Schizophrenia Research.* New York: Raven.

Thelen, M., Farmer, J., Wonderlich, S., and Smith, M. (1991). "A Revision of the Bulimia Test: The BULIT-R." *Psychological Assessment, 3,* 119–124.

Tien, A., and Eaton, W. (1992). "Psychopathologic Precursors and Sociodemographic Risk Factors for the Schizophrenia Syndrome." *Archives of General Psychiatry, 49,* 37–46.

Trethvithick, L., and Hosch, H. (1978). "MMPI Correlates of Drug Addiction Based on Drug of Choice." *Journal of Consulting and Clinical Psychology, 46,* 180.

Trull, T. (1991). "Discriminant Validity of the MMPI-Borderline Personality Disorder Scale." *Psychological Assessment, 3,* 232–238.

Tsushima, W., and Wedding, D. (1979). "MMPI Results of Male Candidates for Transsexual Surgery." *Journal of Personality Assessment, 43,* 385–387.

Turkat, D. (1990). *The Personality Disorders.* New York: Pergamon.

United States v. Freeman, 357 F.2d 606 (1966).

United States v. Lions, 731 F.2d 243 (1984).

United States v. Tonero, 735 F.2d 725 (1984).

Valenstein, E. (1986). *Great and Desparate Cures: The Rise and Decline of Psychosurgery and Other Radical Treatments for Mental Illness.* New York: Basic Books.

Van Gorp, W., and Meyer, R. (1986). "The Detection of Faking on the Millon Clinical Multiaxial Inventory (MCMI)." *Journal of Clinical Psychology, 42,* 742–748.

Van Gorp, W., Satz, P., Kiersch, M., and Henry, R. (1986). "Normative Data on the Boston Naming Test for a Group of Normal Older Adults." *Journal of Clinical and Experimental Neuropsychology, 8,* 702–705.

Virkkunen, M., and Linnoila, M. (1991). "How to Predict Impulsive Violence: The Biochemical Findings Among Habitually Violent Offenders." Abstracts of Ninth Biennial World Meeting of the International Society for Research on Aggression. Banff, Alberta, Canada. *Aggressive Behavior, 17,* 101.

Vogel, G., Vogel, F., McAbee, R., and Thurmond, A. (1980). "Improvement of Depression by REM Sleep Deprivation." *Archives of General Psychiatry, 37,* 247–253.

Wagner, E., and Heise, M. (1981). "Rorschach and Hand Test Data Comparing Bipolar Patients in Manic and Depressive States." *Journal of Personality Assessment, 45,* 240–249.

Wagner, E., and Wagner, C. (1981). *The Interpretation of Psychological Test Data.* Springfield, IL: Charles Thomas.

_____ (1978). "Similar Rorschach Patterning in Three Cases of Anorexia nervosa." *Journal of Personality Assessment, 42,* 426–429.

Walker, G. (1985). "The Brief Therapy of a Compulsive Gambler." *Journal of Family Therapy, 7,* 1–8.

Walker, J., Norton, G., and Ross, C., Eds. (1991). *Panic Disorder and Agoraphobia.* Pacific Grove, CA: Brooks/Cole.

Ward, C. (1991). "A Comparison of T Scores from the MMPI and the MMPI-2. *Psychological Assessment, 3,* 688–690.

Washton, A. (1991). *Cocaine Addiction: Treatment, Recovery, and Relapse Prevention.* New York: W. W. Norton.

Washton, A., and Gold, M. (1987). *Cocaine: A Clinician's Handbook.* New York: Guilford.

Watson, C. (1990). "Psychometric Posttraumatic Stress Disorder Measurement Techniques: A Review." *Psychological Assessment, 2,* 460–469.

Watson, C., Plemel, D., and Jacobs, L. (1978). "An MMPI Sign to Separate Organic from Functional Psychiatric Patients." *Journal of Clinical Psychology, 34,* 398–432.

Webb, J., McNamara, K., and Rodgers, D. (1981). *Configural Interpretations of the MMPI and CPI.* Columbus: Ohio Psychology Publishing.

Wechsler, D. (1981). *WAIS-R Manual.* Cleveland: The Psychological Corporation.

Weeks, D., Freeman, C., and Kendall, R. (1980). "ECT: III. Enduring cognitive defects?" *The British Journal of Psychiatry, 137,* 26–37.

Welsh, G. (1948). "An Extension of Hathaway's MMPI Profile Coding System." *Journal of Consulting Psychology, 12,* 343–344.

Wettstein, R. (1989). "Psychiatric Malpractices." In A. Tasman, R. Hales, and A. Frances, Eds. *Review of Psychiatry,* Vol. 8, pp. 392–394, 398, 401. Washington, DC: American Psychiatric Press.

Wettstein, R., Mulvey, E., and Rogers, R. (1991). "A Prospective Comparison of Four Insanity Defense Standards." *American Journal of Psychiatry, 148,* 21–27.

Wetzler, S., Ed. (1989). *Measuring Mental Illness.* Washington, DC: American Psychiatric Press.

Wicksramasekera, I. (1976). "Aversive Behavior Rehearsal for Sexual Exhibitionism." In I. Wicksramasekera, Ed. *Biofeedback, Behavior Therapy, and Hypnosis.* Chicago: Nelson-Hall.

Wicksramasekera, I. (1988). *Clinical Behavioral Medicine.* New York: Plenum.

Widiger, T., Frances, A., Warner, L., and Bluhm, C. (1986). "Diagnostic Criteria for the Borderline and Schizotypal Personality Disorders." *Journal of Abnormal Psychology, 95,* 43–51.

Widiger, T., Frances, A., Pincus, H., Davis, W., and First, M. (1991). "Toward an Empirical Classification for the DSM-IV." *Journal of Abnormal Psychology, 100,* 280–288.

Widiger, T., and Sanderson, C. (1987). "The Convergent and Discriminant Validity of the MCMI as a Measure of the DSM-III Personality Disorders." *Journal of Personality Assessment, 51,* 228–242.

Wiener, D., and Harmon, L. (1946). "Subtle and Obvious Keys for the MMPI." (Advisement Bulletin 16.) Minneapolis: Regional Veteran's Administration Office.

Wiggins, E., and Brandt, J. (1988). "The Detection of Simulated Amnesia." *Law and Human Behavior, 12,* 57–79.

Wilson, T., and Walsh, B. (1991). "Eating Disorders in the DSM-IV." *Journal of Abnormal Psychology, 100,* 362–365.

Winder, P., O'Dell, J., and Karson, S. (1975). "New Motivational Distortion Scales for the 16 PF." *Journal of Personality Assessment, 39,* 532–537.

Winer, D. (1978). "Anger and Dissociation: A Case Study of Multiple Personality." *Journal of Abnormal Psychology, 87,* 368–372.

Winters, K., Weintraub, S., and Neale, V. (1981). "Validity of MMPI Codetypes in Identifying DSM-III Schizophrenics, Unipolars, and Bipolars." *Journal of Consulting and Clinical Psychology, 49,* 486–487.

Wolf, M., and Mosnaim, A., Eds. (1990). *Posttraumatic Stress Disorder: Etiology, Phenomenology and Treatment.* Washington, DC: American Psychiatric Press.

Wolpe, J. (1987). "Carbon Dioxide Inhalation Treatments of Neurotic Anxiety." *The Journal of Nervous and Mental Disease, 175,* 129–133.

Woody, J. (1992). *Treating Sexual Distress.* Newbury Park, CA: Sage.

World Health Organization (1979). *Schizophrenia: An International Follow-up Study.* New York: Wiley-Interscience.

Woychyshyn, C., McElheran, W., and Romney, D. (1992). "MMPI Validity Measures." *Journal of Personality Assessment, 58,* 138–148.

Yablonsky, L. (1976). *Psychodrama: Resolving Emotional Problems Through Role Playing.* New York: Basic Books.

Yager, J., Gwirtsman, H., and Edelstein, C. (1991). *Special Problems in Managing Eating Disorders.* Washington, DC: American Psychiatric Press.

Yudofsky, S., Williams, D., and Gorman, V. (1981). "Propranolol in the Treatment of Rage and Violent Behavior in Patients with Chronic Brain Syndrome." *American Journal of Psychiatry, 138,* 218–220.

Zeig, J., Ed. (1987). *The Evolution of Psychotherapy.* New York: Brunner/Mazel.

Zigler, E., and Glick, M. (1988). "Is Paranoid Schizophrenia Really Camouflaged Depression?" *American Psychologist, 43,* 284–290.

Zimmerman, I., and Woo-Sam, J. (1973). *Clinical Interpretation of the Wechsler Adult Intelligence Scale.* New York: Grune and Stratton.

Ziskin, J., and Faust, D. (1988). *Coping with Psychiatric and Psychological Testimony,* 4th ed. Marina del Rey, CA: Law and Psychology Press.

Zook, A., and Sipps, G. (1985). "Cross-Validation of a Short Form of the Marlowe-Crowne Social Desirability Scale." *Journal of Clinical Psychology, 41,* 236–238.

Zuckerman, M., Buchsbaum, M., and Murphy, D. (1980). "Sensation Seeking and Its Biological Correlates." *Psychological Bulletin, 88,* 187–214.

# Name Index

# Subject Index